Frontiers in Colorado Paleoindian Archaeology

Frontiers in Colorado

Paleoindian Archaeology
From the Dent Site to the Rocky Mountains
Edited by Robert H. Brunswig and Bonnie L. Pitblado

UNIVERSITY PRESS OF COLORADO

© 2007 by the University Press of Colorado

Published by the University Press of Colorado
5589 Arapahoe Avenue, Suite 206C
Boulder, Colorado 80303

All rights reserved
First paperback edition 2014

 The University Press of Colorado is a proud member of
the Association of American University Presses.

The University Press of Colorado is a cooperative publishing enterprise supported, in part, by Adams State College, Colorado State University, Fort Lewis College, Mesa State College, Metropolitan State College of Denver, University of Colorado, University of Northern Colorado, and Western State College of Colorado.

Library of Congress Cataloging-in-Publication Data

Frontiers in Colorado Paleoindian archaeology : from the Dent Site to the Rocky Mountains / edited by Robert H. Brunswig and Bonnie L. Pitblado.
  p. cm.
  Includes bibliographical references and index.
  ISBN 978-0-87081-890-5 (hardcover : paper) — ISBN 978-1-60732-354-9 (pbk. : paper)
1. Paleo-Indians—Colorado. 2. Paleoanthropology—Colorado. 3. Land settlement patterns, Prehistoric—Colorado. 4. Colorado—Antiquities. I. Brunswig, Robert H. II. Pitblado, Bonnie L., 1968–
  E78.C6F76 2007
  970.01—dc22

                                                                            2007030395

Design by Daniel Pratt

Bob Brunswig

I dedicate this book to my wife, Becky, and my children, Michael and Andrew, who, over the years, have had to sacrifice so much of my time and attention to my pursuit of a career in archaeology and to my other family of valued students and colleagues.

Bonnie Pitblado

I dedicate this volume to my mom, Nancy Pitblado, who has supported me in so many ways through the years. She has set a great example for how a person can enjoy both a loving family and a challenging career, an example I now strive to set for the students I am privileged to mentor.

CONTENTS

List of Illustrations	*ix*
List of Contributors	*xiii*
Preface	*xv*
Acknowledgments	*xvii*

Introduction—*Robert H. Brunswig and Bonnie L. Pitblado*   1

Part 1: Environmental and Archaeological Context

1 Late Quaternary Prehistoric Environments of the Colorado Front Range—*James P. Doerner*   11

2 That Was Then, This Is Now: Seventy-Five Years of Paleoindian Research in Colorado—*Bonnie L. Pitblado and Robert H. Brunswig*   39

Part 2: New Research at the Dent Clovis Site, Northeastern Colorado Plains

3 New Interpretations of the Dent Mammoth Site: A Synthesis of Recent Multidisciplinary Evidence—*Robert H. Brunswig*   87

4 Season of Death of the Dent Mammoths: Distinguishing Single from Multiple Mortality Events—*Daniel C. Fisher and David L. Fox*   123

5 Processing Marks on Remains of *Mammuthus columbi* from the Dent Site, Colorado, in Light of Those from Clovis, New Mexico: Fresh-Carcass Butchery Versus Scavenging?—*Jeffrey J. Saunders*   155

6 Phytolith and Starch Analysis of Dent Site Mammoth Teeth Calculus: New Evidence for Late Pleistocene Mammoth Diets and Environments—*Linda Scott Cummings and Rosa María Albert*   185

Part 3: New Research in the Colorado Rocky Mountains

7 Building a Picture of the Landscape Using Close-Interval Pollen Sampling and Archaeoclimatic Modeling: An Example from the KibRidge-Yampa Paleoindian Site, Northwestern Colorado—*Linda Scott Cummings, R. A. Varney, and Reid A. Bryson*   195

8 Folsom Hearth-Centered Use of Space at Barger Gulch, Locality B—*Todd A. Surovell and Nicole M. Waguespack*   219

9 Paleoindian Cultural Landscapes and Archaeology of North-Central Colorado's Southern Rockies—*Robert H. Brunswig*   261

10 Angostura, Jimmy Allen, Foothills-Mountain: Clarifying Terminology for Late Paleoindian Southern Rocky Mountain Spear Points—*Bonnie L. Pitblado*   311

Afterword: A Wyoming Archaeologist's Past and Present View of Wyoming and Colorado Paleoindian Archaeology—*George C. Frison*   339

Index   357

ILLUSTRATIONS

1.1.	Map showing major physical features of Colorado	12
1.2.	Map showing major air mass trajectories into the Colorado Front Range	13
1.3.	Schematic diagram comparing till of Pinedale, Bull Lake, and pre–Bull Lake glaciations	17
1.4.	Shaded relief map of Colorado Front Range region showing the locations of glacial and paleoecological sites	18
1.5.	Echo Lake pollen diagram	23
1.6.	Correlation of cultural/chronological periods with paleoenvironmental reconstructions from the Colorado Front Range	30
2.1.	Map of key Paleoindian sites mentioned in Chapter 2	43
2.2.	Contemporary Colorado Paleoindian research program areas discussed in Chapter 2 and the remaining chapters of this volume	54
3.1.	Geographic location of the Dent site	88

ILLUSTRATIONS

3.2. Dent geologic context	93
3.3. Aerial view of Dent showing the site's drainage fan draw	93
3.4. Stratigraphic profile of Dent	94
3.5. Locations of cores and upper draw test trench at Dent	97
3.6. Profile of UNC's Dent upper (southeast) gulley test trench	98
3.7. Hypothesized paleolandscape of Dent kill locality	99
3.8. Aerial view of Dent locality showing a now-abandoned South Platte River channel	100
3.9. Photograph of the Dent artifacts	106
4.1. Hierarchy of dentin increments in mammoth tusks and cheek teeth	125
4.2. Transverse sections through Dent tusk and cheek tooth dentin	131
4.3. Oxygen isotope sampling from Dent tusk (DMNH 1450)	133
4.4. Oxygen isotope sampling from root of dP_4 (DMNH 1895)	137
4.5. Oxygen isotope sampling from root of dP_3 (DMNH 1897)	138
4.6. Oxygen isotope variation in tusk and cheek tooth dentin and present precipitation	139
5.1. Photograph of lateral view of EPV.3928, right scapula	163
5.2. Photograph of EPV.3928, right scapula: distal insertion on the scapular neck viewed from the caudal side	164
5.3. Photograph of EPV.3928, right scapula: distal insertion of the spine on the scapular neck viewed from the cranial side	164
5.4. Photograph of EPV.3928, right scapula: hackle marks on the distal scapula showing extensive damage to the lateral glenoid during dismemberment	165
5.5. Photograph of lateral view of EPV.3931, left scapula: spine dismemberment and dismemberment of pre-spinous fossa from the remainder of the scapular blade	166
5.6. Photograph of EPV.3931, left scapula: distal insertion of the spine on the scapular neck seen vertically and showing a shear-fracture scar	166
5.7. Close-up view of EPV.3931, left scapula: fracture through which pre-spinous fossa was dismembered from the remainder of the scapular blade	167
5.8. Proximal medial view of EPV.3937, left ulna, showing a crescentic gouge attributed to dismemberment	168
5.9. Photograph of EPV.3992, left femur: prominent gouge in medial head associated with dismemberment of the hip joint	168
5.10. Close-up view of EPV.3992, left femur: weathered, filleting cut marks on distal medial surface associated with defleshing	169
5.11. Photograph of EPV.3992, left femur: anterior distal view of femur showing two depressions that are probable damages attributed to foreshaft pry bars	170
5.12. Photograph of distal anteromedial view of EPV.3995: right femur diaphysis, showing weathered, filleting cut marks	171

ILLUSTRATIONS

6.1. Phytolith frequency diagram of Dent mammoth teeth	189
7.1. Location of KibRidge-Yampa site in northeastern Colorado	198
7.2. Combined stratigraphic pollen diagram from KibRidge-Yampa site	199
7.3. Comparison of pollen sampling strategies	202
7.4. Monthly and annual insolation, last glacial maximum through the present	206
7.5. Modeled water balance history, Dinosaur National Monument, Colorado	209
7.6. Modeled water balance history, Dinosaur National Monument, Colorado, compared to portions of the pollen diagram	210
7.7. Modeled temperature history, Dinosaur National Monument, Colorado	211
7.8. Modeled snowfall history, Dinosaur National Monument, Colorado	211
7.9. Modeled precipitation history, Dinosaur National Monument, Colorado	212
7.10. March of precipitation from 10,000 to 11,200 RCYBP and modern	213
8.1. Two conjoining biface fragments in situ within main excavation block	225
8.2. Distributions of burned materials from main excavation block of Barger Gulch, Locality B	227
8.3. Plan maps of excavation block	230
8.4. Map of cores and core fragments recovered from primary excavation area	233
8.5. Plan maps of two bifurcated flake concentrations relative to the hearth	235
8.6. Maps of the pit feature located to the southeast of the hearth	236
8.7. Schematic representation of divisions of space used in ring and sector analysis	237
8.8. Ring diagrams by sector for hearth area showing artifact counts as a function of distance from the hearth	239
8.9. Plan map of hypothesized barrier effect	240
8.10. Plan maps of excavation block showing spatial congruence of the possible shelter reconstructed by ring and sector analysis and artifact clusters	242
8.11. Sector diagrams of piece-plotted debitage, bifaces, flake tools, points and preforms, and cores	243
8.12. Sector diagrams of piece-plotted artifacts by size class	246
8.13. Modified ring diagrams for piece-plotted debitage and flake tools	249
8.14. Plan map of all piece-plotted flake tools mapped onto reconstructed structural walls	250
9.1. Physiographic map showing Colorado's north-central and central mountain regions	262

9.2. GIS map showing locations of all Paleoindian components in the project area   269
9.3. GIS map distribution of early Paleoindian components in the project area   271
9.4. Locations of earlier late Paleoindian sites and isolated finds in the project area   284
9.5. Site distribution of Cody components in the project area   285
9.6. Site distribution of post-Cody late Paleoindian components in the project area   287
9.7. Distribution of late Paleoindian cultural components in Rocky Mountain National Park   291
9.8. Sites with late Paleoindian components in the Bighorn Flats hunting territory   293
9.9. Distribution of prehistoric sites in the Mount Ida Ridge hunting territory   294
9.10. Bar chart showing relative percentages of local versus nonlocal projectile point materials by projectile point type/complex   298
10.1. Angostura point tip and base from the type (Ray Long) site, Black Hills, South Dakota, and Angostura projectile point from 5MF625, Moffat County, Colorado   316
10.2. Basal convexity/concavity as expressed in specimens with convergent basal sides   317
10.3. Jimmy Allen projectile points from the type-site, Laramie Basin, southern Wyoming, and from Rocky Mountain National Park   319
10.4. Scatterplot of basal and maximum widths of Angostura and Jimmy Allen points in the Colorado-Utah sample   322
10.5. Scatterplot showing the BW and MW of Angostura and Jimmy Allen points in the original sample and the test assemblage of twenty-one points assigned to "Angostura" from the Chance Gulch site (5GN817), Gunnison Basin, Colorado   323
10.6. Diagnostic artifacts from the Medicine Lodge Creek site, Bighorn Basin, Wyoming   327

CONTRIBUTORS

Rosa María Albert
Department of Prehistory, Ancient History, and Archaeology
Catalan Institution for Research and Advanced Studies

Robert H. Brunswig
Anthropology Program
School of Social Sciences
University of Northern Colorado

Reid A. Bryson
Center for Climatic Research
University of Wisconsin

CONTRIBUTORS

Linda Scott Cummings
Paleo Research Institute
Golden, Colorado

James P. Doerner
Geography Program
School of Social Sciences
University of Northern Colorado

Daniel C. Fisher
Museum of Paleontology
University of Michigan

David L. Fox
Department of Geology and Geophysics
University of Minnesota

George C. Frison
Anthropology Department
University of Wyoming

Bonnie L. Pitblado
Anthropology Program
Department of Sociology, Social Work, and Anthropology
Utah State University

Jeffrey J. Saunders
Illinois State Museum
Research and Collections Center
Springfield, IL

Todd A. Surovell
Anthropology Department
University of Wyoming

R. A. Varney
Paleo Research Institute
Golden, Colorado

Nicole M. Waguespack
Anthropology Department
University of Wyoming

PREFACE

The earliest inspirations for this book sprang from a burgeoning interest in the Dent site and my contact in 1986 with Frank Frazier, discoverer or co-investigator of many well-known Paleoindian sites in the Greeley, Colorado, area during the 1960s and 1970s. Without Frank's generous help and provision of undocumented research records from the 1973 University of Colorado site testing, the Dent site research reported in Part 2 of this volume would never have transpired. Likewise, the collaborations reflected in the Dent chapters and the book in general came about through various serendipitous encounters. I met Dan Fisher (Chapter 4's "season of death" study of the Dent mammoths), for example, in 1988 on a Geological Society of America conference tour. I was privileged to work with Vance Haynes in his 1992 Kersey Terrace investigations near the Dent site. In 1993 I met and began what approaches fifteen years of collaboration with this volume's co-editor, Bonnie Pitblado, when she was completing a master's thesis on late Paleoindians in Southwest Colorado and working seasonally as an archaeologist for the Pawnee National Grassland of northeastern Colorado.

A more concrete foundation for this volume was set in 1995 when I organized and chaired a symposium titled "Current Research on Paleoindian Archaeology and Geoarchaeology of the Central High Plains and Rocky Mountains" for the 60th annual meeting of the Society for American Archaeology in Minneapolis. Participating scholars included Dan Fisher, Linda Scott Cummings and Rosa María Albert, Michael McFaul, Marcel Kornfeld and George Frison, Bonnie Pitblado, and Jim Dixon. Jim Dixon and I subsequently organized many of the symposium papers into the first incarnation of this book and worked to publish it through the University Press of Colorado. For a variety of reasons, mostly bureaucratic, the project was temporarily tabled, but it re-emerged several years later when the Press's newly hired director, Darrin Pratt, excavated the file from the Press archives—together with reviewer recommendations to publish—and resurrected the project. At that point my original co-editor, Jim Dixon, elected not to continue in that capacity, but Bonnie Pitblado agreed to step into his shoes.

For understandable reasons, some of the contributors to the original iteration of the book published their excellent work elsewhere in the intervening years. I believe, however, that this new version is even stronger, more diverse, and more reflective of the significant changes occurring in Colorado (and American western) Paleoindian archaeology than was the original. The new volume particularly benefits from and illustrates recent major advances in Paleoindian research in Colorado's Rocky Mountains. I am greatly appreciative of editor Darrin Pratt's support throughout the book's new incarnation and delight in my collaboration with my longtime colleague, friend, and co-editor, Bonnie Pitblado. I am also grateful to those original contributors who remained loyal to the volume, despite the long and winding road we all followed to finally bring it to press.

—Robert H. Brunswig
University of Northern Colorado

ACKNOWLEDGMENTS

We see this book as in no small part a tribute to our many friends and colleagues who have contributed both to the success of this volume and to Colorado archaeology. Bob expresses special gratitude to Bill Butler, Jim Benedict, Jim Doerner, Darrin Pratt, and Frank Rupp at the academic end of the spectrum. At the personal end, he thanks his wife, Becky, for putting up with an absent (mentally and physically) husband in pursuit of his passion.

Bonnie acknowledges the contributors to this volume for their patience with the editing process and her anthropology colleagues and students at Utah State University for indulging her many moments spent formatting (yet again) errant margins and nonconforming citations. Bonnie also thanks for their indulgence her wonderful family: loving husband, Joe; four-year-old son Ethan (okay, so patience wasn't really his forte, but his cheerful spirit works wonders on cloudy days); and her "Renaissance Man" stepson Derek. Finally, Bonnie tips her hat to the Rocky Mountain archaeologists who have inspired her the most: Jim Benedict, George Frison, and as we emphasize below, Wil Husted.

Both Bob and Bonnie thank the two anonymous reviewers who helped make this last iteration of our book the best possible iteration. Their many concrete suggestions were enormously helpful. We wish to particularly recognize and thank our colleague Wil Husted, who blazed the trail for us and for mountain archaeologists in Colorado and the rest of the Rockies. From your master's thesis in Rocky Mountain National Park to the Mountain Branch of the Western Macrotradition, you started something special, Wil, and you inspired a whole lot of us along the way. Finally, we would like to acknowledge Eric Carlson's very fine artwork for our book cover and chapter title illustrations. For possibly the first time, that art depicts the interactive roles of Paleoindian men and women many millennia ago.

Frontiers in Colorado Paleoindian Archaeology

Robert H. Brunswig and Bonnie L. Pitblado

Introduction

The state of Colorado has, since the dawn of Paleoindian archaeology, occupied a central position in the field, both geographically and intellectually. Several Paleoindian "firsts," a suite of archaeological characters in the discipline's colorful cast, and many methodological and theoretical innovations can all be linked to three-quarters of a century of Colorado Paleoindian archaeology. Advances in Colorado Paleoindian archaeology often either presaged or unfolded in lockstep with developments in North American Paleoindian archaeology as a whole.

It is true that Blackwater Draw's Locality 1, near Clovis, New Mexico, won the right to name the continent's earliest sustained human culture by virtue of the clear association there of large, fluted spear points and megafauna remains. However, the Dent site, located near present-day Greeley, Colorado, had yielded similar evidence several years earlier. But because in 1932 archaeologists had not yet distinguished chronologically later Folsom fluted points from what would soon be forever known as "Clovis," the Dent site—and Colorado—ceded the honor of labeling the first named Paleoindians to New Mexico. This accident of fate, however, does not change the fact that the earliest scientific excavation of a Clovis site is rightfully attributed to Father Conrad Bilgery of Denver's Regis College (now Regis University) and occurred in Colorado.

If we were to poll a roomful of archaeologists, asking them to name Paleoindian archaeology's most noteworthy forefathers and mothers, we would likely engender substantial debate with regard to the former but virtually none with regard to the latter. Marie Wormington was born in Denver in 1914, studied archaeology under the University of Denver's E. B. Renaud, and served as curator of archaeology at the Denver Museum of Natural History for over thirty years. She undertook excavations at such important Colorado Paleoindian sites as Frazier, mentored future Paleoindian scholars like Henry and Cynthia Irwin, and wrote the still-cited classic book *Ancient Man in North America* (1957). Marie Wormington was Colorado born and bred, and she embodies Paleoindian archaeology to this day.

As early as the 1930s, Wormington's own mentor, E. B. Renaud, recognized the importance of systematically cataloging diagnostic Paleoindian artifacts from private collections and very large survey projects—a methodology alive and well today in Colorado and beyond. Renaud had a profound effect on the future of Paleoindian archaeology by training such well-known scholars as John Cotter, who would later put Blackwater Draw on the map (and seal Dent's fate as a Clovis type-site also-ran) and, of course, Wormington herself, who passed along her knowledge to so many others.

In the 1950s–1970s, Joe Ben Wheat pioneered meticulous excavation techniques and taphonomic studies while advancing new assessments of Paleoindian projectile point typology and reinforcing the importance of collaborative efforts with paleoecologists, geologists, and others. We suspect that few scholars who today excavate Paleoindian sites in Colorado—or anywhere in the Western Hemisphere—would or could deny the influence Wheat's work at Olsen-Chubbuck and Jurgens had on their field methodologies and interpretations. Wheat, like Wormington and Renaud, also helped advance the careers of many other scientists, including, for example, Colorado's preeminent paleoecologist, Linda Scott Cummings, who collaborated with him at Jurgens in the 1970s as Linda Scott and coauthored two chapters for this book.

In 1962, Wilfred Husted completed a master's thesis that developed an archaeological chronology for Colorado's Rocky Mountain National Park. Just a few years later, he proposed the then-revolutionary idea that mountain Paleoindian people were different from those in other regions—and worth studying. Colorado-based James Benedict took Husted's idea to heart, as he eventually became one of the founders and—for the past several decades—best practitioners of high-altitude archaeology in North America. The recognition that the Rocky Mountains were far more to Paleoindian people than a physical impediment that kept them from traveling between the Plains and the Great Basin (both with better-known records) changed Paleoindian archaeology in the western United States. Prominent archaeologists like George Frison soon initiated hunts for mountain Paleoindian sites, and, in Frison's case, his interest in the Rockies continues, as he explains in the afterword to this volume. In Colorado, the change in geographic focus was so profound that today, nearly *all* Paleoindian research is taking place in mountain settings. The research of the classic Dent, Lindenmeier, Jones-Miller, Olsen-Chubbuck, Jurgens, Frazier, Claypool, and other plains sites has largely given way to work in Colorado's major parks and high mountains. Archaeologists in other states—Frison is one; others include Marcel Kornfeld, Mary Lou Larson, and many of their students—are also following this Colorado-centered trend, placing new emphasis on the mountains in their neighborhoods as well.

In many ways, Colorado has long been a trend-setting center of Paleoindian archaeology in the western United States. What happens in Colorado is often cutting-edge, both methodologically and theoretically. At a bare minimum, Colorado Paleoindian archaeology can, at any given moment, be viewed as a snapshot of Paleoindian archaeology in general, certainly of Paleoindian archaeology in the West. This is as true today as it ever was, and it forms the fundamental rationale for this book. This volume showcases recent work on Colorado Paleoindian sites and paleoenvironments, ca. 11,800–7,500 radiocarbon years ago (RCYBP)—work that is important not only for its new and emerging methods, interpretations, and theoretical shifts but also as a representation of the "state of the art" of Paleoindian archaeology today in the western United States and perhaps beyond. In reviewing this book's chapters, readers will learn about the latest Clovis through late Paleoindian research in Colorado but will also detect the pulse of the larger discipline.

In a very real sense, *Frontiers of Colorado Paleoindian Archaeology* rests on a foundation built by another volume of collected Paleoindian studies published fifteen years ago and also focusing on the mountains of the American West: *Ice Age Hunters of the Rockies* (1992), edited by Jane Day and prominent Colorado Paleoindian archaeologist Dennis Stanford. *Ice Age Hunters of the Rockies* was based on a 1988 symposium held at the Denver Museum of Natural History and, like this volume, was produced by the University Press of Colorado.

The first of three major parts of this volume, "Environmental and Archaeological Context," weaves together these threads of historical contextual data, establishing in detail the scientific foundations of Paleoindian research that archaeological and paleoecological research has built over the past seventy-five or so years. The second part, "New Research at the Dent Clovis Site, Northeastern Colorado Plains," presents four recent, interrelated studies of the seminal Dent Clovis site, located on the short-grass prairie of northeastern Colorado. The Dent studies are important for several reasons, among them that earlier interpretations of this earliest-excavated Clovis site have always been highly controversial, and new lines of investigation have been sorely needed for decades; that the part's studies showcase innovative methodologies for studying faunal remains; and that its studies represent the only substantial new body of work in Paleoindian archaeology on the Colorado plains in the past two decades. The final section of the book, "New Research in the Colorado Rocky Mountains," assembles four studies set in Colorado's southern Rocky Mountains—as we have noted, the new research area of choice for most Paleoindian scholars working in the state today.

The structure of this volume intentionally reflects and reinforces content shifts, even paradigm shifts, through seven-plus decades of research in Colorado Paleoindian archaeology: from building foundations for the discipline, to a mid-twentieth-century focus on the classic plains megafauna kill and camp sites that put Colorado on the archaeological map (represented by Dent), to the current preoccupation of most Colorado Paleoindian archaeologists with the Rocky Mountains. In the remaining paragraphs, we briefly overview what readers will find in each chapter, and, in the interest of our historical perspective, we take the opportunity, as appropriate, to comment on obvious earlier Colorado influences on the researchers.

Part 1 of the volume consists of two chapters, one summarizing what we have learned to date about Colorado paleoenvironments, the other what we have learned about the Paleoindians who experienced them. James Doerner's Chapter 1 contribution, "Late Quaternary Prehistoric Environments of the Colorado Front Range Rocky Mountains," casts the widest net of any chapter in the volume. Doerner provides a review of over thirty years of glacial chronology and paleo-ecological research that have revealed how environmental conditions shifted in Colorado during the latest Pleistocene and Holocene. His geographic scope and time frame encompass those of all other contributors to the volume, so readers may cross-reference archaeological data with Doerner's paleoenvironmental reconstructions. Doerner's chapter also provides a point of departure for Linda Scott Cummings and colleagues' Chapter 7 evaluation of methodological problems with some paleoenvironmental studies—including some mentioned by Doerner—and suggestions for resolving them.

The second chapter in Part 1 serves as an archaeological counterpoint to Doerner's paleoenvironmental overview and expands thoughts offered earlier in this introduction. In Chapter 2, "That Was Then, This Is Now: Seventy-Five Years of Paleoindian Research in Colorado," we provide a comprehensive discussion of the "who, what, where, why, and how" of Colorado Paleoindian archaeology from its inception in the 1930s through today. We present this information chronologically, from earliest to most recent investigations. We touch on major survey projects, excavations, and studies of assemblages; address work in the state's eastern plains and the Rocky Mountains in the west and note the profound shift in research emphases through time from the former to the latter; and point out similar shifts in research interests and methodologies through time. In so doing, we provide intellectual context that spotlights the influences upon, and inspirations for, research presented in the book's next eight chapters.

Part 2's chapters cumulatively represent results of new work at the Dent Mammoth Site. Robert Brunswig begins his Chapter 3 by expanding upon the history of work at the site, briefly described in Chapter 2. He follows with a discussion of the scope of recent fieldwork and laboratory studies and concludes with a litany of geoarchaeological and archaeological conclusions drawn by him and his collaborators. The three chapters that follow—written by those collaborators, and very much in the methodologically innovative and interdisciplinary-focused spirit of Joe Ben Wheat decades earlier—provide much of the evidence for Brunswig's and his colleagues' interpretations regarding season(s) of mammoth death, degree of human involvement in the deaths, number of kill events, and even mammoth land-use strategies.

Daniel Fisher and David Fox's "Season of Death of the Dent Mammoths: Distinguishing Single from Multiple Mortality Events" (Chapter 4) addresses the enduring question of whether the fourteen mammoths at Dent represent one or multiple kills. Their methodology combines analysis of tooth-dentin accretion and oxygen isotopes. Jeffrey Saunders's Chapter 5 reports his evaluation of mammoth bone modification as the means for inferring the number of kill events at Dent and the manner of processing the bones. Finally, Linda Scott Cummings—long ago a Joe Ben Wheat collaborator—and Rosa María Albert offer in Chapter 6 their study of phytoliths extracted from Dent mammoth teeth, which inform the other chapters' interpretations of season of death and mammoth foraging strategies.

Like the Dent mammoths, which both Brunswig and Cummings and Albert suggest may have spent part of the year grazing in the Front Range foothills and mountains, Part 3 chapters report on new investigations relating to Paleoindian use of the Colorado Rocky Mountains. Cummings, in collaboration with R. A. Varney and Reid Bryson, contributes Chapter 7, which points out that many studies attempting to reconstruct paleoenvironments are methodologically flawed because they fail to sample sediments (and pollen therein) at sufficiently frequent intervals. Cummings, a pioneer not only in paleoecological reconstructions but in Colorado archaeology generally, has teamed with Varney and Bryson to offer practical solutions to this problem and illustrates their suggested methodology and comparison with Bryson's innovative archaeoclimatic modeling through her recent work at the KibRidge-Yampa Paleoindian site in the rugged uplands of northwestern Colorado. Cummings, Varney, and Bryson build neatly on the synthetic overview of earlier paleoecological studies presented by Doerner in Chapter 1, ultimately providing cutting-edge ideas for how to improve paleoenvironmental investigations in general—that is, worldwide—henceforth.

Todd Surovell and Nicole Waguespack's Chapter 8 presents detailed spatial analyses of cultural deposits at the Barger Gulch Folsom site in Middle Park. Their work, which convincingly argues for the presence of a hearth in the absence of obvious remnants thereof in the field, is clearly inspired in part by groundbreaking work at Cattleguard and other San Luis Valley, Colorado, Folsom sites by Margaret (Pegi) Jodry, herself influenced by Colorado Paleoindian icons like Wormington,

Wheat, and Stanford. Surovell and Waguespack's exploration of whether there may have been a structure at Barger Gulch during Folsom time is both timely—given recent claims for a wintertime residential structure at the Mountaineer site, further south in the Gunnison Basin—and exemplary in the attempt they make to scientifically demonstrate the presence of a structure. Surovell and Waguespack provide methodological blueprints adapted from recent European Paleolithic archaeology that will be immediately useful to any archaeologist looking to substantiate the presence of features at ephemeral hunter-gatherer sites where evidence is subtle at best. That describes most, if not all, Paleoindian sites in the Rockies and everywhere else, but also many other sites of various ages and in various environments around the world.

Our respective Chapters 9 and 10, finally, focus on what finds of Paleoindian spear points in the Colorado Rocky Mountains "mean" and can tell us about the people who used them. Our work harkens back to the early surveys of E. B. Renaud and his students in the 1930s, with other inspirations ranging from Wheat's suggested Paleoindian projectile point typologies of the 1960s–1970s to James Benedict's work in the high country of the Indian Peaks Wilderness Area over the past three decades. Brunswig's Chapter 9 examines distributions of Paleoindian points and sites in the north-central Colorado Rocky Mountains, utilizing a synthesis of published and unpublished archaeological reports and Geographic Information System (GIS) technology to model settlement pattern evolution from earliest to latest Paleoindian times. Pitblado's Chapter 10 attempts to clarify what she sees as rampant confusion over how researchers should label mostly parallel-obliquely flaked late Paleoindian spear points found in the Colorado Rockies. Pitblado evaluates Brunswig's Chapter 9 findings as a case study to demonstrate why archaeologists working in the Rockies would benefit from a clearer understanding of variability in the late Paleoindian point types most commonly found there.

While in virtually every case Paleoindian researchers working in Colorado today can point to concrete inspirations in the past for their work in the present, they also bring a plethora of new techniques, technologies, and ideas to the table. Where early archaeologists worked alone, we now almost universally work in teams of sometimes dozens of interdisciplinary collaborators. Where once researchers organized their archaeological pursuits around the latest find of a Colorado rancher, current research programs operate deductively, locating and excavating sites on the basis of larger research questions. Where E. B. Renaud recorded points and private collections and plotted them on maps, we import those data into GIS programs and perform detailed spatial analyses of their locations on the landscape and their relationship to topographic variables and natural resources. Early excavators relied on tape measures and transits; we map our finds with total stations and high-resolution Global Positioning System (GPS) instruments, download the data into our computers, and manipulate them with powerful mapping and statistical software. Even our writings benefit from the advent of computer programs like *Adobe Illustrator*, which permit us to readily produce crisp, publication-ready images of our finds.

We invite readers to enjoy Chapters 1 and 2, which are a tribute to the researchers who have brought us to where we are today, and then to read the rest of the book, where we—researchers of today—blend the lessons of our archaeological forefathers and foremothers with the suite of new research tools at our disposal. Collectively, the authors of this volume are part of a much larger community of archaeologists and specialists in allied disciplines who are striving to advance the science of Paleoindian archaeology in Colorado and beyond. The book's contributions reflect the "state of the art" of Paleoindian archaeology generally and offer new methodologies that we hope will inform and stimulate both our colleagues and the knowledgeable public intrigued by the unfolding story of America's first colonists.

PART ONE

ENVIRONMENTAL AND ARCHAEOLOGICAL CONTEXT

CHAPTER ONE

James P. Doerner

Late Quaternary Prehistoric Environments of the Colorado Front Range

This chapter examines the prehistoric environments of the Colorado Front Range during the past 25,000 years, the interval encompassing the most recent glacial-interglacial cycle (Porter 1983). This interval is generally referred to as the late Quaternary Period and is a critical time in both human and earth history. It was during this time that humans first arrived in North America, large-scale extinctions of Pleistocene mammals occurred, and boreal vegetation consisting mainly of tundra plants and spruce woodlands covered large areas of North America south of the continental ice sheets (Holloway and Bryant 1985). The interval also includes the termination of the Pleistocene and establishment of a new post-glacial macroclimate during the Holocene. These new environmental conditions meant that old plant associations and distributions had to adjust to remain in equilibrium with the changing environment (Baker 1983). As glacial

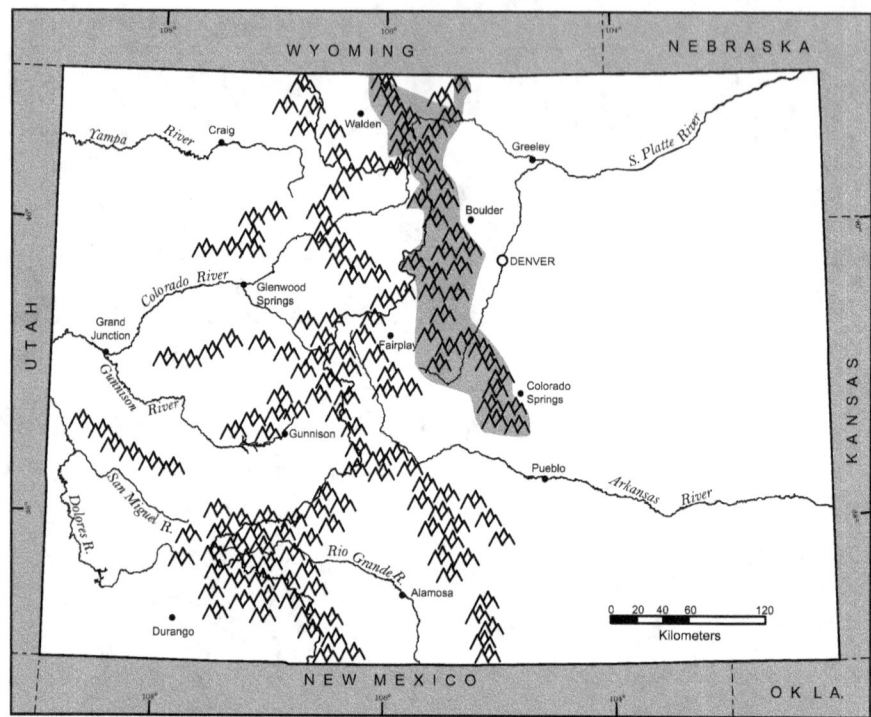

1.1. *Map showing major physical features of Colorado. Shaded area shows the generalized location of the Colorado Front Range in north-central Colorado.*

conditions ameliorated and alpine glaciers melted away, vegetation zones apparently responded by advancing upslope from the plains and the lower montane zones to reclaim the higher elevations (Elias 1988).

Environmental changes during the late Quaternary have been substantial. Climate is probably the most important environmental factor, controlling growth and decay of ice sheets, distributions of flora and fauna (including human populations), development of soils, and erosion and sedimentation processes on the landscape (Wright 1983). The reconstruction of past environments is essential for interpreting past human occupations and cultural landscape modeling.

The remainder of this chapter is divided into four sections: (1) a description of the regional setting, (2) a review of climate reconstructions based on glacial chronologies, (3) an overview of paleoecological studies derived from pollen and fossil beetle investigations, and (4) a summary of late Quaternary climate change in the Colorado Front Range.

REGIONAL SETTING

The Colorado Front Range (Figure 1.1) is made up of the easternmost mountain ranges that comprise the Southern Rocky Mountain physiographic province

1.2. *Map showing major air mass trajectories into the Colorado Front Range.*

(Hunt 1967). The Front Range is about 300 km long, extending from the Arkansas River in the south to the Colorado-Wyoming border in the north (Short 1985). The eastern margin of the Front Range is clearly defined by steeply dipping sedimentary layers that mark the contact with the Great Plains. Along the western margin, the Front Range is bordered by other mountain ranges and intermontane basins (Marr 1967). The topography throughout most of the area is rugged and steep, with broad glaciated valleys prominent above 2,800 m (Veblen and Lorenz 1986).

The modern climate is classified as highland continental, with short cool summers, long cold winters, and relatively dry conditions throughout the year (Griffiths and Rubright 1983). Dramatic changes in average temperature and precipitation occur with increased elevation (Barry 1972). Marr (1967) notes that the area is subject to extreme changes in atmospheric conditions, which can occur from hour to hour, day to day, season to season, and year to year. Climate is also strongly influenced by its position relative to prevailing air mass trajectories (Figure 1.2).

During winter months, westerly circulation brings cool, moist Pacific air masses to the mountains. This can produce heavy snowfalls for the mountains west of the Continental Divide, while the east slope of the divide experiences relatively little precipitation (Veblen and Lorenz 1991). The western slope has a wet season during winter months when the westerlies are the strongest, while the eastern slope is relatively dry during winter (Rink and Kiladis 1986). The Front Range receives most of its annual precipitation from storm systems originating in the Gulf of Mexico (Marr 1967). Maximum precipitation on the east slope usually occurs during the spring (Rink and Kaladis 1986). A secondary peak

Table 1.1. Climatic Parameters and Ecosystem Vegetation for the East Slope of the Colorado Front Range (Barry 1972; Marr 1967; Veblen and Lorenz 1991).

Elevational Range (m)	Mean Annual Precipitation (mm)	Mean Annual Temperature (°C)	Vegetation Zone
1,800 to 2,350	590	8.3	Lower montane
2,350 to 2,800	590	5.6	Upper montane
2,800 to 3,350	770	1.6	Subalpine
> 3,550	1,025	−3.3	Alpine

occurs in July and August, reflecting the influence of summer convective storms (Barry 1972). Elevation can also influence the timing of the precipitation peak for east slope locations in the Front Range (Barry 1973). Elevations at 3,000 m have a spring precipitation maximum, whereas areas above 3,750 m have a winter precipitation peak (Barry 1973).

Elevations in the Front Range vary from about 1,700 m at the base of the mountains to over 4,300 m on the highest peaks. This elevational gradient creates distinct climatic and vegetation zones, which roughly correspond to altitude (Table 1.1). In general, with an increase in elevation, there is a decrease in temperature and an increase in precipitation (Barry 1973, 1981). This provides more available moisture but shorter growing seasons in the mountains. As a result, the mountains have extensive forests compared with the grasslands on the surrounding plains and intermontane basins (Rink and Kiladis 1986).

In Colorado's mountains, grasses and herbs dominate vegetation at the highest and lowest elevations (Mutel and Emerick 1992). Forests in the Front Range are restricted to elevations between 1,800 and 3,350 m. This results in an upper and a lower tree line. At the highest elevations, trees are limited by cold, drought, and wind. For elevations below 1,800 m, trees are limited by drought. Needle-leafed conifers dominate the Front Range forests. Except for areas where disturbance has allowed aspen to invade, broad-leafed deciduous trees are limited to riparian habitats.

Forests in the Rocky Mountains exhibit altitudinal zonation, which can be seen in the vegetation of the Front Range. Marr (1967) divided the vegetation of the eastern slope of the Front Range into four major zones: (1) the lower montane zone, (2) the upper montane zone, (3) the subalpine zone, and (4) the alpine zone. Each of these zones is characterized according to a given range of temperature, humidity, type and amount of precipitation, growing season length, wind, and soil conditions. Boundaries between zones are not sharply defined; instead, there are ecotonal transitions between zones in which plant species from adjacent zones are intermixed.

The Lower Montane Zone

The vegetation in the lower montane zone is an open forest of broad-crowned evergreen trees frequently interrupted by grasslands (Marr 1967). The dominant tree species are ponderosa pine and Douglas fir, with Rocky Mountain juniper common on dry sites. Mountain mahogany, blue gramma and other grasses, shrubs, and herbs form the understory. Narrow-leaf cottonwood, Colorado blue spruce, river birch, and willow are common along stream courses. North-facing slopes support dense forests of Douglas fir and ponderosa pine. Douglas fir is more common on steeper slopes, while higher percentages of ponderosa pine may indicate the presence of coarse soils. On south-facing slopes, the forests are less dense and ponderosa pine is favored over Douglas fir.

The Upper Montane Zone

The vegetation in this zone is similar to that of the lower montane, but the overall density of the forest is greater. Douglas fir and ponderosa pine are still the dominant tree species. Limber pine is present where strong winds persist, soils are coarse, or both (Marr 1967). Aspen and lodgepole pine form dense secondary successional forests after fires, logging, or other disturbances (Windell, Willard, and Foster 1986). Aspen stands typically have a well-developed understory of forbs and grasses, in contrast to ponderosa pine stands, which have a sparse understory (Peet 1988). Aspen is generally found on wetter sites and lodgepole pine on drier sites (Griffths and Rubright 1983). Narrow-leaf cottonwood and Colorado blue spruce are the dominant tree species on the valley floors, with willow, alder, and birch forming complex stands along stream banks (Marr 1967).

The Subalpine Zone

The subalpine zone forms the highest, most continuous and pristine forests in Colorado (Mutel and Emerick 1992). Engelmann spruce and subalpine fir trees occur as dense unbroken forests (Marr 1967). These spruce-fir forests are replaced by stands of bristlecone pine on open, dry, south-facing slopes (Peet 1978) and by limber pine on windy, rocky, and exposed sites (Arno and Hammerly 1984). Dwarf juniper occur throughout this zone (Short 1985). Disturbance areas are indicated by stands of quaking aspen and lodgepole pine.

Spruce and fir have somewhat different ecological characteristics, with spruce more tolerant of extreme conditions than fir (Peet 1988). Spruce is the dominant species on very wet or boggy sites, as well as on the driest sites (Peet 1981). Where conditions are the driest, fir is absent from the subalpine zone (Peet 1988). Spruce is more successful at establishing itself on mineral soils following fires (Alexander 1974; Peet 1981), whereas fir is more successful at establishing itself in the shade and on organic substrates (Knapp and Smith 1982). In areas where stands are mixed, the forest canopy is usually dominated by spruce, but most of the seedlings and saplings in the understory are fir (Peet 1988).

The Krummholz ecotone is the transition between the subalpine and alpine zones. The trees in this region are stunted and dwarfed by the harsh environmental conditions. The lower boundary of the Krummholz ecotone is called timberline, the upper elevational limit of upright, erect trees. The upper boundary of this ecotone is termed tree line, the upper limit of any tree establishment. Trees here rarely grow taller than a meter or two and are often flagged, that is, they lack branches on the windward side because of desiccation by the wind.

The Alpine Zone

The alpine zone consists of low-growth shrubs, cushion plants, small forbs, sedges, and grasses (Mutel and Emerick 1992). Trees are completely absent in this zone. The majority of the plants are perennial, and there is less species diversity than in the subalpine. Most of the shrubs are in the willow family (Thilenius 1975). The important herb families include saxifrage, pink, rose, and buckwheat (Short 1985).

GLACIAL CHRONOLOGIES

The Late Pleistocene

In the Rocky Mountains, at least three distinct periods of Pleistocene glaciation (pre–Bull Lake, Bull Lake, and Pinedale) are recognized (Madole 1976; Table 1.2). Each glaciation can be distinguished based upon moraine morphology, soil development, and surface weathering characteristics (Madole, VanSistine, and Michael 1998; Figure 1.3). The most recent episode of Pleistocene glaciation, the Pinedale, is named after terminal moraines first studied near the town of Pinedale, Wyoming (Blackwelder 1915). The term Pinedale is now widely accepted for both the time and the deposits of the last extensive glaciation in the Rocky Mountains (Benson et al. 2005).

In Colorado, both early and late glacial advances occurred during the Pinedale; however, the chronology of the earlier advance(s) is not well defined by numerical age (radiocarbon dates) determinations. All ages discussed in this chapter are given in radiocarbon years (RCYBP) unless otherwise noted. Madole and Shroba (1979) showed that early Pinedale advances were more extensive than late Pinedale advances. Porter and colleagues (1983) noted that, during the late Pinedale, glaciers were at or near their maximum extent ca. 20,000 RCYBP. Madole (1986) has suggested that the maximum extent of the late Pinedale advance occurred between ca. 23,500 and 19,000 RCYBP. Benson and colleagues (2004) also concluded that glaciers in the Front Range reached their maximum extent by ca. 22,000 RCYBP.

Madole and colleagues (1998) mapped the extent of Pinedale glaciation in the Upper Platte River Basin and found that in the Front Range the maximum length of most glaciers was between 12 and 20 km, with maximum thicknesses between 180 and 350 m. Most large glaciers in the Front Range terminated in deep valleys at elevations between 2,500 and 2,700 m. None of the Front Range glaciers reached as far east as the mountain front, terminating between 17 and 40 km west of eastern foothills and piedmont.

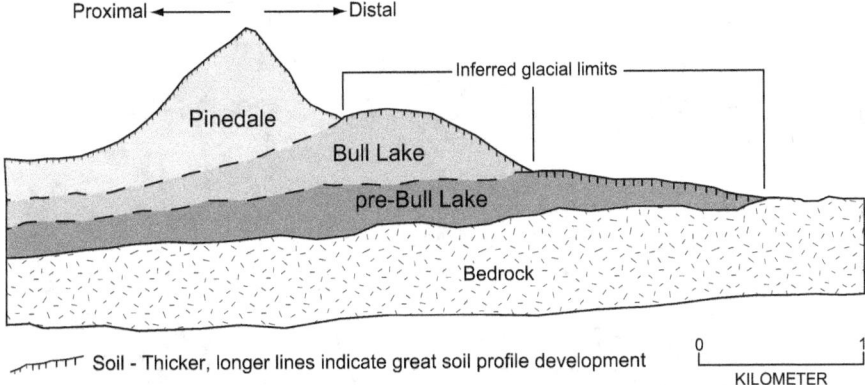

1.3. Schematic diagram showing how till of Pinedale, Bull Lake, and pre–Bull Lake glaciations differ in position, topographic expression, and degree of weathering and soil development (Madole, VanSistine, and Michael 1998).

Table 1.2. Quaternary Time Chart and Provisional Ages of Glaciations (Madole, VanSistine, and Michael 1998).

Formal Time Division	Informal Time Division		Glaciations	Age
Quaternary Period				
	Holocene Epoch			10,000
	Pleistocene Epoch			
	late Pleistocene		Pinedale	~30,000
	middle Pleistocene	late	Bull Lake	~130,000
				~300,000
		middle	pre–Bull Lake	
				~620,000
		early		
				~788,000
	early Pleistocene			
				~1,800,000

Pierce (2004) provides a comprehensive discussion of Pleistocene glaciation studies from the Rocky Mountains. Additional reviews of the glacial history of the Colorado Front Range are provided by Madole (1972, 1976, 1986), Meierding and Birkeland (1980), and Benson and colleagues (2004). Studies from the Front Range (Table 1.3; Figure 1.4) show spatial variability in the timing of Pinedale deglaciation. Madole (1980) used geologic and radiocarbon analyses of samples from sites at La Poudre Pass and near Buffalo Pass in the Park Range to suggest that the termination of Pinedale glaciation occurred by ca. 11,000 RCYBP. In a

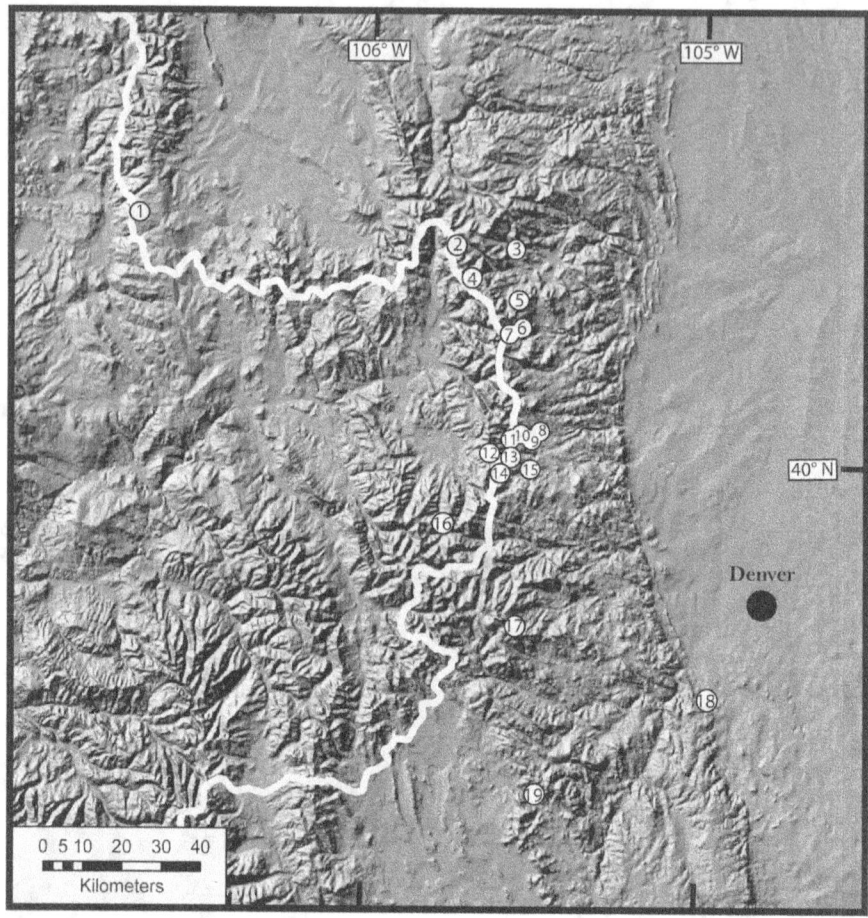

1.4. Shaded relief map of Colorado Front Range region showing locations of glacial and paleoecological sites discussed in this chapter. Circled numbers refer to sites listed in Table 1.3. Solid white line shows the Continental Divide.

study from Lake Devlin, Madole (1986) suggested deglaciation occurred sometime between ca. 15,000 and 12,000 RCYBP.

Nelson and colleagues (1979), working at the Mary Jane site (Frazier River Valley) on the west slope of the Front Range, concluded that Pinedale deglaciation began just prior to ca. 13,000 RCYBP. In the Mount Evans region, sediments from a high-altitude lake (Echo Lake) suggest deglaciation started as early as ca. 15,000 RCYBP and was completed by ca. 13,000 RCYBP (Doerner, Sullivan, and Briles 1998). Benson and colleagues (2004) concluded that Pinedale glaciers in the Front Range had disappeared from all but the highest elevations by 14,000 RCYBP.

There is also evidence for late Pleistocene glacial advances following Pinedale deglaciation and climatic warming. Benedict (1973, 1981) found evidence of ice

Table 1.3. Late Quaternary Glacial and Paleoecological Sites and References from the Colorado Front Range. Site numbers are keyed to Figure 1.4.

Site Number	Site Name	Elevation (m)	Reference(s)
1	Buffalo Pass	3,146	Madole 1980
2	La Poudre Pass	3,103	Madole 1980 Elias 1983, 1985 Short 1985
3	Lawn Lake Fen	3,357	Doerner, Brunswig, and Sanborn 2002
4	Mount Ida Pond	3,520	Elias 1983, 1985
5	Beaver Meadows	2,530	Doerner, Brunswig, and Lane 2001 Doerner 2004
6	Lock Vale	3,322	Nash 2000
7	Sky Pond	3,320	Reasoner and Jodry 2000
8	Redrock Lake	3,100	Pennak 1963 Maher 1972
9	Lefthand Reservoir	3,224	Elias 1983, 1985
10	Long Lake	3,210	Short 1985
11	Lake Isabelle Bog	3,310	Elias 1983, 1985 Short 1985
12	Caribou Lake Valley	3,410	Benedict 1973, 1981 Davis and Osborn 1987
13	Arapaho Valley (Butterfly and Triple lakes)	3,474	Benedict 1973, 1981 Davis and Osborn 1987
14	Fourth of July Valley	3,415	Benedict 1973, 1981 Davis and Osborn 1987
15	Devlin Lake	2,953	Legg and Baker 1980 Madole 1986
16	Mary Jane (Frazier River Valley)	2,882	Nelson et al. 1979 Short and Elias 1987
17	Echo Lake (Mt. Evans)	3,230	Doerner 1994 Doerner, Sullivan, and Briles 1998
18	Lamb Spring	1,713	Elias 1986, 1996a Elias and Toolin 1990
19	Lost Park Meadow	3,079	Vierling 1998

advancement in the Indian Peaks region estimated to have occurred between ca. 12,000 and 11,000 RCYBP. Locally, this advance is known as the 'Satanta Peak' advance. Menounos and Reasoner (1997) also provide evidence from Sky Pond (3,320 m) in Rocky Mountain National Park for a limited glacial advance that correlates to the 'Satanta Peak' advance. They attribute this advance to a short-term cooling associated with the Younger Dryas chronozone. This conclusion is supported by a recent geomorphic study by Nash (2000), working in the nearby Loch Vale area of Rocky Mountain National Park. He used geomorphic mapping and clast analysis to infer that glacial advances associated with the Younger Dryas chronozone in the Loch Vale area (approximately 3,322 m) were between a few meters to 0.5 km in extent.

The Holocene

Holocene glacial deposits are found in many cirques throughout Colorado (Burke and Birkeland 1983). Davis (1988) suggested that alpine areas in Colorado provide some of the best-dated and most detailed Holocene glacial chronologies in the American Cordillera. The majority of the Colorado chronologies are from northern Colorado sites whose chronologies are briefly discussed below.

Benedict (1973, 1981) reconstructed a chronology of Holocene advances for cirques in the Front Range. Working at three sites (Caribou Lake Valley, Fourth of July Valley, and Arapaho Valley) in the Indian Peaks region, Benedict found evidence of at least four intervals of glacier expansion. The first is termed the 'Ptarmigan' advance, dating to ca. 7,500 to 6,400 RCYBP. The second advance is the 'Triple Lakes,' which occurred between ca. 5,000 and 3,000 RCYBP. The 'Audubon' advance was the third expansion, which occurred between ca. 1,850 and 950 RCYBP. The most recent advance was the 'Arapaho Peak' advance, dated between ca. 350 and 150 RCYBP.

Birkeland and Shroba (1974) used relative-dating methods to suggest that the Triple Lakes advance could be as old as the Satanta Peak advance. Davis (1988) pointed out that the radiocarbon ages described by Benedict are only minimum-limiting ages. Davis and Osborn (1987) used radiocarbon dates obtained from Butterfly Lake, inside the Triple Lakes moraine, to suggest that the Triple Lakes advance in the Arapaho Valley could be equivalent in age to the Satanta Peak advance in the Caribou Lake Valley.

The most common Holocene glacial deposits occurring in the Front Range date to the "Little Ice Age" (ca. A.D. 1350–1850) period. These glacial advances reached their maximum extent by the mid-nineteenth century and have been retreating ever since (Elias 2001). Despite some of the best-dated (radiocarbon) glacial chronologies in the Rocky Mountains, the nature of Holocene glacier fluctuations in Colorado remains unresolved.

PALEOECOLOGICAL STUDIES

Environmental changes during the late Quaternary were substantial. Paleoenvironmental research is essentially an interdisciplinary endeavor, drawing from fields as diverse as archaeology, botany, climatology, geography, and geomorphology. The ultimate aim of such research is to collect and synthesize information in an effort to reconstruct the past and explain the present. In this section, results of paleoecological studies conducted in the Front Range are summarized (Table 1.3; Figure 1.4).

The Late Pleistocene

Limited information is available concerning vegetation and climate from Colorado during and subsequent to Pinedale glaciation (Pennak 1963; Maher 1972; Legg and Baker 1980; Elias 1983, 1985; Short 1985; Short and Elias 1987).

This is the case in part because of the absence of research sites (lakes and fens) with a continuous record of deposition extending from the late Pleistocene to the present. Organic-rich deposits are relatively scarce in Colorado (Elias 2001). At lower elevations, Holocene aridity has resulted in desiccation of natural lakes and wetlands. In alpine regions, organic deposits were stripped and drainages were reconfigured as glaciers advanced and retreated. Additionally, basins dammed by terminal moraines were directly influenced by upstream glaciers. Glacial ice tends to collect significant amounts of pollen over time, and as glaciers melted, pollen was released into meltwater streams and transported downstream. Lakes, which received glacial runoff, were consequently loaded with anomalously high concentrations of pollen. This effect has tended to dilute the climatic signal, and, as a result, it is frequently difficult to separate "noise" from the true signal. In addition, glacial sediments may be reintroduced into basins long after glaciers have retreated, thus complicating their stratigraphic records.

At Devlin Lake in the Indian Peaks Wilderness Area, Legg and Baker (1980) analyzed a sediment core recovered from a late-glacial–aged lake. The core contained pollen and a sequence of varved sediments with radiocarbon dates from ca. 22,400 to 12,200 RCYBP. The date of ca. 12,200 RCYBP was interpreted to be the minimum age for the retreat of glacial ice in the area. The pollen from this core was dominated by sagebrush (40–60 percent) and pine (10–25 percent). Other pollen types that were consistently present but in lesser amounts included grass (5–17 percent), goosefoot and amaranth (3–17 percent), daisy (5–10 percent), juniper (2–10 percent), and spruce (1–4 percent). The pollen data indicate that an open tundra environment prevailed during the full-glacial period. During this time, Devlin Lake was about 100 m above tree line. This implies that tree line was about 500 m lower than its present elevation during the last glacial maximum.

Elias (1986, 1996a, 1996b) and Elias and Toolin (1990) used fossil beetle assemblages to reconstruct late Pleistocene temperature parameters for the Lamb Spring site (1,713 m), located 3 km east of the mountain front on the piedmont zone just south of Denver. A beetle assemblage dated to ca. 14,500 RCYBP was found to reflect full-glacial conditions. The reconstructed mean July temperatures were estimated as 10–11°C colder than present, while reconstructed mean January temperatures were 26–30°C colder than present.

At the Mary Jane site (2,882 m), Short and Elias (1987) used fossil insects and pollen from a series of alternating lake sediments and glacial tills to reconstruct late-glacial conditions. The oldest lake sediments were dated to ca. 30,000 RCYBP (Nelson et al. 1979) and were overlain by glacial till. The next-youngest lake bed deposits yielded a radiocarbon age of ca. 13,750 RCYBP. Prior to the last Pinedale glacial advance (ca. 30,000 RCYBP), the vegetation was characterized as an open spruce-fir forest (Elias 2001). This was followed by a colder phase, in which alpine tundra replaced the subalpine forest. The existence of tundra vegetation at the site translates into a depression of upper tree line by more than 500 m. Late-glacial warming at Mary Jane appears to have begun sometime between ca. 13,800 to

12,300 RCYBP (Short and Elias 1987). Its fossil assemblages indicate that summer temperatures had risen well above full-glacial levels by this time and were only 3–4°C cooler than modern values (Elias 1996b).

In the Mt. Evans region, Doerner (1994) used pollen and sediment analysis from Echo Lake (3,230 m) to reconstruct an 18,500-year record of paleoenvironmental change. The pollen diagram from this site indicates that during the last glacial maximum, sagebrush along with other shrubs and herbs dominated the vegetation (Figure 1.5). The limited representation of tree pollen (pine 15 percent, spruce 5 percent) indicates that tundra was probably much more extensive than at present. Colder temperatures depressed tree line by at least 300 m. By ca. 14,000 RCYBP, pollen data show a subtle change in response to climatic warming. A decrease in sagebrush pollen signals the onset of deglaciation and change toward post-glacial environmental conditions. At that time, tree line was still well below the elevation of the lake, and tundra plants continued to dominate the landscape.

The climatic warming that characterized the terminal Pleistocene was interrupted by a brief but intense cool period. Reasoner and Jodry (2000) provide paleobotanical evidence from Sky Pond (3,320 m) that shows a clear and immediate response to cooling associated with the Younger Dryas chronozone (ca. 10,800 and 10,100 RCYBP). They found that tree line was displaced downward between 60 and 120 m in elevation. This change in the position of tree line resulted from a cooling of about 0.4–0.9°C in summer temperature. The Younger Dryas oscillation was expressed in the percentages and accumulation rates of both spruce and fir pollen. In addition, this oscillation was reflected in the signal from two other taxa, oak and pine, which represent regional conditions.

The Holocene

Vierling (1998) analyzed the pollen in a sediment core extracted from Lost Park (3,079 m), a dry meadow in the Tarryall Mountains. This core was divided into three pollen zones and produced a 12,000-year record of environmental change. The lowest zone (ca. 12,000 to 9,000 RCYBP) is characterized by relatively high values of spruce, pine, and sedge. The high percentages of conifer pollen indicate the presence of a spruce-pine forest in the region. Stratigraphy in this zone suggests a wetland existed in the valley bottom, and the high values of sedge pollen support this idea. Vierling concluded that during this period temperatures were cooler than present, with a winter-dominated precipitation regime. The middle zone (ca. 9,000 to 1,800 RCYBP) shows increasing percentages of pine and Chenopodiaceae-type (goosefoot family) pollen. Beginning around 9,100 RCYBP there was a shift to warmer conditions accompanied by an increase in summer (monsoonal) precipitation. There was also a general decline in sedge pollen along with a stratigraphic change from peaty to alluvial sediments. This implies an increase in fluvial activity that resulted in scour and fill of the valley floor. Pine pollen percentages peaked between ca. 7,800 and 6,000 RCYBP,

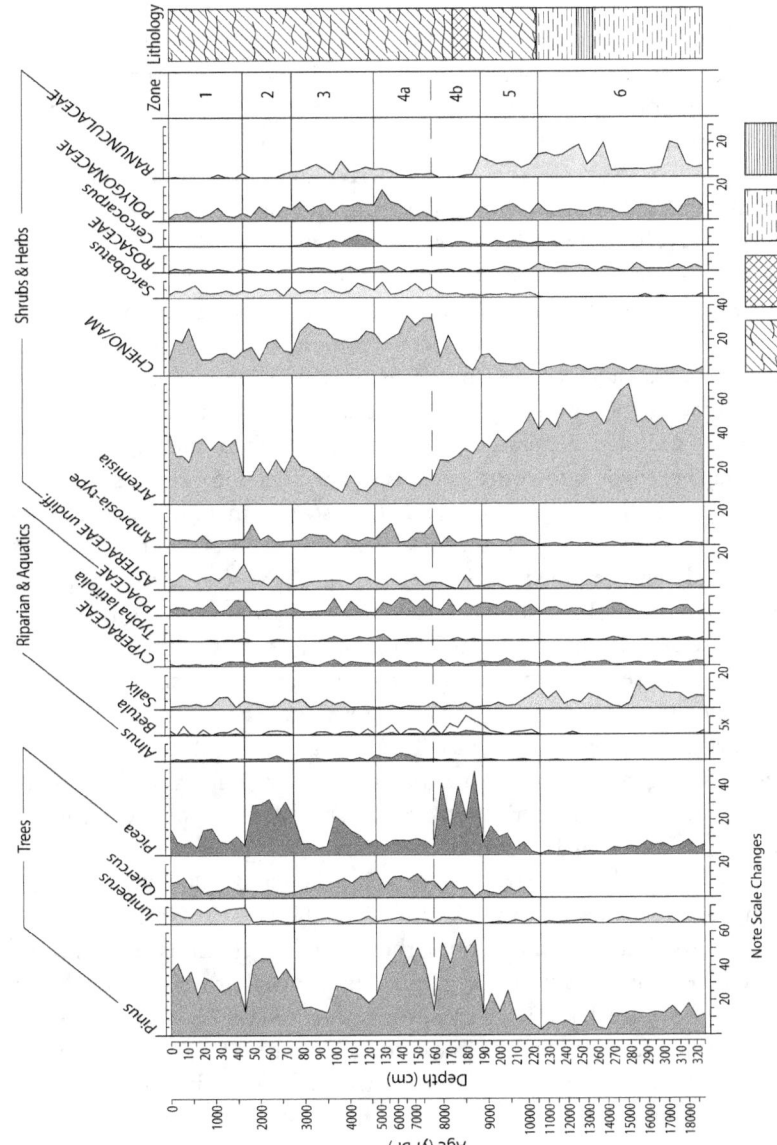

1.5. Echo Lake pollen diagram.

indicating that maximum Holocene temperatures occurred at this time. The period between ca. 6,000 and 4,000 RCYBP was characterized by drier summers, less monsoonal precipitation, and frequent occurrences of charcoal fragments in the sediment. This suggests the onset of drier summer conditions accompanied by a weakening of summer monsoonal circulation. The upper zone (ca. 1,800 RCYBP to the present) represents the establishment of modern climate conditions. Spruce becomes a more important taxon, as indicated by rising ratios of spruce to pine pollen. Sagebrush pollen percentages also increased in this zone. Sedge percentages remained low; however, the core's stratigraphy shows that peat replaced the alluvial sediments of the prior zone. Sedge percentages may be artificially low because of an increase in the percentage of spruce and sagebrush pollen. The late Holocene Period is characterized by cooler conditions.

The Echo Lake site (3,230 m) shows significant post-glacial warming had begun by about ca. 10,200 RCYBP (Doerner 1994). Warming is indicated by increases in arboreal (tree) pollen percentages with concomitant declines in non-tree pollen types, reflecting expansion of coniferous forests at the expense of tundra (Figure 1.5). Between ca. 10,200 and 9000 RCYBP, pine and spruce pollen increased as sagebrush pollen declined. Sagebrush along with plants from the goosefoot and amaranth group are shade-intolerant species, and their decline indicates a gradual reduction in the spatial extent of tundra and the establishment of an open pine-spruce forest. The increase in pine and spruce pollen suggests that tree line was near the lake but likely remained below its elevation. There were also increases in oak and mountain mahogany pollen, which indicates warmer conditions at lower elevations. These taxa do not grow at higher elevations in the Front Range; therefore, they likely represent upslope transport of pollen into the basin. The change in the pollen spectra was accompanied by a depositional change (from inorganic silty clay to organic-rich lake sediment). The increase in organic-rich sediment is interpreted as a signal of increased temperatures. As conditions became more favorable (i.e., warmer and wetter), there was greater organic productivity in the lake and on the surrounding landscape.

The Echo Lake pollen spectra between ca. 9,000 and 4,800 RCYBP suggest that the climate of this period was warmer than the present climate because pine dominates the pollen rain and non-arboreal pollen types have the lowest values in the core. The reduction of sagebrush indicates that tree line had risen to an elevation above the lake. The expansion of spruce and the decline in sagebrush suggest that warmer conditions existed at higher elevations. Maximum warming, as indicated by peaks in tree pollen (spruce and pine), occurred between ca. 9,000 and 7,800 RCYBP. After that time, conditions became slightly cooler and drier, but temperatures remained warmer than the present. Another significant change occurred between ca. 4,800 to 2,900 RCYBP and marked the onset of regional climatic cooling. Pine pollen dropped sharply in this zone, and spruce percentages showed an initial increase, followed by a significant decline. Chenopodiaceae-type percentages remained high (about 20 percent), and cattail

Table 1.4. Echo Lake Vegetation and Climate History.

Pollen Zone	Age Range (RCYBP)	Vegetation	Inferred Climate
1	ca. 1,600 to present	Modern forest (pine and spruce decrease, sagebrush and juniper increase)	Cool and dry
2	ca. 3,000 to 1,600	Forest expansion/higher tree line (pine and spruce increase)	Warm
3	ca. 4,800 to 3,000	Forest thinning (oak and sagebrush increase)	Cool
4a	ca. 7,800 to 4,800	Open pine forest (pine increases, spruce declines)	Warm and dry
4b	ca. 9,000 to 7,800	Tree line expansion (spruce increases)	Maximum warming
5	ca. 10,200 to 9,000	Establishment of subalpine forest	Cool and moist (with increasing temperatures)
6	ca. 18,500 to 10,200	Tundra (sagebrush dominated)	Cold and dry

pollen peaked. Increases in pollen from these taxa suggest dry conditions, fluctuations in lake levels, or both. There were also increases in sagebrush pollen along with pollen from plants in the buckwheat, buttercup, and rose families. Increases in pollen from these plants suggest cooler conditions and the lowering of tree line, the thinning of the forest, or both. Pollen from oak and mountain mahogany also increased at this time. These taxa are not local, and their expansion probably represents a change to more favorable environmental conditions in the foothills to the east of the site.

Climatic warming occurred between ca. 2,900 to 1,500 RCYBP, as the percentages and absolute influx rates of pine and spruce rise rapidly. Sagebrush pollen declines slightly, as does the pollen from the buckwheat, buttercup, and rose families. The decline in these taxa implies either forest expansion or higher tree line. During the last 1,500 RCYBP, the pollen spectra indicate a general cooling trend. Pine and spruce frequencies decline while sagebrush pollen increases. This indicates cooler or drier conditions and the possible retreat (lowering) of tree line to its modern position. Juniper pollen achieves maximum representation during this time. This period represents the establishment of modern conditions for the Mt. Evans region. Table 1.4 summarizes the vegetation and climatic changes reconstructed from the Echo Lake site.

Pennak (1963) analyzed pollen from four sites in the Front Range, ranging in elevation from 2,617 to 3,247 m. Two of the sites were mountain lakes and two were dry meadows. The most complete pollen data were recovered from Redrock Lake (3,100 m), which yielded a 7,000-year record of environmental change. Because results from all four sites are consistent, only the Redrock Lake record is discussed here. The pollen assemblage recovered from this site is relatively simple, with pine, spruce, sagebrush, and grass usually accounting for more than 90 percent of all pollen grains. An open mesic (moist) forest surrounded the lake at ca. 7,000 RCYBP. Five hundred years later there was a dry boreal interval in which climatic conditions were considerably drier than at present. This interval was quickly replaced by a sharply defined warm, dry period that extended from ca. 6,000 to 3,000 RCYBP. Pennak interprets this period as the post-glacial interval, also known as the *Altithermal* (Antevs 1948). This period is notable for the dominance of grasses (35–40 percent), fewer pines (30 percent), and only about 10 percent spruce. Modern vegetation cover became established about 3,000 RCYBP and has remained essentially unchanged.

Maher (1972) reanalyzed the Redrock Lake site and was able to extend the Holocene record back to ca. 9,500 RCYBP. Maher's analysis suggests that between ca. 10,000 and 7,600 RCYBP, the climate was cooler, wetter, or both than the present, with tree line about 150 m lower. From ca. 7,600 to 6,700 RCYBP, both climate and the location of tree line were similar to present conditions. During the period from ca. 6,700 to 3,000 RCYBP, tree line was lower and the climate was cooler, wetter, or both than the present. Establishment of the modern vegetation cover and climate occurred at about 3,000 RCYBP.

Elias (1983, 1985) used fossil insect evidence from La Poudre Pass Bog (3,103 m), Lefthand Reservoir (3,224 m), Lake Isabelle Bog (3,310 m), and Mount Ida Pond (3,520 m) to establish a chronology of Holocene environmental change. Elias found that summer temperatures were warmer than the present during the early Holocene. Maximum ratios of forest-tundra taxa suggest that Holocene temperatures peaked between ca. 9,000 and 7,000 RCYBP. The climate remained warmer than the present until 4,500 RCYBP. At that time, the macrofossil records suggest cooling that lasted from 4,500 to 3,100 RCYBP. The climate warmed from ca. 3,000 to 2,000 RCYBP, followed by a general cooling trend that extends to the present.

Short (1985) analyzed the fossil pollen from three sites in the northern Front Range to test Maher's (1972) climatic reconstruction. Her sites included La Poudre Pass Bog (3,103 m), Lake Isabelle Bog (3,310 m), and Long Lake (3,210 m). The climatic signal from these three sites is consistent. Short interprets the period from ca. 12,000 to 10,500 RCYBP as a tundra environment dominated by sagebrush and grasses, with some birch and willow. Spruce and fir arrived by ca. 10,500 RCYBP at Long Lake and were present at La Poudre Pass by ca. 9,800 RCYBP, when peat accumulation started. Despite the presence of trees in the region, tundra vegetation was still dominant until ca. 9,000 RCYBP. From ca. 9,000 to 6,500 RCYBP, a spruce-fir forest replaced the tundra vegetation, and the climate was similar to or warmer than the present. At Lake Isabella Bog the climate was suitable for the initiation of peat growth and accumulation between ca. 8,000 and 7,000 RCYBP. Short suggests that an increase of lodgepole pine during this period indicates warmer temperatures. Maximum upward extension of the tree line and maximum temperatures for the region occurred between ca. 6,500 and 3,500 RCYBP, when pine achieved its maximum representation. After ca. 3,500 RCYBP, there was a decrease in arboreal pollen representation and an increase in shrub and herb pollen (especially sagebrush and grass). This suggests that tree line was either lowered slightly or that forests thinned and that the decrease in pine may have resulted from a climatic cooling. Modern vegetation distributions were established sometime after ca. 3,500 RCYBP.

Paleoecological studies from Rocky Mountain National Park also provide evidence of Holocene environmental change (Doerner, Brunswig, and Lane 2001; Doerner, Brunswig, and Sanborn 2002). These pollen studies are in broad agreement. The middle Holocene Period (ca. 7,400 to 5,400 RCYBP) was characterized by warm and possibly dry conditions as compared to the present day. At higher elevations (Lawn Lake Fen, 3,357 m), warmer summers and longer growing seasons resulted in rapid peat growth. At lower elevations (Beaver Meadows, 2,530 m), increased temperatures and lower effective precipitation led to the disappearance of wetlands from valley bottoms. After ca. 5,400 RCYBP, regional climate change brought cooler conditions to the area. Modern vegetation associations and climate conditions were likely established by ca. 1,800 RCYBP. Tree-ring studies from the park show that tree invasion and establishment at upper tree line (about 3,414–3,511 m) are likely related to the development of favorable climatic conditions (warmer and wetter) since the end of the "Little Ice Age" (ca. A.D. 1850) (Hessl and Baker 1997a, 1997b; Hessl, Baker, and Weisberg 1996).

Maher's early and middle Holocene reconstruction contrasts with other paleoecological records from the region. An alternative interpretation is offered by Nichols (1982), who notes that a peak in the absolute influx of spruce pollen occurred at 8,500 RCYBP in the Redrock Lake core. High spruce values at this time are also reported at other sites in Colorado (Andrews et al. 1975; Peterson and Mehringer 1976; Short 1985; Doerner 1994). Temperatures during this period are interpreted as warmer than the present. Nichols remarked that spruce values in the Redrock Lake core fluctuated during the middle Holocene until a marked decline occurred between 4,000 and 3,000 RCYBP. This suggests that cooler conditions were established at that time. If one accepts Nichols's reinterpretation of Maher's data, then the Redrock Lake record is in agreement with other Front Range reconstructions.

DISCUSSION

The Late Pleistocene

The late-glacial paleoecological records from the Front Range reflect high sagebrush pollen with moderate values of pine, grass, and other herb taxa. These records are in general agreement with many of the pollen records from the western United States, which are characterized by high frequencies of non-arboreal pollen taxa, including sagebrush, juniper, and grass (Beiswenger 1991; Davis and Pitblado 1995; Doerner and Carrara 2001; Fall, Davis, and Zielinski 1995; Mehringer 1985; Whitlock 1993). The vegetation reconstructions for this period indicate that an open tundra environment existed throughout the Front Range

(Legg and Baker 1980; Short and Elias 1987; Doerner 1994). Elias (1995) suggests this vegetation likely developed under cold, dry conditions similar to the climate found in parts of northern Siberia today.

Paleotemperature reconstructions developed from fossil beetle assemblages suggest that during the full glacial (ca. 14,500 RCYBP), mean July temperatures were as much as 10–11°C colder and mean January temperatures were depressed by 26–29°C compared with modern parameters (Elias 2001). Temperatures were cold enough to support the growth of glacial ice, but there was likely insufficient winter precipitation to allow for glacier expansion. Colder summer temperatures depressed the upper tree line by as much as 300 m below present-day limits on Mt. Evans (Doerner 1994). At the Devlin Lake and Mary Jane sites, upper tree line was depressed by 500 m below modern limits.

While complete agreement is lacking, it appears deglaciation in the Front Range began between ca. 15,000 and 12,000 RCYBP (Nelson et al. 1979; Legg and Baker 1980; Short 1985; Madole 1986). The transition from full-glacial conditions to warmer post-glacial conditions began sometime after ca. 14,000 RCYBP. Fossil insect assemblages from the Mary Jane site indicate that summer temperatures had risen well above full-glacial levels by ca. 13,000 and were only 3–4°C cooler than modern values (Short and Elias 1987; Elias 1996b). Pollen data from several sites indicate that vegetation was responding to climatic warming, but tundra plants still dominated the landscape (Short 1985; Doerner 1994).

Post-glacial warming that began after ca. 14,000 RCYBP was interrupted by a dramatic but short-term period of renewed glaciation and cooling soon after 11,000 BP (Benedict 1973, 1981; Birkeland and Shroba 1974; Davis and Osborn 1987; Menounos and Reasoner 1997; Nash 2000; Reasoner and Jodry 2000). This climatic oscillation is associated with the Younger Dryas chronozone, a pronounced 1,000-year cool period beginning about 11,000 radiocarbon years ago. Termination of this event appears to have resulted in rapid warming and the appearance of essentially modern-equivalent climatic conditions associated with the Holocene.

The Holocene

During the Holocene, Colorado experienced a series of climatic fluctuations. Strong evidence suggests the time interval from 10,000 to 8,000 BP was the warmest period of the Holocene. Research from numerous sites in western North America supports this premise (e.g., Kearney and Luckman 1983; Ritchie, Cwynar, and Spear 1983; Hebda and Mathewes 1984; Davis, Sheppard, and Robertson 1986; Carrara, Trimble, and Rubin 1991; Doerner and Carrara 1999). This period has been named the "early Holocene Xerothermic" (Hebda and Mathewes 1984). A possible explanation for the early Holocene thermal maximum is provided by Kutzbach (1983). From about 10,000 to 9,000 BP, orbital variations produced a solar radiation maximum during the Northern Hemisphere summer. Kutzbach (1983: 274) states that "about 9000 RCYBP, obliquity was 24.23° (compared to 23.45°

at present), perihelion was in Northern Hemisphere summer (July 30 compared to January 3 at present), and eccentricity was 0.0193 (compared to 0.0167 at present). These factors combined to produce increased solar radiation for July and decreased radiation for January."

July insolation was more than 8 percent higher than today, resulting in temperatures in the interior of North America 2–3°C higher than at present (Kutzbach and Guetter 1984, 1986). This greater summer radiation increased temperatures and decreased effective moisture, producing vegetation assemblages more xerothermic than those of present-day environments (Barnosky 1989). Trees responded to this warming by migrating upslope to higher elevations. By ca. 9,000, subalpine forests were well established throughout the Front Range, and tree line reached up to and perhaps beyond modern-day limits.

The period from ca. 8,000 to 4,500 RCYBP was warm, with possibly dry summers; however, this period was not as warm as the early Holocene. This contradicts the traditional view that the middle Holocene (ca. 7,000 to 4,000 RCYBP) was the warmest period of the Holocene. Drier summer conditions during the middle Holocene are indicated by changes in pollen assemblages and meadow stratigraphy. Lower-elevation sites in the Front Range (i.e., Lost Park Meadow [Vierling 1998], Beaver Meadows [Doerner 2004; Doerner, Brunswig, and Lane 2001], and Doolittle Ranch [Doerner 1994]) contain stratigraphic sequences in which peaty sediments overlie alluvial sediments. This suggests that scour and fill was occurring on the valley floors, as summer moisture levels were not high enough to support wet meadows. Less effective precipitation (e.g., greater evaporation rates) at lower elevations could account for the disappearance of the wet meadows.

Warmer-than-modern conditions prevailed in the Front Range until the late Holocene (ca. 4,800–4,500 RCYBP), when regional climate change brought cooler conditions to the area. The regional pollen signal shows a decrease in tree pollen and an increase in shrub and herb pollen (especially sagebrush and grasses). This suggests that either tree line lowered or forests thinned in response to colder summer temperatures. Echo Lake pollen data indicate that this cooler interval lasted from ca. 4,800 to 2,900 RCYBP; however, fossil beetle data suggest the cooling occurred between ca. 4,500 and 3,100 RCYBP. This timing difference may be a result of the interpolation of radiocarbon ages between well-dated intervals in the cores or of differences in response times to environmental change between plants and insects. This cold period was interrupted by a warm interval that lasted between 1,000 and 1,400 years (pollen data, ca. 2,900 to 1,500 RCYBP; fossil beetles, ca. 3,000 to 2,000 RCYBP). Cooler conditions again returned to the Front Range sometime between ca. 2,000 and 1,500 RCYBP, as modern conditions were likely established. The most recent millennium is characterized by warmer than modern ("Medieval" warming), to cooler than modern ("Little Ice Age" cooling), and back to warmer temperatures. Most of the proxy data regarding these most recent climatic reversals is derived from fossil insect assemblages,

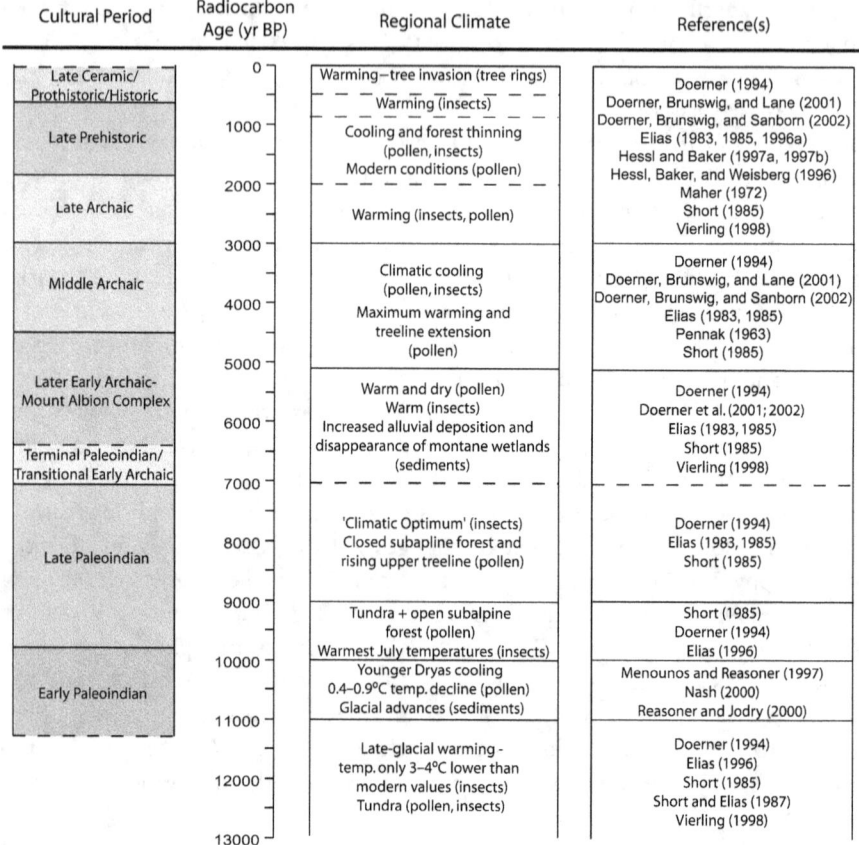

1.6. *Correlation of cultural-chronological periods with paleoenvironmental reconstructions from the Colorado Front Range.*

glacial reconstructions, and tree-ring studies, as the pollen records from the Front Range have generally been insensitive to these short-term fluctuations.

CONCLUSION

From this review of paleoenvironmental studies of the Colorado Front Range, it is clear that substantial changes in climate and vegetation occurred during the late Quaternary. Figure 1.6 provides a summary of paleoenvironmental conditions from the terminal Pleistocene to Historic times correlated with cultural-chronological periods for the Front Range region.

During the late Pleistocene, climate in the Front Range was cold and dry, and vegetation was dominated by tundra. Global cooling associated with full-glacial times gave way to warming between ca. 14,000–11,000 years ago, when glaciers in Colorado began to melt and retreat. This warming was interrupted by a brief but intense cool period known as the Younger Dryas. This nearly 1,000-year event displaced tree line downward between 60 and 120 m and allowed cirque glaciers to re-advance. Post-glacial warming resumed by ca. 10,000 RCYBP, and vegetation responded by advancing upslope. About 9,000 years ago, warming intensified in response to increases in summer insolation. By ca. 8,000 years ago, warmer conditions were well entrenched in the region, with cycles of intense to more moderate warming and aridity, nearly always warmer and drier than the present. Eventually, by the late Holocene (ca. 4,500 years ago), broadly modern climatic parameters were established, although several less intense cycles of cooling ("neo-glaciations") and warming are known to have existed at various times throughout this period. The most recent cold phase was that of the so-called Little Ice Age that began in the fourteenth century A.D. and only ended in the mid-nineteenth century A.D., with increasingly warm conditions of the modern era.

REFERENCES CITED

Alexander, R. R.
    1974   Silviculture of Subalpine Forests in the Southern Rocky Mountains: The Status of Our Knowledge. *United States Forest Service Research Paper* RM-121, Fort Collins, CO.

Andrews, J. T., P. E. Carrara, F. B. King, and R. Struckenrath
    1975   Holocene Environmental Changes in the Alpine Zone, Northern San Juan Mountains, Colorado: Evidence from Bog Stratigraphy and Palynology. *Quaternary Research* 5:173–197.

Antevs, E. V.
    1948   The Great Basin, with Emphasis on Glacial and Postglacial Times. *University of Utah Bulletin* 38:168–191.

Arno, S. F., and R. P. Hammerly
    1984   *Timberline: Mountain and Arctic Forest Frontiers*. The Mountaineers, Seattle.

Baker, R. G.
    1983   Holocene Vegetational History of the Western United States. In *Late-Quaternary Environments of the United States, vol. 2, the Holocene*, ed. H. E. Wright Jr., 109–127. University of Minnesota Press, Minneapolis.

Barnosky, C. W.
    1989   Postglacial Vegetation and Climate in the Northwestern Great Plains of Montana. *Quaternary Research* 31:57–73.

Barry, R. G.
    1972   *Climatic Environment of the East Slope of the Colorado Front Range*. Institute of Arctic and Alpine Research, University of Colorado, Boulder, Occasional Paper 3.
    1973   A Climatological Transect on the East Slope of the Front Range, Colorado. *Arctic and Alpine Research* 5:89–110.
    1981   *Mountain Weather and Climate*. Methuen, London.

Beiswenger, J. M.
1991   Late Quaternary Vegetational History of Grays Lake, Idaho. *Ecological Monographs* 61:165–182.

Benedict, J. B.
1973   Chronology of Cirque Glaciation, Colorado Front Range. *Quaternary Research* 3:584–599.
1981   *The Fourth of July Valley: Glacial Geology and Archeology of the Timberline Ecotone.* Center for Mountain Archeology Research Report 2, Ward, CO.

Benson, L. V., R. Madole, G. Landis, and J. Gosse
2005   New Data for Late Pleistocene Pinedale Alpine Glaciation from Southwestern Colorado. *Quaternary Science Reviews* 24:49–65.

Benson, L. V., R. Madole, W. Phillips, G. Landis, T. Thomas, and P. Kubik
2004   The Probable Importance of Snow and Sediment Shielding on Cosmogenic Ages of North-Central Colorado Pinedale and Pre-Pinedale Moraines. *Quaternary Science Reviews* 23:193–206.

Birkeland, P. W., and R. R. Shroba
1974   The Status of the Concept of Quaternary Soil-Forming Intervals in the Western United States. In *Quaternary Environments: Proceedings of a Symposium*, ed. W. C. Mahaney, 241–276. Geographical Monographs 5. York University–Atkinson College, Toronto.

Blackwelder, E.
1915   Post-Cretaceous History of the Mountains of Central Western Wyoming. *Journal of Geology* 23:307–340.

Burke, R. M., and P. W. Birkeland
1983   Holocene Glaciation in the Mountain Ranges of the Western United States. In *Late-Quaternary Environments of the United States, vol. 2, the Holocene,* ed. H. E. Wright Jr., 3–11. University of Minnesota Press, Minneapolis.

Carrara, P. E., D. A. Trimble, and M. Rubin
1991   Holocene Treeline Fluctuations in the Northern San Juan Mountains, Colorado, U.S.A., as Indicated by Radiocarbon-Dated Conifer Wood. *Arctic and Alpine Research* 23:233–246.

Davis, O. K., and B. L. Pitblado
1995   Late Glacial Aridity in the Southern Rocky Mountains. In *Climate Change in the Four Corners and Adjacent Regions: Implications for Environmental Restoration and Land-Use Planning*, ed. W. J. Waugh, K. L. Petersen, P. E. Wigand, B. D. Louthan, and R. D. Walker, 9–23. U.S. Department of Energy, CONF-9409325. National Technical Information Service, Springfield, VA.

Davis, O. K., J. C. Sheppard, and S. Robertson
1986   Contrasting Climatic Histories for the Snake River Plain, Idaho, Resulting from Multiple Thermal Maxima. *Quaternary Research* 26:321–339.

Davis, P. T.
1988   Holocene Glacier Fluctuations in the American Cordillera. *Quaternary Science Reviews* 7:129–157.

Davis, P. T., and G. Osborn
　1987　Age of Pre-Neoglacial Cirque Moraines in the Central North American Cordillera. *Géographie Physique et Quaternaire* 41 (3):365–375.

Doerner, J. P.
　1994　*The Late-Quaternary Environmental History of Mt. Evans: Pollen and Stratigraphic Evidence from Clear Creek, Colorado.* Unpublished Ph.D. dissertation, University of Denver.
　2004　Paleoenvironmental Interpretation of Holocene Records from Rocky Mountain National Park. In *Ancient and Historic Lifeways in North America's Rocky Mountains: Proceedings of the 2003 Rocky Mountain Anthropological Conference, Estes Park, Colorado*, ed. R. H. Brunswig and W. B. Butler, 168–177. University of Northern Colorado, Department of Anthropology, Greeley.

Doerner, J. P., R. H. Brunswig, and C. Lane
　2001　Holocene Climate and Vegetation Change in Rocky Mountain National Park. *2001 Abstract Volume*, Association of American Geographers 97th Annual Meeting, New York, NY.

Doerner, J. P., R. H. Brunswig, and W. Sanborn
　2002　Vegetation and Climate Change in Rocky Mountain National Park: Pollen Evidence from Lawn Lake Fen. *2002 Abstract Volume*, Association of American Geographers 98th Annual Meeting, Los Angeles, CA.

Doerner, J. P., and P. E. Carrara
　1999　Deglaciation and Postglacial Vegetative History of the West Mountains, West-Central Idaho. *Arctic, Antarctic, and Alpine Research* 31 (3):303–311.
　2001　Late Quaternary Vegetation and Climatic History of the Long Valley Area, West-Central Idaho, U.S.A. *Quaternary Research* 56 (1):103–111.

Doerner, J. P., D. G. Sullivan, and C. Briles
　1998　Late Quaternary Eolian Deposition in Colorado Subalpine Lakes. In *Dust Aerosols, Loess Soils and Global Change*, ed. A. J. Busacca, 135–138. Washington State University College of Agriculture and Home Economics, Miscellaneous Publication MISC0190, Pullman.

Elias, S. A.
　1983　Paleoenvironmental Interpretations of Holocene Insect Fossil Assemblages from the La Poudre Pass Site, Northern Colorado Front Range. *Paleogeography, Paleoclimatology, Paleoecology* 41:87–102.
　1985　Paleoenvironmental Interpretations of Holocene Insect Fossil Assemblages from Four High Altitude Sites in the Colorado Front Range, U.S.A. *Arctic and Alpine Research* 17:31–48.
　1986　Late Pleistocene and Holocene Seasonal Temperatures Reconstructed from Fossil Beetle Assemblages in the Rocky Mountains. *Quaternary Research* 36: 311–318.
　1988　Late Pleistocene Paleoenvironmental Studies from the Rocky Mountain Region: A Comparison of Pollen and Insect Fossil Records. *Geoarchaeology* 3 (2):147–153.
　1995　*Ice Age History of Alaskan National Parks.* Smithsonian Institution Press, Washington, DC.

1996a   Fossil Insect Evidence for Late Pleistocene Paleoenvironments of the Lamb Spring Site, Colorado. *Geoarchaeology* 1 (4):381–387.

1996b   Late Pleistocene and Holocene Seasonal Temperatures Reconstructed from Fossil Beetle Assemblages in the Rocky Mountains. *Quaternary Research* 46:311–318.

2001   Paleoecology and Late Quaternary Environments of the Colorado Rockies. In *Structure and Form of an Alpine Ecosystem: Niwot Ridge, Colorado*, ed. W. D. Bowman and T. R. Seastedt, 285–303. Oxford University Press, New York.

Elias, S. A., and L. J. Toolin

1990   Accelerator Dating of a Mixed Assemblage of Late Pleistocene Insect Fossils from the Lamb Spring Site, Colorado. *Quaternary Research* 33:122–126.

Fall, P. L., P. T. Davis, and G. A. Zielinski

1995   Quaternary Vegetation and Climate of the Wind River Range, Wyoming. *Quaternary Research* 43:393–404.

Griffiths, M., and L. Rubright

1983   *Colorado*. Westview, Boulder.

Hebda, R. J., and R. W. Mathewes

1984   Holocene History of Cedar and Native Indian Cultures of the North American Pacific Coast. *Science* 225:711–713.

Hessl, A. E., and W. L. Baker

1997a   Spruce-Fir Growth Form Changes in the Forest-Tundra Ecotone of Rocky Mountain National Park, Colorado, U.S.A. *Ecography* 20:356–367.

1997b   Spruce and Fir Regeneration and Climate in the Forest-Tundra Ecotone of Rocky Mountain National Park, Colorado, U.S.A. *Arctic and Alpine Research* 29:173–183.

Hessl, A. E., W. L. Baker, and P. J. Weisberg

1996   Spatial Variability of Radial Growth in the Forest-Tundra Ecotone of Rocky Mountain National Park, Colorado. *Bulletin of the Torrey Botanical Club* 123:206–212.

Holloway, R. G., and V. M. Bryant Jr.

1985   Introduction. In *Pollen Records of Late-Quaternary North American Sediments*, ed. V. M. Bryant Jr. and R. G. Holloway, xi–xii. American Association of Stratigraphic Palynologist Foundation, Dallas, TX.

Hunt, C. B.

1967   *Natural Regions of the United States and Canada*. W. H. Freeman, San Francisco.

Kearney, M. S., and B. H. Luckman

1983   Holocene Timberline Fluctuations in Jasper National Park, Alberta. *Science* 221:261–263.

Knapp, A. K., and W. K. Smith

1982   Factors Influencing Understory Seeding Establishment of Engelmann Spruce (*Picea engelmannii*) and Subalpine Fir (*Abies lasiocarpa*) in Southeast Wyoming. *Canadian Journal of Botany* 60:2753–2761.

Kutzbach, J. E.
  1983 Modeling of Holocene Climates. In *Late-Quaternary Environments of the United States, vol. 2, the Holocene*, ed. H. E. Wright Jr., 271–277. University of Minnesota Press, Minneapolis.

Kutzbach, J. E., and P. J. Guetter
  1984 The Sensitivity of Monsoon Climates to Orbital Parameter Changes for 9,000 Years BP: Experiments with the NCAR General Circulation Model. In *Milankovitch and Climate, Part 2*, ed. A. J. Berger, J. Imbrie, J. Hays, G. Kukla, and B. Saltzman, 801–820. Reidel, Boston.
  1986 The Influence of Changing Orbital Parameters and Surface Boundary Conditions on Climate Simulations for the Past 18,000 Years. *Journal of the Atmospheric Sciences* 43:1726–1759.

Legg, T. W., and R. G. Baker
  1980 Palynology of Pinedale Sediments, Devlins Park, Boulder County, Colorado. *Arctic and Alpine Research* 12:319–333.

Madole, R. F.
  1972 Neoglacial Facies in the Colorado Front Range. *Arctic and Alpine Research* 4: 119–130.
  1976 Glacial Geology of the Colorado Front Range. In *Quaternary Stratigraphy of North America*, ed. W. C. Mahaney, 297–318. Dowden, Hutchinson and Ross, Stroudsburg, PA.
  1980 Time of Pinedale Deglaciation in North-Central Colorado: Further Considerations. *Geology* 8:118–122.
  1986 Lake Devlin and the Pinedale Glacial History of the Colorado Front Range. *Quaternary Research* 25:43–54.

Madole, R. F., and R. R. Shroba
  1979 Till Sequences and Soil Development in the North St. Vrain Drainage Basin, East Slope, Front Range, Colorado. In *Guidebook for Post-Meeting Field Trips Held in Conjunction with the 32nd Annual Meeting of the Rocky Mountain Section of the Geological Society of America, May 26–27, 1979*, ed. F. G. Ethridge, 123–178. Geological Society of America, Colorado State University, Fort Collins.

Madole, R. F., D. P. VanSistine, and J. A. Michael
  1998 Pleistocene Glaciation in the Upper Platte River Drainage Basin, Colorado. *United States Geological Survey, Geological Investigations Series* I-2644, Denver.

Maher, L. J., Jr.
  1972 Absolute Pollen Diagram of Redrock Lake, Boulder County, Colorado. *Quaternary Research* 2:531–553.

Marr, J. W.
  1967 *Ecosystems of the East Slope of the Front Range in Colorado*. University of Colorado Studies, Biology 8, Boulder.

Mehringer, P. J., Jr.
  1985 Late-Quaternary Pollen Records from the Interior Pacific Northwest and Northern Great Basin of the United States. In *Pollen Records of Late-Quaternary North American Sediments*, ed. V. M. Bryant Jr. and R. G. Holloway, 167–189. American Association of Stratigraphic Palynologist Foundation, Dallas.

Meierding, T. C., and P. W. Birkeland
    1980   Quaternary Glaciation of Colorado. In *Colorado Geology*, ed. H. C. Kent and K. W. Porter, 165–173. Rocky Mountain Association of Geologists, Denver.

Menounos, B., and M. A. Reasoner
    1997   Evidence for Cirque Glaciation in the Colorado Front Range during the Younger Dryas Chronozone. *Quaternary Research* 48:38–47.

Mutel, C. F., and J. C. Emerick
    1992   *From Grassland to Glacier*. Johnson Books, Boulder.

Nash, G. R.
    2000   The Younger Dryas Climate Oscillation and Its Impact on Glacial Margins in the Rocky Mountain National Park, Colorado, USA. Unpublished undergraduate dissertation, University of Edinburgh, Edinburgh.

Nelson, A. R., A. C. Millington, J. T. Andrews, and H. Nichols
    1979   Radiocarbon-Dated Upper Pleistocene Glacial Sequence, Fraser Valley, Colorado Front Range. *Geology* 7:410–414.

Nichols, H.
    1982   Review of Late Quaternary History of Vegetation and Climate in the Mountains of Colorado. In *Ecological Studies in the Colorado Alpine: A Festschrift for John W. Marr*, ed. J. C. Halfpenny, 27–33. Institute of Arctic and Alpine Research Occasional Paper 37, Boulder.

Peet, R. K.
    1978   Latitudinal Variations in Southern Rocky Mountain Forests. *Journal of Biogeography* 5:275–289.
    1981   Forest Vegetation of the Colorado Front Range: Composition and Dynamics. *Vegetation* 45:3–75.
    1988   Forests of the Rocky Mountains. In *North American Terrestrial Vegetation*, ed. M. G. Barbour and W. D. Billings, 63–102. Cambridge University Press, New York.

Pennak, R. W.
    1963   Ecological and Radiocarbon Correlations in Some Colorado Mountain Lake and Bog Deposits. *Ecology* 44:1–15.

Peterson, K. L., and P. J. Mehringer Jr.
    1976   Postglacial Timberline Fluctuations, La Plata Mountains, Southwestern Colorado. *Arctic and Alpine Research* 8:275–288.

Pierce, K. L.
    2004   Pleistocene Glaciation of the Rocky Mountains. In *The Quaternary Period in the United States*, ed. A. R. Gillespie, S. C. Porter, and B. F. Atwater, 63–76. Elsevier, Amsterdam.

Porter, S. C.
    1983   Introduction. In *Late-Quaternary Environments of the United States, vol. 1, the Late Pleistocene*, ed. S. C. Porter, xi–xiv. University of Minnesota Press, Minneapolis.

Porter, S. C., K. L. Pierce, and T. D. Hamilton
　1983　Late Wisconsin Mountain Glaciation in the Western United States. In *Late-Quaternary Environments of the United States, vol. 1, the Late Pleistocene*, ed. S. C. Porter, 71–111. University of Minnesota Press, Minneapolis.

Reasoner, M. A., and M. A. Jodry
　2000　Rapid Response of Alpine Timberline Vegetation to the Younger Dryas Climate Oscillation in the Colorado Rocky Mountains, USA. *Geology* 28:51–54.

Rink, L. P., and G. N. Kiladis
　1986　Geology, Hydrology, Climate, and Soils of the Rocky Mountains. An Ecological Characterization of Rocky Mountain Montane and Subalpine Wetlands. *United States Fish and Wildlife Service, Biological Report* 86 (11):42–65.

Ritchie, J. C., L. C. Cwynar, and R. W. Spear
　1983　Evidence from Northwest Canada for an Early Holocene Milankovitch Thermal Maximum. *Nature* 305:126–128.

Short, S. K.
　1985　Palynology of Holocene Sediments, Colorado Front Range: Vegetational and Treeline Changes in the Subalpine Forest. *American Association of Stratigraphic Palynologist Contribution Series* 16:7–30.

Short, S. K., and S. A. Elias
　1987　New Pollen and Beetle Analyses at the Mary Jane Site, Colorado: Evidence for Late Glacial Tundra Conditions. *Geological Society of America Bulletin* 98:540–548.

Thilenius, J. F.
　1975　Alpine Range Management in the Western United States—Principles, Practice, and Problems: The Status of Our Knowledge. *United States Forest Service Research Paper* RM-157, Fort Collins, CO.

Veblen, T. T., and D. C. Lorenz
　1986　Anthropogenic Disturbance and Recovery Patterns in Montane Forests, Colorado Front Range. *Physical Geography* 7:1–24.
　1991　*The Colorado Front Range—A Century of Ecological Change*. University of Utah Press, Salt Lake City.

Vierling, L. E.
　1998　Palynological Evidence for Late- and Post-Glacial Environmental Change in Central Colorado. *Quaternary Research* 49:222–232.

Whitlock, C.
　1993　Postglacial Vegetation and Climate of Grand Teton and Southern Yellowstone National Parks. *Ecological Monographs* 63:173–198.

Windell, J. T., B. E. Willard, and S. Q. Foster
　1986　Introduction to Rocky Mountain Wetlands. An Ecological Characterization of Rocky Mountain Montane and Subalpine Wetlands. *United States Fish and Wildlife Service, Biological Report* 86 (11):1–41.

Wright, H. E., Jr.
   1983   Introduction. In *Late-Quaternary Environments of the United States, vol. 2, the Holocene*, ed. H. E. Wright Jr., xi–xvii. University of Minnesota Press, Minneapolis.

CHAPTER TWO

Bonnie L. Pitblado and Robert H. Brunswig

That Was Then, This Is Now

SEVENTY-FIVE YEARS OF PALEOINDIAN RESEARCH IN COLORADO

The origins of Colorado's Paleoindian studies are virtually synonymous with the foundations of Paleoindian archaeology in the United States. In fact, two of the state's earliest, albeit poorly and incompletely reported, discoveries, the Dent Clovis and Lindenmeier Folsom sites (1924–1931), pre-date discoveries and early investigations of their respective cultures' type-sites: New Mexico's (Blackwater Draw) Clovis and Folsom sites. As we explain later, "Clovis" culture should have, on the basis of historical precedent, been known as the "Dent" culture.

Certainly, when myriad archaeologists and artifact hunters took to the field in Colorado in the early twentieth century, little was known of the chronology, material nature, and paleoenvironmental contexts of the state's colonizing residents. Understanding of early human occupations evolved slowly in the earliest decades of the 1900s but accelerated with important discoveries in the 1960s–1980s, keeping pace with and contributing to the overall evolution of North American Paleoindian studies. Now, in the early twenty-first century, archaeologists are developing increasingly sophisticated and productive approaches to interpreting Paleoindian adaptations to ancient Colorado's diverse and dynamic ecosystems.

This chapter reviews Colorado's Paleoindian research history as divided into three general developmental phases: (1) early exploratory surveys and excavations through roughly 1960, (2) site-focused research conducted from the 1960s through the 1980s, and (3) increasingly sophisticated, multidisciplinary research programs based almost exclusively in the state's mountainous regions from the end of the 1980s to the present day.

We do not overview every Paleoindian-related undertaking in Colorado history; rather, we highlight the state's best-reported Paleoindian investigations to give a flavor for how they have evolved. This chapter's reference section provides a foundation for anyone wishing to delve deeper into any aspect of Colorado Paleoindian archaeology. Additional sources of background information can be found in E. Steve Cassells's *The Archaeology of Colorado* (1997), the five (1999) *Colorado Prehistory Contexts* (Gilmore et al.; Lipe, Varien, and Wilshusen; Martorano et al.; Reed and Metcalf; Zier and Kalasz), and the Colorado State Historic Preservation Office site database (a 2006 search of which yielded 715 recorded "Paleoindian" sites and isolated finds in the state). George Frison's Afterword to this volume is also most interesting for the personal perspective he brings to both early and contemporary Colorado Paleoindian archaeology.

EARLY EXPLORATORY SURVEYS AND EXCAVATIONS (ca. 1930–1960)

Colorado's earliest ventures into what eventually became known as Paleoindian archaeology occurred during the 1930s and 1940s with a long-term survey program by the University of Denver (DU) and several important site excavations from 1932 through the late 1950s by the Colorado Museum of Natural History (known as of 1948 as the Denver Museum of Natural History and since 2000 as the Denver Museum of Nature and Science), the Smithsonian Institution, and the University of Colorado. During that time, Colorado archaeologists and sites were at the forefront of North American archaeology's attempts to define an interpretive framework for the continent's earliest prehistoric occupants.

E. B. Renaud and the High Plains Archaeology Survey Program

Some of Colorado's most significant early work in Paleoindian studies came from a series of field surveys conducted by E. B. Renaud of DU from 1930 to 1946. Renaud was a French-trained romance language professor who developed an interest in archaeology. After obtaining a doctorate from DU in 1920, Renaud was appointed full professor of anthropology in 1924. He acquired archaeological field skills in France during the 1920s while also participating in field projects in southwestern Colorado.

In 1930 Renaud initiated a long-term archaeology survey program known variously as the "Eastern Survey of Colorado," the "Archaeological Survey of Colorado," and the "High Plains Archaeological Survey." He documented sites in eastern Colorado's foothills and plains, visiting nearly every county therein at least once. Within two years his Colorado research branched out to include higher portions of the Colorado Rockies, including Rocky Mountain National Park, South Park, the San Luis Valley, and the upper Rio Grande drainage. His methodology entailed making contact with local landowners and artifact collectors, examining their collections, and then tracking down the originating sites. Renaud's students completed graduate theses based on their findings during the survey program, and some made important contributions to Paleoindian studies at the national level.

John Cotter (1935), for example, produced an early summary of Folsom and late Paleoindian projectile points documented by project surveys from 1930 to 1934—roughly the time frame of his excavations at the Clovis type-site, Blackwater Draw, New Mexico. In her thesis, Mary Elizabeth (Betty) Yelm (1935; Yelm and Beals 1934) examined private point collections from Colorado's northern foothills to the Continental Divide. She documented about a dozen "Yuma-type" points and Paleoindian sites, including three very high-altitude localities revisited in 1998–2002 by the University of Northern Colorado (Benedict 2001; Brunswig 2001b, 2001c, 2003a, 2003b, 2004a, Chapter 9, this volume).

When the DU project began, the archaeological community recognized one Paleoindian culture: Folsom. Neither older Clovis nor any late Paleoindian cultures or projectile points had yet been distinguished from Folsom, although some scholars (Cook 1927; Figgins 1927) suggested that lanceolate projectiles with parallel flaking patterns were associated with very ancient human occupations. In the early 1930s, while working with amateur archaeologists Perry and Harold Anderson (e.g., Anderson 1988; LaBelle 2002), Renaud and others adopted the term "Yuma" to describe non-Folsom lanceolate projectile points collected in the vicinity of Yuma, a town in northeastern Colorado. Renaud was by now keenly aware of the significant antiquity of both Folsom and Yuma spear points, and he highlighted their distinctiveness in reports and articles (Renaud 1931, 1932b, 1934, 1935b, 1935c, 1937, 1941, 1960a, 1960b).

With the subsequent discovery at the Lindemeier site of Yuma (later determined to be Cody Complex) occupations *overlying* Folsom camp deposits, the chronological relationship between Folsom and Yuma was definitively established (Roberts 1935, 1937b; Wilmsen and Roberts 1978). Moreover, Renaud, his students, and others (see *Southwestern Lore* editorial 1941) noted the significant stylistic variability of projectile point types then lumped within the Yuma classification. One student, H. Marie Wormington (1949, 1957), was instrumental in developing a generalized system of Yuma "subtypes" in the 1940s and 1950s. Her work presaged the development of more formal late Paleoindian typologies in the 1960s, when radiocarbon dating increased chronological control and the site database was more robust.

In 1935, Renaud (1935a:21) reported 190 Folsom and 662 Yuma points representing "a phase of the American Paleolithic culture" from private artifact collections in Colorado's mountains, eastern foothills, and plains. Many sites identified on the basis of points in those collections and on file in project catalogs in DU's anthropology museum were later entered into the state's site database. In the end, Renaud, his students, and a few others observed and recorded dozens of sites with Paleoindian points or components from eastern Colorado's foothills-plains (Cotter 1935; Gebhard 1949; Renaud 1932a, 1932b, 1933, 1934, 1935a, 1937) and high mountains (Cotter 1935; Potts 1934; Renaud 1933, 1934, 1935a, 1937, 1942; Yelm 1935). In so doing, they established a comprehensive foundation for future Paleoindian research in the state. For more detail on Renaud's contributions to Colorado Paleoindian archaeology, we refer readers to George Frison's Afterword (this volume).

Early Paleoindian Site Excavations

Aside from occasional, limited test excavations, the DU research program involved no major excavations. In fact, in the early decades of Colorado Paleoindian research, substantial professional excavations were conducted at just five sites: the Dent mammoth (Clovis) site and four Folsom localities (Lindenmeier, Powars, Linger, and Zapata) (see Figure 2.1 for site locations). The multicomponent (Clovis–late Paleoindian) Claypool site was subjected to very limited excavations during the 1950s. Because Chapter 3 presents a detailed history of Dent site research, we only briefly overview its early discovery and investigation here. We likewise highlight here only the earliest excavations at Lindenmeier, Linger, and Zapata—all of which were subsequently re-examined in investigations we reference, as appropriate, later in this chapter.

Clovis (Dent). In response to a 1932 report from a student, Saint Regis College geology professor Father Conrad Bilgery excavated the Dent Mammoth Site that autumn (Bilgery 1935). Jesse Figgins, a curator at the Colorado Museum of Natural History, studied the mammoth remains and continued the Dent excavations in 1933. Figgins, who had excavated the Folsom type-site a few years earlier, found at least ten mostly juvenile and infant mammoths coupled with two fluted points. Calling upon his experience at Folsom, Figgins characterized the points as "Folsomoid" but not sufficiently distinct to warrant a new label. A few years later, specimens like the Dent points were recovered *below* Folsom at Blackwater Draw, New Mexico, demonstrating that "Clovis" points (as they were thenceforth known) pre-date Folsom (Meltzer 1993; Sellards and Evans 1960). For decades the Dent site, which through historical accident lost naming rights for the first universally recognized culture in the Americas, remained an enigma—one tackled by contemporary archaeologists and explored in Chapters 3–6 of this volume.

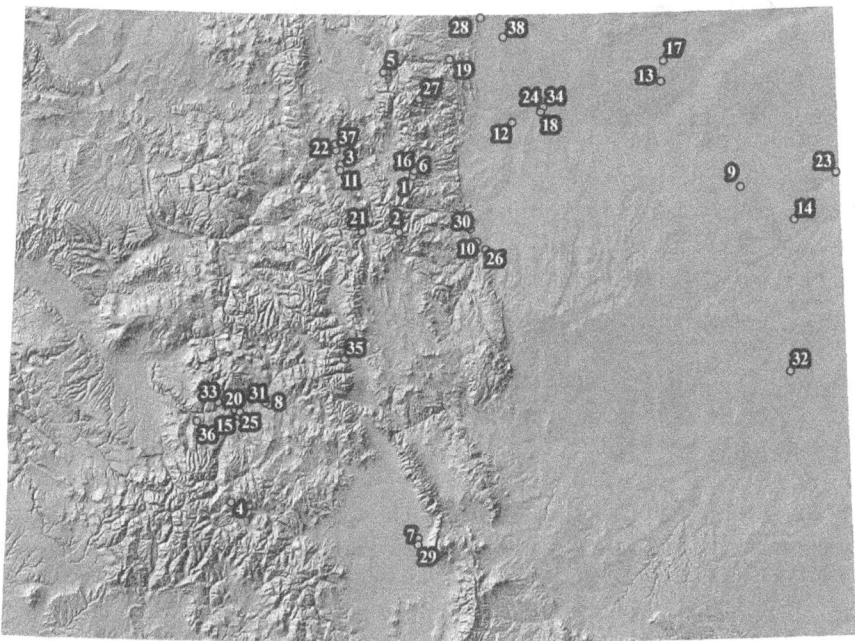

2.1. Map of key Paleoindian sites mentioned in Chapter 2. (1) 5BL3440; (2) Argentine Pass; (3) Barger Gulch; (4) Black Mountain; (5) Carey Lake; (6) Caribou Lake; (7) Cattle Guard; (8) Chance Gulch; (9) Claypool; (10) Crescent Rockshelter; (11) Crying Woman; (12) Drake; (13) Dutton and Selby; (14) Dent; (15) Elk Creek; (16) Fourth of July Valley; (17) Frasca; (18) Frazier; (19) Gordon Creek; (20) Haystack Cave; (21) Hourglass Cave; (22) Jerry Craig; (23) Jones-Miller; (24) Jurgens; (25) Kezar Basin; (26) Lamb Spring; (27) Lawn Lake; (28) Lindenmeier; (29) Linger, Reddin, Zapata Folsom, Zapata Mammoth; (30) LoDaisKa; (31) Mountaineer; (32) Olsen-Chubbuck; (33) Ponderosa/Soap Creek; (34) Powars; (35) Runberg; (36) Soderquist Ranch; (37) Upper Twin Mountain; (38) Wilbur Thomas.

Folsom (Lindenmeier, Powars, Linger, and Zapata). The Lindenmeier site, located in a northern Front Range foothills creek valley, is an extensive, relatively deeply buried campsite with highly visible cultural deposits exposed in an arroyo. Lindenmeier was discovered in 1924—two years before formal excavations began at the Folsom type-site—during an amateur artifact-collecting expedition by Judge Claude C. Coffin, his son A. Lynn, and C. K. Collins (Coffin 1937, 1960; Greenway 1960; Renaud 1932b:27–28). The Coffins spent nearly a decade surface collecting artifacts and conducting small test excavations before learning from E. B. Renaud that many of the specimens in their possession belonged to the newly defined Folsom Complex.

The Coffins eventually contacted scientists at the Smithsonian's Bureau of American Ethnology to report Lindenmeier. Frank H.H. Roberts, a field archaeologist with the Smithsonian, responded, visiting the site in September 1934 with

Roy C. Coffin (a geologist and relative of the site's discoverers). Impressed with the site's potential, Roberts conducted excavations from 1935 through 1940 (Reed 1940; Roberts 1935, 1936a, 1936b, 1937a, 1937b, 1938, 1940a, 1940b, 1941). The first year's investigations involved joint work by the Smithsonian and the Colorado Museum of Natural History, the latter led by former Renaud student John Cotter (1978). Subsequently, Roberts worked alone, although he engaged in interdisciplinary collaborations that produced results revolutionary for the time (Bryan and Ray 1940). Although not immediately published, Roberts's records eventually yielded valuable information when the final site report was produced several decades after the 1930s excavations, after Roberts's death (Wilmsen and Roberts 1978). Even later, Colorado State University student Erik Gantt (2002) wrote a master's thesis on the artifacts in the Coffins' private collections.

The Powars site, identified in the 1930s by local artifact collector John Powars, was discovered on an abandoned terrace of the South Platte River east of Greeley. After a quick test excavation, Powars contacted Frank H.H. Roberts (1937a, 1940b), then directing excavations at Lindenmeier. Roberts conducted a brief excavation at Powars in 1936, recovering Folsom point fragments and other tools suggestive of a small, short-term hunting camp. The site overlooks what was then the South Platte's main floodplain, an ideal location for spotting and hunting game. Powars was never reinvestigated and was destroyed by construction of a private home.

Two San Luis Valley Folsom sites, Linger and Zapata, stand as the state's earliest Rocky Mountain (albeit parkland-setting) Paleoindian excavations. Both sites were discovered by local resident Gene Sutherland in the 1930s, and both were subjected to limited excavations in the 1940s and 1950s. C. T. Hurst (1941, 1943), professor of anthropology at Western State College in Gunnison, conducted test excavations of Linger in 1940–1941. The site yielded what Hurst (1941:31) described as a "definite association (of Folsom artifacts) with the remains of what may be *Bison taylori*." F. V. Worman, an Alamosa State College professor, tested (but never reported) the Zapata site, an endeavor that yielded an artifact assemblage similar to but smaller than that recovered at Linger (Jodry 1999b; Wormington 1957). Both Linger and Zapata saw expanded excavations by the Smithsonian Institution in the 1970s and 1980s.

Late Paleoindian (Claypool). Claypool, a multicomponent Paleoindian site, was discovered in the mid-1930s by Perry and Harold Anderson in the state's easternmost plains (Dick and Mountain 1960; Wormington 1957). Another area resident, Bert Mountain, subsequently recovered two Clovis points and portions of a mammoth skeleton eroding from a terrace creek bank and in 1953 assisted in a brief University of Colorado (CU) site excavation (Dick and Mountain 1960). The CU tests suggested Claypool's cultural deposits consisted of naturally deflated (and thus mixed) Clovis and Cody Complex camp assemblages. Two decades later a Smithsonian Institution team led by Dennis Stanford conducted additional test excavations at Claypool and reached similar conclusions about the integrity and interpretation of the deposits (Stanford and Albanese 1975).

SITE-FOCUSED RESEARCH (1960s–1980s)

Compared with preceding decades, Colorado Paleoindian studies became increasingly diverse, more productive, and technically sophisticated in the 1960s, 1970s, and 1980s, with radiocarbon dating providing chronological data of a resolution previously unknown. Here we highlight excavations conducted at sites representative of the Paleoindian era, beginning with pre-Clovis contenders and ending with late Paleoindian localities (Figure 2.1). In addition to producing a wide array of well-collected data, this period of Paleoindian investigations was also important for expanding investigations from the eastern plains and large, open mountain basins to essentially all of the highly varied environmental settings that make up the state of Colorado.

Pre-Clovis

Mirroring intense interest in the subject throughout North America, Colorado archaeologists of the post-1950s began exploring the possibility that their state supported human groups even prior to the arrival of Clovis people. A local rancher discovered the Lamb Spring site near a natural spring in the foothills west of Denver when he excavated a livestock pond and exposed the bones of Pleistocene mammals. Excavations by Smithsonian archaeologist Waldo Wedel (1960–1961) recovered the remains of at least seven mammoths along with camel bone, some with what Wedel interpreted to be cultural flaking. The bones overlaid a silt-clay layer dated to around 13,000 radiocarbon years before present (RCYBP) (Wedel 1965). In 1979–1981, Dennis Stanford and a new team from the Smithsonian returned to Lamb Spring. Their work (Stanford, Wedel, and Scott 1981) revealed remains of five additional mammoths, more potential evidence of cultural bone modification, and a 33 kg river boulder transportable only through human effort. Additional analysis of the site's faunal assemblage proved inconclusive, however, and the site's pre-Clovis status is regarded as unlikely (Fisher 1992; Stanford 1983a).

Two other Colorado localities, Dutton and Selby, located in the northeastern Colorado plains near Wray, have been proposed as possible pre-Clovis sites. Both were encountered when ranchers in the mid-1970s enlarged natural pond hollows for livestock watering, exposing bones of Ice Age megafauna. Smithsonian archaeologists working at the nearby Jones-Miller bison kill site excavated the localities, which yielded the remains of mammoth, horse, camel, and now-extinct bison (some with possible human modification), as well as—at Dutton—a Clovis point in backhoe dirt excavated prior to the professional investigation (Stanford 1979). Although the sediment adhering to the Clovis point resembled buried sediments dated to 11,170 RCYBP, neither Selby nor Dutton is now viewed as definitively pre-Clovis (Stanford 1979).

Investigation of Colorado's only Rocky Mountain site with potential pre-Clovis cultural deposits, Haystack Cave in western Colorado's Upper Gunnison Basin, occurred in the 1970s. First recorded as a jasper quarry in 1935 by Betty and Harold Huscher, Euler and Stiger (1981) conducted test excavations at the site, reporting deposits over 1.5 m deep. Excavators reported that the cave's lower strata yielded chipped stone of possible cultural origin and the remains of late Pleistocene fauna with reported radiocarbon dates of 12,154 $\pm$ 1,700 RCYBP and 14,935 $\pm$ 610 RCYBP (Emslie 1986; Euler and Stiger 1981; Nash 1987). Subsequent sporadic excavations yielded additional flakes and an expanded collection of Pleistocene fauna (Binford and Nash 1984; Emslie 1986, 1998a, 1998b, 1998c; Nash 1987, in prep). Nash (Emslie 1998c:Part IV-4; Nash in prep) considers Haystack Cave to have yielded positive evidence for a pre-12,000 RCYBP occupation, but most do not view Haystack Cave as a strong pre-Clovis contender.

Clovis

Clovis archaeology since early investigations at the Dent Mammoth Site in 1932–1933 has met with limited success in Colorado, likely a joint function of the low density of Clovis sites and the long period of time they have been subjected to burial and erosion. Nonetheless, Colorado archaeologists explored several Clovis sites in the 1960s–1980s. The Drake site, named for finder Orvil Drake, is a cache of thirteen complete Clovis points from the plains east of Greeley. After tests by the University of Northern Colorado's Bruce Lutz, Dennis Stanford and Margaret (Pegi) Jodry (1988b) excavated the area that yielded the points, locating ivory fragments and a hammerstone. Stanford and Jodry (1988) reported that about half the points were unused while the others were reworked—evidence, they argued, of a utilitarian function.

West of the Great Sand Dunes in the San Luis Valley, the Zapata Mammoth Site was reported in 1943 by Western State College professor C. T. Hurst. A quarter-century later, Dennis Stanford and a Smithsonian Institution team tested the locality (Lyons 1978). According to Jodry (1999b), the tests indicated that the site's original stratigraphy had been disturbed by alternating episodes of wind erosion and reburial, limiting its interpretive potential. However, a local collector reported recovering two Clovis points from a deflated scatter of mammoth bone at the site, and the Smithsonian crew recovered chipped-stone artifacts indicative of Clovis technology. Jodry (1999b) concluded that the Zapata Mammoth Site probably resulted from either a successful Clovis mammoth hunt or Clovis scavenging of an already-dead mammoth.

Over the past two decades, other Clovis finds have been documented in the same general vicinity as the Zapata Mammoth Site, but none has been fully investigated. As summarized in Jodry's (1999b) overview of San Luis Valley Paleoindian archaeology, these localities include the Little Clovis site, an open camp lithic scatter with Clovis and Folsom points (Button 1987); the multicomponent One-Two-Three site with two lithic and ground-stone tool concentrations, a single hearth feature, a Clovis point, and Archaic and late Prehistoric projectile points; and several isolated Clovis point finds.

Folsom

The San Luis Valley is best known for its Folsom sites, the focus of four decades of Smithsonian Institution field investigations. Processual-era excavations of these sites began in the late 1960s when a University of New Mexico anthropology student from the area, Jerry Dawson, conducted a limited excavation of the Linger Folsom site first visited by C. T. Hurst in the 1940s. Dawson later contacted the Smithsonian's Dennis Stanford and persuaded him to visit the site in 1968 (Dawson and Stanford 1975; Jodry 1999b). Stanford returned and supervised excavations at Linger from 1977 through 1979, recovering evidence for three distinct activity areas: a bison kill area and two bison processing areas (Jodry 1998, 1999a, 1999b).

Additional Smithsonian investigations in the San Luis Valley included a joint 1978 Smithsonian Institution–Colorado Archaeological Society test excavation of the Zapata Folsom site (Jodry 1999b; Lyons 1978), surface collection of the Reddin Folsom site in 1979 and 1983 (Jodry 1999b; Stanford 1983b), and a series of post-1980s research projects that constitute a long-term multidisciplinary research program discussed later in this chapter. The Zapata excavation revealed an area of bison butchery with a Folsom preform (Jodry 1999a, 1999b; Lyons 1978). Studies of surface collections showed that a high proportion of San Luis Valley Folsom artifacts are made of Edwards Plateau chert (Texas), sources for which are hundreds of miles to the southeast (Jodry 1999a, 1999b). Stewart's Cattle Guard, finally—reported by local resident Duane Martin and test excavated in 1981—showed from the start an array and distribution of artifacts indicative of a short-term summer camp (Emery and Stanford 1982). The site would later become synonymous with Pegi Jodry, who conducted meticulous excavations that led to a master's thesis, a dissertation, and other writings (1987, 1992, 1996, 1999a, 1999b).

North of the San Luis Valley but in a similar ecological setting, cultural resource management (CRM) surveys by Colorado State University (CSU) in the 1980s documented a significant Folsom presence in Middle Park. Follow-up work by then-CSU graduate student Brian Naze expanded earlier survey-identified sites by consulting with local landowners and identifying Paleoindian (mainly Folsom) artifacts from their collections. Naze later identified site clusters north and southwest of Kremmling in the lower Middle Park Valley (Naze 1986). In 1994, Naze's research culminated in a master's thesis reporting test excavations at the Crying Woman site in the uplands south of the Colorado River, with evidence for Folsom and Jimmy Allen (late Paleoindian) occupations. Naze's work later served as a springboard for an ongoing, long-term Middle Park Paleoindian research program conducted by the University of Wyoming.

The Lindenmeier site east of Middle Park on the Colorado Plains saw renewed archaeological interest in the 1960s to 1980s. After original excavator Roberts's death in 1962, University of Arizona graduate student Edwin Wilmsen wrote his doctoral dissertation using Roberts's detailed field records and Smithsonian artifact collections. He concluded that the main Lindenmeier camp sheltered two distinct Folsom social groups (Wilmsen 1967, 1974; Wilmsen and Roberts 1978). In 1959 archaeologists gained chronological control at Lindenmeier when Vance Haynes and George Agogino (1960) dated deposits to 10,780 ± 375 RCYBP, results confirmed thirty years later with additional radiocarbon assays (Haynes 1992). Finally, in a study yielding similar results to those of Smithsonian archaeologists in the San Luis Valley, Jack Hofman, Larry Todd, and Michael Collins (1991) subjected Lindenmeier chipped-stone artifacts to source analysis that indicated some material originated as far away as west Texas.

Late Paleoindian

In addition to important work on early Paleoindian sites, the 1960s to 1980s stand out as the period when Colorado archaeologists began turning their attention to the post-Folsom Paleoindian era, ca. 10,000 to 7,500 RCYBP. Important late Paleoindian sites of this time frame, beginning with Agate Basin and ending with terminal Paleoindian complexes—in both plains and Rocky Mountain settings—were investigated by archaeologists from the Denver Museum of Natural History, the Smithsonian, the University of Colorado, the Center for Mountain Archeology, and others. The 1960s–1980s also saw the beginnings of CRM, a source of archaeological data for Paleoindian studies, including poorly known late Paleoindian site components. To reinforce the dual geographic focus of this era, we divide our discussion by region: plains work first, then research in the Colorado Rockies.

Colorado Plains. In 1965, geologist Frank Frazier located the Agate Basin Paleoindian site that bears his name about 12 km east of Greeley on the Kersey Terrace. He reported finds of bison bone and Agate Basin projectile points to Marie Wormington, who conducted a test excavation at the locality and recovered additional bison bones, debitage, and one in situ Agate Basin point (Malde 1984; Wormington 1984). She completed additional excavations in 1966–1967, concluding Frazier was a secondary bison butchering and processing area (Wormington 1984). Radiocarbon dates on humate extractions from a soil sample overlying the Agate Basin deposits yielded ages of 9,550 ± 130 and 9,650 ± 130 RCYBP (Malde 1984; Wormington 1984). The most recent Frazier research is a CSU master's thesis study of its lithic assemblage (Slessman 2004).

The Jones-Miller Hell Gap site, located east of Frazier on the Colorado Plains near Wray, was discovered in 1972 when local resident Robert Jones Jr. excavated a livestock watering pond. Jones observed bison bones and projectile points, which he reported to Jack Miller, an archaeologist formerly affiliated with CSU. After testing the site and discovering more bison bone, Miller contacted Jim Judge (then of the University of New Mexico), who in turn alerted the Smithsonian's

Dennis Stanford. Stanford (1974) conducted excavations at the site from 1973 to 1975, exposing an extensive bone bed, 3 fire hearths, 91 chipped-stone artifacts, 61 Hell Gap projectile points and fragments, and 136 bone artifacts. Jones-Miller charcoal yielded an age of 10,020 ± 320 RCYBP (Graham 1987), consistent with other Hell Gap site dates. Stanford (1974) concluded that the Jones-Miller bone bed, like Frazier, was a secondary butchering locus.

In 1947, when Paul Forward began farming land just southeast of the town of Firstview, Cheyenne County, Colorado, he noticed scattered bone fragments. Amateur archaeologist Jerry Chubbuck collected a Paleoindian projectile point and scraper from among the bones, reporting his find to fellow avocational archaeologist Sigurd Olsen, who had collected a similar point from the same area, and to Joe Ben Wheat of the University of Colorado. Olsen and Chubbuck first excavated the site, obtaining twenty-four projectile points, stone tools, and bison bones (Chubbuck 1959). In 1958 and 1960, Wheat (1967, 1972, 1978) excavated a "river" of 192 bison from the locality, by then named for Olsen and Chubbuck. In the process, he set new standards for interdisciplinary collaboration, meticulous excavation, attention to taphonomy, and projectile point typology. Wheat dated hoof collagen from the site to 10,150 ± 500 RCYBP. However, Holliday, Johnson, and Stafford (1999) obtained seven bone gelatin ages between 9,290 ± 60 and 9,480 ± 60 RCYBP—more in line than Wheat's date with the Cody Complex elsewhere (Pitblado 2003).

Like the Frazier site, Jurgens, named for the landowner, was discovered by geologist Frank Frazier, who reported his find to Marie Wormington. In 1967, Frazier, Henry Irwin, William Biggs, and Robert Burton excavated several test pits at Jurgens, uncovering a bone bed and projectile points. In 1967, Joe Ben Wheat visited Jurgens with Wormington and then partnered with her to excavate the site in 1968 and 1970 (Wheat 1979). Wheat's Jurgens research again involved interdisciplinary collaboration, including with pollen analyst Linda Scott (Cummings), who continues working today as Colorado's premier palynologist (see Chapters 6 and 7, this volume). Cody Complex occupation at Jurgens—there has long been debate over *which* manifestation of the Cody Complex the Jurgens projectile points represent—has been dated to 9,070 ± 90 RCYBP, consistent with other Cody site ages.

Around the time Forward observed bison bones near Firstview, rancher Charles Frasca noted large bones eroding out of a bank of Pawnee Creek, twenty miles northwest of Sterling in northeastern Colorado. In 1978, Frasca gave Wayne and his daughter Becky Dreier permission to collect some of the bones for a science project, which led to the discovery of a spear point. The Dreiers contacted the Colorado State archaeologist and the Smithsonian Institution, which excavated the site in 1979–1980. Dennis Stanford led the excavations with a team that included future Paleoindian scholars Pegi Jodry, Larry Todd, Mary Lou Larson, and Marcel Kornfeld. According to Fulgham and Stanford (1982), Frasca was created when hunters killed and butchered at least fifty-six bison at 8,910 ±

90 RCYBP. Fulgham and Stanford (1982) rejected Wheat's term "Kersey" (which Wheat applied to similar-looking projectile points from Jurgens), assigning to the Frasca specimens a generalized "Cody" affiliation.

The Colorado Rocky Mountains. All the post-Folsom Paleoindian sites discussed to this point are located on the plains of eastern Colorado. However, an important theoretical development in the 1960s opened the door for archaeologists to focus on late Paleoindian sites in mountain settings as well. Wilfred Husted (1969, 1995; Husted and Mallory 1968) first proposed that post-Folsom prehistoric occupants of the Rocky Mountains developed adaptations to high-altitude environments that differentiated them from groups on the adjacent plains and other lowland regions. Shortly thereafter, and in many subsequent publications, George Frison (e.g., 1973, 1976, 1988, 1991, 1992, 1997) supported Husted's model with his notion of "foothills-mountain traditions" occupying the Rockies by 10,000 RCYBP. Others (e.g., Black 1991) have since subscribed to this view, a point elaborated and illustrated later in this chapter and volume (e.g., Chapters 9 and 10).

Consistent with and supporting Husted's mountain-focused perspective, the 1960s–1980s saw the beginning of an increasingly substantial body of work focusing on Paleoindian occupation of the Colorado Rocky Mountains. The archaeologist most intimately associated with an emphasis on early human use of the high country is James Benedict of the Center for Mountain Archeology, headquartered in Ward, Colorado. Benedict's meticulous geological and archaeological investigations in the alpine and subalpine region west of Boulder span more than four decades and continue unabated today. Two sites excavated in the early 1970s, Caribou Lake and Fourth of July Valley, represent some of Benedict's earliest work and are therefore discussed here (his more recent work is discussed later).

In 1970–1971, Benedict excavated the Caribou Lake site, located at 3,400 m asl in a cirque valley north of Arapaho Pass, exposing a fire hearth dated to 8,460 ± 140 RCYBP and a projectile point base with a parallel-oblique flaking pattern (1974, 1985). Benedict compared the point to Cody Complex specimens found at Jurgens on the plains to the east. At roughly the same elevation and just 2 km south-southeast of Caribou Lake, Husted reported the Fourth of July Valley site in 1965. Benedict excavated the site in 1971, recovering two types of late Paleoindian projectile points, Jimmy Allen and Pryor Stemmed, and hearth charcoal dated to an anomalously late 6,045 ± 120 B.P. and 5,880 ± 120 B.P. Benedict (1981:92) concluded that the late age of this hunting camp "indicated the persistence of an important late Paleo-Indian complex at the moist western periphery of the plains long after its disappearance from the drier, shortgrass environment." However, new work at Fourth of July Valley in the early 2000s by Benedict (discussed later) has prompted him to alter his interpretation.

Like Benedict, Elizabeth Morris conducted decades of important research in the high Colorado Rockies. In the Rawah Wilderness of northern Colorado, Morris (1990; Morris and Metcalf 1993) repeatedly surface collected the 3,397 m asl–elevation Carey Lake site, netting late Paleoindian projectile point fragments (Cody Complex and Jimmy Allen) and other artifacts. Although Carey Lake has not been tested for subsurface cultural deposits, the surface assemblage suggests that like Caribou Lake and Fourth of July Valley, the site served as a short-term hunting camp. Morris also conducted research at the 3,597 m asl–elevation Argentine Pass site in Summit County (Marcotte and Mayo 1978). Although she did not excavate Argentine Pass, she monitored construction of a transmission line on-site, identifying as she did subsurface artifacts that included an early Archaic point fragment. Subsequent surface collection yielded two Jimmy Allen projectile point fragments, perhaps indicating buried late Paleoindian deposits.

In 1988, spelunkers discovered one of Colorado's two sets of Paleoindian human remains in Eagle County at 3,400 m asl. Known as Hourglass Cave Man and representing the highest occurrence of early human remains in North America, the find consists of a partial, disarticulated skeleton of a man in his early forties, with no grave goods or signs of deliberate burial (Hildebolt et al. 1994; Kight, Frost, and Wilson 1996; Mosch and Watson 1993, 1997a, 1997b; Stone and Stoneking 1997). The 1.5 m (5'4")–tall man crawled into Hourglass Cave through a restrictive corridor between $8{,}170 \pm 100$ and $7{,}714 \pm 84$ RCYBP (Mosche and Watson 1997b). His well-preserved DNA suggests a general genetic link with modern Native Americans, and his mitochondrial DNA indicates genetic connections with contemporary indigenous groups of South and Central America (Stone and Stoneking 1997).

In 1984–1985, Elizabeth Morris's student and later collaborator Michael Metcalf served as P.I. for excavations conducted by his CRM firm at the 2,173 m asl Runberg site, south of Hourglass Cave and Argentine Pass in the eastern foothills of the Sawatch Range, Chaffee County. The excavations yielded evidence for at least three late Paleoindian occupations, all probably by hunting bands (Black 1986). The earliest was ascribed an age between 10,000 and 8,800 radiocarbon years on the basis of lanceolate projectile point morphology and a radiocarbon date from an overlying level. In stratigraphic levels above the one that produced the projectile point, the site yielded four late Paleoindian dates ranging from $8{,}840 \pm 100$ RCYBP to $7{,}740 \pm 140$ RCYBP and representing two distinct occupations (Black 1986).

Even farther south, excavations in the Gunnison Basin during the 1960s to 1980s yielded several sites of late Paleoindian affiliation. Ponderosa/Soap Creek (Dial 1984; Jones 1984a, 1984b) is located on a gentle, sagebrush-covered slope and yielded hearths, a structure, and three late Paleoindian radiocarbon dates between $8{,}540 \pm 140$ B.P. and $7{,}450 \pm 330$ B.P. The multicomponent Kezar Basin site (Euler and Stiger 1981; Mueller and Stiger 1983), on a sagebrush-covered bench intermittently submerged by Blue Mesa Reservoir, yielded eighty-seven fire features, most early Archaic in age. The two earliest assays, however, are $8{,}543 \pm 100$ RCYBP and $7{,}653 \pm 240$ RCYBP, from a boiling pit and an unlined hearth, respectively (Jones 1984b). Based on the recovery of bone fragments and chipped-stone tools and flakes, Mueller and Stiger (1983) suggested Kezar Basin functioned as a bighorn hunting and butchering camp.

The 30-acre Elk Creek site (Mueller and Stiger 1983) is located on a ridgetop at 2,318 m asl. Like Kezar Basin and Ponderosa/Soap Creek, Elk Creek is multi-component, with dates on hearths ranging from about 9,800 to 4,300 RCYBP (Jones 1984b). Only the earliest date, 9,791 ± 830 B.P., obtained from an unlined fire hearth at this multi-use site, falls within the late Paleoindian period (Mueller and Stiger 1983). A final 1980s-vintage Gunnison Basin late Paleoindian site is Soderquist Ranch, located on a mesa slope in southwest Gunnison County. Discovered during a CRM survey, surface artifact collection and limited test excavations revealed shallowly buried camp deposits. The deepest level produced a Jimmy Allen projectile point and another specimen interpreted to be Hell Gap or Great Basin Stemmed (Liestman and Gilmore 1988; Pitblado 1993; Reed and Metcalf 1999). Although excavators did not encounter late Paleoindian features, charcoal collected at the level of the projectile points was dated to 7,670 ± 70 RCYBP (Liestman and Gilmore 1988; Reed and Metcalf 1999).

Caribou Lake, Fourth of July Valley, Carey Lake, Argentine Pass, and Hour-glass Cave are all very high-altitude late Paleoindian sites located in the subalpine-alpine zones at elevations of 3,400 m asl or higher. All but the Hourglass Cave skeleton produced projectile points of the Jimmy Allen type, which have been dated at plains and Rocky Mountain sites to between 9,350 and 7,900 RCYBP (Pitblado 2003). At 2,713 m asl, Runberg is lower than the aforementioned sites, and the Gunnison Basin localities of Ponderosa/Soap Creek, Kezar Basin, Elk Creek, and Soderquist are all located in parkland settings in the 2,200–2,350 m asl–elevation range. The lowest environmental settings of the Rockies are the foothills that transition to the plains as one moves eastward through Colorado. Like the higher regions, the Front Range foothills are home to archaeological sites with late Paleoindian components explored in the 1960s to 1980s.

At the stratified Lamb Spring site, two miles east of the Front Range in Douglas County, a Cody Complex occupation occurred above the potentially pre-Clovis mammoth bone bed (Rancier, Haynes, and Stanford 1982; Stafford et al. 1997; Stanford, Wedel, and Scott 1981; Wedel 1965). Artifacts representing the Cody occupation include two projectile points, a scraper, and a graver, used, Stanford, Wedel, and Scott (1981) argued, during the summer months. Radiocarbon dates obtained on bone collagen from the Cody level—8,870 ± 350 B.P. and 7,870 ± 240 B.P. (Stanford, Wedel, and Scott 1981:24)—reflect a late Cody occupation of the locality.

In 1968–1969, David Breternitz (1971) and a team from CU-Boulder excavated the Wilbur Thomas Shelter, four miles southwest of Carr. This multicomponent rockshelter yielded just one artifact diagnostic of the late Paleoindian period: a Scottsbluff projectile point base. This find, plus one associated artifact thought to be a knife, constitute only a minimal Cody presence at the site and possibly curation of Cody artifacts by later occupants. On the other hand, because the

Scottsbluff point base emerged from the lowest of four stratigraphic levels, it may have been deposited during the late Paleoindian period (Zimmerman 1971). A lack of radiocarbon dates from the level leaves the issue unresolved.

Excavated by the CU-Denver field school, Crescent Rockshelter, southwest of Denver in the Hogback Valley, contained primarily Archaic-era materials in stratigraphic context (Stone 1994; Stone and Mendoza 1994). However (Stone 1994:6), midden deposits in the southern part of the site produced "points indicative of Paleoindian/Archaic transition, including a Jimmy Allen point and a Cody Knife fragment." No accompanying features were found, and no radiocarbon dates were obtained for this level. Nonetheless, as at Wilbur Thomas, the stratigraphic position of Paleoindian artifacts beneath well-dated Archaic materials suggests they could represent late Paleoindian occupation of the rockshelter.

LoDaisKa (Irwin and Irwin 1959) is also located in Colorado's Hogback region. The site is twelve miles north of and at a slightly higher elevation than Crescent Rockshelter, but it shows a similar sequence of Holocene occupations. Excavators recovered one late Paleoindian projectile point from sands and gravels of late Wisconsin outwash. Charcoal, ash, and burned bone occurred in the same level, but in the early days of radiocarbon dating they proved insufficient to date. Irwin and Irwin (1959:146) initially compared the projectile point with the Plainview type on the basis of its lanceolate shape and parallel flaking. However, they wrote elsewhere (1959:31) that the flaking pattern is parallel-oblique, not characteristic of Plainview (e.g., Knudson 1983; Wormington 1957).

A final site located in the Colorado Front Range foothills, Gordon Creek, yielded the second of Colorado's two sets of Paleoindian-aged human remains, these at a lower elevation than those of Hourglass Cave Man. In 1965 the Gordon Creek burial was found eroding from a foothills creek bank northwest of Fort Collins (Anderson 1966; Breternitz, Swedlund, and Anderson 1971; Gillio 1970). Excavations by the University of Colorado recovered the partial skeleton of a young woman believed to be twenty-six to thirty years old and about 1.5 m (4'11") tall. Her body, covered with powdered red hematite, was flexed and interred with her head oriented north. Grave goods included three bifacial knives, an end scraper, a hide abrader, a hammerstone, several utilized flakes, two artiodactyl ribs stained with hematite, and three elk teeth (one perforated). Bone collagen from the remains yielded a radiocarbon date of $9,700 \pm 250$ B.P. Mark Muniz (2004) recently dated carbonized sap from the site and provides a best-estimate age for the burial of $9,620 \pm 45$ B.P. Muniz (2004) also studied the reduction strategy used to knap the bifaces in the burial, concluding it is consistent with Hell Gap—as is the radiocarbon date.

COLORADO PALEOINDIAN RESEARCH PROGRAMS (LATE 1980s TO THE PRESENT)

In this final section, we identify and discuss the state's major research programs currently investigating Paleoindian occupations of Colorado (Figure 2.2). We also

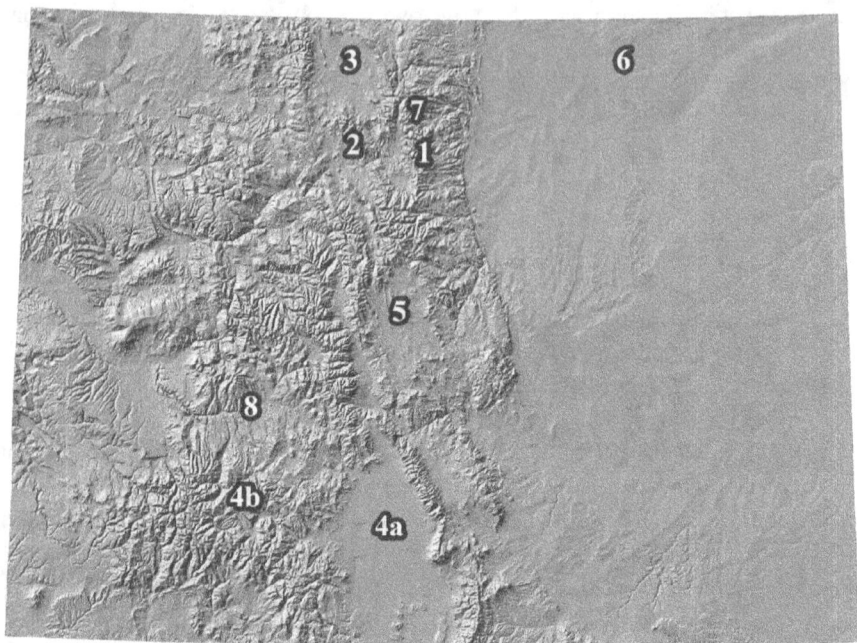

2.2. Contemporary Colorado Paleoindian research program areas discussed in Chapter 2 and the remaining chapters of this volume. (1) Indian Peaks Wilderness, (2) Middle Park, (3) North Park, (4a) San Luis Valley, (4b) Upper Rio Grande Drainage, (5) South Park, (6) South Platte, (7) Rocky Mountain National Park, (8) Upper Gunnison Basin.

touch on one other recent trend in Colorado Paleoindian research: the systematic study of extant artifact collections, primarily projectile points, as sources of data to address questions at broad interpretive scales.

The San Luis Valley/Upper Rio Grande Paleoindian and Paleoecology Program

The Smithsonian Institution's research in the San Luis Valley is the state's earliest and longest-sustained multidisciplinary research program in Paleoindian archaeology. Although the Smithsonian's investigations in the northeastern Colorado foothills and plains in the 1970s and 1980s reflected a commitment to those areas, they never coalesced into a coordinated research program like that in the San Luis Valley, remaining instead site-focused and opportunistic in sites selected for excavation. The Smithsonian's earliest field investigations in the San Luis Valley were also typically site-specific. However, by the late 1980s, research was taking the form of a sustained, long-term effort designated the "Smithsonian Paleoindian/Paleoecology Program" (Jodry 1999c:12). Of all the investigations contributing to and embodying that evolution, excavations at Stewart's Cattle Guard stand out as most significant.

After testing in 1981 (Emery and Stanford 1982), then-graduate student Pegi Jodry undertook excavations of Cattle Guard for her master's thesis (1987) and proceeded in a vein similar to earlier site-based excavations. However, Jodry's decision to expand her research into a multiyear project—one product of which was her Ph.D. dissertation (Jodry 1999a)—set the stage for ongoing, multidisciplinary studies of Folsom cultural adaptations in the region. Cattle Guard excavations from 1987–1996 resulted in the mapping and analysis of more than 1,400 m^2 of deposits (Jodry 1999a). Jodry (Ahler and Jodry 1997; Jodry 1998, 1999a, 1999b) conducted refitting, stone use-wear, and other analyses, concluding that the site contained three distinct areas (a short-term camp, lithic workshop, and late-summer or early-fall bison kill)—each characterized by a suite of unique activities undertaken by a single Folsom group. Inspired by innovators like Joe Ben Wheat before her, Jodry's (1987, 1999a) reconstructions of spatial organization and economic activities at Cattle Guard set new interpretive standards for hunter-gather archaeology that have, in turn, influenced others (e.g., Surovell and Waguespack, Chapter 8, this volume).

During the later stages of her Cattle Guard excavations, Jodry and Vince Spero (Rio Grande National Forest) initiated excavations at the nation's highest excavated Folsom site, Black Mountain (Jody 1993, 1999b:49–55; Jodry et al. 1996). Located in a subalpine valley west of the San Luis Valley at 3,096 m asl, the Black Mountain site's buried Folsom occupations extend for ca. 120 m along a creek terrace bench and represent what Jodry believes to have been two distinct short-term, open camps used as bases for hunting, waypoints in migrations to or from higher elevations, or both. Stratified organic sediment from Black Mountain's Folsom-associated buried A horizon yielded a date of 10,631 ± 84 RCYBP.

An essential element of Jodry and the Smithsonian's contemporary Paleoindian research program is paleoenvironmental reconstruction (Jodry 1999c). With palynologist Owen Davis (University of Arizona) and the University of Colorado's Institute of Arctic and Alpine Research, Jodry (1999c) and her colleagues have cored a series of lakes and bogs from subalpine to San Luis Valley bottom ecosystems to explore relationships between climatic oscillations and Paleoindian use of the region. This research complements that which has engaged Colorado paleoecologist Linda Scott Cummings for several decades and which lies at the heart of Cummings's and her colleagues' Chapter 6 and 7 contributions to this volume.

Paleoindian Investigations in the Upper Gunnison Basin

North of the Black Mountain Folsom site, the Gunnison Basin has shown in the last decade that it may have been as attractive to Paleoindian people as Colorado's other, better-known mountain parks. Three institutions are actively conducting Paleoindian research in the Gunnison Basin, two focusing on the earlier end of the Paleoindian spectrum (Southern Methodist University [SMU] and Western State College [WSC]) and one on the later end (Utah State University). Southern

Methodist's Gunnison Basin research falls under the auspices of the "Quest" Paleoindian Research Program, headed by David Meltzer; Utah State's "Rocky Mountain Paleoindian Research Program" is directed by Bonnie Pitblado; and WSC has a long history of archaeological fieldwork in the Gunnison Basin (Stiger 2001).

Southern Methodist's and Western State's contributions to Paleoindian archaeology have been made to date primarily at the Mountaineer Folsom site, set on the mesa top of Tenderfoot Mountain at an elevation of 2,620 m asl. Recorded in 1994 by CRM firm Alpine Archaeology, the Mountaineer site was surface-collected in 2000 and excavated beginning in 2001 by a WSC team led by Mark Stiger (Dold 2004; Stiger 2002, 2004, 2006). Stiger (2006) reported finding dozens of Folsom points, preforms, and channel flakes; over 35,000 pieces of debitage; bison and other bone fragments; and a structure. Despite the interpretation—seized upon and widely circulated in the popular press (e.g., Lofholm 2002)—that radiocarbon dates of around 7,000 B.P. from the site represent a "relict" Folsom population, recent radiocarbon dating by expert Thomas Stafford suggests a more conventional radiocarbon age for Mountaineer's Folsom occupation of about 10,400 RCYBP (Stiger 2006).

David Meltzer and an SMU team undertook their own excavations at Mountaineer in 2002. In the most recent report on the work, Ph.D. candidate and field director Brian Andrews (2003) outlined the results of excavation of 77 m^2 just northeast of the WSC excavation area. He noted that Folsom-era activities represented in the SMU excavation area differed from those proposed for the WSC block (Stiger 2002, 2006) and primarily included monitoring game in the valley below and retooling. Andrews (2003) also characterized the Folsom occupation in the Quest block as less intensive than that in the WSC area and as the product of warm-season usage rather than winter occupation, as Stiger (2002, 2006) proposed. Whether Mountaineer was used as a long-term winter camp or as a shorter-term game overlook or both, investigations at the site are expanding Colorado's Folsom horizons. They also provide the basis for an intriguing comparison to a possible structure at the Barger Gulch Folsom site in Middle Park (Surovell and Waguespack, Chapter 8, this volume).

Two kilometers southeast of Tenderfoot Mountain, the Chance Gulch late Paleoindian site was tested and excavated by Bonnie Pitblado in 1999–2002 (McFaul 2004; Pitblado 2001a, 2001b, 2002; Pitblado and Camp 2003; Pitblado, Camp, and Stamm 2001; Stamm, Pitblado, and Camp 2004). The late Paleoindian level of this multicomponent campsite, located adjacent to a spring and quartzite quarries, produced a fire-cracked rock feature with charcoal dated to 7,990 ± 50 and 8,050 ± 40 RCYBP (Pitblado and Camp 2003), Angostura projectile points (Pitblado 2002), chipped-stone tools and thousands of debitage fragments (e.g., Ahler 2002), groundstone, animal bones (Walker 2001), and pollen for paleoecological reconstructions (Davis 2002; Varney and Cummings 2004). Pitblado (2003, Chapter 10, this volume) has argued that Angostura points index late Paleoindians who used the Rocky Mountains year-round, and Chance Gulch is probably no exception. Interpretation of the Chance Gulch assemblage continues, and Pitblado's research program recently expanded to include experiments that show promise for sourcing Gunnison Basin quartzite (Pitblado, Dehler, and Nelson 2006).

Paleoindian Research in the Middle and Northern Colorado Rockies

University of Northern Colorado South Park and South Platte Research Programs. East of the Gunnison Basin, Robert Brunswig and the University of Northern Colorado (UNC) sponsored the South Park Archaeology Project in 2001–2003, surveying 3,000 acres in South Park (Bender 2002, 2003; Brunswig 2002b, 2003b; Della Salla in prep; Friedman and Brunswig 2002; Friedman and Lincoln 2003; Friedman, Lincoln, and Tigner 2001, 2003a, 2003b; Lincoln et al. 2003). The survey documented more than a dozen late Paleoindian sites and isolated finds, primarily Cody and Jimmy Allen; however, private collections also contain Clovis points (Della Salla in prep; Lincoln et al. 2003). South Park sites with Paleoindian components were typically dense, complex palimpsests of artifacts and tool-manufacturing debris, almost always located on river terraces and secondary hill ridge spurs. Brunswig (2002b, 2003b) has suggested that such sites represent many generations of primarily summer hunting base camp and lithic procurement-reduction activities extending from early Paleoindian through historic times.

UNC's second major research program, the South Platte Archaeological Project, began with surveys and site excavations in the Front Range foothills in the mid-1980s. Brunswig and his research team subsequently conducted test excavations and surveys along the South Platte River southwest of Greeley and in three large survey blocks of the Pawnee Grassland northeast of Greeley. While the project's plains-based research documented only a few new sites with Paleoindian components (Brunswig 1999b), it was significant for two reasons. First, it represents the only sustained research into Paleoindian use of the Colorado plains during this time frame (the rest was—and remains—mountain-based). Second, it included reinvestigation of the Dent site, as reported in detail in Chapters 3–6 of this volume (see also Fisher 1995; Fisher and Beld 2003; Hoope 2004; Hoope, Carlson, and Webb 1999).

One of the most recent phases of the South Platte Project was a five-year (1998–2002) archaeological inventory program in Rocky Mountain National Park. This endeavor consisted of the survey of nearly 30,000 acres in the park, including several thousand acres at very high altitudes (tundra and subalpine), which are particularly poorly represented in the archaeological literature. Fieldwork also included excavation of the Lawn Lake site, the Jimmy Allen locality first recorded in the early 1930s by Renaud's student Betty Yelm (1935; Yelm and Beals 1934). The results of the survey, the Lawn Lake excavation, and an associated palynological study of bog cores are reported in Chapter 9 of this volume and other manuscripts (Brunswig 1999a, 1999b, 2000, 2001a, 2001b, 2001c, 2001d, 2002a, 2003a, 2003b, 2004a, 2004b, 2004c; Brunswig and Doerner 2001).

Like other contemporary Colorado Paleoindian research programs, for the past two decades UNC research has involved extensive multidisciplinary collaboration. One example is the study of bog cores in the vicinity of the Lawn Lake site; in fact, six coring localities had been investigated in Rocky Mountain National Park by the end of the five-year project. Other multidisciplinary components of the South Platte Archaeological Project included broad-reaching paleoenvironmental reconstruction (Doerner, Chapter 1, this volume), lithic assemblage and material source analysis, Geographic Information System modeling, and ethnoarchaeological studies (Brunswig 2004a, 2004b, 2004c; Brunswig and Doerner 2001; Brunswig, Elinoff, and Lux 2001; Butler 2004; Doerner 2003a, 2003b; Doerner and Brunswig 2002a, 2002b, in prep; Ellinoff 2002; Lux 2004, 2005; McBeth 2007; Rohe 2003a, 2003b, 2004; Wunderlich 2004; Wunderlich and Brunswig 2004).

Center for Mountain Archeology and Indian Peaks Wilderness Area Research. James Benedict and his Center for Mountain Archeology have made important contributions to Paleoindian archaeology and glacial geology since the 1970s, with ongoing fieldwork in the very high-altitude Indian Peaks Wilderness and Rocky Mountain National Park of northern Colorado. Here, we overview Benedict's recent contributions to Paleoindian studies, most notably game drive sites and systems and new work at the Fourth of July Valley site that prompted him to reevaluate conclusions he drew from his 1971 investigation. We also mention the results of Pitblado's reevaluation of the Caribou Lake site—another site first excavated by Benedict in the 1970s—an undertaking that also yielded new insights about late Paleoindian occupation of the very high Rockies.

In four decades of research, Benedict essentially founded the study of high-altitude game drives in the Indian Peaks and Rocky Mountain National Park areas and in the process demonstrated that at least some of them may have been used by Paleoindians (Benedict 1981, 1985, 2000). The Caribou Lake and Fourth of July Valley sites, for example, have both been interpreted as short-term hunting camps associated with nearby game drives. Benedict (1994, 1997, 1998, 2000) recently conducted fieldwork at 5BL3440, part of the 3,425–3,440 m asl Devil's Thumb game drive and the site of surface finds of late Paleoindian obliquely flaked lanceolate projectile points. Excavations at 5BL3440 yielded microdebitage and radiocarbon dates on naturally occurring charcoal flecks that suggested cultural deposition sometime between $9,560 \pm 65$ RCYBP and $5,960 \pm 85$ RCYBP.

5BL3440 presented a second manifestation of obliquely flaked lanceolate points with potentially late radiocarbon dates; the first was the Fourth of July Valley site in 1971. This second occurrence prompted Benedict (2005) to return to Fourth of July Valley to reevaluate the apparent association of late Paleoindian artifacts with radiocarbon dates of $6,045 \pm 120$ and $5,880 \pm 120$ RCYBP. New excavations yielded nine microflakes in a geological unit that Benedict (2005) dated to $8,290 \pm 50$ RCYBP. Benedict also determined that what he believed in 1971 to be a hearth was instead a natural depression that filled with charcoal when trees burned at the site during a wildfire, ca. 5,960 B.P. As a result of these new data, Benedict (2005:797) now notes that "the association of thermally altered microflakes with 8,290-year-old charcoal in a deeply buried stratigraphic context suggests that the site dates from the early Holocene"—not the early Archaic, as he had surmised on the basis of his original work at Fourth of July Valley. The results also instilled new confidence (Benedict 2005) that Paleoindian occupation of 5BL3440 occurred closer to 9,560 ± 65 RCYBP than to 5,960 ± 85 RCYBP.

In the mid-1990s, Benedict encouraged Bonnie Pitblado to reevaluate the Caribou Lake site he first excavated in the early 1970s. Pitblado's work (1996, 2000; Pitblado and Varney 1997) did not radically alter Benedict's (1974, 1985) conclusions, but it did refine them. Pitblado's team discovered a second hearth with dates of 7,985 ± 75 and 7,940 ± 70 RCYBP—500 years younger than the hearth Benedict documented and indicative of reoccupation. Pitblado (1996, 2000) also recovered several late Paleoindian projectile points not of the Cody type, as Benedict had classified his find, but Jimmy Allen. She later concluded that Benedict's specimen was also more consistent with Jimmy Allen than with Cody. Projectile point typology is significant here because Pitblado (2003) has argued that Jimmy Allen represents seasonal use of the high country by people otherwise adapted to the High Plains. Moreover, this type assignment brings Caribou Lake into line with Fourth of July Valley and Devil's Thumb, both within a few km of Caribou Lake and both sources of Jimmy Allen spear points.

University of Wyoming Middle Park Paleoindian Research. The University of Wyoming's Middle Park Archaeology Project, initiated in 1995, is a long-term archaeological research program that focuses on the Paleoindian period in an intramontane basin north of, but ecologically similar to, the San Luis Valley, Gunnison Basin, and South Park. Over the past decade, Wyoming has conducted archaeological surveys and a series of excavations at camp, lithic quarry, and bison bone bed (kill and processing) sites in the Wolford Mountain and Upper to Lower Twin Mountain areas north of Kremmling and in Barger Gulch west of Kremmling (Hall 1992; Kornfeld 1997, 1998; Kornfeld et al. 1999; Surovell 2003a, 2003b; Surovell et al. 2000, 2001a, 2001b, 2003; also see Frison's Afterword, this volume).

Wyoming's contributions to Paleoindian studies in Colorado have been particularly noteworthy for helping define the role and nature of Goshen-Plainview and Folsom occupations in high basin settings. Wyoming's research program has a rich tradition of multidisciplinary collaboration related to paleoenvironment (Cummings and Moutoux 1998; Kornfeld et al. 1999:658–663; Mayer 2003; Mayer et al. 2005; Miller 1998), site formation processes (Kornfeld et al. 1999:663–666; Surovell 2003a), faunal analysis (Kornfeld et al. 1999:666–669; Logan et al. 1998), lithic tool and source material analysis (Daniele 2003a, 2003b; Kornfeld, Frison, and White 2001; Richings 1998; Surovell, Waguespack, and

Kornfeld 2003; White 1999), and spatial organization (Surovell 2003b; Surovell and Waguespack, Chapter 8, this volume).

Wyoming's most significant Middle Park Paleoindian excavations to date include those at the Upper Twin Mountain, Barger Gulch Locality B, and Jerry Craig sites. Upper Twin Mountain, the first site excavated as part of the long-term research initiative, represents a single-episode Goshen-Plainview kill of fifteen adult bison on a gentle mountain slope. The site yielded butchering tools and flake debitage in association with fragmentary *Bison antiquus* remains (Kornfeld 1998; Kornfeld et al. 1999; Kornfeld and Frison 2000). Bison remains from the site's bone bed produced dates of $10,470 \pm 50$ and $10,240 \pm 70$ RCYBP (Kornfeld et al. 1999; Kornfeld and Frison 2000)—younger than northern plains Goshen sites and older than southern plains Plainview sites (Kornfeld and Frison 2000).

University of Wyoming personnel have excavated Barger Gulch Locality B since 1997 (Daniele 2003a, 2003b; Kornfeld 1998; Kornfeld, Frison, and White 2001; Surovell et al. 2000, 2001a, 2001b, 2003, 2005, Chapter 8, this volume). Although the site's surface artifact scatter extends over an estimated 7,000 m^2, its buried Folsom occupation is shallow and thin and represents no more than two medium-term (one- to two-month) cool-season camps ca. $10,770 \pm 70$ to $10,470 \pm 40$ RCYBP (Surovell et al. 2003). Detailed spatial analysis (Surovell and Waguespack, Chapter 8, this volume) has revealed several discrete activity areas at the site, including one centered on a hearth, and the possible presence of a structure. Future studies of the potential Barger Gulch structure will be particularly fruitful as a comparative case for the Folsom structure Stiger (2006) hypothesizes to have stood at the Mountaineer site in the Gunnison Basin.

Excavations at the Jerry Craig site north of Kremmling, finally, exposed Colorado's only excavated mountain basin Cody Complex bison kill (Hill and Kornfeld 1999; Kornfeld and Frison 2000; Logan et al. 1998; Richings 1998; Richings-Germain 1999; Surovell et al. 2000). Scattered over an erosion-cut slope of Little Wolford Mountain, the site yielded the remains of five bison, dispatched in late summer to early fall; chipped-stone butchering tools; and Cody Complex projectile points. Some of the Jerry Craig points exhibit the parallel-oblique flaking pattern characteristic of chronologically equivalent—and, in the Colorado Rockies, more prevalent—Jimmy Allen and Angostura types (Pitblado 2003). Brunswig (2004b) has suggested that the presence of parallel-oblique flaked Eden points could represent an initial indigenous mountain-adapted lifestyle by populations utilizing that projectile point type. Organic sediment from the bone bed yielded an age of $9,310 \pm 50$ RCYBP, an early Cody date (Kornfeld 1998).

Paleoindian Projectile Point Studies: Tapping a Valuable Resource

A final but important development in Colorado Paleoindian research in the past fifteen or so years has been a trend toward increasing and more systematic study of the many early projectile points stored on museum shelves, in private collectors' showcases, and in curation boxes in government repositories. The recording and analysis of artifacts collected from sites as long as seventy or more years ago are often components of the research programs described earlier. At the same time, such studies are the logical extension of a research strategy initiated long ago by archaeologist E. B. Renaud and his students, who visited dozens of ranchers, farmers, and artifact collectors to record their diagnostic artifacts and determine their sites of origin.

An important stimulus for the reinvigoration of artifact collection studies of Paleoindian points in Colorado came with Robert York's (1991) study of Paleoindian projectile points from southwestern Colorado's San Juan National Forest. Pitblado viewed York's work as inspiration for a larger-scale study of 166 Paleoindian projectile point specimens from a geographically larger portion of southwest Colorado, published as a University of Arizona master's thesis and regional journal articles (Pitblado 1993, 1994, 1998). Since then, systematic documentation of projectile points from private, museum, and government repository collections has become standard procedure for many, if not most, Colorado Paleoindian research programs.

In Middle Park, well before the University of Wyoming established its archaeological research program in the region, private collections illuminated the substantial presence of Folsom material throughout that region (Naze 1986, 1994). In fact, without the input of prolific Middle Park–based private collectors, Wyoming might never have targeted the area for Paleoindian research (see Frison's Afterword, this volume, for more on this observation). At the very least, without their strategic collaborations with knowledgeable local avocational archaeologists and collectors and studies of their collections (e.g., Wiesend and Frison 1998), Wyoming is unlikely to have reaped the many archaeological rewards it can now claim.

Other researchers, too, are looking to studies of Paleoindian projectile points for new insights about their study areas. In 1997, Patty Walker-Buchanan, then working for the Bureau of Land Management, wrote an excellent report on a private collection of Paleoindian projectile point specimens from Grand and Summit counties, focusing on the Blue River Valley that forms an important access corridor between Middle Park and South Park. Her work was important for her own archaeological investigations in the region, but it has also had obvious relevance for the Wyoming scholars focusing on Middle Park and University of Northern Colorado personnel working in South Park, North Park, and Rocky Mountain National Park.

Whereas most studies of Colorado Paleoindian projectile points have been undertaken to overview the Paleoindian record of a region or to obtain clues to the locations of sites (e.g., Brunswig 2001a, 2003a, 2004a), some studies, including recent and forthcoming monographs by the editors of this volume (Brunswig 2001b, 2004a, in prep; Pitblado 1993, 1999a, 2003), use them to explore theoretical issues of Paleoindian land use and mobility. In the mid-1990s, Pitblado documented nearly 600 late Paleoindian projectile points from surface contexts all over Colorado and Utah, comparing specimens from Southern Rocky Mountain contexts to those from the Colorado Plains, Colorado Plateau, and Great Basin. She concluded (1999, 2003) that a unique mountain projectile point assemblage indexed year-round use of the Rockies by some groups but that other projectile points represented seasonal use of very high altitudes by plains hunters and sporadic visitation of various environments by lowland-adapted people from the east and west. Pitblado's Chapter 10 (this volume) discusses the parallel-obliquely flaked projectile points she found to be characteristic of late Paleoindian occupations of the Colorado Rockies.

CONCLUSIONS

Beginning in the 1920s and continuing through today, Colorado Paleoindian archaeology both paralleled and contributed to the overall development of Paleoindian archaeology in North America. Early excavations at key Paleoindian sites like Lindenmeier and Dent, for example, presaged the primarily plains site-based work of the 1960s–1980s, as well as the sophisticated new work at Dent undertaken in the 1990s and reported in this volume (Chapters 3–6).

Similarly, E. B. Renaud and his many students in the 1930s–1940s—including seminal Colorado archaeologist Marie Wormington—established a tradition of working closely with artifact collectors that resulted in the earliest systematic recording of Colorado Paleoindian sites. But their work did more than that. It set the stage for and inspired investigations by contemporary scholars like Pegi Jodry and Dennis Stanford; George Frison, Marcel Kornfeld, Mary Lou Larson, and other University of Wyoming personnel; and both editors of this book—all of whom have viewed collectors as critical sources of intimate knowledge of archaeological landscapes and Paleoindian artifacts. Both Brunswig's Chapter 9 and Pitblado's Chapter 10 of this volume are contemporary expressions of research trajectories that date back to Renaud's era.

One of Renaud's students, Betty Yelm, stands as the first "foremother" of high-altitude Colorado Paleoindian archaeology. In the mid-1930s she documented several sites at high elevations in the Colorado Front Range. Wilfred Husted in the 1960s, James Benedict starting in the late 1960s and continuing through today, Elizabeth Morris, and both editors of this book have followed in her footsteps in the research we have undertaken in the uppermost reaches of the Rockies. Similarly, C. T. Hurst's World War II–era work in the San Luis Valley instigated a long tradition of work there by the Smithsonian Institution, as well as in all of Colorado's other major mountain parks: the Gunnison Basin, South Park, Middle Park, and North Park.

One important development not foreshadowed in the earliest decades of Colorado Paleoindian archaeology is the vital role CRM archaeology would play in the growth of the discipline. As privately funded archaeology became increasingly prevalent through the 1960s, archaeologists like Elizabeth Morris (through a CRM arm of Colorado State University), Michael Metcalf (founder of Metcalf Archaeological Consultants), Kevin Black (currently the assistant Colorado state archaeologist), and others conducted important research while also fulfilling CRM mandates. Without their and others' efforts, many of the now 700+ Paleoindian sites in Colorado Historical Society records would never have been documented.

In terms of broad approaches scholars have taken to Colorado Paleoindian archaeology through time, two fundamental shifts differentiate earlier research from more recent iterations. The first shift was from the site-centered approach favored by scholars through the 1980s or so to the regional approach more commonly employed by archaeologists today. Prior to 1990, Paleoindian archaeologists working in Colorado often took an inductive tack in their studies of early sites. They excavated when a potentially early site came along and focused later on drawing broad-scale conclusions about the Paleoindian people who created those sites.

Not surprisingly, this approach helped make the years from about 1960 to 1980 a particularly exciting time in Colorado Paleoindian archaeology. In the Afterword to this volume, George Frison notes that these years were, to him, the "halcyon days" of his career because there were so many new finds and such rich cross-pollination among leading excavators like Dennis Stanford, Marie Wormington, Joe Ben Wheat, and Frison himself. Every site, it seemed, added a dramatic new piece to the puzzle. A detailed chronological picture of Paleoindian prehistory emerged thanks to advances in radiocarbon dating, while studies of lithic technology clarified how projectile points varied and what such variation could mean; and archaeologists began routinely collaborating with other earth scientists.

While necessary for cementing the foundations of Colorado—and broader North American—Paleoindian archaeology, the site-centered orientation of the 1960s–1980s was gradually supplanted by a different approach to the past. Today, most researchers work deductively, creating a theoretical framework for their research teams and choosing geographic areas for survey and sites for excavation on the basis of that framework. For the Smithsonian, for example, Dennis Stanford and Pegi Jodry's central interest is in Folsom use of the San Luis Valley and nearby high-altitude reaches of the Southern Rockies. They carefully craft research strategies to identify and study Folsom sites in their area of interest and to efficiently answer questions they find compelling and believe will contribute to the Folsom database as a whole. Although details of frameworks and research questions vary from researcher to researcher, most currently practicing archaeologists approach their research in broadly similar ways.

A second shift that occurred around the close of the 1980s was the near-complete abandonment of the Colorado Plains in favor of the Rocky Mountains as a geographic area of choice for Colorado Paleoindian scholars (although the 1990s work at Dent reported in this volume is an important exception). Even now, some of us begin conference talks and papers with a statement that the mountains have been marginalized by archaeologists for too long. As should be abundantly clear after reading this volume's Introduction, Chapter 2, and its entire third section, it is time to put to rest what is rapidly becoming a straw-man position.

It is now downright popular to be a Rocky Mountain Paleoindian archaeologist. In fact, almost every active Colorado Paleoindian archaeologist is based to a greater or lesser degree in the mountains. Current geographic centers of Paleoindian archaeology—the San Luis Valley, the Gunnison Basin, South Park, Middle Park, North Park, Rocky Mountain National Park, and the Indian Peaks area—all represent highly variable environmental zones, from rolling sagebrush-filled parklands to alpine meadows; but none is the equivalent of the High Plains. There are a variety of explanations for the geographic shift in research focus, but two factors appear preeminent: (1) pioneering field research by such researchers as Dennis Stanford and Pegi Jodry in the San Luis Valley and James Benedict in the Indian Peaks region convinced others that Paleoindian sites were at least moderately well represented in Colorado's Southern Rockies, and (2) the synergy of vast federally managed land tracts and federal culture resource protection laws ensured a constant source of funding for archaeological inventory and mitigation projects on public lands.

As we noted earlier in this chapter, some Paleoindian complexes that some of us perhaps still intimately associate with the plains—Folsom comes to mind—appear to have been only as plains-based as the Colorado Paleoindian archaeologists who first studied them. A recent glossy magazine article began with the characterization, in large font, that "The Folsom people were believed to be mobile hunter-gatherers who roamed the Great Plains" (Dold 2004:26). It went on to cite David Meltzer as saying: "The stereotypical view of the Folsom is they were out on the High Plains hunting down bison" (Dold 2004:28). It is important now to ask how that stereotype originated and to evaluate its validity. With recent mountain discoveries, it should be dawning on twenty-first-century professionals that we must reconsider that outdated notion in the face not just of new but even of old evidence (see, for example, Surovell 2003c).

As early as the late 1960s to early 1970s, Wilfred Husted (1969; Husted and Mallory 1968) argued that by 10,000 RCYBP (that is, after the end of Folsom time) the Rocky Mountains were home to people who spent the entire year exploiting their environmentally variable resources. Work conducted since then in Colorado and other Rocky Mountain states and excavations undertaken in the last two decades have reinforced the basic tenets of Husted's model. While it is true that pre-10,000 B.P. Folsom sites occur in relative abundance in the mountains, sites have, with the exception of Black Mountain, been restricted to expansive parkland and foothills-plains ecotone settings, possibly as a result of renewed Younger Dryas glacial cooling during much of Folsom time and the presence of bison in those settings, a Folsom staple.

On the other hand, soon after 10,000 radiocarbon years ago, post-Folsom sites like Caribou Lake, Fourth of July Valley, Devil's Thumb, Carey Lake, Lawn Lake,

Chance Gulch, Runberg, LoDaisKa, Crescent Rockshelter, and others—both in Colorado and in other portions of the Southern through Northern Rockies—have been documented in every ecological zone, from the lowest foothills to the highest alpine settings. Recent synthetic research, such as Pitblado's (2003) study of late Paleoindian projectile points from Colorado and Utah and Brunswig's (e.g., 2001c, 2004a) publications on Colorado Paleoindian adaptations, provide a strong empirical record supporting Husted's view that, by at least 10,000 years ago, some groups had committed themselves to a mountain-oriented lifestyle similar to that documented for pre-horse mountain-adapted Shoshone and Ute peoples.

As Colorado Paleoindian archaeology now stands, just a few years into the new millennium it seems clear that the questions that will guide us in coming decades will have less to do with *whether* Paleoindian people used the Rocky Mountains than with *how* they used them and how that use shifted from early to late Paleoindian times and varied across the state's highly variable mountain landscape—issues at the heart of most of the contributions to this volume. We will undoubtedly continue our multidisciplinary efforts to reveal and understand the impact of the paleoenvironmental parameters that confronted Colorado's earliest residents—summarized thoroughly by James Doerner in Chapter 1 of this volume—perhaps using new methods suggested by Linda Scott Cummings and her colleagues in Chapter 7.

Research of Colorado's rich Paleoindian record has come a long way since E. B. Renaud first documented collectors' "Folsom" and "Yuma" projectile points, the only Paleoindian types known in the early 1930s when he began his wide-ranging studies. At the same time, the threads of Renaud's work, and those of his students and his students' students, are with us today, serving as the foundation for seeking answers to new and compelling questions and applying innovative research methodologies by Colorado Paleoindian archaeologists of the twenty-first century.

Acknowledgments. We gratefully acknowledge the suggestions of two anonymous reviewers. They greatly improved the focus and flow of this chapter.

REFERENCES CITED

Ahler, S. A.
    2002   Use-Wear and Functional Analysis of Selected Chipped Stone Artifacts from the Chance Gulch Archaeological Site, Colorado. *PaleoCultural Research Group Contribution 44*, Flagstaff.

Ahler, S. A., and M. A. Jodry
    1997   *Scraper Use-Wear as an Indicator of Folsom Mobility in High-Altitude Southern Colorado.* Paper presented at the 55th annual meeting of the Plains Anthropological Society, Denver, CO.

Anderson, D. C.
   1966   The Gordon Creek Burial. *Southwestern Lore* 32 (1):1–9.

Anderson, H. V.
   1988   History of the Yuma Type Artifacts and the Anderson Collection. *Indian Artifact Magazine* 7 (4):13, 45.

Andrews, B.
   2003   Report 3: Field Research in 2003 at the Mountaineer Site (5GN2477), Gunnison County, Colorado. Ms. on file, Southern Methodist University, Dallas.

Bender, S. J.
   2002   South Park Archaeology Project 2002 Field Work Results. Report prepared for the Colorado Division of Wildlife. Ms. on file, Department of Anthropology, University of Northern Colorado, Greeley.
   2003   Report to the Colorado Division of Wildlife on 2002–2003 Results of Intensive Survey, Mapping, and Artifact Analyses of the Lithic Artifact Assemblage at 5PA2332, South Park, Colorado. Ms. on file, Skidmore College, Saratoga Springs, NY.

Benedict, J. B.
   1974   Occupation of the Caribou Lake Site, Colorado Front Range. *Plains Anthropologist* 19 (63):1–4.
   1981   *The Fourth of July Valley: Glacial Geology and Archeology of the Timberline Ecotone.* Center for Mountain Archeology Research Report 2, Ward, CO.
   1985   *Arapaho Pass: Glacial Geology and Archeology of the Crest of the Colorado Front Range.* Center for Mountain Archeology Research Report 3, Ward, CO.
   1994   Excavations at Site 5BL3440, Devil's Thumb Valley, Indian Peaks Wilderness Area, Colorado. Final Report submitted to Arapaho-Roosevelt National Forests, Fort Collins, CO.
   1997   Devil's Thumb Trail Site: Excavations at 5BL6904, Devil's Thumb Valley, Indian Peaks Wilderness, Boulder County, Colorado. Report submitted to and on file at the U.S. Department of Agriculture, Forest Service, Fort Collins, CO.
   1998   Archaeological Studies in the Devil's Thumb Pass Area, Indian Peaks Wilderness, Summer of 1997. Report submitted to and on file at the U.S. Department of Agriculture, Forest Service, Arapaho-Roosevelt National Forests, Fort Collins, CO.
   2000   Game Drives of the Devil's Thumb Pass Area. In *This Land of Shining Mountains: Archeological Studies in Colorado's Indian Peaks Wilderness Area*, ed. E. S. Cassells, 18–95. Center for Mountain Archaeology Research Report 8, Ward, CO.
   2001   Archaeologists above Timberline: The Early Years. *Southwestern Lore* 67 (2):1–16.
   2005   Rethinking the Fourth of July Valley Site: A Study in Glacial and Periglacial Geoarchaeology. *Geoarchaeology* 20 (8):797–836.

Bilgery, C.
   1935   Evidence of Pleistocene Man in the Denver Basin: A Preliminary Report. Ms. on file at the Office of the State Archaeologist, Denver.

Binford, L. R., and D. T. Nash
    1984   Haystack Cave: A Case for Evolutionary Pre-Clovis Occupation in the Inter-Montane West: Proposal to the National Science Foundation. Department of Anthropology, University of New Mexico, Albuquerque.

Black, K. D.
    1986   Mitigative Archaeological Excavations at Two Sites for the Cottonwood Pass Project, Chaffee and Gunnison Counties, Colorado. Ms. on file, Colorado State Historic Preservation Office, Denver, and at Metcalf Archaeological Consultants, Inc., Eagle, CO.
    1991   Archaic Continuity in the Colorado Rockies: The Mountain Tradition. *Plains Anthropologist* 36 (133):1–29.

Breternitz, D. A. (ed.)
    1971   Archaeological Investigations at the Wilbur Thomas Shelter, Carr, Colorado. *Southwestern Lore* 36 (4):53–99.

Breternitz, D. A., A. C. Swedlund, and D. C. Anderson
    1971   An Early Burial from Gordon Creek, Colorado. *American Antiquity* 36 (2):170–182.

Brunswig, R. H.
    1999a   Report on 1998 Archeological Surveys in Rocky Mountain National Park by the University of Northern Colorado. Ms. on file, Department of Anthropology, University of Northern Colorado, Greeley.
    1999b   Evidence of Mountain Paleoindian Use of the Colorado Piedmont and Plains Territories. *Current Research in the Pleistocene* 16:16–18.
    2000   Report on 1999 Archeological Surveys in Rocky Mountain National Park by the University of Northern Colorado. Ms. on file, Department of Anthropology, University of Northern Colorado, Greeley.
    2001a   Report on 2000 Archaeological Surveys in Rocky Mountain National Park by the University of Northern Colorado. Ms. on file, Department of Anthropology, University of Northern Colorado, Greeley.
    2001b   New Evidence of Paleoindian Occupations in Rocky Mountain National Park, North-Central Colorado. *Current Research in the Pleistocene* 18:10–12.
    2001c   Late Pleistocene/Early Holocene Landscapes and Paleoindian Economic Systems in Colorado's Southern Rocky Mountains. In *Presenting the First Peoples: Proceedings of the 1998 CHACMOOL Conference*, ed. J. Gillespie, S. Tupukka, and C. de Mille, 427–451. The Archaeological Association of the University of Calgary, Alberta.
    2001d   Lawn Lake (5LR318): Results of an Archeological Mitigation Research Project at a High Altitude Prehistoric Site in Rocky Mountain National Park. Ms. on file, Department of Anthropology, University of Northern Colorado, Greeley.
    2002a   Report on 2001 Archaeological Surveys in Rocky Mountain National Park by the University of Northern Colorado. Ms. on file, Department of Anthropology, University of Northern Colorado, Greeley.
    2002b   Summary of Results for University of Northern Colorado Surveys on the Santa Maria Ranch, South Park Colorado, 2002. Report prepared for and on file with the State Historic Preservation Office–State Historic Fund, Denver.

2003a Clovis-Age Artifacts from Rocky Mountain National Park and Vicinity, North Central Colorado. *Current Research in the Pleistocene* 20:7–9.

2003b Results of 2003 Archaeological Survey at Santa Maria Ranch, South Park, Colorado, by the University of Northern Colorado. Ms. on file, Department of Anthropology, University of Northern Colorado, Greeley.

2004a Prehistoric, Protohistoric, and Early Historic Native American Archeology of Rocky Mountain National Park: Final Report of System-Wide Archeological Inventory Program Investigations by the University of Northern Colorado (1998–2002). Ms. on file, Department of Anthropology, University of Northern Colorado, Greeley.

2004b Paleoindian Colonization of Colorado's Southern Rockies: New Evidence from Rocky Mountain National Park and Adjacent Areas. In *Ancient and Historic Lifeways of North America's Rocky Mountains: Proceedings of the 2003 Rocky Mountain Anthropological Conference*, ed. R. H. Brunswig and W. B. Butler, 265–283. Ms. on file and available digitally from the Department of Anthropology, University of Northern Colorado, Greeley.

2004c Hunting Systems and Seasonal Migratory Patterns through Time in Rocky Mountain National Park. In *Ancient and Historic Lifeways of North America's Rocky Mountains: Proceedings of the 2003 Rocky Mountain Anthropological Conference*, ed. R. H. Brunswig and W. B. Butler, 393–410. Ms. on file and available digitally from the Department of Anthropology, University of Northern Colorado, Greeley.

in press End of One World—Beginning of Another: Cultural and Environmental Changes at the Pleistocene-Holocene Boundary in Europe's Western Pyrenees and America's Southern Rocky Mountains. In *Apocalypse Then and Now: Archaeology and Worlds' Ends, Proceedings of the 2002 Chacmool Conference*, ed. L. Steinbrenner and M. Peuramaki-Brown. Department of Archaeology, University of Calgary, Alberta.

Brunswig, R. H., and J. Doerner

2001 *The Lawn Lake Site (5LR318): New Evidence for High Altitude Late Paleoindian Adaptations and Paleolandscapes of Colorado's Southern Rockies in the Early Holocene.* Paper presented at the 5th Biennial Rocky Mountain Archaeological Conference, Waterton, Alberta.

Brunswig, R. H., L. Elinoff, and T. Lux

2001 *Shamans, Spirit Power, and Cultural Landscapes in Mountain Territories: Ute Archaeology and Culture in Rocky Mountain National Park.* Paper presented at the 5th Biennial Rocky Mountain Anthropological Conference, Waterton, Alberta.

Bryan, K., and L. L. Ray

1940 Geological Antiquity of the Lindenmeier Site in Colorado. *Smithsonian Miscellaneous Collections* 99 (2). Washington, DC.

Butler, W. B.

2004 Non-Site Archeology in Rocky Mountain National Park. In *Ancient and Historic Lifeways of North America's Rocky Mountains: Proceedings of the 2003 Rocky Mountain Anthropological Conference*, ed. R. H. Brunswig and W. B. Butler, 453–465. Ms. on file and available digitally from the Department of Anthropology, University of Northern Colorado, Greeley.

Button, V. T.
- 1987 The Closed Basin of Colorado's San Luis Valley: Bureau of Reclamation Archaeological Investigations 1976–1986. Bureau of Reclamation, Closed Basin Division, Alamosa, CO.

Cassells, E. S.
- 1997 *The Archaeology of Colorado*, 2nd ed. Johnson Books, Boulder.

Chubbuck, J.
- 1959 The Discovery and Exploration of the Olsen-Chubbuck Site (CH-3). *Southwestern Lore* 25 (1):4–10.

Coffin, R. C.
- 1937 *Northern Colorado's First Settlers*. Privately printed, Fort Collins, CO.
- 1960 What We Know of Folsom Man. *Southwestern Lore* 26 (3):56–59.

Cook, H.
- 1927 New Geological and Paleontological Evidence Bearing on the Antiquity of Mankind in America. *Natural History* 27:240–247.

Cotter, J. L.
- 1935 *Yuma and Folsom Artifacts*. Unpublished master's thesis, University of Denver.
- 1978 A Report of Fieldwork of the Colorado Museum of Natural History at the Lindenmeier Folsom Campsite. In *Lindenmeier 1934–1974: Concluding Report of Investigations*, by E. N. Wilmsen and F.H.H. Roberts Jr., 181–184. Smithsonian Contributions to Anthropology 24, Washington, DC.

Cummings, L. S., and R. M. Albert
- 1994 Phytolith and Starch Analysis of Tartar from Three Mammoth Teeth from the Dent Site in Colorado. Ms. on file, PaleoResearch Institute, Golden, CO.

Cummings, L. S., and T. E. Moutoux
- 1998 Pollen Analysis at the Jerry Craig (5GA639) and Lower Twin Mountain (5GA186) Sites and a Paleoenvironmental Summary of Paleoindian Period in the Middle Park, Colorado. In *Early Prehistory of Middle Park: The 1997 Project and Summary of Paleoindian Archaeology*, ed. M. Kornfeld, 95–102. University of Wyoming, Department of Anthropology, Technical Report 15a, Laramie.

Daniele, J. R.
- 2003a *The Barger Gulch Locality B Formal Tool Assemblage: A Use-Wear Analysis*. Unpublished master's thesis, University of Wyoming, Laramie.
- 2003b Barger Gulch End Scrapers and Gravers: A Use-Wear Analysis. In *The First Five Field Seasons at Barger Gulch, Locality B, Middle Park, Colorado*, ed. T. Surovell, 109–118. Technical Report 26, George C. Frison Institute of Archaeology and Anthropology, University of Wyoming, Laramie.

Davis, O. K.
- 2002 Pollen Analysis of Chance Gulch. Department of Geosciences, University of Arizona, Tucson. Ms. on file, Department of Sociology, Social Work and Anthropology, Utah State University, Logan.

Dawson, J., and D. J. Stanford
- 1975 The Linger Site: A Re-Investigation. *Southwestern Lore* 41 (4):11–17.

Della Salla, J.
   in prep A Study of Paleoindian Projectile Points in Private Collections, South Park, Colorado (tentative title). Master's thesis in prep, University of Denver.

Dial, J. L.
   1984 *1983 Investigations in Curecanti National Recreation Area: Prehistoric Structural Remains at 5GN42.* Paper presented at the annual meeting of the Colorado Council of Professional Archaeologists, Boulder. Ms. on file, Midwest Archaeological Center, Lincoln, NE.

Dick, H. W., and B. Mountain
   1960 The Claypool Site: A Cody Complex Site in Northeastern Colorado. *American Antiquity* 26 (2):223–235.

Doerner, J.
   2003a *Paleoenvironmental Interpretations of Holocene Records from Rocky Mountain National Park.* Paper presented at the 2003 Rocky Mountain Anthropological Conference, Estes Park, CO.
   2003b A Summary of Paleoenvironmental Research by the University of Northern Colorado in Rocky Mountain National Park, 2000–2003. Ms. on file, Department of Geography, University of Northern Colorado, Greeley.

Doerner, J., and R. H. Brunswig
   2002a *Vegetation and Climate Change in Rocky Mountain National Park: Pollen Evidence from Lawn Lake Fen.* Paper presented at the annual conference of the Association of American Geographers, Los Angeles, CA.
   2002b *Vegetation and Climate Change in Rocky Mountain National Park: Pollen Evidence from Lawn Lake Fen.* Paper presented at the 2002 Rocky Mountain National Park Research Conference, Estes Park, CO.
   in prep Modeling Paleoenvironmental and Archeological Landscapes of Ancient Game Drive Systems in Rocky Mountain National Park, North Central Colorado. Ms. on file, Departments of Geography and Anthropology, University of Northern Colorado, Greeley.

Dold, C.
   2004 This Very Old House. *American Archaeology* 8 (1):26–31.

Elinoff, L.
   2002 *Oral Tradition and the Archaeological Record: An Integral Partnership in Understanding the Human Past of the Rocky Mountain National Park Region.* Unpublished master's thesis, University of Colorado, Denver.

Emery, S., and D. J. Stanford
   1982 Preliminary Report on Archaeological Investigations of the Cattle Guard Site, Alamosa County, Colorado. *Southwestern Lore* 48 (1):10–20.

Emslie, S. D.
   1986 Late Pleistocene Vertebrates from Gunnison County, Colorado. *Journal of Paleontology* 60:170–176.
   1998a Ecology and Paleoecology of the Upper Gunnison Basin, Colorado. Ms. on file, Department of Biological Sciences, University of North Carolina, Wilmington.

1998b Late Holocene Environmental Change in the Upper Gunnison Basin, Colorado. Ms. on file, Department of Biological Sciences, University of North Carolina, Wilmington.

1998c *Nomination of Haystack Cave (5GN189) to the Colorado Register of Historic Properties.* Department of Sciences, Western State College, Gunnison, CO.

Euler, R. T., and M. Stiger
1981 1978 Test Excavations at Five Archeological Sites in Curecanti National Recreation Area, Intermountain Colorado. Ms on file, Midwest Archeological Center, National Park Service, Lincoln, NE.

Figgins, J. D.
1927 The Antiquity of Man in America. *Natural History* 27 (3):220–239.

Fisher, D. C.
1995 *Season of Death of the Dent Mammoths.* Paper presented at the 60th annual meeting of the Society for American Archaeology, Minneapolis, MN.

Fisher, D. C., and S. G. Beld
2003 *Growth and Life History Records from Mammoth Tusks.* Paper presented at the Third International Mammoth Conference, Dawson City, the Yukon, Canada.

Fisher, J. W.
1992 Observations of the Late Pleistocene Bone Assemblage from the Lamb Spring Site. In *Ice Age Hunters of the Rockies,* ed. D. J. Stanford and J. S. Day, 51–82. Denver Museum of Natural History and University Press of Colorado, Denver and Niwot.

Friedman, E., and R. H. Brunswig
2002 Archaeological Inventory Summary and Interim Report for Field Surveys Conducted under Cooperative Agreement 02-CS-1102 1200–045 to the South Park Ranger District, Pike and San Isabel National Forest, U.S. Forest Service, Park County, Colorado. Report prepared for the USDA Forest Service, Pike and San Isabel National Forest. Ms. on file, Department of Anthropology, University of Northern Colorado, Greeley.

Friedman, E., and T. Lincoln
2003 Results of a 2003 Class III Archaeological Survey on Bureau of Land Management Lands, South Park, Colorado. Report prepared for the Bureau of Land Management, Royal Gorge Resource Area. Ms. on file, Department of Anthropology, University of Northern Colorado, Greeley.

Friedman, E., T. Lincoln, and L. Tigner
2001 *The South Park Archaeological Project.* Paper presented at the 2001 annual meeting of the Colorado Archaeological Society, Fort Collins, CO.

2003a Class III Archaeological Survey in the Northeast Sector of South Park, Colorado. Report prepared for the USDA Forest Service, Pike and San Isabel National Forest. Ms. on file, Department of Anthropology, University of Northern Colorado, Greeley.

2003b Summary Results of 2001 and 2002 Field Surveys at the James Mark Jones State Wildlife Area (Formerly Mud Springs State Wildlife Area and Reinecker

Ridge State Wildlife Area), Park County, Colorado. Report prepared for the Colorado Division of Wildlife. Ms. on file, Department of Anthropology, University of Northern Colorado, Greeley.

Frison, G. C.
1973   Early Period Marginal Cultural Groups in Northern Wyoming. *Plains Anthropologist* 18 (62, Parts 1 and 2):300–312.
1976   The Chronology of Paleoindian and Altithermal Cultures in the Big Horn Basin, Wyoming. In *Cultural Change and Continuity, Essays in Honor of James Bennett Griffin*, ed. C. E. Cleland, 147–173. Academic, New York.
1988   Paleoindian Subsistence and Settlement during Post-Clovis Times on the Northwestern Plains, the Adjacent Mountain Ranges, and Intermontane Basins. In *America Before Columbus: Ice-Age Origins*, ed. R. C. Carlisle, 83–106. Ethnology Monographs 12, University of Pittsburgh, Department of Anthropology.
1991   *Prehistoric Hunters of the High Plains*, 2nd ed. Academic, New York.
1992   The Foothills-Mountains and the Open Plains: The Dichotomy in Paleoindian Subsistence Strategies between Two Ecosystems. In *Ice Age Hunters of the Rockies*, ed. D. J. Stanford and J. S. Day, 323–342. Denver Museum of Natural History and University Press of Colorado, Denver.
1997   The Foothill-Mountain Late Paleoindian and Early Plains Archaic Chronology and Subsistence. In *Changing Perspectives of the Archaic in the Northwest Plains and Rocky Mountains*, ed. M. L. Larson and J. E. Francis, 84–105. University of South Dakota Press, Vermillion.

Fulgham, T., and D. J. Stanford
1982   The Frasca Site: A Preliminary Report. *Southwestern Lore* 48 (1):1–9.

Galloway, E., and G. A. Agogino
1961   The Johnson Site: A Folsom Campsite. *Plains Anthropologist* 6 (13):205–208.

Gantt, E. M.
2002   *The Claude C. and A. Lynn Coffin Lindenmeier Collection*. Unpublished master's thesis, Colorado State University.

Gebhard, P. H.
1949   An Archaeological Survey of the Blowouts of Yuma County, Colorado. *American Antiquity* 15 (2):132–143.

Gillio, D. A.
1970   A Reexamination of the Gordon Creek Burial Lithic Materials. *Southwestern Lore* 36 (1):12–14.

Gilmore, K. P., M. Tate, M. L. Chenault, B. Clark, T. McBride, and M. Wood
1999   *Colorado Prehistory: A Context for the Platte River Basin*. Colorado Council of Professional Archaeologists, Denver.

Graham, R. W.
1987   Late Quaternary Mammalian Faunas and Paleoenvironments of the Southwestern Plains of the United States. In *Late Quaternary Mammalian Biogeography of the Great Plains and Prairies*, ed. R. W. Graham, H. A. Semken Jr. and M. A. Graham, 24–86. Illinois State Museum Scientific Papers 22, Springfield.

Greenway, J.
1960 The Coffins: Discoverers of the Lindenmeier Site. *Southwestern Lore* 26 (3):54–55.

Hall, D. A.
1992 Paleoindians Killed Bison in Rockies. *Mammoth Trumpet* 8 (1):1, 6.

Haynes, C. V.
1992 Contributions of Radiocarbon Dating to the Geochronology of the Peopling of the New World. In *Radiocarbon after Four Decades*, ed. R. E. Taylor, A. Long, and R. S. Kra, 355–374. Springer-Verlag, New York.

Haynes, C. V., and G. A. Agogino
1960 Geological Significance of a New Radiocarbon Date from the Lindenmeier Site. *Proceedings of the Denver Museum of Natural History* 9, Denver.

Hildebolt, C. F., W. P. Murphy, D. T. Rasmussen, and A. M. Haeussler
1994 Skeletal Remains of an 8,000-Year-Old American. *American Journal of Physical Anthropology Supplement* 18:107.

Hill, Matthew G., and M. Kornfeld
1999 Inferring Season of Kill for a Cody-Complex Bison Bonebed in Middle Park, Colorado. *Current Research in the Pleistocene* 16:30-32.

Hofman, J., L. C. Todd, and M. B. Collins
1991 Identification of Central Texas Edwards Chert at the Folsom and Lindenmeier Sites. *Plains Anthropologist* 36 (137):297–308.

Holliday, V. T., E. Johnson, and T. W. Stafford Jr.
1999 AMS Radiocarbon Dating of the Type Plainview and Firstview (Paleoindian) Assemblages: The Agony and the Ecstasy. *American Antiquity* 64 (3):444–454.

Hoope, K. A.
2004 Late Mammoth Herd Structure, Migration Patterns and Clovis Hunting Strategies Inferred from Isotopic Analysis of Multiple Death Assemblages. *Paleobiology* 30 (1):129–145.

Hoope, K. A., R. W. Carlson, and S. D. Webb
1999 Tracking Mammoths and Mastodons: Reconstruction of Migratory Behavior Using Strontium Isotope Ratios. *Geology* 27 (5):439–442.

Hurst, C. T.
1941 A Folsom Location in the San Luis Valley, Colorado, a Preliminary Report. *Southwestern Lore* 7 (2):31–34.
1943 A Folsom Site in a Mountain Valley of Colorado. *American Antiquity* 8 (3): 250–253.

Husted, W. M.
1965 Early Occupation of the Colorado Front Range. *American Antiquity* 30 (4):494–498.
1969 *Bighorn Canyon Archeology*. Publications in Salvage Archeology 12. River Basin Surveys, Museum of Natural History, Smithsonian Institution, Washington, DC.

    1995   The Western Macrotradition Twenty-Seven Years Later. *Archaeology in Montana* 36 (1):37–92.

Husted, W. M., and O. L. Mallory
    1968   The Western Macrotradition: Archeology and Language in the Western United States. Ms. in possession of the senior author, Billings, MT.

Irwin, C., and H. Irwin
    1959   Excavations at the LoDaisKa Site in the Denver, Colorado Area. *Proceedings of the Denver Museum of Natural History* 8, Denver.

Jodry, M. A.
    1987   *Stewart's Cattle Guard Site: A Folsom Site in Southern Colorado: Report of the 1981 and 1983 Field Seasons.* Unpublished master's thesis, University of Texas, Austin.
    1992   Fitting Together Folsom: Refitted Lithics and Site Formation Processes at Stewart's Cattle Guard Site. In *Piecing Together the Past: Applications of Refitting Studies in Archaeology*, ed. J. L. Hoffman and J. G. Enloe, 179–209. British Archaeological Reports, International Series, 578, Oxford.
    1993   The Black Mountain Site, 5HN55, Rio Grande National Forest, Colorado, Its Research Significance and History of Investigations. Report to and on file at the San Juan and Rio Grande National Forests, Monte Vista, CO. Department of Anthropology, Smithsonian Institution, Washington, DC.
    1996   Archaeology of Stewart's Cattle Guard Site: Report of the 1995 Field Season. Ms. on file, Department of Anthropology, Smithsonian Institution, Washington, DC.
    1998   The Possible Design of Folsom Ultrathin Bifaces as Fillet Knives for Jerky Production. *Current Research in the Pleistocene* 15:75–77.
    1999a   *Folsom Technological and Socioeconomic Strategies: Views from Stewart's Cattle Guard and the Upper Rio Grande Basin, Colorado.* Unpublished Ph.D. Dissertation, Department of Anthropology, American University, Washington DC.
    1999b   The Paleoindian Stage. In *Colorado Prehistory: A Context for the Rio Grande Basin*, ed. M. A. Martorano, T. Hoefer, M. A. Jodry, V. Spero, and M. L. Taylor, 45–114. Colorado Council of Professional Archaeologists, Denver.
    1999c   Paleoindian Stage Paleoecological Records. In *Colorado Prehistory: A Context for the Rio Grande Basin*, ed. M. A. Martorano, T. Hoefer, M. A. Jodry, V. Spero, and M. L. Taylor, 12–26. Colorado Council of Professional Archaeologists, Denver.

Jodry, M. A., M. D. Turner, V. Spero, J. C. Turner, and D. J. Stanford
    1996   Folsom in the Colorado High Country: The Black Mountain Site. *Current Research in the Pleistocene* 13:25–27.

Jones, B. A.
    1982   The Curecanti Archaeological Project: 1980 Investigations in Curecanti National Recreation Area, Colorado. Ms. on file, Midwest Archeological Center, National Park Service, Lincoln, NE.
    1984a   The Curecanti Archaeological Project: 1981 Investigations in Curecanti National Recreation Area, Colorado. *Midwest Archaeological Society Occasional Studies in Anthropology* 8, Lincoln, NE.

1984b   Radiocarbon Dates from the Gunnison Basin, Curecanti National Recreation Area, Colorado. *Southwestern Lore* 50 (3):14–22.

Kight, W., K. Frost, and P. J. Wilson
1996   *Life and a Death in the Rocky Mountains, 8,000 B.P.* Paper presented at the 61st annual meeting of the Society for American Archaeology, New Orleans, LA.

Knudson, R.
1983   *Organizational Variability in Late Paleo-Indian Assemblages.* Washington State University Laboratory of Anthropology Reports of Investigations 60, Pullman.

Kornfeld, M.
1997   Early Prehistory of Middle Park: The 1997 Project and Summary of Paleoindian Archaeology. Technical Report 5a, Department of Anthropology, University of Wyoming, Laramie.
1998   Summary of Paleoindian Archaeology in the Middle Park. In *Early Prehistory of Middle Park: The 1997 Project and Summary of Paleoindian Archaeology*, ed. M. Kornfeld, 49–55. University of Wyoming, Department of Anthropology, Technical Report 15a, Laramie.

Kornfeld, M., and G. C. Frison
2000   Paleoindian Occupation of the High Country: The Case of Middle Park, Colorado. *Plains Anthropologist* 45 (172):129–153.

Kornfeld, M., G. C. Frison, M. L. Larson, J. C. Miller, and J. Saysette
1999   Paleoindian Bison Procurement and Paleoenvironments in Middle Park of Colorado. *Geoarchaeology* 14 (7):655–674.

Kornfeld, M., G. C. Frison, and P. White
2001   Paleoindian Occupation of Barger Gulch and the Use of Troublesome Formation Chert. *Current Research in the Pleistocene* 18:32–34.

LaBelle, J. M.
2002   Slim Arrow, the Long-Forgotten Yuma Type Site in Eastern Colorado. *Current Research in the Pleistocene* 19:52–55.

Liestman, T. L., and K. P. Gilmore
1988   Archaeological Mitigation of the Soderquist Ranch Site (5GN246), Gunnison County, Colorado. *Colorado Department of Highways Salvage Report* 62, Denver.

Lincoln, T., E. Friedman, R. H. Brunswig Jr., S. Bender, J. Della Salla, and J. Klawon
2003   South Park Archaeology Project: Final Report of Archaeological Investigations Conducted in 2000 and 2001, South Park, Colorado. Ms. on file, Department of Anthropology, University of Northern Colorado, Greeley.

Lipe, W. D., M. D. Varien, and R. H. Wilshusen
1999   *Colorado Prehistory: A Context for the Southern Colorado River Basin.* Colorado Council of Professional Archaeologists, Denver.

Lofholm, N.
2002   Prehistoric Site Raises Questions. *The Denver Post* (September 1), 1B, 4B.

Logan, J., J. Durr, M. G. Hill, C. Lee, and V. McMillan
    1998   Jerry Craig Site, 5GA639, a Cody Complex Site in Colorado. In *Early Prehistory of Middle Park: The 1997 Project and Summary of Paleoindian Archaeology*, ed. M. Kornfeld, 11–24. University of Wyoming, Department of Anthropology, Technical Report 15a, Laramie.

Lux, T. A.
    2004   Archeological Investigation of Ancient Trails in Rocky Mountain National Park, North Central Colorado. In *Ancient and Historic Lifeways of North America's Rocky Mountains: Proceedings of the 2003 Rocky Mountain Anthropological Conference*, ed. R. H. Brunswig and W. B. Butler, 411–424. Ms. on file and available digitally at the Department of Anthropology, University of Northern Colorado, Greeley.
    2005   *Archeological Investigation of Ancient Trails in Rocky Mountain National Park, North Central Colorado*. Unpublished master's thesis, University of Denver.

Lyons, R.
    1978   The People and the Sand Dunes—1978. *All Points Bulletin* 5 (11):2–5. Newsletter of the Denver Chapter, Colorado Archaeological Society.

Malde, H. E.
    1984   Geology of the Frazier Site, Kersey, Colorado. *Field Trip Guide for the American Quaternary Association 1984 Annual Meeting* 2:13–16. Denver.

Marcotte, J. R., and D. Mayo
    1978   Archaeological Surveillance during Construction Activities at the Argentine Pass Site, Summit County, Colorado. *Reports of the Laboratory of Public Archaeology* 19. Department of Anthropology, Colorado State University, Fort Collins.

Martorano, M. A., T. Hoefer III, M. A. Jodry, V. Spero, and M. L. Taylor
    1999   *Colorado Prehistory: A Context for the Rio Grande Basin*. Colorado Council of Professional Archaeologists, Denver.

Mayer, J.
    2003   Preliminary Report of Geoarchaeological Investigations at Barger Gulch, Locality B. In *The First Five Field Seasons at Barger Gulch, Locality B, Middle Park, Colorado*, by T. A. Surovell, N. M. Waguespack, M. Kornfeld, and G. C. Frison, 19–44. Technical Report 26. George C. Frison Institute of Archaeology and Anthropology, University of Wyoming, Laramie.

Mayer, J. H., T. A. Surovell, N. M Waguespack, M. Kornfeld, R. G. Reider, and G. C. Frison
    2005   Paleoindian Environmental Change and Landscape Response in Barger Gulch, Middle Park, Colorado. *Geoarchaeology* 20 (6):599–625.

McBeth, Sally
    2007   *Native American Oral History and Cultural Interpretation in Rocky Mountain National Park: Report to the National Park Service*. Anthropology Program, University of Northern Colorado, Greeley.

McFaul, M. D.
    2004   Geoarchaeological Evaluations 2000 and 2002, Chance Gulch (5GN817). *LaRamie Soils Service Report 6-2-00*, Laramie, WY.

Meltzer, D. J.
    1993   *Search for the First Americans.* Smithsonian Exploring the Ancient World Series, ed. Jeremy A. Sabloff. Smithsonian Books, Washington, DC.

Miller, J. C.
    1998   Latest Pleistocene and Holocene Geology and Geoarchaeology of Middle Park. In *Early Prehistory of Middle Park: The 1997 Project and Summary of Paleoindian Archaeology*, ed. M. Kornfeld, 70–94. University of Wyoming, Department of Anthropology, Technical Report 15a, Laramie.

Morris, E. A.
    1990   Carey Lake, 5LR230, a High Altitude Paleo-Indian Site in Northern Colorado. In *Abstracts of Papers, 55th Annual Meeting, Society for American Archaeology*, 131.

Morris, E. A., and M. Metcalf
    1993   Twenty-Two Years of Archaeological Survey in the Rawah Area, Medicine Bow Mountains, Northern Colorado. In *Abstracts of Papers, 1st Biennial Rocky Mountain Anthropology Conference.* Jackson, WY.

Mosch, C., and P. J. Watson
    1993   Collaborative Research at an Unusual High-Altitude Locale in the Southern Rocky Mountains (Hourglass Site). Report to and on file at the U.S. Forest Service, White River National Forest, New Mexico University, Las Cruces.
    1997a   An Ancient Rocky Mountain Caver. *Journal of Cave and Karst Studies* 59 (1):10–14.
    1997b   The Ancient Explorer of Hourglass Cave. *Evolutionary Anthropology* 5 (4):111–115.

Mueller, J. W., and M. Stiger
    1983   Sheltered Hunter-Gatherers at a Moderately High Altitude: An Interim Summary of Archaeology in Curecanti National Recreation Area. In *High Altitude Adaptations in the Southwest*, ed. J. C. Winter, 69–90. Southwestern Region Report 2. U.S. Forest Service, Santa Fe, NM.

Muniz, M. P.
    2004   Exploring Technological Organization and Burial Practices at the Paleoindian Gordon Creek Site (5LR99), Colorado. *Plains Anthropologist* 49 (191):253–279.

Nash, D. T.
    1987   Archaeological Investigations at Haystack Cave, Central Colorado. *Current Research in the Pleistocene* 4:114–116.
    in prep   Site Formation Processes at Haystack Cave and the Pre-Clovis Debate. Ph.D. dissertation in progress, University of New Mexico, Albuquerque.

Naze, B. S.
    1986   The Folsom Occupation of Middle Park, Colorado. *Southwestern Lore* 52 (4):1–32.
    1994   *The Crying Woman Site: A Record of Prehistoric Human Habitation in the Colorado Rockies.* Unpublished master's thesis, Colorado State University, Fort Collins.

Pitblado, B. L.
    1993   *Paleoindian Occupation of Southwest Colorado.* Unpublished master's thesis, University of Arizona, Tucson.

1994   Paleoindian Presence in Southwest Colorado. *Southwestern Lore* 60 (4):1–20.

1996   The Caribou Lake Site Revisited: 1995 Excavations at a High Altitude Late Paleoindian Campsite. In *Abstracts of Papers*, 61st annual meeting of the Society for American Archaeology, New Orleans, LA.

1998   Peak to Peak in Paleoindian Time: Occupation of Southwest Colorado. *Plains Anthropologist* 43 (166):333–348.

1999a   *Late Paleoindian Occupation of the Southern Rocky Mountains: Projectile Points and Land Use in the High Country.* Unpublished Ph.D. dissertation, University of Arizona, Tucson.

1999b   New ^{14}C Dates and Obliquely Flaked Projectile Points from a High-Altitude Paleoindian Site, Colorado Rocky Mountains. *Current Research in the Pleistocene* 16:65–66.

2000   Living the High Life in Colorado: Late Paleoindian Occupation of the Caribou Lake Site. In *This Land of Shining Mountains: Archeological Studies in Colorado's Indian Peaks Wilderness Area*, ed. E. S. Cassells, 124–158. Center for Mountain Archaeology Research Report 8, Ward, CO.

2001a   *Early Holocene Occupation of the Late Paleoindian Chance Gulch Site, Gunnison Basin, Colorado.* Paper presented at the 5th Biennial Rocky Mountain Anthropological Conference, Waterton Lakes, Alberta.

2001b   Final Report: Test Excavations at Sites 5HN219, 5GN411, 5GN2151 (and Interim Results of Test Excavations of 5GN817). Report to and ms. on file at the Gunnison Field Office, Bureau of Land Management, Gunnison, CO.

2002   The Chance Gulch Late Paleoindian Site, Gunnison Basin, Colorado. *Current Research in the Pleistocene* 19:74–76.

2003   *Late Paleoindian Occupation of the Southern Rocky Mountains.* University Press of Colorado, Boulder.

Pitblado, B. L., and B. A. Camp

2003   2001–02 Excavations at the Chance Gulch Site (5GN817). Report to and ms. on file at the Gunnison Field Office, Bureau of Land Management, Gunnison, CO, and at the Colorado Historical Society, Denver.

Pitblado, B. L., B. A. Camp, and J. Stamm

2001   Final Report: 2000 Test Excavations at the Chance Gulch Site (5GN817). Report to and ms. on file at the Gunnison Field Office, Bureau of Land Management, Gunnison, CO, and at the Colorado Historical Society, Denver.

Pitblado, B. L., C. M. Dehler, and S. T. Nelson

2006   Sourcing Quartzites from the Late Holocene Chance Gulch Site, Gunnison Basin, Colorado: A Pilot Study. *Current Research in the Pleistocene* 23:135–138.

Pitblado, B. L., and R. A. Varney

1997   The Caribou Lake Site in Regional Perspective. In *Abstracts of Papers*, 62nd meeting of the Society for American Archaeology, Nashville, TN.

Potts, B.

1934   Archaeology of the South Park Region. Ms. on file, Office of the State Archaeologist, Denver.

Rancier, J., G. Haynes, and D. J. Stanford

1982   1981 Investigations of Lamb Spring. *Southwestern Lore* 48 (2):1–17.

Reed, A. D., and M. D. Metcalf
  1999   *Colorado Prehistory: A Context for the Northern Colorado River Basin.* Colorado Council of Professional Archaeologists, Denver.

Reed, E.
  1940   Archaeological Site Report on the Lindenmeier Site, Colorado. Ms. on file at the Midwest Archeological Center, National Park Service, Lincoln, NE.

Renaud, E. B.
  1931   Prehistoric Flaked Points from Colorado and Neighboring Districts. *Proceedings of the Colorado Museum of Natural History* 10 (2). Denver.
  1932a Archaeological Survey of Eastern Colorado, 1931 Season. *University of Denver Department of Anthropology Archaeological Report* 2. Denver.
  1932b Yuma and Folsom Artifacts. *Proceedings of the Colorado Museum of Natural History* 11 (2). Denver.
  1933   Archaeological Survey of Eastern Colorado, 1932 Season. *University of Denver Department of Anthropology Archaeological Report* 3. Denver.
  1934   The First Thousand Yuma-Folsom Artifacts. *University of Denver Department of Anthropology Archaeological Series Paper* 1. Denver.
  1935a Archaeological Survey of Colorado, 1933 and 1934 Seasons. *University of Denver Department of Anthropology Archaeological Report* 4. Denver.
  1935b Arrowhead Types of Colorado. *Southwestern Lore* 1 (1):4–6.
  1935c Classification and Description of Arrowheads. *Southwestern Lore* 1 (4):5–8.
  1937   Les Pointes Americaines de Folsom et de Yuma. *Bulletin de la Societe Prehistorique Française* 10:n.p.
  1941   About the "Disappearance" of Folsom Man and Folsom Points. *Southwestern Lore* 11 (1):1–18.
  1942   Reconnaissance Work in the Upper Rio Grande Valley, Colorado, and New Mexico. *Department of Anthropology Archaeological Series Paper* 3. Denver.
  1960a Classification and Description of Indian Stone Artifacts. *Southwestern Lore* 26 (1):1–36.
  1960b Typology of Yuma, Folsom and Other Weapon Points. *Southwestern Lore* 26 (2):37–42.

Richings, S.
  1998   Jerry Craig Site Projectile Point Assemblage. In *Early Prehistory of Middle Park: The 1997 Project and Summary of Paleoindian Archaeology,* ed. M. Kornfeld, 25–33. University of Wyoming, Department of Anthropology, Technical Report 15a, Laramie.

Richings-Germain, S.
  1999   The Jerry Craig Site. In *Abstracts, Fourth Biennial Rocky Mountain Anthropological Conference,* 50–51. Glenwood Springs, CO.

Roberts, F.H.H., Jr.
  1935   A Folsom Complex: Preliminary Report on Investigations at the Lindenmeier Site in Northern Colorado. *Smithsonian Miscellaneous Collections* 94 (4). Washington, DC.
  1936a Additional Information on the Folsom Complex: Report on the Second Season's Investigations at the Lindenmeier Site in Northern Colorado. *Smithsonian Miscellaneous Collections* 95 (10). Washington, DC.

1936b   Problems in American Archaeology. *Southwestern Lore* 1: 8–11.
1937a   New Developments in the Problem of the Folsom Complex. *Explorations and Fieldwork of the Smithsonian Institution in 1936*:67–74. Washington, DC.
1937b   The Material Culture of Folsom Man as Revealed at the Lindenmeier Site. *Southwestern Lore* 2 (4):67–73.
1938   The Lindenmeier Site in Northern Colorado Contributes Additional Data on the Folsom Complex. *Explorations and Field-work of the Smithsonian Institution in 1937*:115–118. Washington, DC.
1940a   Excavations at the Lindenmeier Site Contribute New Information on the Lindenmeier Complex. *Explorations and Field-work of the Smithsonian Institution in 1939*:87–92. Washington, DC.
1940b   Developments in the Problem of the North American Paleo-Indian. *Smithsonian Miscellaneous Collections* 100:51–116. Washington, DC.
1941   Latest Excavations at the Lindenmeier Site Add to Information on the Folsom Complex. *Explorations and Field-work of the Smithsonian Institution in 1940*:79–82. Washington, DC.

Rohe, C. M.
2003a   *Reading the Landscape: A Location Model for Prehistoric Sites in Rocky Mountain National Park*. Unpublished master's thesis, University of Arkansas, Fayetteville.
2003b   Final Report on the Development of Predictive Models for Rocky Mountain National Park. Report submitted to and on file at the Department of Anthropology, University of Northern Colorado, Greeley, and Rocky Mountain National Park, Estes Park, CO.
2004   Use of the Simple Weighting Method in Modeling Prehistoric Site Locations in Rocky Mountain National Park. In *Ancient and Historic Lifeways of North America's Rocky Mountains: Proceedings of the 2003 Rocky Mountain Anthropological Conference*, ed. R. H. Brunswig and W. B. Butler, 425–452. On file and available digitally from the Department of Anthropology, University of Northern Colorado, Greeley.

Sellards, E. H., and G. L. Evans
1960   The Paleo-Indian Culture Succession in the Central High Plains of Texas and New Mexico. In *Men and Culture: Selected Papers of the 5th International Congress of Anthropological and Ethnological Sciences*, ed. A.F.C. Wallace, 639–649. University of Pennsylvania Press, Philadelphia.

Slessman, S. A.
2004   *The Frazier Site: An Agate Basin Occupation and Lithic Assemblage on the Kersey Terrace, Northeastern Colorado*. Unpublished master's thesis, Colorado State University, Fort Collins.

Stafford, T., M. McBrinn, E. J. Dixon, D. Stanford, and E. A. Bettis
1997   Lamb Spring Archaeological Preserve 1996: Geoarchaeological Assessment. In *Abstracts of Papers*, 62nd meeting of the Society for American Archaeology, Nashville, TN.

Stamm, John, B. L. Pitblado, and B. A. Camp
2004   The Geology and Soils of the Chance Gulch Archaeological Site, Near Gunnison, Colorado. *The Mountain Geologist* 41(2):63–74.

Stanford, D. J.
- 1974 Preliminary Report of the Excavation of the Jones-Miller Hell Gap Site, Yuma County, Colorado. *Southwestern Lore* 40 (3-4):29–36.
- 1979 The Dutton and Selby Sites: Evidence for a Possible Pre-Clovis Occupation of the High Plains. In *Pre-Llano Cultures of the Americas: Paradoxes and Possibilities*, ed. R. L. Humphrey and D. Stanford, 101–123. The Anthropological Society of Washington, Washington, DC.
- 1983a Pre-Clovis Occupation South of the Ice Sheets. In *Early Man in the New World*, ed. R. Shutler, 65–72. Sage, Beverly Hills, CA.
- 1983b Report on 1983 Investigations at the Reddin Site (5SH77), Saguache County, Colorado. Ms. on file, Department of Anthropology, Smithsonian Institution, Washington, DC.

Stanford, D. J., and J. Albanese
- 1975 Preliminary Results of the Smithsonian Institution Excavation at the Claypool Site, Washington County, Colorado. *Southwestern Lore* 41 (4):22–28.

Stanford, D. J., and M. A. Jodry
- 1988 The Drake Clovis Cache. *Current Research in the Pleistocene* 5:21–22.

Stanford, D. J., W. R. Wedel, and G. R. Scott
- 1981 Archaeological Investigations of the Lamb Spring Site. *Southwestern Lore* 47 (1):14–27.

Stiger, M. A.
- 2001 *Hunter-Gatherer Archaeology of the Colorado High Country.* University Press of Colorado, Niwot.
- 2002 The Mountaineer Site, a Large Folsom Camp Near Gunnison, Colorado. *Current Research in the Pleistocene* 19:80–81.
- 2004 *The 2003 Field Season at the Mountaineer Site, Gunnison County, Colorado, Folsom Occupation in the Colorado Mountains.* Paper presented at the 2004 annual meeting of the Colorado Council of Professional Archaeologists, Colorado Springs.
- 2006 A Folsom Structure in the Colorado Mountains. *American Antiquity* 71 (2): 321–351.

Stone, A. C., and M. Stoneking
- 1997 Genetic Analysis of an 8,000-Year-Old Native American Skeleton. *Ancient Biomolecules* 1 (1):83–87.

Stone, T.
- 1994 *Shifts in Resource Procurement and Regional Organization during the Archaic Period in the Hogback Valley.* Paper presented at the 59th Annual Meeting of the Society for American Archaeology, Anaheim, CA.

Stone, T., and R. Mendoza
- 1994 Excavations at the Crescent Rockshelter: 1993 Field Season. *Cultural Resources Report* 1. Department of Anthropology, University of Colorado, Denver.

Surovell, T. A.
- 2003a Occupation Span and Site Reoccupation. In *The First Five Field Seasons at Barger Gulch, Locality B, Middle Park, Colorado*, by T. A. Surovell, N. M. Waguespack,

M. Kornfeld, and G. C. Frison, 119–129. Technical Report 26. George C. Frison Institute of Archaeology and Anthropology, University of Wyoming, Laramie.

2003b Spatial Analysis. In *The First Five Field Seasons at Barger Gulch, Locality B, Middle Park, Colorado,* by T. A. Surovell, N. M. Waguespack, M. Kornfeld, and G. C. Frison, 131–157. Technical Report 26. George C. Frison Institute of Archaeology and Anthropology, University of Wyoming, Laramie.

2003c *The Behavioral Ecology of Folsom Lithic Technology.* Unpublished Ph.D. dissertation, University of Arizona, Tucson.

Surovell, T. A., N. M. Waguespack, and M. Kornfeld

2003 A Note on the Function of Folsom Ultrathin Bifaces. *Current Research in the Pleistocene* 20:75–77.

Surovell, T. A., N. M. Waguespack, M. Kornfeld, and G. C. Frison

2001a *The 2000 Field Season at Barger Gulch, Locality B, Middle Park, Colorado.* Technical Report 19c. George C. Frison Institute of Archaeology and Anthropology, University of Wyoming, Laramie.

2001b Barger Gulch Locality B: A Folsom Site in Middle Park, Colorado. *Current Research in the Pleistocene* 18: 58–60.

2003 *The First Five Field Seasons at Barger Gulch, Locality B, Middle Park, Colorado.* Technical Report 26. George C. Frison Institute of Archaeology and Anthropology, University of Wyoming, Laramie.

Surovell, T. A., N. M. Waguespack, J. H. Mayer, M. Kornfeld, and G. C. Frison

2005 Shallow Site Archaeology: Artifact Dispersal, Stratigraphy and Radiocarbon Dating at the Barger Gulch Locality B Site, Middle Park, Colorado. *Geoarchaeology* 20 (6):627–649.

Surovell, T. A., N. M. Waguespack, S. Richings-Germain, M. Kornfeld, and G. C. Frison

2000 *1999 Investigations at the Barger Gulch and Jerry Craig Sites, Middle Park, Colorado.* Technical Report 18a. George C. Frison Institute of Archaeology and Anthropology, University of Wyoming, Laramie.

Varney, R. A., and L. S. Cummings

2004 Pollen Analysis at 5GN817, Chance Gulch, Colorado, with Supporting Archaeoclimatic Models from Gunnison, Colorado. *PaleoResearch Institute Technical Report* 04-29. Golden, CO.

Walker, Danny N.

2001 Faunal Remains from the Chance Gulch Site (5GN817), 2000–2002 Excavations. Ms. on file, Department of Sociology, Social Work and Anthropology, Utah State University, Logan.

Walker-Buchanan, P.

1997 Documentation of a Paleoindian Collection from the Lower Blue River, Summit and Grand Counties, Colorado. Ms. on file, Bureau of Land Management, Glenwood Springs, CO.

Wedel, W. R.

1965 Investigations at the Lamb Spring Site, Colorado. Ms. on file at the National Science Foundation, Washington, DC.

Wheat, J. B.
- 1967 A Paleo-Indian Bison Kill. *Scientific American* 216 (1):43–52.
- 1972 *The Olsen-Chubbuck Site: A Paleo-Indian Bison Kill.* Memoir of the Society for American Archaeology 26, Washington, DC.
- 1978 Olsen-Chubbuck and Jurgens Sites: Four Aspects of Paleo-Indian Bison Economy. In *Bison Procurement and Utilization*, ed. L. B. Davis and M. Wilson, 84–89. Plains Anthropologist Memoir 14. Plains Anthropological Society, Lincoln.
- 1979 *The Jurgens Site.* Plains Anthropologist Memoir 24 (84, pt. 2). Plains Anthropological Society, Lincoln.

White, P. M.
- 1999 *Getting the High Altitude Stone: Lithic Technology at the Barger Gulch Site (5GA195).* Unpublished master's thesis, University of Wyoming, Laramie.

Wiesend, C. M., and G. C. Frison
- 1998 Parallel-Oblique Flaked Projectile Points from the Phillips–Williams Fork Reservoir Site (5GA1955) in Middle Park, Colorado. *Southwestern Lore* 64 (1):8–21.

Wilmsen, E. N.
- 1967 *Lithic Analysis and Cultural Inference: A Paleoindian Case.* Unpublished Ph.D. dissertation, University of Arizona, Tucson.
- 1974 *Lindenmeier: A Pleistocene Hunting Society.* Harper and Row, New York.

Wilmsen, E. N., and F.H.H. Roberts Jr.
- 1978 *Lindenmeier, 1934–1974: Concluding Report on Investigations.* Smithsonian Contributions in Anthropology 24, Washington, DC.

Wormington, H. M.
- 1949 A Proposed Revision of Yuma Point Terminology. *Southwestern Lore* 15 (2):26–40.
- 1957 *Ancient Man in North America.* Denver Museum of Natural History Popular Series 4, Denver.
- 1984 The Frazier Site, Colorado. *AMQUA 1984, Field Trip 2* (Guide):12–15.

Wunderlich, R.
- 2004 *Material Sourcing Studies of Lithic Assemblages in Rocky Mountain National Park.* Undergraduate thesis, University of Northern Colorado, Greeley.

Wunderlich, R., and R. H. Brunswig
- 2004 Material Sourcing Studies of Prehistoric Lithic Assemblages in Rocky Mountain National Park. In *Ancient and Historic Lifeways of North America's Rocky Mountains: Proceedings of the 2003 Rocky Mountain Anthropological Conference*, ed. R. H. Brunswig and W. B. Butler, 214–223. Ms. on file and available digitally from the Department of Anthropology, University of Northern Colorado, Greeley.

Yelm, M.
- 1935 *Archaeological Survey of Rocky Mountain National Park–Eastern Foothill Districts.* Unpublished master's thesis, University of Denver, Denver.

Yelm, M., and R. L. Beals
- 1934 *Indians of the Park Region.* Rocky Mountain Nature Association, Estes Park, CO.

York, R.
    1991   Evidence for Paleoindians on the San Juan National Forest, Southwest Colorado. *Southwestern Lore* 57 (2):5–22.

Zier, C. J., and S. M. Kalasz
    1999   *Colorado Prehistory: A Context for the Arkansas River Basin*. Colorado Council of Professional Archaeologists, Denver.

Zimmerman, J.
    1971   Projectile Point Provenience. In *Archaeological Investigations at the Wilbur Thomas Shelter, Carr, Colorado*, ed. D. A. Breternitz, 81–82. *Southwestern Lore* 36 (4).

PART TWO

NEW RESEARCH AT THE DENT CLOVIS SITE, NORTHEASTERN COLORADO PLAINS

CHAPTER THREE

Robert H. Brunswig

New Interpretations of the Dent Mammoth Site

A SYNTHESIS OF RECENT MULTIDISCIPLINARY EVIDENCE

The Dent Mammoth Site (5WL269) was discovered in the spring of 1932 when flood runoff eroded mammoth bone from a draw draining low sandstone cliffs west of the South Platte River floodplain near Milliken, Colorado (Figure 3.1). A passing railroad foreman, Frank Garner, noted the eroding bones and informed the local Dent depot operator, Michael Ryan, of the find. Ryan's son later reported the discovery to his Regis College geology professor, Father Conrad Bilgery.

In November 1932, Bilgery and several Regis students traveled to Dent and conducted a brief excavation. During the excavation a large, basally fluted projectile point, of a type later named Clovis (after Clovis, New Mexico), was recovered among the bones. In late 1932, after winter closed down Bilgery's excavations, he notified Colorado Museum of Natural History (now the Denver Museum of Nature and Science) paleontology curator, Jesse D. Figgins, of the discovery. At the

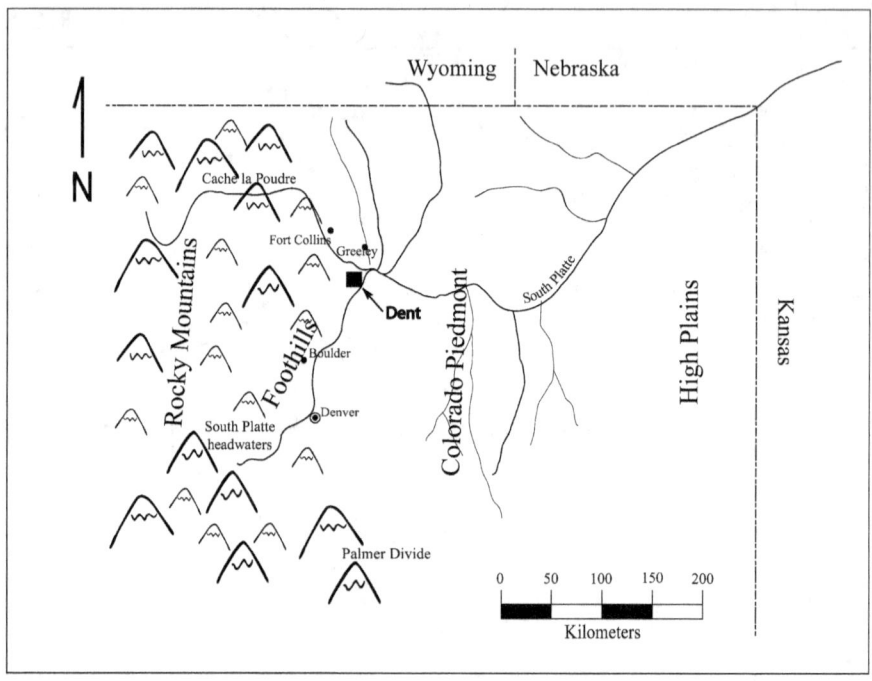

3.1. Geographic location of the Dent site.

same time, he also "most generously extended to the Colorado Museum of Natural History the privilege of removing the remainder of the fossils" (Figgins 1933:4).

The next year, starting on June 13, 1933, a Museum of Natural History field crew excavated at Dent until the work was suspended and the site backfilled in late July. The 1933 excavation was directed by a museum staff member, Frederick Howarter, whose crew consisted mainly of amateur volunteers, including two museum trustees, along with Father Bilgery and several Regis College students. Under Howarter's supervision, the quality of recovery and documentation techniques appreciably improved from the earlier Regis work, although it fell well short of modern standards. The museum's excavation was hampered by Regis College's earlier, less professional excavation that resulted in destruction of much of the bone bed's depositional integrity. In an unpublished letter to Barnum Brown of the American Museum of Natural History, Figgins wrote:

> You will recall that Father Bilgery discovered a fine blade there [Dent] in 1932 and Howarter [the museum's excavation supervisor] uncovered a second when removing the remainder of the skeletons. We will get two skeletons out of the Dent deposit but Regis had removed the major share of the material with College students under Father Bilgery. They made a frightful job of it, and while their entire collection was turned over to us, most of it is useless. There were fourteen pairs of lower jaws in the Dent deposits, from babies to old

examples, but they were mostly wrecked skulls—completely so, and only two skeletons came from the Howarter collecting.

Despite the museum's 1933 professional excavation, little substantial data from the early Dent research were documented, or at least survived. Lack of good field documentation is likely a result of two main factors: (1) the earlier-cited "amateur" excavation by Bilgery and his students, and (2) wholly inadequate site documentation by the subsequent 1933 "professional" excavations. Even accounting for lower standards of field excavation of the day, the lack of all forms of data—including site maps, adequate photographic documentation, and field notes—has severely hampered and confused our understanding of Dent to the present day. Extensive site reconstruction efforts by this author have resulted in a "paper trail" of around thirty-five years of Dent research and correspondence. That research supports a conclusion that original documentation of the early excavations was restricted to only broad descriptions by Bilgery and Figgins and a brief film of the 1933 excavations. The latter visual record of the Dent excavations is a five-minute 16-mm film taken of the July 7, 1933, excavations. The only still photographs of the excavations were made from film negatives. Although very brief, the film does show the location of a recovered Dent Clovis point in association with mammoth bone. On the other hand, it was not sufficiently wide-angled to show the overall bone bed perspective, consisting only of bone bed excavation close-ups.

Once the 1933 excavations were completed, Dent remained untouched until 1973, when graduate students and faculty from the University of Colorado (CU) at Boulder undertook a limited backhoe test of previously unexcavated eastern site margins (Haynes 1974:135–136; Spikard 1972). Several archaeologists and geologists prominent in Paleoindian archaeology at the time were present, including Frank Frazier, Joe Ben Wheat, Marie Wormington, and C. Vance Haynes. The test had been planned as a precursor to a CU graduate thesis project by Linda Spikard. However, once the test determined that the only remaining undisturbed portions of the site lay below active railroad tracks, re-excavation plans were suspended. The 1973 testing did produce valuable new information on Dent, exposing an undisturbed profile of site strata where earlier excavations had stopped along the western margins of the Dent railroad bed. Both geological data and samples were recovered from the test profile, as were mammoth bone fragments and a juvenile mammoth's skull. Bone fragments were retained for later study, but the skull was wrapped in plastic and reburied in its original find context (Frank Frazier personal communication, 1988).

In 1987, I initiated a long-term Dent site study at the University of Northern Colorado (UNC). UNC's Dent research included geological coring, limited test excavations, ground surveys, and lithic analyses, frequently conducted collaboratively with parallel research programs of other scholars (Brunswig 1995; Brunswig and Fisher 1993; Cummings and Albert 1993, Chapter 6, this volume;

Fisher 1995; Fisher and Fox, Chapter 4, this volume; Haynes et al. 1998; Saunders 1999, Chapter 5, this volume).

This chapter describes Dent Mammoth Site research results since 1987. During the past two decades that research has involved multiple lines of scientific inquiry in archaeology, geology, faunal analysis, and paleoclimatology. It has increasingly taken advantage of emerging technologies in such areas as faunal analysis, biochemistry, geoarchaeology, and computer mapping to produce a diverse range of clues, described in this and subsequent chapters, to better understand what occurred at Dent in the waning stages of North America's late Pleistocene.

CHRONOLOGY AT DENT

The earliest estimate of Dent site chronology was based on inferred late glacial gravels underlying its mammoth bone layer. In the mid-1930s the presence of the gravels was thought to indicate a time frame between 10,000 and 12,000 radiocarbon years before present (RCYBP), an excellent estimate under the circumstances. It was not until 1963 that Dent mammoth bone was first radiocarbon dated, yielding a one standard deviation date range between 11,700 and 10,700 RCYBP (Agogino 1963, 1968, 1997; Haynes 1992:362–363). Since the dated bone was originally treated with organic preservative (shellac), its initial dating yielded a younger-than-expected date of 7,200 ± 200 RCYBP (I-473). A second analysis of the same bone treated with an extraction solvent to remove preservative later provided a more plausible date of 11,200 ± 500 RCYBP.

In the 1980s and 1990s, bone from a number of mammoth sites, including Dent, was sampled to test alternate methods of processing mammoth bone for high-resolution atomic accelerator radiocarbon dating (Haynes 1992; Stafford 1988; Stafford et al. 1991). During that study, Tandem Accelerator Mass Spectroscopy (TAMS) dates were run on untreated samples of bone retrieved during 1973 University of Colorado testing. Several different organic bone chemical fractions from Dent bone were TAMS dated, including acetone-insoluble collagen, fulvic acids, O-H apatite, total bone carbon, acid-insoluble collagen, and gelatin. Archaeologically unacceptable dates, based on the currently documented Clovis radiocarbon database (Haynes 1992; Taylor et al. 1996), were derived from the use of acid-insoluble collagen (8,250 ± 520 RCYBP) and unpurified gelatin (9,240 ± 350 RCYBP). Eight additional, more plausible dates were obtained from TAMS radiocarbon dates of weak acid-soluble collagen, aspartic acid, glutamic acid, hyroxyproline, glycine, alanine, and gelatin hydrolyzed and purified with XAD resin. Those dates ranged from 10,980 ± 90 RCYBP at the high end to 10,240 ± 120 RCYBP at the lower end. In 1999, experiments using variations of the Haas and Banewicz (heating extraction) technique of processing bone apatite from mammoth tooth enamel and cortical bone produced a total of twenty-seven individual TAMS dates ranging from 3,095 ± 50 to 10,950 ± 230 RCYBP (Surovell 2000). Only one of the twenty-seven experimental extraction variations actually produced a Clovis-

Table 3.1. Dent Mammoth Bone Radiocarbon Dates, 1960–1999

Uncorrected Bone Date (RCYBP)	Laboratory Number	Dated Organic Component	Primary References
11,200 ± 500	I-622	whole bone	Agogino 1997
8,250 ± 520	AA-830	bone, acid-insoluble collagen	Agogino 1963
9,240 ± 350	AA-831	bone, unpurified gelatin	Haynes 1992
10,590 ± 500	AA-832	bone, weak acids-soluble collagen purified with XAD resins	Stafford 1988; Stafford et al. 1991
10,950 ± 480	AA-833	hydrologized gelatin, purified with XAD resins	Stafford 1988; Stafford et al. 1991
10,980 ± 90	AA-2941	XAD hydrolysate	Stafford 1988; Stafford et al. 1991
10,660 ± 170	AA-2942	aspartic acid	Stafford 1988; Stafford et al. 1991
10,800 ± 110	AA-2943	gutamic acid	Stafford 1988; Stafford et al. 1991
10,600 ± 90	AA-2945	hydroxyproline	Stafford 1988; Stafford et al. 1991
10,710 ± 90	AA-2946	glycine	Stafford 1988; Stafford et al. 1991
10,670 ± 120	AA-2947	alanine	Stafford 1988; Stafford et al. 1991
10,950 ± 250	AA-31319	tooth enamel treated by extraction heating to 620° C	Surovell 2000

age date of 10,950 ± 230 RCYBP. Table 3.1 shows data for radiocarbon-dated Dent materials from 1960 to 1999 that exclude all but the most "reliable" Haas and Banewicz experiment dates.

With ten reasonably acceptable radiocarbon determinations in hand, the Dent mammoths appear securely dated at the end of the twelfth or very early in the eleventh millennium. Stafford and colleagues (1991) suggested that the likely "true age" of the earlier series of five TAMS dates was 10,810 ± 40 RCYBP. A subsequent review (Taylor, Haynes, and Stuiver 1996) of Stafford and colleagues' radiocarbon results proposed a nearly identical age of 10,890 ± 50 RCYBP, based only on the XAD hydrolysate fraction date. With the exception of the experimental Surovell (2000) radiocarbon study, the vast majority of Dent radiocarbon dates strongly suggest its probable age is ca. 11,000 RCYBP.

GEOARCHAEOLOGICAL CONTEXT

Dent's mammoth bones and two Clovis points, excavated in 1932–1933, were described as having been recovered from 5.5 feet below the site's modern surface. The Clovis point found in 1932, excavated by Regis College, was recovered from the upper portion of the bone bed, the latter covered with "a disturbed deposit of fine sand" (Figgins 1933:4). In 1933, during Colorado Museum of Natural History excavations, lower levels of the bone bed were explored. According to Figgins's brief published account of the Dent excavations, the lower third of the bone bed was situated 7 feet below the terrace surface and consisted "of sands, gravels, pebbles and bowlders [sic], the latter occasionally as large as 20 inches or more in circumference . . . long subjected to the action of and . . . unquestionably deposited by water. It rests directly upon uneven, but undisturbed Cretaceous deposits. The overload, varying from three to four feet to ten feet in thickness, consists of fine yellow sands, doubtless secondary deposition of Cretaceous material and carrying occasional pebbles and limy concretions" (Figgins 1933:5).

Although it lasted only two days, the 1973 testing program generated new and important data on Dent that have never been extensively reported. The only available sources of 1973 results are participant recollections, field notes, and a brief section of a journal article by C. V. Haynes (1974). Combining those data with those acquired from post-1973 site coring and excavation of a UNC test trench in the site's upper draw area has made a more comprehensive assessment of Dent's geoarchaeological nature possible.

The Dent site is located within the western margins of the South Platte River of the Colorado Piedmont, immediately east of the Front Range foothills (Figure 3.1). Its immediate location is within and at the base of a fan-shaped draw eroded into low bluffs of late Cretaceous (Foxhills formation) sandstone. The bluffs mark the western boundary of the former late Pleistocene South Platte River floodplain (Figure 3.2). A large, gently rising hill, mantled by mid-Pleistocene Sluocum gravels, descends northeastward to the earlier noted sandstone bluff line. The site's faunal and archaeological remains were found embedded within a drainage cut at the base of the bluff, covered by colluvial sediments and gravel. Its mammoth remains, described in detail later, were found superimposed over an eroded surface of a former late Pleistocene–era South Platte River bed, known regionally as the Kersey Terrace.

Between 11,000 and 10,000 RCYBP, the South Platte River began incising and eventually shifted eastward from its abandoned late Pleistocene streambed below the bluffs. An approximate date of river channel down cutting and floodplain abandonment of ca. 10,105 ± 90 RCYBP has been provided by geological and radiocarbon studies of a terrace cut bank at the Bernhardt site 100 m southeast of Dent (Haynes et al. 1998; Holliday 1987:322). The modern South Platte River channel is now located 2 km to the east and 10 m lower in elevation than the Dent locality. The site itself is embedded in a locally preserved remnant of the late Pleistocene Kersey Terrace. The Dent draw (immediately west of the site's mammoth bone bed) represents a very short, minor drainage tributary into the ancient South Platte that probably allowed access through the bluffs to the river's western edge in Terminal Pleistocene times (Figure 3.3).

Data from the University of Colorado testing program (1973) and sediment cores (hand- and hydraulic-powered) taken by the Universities of Northern Colorado and Arizona between 1987 and 1994 showed Dent's stratigraphy to consist of five depositional units (Brunswig 1995; Haynes et al. 1998). These are designated here as unit K (sandstone bedrock) and units 1 through 4, in accord

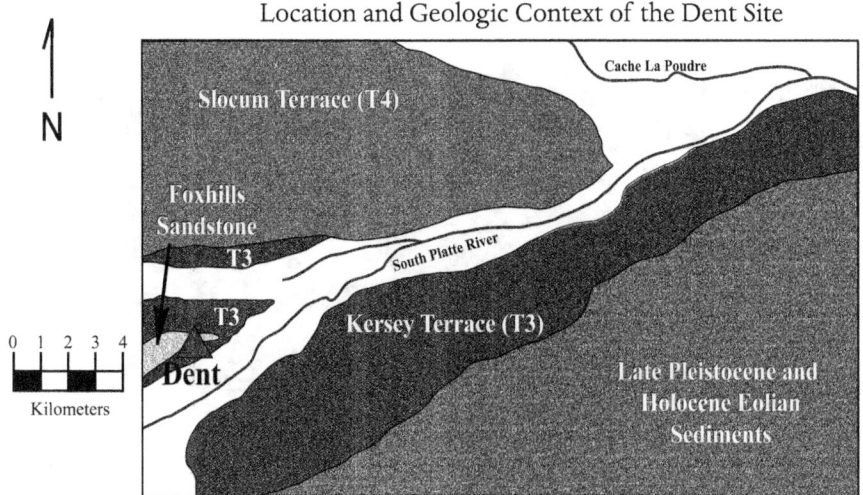

3.2. Dent geologic context.

3.3. Aerial view of Dent showing the site's drainage fan draw as it cuts through its bluff line. Courtesy, Frank Frasier.

with earlier stratigraphic unit designations established in 1973 field notes and profile drawings by Frazier and Haynes (Figure 3.4).

Unit K, the lowest geologic stratum, also appears as exposed bedrock in the adjacent bluffs and in exposed bedrock areas of the Dent draw. It is fine yellow sandstone with occasional shale laminations, belonging to the late Cretaceous Foxhills formation. Overlying K is unit 1, a buried, 10–30-cm-thick riverbed deposit of arkosic sand, gravel, and cobbles. Unit 1 samples recovered from the

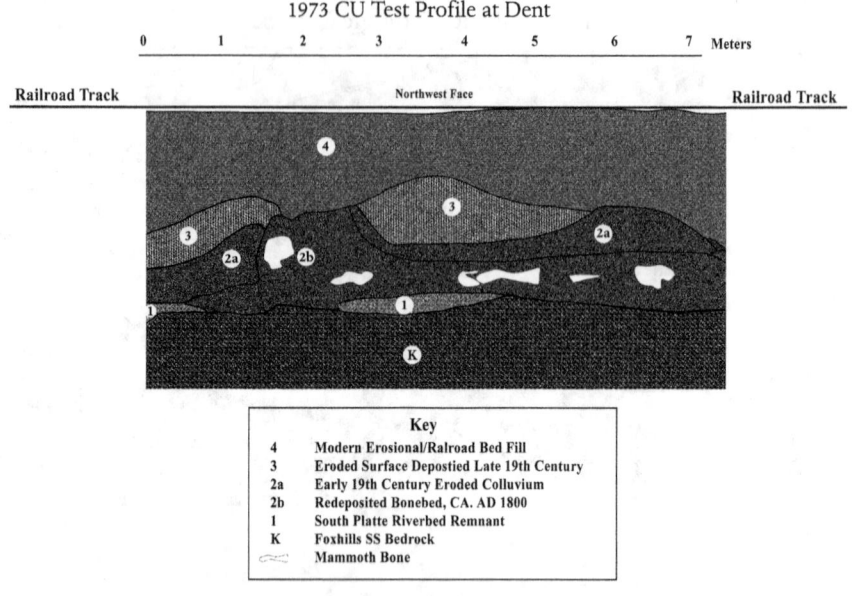

3.4. Stratigraphic profile (adapted from 1973 testing program records).

1973 trench test were analyzed for physical and sediment traits and found to compare with late Pleistocene South Platte alluvial fill retrieved from backhoe trench profiles near Kersey, Colorado (sediment data for upper Kersey deposits are described in Jepson et al. [1994:52–54, figures 16 and 17] and Haynes et al. [1998:204–208, table 1]).

Unit 1 sands and gravels are interpreted as representing primary late and Terminal Glacial deposits of the Kersey strath. Sediment analysis of unit 1 samples suggests high South Platte River sediment load and stream flow velocities prior to terrace abandonment in Terminal Glacial/early Holocene times. Excavation accounts from the 1930s established that unit 1 was thinner on the west (near the cliff margin) and thickened to the east, closer to the ancient South Platte River's main channel. The 1973 backhoe test profile indicated unit 1 alluvial deposits had been partly eroded down to unit K bedrock in several places.

The next-higher stratigraphic unit (2) has been divided into two subunits: 2a and 2b. Stratigraphic and sedimentological arguments for distinguishing the subunits are described in Haynes and colleagues (1998 and later in this chapter). Unit 2a contained most of the mammoth bone and associated soil matrix. Its base extends between 2 and 2.5 m below the modern Kersey Terrace surface (Figure 3.4). The bone bed, documented in 1932–1933 and 1973 tests and excavations, was found near the base of the Dent draw. Unit 2a sediments consist of light yellowish-brown, fine silty sand derived from decomposed, very fine sands of the Foxhills formation. Unit 2a sediments closely match the local Tassel fine sandy loam soil, derived from weathering and chemical decomposition of Foxhills parent material (Crabb 1978:40). The unit's sediments include minor amounts of calcite-encrusted quartz and quartzite sand, pebbles, and rare cobbles, derived from middle Pleistocene Slocum Terrace remnants lying directly on sandstone bedrock.

Geologic data and local topographic clues support the hypothesis that unit 2a is primarily reworked and redeposited colluvium or alluvial fan deposits derived from the adjacent draw. The likelihood of redeposition was noted in a recent study of the Dent area's geoarchaeology (Haynes et al. 1998:207–208). It is likely the unit's mammoth bone was redeposited from an upslope location. Basal portions of subunit 2a lie unconformably on an eroded surface of unit 1 alluvial fill, truncated by post-depositional erosion in its upper area. Haynes (1974), in describing unit 2a's upper contact, noted it was separated from the next overlying deposit, unit 2b, by a "weak erosional contact," indicating that its inclusive bone and sediments had been reburied soon after redeposition (also see Haynes et al. 1998:207).

Subunit 2b, found only in two discrete areas of the 1973 profile, is similar in sediment texture and composition to subunit 2a. Several distinguishing traits were noted as classifying 2b as a distinctive subunit. Test samples of 2b in 1973 contained only small fragments of mammoth bone with no significant bone elements. The subunit is further distinguished by nearly invisible, fine laminations in its upper portion (Haynes 1974). The laminations have been interpreted as representing either sheetwash or alluvial fan deposition conditions. What is not in doubt is the fact that subunit 2b was deposited subsequent to earlier *redeposition of the bone bed matrix* (subunit 2a). While the subunit 2b sedimentation rate remains uncertain, it appears to have occurred fairly rapidly and uniformly over the previously exposed and eroded surface of the primary bone bed subunit (2a).

The next-higher unit (3) in the 1973 profile is distinguished from subunits 2a and 2b by the absence of bone and a darker coloration as a result of slightly greater organic content, resulting in weak A horizon soil development. Development of the unit's weak A horizon is thought to have been a result of relative erosional stability and conditions of greater effective precipitation. The final stratigraphic unit in the profile, designated unit 4, consists of late Historic fill dirt graded over the unit 3 surface when a railroad bed was constructed over most of the site in the early 1900s.

Dent's geological evidence provides a picture of mammoth bone bed redeposition resulting from highly localized, alternating cut and fill episodes. Prior to recent geological studies, the redeposition hypothesis had been suggested by others, including Cassells (1983) and Holliday (1987:324), and proposed by the site's first investigator, Father Conrad Bilgery (1935). Support for the redeposition hypothesis and evidence for its timing are available in historically recent organic material recovered from the subunit 2a bone bed matrix in 1973. During retrieval of 1973 profile samples, it was noted that subunits 2a and 2b contained burned coal or coke (coal burned in a low oxygen atmosphere), plant rootlets, gastropods, and both burned and unburned wood (from unpublished 1973 correspondence among Frank Frazier, Vance Haynes, and Joe Ben Wheat; Haas and Haynes 1975:358; Haynes et al. 1998). The 1973 excavators were convinced that the burned and unburned wood fragments were not introduced from above through biological or mechanical turbation, because no geologically *intrusive* features related to the introduction of the wood and coke were stratigraphically defined in the profile. In fact, the samples were described as having been *well sealed* in naturally inter-bedded silty sand lenses in subunits 2a and 2b (Frank Frazier personal communication, 1988). In 1975, samples of charred wood and coke retrieved from the two subunits were radiocarbon dated (Haas and Haynes 1975). The coke was dated to 32,000 years ago (32,260 ± 2,100 RCYBP [SMU-121]), consistent with the fact that its parent material was ancient coal (the 32,000 RCYBP date was at the outside range of radiocarbon dating technology). More surprising was the charred-wood date of ca. A.D. 1780 (170 ± 50 RCYBP [SMU-120]) (Haas and Haynes 1975:358). With a lack of evidence for stratigraphic mixing, the wood-based radiocarbon date suggests bone bed redeposition no earlier than A.D. 1800 and probably within a half century of that date.

UNC CORING AND TEST EXCAVATION DATA: GEOMORPHIC MODELING

The University of Northern Colorado's Dent research was initiated in 1987 with site-area survey mapping and systematic sediment cores designed to recover column samples of the site's three-dimensional paleo-geomorphology. Sediment cores were drilled in a grid pattern over previously excavated and suspected site areas. Sediment changes in the cores were described and measured with a steel measuring tape, while surface points were transit-surveyed for contour mapping. Samples were retrieved in 20 cm probe sections, separated into unit types, then bagged, marked, and stored for analysis. Coring of the bone bed's upslope draw was done in 1991, following an analysis of core samples collected from the original bone bed vicinity from 1987 through 1990.

Systematic coring of the site area and a test trench in its upper draw provided valuable information on Dent's overall geomorphology and stratigraphy (Figure 3.5). Sediment coring occurred in areas adjacent to the original excavation, in excavation backfill, and in undisturbed sections along the railroad tracks. Unit 1, consisting of eroded remnants of late Pleistocene South Platte stream gravels and sands, was noted through most of the coring area wherever it had not been removed by earlier erosion episodes. Unit K, the underlying sandstone bedrock, was encountered at the bottom of the core, providing a baseline surface on which to plot a subsurface contour map of the site's late Pleistocene South Platte shoreline. In some areas, such as the deep gully that bisected the site immediately southeast of the excavated bone bed, late Pleistocene sandstone bedrock and overlying alluvial and colluvial deposits were found to have been completely removed over the past ten millennia. Remnants of South Platte River sediments encountered below the mammoth bone bed, although eroded and unconform-

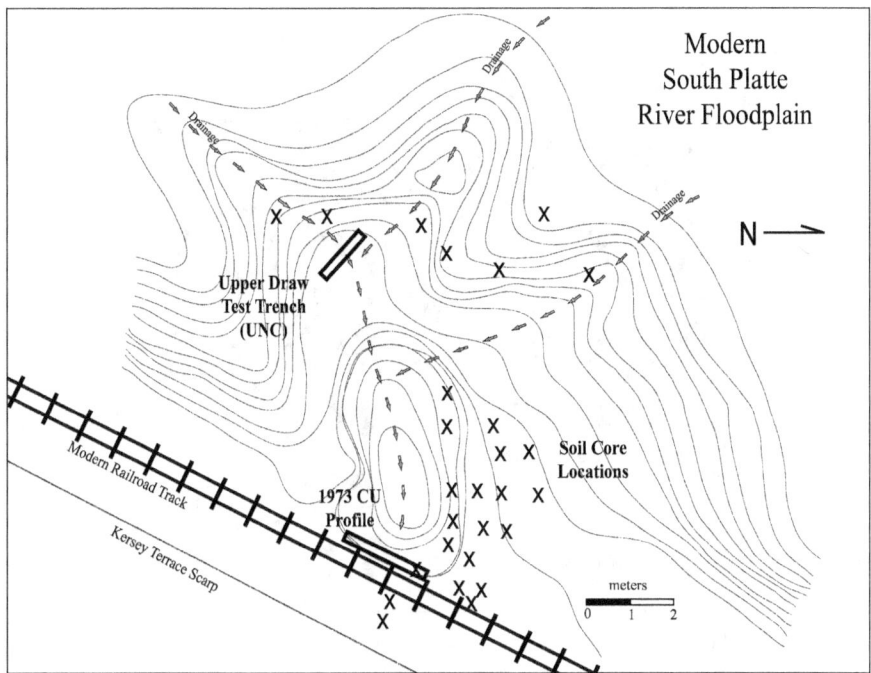

3.5. Locations of cores and upper draw test trench at Dent. Contour lines (at 0.5 meters) represent the modern surface.

able, appeared to provide a reasonable picture of the site's late Pleistocene river margin topography. Although post–bone bed erosion of the unit 1 gravel layer left limited evidence for reconstruction of late Pleistocene riverbed margin contours, the underlying sandstone bedrock surface defined in the grid cores provided a reasonably assured guide for the reconstruction. A similar effort at subsurface contouring of the upper Dent draw area was made using data from grid cores and the single test trench. These provided important baseline information for reconstruction of that portion of the site's overall paleo-topography.

Sediment cores in the site's upper erosional fan area revealed that two (right and center) of the three modern swales in the fan-shaped draw were very shallow, with fine sandy colluvium and Slocum calcite-encrusted gravels extending only 15–20 cm below the surface before encountering sandstone bedrock. Only the southernmost (or left) swale was found to have any depth. Earlier, during 1991 sediment coring of that swale, sediment core penetration was halted by heavy gravel and cobble deposits below 50 cm. In 1993 a 3-m-long by 1.5-m-wide test trench was excavated, revealing a buried, narrow, confining gully more than 1.5 m deep (the test trench location shown in Figure 3.5). The trench profile revealed evidence for three cut and fill episodes, closely matching similar deposits found in the 1973 upper bone bed profile (Figure 3.6). The recent nature of the test trench's

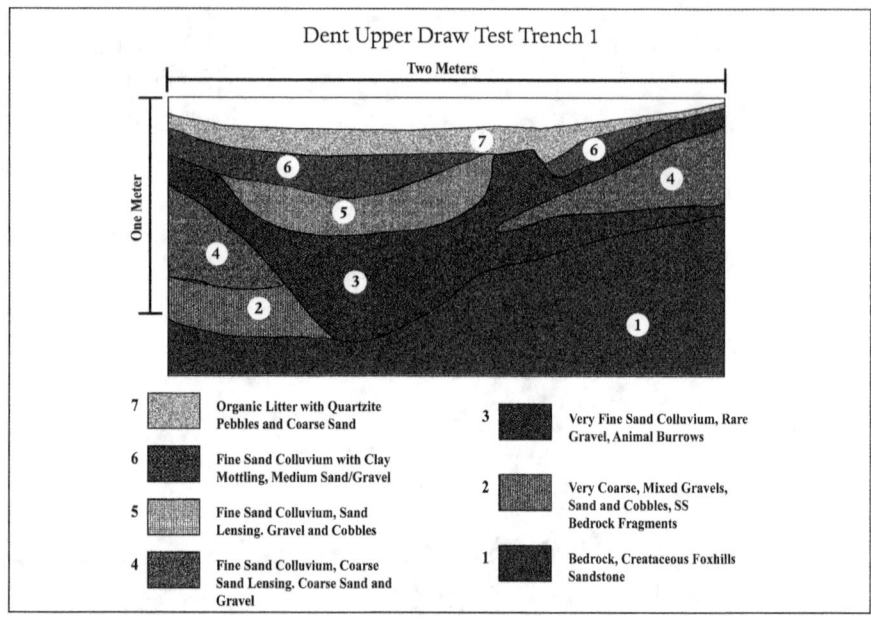

3.6. *Profile of UNC's Dent upper (southeast) gully test trench.*

cut and fill deposits was emphasized by recovery of early-twentieth-century nails and metal artifacts more than halfway down into the stratified units. The trench testing results provide evidence for the recent deposition of upper sedimentary units (2a/2b and 3) of the main bone bed.

In 1993 a hydraulic corer was used to probe for subsurface stratigraphic deposits below the modern railroad track (Haynes et al. 1998:209). The cores revealed a continuation of the site's lower bone bed within an east-west paleo-draw swale under the tracks for a distance of ca. 30 m, with an inferred width of 8–12 m. Fragments of mammoth bone recovered in the cores indicated that elements of the previously described redeposited unit 2a bone bed were present.

Three-dimensional mapping, using a combination of coring, test trench, and topographic surface data, was done to recreate a hypothetical model of Dent's late Pleistocene terrain. A resulting paleo-map (Figure 3.7) suggests that, ca. 11,000 RCYBP, a northward-flowing South Platte River angled west toward the sandstone bluffs (and Dent) from an east-trending river bend just south of the site. Paleo-contour mapping and local floodplain geomorphology indicate that the river angled northward along the bluffs to the base of the modern Dent draw and gradually curved northeast to complete a river bend loop. If accurate, the reconstruction would mean that Dent was located at a river bend where stream flow would have been subject to increased turbulence and sediment load materials settling near the river's western shore, creating a relatively shallow river ford. This scenario is supported by the nature of riverbed sediments recovered

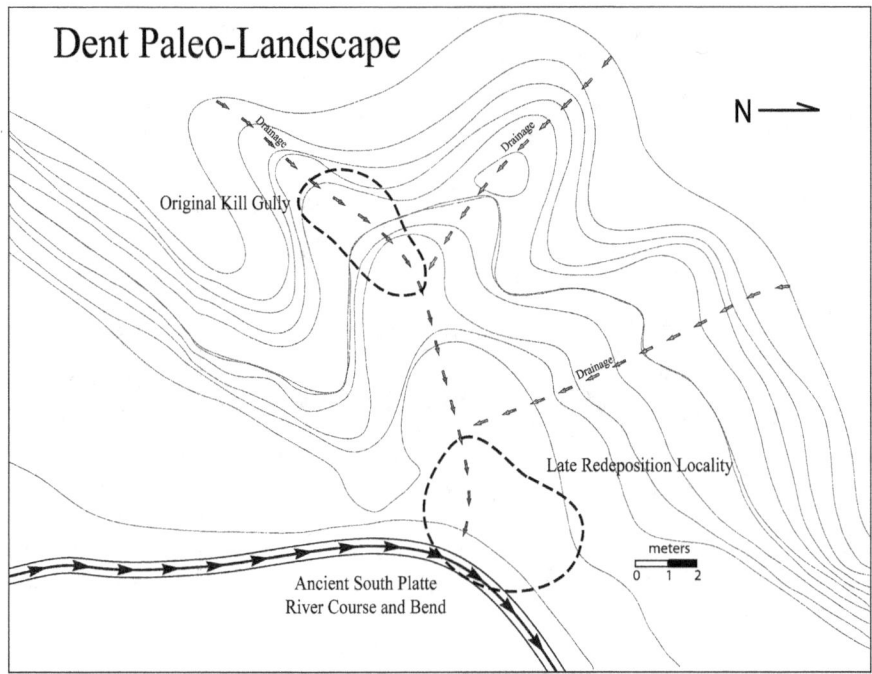

3.7. *Hypothesized paleolandscape of Dent kill locality.*

from the 1973 unit 1 profile, consisting of coarse gravels, pebbles, and large cobbles (up to 13 cm in diameter). It is reasonable to hypothesize that sediment accumulation and stream flow retardation at the Dent locality created a shallow ford where humans and animals could have crossed the river, particularly during fall and winter months when water levels would have been low. As discussed in greater detail later, it is probable the river crossing would have been part of the mammoth herd's seasonal migratory rounds and well-known to locally informed Clovis hunters. Dent's local landscape, in essence, would have consisted of an erosion-incised alluvial fan cut through low sandstone bluffs, allowing animal and human access to a shallow ford in a South Platte River bend (Figure 3.7).

Two additional lines of evidence support the river crossing scenario: a fall-winter season of death finding for the Dent mammoths (discussed later and in Chapter 4, this volume) and the modern presence of an abandoned (although much later) prehistoric/historic channel in the floodplain immediately east of Dent, showing an identical west-looping river bend pattern to that hypothesized for the late Pleistocene site (Figure 3.8).

FAUNAL DATA: THE DENT MAMMOTHS

This section discusses and summarizes historical and recent research associated with Dent's mammoth remains. The section summarizes an impressive

3.8. Aerial view of Dent locality showing a now-abandoned (and much later than Dent) South Platte River channel that may approximate the more ancient Dent-age river course. Courtesy, Frank Frasier.

body of faunal evidence on the animals, including osteological data used to reconstruct their number, ages, genders, social (herd) behavior, and evidence of butchering. Other forms of analysis extracted evidence for season of death (tooth and tusk growth rings), mammoth diet (chemical isotope and micro-botanical data), paleoenvironmental/paleoclimatic conditions, and Dent herd migratory patterns. Three major Dent faunal studies are included in this volume and follow this chapter (Chapters 4–6).

Osteological and Life Composition Data

Until recently, published data on Dent mammoth remains were limited. Figgins (1933:7), in his only report on the site, remarked that fourteen individuals, mainly sub-adults, were recovered from the bone bed. Most of the Dent skeletal remains were curated at the Denver Museum of Natural History through the 1950s (the museum began as the Colorado Museum of Natural History, later adopted the name Denver Museum of Natural History, and was recently renamed the Denver Museum of Nature and Science). However, in 1935 an adult female skeleton had been sent to the Carnegie Museum in Pittsburgh, Pennsylvania. Then, in the 1940s the Denver museum constructed a juvenile mammoth display from bone elements of several individuals, but in the 1960s that display was transported to another institution, the Cleveland Museum, in return for other paleontological specimens. Until recently, little effort had been made to catalog and study Dent mammoth remains. That situation changed in 1978 when Saunders (1980)

Table 3.2. Age Distribution of Dent Mammoths in African Elephant [Equivalent] Years (AEY). Adapted from Saunders (1980:table 2, 1999; Chapter 5, this volume).

Accession Number	AEY Age
Sub-Adults	
EPV/DMNH* 1897	2
EPV/DMNH 1893	3
EPV/DMNH 1898	3
EPV/DMNH 1637	6
EPV/DMNH 1895	9
EPV/DMNH 1899	10
CIMNH2 (Cleveland)	10
EPV/DMNH 1896	14
EPV/DMNH 1901†	16
Adults	
EPV/DMNH 1636	22
CaMNH3 (Pittsburgh)	23
EPV/DMNH 1894	26
DMNH 1450	28
EPV/DMNH 1635	43 ± 2

* EPV/DMNH=Denver Museum of Natural History (second incarnation of the current Denver Museum of Nature and Science). EPV represents a recently introduced accession prefix system.
† Individual recently identified in Denver collections by Saunders (1999).

researched the Dent materials along with mammoth remains from other Clovis sites. From an analysis of Dent materials in Denver, Pittsburgh, and Cleveland, Saunders concluded Dent's minimum number of individuals (MNI) was thirteen. A more recent analysis of Dent skeletal elements revealed an additional juvenile in the Denver Museum collections and established an age distribution (attritional) profile of nine juveniles (sixteen years or younger) and five mature adults (older than twenty-two years) (Saunders 1999; Table 3.2). An additional juvenile skull was discovered in the University of Colorado's 1973 testing program but was reburied in the profile wall pending future re-excavation and study. Discounting potential additional remains existing in yet-unexcavated portions of the site, the current Dent faunal assemblage count (MNI) now stands at fifteen.

Inferred Social Organization and Behavior

Dent's mammoth age distribution is characterized by an adult age cluster between 22 and 28 African Elephant [Equivalent] Years (AEY) and a single adult standing alone at 43 AEY. Saunders (1980:91–93) found a surprisingly close age distribution parallel of the Dent group with matriarchal elephant herd data from Africa and concluded that "the Dent sample compares closely with the Murchison Falls [Uganda] data, which are matriarchal family units."

Modern African elephant herds have multigeneration family units based in mature females and sexually immature offspring of both sexes (Haynes 1992a:65–

74). Both male and female calves are typically weaned between 2½ and 4 years of age and reach sexual maturity between 12 and 15 years. Male elephants, on reaching maturity, generally leave (or are forced to leave) the family herd and live solitary lives or join small male herds. It is only during the annual mating season that males temporarily interact with matriarchal family herds. Matriarchal African elephant family herds are led by their oldest female, known as the matriarch. Matriarchs are mother, grandmother, or eldest sibling to the remaining younger adult females. Gary Haynes's (1992a:66) study of African elephant herds in Zimbabwe's Hwange National Park showed that "groups that contained nine to twenty-nine animals were considered to be of 'medium' size, although fifteen is probably an optimal number for a 'medium' group."

The Dent age distribution supports a demographic pattern of a medium-size matriarchal herd consisting (minimally) of an older female matriarch, four younger (daughter or sister) adult females, and at least ten (including the skull remaining at the site) sub-adults ranging from 2 to 16 AEY. If the modern elephant analogue for Columbian mammoths is accurate, the Dent mammoths would have constituted a herd with an alpha matriarch female, other adult cows, and younger, immature male and female calves. The Dent herd, again if the African elephant social model fits, would also have been socially and genetically related to one or more other such herds in the region that belonged to a larger "clan," closely related family units that would have occasionally aggregated in larger clan gatherings where "[s]eparate matrilines come and go in everyday groupings, attaching themselves to other groups when convenient or preferred" (Haynes 1992a:66).

Aside from the Dent assemblage age profile, fossil and social behavior studies comparing African elephant social behavior and Columbian mammoths suggest both species followed a matriarchal herd social pattern. One source of fossil data has been extracted from sinkhole sediment deposits of South Dakota's Hot Springs Mammoth Site. Hot Springs was an artesian spring-fed sinkhole active in Wisconsin III–late Pleistocene times at ca. 26,000 RCYBP. At Hot Springs, over an estimated 500–1,000-year time span, as many as 100 mammoths (representing two species, *Mammuthus primigenius* and *Mammuthus columbi*) were trapped and died by either drowning or starvation in the site's steep-sided depression (Agenbroad 1984, 1990; Lister and Agenbroad 1994). More than 80 percent of 43 Hot Springs mammoths excavated by 1989 were determined to have been older juveniles or younger adults (probably males), but sex determination on most of the skeletal material was problematic (Agenbroad 1990:34; Lister and Agenbroad 1994). The remaining 18 percent of the Hot Springs mammoths were older, physically declining animals near the end of their life spans. In light of these data, Larry Agenbroad (1990) suggested the majority of Hot Springs mammoths represented young, inexperienced males. Further, these young males are seen as having been either members of African elephant-equivalent male herds or solitary bachelors previously separated from their childhood matriarchal family herds. According to Agenbroad (1990:37), the Hot Springs sinkhole was a fatal attractor for "adventurous 12- to 30-year-old bachelor males," *but* "no infants are known from the Hot Springs Mammoth Site as yet, probably due to the 'baby sitting' efforts of big sisters, aunts and mother [i.e., the matriarchal herd]."

Physical Condition of the Mammoth Bones and Questions of In Situ Articulation

Museum studies by myself and others have determined that the overall physical condition of Dent mammoth bones ranges from excellent to good (see Saunders, Chapter 5, this volume). None exhibits weathering traits greater than early stage two in the Behrensmeyer (1978) weathering scale. Although weathering and minor rodent marks are present, Dent mammoth bones and teeth were apparently preserved by rapid burial at their original death event (or events—discussed later) and later Historic period redeposition. In past discussions on Dent, it has been suggested that some of its skeletal elements may have been recovered in articulated positions. If true, it would indicate that those elements remained attached by muscle and ligaments by the time of burial. However, a much later redeposition of the remains long after death, as indicated earlier, would have rendered any semblance of articulation extremely unlikely. Further, visual analysis of a short film clip of the 1933 excavation provides no obvious evidence of skeletal articulation.

Season-of-Death Analysis

Season-of-death studies were conducted on a Dent mammoth tusk and teeth by Dan Fisher (Brunswig and Fisher 1993; Fisher 1995; Fisher and Beld 2003; Fisher and Fox, Chapter 4, this volume) in tandem with UNC's geoarchaeological research, discussed earlier. They indicated a possible simultaneous or near-simultaneous late-fall kill of two of the three sampled individuals (an older female, based on season-of-death analysis of the DMNH 1450 tusk, possibly the herd's ca. 43 ± 2 AEY-old matriarch) and a young (ca. 9 AEY, based on analysis of the DMNH 1895 pre-molar) juvenile. The third animal, a 2-AEY-old infant (based on analysis of the DMNH 1897 pre-molar), yielded tooth laminae and oxygen isotope results consistent with a slightly later early-winter kill. Fisher and Fox (Chapter 5, this volume) observed strong similarities, but also some variations, in oxygen isotope values between the adult female and the 9-year-old juvenile (whose deaths were considered late fall and may or may not have been contemporaneous), but a more marked difference in oxygen isotope values was seen between that older female and the youngest mammoth (2 AEY) whose death appears to have occurred slightly later in time (early winter). Fisher and Fox (Chapter 4, this volume, pp. 146) suggested that the difference could be related to changes induced by nursing and "[m]ay be compatible with interpreting the latter (DMNH 1897 [the two-year-old]) as belonging to a nursing calf of the adult female that produced the tusk, but regardless of the likely milk intake of a calf this age (and a consequent shift in isotope profile), the different seasons of death for these two individuals imply they did not comprise a mother-calf pair at death."

Fisher and Fox also suggest that the other sampled individual (DMNH 1895), at 9 AEY, was too old to be nursing and that modest oxygen isotope differences between it and the older individual "probably [imply] memberships in [a] different family," although both appear to have died around the same time. The possibility of multiple death events (two or even three) at the site is also suggested by a more recent study of Dent mammoth tooth carbon, oxygen, and strontium isotope ratios that indicate it, along with four other mammoth sites (Blackwater Draw, Friesenhahn, Miami, and Waco), may represent an "accumulated" faunal assemblage (Hoope 2004:139–140). Saunders's analyses of butchering marks on Dent bone also support the probability of serial processing of mammoth remains over a limited period of time (Chapter 5, this volume). Implications of the potential multiple death event findings are discussed in greater detail later.

Micro-botanical Evidence for Diet and Paleoenvironment

Another Dent research effort consisted of extraction of plant opal phytoliths from tartar deposits on mammoth molars. While the research has been successful in extracting phytoliths, the main type of plant represented in the first molar tested, prickly pear cactus (*Opuntia* sp.), was puzzling (Cummings 1993; Cummings and Albert 1993, Chapter 6, this volume). However, other micro-botanical remains from that molar were within expectations, including the presence of grass phytoliths, a fragment of conifer bark, and river-based sponge spicules, which suggest a mixed grazing-browsing diet within a range of regional micro-environments. Subsequent tartar extractions of three additional Dent molars provided further evidence of mammoth grazing across a wide range of ecozones and data suggesting late Pleistocene climatic conditions at least marginally cooler and wetter than at present (Cummings and Albert 1993, Chapter 6, this volume). The existence of cooler seasonal temperatures in the Dent time period, on the range of 2–4°C cooler than at present, is indicated by oxygen isotope ratios of Dent mammoth molars (Fisher and Fox, Chapter 4, this volume). This conclusion is further supported by a recent chemical study of Dent mammoth teeth and bone that compared carbon isotope, oxygen isotope, and strontium isotope ratios, concluding the animals lived in a region with a cooler-than-present climate and drank water produced in a cold climate regime (Hoope 2004:140–141: Hoope, Carlson, and Webb 1999). Chemical evidence of a cooler and possibly moister climate regime in the late Clovis Period appears to run counter to Haynes's (1989) North American Clovis-age drought.

DENT ARCHAEOLOGICAL EVIDENCE

Dent was one of the earliest excavated Clovis sites in the United States, but it was not initially recognized as such. The Clovis culture derives its name from the town of Clovis, New Mexico, where Clovis points were discovered in association with mammoth remains in 1936. Figgins's 1933 article on Dent referred to its projectile points as a "crude" version of the then-newly recognized Folsom projectile point type. Figgins's identification of Dent points as Folsom is interesting in light of the fact he had previously suggested the point recovered by Bilgery in 1932 was *pre-Folsom*. In a letter to Bilgery on November 13, 1932 (letter on file at the Denver Museum of Nature and Science), Figgins, having examined a point discovered in Regis College's first excavation, noted, "It must be regarded as antedating the true Folsom culture. Indeed, the rather crude workmanship it exhibits is suggestive of its being earlier than our examples of pre-Folsom culture."

Dent archaeological evidence is confined to two complete Clovis points and one partial Clovis point, the latter reworked into a knife. The two complete points were recovered in situ during the 1932 and 1933 excavations. The third artifact, possibly a reworked Clovis point upper blade section or (as discussed later) a Clovis-era Sandia knife, was found during the 1932–1933 excavations and removed from the site by the site's initial discoverer, Frank Garner, an action then unknown to the Dent excavators. In 1954, geologist Harold Malde, Denver Museum of Natural History archaeologist H. Marie Wormington, and George Volk (Wormington's husband) traveled to Dent to re-examine the site and interview local residents who had participated in or visited the original excavations (Malde 1954). Among those interviewed was Frank Garner, the railroad foreman who first reported the site to the Dent station master. After completing the interviews and returning to Denver, Wormington was contacted by Garner, who informed her he had picked up an artifact from near a mammoth tooth during Bilgery's 1932 excavations and kept it, not thinking to tell anyone. He subsequently contributed the reworked upper Clovis blade to the Denver Museum, where it remains on display.

I assessed all three artifacts in their cast or original forms for manufacturing and use-wear characteristics. Figure 3.9 shows a photograph of two of the original artifacts and a cast of the third.

Bilgery and his crew recovered projectile point A, designated here as 5WL269-001, in November 1932 from 1.69 m below the surface in the main bone bed (subunit 2a). It was found lying just beneath and between two metapodial (cannon) bones in the bone matrix. Unfortunately, the original point was lost or stolen from the (then-named) Denver Museum of Natural History in the early 1940s. Fortunately, several plaster casts and a physical description of the point survived. My analysis of the tools also included the consultation of descriptive notes and illustrations made by Joe Ben Wheat (University of Colorado) in the early 1970s and descriptive notes graciously provided by Frank Frazier (a geologist who participated in the 1973 testing program).

Since the earliest discovered point (A-001) was lost, its actual weight cannot be known. However, reasonably accurate attribute measurements were obtained from plaster casts and are presented in Table 3.3. Source information on the Dent

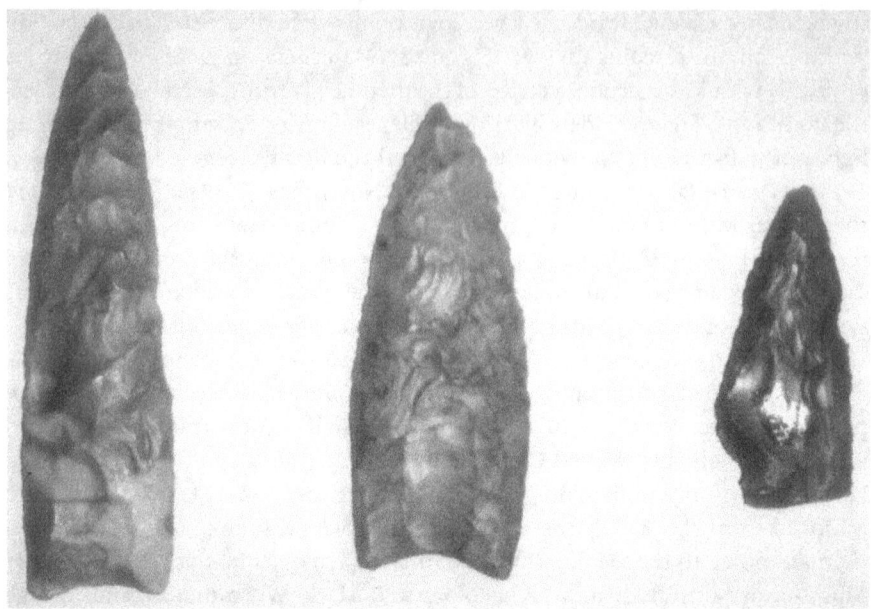

3.9. Photograph of Dent artifacts. Left (001), center (002), right (003).

A-001 lithic material type is taken from a brief description by Figgins (1933:5), who indicates it was made of either a semitranslucent, fine-grained chert or chalcedony, probably containing inclusions of both closely related materials. Figgins, using the Ridgeway Color Standards and Color Nomenclature, described the material as deep brownish drab, with irregular inclusions of pale brownish drab to creamy white. The most appropriate Munsell soil color chart analog for the primary (deep brownish drab) color is 10R 4/2 (weak red). Texture, material type, and colorations correspond to a regional lithic material known as Flattop Chert, which outcrops in northwestern Logan County, Colorado. Examination of the casts suggests manufacturing consisted of primary flaking of a large flake or core preform with soft hammer percussion, with pressure flaking shaping of the point's basal and lateral blade edges. Pressure flaking retouch was subsequently done to rejuvenate dulled or broken blade edge areas. Lower lateral blade and base edges were heavily ground, presumably to facilitate hafting and prevent cutting of haft bindings.

Use-wear traits of the lost projectile point were reconstructed through a close examination of extremely high-quality plaster museum casts (multiples were made) made prior to its loss. The casts show evidence of heavy lateral grinding of the point's lower basal blades, extending around 280 mm upward from its base. Moderate to heavy basal concavity grinding was also noted. Pressure flake removals form a serrate pattern on the upper half of both upper blade side areas, suggesting sharpening retouch. Midsections of both blade edges show evidence of heavy downward cutting pressure, with obvious edge crushing and step fracture. There is also minor faceting (step fracturing) on the upper tip area of the right-hand blade, possibly as a result of use of the tool in cutting or sawing. This latter action resulted in the creation of a burinated tip.

Dent point B-002 was originally discovered during Colorado Museum of Natural History excavations on June 13, 1933. It was found embedded in the subunit 2a bone-soil matrix near a heavy concentration of mammoth bone. The point is both shorter and broader than point A but well within the morphological range of known Clovis points. It was recovered at a depth of 2.13 m, about 60 cm from a mammoth long bone. Surviving 16 mm film of the 1933 excavation provides a close-up of the point's discovery context. Its physical attributes are given in Table 3.3. Based on comparative lithic samples, the point's material traits are closely comparable with those of Hartville Chert found in southeastern Wyoming. Its primary colors range from yellowish brown (10YR 5/6) to brown (7.5YR 5/6), and it contains black (N 2/0) inclusions. Its luster is dull and waxy, and the material is translucent to a depth of approximately 1.5 mm. Primary flaking was accomplished by soft hammer percussion, with pressure flaking used to form basal and lateral blade edges. In places, pressure flaking retouch had been used to rejuvenate dulled or broken blade edge areas. Lower lateral blade and base edges were heavily ground to facilitate hafting. The point has a tip section broken off on one side, but freshness of the flake scar suggests the break is recent. The unbroken tip side has two burinated facets with evidence of crushed and heavily worn edges, which suggests the tip area was used for wedging, prying, cutting, or some combination.

Saunders's analysis of Dent mammoth bone revealed evidence of tool pry marks, which, combined with the point's use-wear patterning, supports its final stage of utilization as a processing tool. Its upper blade edges are pressure flake serrated, particularly on the right blade, and serrated edge areas show evidence of heavy crushing across raised surface projections. Heavy step fracturing from intense downward cutting is evident on the right blade side immediately below and at its burinated tip. During cutting, deep conchoidal flakes spalled off along the upper half to two-thirds of both blade edges. Thinner areas of the blade margins are broken or crushed from use, producing high flaking angles (dulling). In the center of both blades, there is also rounding and smoothing of retouched edges, with moderate polish evident in flake scar valleys. Haft polish is evident in the flute scars of both lower blade areas. Moderate impact crushing and microflake removal also occur in the center of the point's basal cavity, suggesting wear stemming from its use as a weapon as well as a processing tool.

Physical examination of the original point allowed its manufacturing sequence to be reconstructed in detail. That sequence is described next, based in part on handwritten notes by Joe Ben Wheat (unpublished notes in possession of the author) and in part on my own observations. The flute-area flaking sequence in the lower part of side A is reconstructed as follows:

1. A wide, flat, thin fluting flake was removed from the exterior of the point base.
2. A second and narrower, deeper flute was then removed from near the present base area.

The flute-area flaking sequence continued in the lower part of side B and can be reconstructed as follows:

3. A wide, flat, fluting flake was removed from the corner of the base.
4. A second and narrower, deeper flute flake was then removed cutting through part of the third-stage flake scar.
5. Finally, just before basal and lateral grinding occurred, a series of fine pressure flakes were removed from the basal portion of the stage 2 flute scars.

Point C-003 is a knife and cutting tool, once probably hafted to a bone or wood handle. Macroscopic and microscopic analyses indicate it may be a substantially reworked upper portion of a Clovis point that, prior to reworking, was snapped off in use or by accident. However, morphologically, the artifact, with the exception of its unshaped, hinge fractured base, resembles type II "points" from Sandia Cave, New Mexico (Hibben 1941, 1946; Stevens and Agogino 1961:39–44; Willey 1966:41). Its different blade angles, in particular, suggest it was manufactured (or reworked) for use as a cutting tool rather than simply being a snapped-off Clovis point section. After two decades of geoarchaeological studies at Sandia Cave, Haynes and Agogino (1986:29) concluded that Sandia points were likely specialized Clovis or (less likely) Folsom tools.

As noted earlier, whether the Dent artifact is typologically related to Sandia points or not, we do know it was originally discovered by railroad worker Frank Garner in 1932 during Regis College excavations at Dent and (much) later reported to Marie Wormington in a 1955 interview prior to Garner's death (Wormington 1957:44; Wormington Interview Notes 1955, on file at the Denver Museum of Nature and Science). Garner described the point as having been recovered from the unit 2a bone bed about 30 cm from a mammoth molar. Physical attributes of the tool are given in Table 3.3. Point 003's lithic material is a fine-quality chert. The actual material source is undetermined, but its physical attributes resemble those of Knife River flint from the Dakotas, although the color is darker and blacker than most samples of that material, which tends to be dark brown in color. A second possible source is a dark gray chert found in Mississippian formations of Wyoming's Hartville uplift. The tool's primary Munsell color is very dark gray (N 3/0), with darker areas of dark gray (N 4/0) and occasional, minor inclusions of black (N 2/0).

Use-wear analysis shows the tool's tip to have one side with an angled burination, with evidence of crushing and use in downward cutting. Its burinated edge shows extremely heavy wear. Both blade edges show evidence of heavy wear and crushing in raised flake scar sections. In some flake scars, percussion lines are

Table 3.3. Metric Attributes of Dent Tools.

Attributes	001	002	003
Weight (gms)	unknown	28.87	14.84
Maximum thickness (mm)	8.75	8.2	7.4
Total length (mm)	114.5	92.7*	62.8
Blade length (mm)	115.5	91.6	60.1
Maximum blade width (mm)	31.0	37.0	31.0
Blade tip angle (o)	70	75	61
Blade edge angle (o)	12.5	17	29[†]
			27.5[‡]
Blade edge cross-section angle (o)	28.5	20	26.5[†]
			10[‡]
Maximum base concavity depth (mm)	2.5	4.2	NA
Base width (mm)	28.9	30.4	26.1
Flute width (side A) (mm)	16.0	15.5	NA
Flute width (side B) (mm)	14.5	16.4	NA
Flute length (side A) (mm)	15.7	31.2	NA
Flute length (side B) (mm)	27.1	40.0	NA
Lower blade basal grinding edge width (right on side A) (mm)	33	35.8	NA
Lower blade basal grinding edge width (left on side A) (mm)	31	38.0	NA

* Tip broken after discovery. Estimated original length is 94 mm.
† Long blade side.
‡ Short blade side.

smoothed, and some interior flake valleys show evidence of retouch with step fracturing. Also present are conchoidal fractures resulting from heavy downward cutting pressure. In the lower left-hand corner of the tool, there is a concave notch with evidence of moderate wear. The artifact's area of heaviest and most persistent wear is on the longer blade edge. The basal area has prominent snap-hinge fracturing, suggesting that the reworked tool had once been hafted and snapped off in the upper haft area while in use. Evidence for hafting is present in polish over the basal flute scars. Lower flake scar remnants, present on both basal areas of dorsal and ventral faces, are well polished, supporting the probability that fluting flakes were removed to facilitate hafting. However, the "snapping off" of the hafted tool left only the uppermost portion of the fluting flake scars intact, preventing more complete haft-wear analysis. This evidence indicates the artifact served as a hafted knife and had been manufactured from the upper two-thirds of a Clovis point that, on having been snapped off at the upper end of its flute, was reworked. Reworking appears to have included refluting the broken piece for a second, post-break hafting.

Aside from the Clovis tools, other possible Dent artifacts have been cited in the presence of large river cobbles. In 1933, Figgins described "bowlders" within the unit C bone bed as "occasionally as large as 20 inches or more in circumference" (1933:5). He suggested they could have been used as hammers or stunning projectiles in the mammoth kill and later butchering activity. He also noted that such "bowlders" were uncommon to the Dent area and must have been transported to the site by hunters. As Cassells (1998:61–62), in a review of Dent archaeology, pointed out, cobbles up to 6 inches in diameter, equivalent to Figgins's 20-inch circumference, are common on the adjacent, eroded remnants of the western, higher Slocum Terrace. Further, this author has noted the existence of similar cobbles in the modern Dent upper draw area. The presence of large Slocum-derived cobbles in the upper draw area makes it likely that some of Figgins's "bowlders" were washed in with the redeposited bone bed from an upslope location. Whether those cobbles played a role in processing the mammoth carcasses will likely remain a mystery, although Saunders, in his study (Chapter 5, this volume, and later discussion in this chapter) of butchering marks on the Dent bones, suggests large cobbles could well have been employed as hammers during processing.

EVIDENCE OF HUMAN MODIFICATION OF DENT MAMMOTH BONE

In the past two decades, a number of researchers have examined Dent mammoth bone for evidence of deliberate human modification, either as tool cut marks or intentional flaking and smashing of bone (e.g., D. Fisher 1988). Recent investigation of the Dent material by Saunders (1999, Chapter 5, this volume) established the presence of butchering modifications on a number of bones, suggesting both primary (fresh) and secondary (scavenging) butchering activities. That study documented several bone modifications traceable to human agency. Although its observed modifications might seem relatively few for processing up to fifteen mammoths, it should be noted that, while some mammoth kill sites present reasonably good evidence of butchering activity on bone, others do not.

Cut marks and bone modifications in the form of punctates and a human-like design have been documented elsewhere on two adult mammoths from New Mexico's Clovis type-site (Saunders 1992; Saunders and Daeschler 1994). Another Clovis site, Lange-Ferguson, is directly associated with Clovis artifacts (Hannus 1990) and included evidence of extensive butchering marks at strategic bone locations and bone breakage consistent with deliberate flaking of fresh bone to create tools used in processing.

Saunders (Chapter 5, this volume) identified carcass processing markings on several Dent mammoth scapulae and long bones (ulnas, tibias, and femurs). The most extensive cultural modifications, on scapulae, were medium to heavy cut mark striations, tool indentations, and chatter marks consistent with manual defleshing, chopping, and prying. Light to heavy cut marks, as well as gouge and pry marks, were noted on ulnas, tibias, and femurs. Saunders (Chapter 5, this volume) cites a number of mainly transverse, fine to medium cut marks on these bone elements as morphologically consistent with ones ethnographically documented in the filleting of meat from bone during game butchering. Saunders also found evidence of delayed post-kill processing that likely occurred "when the carcasses were no longer fresh," an activity that could have ranged from days to weeks after death depending on carcass preservation conditions, particularly seasonal temperatures.

Despite the presence of processing marks on some Dent bones, their overall evidence is relatively limited compared with butchering evidence often found on smaller species in archaeological contexts. However, research suggests that clear and abundant butchering evidence of such large game species as proboscideans (including mammoths, mastodons, and modern elephants) is unlikely to occur (discussed later). The relative lack of such evidence appears to be a result of at least two factors: (1) the physical characteristics of proboscidean (in this case mammoth) anatomical elements, and (2) the likelihood of only partial, selective processing of selected carcass elements and not others. Insight into the first factor comes from experiments with stone-tool butchering by archaeologists on dead zoo elephants and African elephants culled from wild game preserves, which infrequently leave tool marks on freshly butchered elephant bone (Frison 1989). Frison and Todd (1986:42), noting the lack of cut marks on clearly butchered mammoths at the Wyoming Colby site, suggested that, in the Colby case: "The bone surfaces here are well-preserved, but there are no cutting or chopping marks to indicate the process or processes that were involved. The absence of such marks is not surprising based on experimental evidence. The identical separation [of bone ligament attachments] was done on the front leg of a mature Indian elephant. The joint capsule was too thick for the cutting tools to penetrate and leave marks on the bone even though the cutting of the ligaments required heavy pressure on the tools. Even so, the separation was accomplished without undue difficulty."

The Colby interpretation provides only a partial explanation for limited butchering evidence on the Dent mammoths. A corollary factor may be present in the nature of the site itself. Dent, unlike known or inferred individualized kill events at the Clovis, Lange-Ferguson, and Colby sites, appears to represent at least two closely spaced but separate kill events involving one or more ambushes of mammoth family herds or returning elements of the same herd (discussed later). The sheer volume of subsistence resources represented by multiple mammoths killed in a single hunting event would have presented a substantial butchering and processing task for Clovis hunter-gatherers, even with additional, slightly later scavenging of the mammoth carcasses (as suggested by Saunders in Chapter 5, this volume). Selective and incomplete butchering of the Dent mammoths, resulting in a relatively low representation of butchering modifications, could be related to conditions surrounding the closely spaced autumn–early-winter kills—particularly given the site's confined arroyo topography. Conditions under which the kills took place presented a surfeit of subsistence wealth and, at the same time, a logistical problem for the hunters: how to process the animals before advanced physical deterioration made processing of the remains impractical. Exacerbating the problem is the likelihood that the Dent kills likely took place in a confined space, in a sloping, narrow paleo-gully that transects the bluff top to the river. Although a good location for a kill, a hypothesized Dent gully trap would have ended up being densely packed with bunched mammoth family carcasses after each kill. Wholesale, complete butchering of multi-ton animals in such a context would have been difficult in such closed circumstances and may have discouraged other mammoth groups, if present in the area, from using the same corridor for some time afterward.

Dent faunal data (see Chapters 4 and 5, this volume) support the hypothesis that the site's bone bed represents a series of at least two closely spaced kill and processing events by one or more bands of Clovis hunter-gatherers. Those hunters would have likely concentrated on more physically accessible mammoth body parts immediately after the kill and later returned for final scavenging of remaining meat scraps, bone, and bone marrow. Another important clue to what may have transpired at Dent is found in the physical condition of the bones on excavation. While some postmortem rodent tooth marks have been identified along with minimal weathering evidence, the bones are in remarkably good condition and lack substantial evidence of carnivore gnawing. Saunders (1999, Chapter 5, this volume) interprets generalized weathering patterns of the Dent bone as early stage 2, suggesting they had been exposed on the surface for under two years. Both bone weathering and animal gnawing evidence indicate that the Dent mammoths were likely to have been buried soon after death and processing. A scenario of rapid carcass burial provides a logical corollary to the earlier-proposed model suggesting the mammoth kills took place in a narrow arroyo in the upper draw, with resulting concentrated mammoth bodies trapping large amounts of sediment, covering the remains relatively quickly and efficiently.

THE DENT MAMMOTH DEATH EVENT: HUMAN OR NATURAL AGENCY?

For many decades, controversy has surrounded the nature of the Dent Mammoth Site. Three hypotheses have been proposed to explain what occurred at the site 11,000 years ago. The earliest formal hypothesis, a bluff kill, was proposed by Haynes (1966:111–112), who considered it "plausible that . . . Clovis hunters had stampeded a mammoth herd over the edge of the bluff. Some of the animals may have been killed by the fall; others may have escaped. Those that were too badly hurt to fight free of the narrow gully may then have been stunned with boulders—an assumption that helps explain the presence of these misplaced stones among the mammoth bones—and finally dispatched with spears."

The bluff-kill hypothesis has a number of weaknesses, particularly in assuming that the Dent topography would have been conducive to such a drive, that is, that it would have generated sufficient herd momentum through panic to force the animals into the site's adjacent bluff erosion fan. The low bluffs immediately above Dent's bone bed erosion cut do not precipitously drop into the fan but descend with fairly gradual slopes of $25°–35°$ through the bluff's fine sandstone channeled by three narrow drainage channels. The longest and deepest of the fan channels (described earlier) runs along a southwest to northeast line and provides a gentle 10°–12° slope access from the bluff scarp line to the former late Pleistocene shoreline of the South Platte River. Geomorphic analysis of the Dent draw topography, described earlier, indicates it would have provided easy access through the bluffs to the river, a circumstance conducive to a restricted area ambush of migrating animals (and not requiring that they be driven over the bluff). A bluff drive would have also been made more difficult by the mammoths' hypothesized matriarchal herd bunching behavior, with the animals forming a protective circle rather than running headlong over the low bluffs.

It has also been suggested that Dent represents a natural death event, either as a single event or a longer-term accumulation of naturally killed animals. In a letter written on August 2, 1935, by Conrad Bilgery to J. D. Figgins (on file at the Denver Museum of Nature and Science), Bilgery remarked, "I wish to draw your attention to my conviction that the flint-blades of Dent were simply washed in with the bones of the mammoth."

Possible variations of the natural death hypothesis, if true, would include the animals being trapped between a rising, flooded South Platte and an insurmountable, steep stream bank and drowned together at the Dent location or washed into the site from upstream drowning locations, resulting in carcass accumulations over several months or years. The matriarchal herd age profile of the Dent mammoths and essentially identical weathering condition of the bones, however, point to a limited number of closely spaced death events (possibly no more than two) rather than an extended accumulation of remains at the current site location. Frank Frazier (participant in the 1973 University of Colorado test excavation) is quoted by Cassells (1983:47) as saying it was unlikely, given a lack of evidence for bone polish, rounding, and sorting normally resulting from long-distance water transport, that the mammoth bones had been transported very far. Having closely examined Dent bone at the Denver Museum, I agree with Frazier's conclusions. Further evidence against the distant transport hypothesis and contrary to the natural death scenario includes previously described geological and historic wood radiocarbon data that support an alternative hypothesis (discussed later) that a closely spaced, small number (perhaps only two) of death events produced a rapidly buried bone bed that was (much) later washed down from the upper Dent draw to its 1930s find locality. Even the presence of Clovis tools with the Dent mammoths has been excused as an example of previously wounded animals carrying weapons tips in their bodies until they died through an "unknown catastrophic cause" (Cassells 1983:49). For instance, the Escapule and Naco Mammoth Sites in southeastern Arizona are associated with Clovis points and were provisionally classified as unbutchered mammoths and interpreted as examples of "ones who got away" (Haury 1953; Hemmings and Haynes 1969). Heavy use-wear patterns on both Dent Clovis points, existence of reworked point butchering tool, butchering marks, and geologic evidence that Dent's mammoth remains were redeposited downslope from an original death locality make a natural death scenario implausible.

A third Dent hypothesis, the confrontational herd kill (Saunders 1980, 1992:138–140), better fits available evidence, with some caveats. Geological analysis of the site, the nature of its surrounding terrain, and faunal and archaeological data suggest good topographic circumstances for mammoth herd ambushes. The narrow, deep gully in the southeast portion of the site's erosion fan would have provided access through the bluffs to a South Platte River ford or a downstream trail on the river's western bank. Based on analogy with African elephants whose social and economic behaviors are often compared with Columbian mammoths (Haynes 1992a:112–115; Saunders 1980, 1992), the Dent mammoths likely represented a medium-size matriarchal herd, part of a larger regional mammoth clan that practiced nomadic foraging journeys through a well-established resource territory in the Colorado Front Range foothills and piedmont. I suggest that, based on modern proboscidean behavior, mammoths in the Colorado Front Range were seasonally migratory, although their territorial ranges may have been limited in area (see Haynes 1992a:94–99 for a discussion on inferred mammoth migration; also see Hoope, Carlson, and Webb 1999; Hoope 2004, and this chapter's subsequent discussion on isotopic data evidence for mammoth seasonal migration). In fact, the current Dent evidence, cited previously (and later), supports the hypothesis of its animals having engaged in at least a limited-range migratory pattern, with the site's local river ford making up part of a mammoth herd migration route. Clovis hunters, familiar with local mammoth herd habits (knowledge important for hunting band survival), could easily have planned an ambush in Dent's bluff erosion fan. The animals, once in the fan gully, could have been trapped in a narrow, possibly water-slicked drainage gully and dispatched. The animals may have been further condemned by a common African elephant social behavior, matriarchal herd protective instincts, as well as the local Dent topography and the skills of its Clovis hunters.

African elephant matriarchal herds exhibit an instinctive social response to predators known as *bunching* (Douglas-Hamilton and Douglas-Hamilton 1975; Laws, Parker, and Johnstone 1975:161–163). Bunching consists of older adult females, taking their lead from the herd matriarch, forming an outward-facing circle with immature young remaining in its center when threatened by a predator or predators. African male elephant herds, without slow, defenseless young to protect, habitually scatter when threatened. Matriarchal herd members have been known to maintain protective circles for hours, even to defend dead or dying family members. If Columbian mammoth matriarchal herds exhibited similar behavior, as also suggested at the Waco Mammoth Site (Fox, Smith, and Lintz 1992; cf. Haynes 1992b), Dent's Clovis hunters could have trapped the animals in the narrow draw gully where they would have formed a defensive formation. The hunters would only have had to patiently maneuver around the tightly bunched herd from the sides and ends of the arroyo, dispatching the animals individually. One important potential flaw, and a continuing part of Dent's mystery, is the limited number of Clovis points (2) and dedicated butchering tools (1) at the site, although use-wear analysis showed all three artifacts to have been used for butchering. One explanation may be that more artifacts remain to be discovered, still buried in the site's upper draw and unexcavated railroad bed deposits. Another factor may be that artifacts were removed from the site by visitors or even members of the two (Regis and Denver Museum) excavation teams and never reported. It took thirty years to ascertain the existence of the gray chert knife (Dent artifact C), which had been retrieved during excavations by the site's discoverer, Frank Garner, and remained unreported until 1955 (Wormington 1957:44).

An ambush kill, whether in a single or multiple phases, would have been facilitated by environmental and climatic changes occurring in the Colorado Front Range during the late Pleistocene. Gary Haynes (2002:404), in a review of Clovis Mammoth Site data, saw clear evidence for a megafaunal subsistence strategy that at least partially focused on "opportunistic specialization in proboscideans," which would have been "a viable strategy when prey diversity is low, and prey [such as mammoths] tend to aggregate in herds that feed nomadically [and] were distributed non-randomly in different habitats. Not only were megamammals found in clustered aggregations, but they were also reordering their range distributions as climatic changes altered floral community spatial distributions and area coverage. The main changes in vegetation involved a reduction in mosaic cell sizes . . . or areal extent of different floral communities contacting each other."

The Dent kill, coming near the end of the late Pleistocene, was among the most recent of all North American mammoth sites, at ca. 10,900 RCYBP (Graham, Stafford, and Semken 1997; Haynes 1992a; Stafford et al. 1999), and within the late Pleistocene's transition of ecosystems from Ice Age to modern climates and environments when ancient foraging territories were being altered in time and space. Growing geographic restrictions and tightening ecological mammoth patches would have made it easier for Clovis hunters to anticipate mammoth herd movements.

Evidence that decreasing mammoth patch territories may have contributed to the demise of the Dent mammoths can be found in recent strontium studies of several mammoth assemblages in the southern and central plains. Those studies compared strontium ($^{87}SR/^{86}SR$) ratios among five Clovis mammoth assemblages, including Dent (Hoope, Carlson, and Webb 1999; Hoope 2004). Strontium, reflective of different geographically distinct bedrock-derived soils, enters herbivore, in this case mammoth, skeletal elements (bone and teeth) through the ingestion of plant foods. Ratios in those elements vary in relation to the areas where the animal has forged. Analysis of strontium ratios in mammoth bone and teeth provides a form of proxy data for whether the analyzed animal has persistently grazed in a particular region or seasonally migrated between regions with differing strontium signatures. Hoope and colleagues (1999) and Hoope (2004) found that strontium ratios in Dent tooth enamel indicated they likely derived from a distinctly localized population that did not migrate far outside its immediate foraging patch territory.

The confrontation-kill hypothesis, based on available evidence, provides the best available explanation for what happened to the Dent mammoths around 11,000 years ago. Projectile points and a hafted tool discovered with the bones show distinctive edge wear patterning consistent with heavy butchering. Saunders's discovery of even limited evidence of cultural processing provides a strong suggestion of postmortem butchering of newly dead animals and, possibly, subsequent scavenging. However, since season-of-death and chemical isotope data appear to suggest at least two (and possibly three) closely spaced kill events, they potentially represent an important caveat to the confrontational herd scenario. There may be at least two possible explanations for the multiple death event evidence. Either more than one herd and/or individual kill is represented, or some animals of a single herd—including the youngest Dent mammoth described earlier—escaped the first ambush, only to return later and be dispatched at the same locality. The latter explanation is attractive if mammoth social behavior resembled that of African elephants in expressing a reluctance to abandon their dead. African elephants, particularly those belonging to matriarchal herd groups, often remain in the vicinity of dead relatives for days or even weeks, reluctant to be separated from them even in death (Joubert 1991; Moss 1988). This is particularly true of nuclear family units, such as mothers and calves. If Dent mammoths escaping the first kill exhibited a similar familial loyalty, the site's multiple death events could have been the result of mammoth-savvy Clovis hunters maintaining a watch over the site and setting up later ambushes to "polish off" herd survivors returning to grieve their dead family members. It is also possible that one or more slightly later ambushes of members of another clan-related matriarchal herd occurred at the same location, perhaps drawn to the site by the presence of their dead relatives.

CONCLUSION

In light of the evidence presented in this chapter, I believe the most plausible interpretation of the Dent Mammoth Site is that it represents two or more closely spaced Clovis ambush kills, possibly of elements of the same herd. A second, less likely possibility is that it represents two or more closely spaced Clovis hunter scavenging events. Accumulated carcasses, based on minimal bone weathering and a relative lack of scavenger gnawing evidence, appear to have been rapidly buried—within weeks or at most a few months—in their gully kill location, a gully that had long provided migratory access through low bluffs to a Colorado Piedmont river ford. The demise of the Dent mammoths appears to have resulted from two closely timed, well-planned late-fall and early-winter ambush kills of one or more migrating matriarchal mammoth families in very late Clovis times around 11,000 years ago. Butchering and season-of-death evidence and knowledge of modern proboscidean behavior present the possibility that escaped animals of the initial kill may have later returned to the site and, in turn, been killed by Clovis hunters anticipating such a return.

Acknowledgments. Many individuals contributed to this chapter's research. My interest in the Dent site was encouraged and supported by Frank Frazier, an original 1973 Dent investigator, who generously made available his personal notes, photographs, and excavated geological samples. Aerial photographs of Dent shown in Figures 3.3 and 3.8 were provided courtesy of Frank. Map figures in the text were partly produced by Tabbatha Sandoval, a former student at the University of Northern Colorado. Vance Haynes, also an earlier investigator of Dent, has been an invaluable source of information, advice, and encouragement. He returned to Dent in 1995 to study the local terrace sequence and graciously included me in his research. Others who conducted their own parallel or supporting research on Dent and contributed greatly to our understanding of the site are Dan Fisher of the University of Michigan, Jeffrey Saunders of the Illinois State Museum, and Linda Scott Cummings of Paleo Research Laboratories. I would also like to thank the Denver Museum of Nature and Science staff who assisted me in too many ways to count, notably Jim Dixon, the museum's former curator of archaeology. Finally, I owe a great deal to the Bernhardt family, which provided continuous access to the site for many years and have been good and kind friends as we tromped over, poked, and prodded Dent in an attempt to reveal its long-held secrets. Thanks, Reuben and Tim.

REFERENCES CITED

Agenbroad, L. D.
- 1984 Hot Springs South Dakota: Entrapment and Taphonomy of Columbian Mammoth. In *Quaternary Extinctions: A Prehistoric Revolution*, ed. P. S. Martin and R. G. Klein, 90–108. University of Arizona Press, Tucson.
- 1990 The Mammoth Population of the Hot Springs Site and Associated Fauna. In *Megafauna & Man*, ed. L. D. Agenbroad, J. I. Mead, and L. W. Nelson, 32–39. Mammoth Site of Hot Springs, South Dakota, Inc., Hot Springs, and Northern Arizona University, Flagstaff.

Agogino, G.
- 1963 Progress Report on the Chemical Removal of Preservative from Radiocarbon Samples. *La Conquista* 2:n.p.
- 1968 The Experimental Removal of Preservative from Radiocarbon Samples. *Plains Anthropologist* 13 (40):146–147.
- 1997 An Early Attempt to Remove Preservatives from Bone. *Southwestern Lore* 63 (3):42–43.

Behrensmeyer, A.
- 1978 Taphonomic and Ecological Information from Bone Weathering. *Paleobiology* 4 (2):150–162.

Bilgery, C.
- 1935 *Evidence of Pleistocene Man in the Denver Basin: A Preliminary Report.* Ms. on file at the Office of the Colorado State Archaeologist, Denver.

Brunswig, R. H., Jr.
   1995   *The Dent Mammoth Site: Directions in Current Research*. Paper presented at the 60th Annual Society for American Archaeology Conference, Minneapolis, MN.

Brunswig, R. H., Jr., and D. C. Fisher
   1993   Research on the Dent Mammoth Site. *Current Research in the Pleistocene* 10:63–65.

Cassells, E. S.
   1983   *The Archaeology of Colorado*, 1st ed. Johnson Books, Boulder.
   1998   *The Archaeology of Colorado*, 2nd ed. Johnson Books, Boulder.

Crabb, J.
   1978   *Soil Survey of Weld County, Colorado: Southern Part*. U.S. Government Printing Office, Washington, DC.

Cummings, L. S.
   1993   *Phytolith Analysis of a Mammoth Tooth from the Dent Site, Colorado*. Ms. on file at Paleo Research Laboratories, Golden, CO.

Cummings, L. S., and R. M. Albert
   1993   *Phytolith and Starch Analysis of Tartar from Three Mammoth Teeth from the Dent Site in Colorado*. Ms. on file, Paleo Research Laboratories, Golden, CO.

Douglas-Hamilton, I., and O. Douglas-Hamilton
   1975   *Among the Elephants*. Viking, New York.

Figgins, J. D.
   1933   A Further Contribution to the Antiquity of Man in America. *Proceedings of the Colorado Museum of Natural History* 12 (2):4–10.

Fisher, D. C.
   1995   *Season of Death of the Dent Mammoths*. Paper presented at the 60th Annual Society for American Archaeology Conference, Minneapolis, MN.

Fisher, D. C., and S. G. Beld
   2003   *Growth and Life History Records from Mammoth Tusks*. Paper presented at the Third International Mammoth Conference, Dawson City, Canada.

Fisher, D. C., and D. L. Fox
   1998   *Season of Death of the Dent Mammoths: Distinguishing Single from Multiple Mortality Events*. Ms. on file, Department of Geology, University of Michigan, Ann Arbor.

Fisher, J.
   1988   *The Dent Site Mammoth Bones: Comments on My System of Description*. Ms. on file, Denver Museum of Natural History, Denver.

Fox, J. W., C. B. Smith, and D. O. Lintz
   1992   Herd Bunching at the Waco Mammoth Site: Preliminary Investigations, 1978–1987. In *Proboscidean and Paleoindian Interactions*, ed. J. W. Fox, C. B. Smith, and K. T. Wilkins, 51–74. Baylor University Press, Waco.

Frison, G. C.
    1989   Experimental Use of Clovis Weaponry and Tools on African Elephants. *American Antiquity* 54 (4):766–783.

Frison, G. C., and L. C. Todd
    1986   *The Colby Mammoth Site: Taphonomy and Archaeology of a Clovis Kill in Northern Wyoming.* University of New Mexico Press, Albuquerque.

Graham, R. W., T. W. Stafford Jr., and H. A. Semken Jr.
    1997   *Pleistocene Extinction: Chronology, Non-Analog Communities, and Environmental Change.* Paper presented at the 1997 Symposium on Humans and Other Catastrophes, American Museum of Natural History, New York, NY.

Haas, H., and C. V. Haynes
    1975   Southern Methodist University Radiocarbon Date I. *Radiocarbon* 17 (3):358–359.

Hannus, A.
    1990   The Lange-Ferguson Site: A Case for Bone Butchering Tools. In *Megafauna and Man*, ed. L. Agenbroad, J. I. Mead, and L. W. Nelson, 86–99. Mammoth Site of Hot Springs, South Dakota, Inc., Hot Springs.

Haury, E. W.
    1953   Artifacts with Mammoth Remains, Naco, Arizona. *American Antiquity* 19:1–14.

Haynes, C. V.
    1966   Elephant Hunting in North America. *Scientific American* 214:104–112.
    1974   Archaeological Geology of Some Selected Paleo-Indian Sites. *The Museum Journal* 15:133–139.
    1989   Geoarchaeological and Paleohydrological Evidence for a Clovis-Age Drought in North America and Its Bearing on Extinction. *Quaternary Research* 35:438–450.
    1992   Contributions of Radiocarbon Dating to the Geochronology of the Peopling of the New World. In *Radiocarbon after Four Decades: An International Perspective*, ed. R. E. Taylor, A. Long, and R. S. Kra, 355–374. Springer-Verlag, New York.

Haynes, C. V., and G. A. Agogino
    1986   Geochronology of Sandia Cave. *Smithsonian Contributions to Anthropology* 32, Washington, DC.

Haynes, C. V., M. McFaul, R. H. Brunswig Jr., and K. D. Hopkins
    1998   Kersey and Kuner Terrace Investigations at the Dent and Bernhardt Sites, Colorado. *Geoarchaeology* 13 (2):201–218.

Haynes, G.
    1992a   *Mammoths, Mastodonts and Elephants.* Cambridge University Press, Cambridge.
    1992b   The Waco Mammoths: Possible Clues to Herd Size, Demography, and Reproductive Health. In *Proboscidean and Paleoindian Interactions*, ed. J. W. Fox, C. B. Smith, and K. T. Wilkins, 111–122. Baylor University Press, Waco.
    1999   The Role of Mammoths in Rapid Clovis Dispersal. *Deinsea* 6:9–38.

2002   The Catastrophic Extinction of North American Mammoths and Mastodons. *World Archaeology* 33 (3):391–416.

Hemmings, E. T., and C. V. Haynes
1969   The Escapule Mammoth and Associated Projectile Points, San Pedro Valley, Arizona. *Journal of the Arizona Academy of Sciences* 5:184–188.

Hibben, F. C.
1941   Evidence of Early Occupation in Sandia Cave, New Mexico, and Other Sites in the Sandia-Manzano Region. *Smithsonian Miscellaneous Collections* 99 (23), Washington, DC.
1946   The First Thirty-Eight Sandia Points. *American Antiquity* 11 (4):257–258.

Holliday, V. T.
1987   Geoarchaeology and Late Quaternary Geomorphology of the Middle South Platte River, Northeastern Colorado. *Geoarchaeology* 2 (4):317–329.

Hoope, K. A.
2004   Late Mammoth Herd Structure, Migration Patterns and Clovis Hunting Strategies Inferred from Isotopic Analysis of Multiple Death Assemblages. *Paleobiology* 30 (1):129–145.

Hoope, K. A., R. W. Carlson, and S. D. Webb
1999   Tracking Mammoths and Mastodons: Reconstruction of Migratory Behavior Using Strontium Isotope Ratios. *Geology* 27 (5):439–442.

Jepson, D. A., C. J. Zier, M. McFaul, K. L. Traugh, G. D. Smith, and W. Doering
1994   *Archaeological and Geomorphic Investigations along U.S. Highway 34 between Greeley and Kersey, Weld County, Colorado.* Ms. on file, Centennial Archaeology, Inc., Fort Collins, CO, and Laramie Soils Service, Laramie, WY.

Joubert, Derek
1991   Eyewitness to an Elephant Wake. *National Geographic* 179(5):39–49.

Laws, R. M., I.S.C. Parker, and R.C.B. Johnstone
1975   *Elephants and Their Habitats.* Clarendon, London.

Lister, A., and L. Agenbroad
1994   Gender Determination of the Hot Springs Mammoths. In *The Hot Springs Mammoth Site*, ed. L. D. Agenbroad and J. I. Mead, 208–214. Mammoth Site of Hot Springs, South Dakota, Hot Springs.

Malde, H. E.
1954   *Memorandum for the Record (Notes of a Conversation with Albert [Frank] Garner on the Dent Site).* Ms. on file at the Denver Museum of Natural History, Denver.

Moss, C.
1988   *Elephant Memories: Thirteen Years in the Life of an Elephant Family.* Morrow, New York.

Saunders, J. J.
1980   A Model for Man-Mammoth Relationships in Late Pleistocene North America. *Canadian Journal of Anthropology* 1 (1):87–98.

1992 Blackwater Draws: Mammoths and Mammoth Hunters in the Terminal Pleistocene. In *Proboschean and Paleoindian Interactions*, ed. J. W. Fox, C. B. Smith, and K. T. Wilkins, 123–147. Baylor University Press, Waco.

1999 Morphological Analysis of *Mammathus columbii* from the Dent Site, Weld County, Colorado. *Deinsea* 6:55–78.

Saunders, J. J., and E. B. Daeschler

1994 Descriptive Analyses and Taphonomical Observations of Culturally Modified Mammoths Excavated at "The Gravel Pit," near Clovis, New Mexico in 1936. *Proceedings of the Academy of Natural Sciences of Philadelphia* 145:1–28.

Spikard, L.

1972 *A Proposal to the Union Pacific Railroad for Permission to Stratigraphically Test the Dent Site, Colorado*. Ms. on file at the Office of the Colorado State Archaeologist. Denver.

Stafford, T. W.

1988 Late Pleistocene Megafauna Extinctions and the Clovis Culture: Absolute Ages Based on Accelerator ^{14}C Dating of Skeletal Remains. In *Megafauna and Man*, ed. L. D. Agenbroad, J. I. Mead, and L. W. Nelson, 118–122. Mammoth Site of Hot Springs, South Dakota, Inc., Hot Springs, and Northern Arizona University, Flagstaff.

Stafford, T. W., Jr., P. E. Hare, L. Currie, A.J.T Jull, and D. J. Donahue

1991 Accelerator Radiocarbon Dating at the Molecular Level. *Journal of Archaeological Science* 18:35–72.

Stafford, T. W,, Jr., A. Holmes, H. A. Semken, R. W. Graham, W. I. Klippel, A. K. Markova, N. G. Smirnov, and J. Sothen

1999 First Accelerator Mass Spectrometry ^{14}C Dates Documenting Contemporaneity of Non-Analog Species in Late Pleistocene Mammal Communities. *Geology* 27:903–906.

Stafford, T. W., Jr., A.J.T. Jull, K. Bredel, K. Duhamel, and D. J. Donahue.

1985 Study of Bone Dating Accuracy at the University of Arizona NSF Accelerator Facility for Radioisotope Analysis. *Radiocarbon* 29 (1):29–44.

Stevens, D. E., and G. A. Agogino

1961 Sandia Cave: A Study in Controversy. *Eastern New Mexico University Contributions in Anthropology* 7 (1). Portales.

Surovell, T. A.

2000 Radiocarbon Dating of Bone Apatite by Step Heating. *Geoarchaeology* 15 (6): 591–608.

Taylor, R. E., C. V. Haynes, and M. Stuiver

1996 Clovis and Folsom Age Estimates: Stratigraphic Context and Radiocarbon Calibration. *Antiquity* 70 (269):515–525.

Willey, Gordon R.

1966 *An Introduction to American Archaeology*. Prentice-Hall, Englewood Cliffs, NJ.

Wormington, H. M.

1957 *Ancient Man in North America*. Denver Museum of Natural History, Denver.

CHAPTER FOUR

Daniel C. Fisher and David L. Fox

Season of Death of the Dent Mammoths

DISTINGUISHING SINGLE FROM MULTIPLE MORTALITY EVENTS

The Dent site, in northeastern Colorado, is the first discovered, and still one of the most influential, of the sites that document association of Paleoindians with late Pleistocene mammoths (*Mammuthus columbi*) in North America (see Brunswig, Chapter 3, this volume for an overview of site history). Yet the nature of this association remains a matter of debate. Open questions include whether the deaths of the mammoths were brought about directly by human hunting activity or by some other cause and whether the association represents a single, temporally coherent event or more than one event occurring at the same site. The study reported here is an attempt to answer these questions through data bearing on the season of death of individual mammoths. Season of death of faunal elements at archaeological sites has often been used to constrain interpretation of human subsistence behavior (e.g., Pike-Tay 1991; Spiess 1979). However, the techniques used here offer greater temporal resolution than is available through analyses of stages of tooth eruption and wear (e.g., Frison and Reher 1970) or cementum annuli (Lieberman 1994). Beyond showing the timing of death within the seasonal cycle, these techniques can provide paleoenvironmental data covering an extended portion of an organism's life.

Saunders (1977, 1980) has argued that, based on assemblage age structure, the Dent mammoths represent a matriarchal family unit confronted by Paleoindians and killed within a short span of time. He evaluated ages of the Dent mammoths using Laws's (1966) relative age categories, based on cheek tooth succession in African elephants. He showed that the distribution of relative ages in the Dent assemblage resembled the relative age distributions of African elephant matriarchal family units. This corroborated his identification of the Dent assemblage as a matriarchal unit without necessarily ruling out alternative hypotheses, but it did not directly address the issue of simultaneity of death. Taking on both issues together, Conybeare and Haynes (1984) and Haynes (1985) pointed out that a series of deaths, affecting members of one or more matriarchal groups, independent of individual age, might produce a composite assemblage with an age structure like that of a single matriarchal unit.

We evaluate these competing interpretations by determining season of death for three of the fourteen Dent mammoths based on the structure and composition of incrementally deposited tooth tissues. Although this approach is not a direct assay of simultaneity of death, simultaneity can be ruled out if a clear disparity in season of death is observed. Moreover, the data obtained could in principle be pushed to a level of resolution that would allow matching of time intervals recorded in different individuals, which would in this special case provide direct evaluation of simultaneity of death. In this chapter we utilize two approaches to determining season of death: measurement of growth increments in tusk and cheek tooth dentin, and oxygen isotope analysis of hydroxyapatite in tusk and cheek tooth dentin. In each case, we are interested in the pattern of variation in a time series leading up to the time of death. The oxygen isotope approach offers the additional prospect of using compositional comparisons to evaluate the hypothesis of membership in a single matriarchal unit. To be clear from the outset, our results support the view of Conybeare and Haynes (1984) and run counter to expectations based on Saunders (1980).

INCREMENTAL FEATURES IN PROBOSCIDEAN DENTIN

Proboscidean dentin is characterized by a hierarchical system of incremental features (Figure 4.1). The most inclusive level in the hierarchy consists of features referred to as first order, and on many specimens, especially from environments with high seasonality (intra-annual, seasonal contrast), these are very conspicuous. They are sometimes expressed as regular undulations of the dentin-cementum interface, producing circumferential annuli ("periradicular bands") evident externally without sectioning. Cross-sectional views of well-preserved

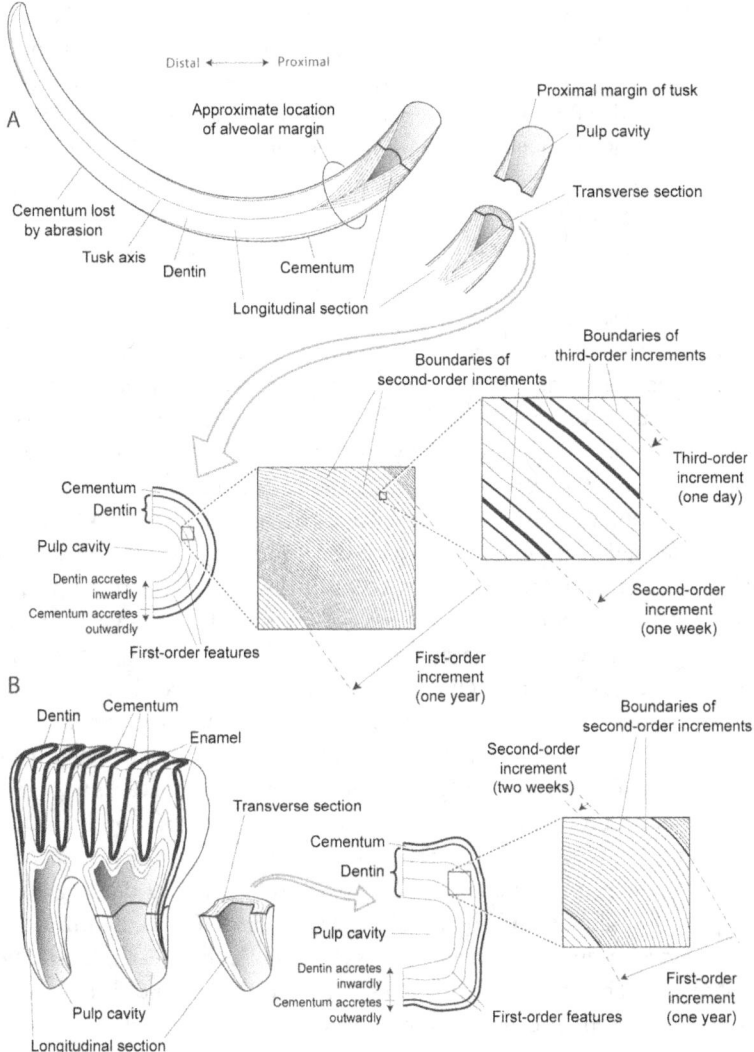

4.1. Hierarchy of dentin increments in mammoth tusks and cheek teeth. (a), longitudinally sectioned right tusk, showing major structural features and, near the proximal extremity, the trace of a transverse plane of section; displaced to the right is the specimen after transverse sectioning; successive enlargements illustrate idealized first-, second-, and third-order increments. (b), longitudinally sectioned cheek tooth, showing major structural features and, across the posterior root, the trace of a transverse plane of section; displaced to the right is the proximal (apical) portion of the root; successive enlargements illustrate idealized first- and second-order increments.

dentin, including specimens from extant elephants, usually show only subtle first-order color variation with one dark-light couplet per first-order feature, but on specimens preserved in wet, organic-rich sediments, post-depositional

125

staining may enhance the visibility of underlying structural variation, yielding pronounced color bands (Fisher 1984). Low seasonality of conditions controlling growth may make first-order features difficult to distinguish, but detailed evaluations of first-order features have consistently shown them to be annual (Fisher 1987, 1988, 1996; Koch 1989; Koch, Fisher, and Dettman 1989). They are generally comparable to annual increments in the dentin of many mammals (e.g., Klevezal and Kleinenberg 1969).

Second-order incremental features are the most problematic aspect of this growth system. We do not know what cyclic process they record, and their period is not the same for all teeth and taxa. Second-order features are expressed at the dentin-cementum interface as minor topographic discontinuities. In thin section, they are bounded by relatively dark growth lines. In mastodon (*Mammut americanum*) tusk dentin, second-order features generally represent fortnightly increments, of which there are usually 26 ± ca. 2 per first-order feature. However, in mastodon molar dentin, second-order features appear to be lunar monthly, numbering about 13 ± 1 per first-order feature. In contrast, weekly increments (i.e., ca. 52 second-order features per first-order feature) have been traced in tusk dentin of Miocene gomphotheres (Fox 1995a, 1995b, 2000) and are present also in mammoth tusk dentin, punctuating the fortnightly (two-week) increments previously described for mammoths (e.g., Koch, Fisher, and Dettman 1989). Replicating the twofold difference in period between mastodon tusk and cheek tooth dentin, second-order features in mammoth cheek teeth appear to be fortnightly. Recent work on woolly mammoth (*Mammuthus primigenius*) tusks from Alaska and the Siberian Arctic suggests that second-order features may reflect an interaction between circadian rhythms and some other, still poorly understood, periodic aspect of tusk mineralization (Fisher 2001b).

Third-order increments are the faintest and finest-scale dark-light couplets observed in thin section and are not expressed at the dentin-cementum interface. They are more often recognizable in tusks than in cheek teeth, if only because tusks show a higher rate of dentin apposition (accretion and mineralization of new tissue) and thus greater increment thicknesses. Although not always well preserved, when present they show a characteristic hierarchic relation to other incremental features. Their numerical relations to both first- and second-order increments indicate that they represent daily features. Although difficult to count in the lunar monthly second-order features of mastodon cheek teeth, we routinely observe ca. 14 third-order increments per second-order feature when the latter represent fortnights and ca. 7 third-order increments per second-order feature when the latter represent weeks. Comparable features are well documented in other mammals (e.g., Miani and Miani 1972; Rosenberg and Simmons 1980) and probably reflect some aspect of circadian rhythms.

Living elephants show dentin increments broadly similar to those of mammoths, but because of the logistic complexities of conducting research on CITES-regulated species, they have not yet provided the type of "ground truth" for interpretation of increment patterns that would clearly be desirable. Instead, interpretations of the season represented by a given portion of a dentin sequence in a fossil proboscidean are based on less direct arguments: (1) analogy with extant non-proboscidean mammals, in which the relatively thin, dark portion of an annual dark-light couplet usually forms in winter (Klevezal and Kleinenberg 1969); (2) spacing of second-order incremental features, in which thinner periodic increments indicative of lower rates of dentin apposition are expected in winter (Fisher 1987); and (3) oxygen isotope variation, in which lower $\delta^{18}O$ values are expected in winter (Koch, Fisher, and Dettman 1989). Use of incremental features in proboscidean dentin to determine season of death requires assessment of a dentin sequence long enough to achieve confirmation of the seasonal identity of the last-formed dentin, located adjacent to the pulp cavity, in a tooth undergoing dentin apposition at the time of death. This involves looking for annual, seasonal variation in the thickness of second-order features and locating the time of death relative to such fluctuations. This may be attempted even on short dentin sequences, but results are more susceptible to multiple, independent tests when an interval on the order of several years is available for analysis.

OXYGEN ISOTOPE VARIATION IN PROBOSCIDEAN DENTIN

The oxygen isotope composition of hydroxyapatite in dental tissues reflects various inputs, outputs, and fractionation factors, but in a large mammal it is influenced mostly by the composition of drinking water (Bryant and Froelich 1995; Koch 1989). To the extent that drinking water is derived from local precipitation, which typically shows seasonal variation in isotope composition (Dansgaard 1964), an appositional sequence of hydroxyapatite may show a correlated seasonal isotope signal. Several factors could complicate analysis of such patterns (e.g., diagenetic alteration, or animals drinking from multiple water sources representing different hydrologic systems, histories of fractionation, or both). However, if a consistent pattern of isotope variation is observed within an appositional sequence independently recognizable as annual (e.g., by incremental features), it probably reflects seasonal variation in the composition of locally available water.

The broad area of research known as sclerochronology (Steuber 1996) is based on recognition that many biological systems that grow by accretion preserve records of changing organismal and environmental conditions. An extensive literature (e.g., Arthur, Williams, and Jones 1983) documents such variation in calcium carbonate skeletons of various invertebrate groups, where the signal is influenced by both water composition and water temperature. A comparable vertebrate system, also calcium carbonate–based, is provided by fish otoliths (Patterson, Smith, and Lohmann 1993). Recently, mammalian teeth have been recognized as providing useful data on the isotope composition of local precipitation, relatively uncomplicated by temperature effects (because body temperature is held relatively constant in most mammals). Some of this work (e.g., Koch, Fisher, and Dettman 1989) focused on the carbonate fraction of hydroxyapatite because the chemical treatment necessary for measuring oxygen isotope composition in carbonate was relatively straightforward. However, concern over diagenetic (post-depositional) alteration of original compositions (Land, Lundelius, and Velastro 1980) has led many workers dealing with hydroxyapatite to favor analyses of phosphate oxygen because it is more resistant to isotope exchange with groundwater (Ayliffe, Chivas, and Leakey 1994). Likewise, most workers have used enamel, rather than dentin, because its larger crystallites reduce the surface area over which isotope exchange might occur during diagenesis (e.g., Bryant, Luz, and Froelich 1994; Fricke and O'Neil 1996).

In the work reported here, we accept the importance of focusing on phosphate oxygen, but we cannot restrict our analyses to enamel. Mammoth tusks only have enamel at their tips, and this is lost by abrasion soon after eruption. Mammoth cheek teeth have extensive enamel, but most of it is laid down prior to fusion of the initially separate tooth plates into a complete, lophodont molar. When a developing molar is still in its alveolus, the appositional surface of enamel is sequestered within surrounding bone, and when molars occur as isolated specimens (removed from an alveolus), they frequently have lost unfused tooth plates or suffered damage to the appositional surface of enamel, if indeed they were still undergoing enamel apposition at the time of death. This means the appositional surface of enamel is either hard to get at, subject to damage, or no longer active and therefore irrelevant to determination of season of death.

In contrast, proboscideans deposit dentin throughout a longer interval than is committed to enamel production, considering both individual teeth and the dentition as a whole. Further, dentin apposition occurs within the relatively protected space of the pulp cavity, making it less subject to postmortem abrasion. Although dentin may be more susceptible to diagenetic alteration than enamel, Koch and colleagues (1989) pointed out that this is unlikely to generate artifactual variation that would mimic seasonal variation in isotope composition. Profiles of variation in oxygen isotopes from cheek tooth root and tusk dentin will therefore be used as our source of data on season of death.

As with profiles of growth increment thickness, this method of determining season of death requires access to the last-formed tissue, adjacent to the pulp cavity, and requires evaluation of a transect through an appositional sequence long enough to provide a context for distinguishing one season from another. Sampling resolution limits the precision of any determination, but the pattern of compositional change approaching the end of an appositional sequence and the final value attained fix the time of death within the seasonal cycle. Koch and colleagues (1989) reported the lowest oxygen isotope values in late winter (Pleistocene proboscideans and Pleistocene and Recent bears), and similar work on modern beaver (*Castor canadensis*) shows the same pattern (Stuart-Williams and Schwarcz 1997).

MATERIALS AND METHODS

Given the exploratory nature of this study and its requirement for sectioning, we restricted our attention to specimens not on display. Tusks are ideal for this analysis. Although most retain no enamel and their cementum increments provide little temporal resolution, they have a large mass of dentin that usually shows clear growth increments. The relatively simple, conical geometry of dentin increments in tusks and the high rate of apposition of tusk dentin maximize temporal resolution, whether we are measuring growth increment thicknesses or variation in composition.

The only Dent mammoth tusk in the Denver Museum of Natural History (DMNH) (now the Denver Museum of Nature and Science) collection not on exhibit (DMNH 1450) is broken but has an estimated length of 185 cm and a well-preserved pulp cavity at its proximal end, where it measures 38.8 cm in circumference. Circumference is relatively constant throughout the proximal half of the specimen. Comparison with other circumference-length profiles suggests this tusk is attributable to an adult female (Fisher 1996; Osborn 1936; Sher and Fisher 1995). An adult male would have a tusk of larger diameter and, at this length, might still be increasing in girth proximally. Collection data did not associate this tusk with any other particular specimens from the site, but its size suggests an individual in a Laws age category of XX or greater. It could belong to the oldest individual Saunders (1980) recognized at Dent, DMNH 1635, in Laws age category XXIII (43 $\pm$ 2 African Elephant [Equivalent] Years [AEY]). For analysis, a sample of tusk dentin ca. 15 cm long and 3.5 cm wide, including part of the pulp cavity surface, was removed using a flexible-shaft grinder and carbide burr. The last-formed dentin comprised the pulp cavity surface itself, and the sample location was chosen to provide a contiguous thickness of 1–3 cm of dentin.

Selection of additional individuals focused on cheek teeth (deciduous premolars and molars). Those that could be sampled most easily, minimizing impact on other specimens, were ones recovered as isolated teeth. However, it was important that we not unwittingly duplicate analyses of season of death on material from the same individual. We therefore considered only teeth for which position and state of wear ruled out derivation from the same individual. To avoid cheek teeth that might have belonged to the same adult female whose tusk we sampled, and to give the best chance of corroborating Saunders's family unit hypothesis (e.g., finding an associated mother and calf), we focused on teeth of juveniles. Additional criteria were quality of preservation, access to tissue undergoing apposition at the time of death, and minimization of the amount of "dissection" each specimen would require. Two teeth were selected, both showing patent pulp cavities and an adequate thickness of dentin associated with a partly formed root: a right dP_3 (DMNH 1897) and a right dP_4 (DMNH 1895). Saunders (1980) recognized the first of these as representing the youngest individual (Laws age category IV; 2 AEY) at the site and the second as a somewhat older individual (Laws age category VIII/IX; 9 AEY).

To ensure that the last-formed dentin did not spall off during sample preparation, pulp cavity surfaces were protected by embedding with polyester resin. Impregnation by resin was avoided, as it tends to obscure incremental features (Fisher 1988). The pulp cavity of the dP_4 was mostly filled with resin through the larger, posterior root before cutting. However, the posterior root of the dP_3 was not thick enough to record an adequate interval of time, so the anterior root was chosen for sectioning. Its apical foramen was too nearly occluded to give clear access to the pulp cavity, so it was cut off some distance from the base of the crown. Unconsolidated sediment was then removed and replaced by resin. Dentin samples from each tooth were removed from near the base of the crown (where dentin was thickest) using abrasive cutoff wheels mounted on a flexible-shaft grinder. Root segments thus produced were embedded for further support, and samples of both tusk and cheek tooth dentin were sectioned transversely with a Buehler Isomet low-speed saw. Thin sections were prepared following methods outlined by Fisher (1988) and examined with a Lietz Laborlux 12-Pol polarizing microscope. Data on the thicknesses of second-order increments were collected using Optimas™ image analysis software.

Samples for isotope analysis were collected under stereomicroscopic observation in the Stable Isotope Laboratory of the University of Michigan's Department of Geological Sciences. The procedure resembled that of Dettman and Lohmann's (1993) high-resolution, computer-driven sample stage, but our greater sample size needs (for studying phosphate oxygen rather than carbonate oxygen) made a higher-speed, operator-driven system preferable. Some second-order increments were visible in reflected light on surfaces polished with 600-grit abrasive, and these guided sample removal. A dental drill with a 0.5-mm-diameter carbide bit was clamped vertically over a specimen stage that could be raised to allow the bit to plunge below the polished surface of a specimen, mounted with incremental laminae oriented vertically. After plunging to an appropriate depth (ca. 1 mm per pass), the specimen was moved horizontally, following a second-order incremental feature and routing out a narrow groove in the dentin. The powder from each pass was tapped onto a clean sheet of weigh-paper and transferred to a sample vial. Additional passes were taken at successively greater depths until an estimated 20–30 mg sample had been collected. Any remaining powder was dislodged with a blast of compressed air before beginning the next sample. Sample collection was usually preceded by drilling out polyester resin adjacent to the pulp cavity surface because it was otherwise difficult to remove sample powder from the single, narrow groove of the first sample. By starting at the pulp cavity surface, we hoped to maximize temporal resolution for the last-formed dentin. In a later phase of the study, replicate samples were drilled from fresh areas of each specimen. On the dP_3, in areas difficult to sample with the fixed grinder, replicate sampling was done with a handheld grinder.

Sampling for isotope analysis was conducted after measuring growth increments in thin section. Working hypotheses on the amount of time represented

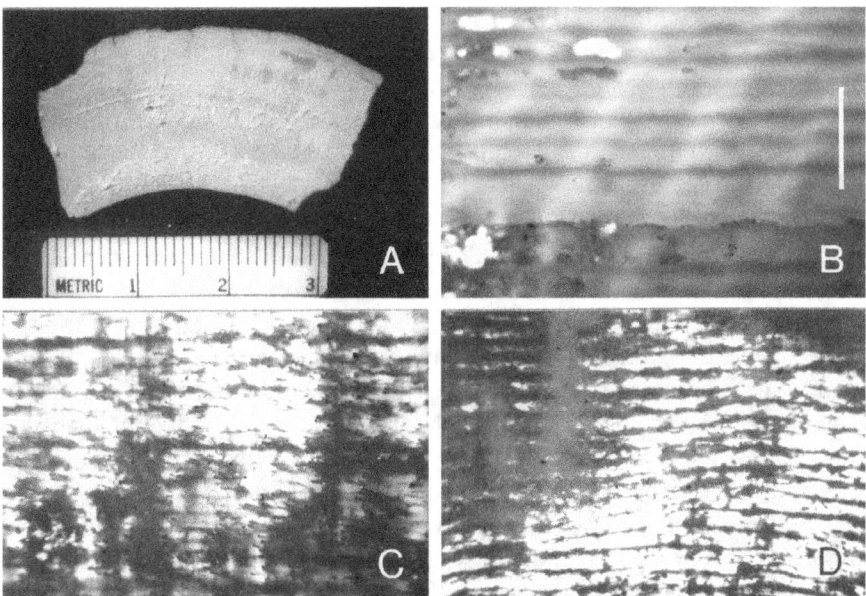

4.2. Transverse sections through Dent tusk and cheek tooth dentin (all oriented with pulp cavity toward bottom). (a), polished section (incident light) through sample block removed from proximal portion of tusk (DMNH 1450); Schreger bands (diagonal pattern) appear over much of the central region and indicate areas of better preservation; irregular zones of porous material appear as lighter areas with coarse relief; cementum, dentin, and pulp cavity identified in Figure 4.3a. (b), photomicrograph of tusk dentin, showing second-order (and some third-order) increments; primary structure preserved over most of this area but with a porous, chalky zone at left and along lower edge; scale bar = 1 mm. (c), second-order increments (transmitted light, crossed polars) in root dentin of dP_4 (DMNH 1895); scale as in b. (d), second-order increments (transmitted light, crossed polars) in root dentin of dP_3 (DMNH 1897); scale as in b.

in each dentin sequence thus guided determination of the number and spacing of isotope samples likely to yield acceptable resolution of seasonal variation in isotope values. For example, the entire thickness of tusk dentin illustrated in Figure 4.2a appeared to span about three years. To get season of death from isotopes and also some evaluation of inter-annual variability, we targeted recovery of about two years of data, which we expected to be recorded in about the 11 mm of dentin nearest the pulp cavity. Sample spacing was usually on the order of bit diameter (plus some wobble), but samples could be spaced more closely by working along the margin of a previously drilled area. Actual spacing was measured along a single radial transect after each sample was collected. Spacing varied, even along the reference transect, because the incremental features used to guide sample extraction were picked opportunistically (favoring those easiest to follow) to minimize sample overlap. Sample spacing also varied along strike (i.e., measured at different radial transects) because increments typically thin or thicken in a regular fashion with change in radial position on a tusk or cheek tooth root. Temporal discreteness of adjacent samples was the objective, not a sample groove of constant width.

Sampling strategy and examples of contingencies encountered are illustrated in Figure 4.3. Isotope sample numbers in Figures 4.3–4.6 record [sample series]-[sample number within series]; in each case, sample series 1 is the first and most complete study, and sample series >1 represent replicate studies, undertaken to check results of initial studies. The side of the tusk sample block in Figure 4.3a (shown also in Figure 4.2a) offered best preservation of the few millimeters of dentin near the pulp cavity, so sampling began there. Sample 1-1 removed some polyester resin from the pulp cavity itself (solid black area in Figure 4.3a), along with a narrow, well-constrained zone of dentin adjacent to the pulp cavity. Sampling continued on this side through sample 1-6, but beyond this point better material was found on the side shown in Figure 4.3b. Before drilling sample 1-7, the most friable of the dentin located between this position and the pulp cavity was predrilled, partly to facilitate removal of sample 1-7 and partly to ensure that this material would not crumble and contaminate samples 1-(7–21).

Strategies for cheek teeth were similar. Based on the number of second-order increments, dentin exposed in dP_4 sections seems to record only about two years, and dP_3 dentin shows little more than one year. Second-order increments were less clear on these specimens, so although sample paths still followed the nearest prominent growth line, the line selected was less often adjacent to the sample groove. With greater reliance on bit diameter as a reference for sample spacing, we chose to use about the same spacing as on the tusk, even though this provided fewer samples per year and per specimen. Replicate studies followed the pattern of originals, but the small size of dP_3 posed some limits. To obtain replicates and still leave prime sampling locations undisturbed and available for any follow-up analysis, we sampled less ideal locations extending onto the roof of the pulp cavity. With a handheld grinder, a portion of the polyester resin filling the pulp cavity was ground out, and then isotope samples were stripped from this surface, using only the diameter of the burr as a reference dimension.

The method used for oxygen isotope analyses was that of O'Neil and colleagues (1994), with only minor changes in protocol that have evolved through subsequent trials. After sample dissolution, phosphate was isolated from precipitates by filtration rather than by centrifugation. Silver phosphate crystals were heated to 525°C (rather than 550°C) during degassing. And the reaction to produce CO_2 gas from silver phosphate and graphite was run at 1,400°C for 1.75 minutes (rather than 1,200°C for 3 minutes). The isotope composition of phosphate oxygen ($\delta^{18}O_p$) was measured with a Finnigan Mat Delta S mass spectrometer. Reproducibility of analyses reported by O'Neil and colleagues (1994) was better than 0.2‰ (per mille notation used to report isotope compositions; $\delta^{18}O = ((R_{sample}/R_{standard}) - 1) \times 1,000$, where R is the measured $\delta^{18}O/\delta^{16}O$ ratio of the sample or standard; standard is VSMOW, Vienna Standard Mean Ocean Water). We confirmed similar precision

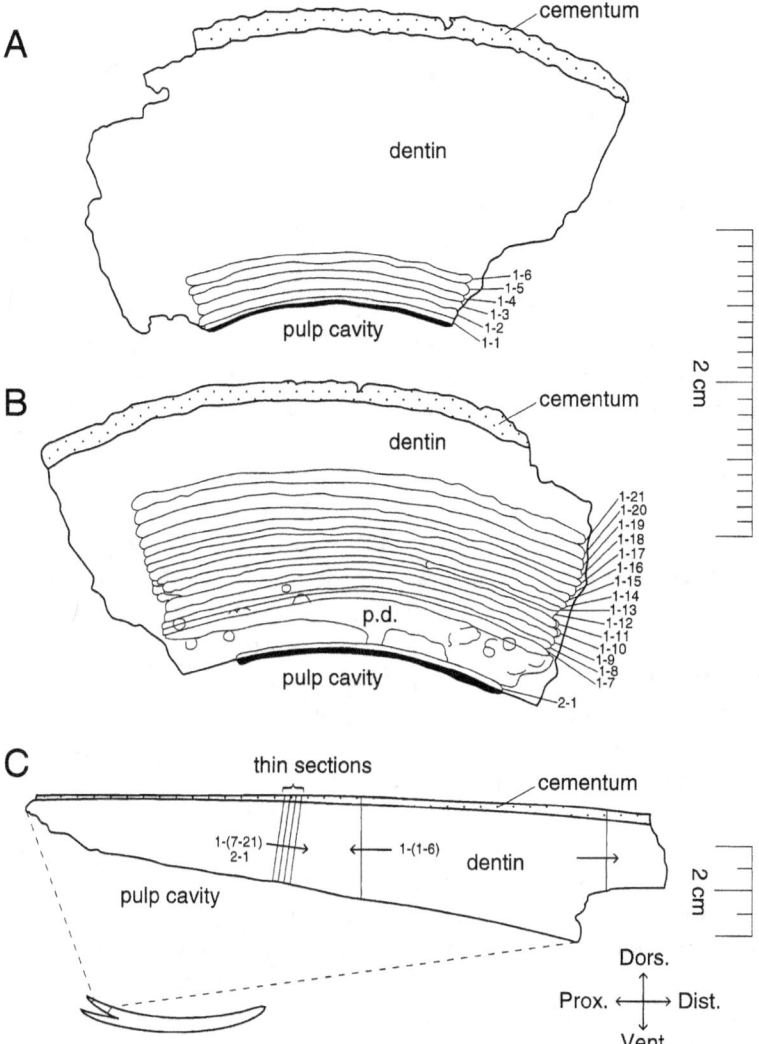

4.3. Oxygen isotope sampling from Dent tusk (DMNH 1450); cementum, dentin, and pulp cavity indicated on each drawing; p.d., predrilled area of chalky dentin, removed to avoid contamination of samples 1-(7–21); solid black, polyester resin from pulp cavity, removed with first dentin sample in series (1-1 and 2-1). (a), camera lucida drawing of distal aspect of block from which sample series 1-(1–6) was drilled (arrow in c). (b), camera lucida drawing of proximal aspect of block from which sample series 1-(7–21) and 2-1 were drilled (arrow in c); irregular circular marks in predrilled region mark deeper penetration of bit following sample removal (recorded here as landmarks along sample paths and indications of bit diameter + wobble). (c), index drawing of sample block and its location on tusk; lines show positions of transverse cuts (and thin sections); arrows indicate source of isotope samples (head toward end of bit); gnomon shows anatomical orientation. [Parts a and b appeared previously in figure 13.3 of Fisher 2001a, where they were attributed to this work, "Fisher and Fox, in press".]

for our protocol by analyses of four aliquots of a homogenized sample of dentin from the position of the arrow on the right in Figure 4.3c. Three of these measurements were within 0.1‰ of the mean value for this sample.

RESULTS

Appositional Increments in Dentin

On the anterior root of DMNH 1895 (dP_4), where cementum has spalled off the tooth, revealing a portion of the dentin-cementum interface, subtle topographic annulations (periradicular bands) mark what are probably annual increments of root elongation. However, this root had been broken apically, preventing use of this pattern for estimating season of death. These specimens show no other topographic or color patterns on the scale expected of first-order increments.

Structurally, dentin from these specimens is chalky and friable, indicating less-than-optimal preservation, but despite this appearance a great deal of primary structure is retained (Figure 4.2). On polished surfaces, differences in hardness (judged from quality of polish or micro-relief) are good predictors of the degree of retention of structure at the histological level. Harder zones, with a more amber color, characterize most of the thickness of the tusk specimen. This style of preservation retains clear dentinal tubules, Schreger bands (curved, diagonally crossing, dark-light bands that reflect patterns of dentinal tubule undulation in proboscidean dentin; see Espinoza and Mann 1992), and incremental features. The latter are mainly second-order, and many are visible in both reflected and transmitted light, either with or without crossed polars. Cutting across such material are regions of softer, whiter dentin in which little primary structure is visible. The incremental features visible in the harder zones tend to be lost in the softer, whiter zones, although with crossed polars they can often be traced across this preservational discontinuity. This suggests that the preservational transformation has occurred in situ, with no wholesale displacement of material, at least on the scale of these increments. At the microscopic scale, much of the loss of structure is attributable to extensive postmortem development of porosity. The contact between these two styles of preservation may be sharp macroscopically but becomes more diffuse and irregular at microscopic scales. The appearance is suggestive of a bacterially or fungally mediated transformation, with the softer, whiter material a degradation product of the harder, more yellow-colored material.

Second-order features are evident on transverse sections and were counted and measured microscopically. Third-order increments are inconsistently preserved, even in the best areas, and are completely obliterated in the softer zones. We were thus unable to check identifications of second-order increments based on the number of included third-order increments. Rather, we used the greater continuity and contrast of second-order features (enhanced in the cheek teeth by use of crossed polars) to distinguish them from third-order increments.

Variation in second-order increment thickness in these specimens was less conspicuous and less clearly organized on an annual basis than has been observed in other proboscideans (e.g., Fisher 1987, 1988, 1996, 2001a; Koch 1989; Koch, Fisher, and Dettman 1989). Most dentin sequences displayed no sustained pattern of variation (Figure 4.2c, d). Weekly second-order increments in the tusk specimen average ca. 0.11 mm in thickness, ranging from ca. 0.05 mm to ca. 0.17 mm. Fortnightly second-order increments in the cheek teeth average ca. 0.12 mm in dP_3 and 0.08 mm in dP_4. Complicating quantitative analysis of these patterns, dentin sequences are broken in several places, especially in the cheek teeth, by zones in which preservation is inadequate to identify second-order increments. The number of increments obscured in such zones can be estimated based on mean increment thickness, but the record is still incomplete. These problems notwithstanding, each time series of increment thicknesses did offer a best candidate for a winter interval, an interval with relatively thin increments, lasting for what might have been several months. Taking the end of the thinnest increment in such a series (Fisher 1987) as a working hypothesis for the location of a winter-spring boundary, and scanning before and after at intervals of 20–30 (i.e., ca. 26) second-order increments in the cheek teeth and 45–60 (i.e., ca. 52) second-order increments in the tusk, further candidates for winter-spring boundaries were found. Evaluation of season of death for each individual relative to the last winter-spring boundary preceding death revealed that all three specimens appeared to represent autumn deaths, as reported by Brunswig and Fisher (1993). Subsequent work has broadly confirmed this result, but given the difficulties discussed earlier, we were not satisfied to rest the case on this evidence and will not present or attempt to interpret profiles of increment variation in this report.

Despite our reservations about determining season of death from second-order increment profiles for these individuals, the increment pattern did yield working hypotheses about rates of dentin apposition. From these we can infer the spatial scale on which annual variation in any other relevant parameter can be expected to occur. This constitutes an independent reference against which patterns of oxygen isotope variation may be judged.

Profiles of Oxygen Isotope Variation in Dentin

Figures 4.3–4.5 provide maps of sample paths and index drawings showing locations of areas sampled for isotope analysis. Some overlap between adjacent samples occurred with a given path straying slightly into the right-of-way reserved for its neighbor, but each successive sample is dominated volumetrically by material representing a separate interval of time. Since incremental laminae were oriented to extend vertically into the specimen, material removed at depth generally represented the same time interval encountered at the surface, although some replicate samples that failed to reproduce a previously measured profile appear to have encountered curved laminae that shifted their representation of growth history. Of the sixty samples of dentin collected, two (neither from a position close to the pulp cavity) were lost by fracture of sample tubes during quenching of the CO_2-generating reaction. When viewed in the context of other data (Figure 4.6), neither of these two samples seems likely to have represented a local maximum or minimum, so no effort was made to resample these portions of the tusk. The lost samples are indicated by question marks at an interpolated position relative to the y-axis, and the line connecting successive sample values is dashed across them.

Results of oxygen isotope analysis are given in Table 4.1 and are plotted in Figure 4.6a–c vs. distance (in mm) from the pulp cavity (at 0 mm, on the right). In general, the pattern conforms well to expectations. The profile from tusk dentin includes two cycles of variation that correspond closely to the scale interpreted as annual, based on second-order growth increments. The amplitudes (>> analytical error) and the slopes of these curves are similar between the two years, and a broadly similar pattern is seen in each of the cheek teeth. The isotope values measured for these samples differ from those of recent precipitation (Figure 4.6d) by an amount that mainly reflects the fractionation factor for phosphate oxygen relative to drinking water but that would also have been influenced by differences in mean annual temperature and patterns of atmospheric circulation. They differ from reported values of carbonate oxygen (Koch, Fisher, and Dettman 1989) because of the difference in fractionation factors for oxygen in carbonate and phosphate. However, they are compatible with other results reported for phosphate oxygen (e.g., Ayliffe, Chivas, and Leakey 1994; Bryant, Luz, and Froelich 1994; Fricke and O'Neil 1996). We interpret these profiles as representing seasonal fluctuations in the composition of drinking water available to these mammoths and as useful for indicating the season of apposition of their last-formed dentin.

The isotope profiles for the two cheek teeth occupy about the same range of $\delta^{18}O$ variation. The tusk curve shows similar amplitude but is shifted downward by about 2‰. This suggests some difference in water composition, physiology, or both. The observed ranges of values for the cheek teeth appear compatible with an interpretation that they represent the same calendar year in two members of the same matriarchal unit, but the compositional difference between tusk and cheek teeth poses some challenge to the single-matriarchal-unit hypothesis.

The seasons of death shown by the tusk (DMNH 1450) and dP_4 (DMNH 1895) are very similar (Figure 4.6a, b), especially comparing the first sample series for each (1-[1–21] for the tusk and 1-[1–9] for dP_4). The last $\delta^{18}O$ value before the pulp cavity in each comes near the apparent end of a rising phase (i.e., it shows a value comparable to prior maxima). This point on a curve describing seasonal variation in oxygen isotope composition of precipitation (Figure 4.6d) comes near the middle or end of summer, but because of mixing of precipitation with surface water and ingested water with body water, the maximum value in tooth composition typically lags by as much as three months (Koch, Fisher, and Dettman 1989; Stuart-Williams and Schwarcz 1997). Thus, the tusk and dP_4 are

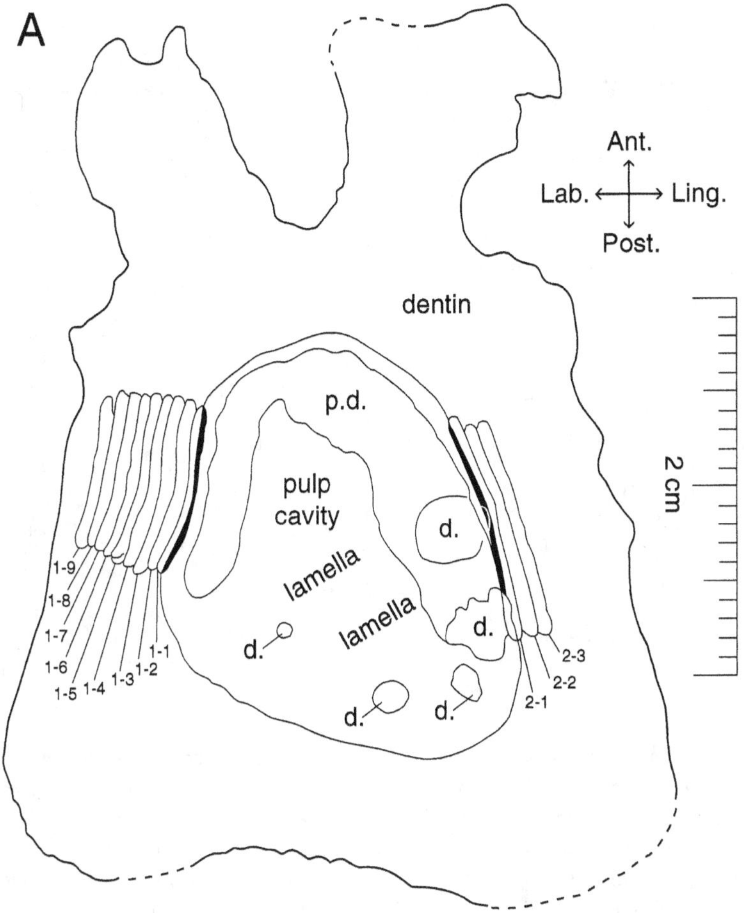

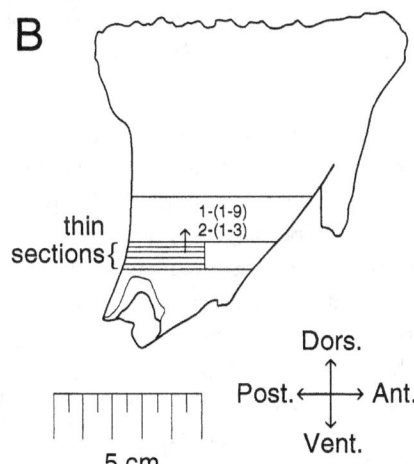

4.4. Oxygen isotope sampling from root of dP_4 (DMNH 1895); location of dentin (d.), pulp cavity, and areas of apical fusion between adjacent toothplates (lamellae) shown in a; p.d., predrilled area of pulp cavity removed to check positions of tooth lamellae; gnomons show anatomical orientation. (a), ventral (apical) aspect of crown-root transition, showing surface from which sample series 1-(1–9) and 2-(1–3) were drilled (see arrow in b). (b), index drawing of whole tooth; lines show positions of transverse cuts (and thin sections); arrow indicates source of isotope samples (head toward end of bit).

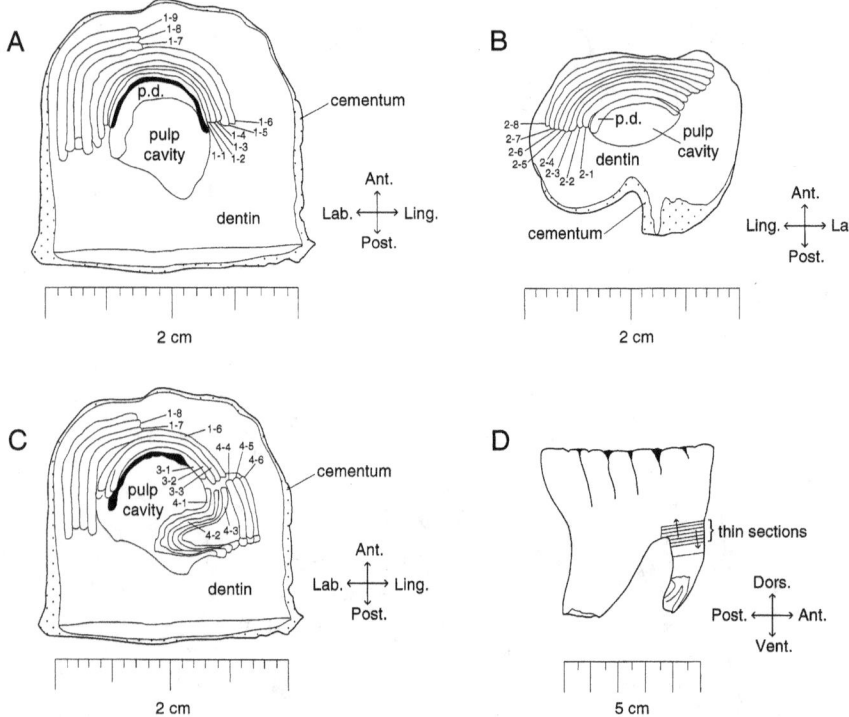

4.5. Oxygen isotope sampling from root of dP_3 (DMNH 1897); cementum, dentin, and pulp cavity shown in a–c; p.d., predrilled area of pulp cavity removed to facilitate sampling; gnomons show anatomical orientation. (a), ventral (apical) aspect of crown-root transition, showing surface from which sample series 1-(1–9) was drilled (before further sampling; upper arrow in d). (b), dorsal (abapical) aspect of anterior root, showing surface from which sample series 2-(1–8) was drilled (lower arrow in d). (c), ventral (apical) aspect of crown-root transition, showing surface from which sample series 1-(6–9), 3-(1–3), and 4-(1–6) were drilled (after completion of sampling; upper arrow in d). (d), index drawing of whole tooth; lines show positions of transverse cuts (and thin sections); arrows indicate source of isotope samples (heads toward end of bit).

each ascribed an autumn death. This agrees with the dentin increment study reported in Brunswig and Fisher (1993). The initial sample series (1-[1–9]) of dP_3 (DMNH 1897) looks different in that the final value occurs on a falling phase of the cycle, perhaps as much as halfway to a minimal value. This isotope pattern appears to represent an early-winter death. Although this differs from the increment-based result reported in Brunswig and Fisher (1993), the difference is too small to be resolved by most approaches to season-of-death determination. Given the uncertainties in dentin increment analysis posed by mediocre preservation and low variability of increment thicknesses in this tooth, the oxygen isotope determination is clearly more compelling. Season-of-death determinations thus suggest at least two mortality events are recorded by these three individuals.

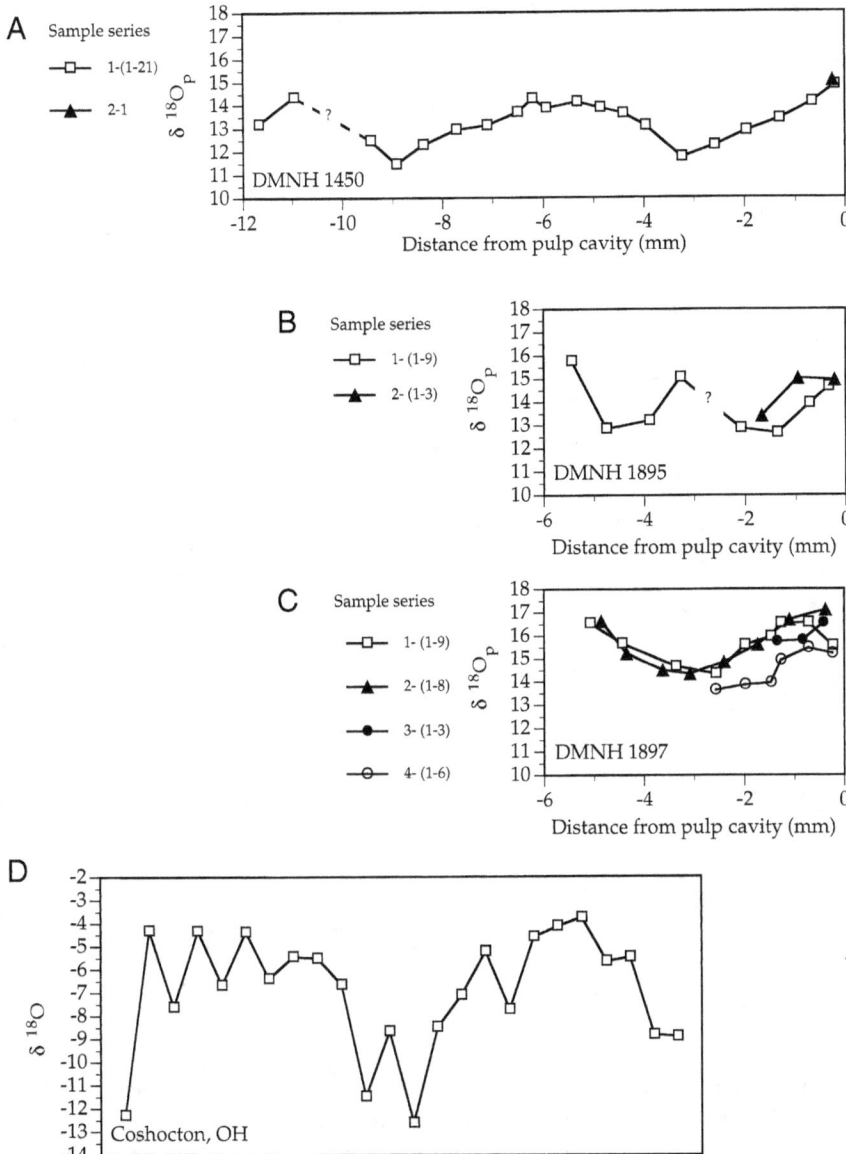

4.6. Oxygen isotope variation in tusk and cheek tooth dentin and present precipitation; dentin graphs right-justified along surface of pulp cavity (0 mm), representing last-formed dentin and time of death; original and replicate sample series plotted with different symbols (see legends). (a), phosphate oxygen profile from Dent tusk (DMNH 1450) [the same data were graphed previously in figure 13.3 of Fisher 2001a, where they were attributed to this work, "Fisher and Fox, in press"]. (b), phosphate oxygen profile from root of dP_4 (DMNH 1895). (c), phosphate oxygen profile from root of dP_3 (DMNH 1897). (d), seasonal variation in oxygen isotope composition of modern precipitation near Coshocton, Ohio.

Table 4.1. Tusk and Molar Specimens, Isotope Samples, Distances (mm) from Respective Pulp Cavities, and $\delta^{18}O$ Values (relative to VSMOW).

Specimen	Sample	Distance (mm)	$\delta^{18}O_p$	Specimen	Sample	Distance (mm)	$\delta^{18}O_p$
DMNH 1450	1-1	−0.20	14.9	DMNH 1897	1-1	−0.24	15.6
	1-2	−0.66	14.1		1-2	−0.72	16.6
	1-3	−1.31	13.4		1-3	−1.28	16.5
	1-4	−1.96	12.9		1-4	−1.48	15.9
	1-5	−2.58	12.2		1-5	−1.99	15.6
	1-6	−3.24	11.7		1-6	−2.56	14.3
	1-7	−3.96	13.1		1-7	−3.36	14.7
	1-8	−4.41	13.6		1-8	−4.44	15.7
	1-9	−4.86	13.9		1-9	−5.08	16.5
	1-10	−5.32	14.1		2-1	−0.38	17.1
	1-11	−5.94	13.9		2-2	−1.11	16.7
	1-12	−6.21	14.3		2-3	−1.74	15.6
	1-13	−6.50	13.7		2-4	−2.40	14.9
	1-14	−7.10	13.1		2-5	−3.08	14.3
	1-15	−7.72	12.9		2-6	−3.63	14.5
	1-16	−8.38	12.3		2-7	−4.36	15.2
	1-17	−8.92	11.5		2-8	−4.86	16.6
	1-18	−9.44	12.5		3-1	−0.24	16.5
	1-19	−10.96	14.3		3-2	−0.72	15.8
	1-20	−11.68	13.2		3-3	−1.28	15.7
	2-1	−0.25	15.1		4-1	−0.24	15.2
					4-2	−0.72	15.5
DMNH 1895	1-1	−0.34	14.7		4-3	−1.28	14.9
	1-2	−0.72	13.9		4-4	−1.48	13.9
	1-3	−1.37	12.7		4-5	−1.99	13.9
	1-4	−2.09	12.9		4-6	−2.56	13.6
	1-5	−3.28	15.1				
	1-6	−3.90	13.2				
	1-7	−4.76	12.9				
	1-8	−5.44	15.8				
	2-1	−0.23	14.9				
	2-2	−0.96	15.0				
	2-3	−1.68	13.4				

The easiest exit at this point would have been to call the project complete, report the refutation of Saunders's (1980) single-event hypothesis, and move on. However, we were concerned to give the hypothesis a thorough evaluation, including consideration of the replicability of these analyses. Is the pattern clear enough that replicate analyses would give the same result?

The first attempted replication of these analyses targeted the last-formed dentin on the tusk specimen. Despite poor preservation of nearby material, a narrow zone adjacent to the pulp cavity on the side shown in Figure 4.3b was well preserved and had not been predrilled. Sample 2-1 closely replicated the provenience of sample 1-1, judging post hoc from drill paths, and yielded a value within measurement error of sample 1-1. This concordance of terminal values corroborates the first determination at its most critical point. When appositional geometry (the regular, conical increments typical of tusks) is this simple and successive values (Figure 4.6a) show such smooth intermediacy, adjacent values in the time series become their own best controls, and repetition of the entire profile is unnecessary.

The clearest indication of inconsistency with Saunders's (1980) hypothesis is the different season of death attributed above to the individual represented by dP_3 (DMNH 1897). To be as certain as possible that this did not result from a sampling or analytical problem, we attempted to replicate our entire analysis of this individual, sampling a more apical level on the anterior root of the tooth. The sampling map for this attempt is shown in Figure 4.5b, and the results (sample series 2-[1–8]) are plotted with solid triangles in Figure 4.6c. Most of the profile matches the original curve very closely, but the first sample, recording the last-formed dentin, now appears at the end of a rising phase, like the pattern seen in the other two individuals. The close match between most parts of these curves confirmed the robustness of our approach, but the disparity between these two terminal values, supposedly recording the same time interval on the same individual, posed a serious challenge. The resolution of this discrepancy, however, was discovered on close inspection of the drill paths. Pre-drilling prior to sample 1-1 (Figure 4.5a) had removed only polyester resin, and sample 1-1, by design, removed some additional polyester resin (solid black in Figure 4.5a) and a narrow zone of dentin adjacent to the pulp cavity. However, pre-drilling prior to sample 2-1 (Figure 4.5b) inadvertently cut into the last-formed dentin at both the lingual and labial ends of the path. In addition, from examining the walls of the sampled area after the fact, it appears that the pulp cavity surface curved as it plunged into the specimen block, such that an even larger portion of the last-formed dentin may have been removed by pre-drilling than is evident from Figure 4.5b. This was not observed during sampling because of difficult visual access to the sampled area, and the predrilled material was discarded. Finally, sample 2-1 can be seen in Figure 4.5b to have recovered a thicker zone of dentin than sample 1-1, reaching into an earlier portion of the sequence where, according to the composition measured for sample 1-2, the $\delta^{18}O_p$ value is expected to be higher. The fact that the value for sample 2-1 is higher than that for sample 1-2 may simply reflect a short-term peak in isotope value that was diluted by mixing with lower-valued material in samples 1-1 and 1-2.

Although these observations account for the different terminal portions of the first two isotope profiles from this individual, the goal of checking initial determinations of season of death was still not attained. We therefore undertook another round of sampling on both cheek teeth, collecting sample series 2-(1–3) from DMNH 1895 and 3-(1–3) from DMNH 1897. The samples from dP_4 (Figure 4.4a) were collected easily and, on examination of drill paths, seemed to present a good series. Pre-drilling encountered denticles located along the area of fusion of initially separate tooth plates (or lamellae) making up the tooth crown, and sample 2-1 stripped some dentin from the surface of two of these, but this should have been some of the last-formed dentin, and its inclusion in sample 2-1 was not judged to be problematic. The predrilled area was extended around to the vicinity of sample series 1-(1–9) on this tooth, but lamellar denticles did not reach the sampled level on this side.

DMNH 1897 (dP_3) presented greater problems. Samples 1-(1–4) had been relatively thin and extended well around the pulp cavity and up into the base of the tooth crown (Figure 4.5a). At the level in the tooth now available for sampling, the pulp cavity surface was already curving to form its roof, making design and control of sample paths uncertain. Because of this curvature, sample paths for the third series (samples 3-[1–3]) from this specimen did not exactly follow those from the first series. Most such differences were planned, but sample 3-1 went farther than expected into the pulp cavity toward its labial end and into earlier-formed dentin toward its lingual end, making it effectively more similar to sample 2-1 than to sample 1-1, from the same tooth.

When Ag_3PO_4 crystals were precipitated for samples 2-(1–3) from dP_4 and 3-(1–3) from dP_3, an abnormal, light-colored material appeared. Samples analyzed by others in the laboratory at the same time behaved similarly. Observations by H. C. Fricke (pers. comm.) suggested that an additional phase (other than pure silver phosphate) was present that did not interfere with isotope analysis directly but that did constitute a potential problem. In the O'Neil and colleagues (1994) method, an accurate, stoichiometric amount of graphite (i.e., just enough to react with the silver phosphate) is added prior to initiating the reaction that evolves the CO_2 admitted to the mass spectrometer to measure an oxygen isotope ratio. If the right amount of graphite is added, the analysis produces an accurate result (too much or too little biases the result), but the presence of the additional phase prevented accurate weighing of Ag_3PO_4, which is generally required to determine the right amount of graphite. Attempting to salvage these samples, we approached the problem in a different way. The amount of graphite needed was estimated, based on the original mass of sample powder and a yield factor calculated from prior analyses. These problems were later determined to have resulted from contamination of our distilled water source, stemming from recent building renovations.

Because of this contamination, our attempted replication of the original profiles is compromised but perhaps not thoroughly invalidated. Any value measured in this series of analyses is a function of both the material sampled and our nonstandard analytical procedure. If we observe disparate values for ostensibly comparable material, we would probably reject the value derived from the contaminated sample rather than question the original value, and if such an outcome protects the original values from refutation, they will not have been fully tested. However, if original and replicate values agree, again sampling ostensibly comparable material, either (1) they both reflect the same, true value, and, by careful estimate of silver phosphate yield, we avoided analytical error in the contaminated sample; (2) both values are identically erroneous for some reason unrelated to contamination of the water supply, but, by careful estimate of silver phosphate yield, we avoided further error in the contaminated sample; or (3) the original and replicate values are erroneous to different degrees, but the contaminated sample engendered an analytical error that just happened to offset the disparity. Both (2) and (3) have ad hoc elements not required by (1), making (1) the more parsimonious interpretation. In this sense, if original and replicate values agree despite the contamination of replicate samples, we can claim some level of corroboration of original values.

For dP_4 (DMNH 1895; solid triangles, Figure 4.6b), samples 2-1 and 2-3 are very close to the values they were expected to replicate. Sample 2-2 differs from the value it was expected to replicate, but this probably reflects only an improper amount of graphite, and we interpret sample series 2-(1–3) as (at least approximate) confirmation of the original profile. For dP_3 (DMNH 1897; solid dots, Figure 4.6c), samples 3-1 and 3-3 are close to other values at similar positions relative to the pulp cavity on this specimen. Only sample 3-2 differs substantially from expectation, and this may again reflect a problem with graphite addition. Such an explanation is awkward, however, because if this profile were taken at face value, it would appear (contrary to our earlier result) to bring all three specimens into conformity as autumn deaths (although differences in the range of values would still complicate interpreting them as members of a single family unit). Such an interpretation is unlikely, in part because sample 3-1 clearly included material at some distance from the pulp cavity (as noted earlier, it replicates sample 2-1 rather than 1-1), but we hesitate to rule it out without independent data confirming our original result. Unfortunately, the abnormal chemistry encountered during these analyses precludes any firm conclusion from these results alone.

After we secured an uncontaminated water source, testing resumed on dP_3 (DMNH 1897). We had already used the most accessible sampling locations and wanted to protect a generous portion of remaining material for potential future analyses. In particular, we were concerned to leave the dentin around the base of the other root intact. We therefore selected the curving wall and roof of the pulp cavity above the anterior root. With a handheld grinder, polyester resin was removed from most of the pulp cavity, and samples were stripped sequentially from its surface, leaving narrow, peripheral terraces to mark depth (disjunct, curved traces for samples 4-[1–3]). Removal of the last portions of sample 4-3 encountered some resistant areas that were probably enamel, so samples 4-(4–6) were limited to vertically oriented paths on the lingual side of the pulp cavity. No second-order increments could be followed in this area, so although we are confident that sample 4-1 represents the end of life, temporal control on all succeeding samples declines, especially for samples 4-(4–6).

The oxygen isotope value measured for sample 4-1 is a close match for that of sample 1-1, and the values for 4-2 and 4-3, although possibly affected by temporal mixing, again show a pattern in which death is associated with a declining phase of oxygen isotope variation, providing replication of the original analysis. The spatial scale and range of this variation differs from that of the original profile, but this probably reflects lower rates of dentin apposition, and therefore greater time averaging, associated with the difference in location on the tooth. In summary, these results confirm an early-winter death for DMNH 1897 (dP_3) and, in conjunction with results for DMNH 1450 (tusk) and DMNH 1895 (dP_4), demonstrate more than one mortality event at the Dent site.

DISCUSSION

The isotope profiles described previously in this chapter (and summarized earlier by Fisher 1995, 2001a) resemble present-day, and presumed ancient, patterns of seasonal change in composition of precipitation, but their relation to atmospheric conditions is no doubt inexact. We do not expect ancient climate to be identical to modern climate, but comparisons between ancient and modern isotope data can help assess the meaning and integrity of the ancient data. Figure 4.6d shows two years of data (at monthly intervals) on oxygen isotope composition of precipitation at a recording station near Coshocton, Ohio (similar in latitude, if not longitude, to Dent; IAEA data available at http://www.iaea.or.at/). The y-axis shows measured values for precipitation, but these values would be shifted in mammalian phosphatic tissues by a fractionation factor of ca. +23‰ (Ayliffe, Lister, and Chivas 1992; Stuart-Williams and Schwarcz 1997). The small residual difference in mean value between this profile and that of the Dent teeth suggests a mean annual temperature 2–4°C lower at Dent or else some combination of differences involving mean annual temperature, altitudinal effects, and air mass histories. It is difficult to ascribe such differences to any particular factor, but the differences are of a degree easily explained by numerous factors. As a result, they are entirely compatible with the proposed interpretation of seasonal cycles.

Another difference from the Dent isotope data is the higher amplitude of the recent curve. This does not mean the Dent data could not reflect an annual isotopic cycle. On the contrary, the amplitude of seasonal cycles in oxygen isotope composition has been recognized as a potential measure of seasonality (Koch, Fisher, and Dettman 1989), and the seasonality of late Pleistocene northeastern Colorado could have been less pronounced than observed in Ohio today. Indeed, workers who interpret late Pleistocene climate change as a cause of megafaunal extinctions often propose that increase in seasonality was a major factor during the Pleistocene-Holocene transition (e.g., Graham and Lundelius 1984; King and Saunders 1984). If the Dent mammoths, at ca. 10,800 radiocarbon years before present (RCYBP) (Brunswig, Chapter 3, this volume; Stafford et al. 1991), were still recording low seasonality, the shift to high seasonality must have been particularly rapid to bring about extinction by ca. 10,400 RCYBP (Beck 1996). However, other factors could have affected isotope profiles as well. If the Dent mammoths migrated seasonally between summer, high-altitude habitats and winter, lower-altitude habitats (as suggested by Cummings and Albert, Chapter 6, this volume), their tusks would record a damped representation of the seasonal variation they would have experienced had they stayed year-round in one place (as a recording station does). Topographic relief within 100 km of Dent could account for a 4–8‰ damping effect (Siegenthaler and Oeschger 1980). Seasonal shifts between water sources pose a further possible complication. The potential contributions of such factors could be evaluated by comparing isotope data from several contemporaneous, sympatric taxa that differ in inferred behavior and habitat. Pending such comparisons, we must not assume that isotope profiles from the Dent mammoths are uncompromised records of local climate, but it is unlikely that complicating factors would neatly invert a seasonal signal, resulting in gross error in determining season of death.

The possibility that behavior and habitat might interact to determine details of the isotope profile expressed in individual mammoths gives this system unusual potential for testing the hypothesis of membership in a single social group of the sort observed in extant elephantids. Members of the same matriarchal family unit would be expected to drink together from the same water sources, have access to the same food, and produce parallel records of environmental fluctuations that might distinguish one year from another (Moss 1988). Nursing calves might show some fractionation relative to their lactating mothers (Roberts et al. 1988), to a degree reflecting the portion of their fluid intake derived from milk, but it is difficult to predict how great this effect should be. In any case, temporally equivalent dentin sequences of members of the same family unit should usually show an identity greater than would be expected for different years recorded in members of the same family unit. Likewise, isotope profiles from the same years among family members should be more similar to each other than either the same or different years between non-family members. Secure correlation of time intervals among individuals, however, will probably require increased spatial resolution of sampling, which would in turn require a decrease in minimum sample size. Current samples homogenize material deposited over periods of weeks to months, preventing higher frequency shifts in isotope value from being resolved. For this reason, we are currently unlikely to observe the exact profile, or the full amplitude, of variation in isotope composition. Discrepancies such as the differences in profile between the original data for dP_3 (DMNH 1897) and subsequent attempts at replication are indicative of how details of sample provenience limit recovery of an isotope profile. Of the specimens analyzed here, the smallest, where dentin laminae curved most sharply, presented the greatest problem.

Despite the difficulties of comparing independently sampled profiles, it seems well established that the individuals represented by the tusk and by dP_4 died at or near the ends of rising phases of the annual curve recording seasonal variation in oxygen isotopes from dentinal phosphate. In contrast, two analyses from DMNH 1897 (samples 1-1 and 4-1) confirm that the individual represented by dP_3 died on a declining (cooling) phase of isotope variation. DMNH 1897 is thus confirmed as showing survival to a more advanced stage in the seasonal cycle than the time of death shown by the other two specimens. The difference in range of isotope values between the tusk and dP_3 (DMNH 1897) may be compatible with interpreting the latter as belonging to a nursing calf of the adult female that produced the tusk, but regardless of the likely milk intake of a calf this age (and the consequent shift in isotope profile), the different seasons of death for the two individuals imply that they do not represent a mother-calf pair that died at the same time. Brunswig (Chapter 3, this volume) raises the possibility that the two-year-old calf's mother could have been one of the younger adults found at the site and that they could have survived the older matriarch's death, only to become victims at the same site several months later. This is indeed possible, but to have strong evidence favoring such an interpretation, we would like to see longer profiles, with some distinctive annual feature supporting correlations between the last years of these individuals.

DMNH 1895 (dP_4), ca. 9 AEY, clearly comes from an individual too old to be still nursing, so the difference between its range of isotope values and that of the tusk cannot be taken as evidence of a mother-calf pair. The difference probably implies membership in different family units (and thus different timing of mortality), despite the similar season of death of these two individuals. In other words, the death of each individual studied here appears to have been a separate event. We therefore believe a single mortality event is ruled out as the cause of accumulation of the entire Dent mammoth assemblage. Although it is still possible that some of the mammoths at Dent (i.e., others not studied here) are family members that died together, these results refute the simplest version of Saunders's (1980) model of site origin. In view of widespread interest in the nature of this site, it would be worthwhile to extend this work to other individuals.

These results do not definitively indicate death by human vs. nonhuman causation. However, considering the generally low probability of death by natural causes in autumn–early winter for large mammals and the seasonal distribution of mortality and butchery in Great Lakes–region mastodons (Fisher 1987), the pattern observed at Dent seems more likely under (and, to that extent, more consistent with) a model of hunting-induced mortality than under a hypothesis of natural mortality. Relatively few agents of mortality other than human activity tend to affect large mammals at this time of year. In a sense, it would have been easier to attribute mammoth mortality at Dent to natural causation if all deaths had turned out to result from a single event because in a species that is normally gregarious, even an unusual event might affect a group of individuals at once, yielding a single assemblage with a single season of death. On the other hand, if multiple mortality events are demonstrated, showing even approximate similarity in season of death, we are left wondering how to explain their seasonal selectivity and the spatial association of carcasses produced by separate events. That is, what agent would kill a number of mammoths in autumn–early winter and act repeatedly at the same locale? Geologic investigations at Dent (Chapter

3, this volume) suggest limited transport as a debris flow or landslide, but this would not produce a significant concentration of carcasses from disparate original settings, so site fidelity as well as seasonal selectivity must still be explained. Some natural traps yield localized concentrations of carcasses produced through separate mortality events that may nonetheless be seasonally selective (based on the mechanism of entrapment; Fisher, Fox, and Agenbroad 2003). However, nothing about the geological context of the Dent site suggests a natural trap, operating without mediation by human activity.

For these reasons, the larger the number of separate mortality events observed at Dent, and the more they tend to cluster at one general time of year, as the three deaths evaluated here suggest, the more likely it is that some single process, even if it acted on numerous occasions, is responsible for the entire Dent assemblage. As for what that single process might be, human activity, taking advantage of strategic attributes of this site, could explain such a pattern in a way that seems at present less effectively explained by natural alternatives. We therefore infer that Paleoindians hunted mammoths on at least three occasions in the immediate vicinity of Dent.

Subsequent to our completion of this project, Hoppe (2004) began a study of carbon, oxygen, and strontium isotope compositions of enamel from mammoth teeth from various late Pleistocene sites, including Dent. Hoppe's study also had the objective of determining whether the Dent assemblage (and that at the Miami site, Roberts County, Texas) represented a single event, and she concluded that it did not. Despite the apparent similarity of our results, our studies are quite different. Rather than sample time series from each individual, Hoppe (2004:135) collected bulk samples of enamel representing "at least a year of growth," although she gives no information on how this was accomplished or the likelihood that it was consistently achieved. The hypothesis that a single event was responsible for the entire assemblage was evaluated by comparing the variation between bulk sample compositions at the Dent site to variation observed at another site thought to represent a single event (Waco, Texas, interpreted as preserving a family group of mammoths overcome by a flood). Single-event, family unit assemblages were expected to be characterized by low levels of inter-individual variation, whereas higher levels of variation between individuals were expected for multi-event assemblages. Note that this approach requires no access to the last-formed tissue of any kind but also yields no insight on season of death. Whether family unit assemblages would always conform to the expected pattern of restricted inter-individual variation depends on issues such as temporal control of sampling and the pattern of seasonal and inter-annual variation in isotope composition, which would be expected to vary among environments and regions.

Another study that relates to ours is Saunders's report of new observations on processing marks on bones of the Dent mammoths (Chapter 5, this volume). Saunders is not attempting to distinguish between single- and multiple-event models of site formation; indeed, his results are compatible with both. However, his work does provide additional detail for the fundamental inference that human activity is recorded at this site, a conclusion that our results support as well.

As discussed earlier, our current interpretation is that analysis of oxygen isotope profiles from three individuals has demonstrated at least two, and probably three, separate mortality events, but what does this mean for the origin of the Dent site as a whole? Were all of the mammoths found at Dent victims of separate mortality events, or do we simply scale back Saunders's (1980) "herd confrontation hypothesis" and envision a small number of such events, still with several members of family units killed in each, as suggested by Brunswig's (Chapter 3, this volume) summary and synthesis of Dent data? Data in hand do not allow us to answer this question definitively, but we can think about the problem from a probabilistic perspective. What is the probability of choosing three individuals to analyze and discovering three mortality events if as few as three such events are actually responsible for the whole assemblage? The answer would depend on the distribution of individuals among the three events, and this outcome would be more probable for more even distributions (i.e., equal numbers of victims in each group). Still, with only three events, finding an example of one of each in only three tries is not the most likely outcome. However, this outcome becomes more likely the larger the number of events, suggesting to us that there were probably more than three. In considering this multiplicity of events, it is clearly necessary to maintain consistency with other taphonomic data; for example, victims of each event must have been buried relatively quickly to explain the lack of weathering on the bones, but the geomorphic context of the site seems adequate to accomplish this. In any case, we agree with Brunswig that the site context, together with our data, argue against fluvial transport of the assemblage from some upriver location, and we agree that an ambush scenario is the best explanation for seasonal selectivity and site fidelity.

One way to improve resolution on our reconstruction of events at Dent is to extend the type of study conducted here to additional individuals, maintaining the maximum possible resolution in seasonal profiles of variation in isotope composition. It would also be useful to extend the isotope records to a larger number of years per individual to allow more severe testing of year-to-year correlations between individuals (i.e., checking whether a given year in one individual is likely the same as a year in another individual). Such a study would be a major analytical effort, and its results would be dependent on the spatiotemporal control achieved in milling consecutive samples, but it would hold out the prospect of adding greatly to our understanding of the paleobiology and environment of the Dent mammoths. Even better would be to add other isotope systems to compare profiles in other modalities. For instance, strontium isotope time series (rather than bulk samples, as studied by Hoppe 2004) could help greatly (although at considerable effort and expense). There is much still to be learned about this site, but analyses that tap information locked in the remarkable record of tusks and cheek teeth show great promise for constraining interpretations of site history.

Acknowledgments. We are grateful to Robert Brunswig for inviting this contribution and for introducing us to many aspects of research on the Dent site and to Bonnie Pitblado for her comments on the manuscript and for facilitating final revisions. We appreciate Richard Stucky's assistance in surveying DMNH collections and granting permission to analyze these specimens. We would have been unable to undertake the isotope component of this study without help from James O'Neil and Henry Fricke, who developed the approach to analyzing phosphate oxygen utilized here and trained DLF in the necessary procedures. Bonnie Miljour assisted with illustrations. This research was supported by NSF grant SBR-9211984 to DCF.

REFERENCES CITED

Arthur, M. A., D. F. Williams, and D. S. Jones
    1993   Seasonal Temperature-Salinity Changes and Thermocline Development in the Mid-Atlantic Bight as Recorded by the Isotope Composition of Bivalves. *Geology* 11:655–659.

Ayliffe, L. K., A. R. Chivas, and M. G. Leakey
    1994   The Retention of Primary Oxygen Isotope Compositions of Fossil Elephant Skeletal Phosphate. *Geochimica et Cosmochimica Acta* 58 (23):5291–5298.

Ayliffe, L. K., A. M. Lister, and A. R. Chivas
    1992   The Preservation of Glacial-Interglacial Climatic Signatures in the Oxygen Isotopes of Elephant Skeletal Phosphate. *Palaeogeography, Palaeoclimatology, and Palaeoecology* 99:179–191.

Beck, M. W.
    1996   On Discerning the Cause of Late Pleistocene Megafaunal Extinctions. *Paleobiology* 22 (1):91–103.

Brunswig, R. H., Jr., and D. C. Fisher
    1993   Research on the Dent Mammoth Site. *Current Research in the Pleistocene* 10: 63–65.

Bryant, J. D., and P. N. Froelich
    1995   A Model of Oxygen Isotope Fractionation in Body Water of Large Mammals. *Geochimica et Cosmochimica Acta* 59 (21):4523–4537.

Bryant, J. D., B. Luz, and P. N. Froelich
    1994   Oxygen Isotopic Composition of Fossil Horse Tooth Phosphate as a Record of Continental Paleoclimate. *Palaeogeography, Palaeoclimatology, Palaeoecology* 107:303–316.

Conybeare, A., and G. Haynes
    1984   Observations on Elephant Mortality and Bones in Water Holes. *Quaternary Research* 22:189–200.

Dansgaard, W.
    1964   Stable Isotopes in Precipitation. *Tellus* 16:436–468.

Dettman, D. L., and K. C. Lohmann
  1993   Seasonal Change in Paleogene Surface Water $\delta^{18}O$: Freshwater Bivalves of Western North America. In *Climate Change in Continental Isotopic Records*, ed. P. K. Swart, K. C. Lohmann, J. McKenzie, and S. Savin, 153–163. Geophysical Monograph 78, American Geophysical Union, Washington, DC.

Espinoza, E. O., and M-J. Mann
  1992   *Identification Guide for Ivory and Ivory Substitutes*. World Wildlife Fund, Washington, DC.

Fisher, D. C.
  1984   Taphonomic Analysis of Late Pleistocene Mastodon Occurrences: Evidence of Butchery by North American Paleo-Indians. *Paleobiology* 10:338–357.
  1987   Mastodont Procurement by Paleoindians of the Great Lakes Region: Hunting or Scavenging? In *The Evolution of Human Hunting*, ed. M. H. Nitecki and D. V. Nitecki, 309–421. Plenum, New York.
  1988   Season of Death of the Hiscock Mastodonts. In *Late Pleistocene and Early Holocene Paleoecology and Archeology of the Great Lakes Region*, ed. R. S. Laub, N. G. Miller, and D. W. Steadman, 115–125. Bulletin of the Buffalo Society of Natural Sciences 33.
  1990   Age, Sex, and Season of Death of the Grandville Mastodont. In *Pilot of the Grand: Papers in Tribute to Richard E. Flanders*, ed. T. J. Martin and C. E. Cleland. *Michigan Archaeologist* 36 (3–4):141–160.
  1995   Season of Death of the Dent Mammoths. In *Society of American Archaeology Abstracts*, Sixtieth Annual Meeting, Minneapolis, MN, 76.
  1996   Proboscidean Extinctions in North America. In *The Proboscidea: Evolution and Paleoecology of Elephants and Their Relatives*, ed. J. Shoshani and P. Tassy, 296–315. Oxford University Press, Oxford.
  2001a Season of Death, Growth Rates, and Life History of North American Mammoths. In *Proceedings of the International Conference on Mammoth Site Studies*, ed. D. West, 121–135. *Publications in Anthropology* 22, University of Kansas, Lawrence.
  2001b Entrained vs. Free-Running Physiological Rhythms and Incremental Features in the Tusks of Woolly Mammoths. *Journal of Vertebrate Paleontology* 21 (suppl. to 3):49A–50A.

Fisher, D. C., D. L. Fox, and L. D. Agenbroad
  2003   Tusk Growth Rate and Season of Death of *Mammuthus columbi* from Hot Springs, South Dakota, USA. In *Advances in Mammoth Research* (Proceedings of the Second International Mammoth Conference, Rotterdam, May 16–20, 1999), ed. J.W.F. Reumer, J. De Vos, and D. Mol. *Deinsea* 9:117–133.

Fox, D. L.
  1995a Incremental Growth in *Gomphotherium* Tusks. *Journal of Vertebrate Paleontology* 15 (suppl. to 3):30A.
  1995b *Growth Increments in Gomphotherium Tusks and Implications for Miocene Climate Change*. Unpublished master's thesis, University of Michigan, Ann Arbor.
  2000   Growth Increments in *Gomphotherium* Tusks and Implications for Late Miocene Climate Change in North America. *Palaeogeography, Palaeoclimatology, Palaeoecology* 156:327–348.

Fricke, H. C., and J. R. O'Neil
  1996   Inter- and Intra-Tooth Variation in the Oxygen Isotope Composition of Mammalian Tooth Enamel: Some Implications for Paleoclimatological and Paleobiological Research. *Palaeogeography, Palaeoclimatology, Palaeoecology* 126:91–99.

Frison, G. C., and C. A. Reher
  1970   Age Determination of Buffalo by Teeth Eruption and Wear. In *The Glenrock Buffalo Jump, 48CO304*, ed. G. C. Frison. *Plains Anthropologist Memoir* 7:46–50.

Graham, R. W., and E. L. Lundelius
  1984   Coevolutionary Disequilibrium and Pleistocene Extinctions. In *Quaternary Extinctions: A Prehistoric Revolution*, ed. P. S. Martin and R. G. Klein, 223–249. University of Arizona Press, Tucson.

Haynes, G.
  1985   Age Profiles in Elephant and Mammoth Bone Assemblages. *Quaternary Research* 24:333–345.

Hoppe, K. A.
  2004   Late Pleistocene Mammoth Herd Structure, Migration Patterns, and Clovis Hunting Strategies Inferred from Isotopic Analyses of Multiple Death Assemblages. *Paleobiology* 30:129–145.

King, J. E., and J. J. Saunders
  1984   Environmental Insularity and the Extinction of the American Mastodont. In *Quaternary Extinctions: A Prehistoric Revolution*, ed. P. S. Martin and R. G. Klein, 315–339. University of Arizona Press, Tucson.

Klevezal, G. A., and S. E. Kleinenberg
  1969   Age Determination of Mammals from Annual Layers in Teeth and Bones. *Israel Program of Scientific Translations, Jerusalem* TT 69-55033:1–128.

Koch, P. L.
  1989   *Paleobiology of Late Pleistocene Mastodonts and Mammoths from Southern Michigan and Western New York*. Ph.D. dissertation, University of Michigan, Ann Arbor.

Koch, P. L., D. C. Fisher, and D. L. Dettman
  1989   Oxygen Isotope Variation in the Tusks of Extinct Proboscideans: A Measure of Season of Death and Seasonality. *Geology* 17:515–519.

Land, L. S., E. L. Lundelius Jr., and S. Velastro
  1980   Isotopic Ecology of Deer Bones. *Palaeogeography, Palaeoclimatology, Palaeoecology* 32 (1–2):143–151.

Laws, R. M.
  1966   Age Criteria for the African Elephant, *Loxodonta africana*. *East African Wildlife Journal* 4:1–37.

Lieberman, D. E.
  1994   The Biological Basis for Seasonal Increments in Dental Cementum and Their Application to Archaeological Research. *Journal of Archaeological Science* 21:525–539.

Miani, A., and C. Miani
    1972   Circadian Advancement Rhythm of the Calcification Front in Dog Dentin. *Panminerva Medica* 14:127–136.

Moss, C.
    1988   *Elephant Memories: Thirteen Years in the Life of an Elephant Family*. William Morrow, New York.

O'Neil, J. R., L. J. Roe, E. Reinhard, and R. E. Blake
    1994   A Rapid and Precise Method of Oxygen Isotope Analysis of Biogenic Phosphate. *Israel Journal of Earth Science* 43:203–212.

Osborn, H. F.
    1936   *Proboscidea, Volume I*. American Museum of Natural History, New York.

Patterson, W. P., G. R. Smith, and K. C. Lohmann
    1993   Continental Paleothermometry and Seasonality Using the Isotopic Composition of Aragonitic Otoliths of Freshwater Fishes. In *Climate Change in Continental Isotopic Records,* ed. P. K. Swart, K. C. Lohmann, J. McKenzie, and S. Savin, 191–202. Geophysical Monograph 78, American Geophysical Union, Washington, DC.

Pike-Tay, A.
    1991   Red Deer Hunting in the Upper Paleolithic of South-West France: A Study in Seasonality. *BAR International Series* 569, Oxford.

Roberts, S. B., W. A. Coward, G. Ewing, J. Savage, T. J. Cole, and A. Lucas
    1988   Effect of Weaning on Accuracy of Doubly Labeled Water Method in Infants. *American Journal of Physiology* 254:R622–R627.

Rosenberg, G. D., and D. V. Simmons
    1980   Rhythmic Dentinogenesis in the Rabbit Incisor: Circadian, Ultradian, and Infradian Periods. *Calcified Tissues International* 32:29–44.

Saunders, J. J.
    1977   Lehner Ranch Revisited. In *Paleo-Indian Lifeways,* ed. E. Johnson. *The Museum Journal* 17:48–64.
    1980   A Model for Man-Mammoth Relationships in Late Pleistocene North America. *Canadian Journal of Anthropology* 1:87–98.

Sher, T. M., and D. C. Fisher
    1995   Sexual Dimorphism in *Mammut americanum*. *Journal of Vertebrate Paleontology* 15 (suppl. to 3):53A.

Siegenthaler, U., and H. Oeschger
    1980   Correlation of ^{18}O in Precipitation with Temperature and Altitude. *Nature* 285:314–317.

Spiess, A. E.
    1979   *Reindeer and Caribou Hunters: An Archaeological Study*. Academic, New York.

Stafford, T. W., Jr., P. E. Hare, L. Currie, A.J.T. Jull, and D. J. Donahue
    1991   Accelerator Radiocarbon Dating at the Molecular Level. *Journal of Archaeological Science* 18:35–72.

Steuber, T.
   1996   Stable Isotope Sclerochronology of Rudist Bivalves: Growth Rates and Late Cretaceous Seasonality. *Geology* 24 (4):315–318.

Stuart-Williams, H. L., and H. P. Schwarcz
   1997   Oxygen Isotopic Determination of Climatic Variation Using Phosphate from Beaver Bone, Tooth Enamel and Dentine. *Geochimica et Cosmochimica Acta* 61 (12):2539–2550.

CHAPTER FIVE

Jeffrey J. Saunders

Processing Marks on Remains of Mammuthus columbi *from the Dent Site, Colorado, in Light of Those from Clovis, New Mexico*

FRESH-CARCASS BUTCHERY VERSUS SCAVENGING?

In 1978 I examined skulls, mandibles, and teeth of the Dent site mammoth sample in storage at the Denver Museum of Natural History (DMNH)—now the Denver Museum of Nature and Science—and on exhibit in museums in Cleveland, Ohio, and Pittsburgh, Pennsylvania. Skulls, mandibles, and isolated teeth in the DMNH were assembled into dentitions that, with the skeletons in Cleveland and Pittsburgh, represented thirteen individuals. Age at death for these individuals was assigned on the basis of cheek tooth progression through the jaw and occlusal wear, using criteria for *Loxodonta africana* (African elephant) provided by Laws (1966). Individual ages of Dent mammoths were thus reported in African Elephant [Equivalent] Years (AEY) (Saunders 1980).

From comparison of the Dent age profile with age profiles of other Clovis-associated mammoth samples, I concluded (Saunders 1980) that those from Dent and the Lehner (Arizona) site, and probably those of mammoth samples from the Miami (Texas) and Colby (Wyoming) sites as well, were consistent with natural matriarchal family groups as observed in modern elephantids. In conjunction with gender-determination studies of the Hot Springs (South Dakota) mammoth sample, Lister and Agenbroad (1994) examined two incomplete adult pelvises from Dent in the DMNH. On the bases of oblique aperture height and ilium shaft width, these pelvises are attributed to female individuals. In their view, this finding corroborated the conclusion previously drawn on the basis of age profiles that the Dent mammoths represent one (or more) matriarchal family group(s) (Saunders 1980).

It was suggested that "natural" age samples like Dent represented catastrophic mass kills of matriarchal groups by Clovis hunters (Saunders 1980). Results of renewed research at Dent concluded, from studies of dentinal banding in tusks and cheek teeth, two closely spaced late-fall and early-winter season-of-death events (Fisher and Fox, Chapter 4, this volume). This determination supported the view that the Dent individuals had been hunted but lessened the likelihood that a single event was represented.

Contrast between "natural" age profiles and "non-natural" (i.e., nonfamily) mammoth age profiles like Murray Springs (Arizona) and Blackwater Draw (New Mexico; the El Llano Dig, Warnica 1966) suggested the latter two samples represented carcasses found and scavenged by Clovis foragers (Saunders 1980). The scavenging hypothesis was supported in a study of the remains of Mammoth 1 and Mammoth 2 recovered in 1936 at the Clovis type-site (Cotter 1937) in Blackwater Draw (Saunders and Daeschler 1994).

The analysis of Mammoth 1 and Mammoth 2 (Saunders and Daeschler 1994) from the Clovis type-site forms the basis for a comparative bone modification data set against which the Dent sample is viewed. Other than Mammoth 1 and Mammoth 2 from Clovis, butchery discussions have centered primarily on samples from Lange-Ferguson, South Dakota (Hannus 1989), Duewall-Newberry, Texas (Steele and Carlson 1989), some sites on the southern High Plains of New Mexico and Texas (Johnson 1989), and the northern High Plains at Colby, Wyoming (Frison and Todd 1986). The Colby discussions were limited, however, in part because of the poor preservation of the Colby bone (Frison and Todd 1986:33–43). Mammoth remains from Clovis and Dent, on the other hand, are well preserved. In addition, the Clovis material is extensively modified, and these modifications have been reported and several have been illustrated. For these reasons Clovis is currently the most suitable comparative sample available. The objectives of this chapter are to (1) document the patterns of modifications to mammoth postcranial elements from Dent, (2) compare these patterns with modification patterns previously recognized on corresponding material at the Clovis type-site, and (3) suggest possible explanations for differences, if differences are noted.

DESCRIPTION OF THE STUDY AREA

The discovery of the Dent site and descriptions of 1932–1933 and subsequent investigations are described by Figgins (1933), Bilgery (1935), Wormington (1957), Sellards (1952), Spikard (1972), Brunswig and Fisher (1993), and in great detail by Brunswig in Chapter 3 of this volume.

Aspects of the discovery and study area that are of particular importance to this chapter's research results are noted here. The Dent mammoth bone stratum was found to be ca. 4.5 feet (1.5 m) in vertical thickness, with its top extending ca. 4 feet (ca. 1.25 m) beneath the 1930s ground surface (Brunswig, Chapter 3, this volume). Earlier accounts (e.g., Figgins 1933) noted the entombing matrix at Dent as consisting of prominently fine, yellow colluvial sand originating from the degradation of Cretaceous bedrock. In addition to this sand, quartz and granitic pebbles and small boulders comprised a portion of the matrix in the lower third of the bone deposit. It was also noted that numerous large boulders were found with the mammoth remains, although boulders of comparable size are rare elsewhere in the vicinity. Comprehensive studies of the geological and environmental contexts of Dent are described in Brunswig (Chapter 3, this volume) and Haynes et al. (1995, 1998).

Sellards (1952:31) suggested that Dent presents unusual conditions in that the partial skeletons were found within a small area. A photograph of the Dent expedition in 1933 (Haynes 1966) shows exposed remains, in part articulated and in part jumbled, notably a tibia-fibula in a plaster half-jacket, an ulna-? radius, a lower jaw, and a pelvis. Other specimens are set aside for removal. The excavation is conducted quarry-style. Weakly cemented friable matrix in this area of the excavation can be discerned in Haynes's photograph, as it can in two photographs presented by Figgins (1933:plate II). The photograph reproduced by Haynes reveals that three of four excavators are using trowels, of which one trowel is unpointed, and the other excavator holds a two-inch paintbrush and an awl. A shovel handle is in view, and a piece of cardboard or plywood covered with uniformly fine sediment suggests a "dustpan" containing "sweepings" of back dirt. Tool choice (hand tools) and use (brushing) during excavation, as well as excavation methods (nearly complete exposure of remains prior to removal in plaster jackets), have implications for modifications that are subsequently interpreted, as in this study. The tools chosen in 1932–1933 are used currently and, used with care, do not alter bone surfaces during bone recovery. Even so, it appears that not all bones recovered in 1932 were free of excavation damage. Figgins (1933:plate II), for example, illustrates a distal left femur in situ at Dent that appears to have fresh damage to the edges of the patellar surface. Similar fresh damage is seen on the patellar surface of EPV.3992, a left femur ("EPV" is a DMNH acronym for Earth Sciences, Paleontology, Vertebrate and is the prefix in the number denoting cataloged specimens). Considering these cautionary damages, special care is taken to restrict discussion to modified conditions that clearly predate recovery activities.

THE DENT MAMMOTHS

The Dent mammoths are assigned to *Mammuthus columbi* (Falconer 1857) on the basis of standard variates of the M_3, including ridge plate number (20), width (89 mm), enamel thickness (2.1 mm), and lamellar frequency (6.3) (Saunders 1999; typical standard variate values for this species are reported in Saunders 1970 and Madden 1981). An age determination of $10,810 \pm 40$ radiocarbon years before present (RCYBP) for Dent mammoth remains was obtained from dated amino acid fractions in bone collagen (Stafford et al. 1991). This date represents one of the youngest available for *Mammuthus* in North America (terminal date $10,550 \pm 350$ RCYBP, Rawhide Butte, Wyoming; fide Meltzer and Mead 1983).

Evolving from *Mammuthus imperator* (Leidy 1858) by ca. 700,000 years ago (e.g., Webb et al. 1989), *Mammuthus columbi* was the most successful endemic North American mammoth. The species occurred in the western, southern, and northern United States, Mexico, and western Canada. During the late-glacial interval 15,000 to 10,000 RCYBP, *M. columbi* was distributed from Florida westward to Texas, New Mexico, and Arizona and northward to Colorado, Utah, Wyoming, and Nevada (Graham and Lundelius, principal authors 1994:418).

Large individuals of *Mammuthus columbi* were early noted from excavations in Blackwater Draw, New Mexico (Stock and Bode 1936), dating to ca.11,000 RCYBP (C. V. Haynes 1991, 1995). Mammoth 1 and Mammoth 2 excavated at the Clovis type-site in Blackwater Draw in 1936 (Cotter 1937) measured 3.96 m (13 feet) and 3.75 m (12.4 feet) in height while in the flesh, respectively (Saunders and Daeschler 1994).

Following study of Dent skulls, mandibles, and teeth in the DMNH in 1978 (Saunders 1980), I was informed of another mandible in the collections, DMNH 1901, that on the basis of preservation and other likenesses is viewed as part of the Dent sample. This jaw's attributes were recorded from photographs. DMNH 1901 brings to fourteen the number of mammoth individuals I recognized in the Dent collection up to June 1995 (Table 5.1). DMNH 1901 is ninth in age series and was 16 AEY at death (Table 5.1). For the Dent sample available in June 1995, therefore, the oldest individual has an inferred age at death of 43 ± 2 AEY (Saunders 1980, 1999). The sample's mean age is 15 AEY. well above the modal age class (2–4 AEY). Recruitment, by strict definition (calves, i.e., elephants between 0 and 18 months of age that can stand between their mother's front legs; Laws 1966:36), was 0 percent, but sexually immature individuals (those 14 years of age and younger) are numerous (8 of 14 individuals = 57 percent). In these demographic attributes, the Dent mammoth sample agrees with *Loxodonta africana* samples from Murchison Falls, Uganda, that are matriarchal family units (Laws and Parker 1968).

The Dent mammoths, with the exception of the oldest individual, were relatively small. Small size is only partially explained by individual age differences or by relative youth. In stature but not in dentitions (Saunders 1999), they agree with penecontemporary samples of *M. columbi* from the Lehner site (Lance 1959; Saunders 1977, 1995, 1999).

Table 5.1. Age Criteria, Age Groups, and Age at Death of 14 Individuals of *Mammuthus columbi* from the Dent Site, Colorado (Saunders 1980, 1999) (AEY = African Elephant [Equivalent] Years).

Sample #	Age Order	Age Criteria	Age Class[e]	Age (AEY)
EPV.1897[1]	1	dP3 in wear, dP4 beginning wear	IV	2
EPV.1893	2	dP4 with 50 percent ridge plates worn	V	3
EPV.1898	3	left dP3, left & right dP4; comparison with 1893, for which associate upper teeth are available, shows 1898 to be slightly older	V[e]	3[e]
EPV.1637	4	dP4s in wear, M1s in germ cavity	VII	6
EPV.1895	5	dP4s with 100 percent ridge plates worn, M1s 27 percent worn	VIII/IX	9
EPV.1899	6	left and right M1 in early middle wear	IX	10
CLMNH[2]	7	dP4s with 100 percent ridge plates worn, M1s 50 percent worn	IX	10
EPV.1896	8	dP4s eliminated, M1s 86 percent worn, M2s unerupted	X/XI	14
EPV.1901	9	dP4 aveoli closed, M1s 100 percent worn, M2 germ cavity persists	XI/XII	16
EPV.1636	10	M1s with 100 percent ridge plates worn, M2s 40 percent worn	XIV	22
CaMNH[3]	11	M1s nubbin-like, M2s with 50 percent ridge plates worn	XIV/XV	23
EPV.1894	12	M1s nubbin-like, M2s with 67 percent ridge plates worn	XVI	26
DMNH1450[4]	13	M1s nubbin-like, M2s with 72 percent ridge plates worn	XVII	28
EPV.1635	14	M3s with 75 percent ridge plates worn	XXIII	43 ± 2

e estimate; contra Laws 1966, based on wear of upper teeth
1. In 1978 paleontological specimens from Dent in the Denver Museum of Natural History bore the prefix DMNH followed by a four-digit number (e.g., Saunders 1980:table 2). After 1994 and 1995, with the collection's renovation, these specimens were re-recorded with the prefix EPV, followed by the same four-digit number as previously.
2. Cleveland Museum of Natural History.
3. Carnegie Museum of Natural History, Pittsburgh; specimen number CM 12066.
4. DMNH 1450 is as labeled when recorded in 1978; EPV assignment of specimen subsequent to 1978 is not known to me.

Latest Pleistocene Dent mammoths were smaller individuals than those comprising interstadial samples, for example, the Mammoth Site of Hot Springs (ca. 26,000 RCYBP; Agenbroad 1994). Comparison of Dent with Hot Springs, however, is constrained by taphonomic pathways at Hot Springs that preferentially accumulated the remains of reproductively mature male individuals (Lister and Agenbroad 1994). Furthermore, Hot Springs includes the remains of two species, *M. columbi* and *M. primigenius* (Agenbroad et al. 1994). Thus differences (Dent, Lehner, and others versus Hot Springs) are explained primarily by taxonomic, individual age, and sex considerations and only partially by local evolution. The point of interest is that comparison of Dent with Hot Springs supports the view that late Pleistocene mammoths were organized like modern elephantids

(Moss 1988) into (1) matriarchal family units (Dent) representing a kin group of sexually immature males and females of all ages, and (2) units composed exclusively of reproductively mature males (Hot Springs).

The Dent remains were taken to the Colorado Museum of Natural History (later the Denver Museum of Natural History), where parts of the collection were dispersed. Dispersal included skeletons sent to the Cleveland Museum of Natural History (ClMNH) in Ohio (a ten-year-old female; Saunders 1980; Table 5.1) and to the Carnegie Museum of Natural History (CaMNH) in Pittsburgh, Pennsylvania (a twenty-three-year-old female; Saunders 1980; Table 5.1). These skeletons, which are on display, cannot be studied as rigorously as the material in storage in Denver. Joint areas, epiphyseal plates, and taphonomical and zooarchaeological data are obscured, and in Pittsburgh it is doubtful that the skull and jaw are of the same individual.

Representation (the number of expected specimens divided by the number observed in the sample, with distinctive fragments counted as specimens) of cranial, mandibular, and postcranial elements comprising the Dent mammoth sample is given in Table 5.2. Representation is greatest for the mandibles, followed by crania and fibulae. Representation is good for atlases, axes, left scapulae, and right ulnae as well as femora and tibiae. The ectocuneiform is underrepresented in the DMNH material (and like other podial bones is only presumed to exist other than in replicated form in the Cleveland and Pittsburgh skeletons) and is relatively low for other foot bones and caudal vertebrae. Representation is thus selective (Marshall 1989), resulting from differential sorting, differential destruction, and perhaps differential recovery. The first two of these differential processes may in part be cultural.

The Dent bone is well preserved. The majority of bones in Denver exhibit a weathering stage like that described for early stage 2 by Behrensmeyer (1978). In general, outermost concentric thin layers of Dent bones show only shallow cracking associated in some instances with the exfoliation of long, thin flakes of cortical bone (Behrensmeyer 1978:151).

METHODS OF THE STUDY

Cultural versus Noncultural Bone Modifications

The method for distinguishing cultural from noncultural modifications is provided primarily by Binford's (1981) ethnoarchaeological study and analyses of caribou butchery by Nunamiut hunters. These results showed butchery marks to be systematic vis-à-vis form and placement on specific bones, resulting, through intention and by design, in functional-locational patterns. Functional patterns included marks resulting from (1) dismemberment, (2) filleting, and (3) skinning. Dismemberment locations favored joint areas, filleting favored anterior and posterior portions of long bone shafts where muscles originate and insert, and skinning favored the distal parts of distal limb bones.

Table 5.2. Preservation of *Mammuthus columbi* from the Dent Site, Colorado (DMNH, ClMNH, CaMNH).

Element	Expected (right/left)	Observed (right/left)	Ob/Ex (%)
Mandibles[1]	14	13	92.8
Crania[2]	14	8	57.1
Atlases	14	6	42.9
Axes	14	6	42.9
Cervical vertebrae 3–7	70	14	20
Thoracic vertebrae (=19)	266	45 (max 48)	16.9 (18)
Lumbar vertebrae (=4)	56	19 (max 22)	33.9 (39.3)
Sacra (5 fused bodies)	14	4	28.6
Caudal vertebrae (=21)[3]	294	48	16.3
Scapulae[4]	14/14	6/5	42.9/35.7
Humeri	14/14	4/2, 4?	35.7
Ulnae	14/14	5/7	35.7/50
Radii	14/14	5/5, 1?	39.3
Scaphoids	14/14	3/3	21.4/21.4
Lunars	14/14	4/4	28.6/28.6
Cuneiforms	14/14	4/4	28.6/28.6
Pisiforms	14/14	2/3	14.3/21.4
Trapezoids	14/14	2/3	14.3/21.4
Magnums	14/14	3/3	21.4/21.4
Unciforms	14/14	3/2	21.4/14.3
Metacarpal I[5]	14/14	2/2	14.3/14.3
Metacarpal II	14/14	2/2	14.3/14.3
Metacarpal III	14/14	3/3	21.4/21.4
Metacarpal IV	14/14	2/2	14.3/14.3
Metacarpal V	14/14	3/2	21.4/14.3
Innominates[6]	14/14	4/4, ?5	46.4
Femora	14/14	6/6, ?2	50
Tibiae	14/14	9/2, ?3	50
Fibulae	14/14	6/3, ?7	57.1
Astragali	14/14	4/3	28.6/21.4
Calcanea	14/14	2/3	14.3/21.4
Naviculars	14/14	3/3	21.4/21.4
Entocuneiforms	14/14	2/3	14.3/21.4
Mesocuneiforms	14/14	2/2, ?1	17.9
Ectocuneiform	14/14	2/2	14.3
Cuboids	14/14	3/3	21.4/21.4
Metatarsal I[7]	14/14	3/2	21.4/14.3
Metatarsal II	14/14	2/2	14.3/14.3
Metatarsal III	14/14	2/2	14.3/14.3
Metatarsal IV	14/14	2/3	14.3/21.4
Metatarsal V	14/14	4/2	28.6/14.3

1. Maximum, associated but isolated lower teeth are considered to represent mandibles.
2. Maximum, associated but isolated upper teeth are considered to represent crania.
3. The number of caudal vertebrae in *M. columbi* has not been reported (fide Osborn 1942); 21 = the number in *M. primigenius* (fide Zalensky 1903).
4. Fore and hind limb representation is exclusive of phalanges.
5. Metacarpals do not include 6 specimens identified only as metapodial.
6. Does not include 4 innominate fragments, 3 of which are illia epiphyses.
7. Metatarsals do not include 6 specimens identified only as metapodial.

Each functional pattern as it affected the skull, mandible, and postcranial elements of caribou was described and illustrated by Binford (1981:figures 4.06, 4.11, 4.16, 4.20–22, 4.25–32, 4.36–39, table 4.04). His descriptions and illustrations form the methodological bases for causal interpretations (cultural versus noncultural) of the bulk of the modifications in the present instance and for the implied functional meaning of modifications attributed as cultural. Some biases or cautions are introduced, however, by the taxonomic distinction: caribou-mammoth, for example, the presumed necessity of Clovis processors of mammoth to divide larger muscle masses, resulting in cut marks with mid-shaft placements on long bones. These departures from Binford's results are noted later.

Focusing Studies

Broader interpretations and implications of cultural modifications on proboscidean bones are assisted by modern focusing studies, which in essence are guides to this fossil undertaking. Focusing studies of elephant butchery that are relevant for mammoth processing include (1) experimental (Frison 1989; Frison and Todd 1986), (2) ethnoarchaeological (Binford 1981; Crader 1983; Fisher 1992), and (3) actualistic (G. Haynes 1991) analyses, as well as (4) primarily theoretical constraints imposed by carcass conditions (Binford 1984).

Specifically, Frison (1989:778) noted from elephant processing experiments conducted in Zimbabwe that "once the thick joint capsule is cut through . . . the joints literally fall apart. This can be done [with a quartzite reduction flake] leaving no cut marks on the bone." Frison and Todd (1986:42) reached the same conclusion on the basis of experimental butchering of the forelimb of an Asiatic elephant. Crader (1983:135) concluded from observations of elephant processing by the Valley Bisa in Zambia that "if the ethnographic data are meaningful for the . . . Pleistocene, it seems likely that . . . hominids could have butchered large animal carcasses with stone tools without leaving a mark."

In discussion of the Klasies River Mouth faunal assemblage, Binford (1984:72) stated that "(1) patterned properties of placement and orientation to cut marks . . . aid in judging the state of the carcass at the time of dismemberment and (2) dismemberment of parts during a scavenging episode can be expected to cope most often with a carcass that is stiff, with relatively inflexible joints."

RESULTS

Skulls and mandibles of Dent mammoths examined in Denver did not show modifications attributed to butchery. Among 229 postcranial elements examined, 19 (= 8.3 percent) bore processing modifications (as noted fide Binford 1981). Culturally modified specimens included 4 tibiae (EPV.2190–2193), 3 ribs and 3 rib fragments (EPV.3885, 3888, 3893–3895, 3903), 2 scapulae (EPV.3928, 3931), 1 ulna (EPV.3937), and 3 femora (EPV.3992, 3995, 3996). In addition, 1 innominate (EPV.3983) bore good and 1 innominate (EPV.3984) bore probable cut marks, as

5.1. Photo of lateral view of EPV.3928, right scapula. Scale bars for all figures are in centimeters.

did 1 fibula (EPV.4061). The most clearly revealed evidence of processing occurred on the scapula, ulna, femur, and tibia.

Scapula

Of scapulae examined (Table 5.2, with the caveat that individual bones in Cleveland and Pittsburgh could not be closely examined), two (EPV.3928, right scapula; EPV.3931, left scapula) are culturally modified, extensively so. They show a pattern of removal of the acromion, mid-spinous process, and the proximal scapular spine. They also show indication of the dismemberment of the pre-spinous fossa from the scapular blade. While occurring on both EPV.3928, right scapula, and EPV.3931, left scapula, the pattern of spinous dismemberment is most clearly shown by damage to EPV.3928 (Figure 5.1).

Heavy hackle marks reflecting rough cutting (Guralnik and Friend 1964:650) and attributed to chopping commence beneath the caudal-most acromion (Figure 5.2) in the mid-scapular region and continue 386 mm proximally along the spine to a position where the scapula is broken and its proximal and post-spinous portions are missing.

This damage reveals a mammoth processing strategy at Dent, where the spine was dismembered from the scapular blade by chopping. This dismemberment may have been conducted jointly, with the assistance of another processor utilizing a lever to manipulate interfering tissue (gouge marks shown in Figure 5.3).

Although Binford (1981) does not show dismemberment marks in these locations on caribou scapulae butchered by Nunamiut hunters, he shows dismemberment (scapulohumeral joint) marks distally on the lateral glenoid border (Binford 1981:figure 4.29). Dismembering marks on the distal scapula are transverse in Binford's study, but in EPV.3928 the lateral glenoid has been extensively damaged

5.2. EPV.3928, right scapula. Photo showing distal insertion of spine on the scapular neck viewed from the caudal side, showing transverse hackle marks on the distal and near-distal spine.

by primarily normal or vertical, heavy chop marks (Figure 5.4).

As displayed on the lateral glenoid, these are similar to chop marks on the scapular spine. No dismemberment or filleting marks occur on the medial surface of EPV.3928 or on medial surfaces of the other Dent scapula. The large size of mammoth shoulders may have constrained their management by Clovis processors, a consideration already implied by division of the scapula into parts. On the basis of ethnoarchaeological study by Fisher (1992) of elephant butchery by Efe people, such constraints imposed by carcass size do occur.

The acromion, mid-spinous process, and proximal spine are also dismembered from EPV.3931, left scapula. Fewer hack marks, however, attest to this activity on EPV.3931 (Figures 5.5, 5.6). EPV.3931 is of further interest for showing, through hackle marks cranial to the previous location of the mid-spinous process, that Clovis processors also dismembered the pre-spinous fossa from the scapular blade.

The pre-spinous fossa of EPV.3931 is missing from a point 160 mm prox-

5.3. EPV.3928, right scapula. Photo showing distal insertion of the spine on the scapular neck viewed from the cranial side, showing gouges (a) that may be associated with tissue manipulation by bone foreshaft/pry bars (see Saunders and Daeschler 1994:figure 6).

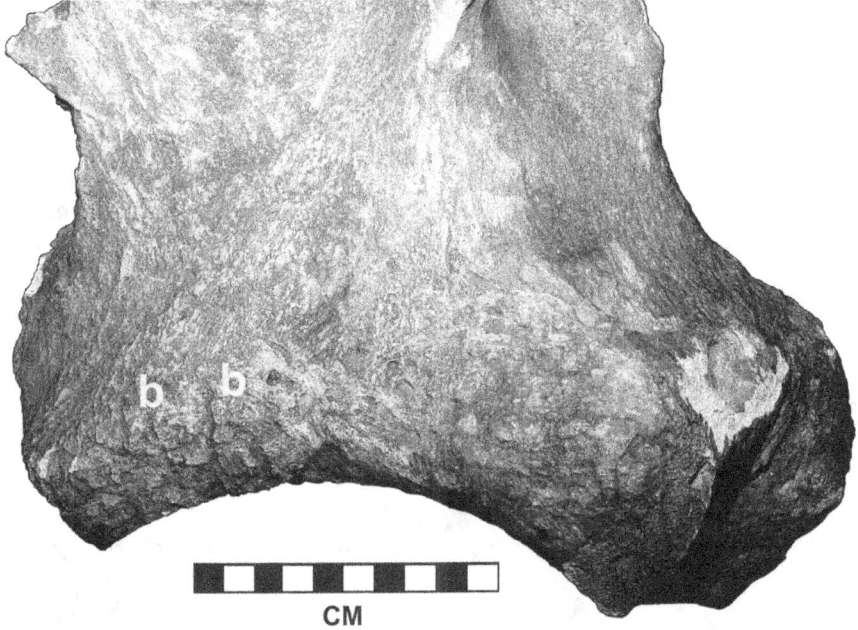

5.4. EPV.3928, right scapula. Photo indicates hackle marks (b) on the distal scapula showing extensive damage to the lateral glenoid during dismemberment. As displayed here, particularly on the caudal portion of the glenoid, these marks are similar to hackle marks along the scapular spine.

imal of the cranial lip of the glenoid fossa (Figure 5.5). The hackle-marked detachment fracture representing the missing portion continues 416 mm proximally along the cranial edge of the spine, to a point where this fracture is lost through modern breakage (Figures 5.5, 5.7).

Contra EPV.3928, no scapulohumeral dismemberment marks, as shown by Binford (1981), occur on the lateral glenoid border of EPV.3931. Gouged depressions, however, including one like those imparted by foreshafts used as levers at the Clovis type-site (Saunders and Daeschler 1994), occur in the glenoid cavity. These depressions may be associated with scapulohumeral dismemberment or may have resulted from post-processing, pre-depositional events (trampling by mammoths or other large animals; e.g., Behrensmeyer, Gordon, and Yanagi 1986; Conybeare and Haynes 1984; Fiorillo 1989; Oliver 1989).

Ulna

EPV.3937, left ulna diaphysis, exhibits a crescentic gouge modification observed elsewhere on Dent material (Figure 5.8).

In contrast to chatter marks, which are small, densely packed, short curved scars, crescentic gouges are larger and have the form of a groove or channel with a somewhat rounded bottom. In geological analogy (e.g., Gary, McAfee,

5.5. *Lateral view of EPV.3931, left scapula. Photo showing spine dismemberment as well as dismemberment of the pre-spinous fossa from the remainder of the scapular blade (extent of the fracture through which the pre-spinous fossa was dismembered from the remainder of the scapular blade is delineated by c-c' on left side of figure).*

and Wolf 1972:164), crescentic gouges are formed by plucking (e.g., by a glacier) on a host (e.g., bedrock) surface. The crescentic gouge on EPV.3937 is culturally attributed on two bases (Figure 5.8): (1) weathering cracks bisect the gouge containing the crescentic ridges as well as the crescentic ridges themselves, a superposition indicating the crescentic gouge was applied while the bone was in a pre-weathered, fresh condition; and (2) the crescentic gouge occurs proximal-medially beneath the olecranon process and posterior to the humeral articular facet, that is, it is appropriately placed to be associated with dismemberment of the elbow joint (Binford 1981:figure 4.31, figure 4.32(a).

The crescentic gouge on EPV.3937 is prominent. Measurements (here and below, in mm; measurements presented for explications and comparisons) of the gouge are length = 34.54, greatest width (proximal) = 21.31, least width (distal) = 6.73, depth = ca. 0.33–0.86. As seen from Figure 5.8, the "horns" of the crescentic ridges are directed proximally, usually not the case if they were chatter marks (fide Gary, McAfee, and Wolf 1972:120) indicating the force producing

5.6. *EPV.3931, left scapula. View of distal insertion of the spine on the scapular neck seen vertically and showing the shear-fracture scar where the distal spine had presumably been snap-broken and freed in dismemberment.*

5.7. *EPV.3931, left scapula. Close-up view of the fracture through which pre-spinous fossa was dismembered from the remainder of the scapular blade (scale rotated to bring the centimeter rule adjacent to fracture trace; view corresponds approximately to c-c' in Figure 5.5.*

the marks would have taken a proximal-to-distal direction. Examination of the gouge by 10x hand lens shows this movement direction to be reasonably the case: the gouging implement (at the Clovis type-site these implements were scrapers [see Saunders and Daeschler 1994:21, citing Wilmsen fide Speth 1983]) "purchases" or "fast holds" (Guralnik and Friend 1964:1181) proximally on the shaft through a steep-sided and conspicuous mark of insertion; the gouge then "feathers out" distally. Longitudinal striae occur on the crescentic ridges, suggesting the gouge was produced by a flaked stone tool (Newcomer 1974:149; Olson 1984:135) applied with great force.

Femur

Cultural modifications occur on three femora (EPV.3992, left femur; EPV.3995, right femur diaphysis; EPV.3996, left femur diaphysis and distal epiphysis). Each bears cut mark evidence of filleting of meat from the distal inner thigh, and one exhibits proximal and distal pry marks.

EPV.3992, a left femur, bears a trough-shaped gouge in the medial head that indicates dismemberment of the hip joint (Figure 5.9; compare with Binford 1981:figure 4.25(a), Fp-2). This gouge measures (here and later, presented as length x width x depth or only as length x width) 56.36 x 20.44 x 6. Dismemberment may be indicated by similar depressions in the distal shaft (see Figure 5.8 and discussion later), or these distal depressions may be a result of filleting.

A series of cut marks on the distal anteromedial diaphysis (Figure 5.10) commences 42 mm above the epiphyseal plate and continues as a scattering of marks ca. 195 mm proximally along the femoral shaft. These marks on EPV.3992 suggest the filleting of deeper muscles from the medial thigh at a position above the knee. Individual cut marks (n = 17), as with other modifications attributed on the criteria of Binford (1981), average 9.24 mm in length (range = 6.51–14.27). They are approximately transverse to the long axis of the diaphysis and carry to

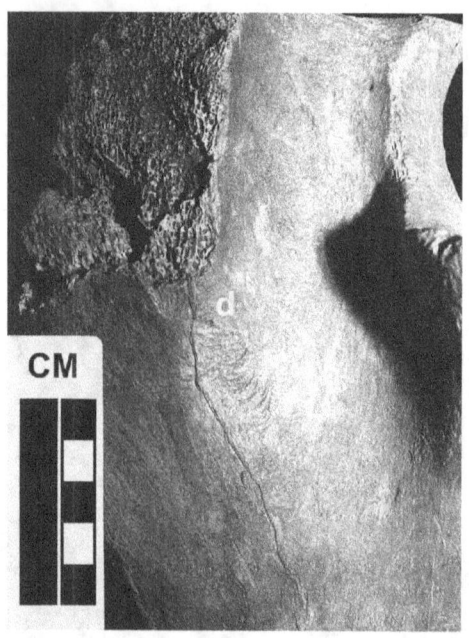

5.8. *Proximal medial view of EPV.3937, left ulna, showing a crescentic gouge attributed to dismemberment. The gouge is prominent, groove or channel shaped, and has a somewhat rounded bottom, features distinguishing crescentic gouges from chatter marks. Ridges within the groove are bisected by a superimposed weathering crack. The crescent horns point proximally (toward the top of the figure), indicating (on the basis of geological analogies and contra the case of these chatter marks) the cutting motion proceeded in a proximal to distal direction. A pit (d) marks the point of purchase for the cutting motion, which feathered distally. Similarities with patterns on the Cotter material from the Clovis type-site suggest the tool used in this activity was a heavy scraper.*

5.9. *EPV.3992, left femur. Photo shows a prominent gouge in the medial head (e) associated with dismemberment of the hip joint. In analogy with the Clovis type-site, the tool employed in this activity was possibly a bone or ivory foreshaft used as a pry bar.*

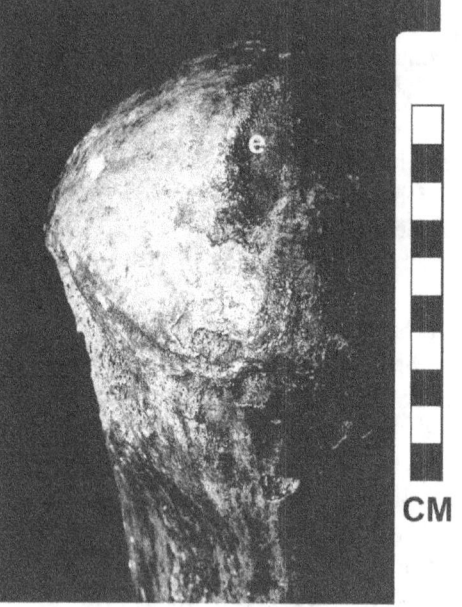

its anterior-medial edge. Although occurring anteromedially on the distal femur, the marks are like filleting cut marks illustrated by Binford (1981:figure 4.38, Fd-4 and Fd-5) for the distal posterior and distal anterolateral femur. Filleting cut marks do not appear distal posteriorly on EPV.3992, nor do they occur on its proximal shaft.

Two depressed pits occurring distal anteriorly on EPV.3992 (Figure 5.11) are compressed through the cortex and expose underlying spongiosa. The pits are each ca. 10.61 mm wide and have depths of 6 and 3 mm, respectively. Delineated in one case by clearly defined walls and a flat floor and in

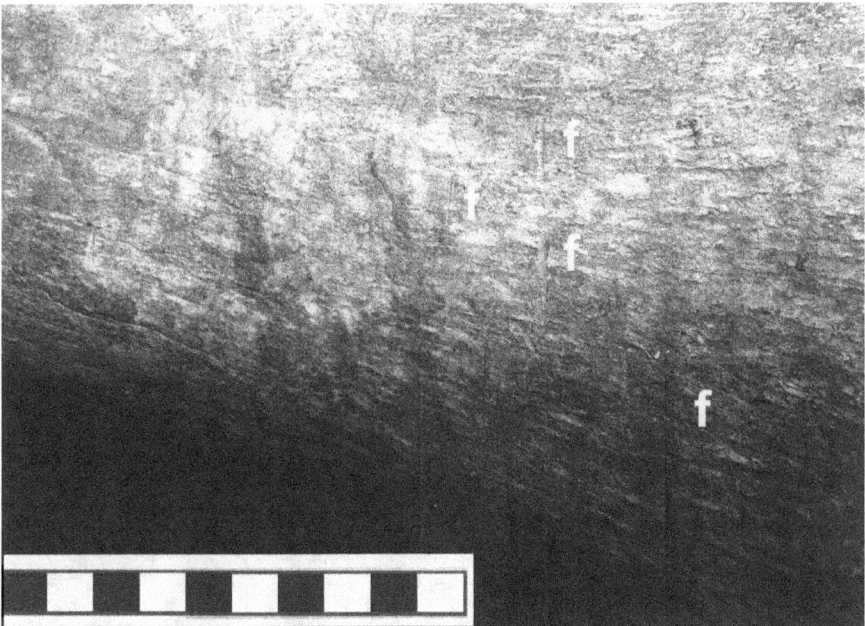

5.10. EPV.3992, left femur. Close-up of weathered, filleting cut marks (e.g., f) on distal medial surface are associated with defleshing the inner thigh above the knee joint.

the other case crater-like, the pits may have been produced by the same tool that gouged the femoral head (Figure 5.9) and of the same tool class used to gouge the distal scapula (Figure 5.4).

At the Clovis type-site, tools responsible for gouges and pits like these were both bi-beveled and pointed bone foreshafts used as pry bars or wedges by Clovis processors in cooperative joint dismemberments (Saunders and Daeschler 1994: e.g., figure 6.6). The distal anterior pits on EPV.3992 occur above the patellar surface and may be associated with filleting, for example, traces of levers used to manipulate deeper muscles or connective tissues. Alternatively, these pits are associated with dismemberment of the knee joint, for example, traces of levers used to manipulate ligaments (compare, however, Binford 1981:figure 4.25 = dismemberment, with Binford 1981:figure 4.38 = filleting, and note better agreement of damage to EPV.3992 with filleting, e.g., Fd-5).

Distal anteromedial filleting cut marks noted on EPV.3992 are repeated on EPV.3996, a left femur diaphysis and distal epiphysis. On EPV.3996, however, filleting cut marks are fewer and seem to be heavier, although they too are approximately transversely oriented. The heavier application of these marks vis-à-vis their expression on EPV.3992 can be explained by a greater force, suggesting a different processor or condition of flesh, or by employment of a dulled implement or different tool, or by a combination of these possibilities.

5.11. EPV.3992, left femur. Anterior distal view of femur showing two depressions that, on the basis of analogy with the Clovis type-site results, are probable damages attributed to foreshaft(s) used as pry bars. One is flat-bottomed (g), as though produced by a bevel-ended foreshaft, and the other (h) is crater-like, as though produced by a pointed foreshaft, perhaps indicating a cooperative activity. The placement of g and h can be functionally associated with either dismemberment of the knee joint or filleting of the thigh, although on the basis of modern ethnographic studies filleting seems most likely by their placement. Damage on the lateral patellar surface is ambiguous but in part clearly modern breakage; my notes do not discuss this damage in the context of butchery. Scale bars are in centimeters.

A third instance of filleting of the distal medial thigh is inferred from cut marks on the distal anteromedial surface of EPV.3995, right femur diaphysis (Figure 5.12). These filleting cut marks on EPV.3995 are "cleaner" and more numerous than on EPV.3996, left femur diaphysis and distal epiphysis, and, although somewhat heavier, they compare more closely in number and staccato-like application with cut marks on EPV.3992, a left femur. Filleting cut marks on EPV.3995 commence proximally to the upper border of the patellar surface, ca. 34 mm above the epiphyseal plate, and continue proximally 165 mm along the anteromedial and anterior diaphysis. Lengths of filleting cut marks on EPV.3995 (n = 9) average 16.93 mm, r: 9.86–23.67; widths of these marks (n = 9) average 2.00 mm, r: 1.6–2.41.

Tibia

Butchery modifications occur on four tibiae (EPV.2190, right diaphysis; EPV.2191, right diaphysis; EPV.2192, right diaphysis fragments; EPV.2193, right tibia). Butchery modifications are of special interest on three of these.

On EPV.2193, right tibia, three heavy, approximately transverse filleting cut marks commence 45 mm above the distal posterior epiphyseal plate and continue proximally for 50 mm along the diaphysis. Measurements of these marks are 11.5 × 2.41 × 0.45; 15.39 × 3.70 × 0.78; and 11.43 × 2.08 × 0.27. Lighter marks on the lateral margin of the bone are in the same distal posterior location and presumably are also filleting cut marks.

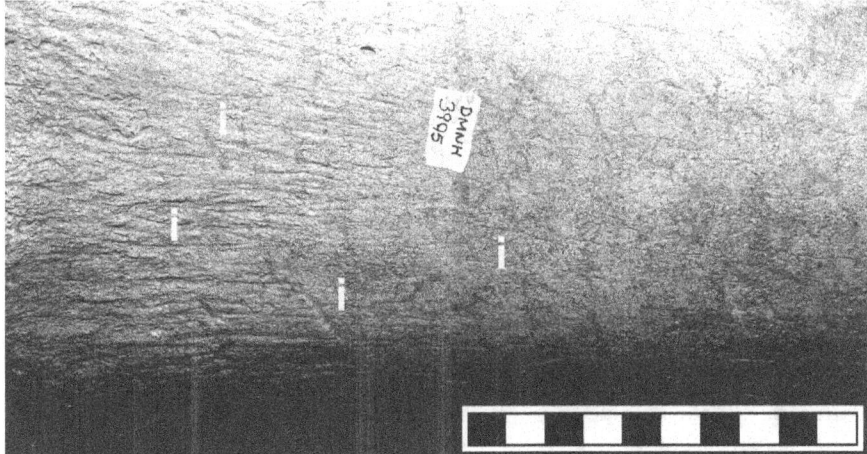

5.12. Distal anteromedial view of EPV.3995, right femur diaphysis, showing weathered, filleting cut marks (e.g., i). As with other Dent femora these marks are associated with defleshing the inner thigh above the knee joint. Scale bar is in centimeters.

EPV.2190, right diaphysis, shows generally lighter modification from processing, including crescentic marks similar to those previously described on EPV.3937, left ulna diaphysis. A heavy, approximately transverse mark occurs posteromedially on the shaft, 64 mm above the epiphyseal plate. Measurements of this mark are 9.44 x 2.46 x 0.58. On the basis of similarity to cut marks described on EPV.2193, right tibia, this too is a filleting cut mark.

EPV.2191, right diaphysis, bears crescentic marks similar to those noted earlier for EPV.2190, right tibia diaphysis, and EPV.3937, left ulna. On EPV.3937 the crescentic mark was a gouge associated with dismemberment, as may also be implied by its proximal lateral location on EPV.2191; alternatively, on EPV.2191 this mark may be associated with filleting. Less equivocal filleting cut marks occur distal posteriorly on EPV.2191, and a series of arcuate cut marks occurs posteriorly on the mid-shaft. The arcuate cut marks are similar to marks on a rib shaft piece recovered in Cotter's excavations at the Clovis type-site (Saunders and Daeschler 1994:figure 9.1), where they were attributed to the scoring of tough meat by Clovis scavengers. It is noteworthy that the frequency of culturally attributed modification decreases from this mid-shaft location proximally along the shaft; that is, more marks attributed to processing occur on distal vis-à-vis proximal tibial surfaces.

DISCUSSION AND COMPARISON OF DENT AND CLOVIS MAMMOTHS
Scapula

The left scapula of Mammoth 1 (regarding Mammoth 1 and Mammoth 2, see introductory material to this chapter), like the Dent scapulae, is fragmentary. The scapular blade is broken transversely 50 cm proximal to the cranial edge of the glenoid fossa, and the spine is shear-fractured (Gary, McAfee, and Wolf 1972:651) where the acromion and mid-spinous processes previously conjoined. Unlike EPV.3928, right scapula, where the acromion and mid-spinous processes were removed by chopping, the acromion and mid-spinous processes on the scapula of Mammoth 1 were removed through a shear-fracture, suggesting snap-breakage by hand or heavy impact, and then manually wrenched free. The acromion and mid-spinous processes in elephantids are large and, if accessible, can be wrenched manually, and the shear-fracture at the distal spinous border of the scapula of Mammoth 1 probably resulted from forelimb processing, as at Dent. In contrast with EPV.3928, dismemberment of the spine on EPV.3931, left scapula, seems like that conducted on the scapula of Mammoth 1, that is, by snap-breakage, with removal of the spine through a shear-fracture (rather than through hackle marks) nearer its base vis-à-vis EPV.3928 (compare Figures 5.2 and 5.6 and those discussed in Saunders and Daeschler 1994:13). This correspondence corroborates the conclusion by Saunders and Daeschler (1994) that the scapula of Mammoth 1 had been processed and suggests further that this processing in New Mexico was a dismemberment strategy shared by Clovis processors at Dent (Table 5.3).

Crader's study (1983) of elephant butchery by the Valley Bisa in Zambia suggested dismemberment occurred so more processors could work on a carcass simultaneously, with the objective of expeditiously removing meat. In light of this rationale, the important result to note from Dent scapulae is not that they were dismembered from the humeri (although one had been) but that Clovis processors dismembered each scapula into parts or "packages." Dismemberment of EPV.3928 and EPV.3931 in the manner interpreted for Dent was presumably to facilitate greater ease of handling large packages (e.g., Fisher 1992), and it seems likely, therefore, that dismembered scapular portions at Dent were passed on with adhering flesh for filleting. It is also possible that such packages were transported from the site. Scapula fragments are poorly represented among Dent materials in Denver (EPV.3932, scapula fragments), which may reflect cultural selection (Marshall 1989).

Other modifications to the scapulae reinforce a New Mexico–Colorado continuity in mammoth processing (Table 5.3). The scapula of Mammoth 1 bears five cut marks on the lateral surface near the glenoid fossa (Saunders and Daeschler 1994:figure 3). These are heavily incised and, wherever occurring, are perpendicular to the glenoid's border. Although they have the longitudinal orientation of filleting cut marks (Binford 1981:figure 4.06, ca. cut marks S-3), their placement is at a dismembering location (Binford 1981:figure 4.29, ca. cut marks S-1). Dismemberment marks (scapulohumeral joint) on the lateral glenoid fossa of EPV.3928 agree in attitude with those on the lateral glenoid of Mammoth 1. On EPV.3928, however, the marks are not applied with a discernible design as on the left scapula of Mammoth 1; the sole motivation for their presence on EPV.3928 seems to have been to free the scapulohumeral joint (compare Figure 5.4 and Saunders and

Table 5.3. Location and Function of Processing Marks on Limb Bones of *Mammuthus columbi* from Dent, Colorado (EVP), and the Clovis Type-Site (M1, M2), New Mexico.

Specimen	Proximal					Middle					Distal				
	ant	post	lat	med	art	ant	post	lat	med	art	ant	post	lat	med	art
Scapula	—	—	—	—	—	—	—	—	—	—	—	—	—	—	—
EVP.3928	—	—	—	—	—	—	—	dd	—	—	—	—	dd	—	—
EVP.3931	—	—	—	—	—	dd	—	dd	—	—	—	—	—	—	?dd
M1	—	—	—	—	—	—	—	?dd	—	—	—	—	dd	—	—
Ulna	—	—	—	—	—	—	—	—	—	—	—	—	—	—	—
EPV.3937	—	—	d	—	—	—	—	—	—	—	—	—	—	—	—
M1	—	f	—	—	dd	—	—	—	—	—	—	—	—	—	—
M2	f	—	—	—	dd	f	—	—	—	—	—	—	—	—	d
Femora	—	—	—	—	—	—	—	—	—	—	—	—	—	—	—
EVP.3992	—	—	—	d	—	—	—	—	—	—	?ff	—	—	ff	—
	—	—	—	—	—	—	—	—	—	—	?dd	—	—	—	—
EVP.3995	—	—	—	—	—	—	—	—	—	—	—	—	—	ff	—
EVP.3996	—	—	—	—	—	—	—	—	—	—	—	—	—	ff	—
M2	—	—	—	f	—	—	—	—	—	—	—	—	—	?ff	dd
Tibiae	—	—	—	—	—	—	—	—	—	—	—	—	—	—	—
EVP.2190	—	—	—	—	—	—	ff	—	—	—	—	f	—	—	—
EVP.2191	—	—	?f	—	—	—	—	—	—	—	—	—	—	—	—
	—	—	?d	—	—	—	ff	—	—	—	—	ff	—	—	—
EVP.2193	—	—	—	—	—	—	—	—	—	—	—	ff	?ff	—	—
M2	—	—	—	—	—	—	—	—	—	—	—	ff	—	ff	d

d   trace of dismemberment (dd = multiple traces)
f   trace of filleting (ff = multiple traces)

Daeschler 1994:figure 3). The geometric ordering of dismembering cut marks on the distal scapula of Mammoth 1 (Saunders and Daeschler 1994:figure 3) and the nondispersal of dismembered parts (left scapula/left humerus, closely adjacent locations shown by Cotter 1937:text-plate 2; Saunders and Daeschler 1994:figure 1) were at a variance with expectation vis-à-vis Crader's study and thus comprised an ambiguous data set. The ordering of the five marks on the distal lateral scapula of Mammoth 1, which is not further clarified by the Dent results, was ascribed to ritualism by Saunders and Daeschler (1994). Saunders and Daeschler (1994) suggested, from evidence of foot dismemberment, that perhaps as few as two cooperating and communicating processors were ultimately involved with the remains of Mammoth 1 and Mammoth 2, a numerical circumstance that in their view explained the relative lack of dispersal of dismembered parts.

Ulna

Although dismemberment (elbow joint) traces occur on EPV.3937, left ulna as a crescentic gouge posterior to the medial humeral articular facet, other dismemberment marks (e.g., RCp-5, Binford 1981:figure 4.32) are absent on the proximal and other surfaces (Table 5.3) [Editors' note: RCp refers to locations of markings on bone drawings]. The lack of additional dismemberment marks on EPV.3937 is consistent with the observations of Crader (1983:135), Frison (1989:778), and Frison and Todd (1986:42) that once the joint area of freshly killed, modern elephant carcasses has been invaded in butchery, the limbs readily dissociate. This implies on the basis of EPV.3937 that the elbow joint of this Dent individual was in relatively fresh condition when dismembered.

Compared to EPV.3937, the ulnae of Mammoth 1 and Mammoth 2 are heavily damaged (Table 5.3). A deeply incised transverse chop mark (29.6 x 7.1 x 3.6) occurs on the proximal posteromedial shaft of the right ulna of Mammoth 1. This mark, 30 cm below the summit of the olecranon, has a filleting placement (Binford 1981:figure 4.39, marks above RCp-7 on upper-right drawing) presumably related to the detachment of ligaments or deeper muscles occurring close to the bone, such as shown for *Elephas* by Nielsen (1965:figure 6). A cut mark (50.6 x 2.1) 6 mm beneath the proximal medial articular border of the right ulna of Mammoth 2 had removed a fragment of the articular rim. Another piece of articular rim was removed from the medial anconeal process. Marks on joint areas and the removal of articular fragments from proximal ulnae indicate dismemberment of the elbow joint (Binford 1981:figure 4.32a–c, ca. marks at RCp-5, Rcp-4).

The right ulna of Mammoth 2 shows processing damage on both proximal and distal articular surfaces (Table 5.3). A heavy dismembering cut mark (46.6 x 2 x 0.8) occurs on the anteromedial surface of the semilunar notch, ca. 9 mm posterior of the anterior border. Broken edges on the anterior coronoid process of this ulna are conarticular (fulcrum) damages (Fisher 1984a, 1984b) to dismembering pry marks on the distal medial humerus of Mammoth 2. Another heavy but distal cut mark (32.13 x 3.13 x 2.45) on the spine between the radial and carpal articular facets is associated with dismemberment of the distal limb and forefoot (e.g., Binford 1981:figure 4.32). Although these damages to proximal and distal articular surfaces of the Clovis ulnae, like the crescentic gouge on the proximal ulna from Dent, are clearly attributed to dismemberment, by lying heavily on the bone comprising articular surfaces the Clovis damages indicate, contra Dent, that greater work was required to dismember the Clovis joints.

A filleting cut mark was also noted on the right ulna of Mammoth 2. A heavily incised cut mark (20.1 x 2 x 1.7) 64 mm below the anterior coronoid process (Saunders and Daeschler 1994:figure 7) is similar to a chop mark on the proximal medial ulna of Mammoth 1, noted previously. This mark on both specimens was attributed to filleting deeper muscles or ligaments. Another chop mark (17.9 x 2.1 x 1.01) occurs anteriorly near mid-shaft. Although not functionally attributed by Saunders and Daeschler (1994), this mid-shaft mark presumably occupies a filleting location in mammoth butchery.

Femur

Compressional pits were noted proximally and distal anteriorly on EPV.3992, left femur (Figures 5.9, 5.11). These are consistent with traces of bone foreshafts, for example, as used to dismember the forefeet of Mammoth 1 and Mammoth 2 and the right knee joint of Mammoth 2 (Saunders and Daeschler 1994:figures 6, 8).

The distal articular surface of Mammoth 2's right femur is heavily modified with marks attributed to scraping and, especially, pry marks from wedge and lever activity (Table 5.3). Dismembering pry marks are prominent on the anterior medial patellar surface where the knee joint is invaded in butchery. These pry marks occur as pits (e.g., one measuring 15.24 x 13.74 x 3.58) and as elongate, arcuate gouges (e.g., one measuring 25.94 x 7.08 x 2.20). The latter are like those on the ventral posterior lunar of Mammoth 1 that could be attributed specifically to foreshaft 9–10 (Saunders and Daeschler 1994). Pitting and grooving were absent on a scraped field on the distal posterior portion of the medial patellar surface, showing that scraper-attributed damage was superimposed on that attributed to foreshafts. This suggested in this instance that foreshafts were first used as levers to lift, and then scrapers were used to cut (for the interpretation of heavy scrapers used as cutting implements, see Saunders and Daeschler 1994:21, citing Cotter 1937 on "scraper" and Wilmsen fide Speth 1983 on the implications of scraper-edge angles as "cutting" edges).

Other cultural modifications on the right femur of Mammoth 2 include a transverse filleting cut mark (2.5 x 2.2) on the medial shaft, 10 cm below the proximal articular surface (Binford 1981:figure 4.37(b), Fp-6, Fp-7). Of perhaps enhanced significance, in light of the Dent results, are two transverse cut marks (17.62 x 1.57 and 19.07 x 1.27) on the anterior shaft, 8.5 to 11.5 cm above the distal articular surface. Although they do not occur on medial or lateral surfaces, they have a suitable distal placement to be possible traces of filleting (Binford 1981: figure 4.38). In spite of this, in comparison to the pattern of filleting cut marks on distal femora from Dent, presumed or possible filleting cut marks on the femur of Mammoth 2 are of lesser significance. Overall, the consistent pattern of filleting the medial thigh on the basis of relatively fine and uniform cut marks on EPV.3992, EPV.3995, and EPV.3996 leaves the impression that these portions were meatier, fresher carcasses when processed compared with either Mammoth 1 or Mammoth 2 from Clovis, where multiple traces of heavier pry and scraper marks indicated dismemberment of stiffened joints (Saunders and Daeschler 1994:figure 8; Table 5.3).

Tibia

Compared with the fine display of filleting cut marks on the distal anteromedial femora, with one exception the patterning of marks to the Dent tibiae is less clearly revealed, and several marks are ambiguous (noted by "?" in Table 5.3). The one exception to light damage to the Dent tibia is the approximately transverse triplet of filleting cut marks occurring distal posteriorly on EPV.2193, right tibia (Table 5.3). Similar but heavier transverse marks affected the right tibia of Mammoth 2, where three sets of three parallel, deeply incised filleting cut marks occurred on distal posterior and distal medial shaft surfaces (Saunders and Daeschler 1994:19; compare with Binford 1981:figure 4.38, ca. marks Td-4). The first set, on the distal posterior shaft, measures 73.5 x 2.1 x 0.54, 58.7 x 2.1 x 0.54, and 9.2 x 2.3 x 0.54. This triplet is ca. 25 mm wide, and the distal-most cut mark terminates 5 cm above the distal articular surface. The second set, on the distal medial shaft, measures 43.6 x 1.7 x 0.6, 50.2 x 2 x 0.6, and 41.4 x 1 x 0.6. This triplet is ca. 40 mm wide, with the distal-most cut mark terminating 13 cm above the distal articular surface. The third set measures 43.8 x 2.1 x 0.25, 18.9 x 2.1 x 0.25, and 15.9 x 1.1 x 0.25. This triplet is ca. 35 mm wide, and its distal-most cut mark terminates 14 cm above the distal articular surface.

These triplets on the right tibia of Mammoth 2 agree in form and placement with the three heavier cut marks on EPV.2193, right tibia. The cut marks on EPV.2193 are shorter than all but one cut mark noted for the tibia of Mammoth 2 and are generally wider as well. The cut marks on EPV.2193 are also applied on a cortex field 10 mm wider than the widest field noted for a triplet on the tibia of Mammoth 2. Of interest is the corresponding placement of each set of marks on the shaft: at Dent the filleting cut marks begin ca. 96 mm above the distal articular surface, while on Mammoth 2 the three triplets commence 50, 130, and 140 mm, respectively (= 107 mm), above the distal articular surface.

For EPV.2193, right tibia, shallowly incised marks at filleting locations on the distal lateral surface are presumed cut marks. Other shallow marks—for example, anteriorly on EPV.2191, right tibia diaphysis (not those noted in Table 5.3), and shallow marks on other specimens—have placements seemingly inconsistent with intentional processing vis-à-vis Binford (1981) and may be incidental or trampling marks. Although all of the patterns noted in results of the Dent study are attributed to Clovis butchery, multiple causal agents of damage cannot be discounted at Dent and frankly are to be expected (see Conybeare and Haynes 1984 and G. Haynes 1991 for discussions of milling activity in modern *Loxodonta africana*). As noted, the bulk of the material in storage in Denver is in Behrensmeyer's (1978) stage 2 of weathering. This stage can indicate two–three years of postmortem exposure on the basis of Crader's (1983) study of modern elephant remains in south-central Africa, ample time for trampling marks to develop on bone surfaces. Even if attributed to processing, these shallow marks on the Dent tibia simply corroborate the suggestion from other data that the Dent carcasses were in fresher condition when processed, compared to the more deeply incised remains of Mammoth 1 and Mammoth 2. Other contrasts between the Dent and Clovis samples support the latter suggestion, for example, (1) a gouge-shaped pry mark (24.7 x 7.0 x 2.24) 55 mm posterior to the anterior border of the lateral condyle of the right tibia of Mammoth 2 that is associated with knee dismemberment (Binford 1981:figure 4.26b, d, marks located at Td-1 [should read Tp-1]), and (2) corresponding, conarticular damage to the distal end of the right femur of this individual. Although pry bar damage occurs elsewhere on Dent bones, including, for example, distal medially on EPV.3992, a left femur, no conarticular damage was noted on the proximal articular surfaces of the Dent tibia.

CONCLUSIONS

Table 5.3 summarizes location and function of processing marks on scapulae and limb bones of *Mammuthus columbi* from Dent and the Clovis type-site. Butchery of Dent scapulae amplifies, and provides additional insight into, the Clovis type-site data. Butchery noted for two Dent scapulae showed a pattern of processing involving both chopping and presumed snap-breakage removal of the acromion, mid-spinous process, and proximal scapular spine. Such snap-breakage identifies a possible role for the large boulders/expedient hammerstones recovered among the mammoth remains at Dent. Snap-breakage at this location mimics butchery strategy applied to Mammoth 1 at the Clovis type-site, where the same portions were dismembered in this manner from the scapular blade. Although Cotter (1937:text-plate 2) clearly shows the right and left scapula of Mammoth 2 on the planimetric map of the Mammoth Pit, neither scapula of Mammoth 2 could be located subsequently by Saunders and Daeschler (1994) in their study of these remains.

Contra the strategy employed at the Clovis type-site, however, the impression received from the dismembered pre-spinous fossa of EPV.3931, left scapula, and from the modified proximal medial ulna, EPV.3937, is that Dent butchery was done by teams. In this model a dismemberment team passed fresh, meaty limbs or dismembered portions on to a filleting team, whose activity, except for the distal femora and middle and distal tibiae (Table 5.3), is only lightly evidenced. If an accurate assumption, the team approach implies coordinated activity and a coordinating individual. Although Saunders and Daeschler (1994:18–19) noted chatter marks on the distal humerus and distal femur of Mammoth 2, they did not observe the more forcefully applied crescentic gouges on the remains of Mammoth 1 and Mammoth 2, which had been scavenged (the head of Mammoth 2 and the forefeet of both Mammoth 1 and Mammoth 2). It is unlikely for interpretation that the crescentic gouge on EPV.3937, a left ulna, resulted from downslope movement of the Dent bone bed indicated for relatively recent times. This traction interpretation is discounted on the bases of the fossilized condition to the crescentic ridges, the placement of the gouge, and the repetition of crescentic modifications on both Dent ulna and tibiae (notably, bones with corresponding fore and hind limb locations). It is possible that prominent crescentic gouges, as on the Dent material, resulted from a different butchering strategy than at Clovis, with differences related to carcass condition.

From similarities in scapula treatment at Dent and Clovis, and from the assumption of dismemberment and filleting teams associated with this activity on the basis of the Dent results, the processing of Mammoth 1 and Mammoth 2 at the Clovis type-site may have been a serial activity by visitors in two episodes. In this serial scenario, filleting marks with anterior and distal placements on long bones at Clovis (Table 5.3) can be attributed to an earlier episode of processing, perhaps by the individuals who hunted these mammoths and were responsible for weaponry in target locations (Saunders and Daeschler 1994:25). These hunter-processors were succeeded at the remains of Mammoth 1 and Mammoth 2 by Clovis scavengers, who focused on heads and feet (Saunders and Daeschler 1994:25) at a time near the Pleistocene-Holocene boundary (C. V. Haynes 1991). In this second, ultimate episode of modification, a team approach, as was possibly used at Dent, was not enacted—there were too few consumables and too few processors, probably only two, accompanied by their companion or pack canids (Saunders and Daeschler 1994).

Serially episodic processing of the Dent remains also seems likely. On the basis of the focusing studies, the Dent results suggest that some dismemberment and possibly even filleting of mammoths occurred there when the carcasses were no longer fresh. This evidence is best revealed on the medial head and distal anterior shaft of EPV.3992, a left femur (Figures 5.9, 5.11). Here a gouge and pits occur that are attributed from the Clovis results to foreshafts used as wedges or pry bars. In the former instance, damage is associated with hip joint dismemberment, and in the latter, knee joint dismemberment may also be indicated. From this evidence, on the basis of focusing studies, Clovis processors at Dent were dealing in this instance with stiff joints. Alternatively, if the distal pitting on EPV.3992 is attributed to filleting, then the interpretation is that Clovis processors were dealing with tenacious tissue close to the bone. In any event, a hind limb that had gone beyond a fresh condition was the focus of these activities at Dent.

It is not possible to know what amount of time is defined in "beyond fresh" in Clovis processing. Perhaps, consistent with constraints imposed by band size, technology, and size and number of available prey, normal processing (in contrast to scavenging) required a span of days or weeks during which, even in the fall of the year, decomposition would have resulted in carcasses' "beyond fresh" conditions. This consideration would lessen the significance of differences between the two Clovis zooarchaeological samples analyzed here and may make both common, vis-à-vis Clovis, practice. Lingering questions such as these, arising from comparison of two of the limited number of available samples, require experimental, actualistic approaches that more precisely target specific issues than do the best-focused, currently available studies.

It is also important to note that a recent article by Hoope (2004) suggested that the culturally associated mammoth remains from Dent, Colorado, as well as those from Miami, Texas, are, *at least in part*, time-averaged, attritional accumulations of unrelated individuals. Since 1975 (in oral presentation and published as Saunders 1977), I had hypothesized these and other Clovis-associated assemblages to be the result of single catastrophic mortality events affecting mammoth family groups. It is now clear from Hoope's work, as foreshadowed from tuskology analysis previously reported by Daniel Fisher (2001, and amplified by Fisher and Fox, Chapter 4, this volume), that at least some of the Dent mammoths died at different times. However, in contrast to Hoope, Brunswig (Chapter 3, this volume) and Fisher and Fox (Chapter 4) propose a relatively short-term attritional pattern for the Dent mammoths that preserves the hypothesis that their remains likely constitute a single family herd of which some members died at modestly spaced time intervals. Catastrophe(s) and attrition aside, the focus of this chapter is on damage conditions exhibited on Dent mammoth bones. These are compared and contrasted with previously reported damages attributed to Clovis mammoth processing (dominantly scavenging) at Blackwater Draw, New Mexico (Saunders and Daeschler 1994). Although contrasts appear, from the broad overlap of similar strategies employed in New Mexico and Colorado, Clovis processors apparently adhered to tradition in utilizing carcasses, including those opportunistically found.

Acknowledgments. Study of remains of *Mammuthus columbi* from the Dent site stored in the Denver Museum of Natural History in 1978 was conducted with the cooperation of K. Don Lindsey, curator of the Paleontology Division. I thank Frank Frazier and C. Vance Haynes Jr. for discussions and information regarding their investigations at the Dent site. Additional study of *M. columbi* remains from Dent in the DMNH in 1994 and 1995 was aided by Richard Stucky, Logan Ivy, Karen Arnedo, and Madeline Harrel. Tatyana Platonova, Zoological Institute, St. Petersburg, Russia, assisted me at the DMNH in 1995. For permitting access to exhibited Dent material in 1978, I thank Harold Mahan and Michael Williams of the Cleveland Museum of Natural History and Craig Black and Ronald Wilson of the Carnegie Museum of Natural History. I also thank James Dwyer of the University of Pittsburgh. The figures were prepared from my 35 mm slides and black-and-white negatives by Marlin Roos, Illinois State Museum. Here, as throughout, clarity issues are mine alone.

REFERENCES CITES

Agenbroad, L. D.
1994 Taxonomy of North American *Mammuthus* and Biometrics of the Hot Springs Mammoths. In *The Hot Springs Mammoth Site: A Decade of Field and Laboratory Research in Paleontology, Geology, and Paleoecology,* ed. L. D. Agenbroad and J. I. Mead, 158–207. Mammoth Site of Hot Springs, Hot Springs, SD.

Agenbroad, L. D., A. Lister, D. Mol, and V. L. Roth
1994 *Mammuthus primigenius* Remains from the Mammoth Site of Hot Springs, South Dakota. In *The Hot Springs Mammoth Site: A Decade of Field and Laboratory Research in Paleontology, Geology, and Paleoecology,* ed. L. D. Agenbroad and J. I. Mead, 269–281. Mammoth Site of Hot Springs, Hot Springs, SD.

Behrensmeyer, A. K.
1978 Taphonomic and Ecologic Information from Bone Weathering. *Paleobiology* 4: 150–162.

Behrensmeyer, A. K., K. D. Gordon, and G. T. Yanagi
  1986   Trampling as a Cause of Bone Surface Damage and Pseudo-Cut Marks. *Nature* 319:768–771.

Bilgery, C.
  1935   *Evidences of Pleistocene Man in the Denver Basin: Preliminary Report.* Ms. on file at the Denver Museum of Nature and Science, Denver.

Binford, L. R.
  1981   *Bones: Ancient Men and Modern Myths.* Academic Press, New York.
  1984   *Faunal Remains from Klasies River Mouth.* Academic Press, Orlando.

Brunswig, R. H., Jr.
  1995   *The Dent Mammoth Site: Directions in Current Research.* Paper presented at the 60th Annual Meeting of the Society for American Archaeology, Minneapolis, MN.

Brunswig, R. H., Jr., and D. C. Fisher
  1993   Research on the Dent Mammoth Site. *Current Research in the Pleistocene* 10:63–65.

Conybeare, A., and G. Haynes
  1984   Observations on Elephant Mortality and Bones in Water Holes. *Quaternary Research* 22:189–200.

Cotter, J. L.
  1937   The Occurrence of Flints and Extinct Animals in Pluvial Deposits near Clovis, New Mexico, Part IV, Report on Excavation at the Gravel Pit, 1936. *Proceedings of the Philadelphia Academy of Natural Sciences* 89:1–16.

Crader, D. C.
  1983   Recent Single-Carcass Bone Scatters and the Problem of Butchery Sites in the Archaeological Record. In *Animals and Archaeology: 1. Hunters and Their Prey*, ed. J. Clutton-Brock and C. Grigson, 107–141. BAR International Series 163, Oxford.

Falconer, Hugh
  1857   Elephas columbi. *Quarterly Journal, Geological Society of London* 12:319.

Figgins, J. D.
  1933   A Further Contribution to the Antiquity of Man in America. *Proceedings of the Colorado Museum of Natural History* 12 (2), Denver.

Fiorillo, A. R.
  1989   An Experimental Study of Trampling: Implications for the Fossil Record. In *Bone Modification*, ed. R. Bonnichsen and M. H. Sorg, 61–72. Center for the Study of the First Americans, University of Maine, Orono.

Fisher, D. C.
  1984a Mastodon Butchery by North American Paleoindians. *Nature* 308:271–272.
  1984b Taphonomic Analysis of Late Pleistocene Mastodon Occurrences: Evidence of Butchery by North American Paleo-Indians. *Paleobiology* 10:338–357.
  2001   Season of Death, Growth Rates, and Life History of North American Mammoths. In *Proceedings of the International Conference on Mammoth Site Studies*,

ed. D. West, 122–135. Publications in Anthropology 22, University of Kansas, Lawrence.

Fisher, J. W., Jr.
1992 Observations on the Late Pleistocene Bone Assemblage from the Lamb Spring Site, Colorado. In *Ice Age Hunters of the Rockies*, ed. D. J. Stanford and J. S. Day, 51–81. Denver Museum of Natural History and University Press of Colorado, Niwot.

Frison, G. C.
1989 Experimental Use of Clovis Weaponry and Tools on African Elephants. *American Antiquity* 54:766–784.

Frison, G. C., and L. C. Todd
1986 *The Colby Mammoth Site: Taphonomy and Archaeology of a Clovis Kill in Northern Wyoming*. University of New Mexico Press, Albuquerque.

Gary, M., R. McAfee Jr., and C. L. Wolf (eds.)
1972 *Glossary of Geology*. American Geological Institute, Washington, DC.

Graham, R. W., and E. L. Lundelius, principal authors.
1994 FAUNMAP: A Database Documenting Late Quaternary Distributions of Mammal Species in the United States. *Illinois State Museum Scientific Papers* 25.

Guralnik, D. B., and J. H. Friend (eds.)
1964 *Webster's New World Dictionary of the American Language, College Edition*. World Publishing, Cleveland.

Hannus, L. A.
1989 Flaked Mammoth Bone from the Lange/Ferguson Site, White River Badlands Area, South Dakota. In *Bone Modification*, ed. R. Bonnichsen and M. H. Sorg, 395–412. Center for the Study of the First Americans, University of Maine, Orono.

Haynes, C. V., Jr.
1966 Elephant Hunting in North America. *Scientific American* (June):104–112.
1991 Geoarchaeological and Paleohydrological Evidence for a Clovis-Age Drought in North America and Its Bearing on Extinction. *Quaternary Research* 35:438–450.
1995 Geochronology of Paleoenvironmental Change, Clovis Type Site, Blackwater Draw, New Mexico. *Geoarchaeology* 10:317–388.

Haynes, C. V., Jr., M. McFaul, R. H. Brunswig Jr., and K. D. Hopkins
1995 Kersey and Kuner Terrace Investigations at the Dent and Bernhardt Sites, Colorado. Paper presented at the 60th Annual Meeting of the Society for American Archaeology, Minneapolis, MN.
1998 Kersey and Kuner Terrace Investigations at the Dent and Bernhardt Sites, Colorado. *Geoarchaeology* 13 (2):201–218.

Haynes, G.
1991 *Mammoths, Mastodonts, and Elephants: Biology, Behavior, and the Fossil Record*. Cambridge University Press, Cambridge.

Hoope, K. A.
2004　Late Mammoth Herd Structure, Migration Patterns and Clovis Hunting Strategies Inferred from Isotopic Analysis of Multiple Death Assemblages. *Paleobiology* 30 (1):129–145.

Johnson, E.
1989　Human Modified Bones from Early Southern Plains Sites. In *Bone Modification*, ed. R. Bonnichsen and M. H. Sorg, 431–471. Center for the Study of the First Americans, University of Maine, Orono.

Lance, J. F.
1959　Faunal Remains from the Lehner Mammoth Site. *American Antiquity* 25:35–42.

Laws, R. M.
1966　Age Criteria for the African Elephant, *Loxodonta A. Africana*. *East African Wildlife Journal* 4:1–37.

Laws, R. M., and I.S.C. Parker
1968　Recent Studies on Elephant Populations in East Africa. In *Comparative Nutrition of Wild Animals*, ed. M. A. Crawford, 319–359. Academic, London.

Leidy, J.
1858　Notices of Remains of Extinct Vertebra. *Proceedings of the Academy of Natural Sciences, Philadelphia* 10:20–29.

Lister, A., and L. D. Agenbroad
1994　Gender Determinations of the Hot Springs Mammoths. In *The Hot Springs Mammoth Site: A Decade of Field and Laboratory Research in Paleontology, Geology, and Paleoecology*, ed. L. D. Agenbroad and J. I. Mead, 208–214. Mammoth Site of Hot Springs, Hot Springs, SD.

Madden, C. T.
1981　*Mammoths of North America*. Ph.D. dissertation, University of Colorado, Boulder. University Microfilms, Ann Arbor, MI.

Marshall, L. G.
1989　Bone Modification and the Laws of Burial. In *Bone Modification*, ed. R. Bonnichsen and M. H. Sorg, 7–24. Center for the Study of the First Americans, University of Maine, Orono.

Meltzer, D. J., and J. I. Mead
1983　The Timing of Late Pleistocene Mammalian Extinctions in North America. *Quaternary Research* 19:130–135.

Moss, C.
1988　*Elephant Memories: Thirteen Years in the Life of an Elephant Family*. William Morrow, New York.

Newcomer, M. H.
1974　Study and Replication of Bone Tools from Ksar Akil. *World Archaeology* 6 (2):138–153.

Nielsen, E. H.
- 1965 Die Muskulatur der Vordergliedmassen bei *Elephas indicus. Anat. Anz.* 117:171–192.

Oliver, J. S.
- 1989 Analogues and Site Context: Bone Damages from Shield Trap Cave (24CB91), Carbon County, Montana, U.S.A. In *Bone Modification*, ed. R. Bonnichsen and M. H. Sorg, 73–98. Center for the Study of the First Americans, University of Maine, Orono.

Olson, S. L.
- 1984 *Analytical Approaches to the Manufacture and Use of Bone Artifacts in Prehistory.* Unpublished Ph.D. dissertation, University of London.

Osborn, H. F.
- 1942 *Proboscidea, a Monograph of the Diversity, Evolution, Migration, and Extinction of the Mastodons and Elephants of the World*, Vol. 2. American Museum of Natural History, New York.

Saunders, J. J.
- 1970 *The Distribution and Taxonomy of Mammuthus in Arizona.* Unpublished master's thesis, University of Arizona, Tucson.
- 1977 Lehner Ranch Revisited. *The Museum Journal* 17:48–64.
- 1980 A Model for Man-Mammoth Relationships in Late Pleistocene North America. *Canadian Journal of Anthropology/Revue Canadienne d'Anthropologie* 1:87–98.
- 1995 The Dent Locality: A Latest Pleistocene Mammoth Assemblage from the American Great Plains. *Abstracts of the First International Mammoth Symposium*, October 16–22, 1995, St. Petersburg, Russia. *Cytology* 37:699–700.
- 1999 Morphometrical Analyses of *Mammuthus columbi* from the Dent Site, Weld County, Colorado. *DEINSEA* 6:55–78.

Saunders, J. J., and E. B. Daeschler
- 1994 Descriptive Analyses and Taphonomical Observations of Culturally Modified Mammoths Excavated at the Gravel Pit, near Clovis, New Mexico in 1936. *Proceedings of the Academy of Natural Sciences of Philadelphia* 145:1–28.

Sellards, E. H.
- 1952 *Early Man in America: A Study in Prehistory.* University of Texas Press, Austin.

Speth, J. D.
- 1983 *Bison Kills and Bone Counts.* University of Chicago Press, Chicago.

Spikard, L.
- 1972 *Progress Report of a Dent Site Investigation.* Unpublished ms. on file at the Denver Museum of Nature and Science, Denver.

Stafford, T. W., Jr., P. E. Hare, L. Currie, A.J.T. Jull, and D. J. Donahue
- 1991 Accelerator Radiocarbon Dating at the Molecular Level. *Journal of Archaeological Science* 18:35–72.

Steele, D. G., and D. L. Carlson
- 1989 Excavation and Taphonomy of Mammoth Remains from the Duewall-Newberry Site, Brazos County, Texas. In *Bone Modification*, ed. R. Bonnichsen and

M. H. Sorg, 413–430. Center for the Study of the First Americans, University of Maine, Orono.

Stock, C., and F. D. Bode
1936   The Occurrence of Flints and Extinct Animals in Pluvial Deposits near Clovis, New Mexico, Part III, Geology and Vertebrate Paleontology of the Late Quaternary near Clovis, New Mexico. *Proceedings of the Philadelphia Academy of Natural Sciences* 88:219–241.

Warnica, J. M.
1966   New Discoveries at the Clovis Site. *American Antiquity* 31:345–357.

Webb, S. D., G. S. Morgan, R. C. Hulbert Jr., D. S. Jones, B. J. MacFadden, and P. A. Mueller
1989   Geochronology of a Rich Early Pleistocene Vertebrate Fauna, Leisey Shell Pit, Tampa Bay, Florida. *Quaternary Research* 32:96–110.

Wormington, H. M.
1957   *Ancient Man in North America*. Denver Museum of Natural History, Popular Series 4, Denver.

Zalensky, V.
1903   *Osteological and Odontological Researches on the Mammoth (Elephas primigenius Blum.) and Elephants (El. indicus L. and El. africanus Blum.). Scientific Results Obtained by the Expedition, Sent Out by the Imperial Academy of Science to Dig for Mammoths, on the River Berezovka*. Printing Works of the Imperial Academy of Science, St. Petersburg, Russia.

CHAPTER SIX

Linda Scott Cummings and Rosa María Albert

Phytolith and Starch Analysis of Dent Site Mammoth Teeth Calculus

NEW EVIDENCE FOR LATE PLEISTOCENE MAMMOTH DIETS AND ENVIRONMENTS

Mammoth (*Mammuthus columbi*) teeth excavated from the Dent site (5WL269) in 1932 and 1933 by the Denver Museum of Natural History (DMNH) (now the Denver Museum of Nature and Science) were examined for phytoliths (Table 6.1). All teeth had been "stabilized" with varnish, which was removed prior to recovering calculus for examination of their phytolith records. One lower mammoth mandible (DMNH 1636) with two intact teeth and two independent mammoth teeth (DMNH 3801 and 3809) provided the calculus that was examined for microbotanical remains to provide dietary and paleoclimatic interpretations.

REVIEW OF PREVIOUS ANALYSIS

Previous analysis of a mammoth tooth from the Dent site (Cummings 1993) yielded dominance of the phytolith record by *Opuntia* sp. calcium oxylate crystals. The

Table 6.1. Provenience Data for Dent Mammoth Teeth Samples. (Note: DMNH is a pre-1994–1995 Denver Museum Catalog code, while EPV is the recent equivalent).

EPV/ DMNH No.	Genus/Species Identification	Probable Age	Provenience	Phytoliths Counted
1636	Mammoth (*Mammuthus columbi*)	22 African Elephant [Equivalent] Years (AEY)	Lower mandible with L and R m1 and L and R 2	51
3801	Mammoth (*Mammuthus columbi*)	Adult, age unknown	Maxillar fragment with intact molar tooth Rm2	75
3809	Mammoth (*Mammuthus columbi*)	Adult, age unknown	Molar tooth, Lm2	109

tooth examined was the second upper-left molar that belonged to an approximately thirty-year old mammoth (*Mammuthus columbi*). The tooth was obtained on loan from the Denver Museum of Natural History for analysis and found coated with varnish. No obvious pockets of sediments were noted while removing the varnish and cleaning the tooth preparatory to removing calculus for phytolith analysis. After completion of the analysis and submission of the report, it was discovered that the tooth had been recovered from a reworked area of the site and was associated with relatively modern sediments (Robert Brunswig personal communication, 1994).

Evidence of probable contamination by more recent sediments pointed to the necessity of reevaluating the earlier-obtained phytolith record from Dent mammoth teeth since it is probable that the varnish sealed in recent sediments. Excavation and curation methods of Dent remains included the use of varnish over an apparently partially cleaned surface, thus sealing any potential sediment contaminants to the tooth. Subsequent work with three additional mammoths from the Dent collection emphasized more thorough cleaning of the teeth to ensure no contaminants from the sediments remained. The three additional mammoth teeth were then examined to identify phytoliths that may represent foods consumed by late Pleistocene mammoths in the Dent area.

METHODS

Prior to removing calculus from the mammoth teeth, varnish used as a preservative, stabilizer, or both was removed from sections of the teeth by wiping and brushing the teeth with mineral spirits. After the varnish had been removed, the tooth surfaces were brushed using mineral spirits to remove any remaining sediment that might have adhered to the surfaces with the varnish. After a thorough brushing and visual inspection, calculus was removed from the teeth with dental picks. As discussed earlier, previous analysis of a mammoth tooth from the Dent site (Cummings 1993) might have included sediment adhering to the tooth beneath the varnish, so extra care was taken during removal of calculus from these teeth to ascertain that absolutely no contaminated material was present. Once removed from the tooth, dental calculus was dissolved using glacial acetic to release any phytoliths and calcium oxylate crystals.

The concentration of phytolith, calcium oxylate crystals, or both was very low in the initial sample, so the process of removing calculus with the dental pick was continued and a second sample gathered. In this sample, dilute (10 percent) hydrochloric acid was used to dissolve the dental calculus. After rinsing with water, organic debris was removed with 30 percent hydrogen peroxide. Phytoliths recovered from the calculus were rinsed first with distilled water, then with alcohol to remove the water. After several alcohol rinses, samples were mounted on a microscope slide using Cinnamaldehyde.

When recovery was compared between the two extraction methods described earlier (using glacial acetic acid and hydrochloric acid), no differences were noted. Therefore, residues were combined into a single sample for microscopic analysis. A light microscope was employed to identify and count phytoliths at a magnification of 400x.

PHYTOLITH REVIEW

Phytoliths are silica bodies produced by plants when soluble silica in the groundwater is absorbed by the roots and carried up to the plant by way of the vascular system. Evaporation and metabolism of this water result in precipitation of the silica in and around the cellular walls. The general term phytoliths, while strictly applied to opal phytoliths, may also be used to refer to calcium oxylate crystals produced by a variety of plants, including *Opuntia* sp. (prickly pear cactus). Opal phytoliths, which are distinct and decay-resistant plant remains, are deposited in the soil as the plant or plant parts die and break down. They are, however, subject to mechanical breakage and erosion and deterioration in high pH soils. Phytoliths are usually introduced directly into the soils in which the plants decay. Transportation of phytoliths occurs primarily by animal consumption, gathering of plants by people, or erosion or transportation of the soil by wind, water, or ice. When phytoliths are trapped in the calculus on animal teeth, they are presumed to represent phytoliths present either in vegetation consumed by the animals or in sediment present on that vegetation or in the immediate vicinity.

The major divisions of grass short-cell phytoliths recovered include festucoid, chloridoid, and panicoid. Smooth elongate phytoliths are currently of no aid in interpreting either paleoenvironmental conditions or the subsistence record because they are produced by a large number of grasses. Phytoliths were tabulated to represent total phytoliths, including all forms representing plants (grasses and dicots). Frequencies for diatoms and starches were calculated by dividing the number of each type recovered by the total phytoliths.

The festucoid class of phytoliths is ascribed primarily to the subfamily Pooideae and occurs most abundantly in cool, moist climates. However, Brown

(1984) noted that festucoid phytoliths are produced in small quantities by nearly all grasses, and, while they are phytoliths produced most commonly by the subfamily Pooideae , they are not exclusive to that subfamily. Some members of the subfamily Pooideae produce bilobate and polylobate forms. Chloridoid phytoliths are found primarily in the subfamily Chloridoideae, a warm-season grass that grows in arid to semiarid areas and requires less available soil moisture. Chloridoid grasses are most abundant in the American Southwest (Gould and Shaw 1983:120). Panicoid phytoliths occur in warm-season or tall grasses that frequently thrive in humid conditions. Twiss (1987:181) also noted that some members of the subfamily Chloridoideae produce both bilobate (panicoid) and festucoid phytoliths. According to Gould and Shaw (1983:110), more than 97 percent of native U.S. grass species (1,026 or 1,053) are divided equally among three subfamilies: Pooideae, Chloridoideae, and Panicoideae (Twiss 1987:181).

DISCUSSION

A *Mammuthus columbi* (mammoth) lower mandible (EPV/DMNH 1636) removed from a current exhibit was described in Denver Museum of Nature and Science accession records as representing an individual age twenty-two years (AEY), probably a female (see also Saunders, Chapter 5, Table 5.1, this volume). The lower mandible contained both molars on the left and right sides. Only the right first molar was sampled for phytoliths because it yielded a sufficient quantity of phytoliths for analysis and it was desirable to leave sufficient calculus on other teeth for future analysis. Because mammoth teeth grew continuously and were continuously worn down, any calculus present on any of the teeth resident in the mouth at the time of death logically represents food consumption during calculus accumulation for a limited time, not for the entire life of the animal.

The second tooth examined was a maxillary fragment (EPV/DMNH 3801) of a right second molar of an adult mammoth. The third tooth (EPV/DMNH 3809) represents the left second molar, also from an adult. No information from museum accession records was found on estimated ages or genders for the latter molars, although both were documented in museum records as coming from the Dent site (Robert Brunswig personal communication, 1994).

RESULTS

Phytoliths were not recovered in great abundance from any of the Dent mammoth teeth examined. The most abundant forms recovered were irregular bulky dicot forms (Figure 6.1), all relatively large. A small quantity of angular dicot forms was observed and probably represents plant silica.

Rovner (1971:350) noted that irregular bulky forms are typical of conifers. Kondo and Sumida (1978:141) noted relatively large irregular forms in conifers and also in *Quercus* and *Magnolia* (Kondo and Peason 1981:226). The angular shapes are more common in *Quercus*. In our reference work we have found similar irregular

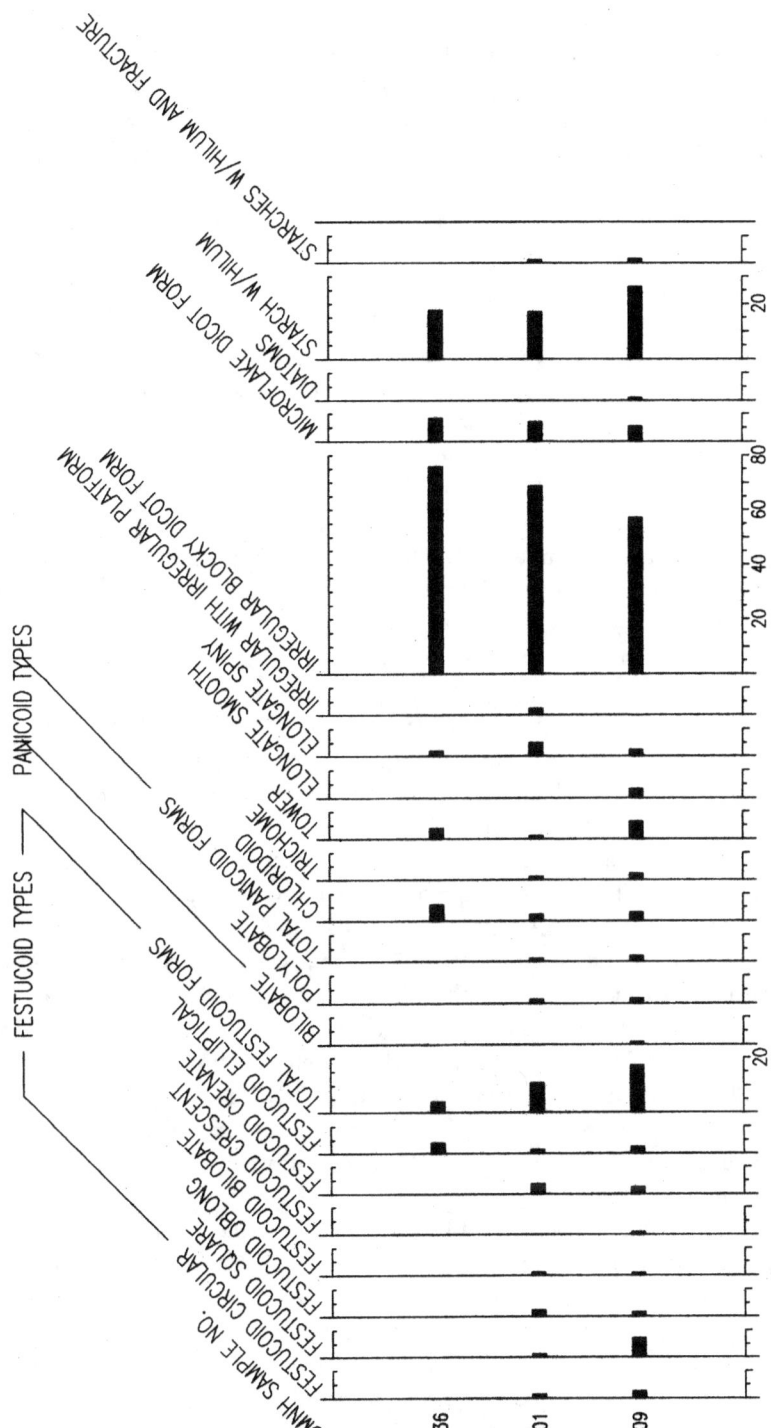

6.1. Phytolith frequency diagram of Dent mammoth teeth.

blocky forms in the roots of grasses, such as *Stipa longiseta*. The frequency with which they were noted indicates that the majority of these irregular blocky forms likely represent dicots, since grass roots would not have been consumed in preference to the entire grass plant. In comparison with the abundance of phytoliths produced in other parts of grasses, these irregular forms noted in grass roots were very rare in the reference material.

Another microscopic remain commonly noted in the Dent samples was starch granules with hila. Starches with hila and starches with hila and fissures are separated in this study in the hope that future reference work will allow refinement of this identification. Both types of starches were angular in shape and exhibited a cross under cross-polar illumination. These crosses, an optical phenomenon, are considered part of a suite of diagnostic characteristics for starches. These starch types are produced by seeds from a variety of grasses. Since no universal key exists for identifying starch granules from grass seeds, they remain identified at the family level. Starches, while most abundant and easily observed in starchy fruits and vegetables, occur in all land plants except possibly the parasite *Thonningia* (Mangenot 1968). They may occur in almost all cells and may be mobile, transported to different parts of the plant during the day or night (Mauseth 1988:31). Starches often are noted in seeds, roots, or tubers, although some woody plants contain starches in the woody stems.

Grass family short-cell phytoliths were also recovered from the calculus of the mammoth teeth. These phytoliths represent silicification inside epidermal tissue of the leaves and stems. The most abundant types of grass short cells recovered belong to the festucoid group, representing cool-season grasses. These grasses are the first to green up in the spring and are usually brown by summer. They also may grow again in the cool autumn months. Often, these grasses produce a large biomass. Panicoid-type phytoliths were observed in two samples, nos. EPV/DMNH 3801 and EPV/DMNH 3809. Panicoid grasses prefer the warmth of summer and also increased moisture. Panicoid-type phytoliths may be produced in certain festucoid grasses. Of the grasses likely to appear in this area, *Aristida* (three-awn), a C-4 grass, is the most likely to produce this form. Many panicoid grasses are found in riparian habitats where their moisture needs are more easily met. Chloridoid short cells were present in all samples but were most abundant in sample EPV/DMNH 1636. Chloridoid phytoliths represent short grasses that grow during the relatively hot, dry months of summer. Examples are grama and buffalo grasses.

Towers, a form of festucoid rondals that are taller than they are wide and always microscopically viewed from the side, were recovered in all samples but were most abundant in sample DMNH 3809. Towers are noted most frequently in festucoid grasses but also may occur in chloridoids and panicoids. Trichomes were observed in samples DMNH 3801 and 3809. These forms represent the silicified hairs on the outside of grass leaves and palea and lemma. Elongates, representing long cells, also are produced in the epidermal tissue of grasses. These forms were recovered in all samples and are distinguished as having either smooth or spiny edges. At present, they are not considered diagnostic as to grass type. A few grass phytoliths with both an irregular base and platform (irregular double-lined grass forms) were identified in sample DMNH 3801.

Sample EPV/DMNH 1636, representing a tooth in the lower mandible of a Dent mammoth, yielded the fewest phytoliths. Irregular forms were dominant, and festucoid, chloridoid, tower, and spine elongate forms were observed. Grass starch granules were recovered.

Sample EPV/DMNH 3801 yielded more abundant phytoliths. Again, irregular forms were most abundant. Within the grass family festucoid forms were most abundant, and only a few panicoid and chloridoid forms were noted. Spiny elongate forms were more abundant in this sample than in others. Starch granules were present in a similar frequency in this sample as in sample EPV/DMNH 1636.

Sample EPV/DMNH 3809 exhibited slightly less irregular forms than the other teeth. Festucoid phytoliths were more abundant, particularly square forms. Chloridoid- and panicoid-type phytoliths were noted in small frequencies. Towers were more abundant in this sample, as were trichomes. Both elongate smooth and elongate spiny forms were observed. Starch granules were more abundant in this sample relative to the total quantity of phytoliths recovered than in any of the other teeth sampled.

INTERPRETATIONS AND CONCLUSIONS

Phytolith analysis of calculus from Dent mammoth teeth exhibited dominance by an irregular form that appears to represent such diverse plants as conifer, *Quercus* (oak), and possibly grass roots. Phytoliths that definitely represent grasses included the short cells. For samples EPV/DMNH 3801 and 3809, festucoid-type phytoliths dominated the grass portion of the record. Chloridoid- and panicoid-type phytoliths were much less abundant. In sample EPV/DMNH 1636, however, nearly equal quantities of festucoid and chloridoid phytoliths were recovered. The general dominance of festucoid phytoliths in the mammoth tooth calculus suggests cool-season grasses played a significant part in the mammoths' diets. Recovery of chloridoid short-cell phytoliths in all calculus samples indicates that short grasses were present in the local vegetation community and were consumed by the mammoths. Recovery of a few bilobate and polylobate forms may represent the presence of a few panicoid grasses or may have been produced in feshicoid grasses. Recovery of grass-type starch granules in the calculus of all the mammoths indicates that grasses were definitely consumed with grass seeds. Recovery of this suite of phytoliths and starch granules indicates that, at a minimum, the mammoths consumed grasses whenever they were available. Dominance of the record by irregular blocky dicot forms indicates that plants other than grasses contributed significantly to mammoths' diet. These irregular forms suggest that mammoths were eating conifers and perhaps oak. Oak is further suggested by the presence of microflake dicot forms, typical of those seen in oak. If the irregular blocky forms were introduced solely from grass roots, they would not be expected in the large frequencies in which they were observed and therefore are interpreted to represent conifers and perhaps oak.

The total phytolith assemblage recovered suggests that these mammoths utilized several environmental zones along the Front Range. Apparently they ranged into the foothills and perhaps to higher elevations, where they might have consumed conifers and probably other woody plants, as well as grasses. While on the plains near the Dent site, their diet probably included grasses as well as plants and woody shrubs supported in the area's riparian communities.

REFERENCES CITED

Brown, D. A.
    1984   Prospects and Limits of Phytolith Key for Grasses in the Central United States. *Journal of Archaeological Science* 11:345–368.

Cummings, L. S.
    1993   *Phytolith Analysis of a Mammoth Tooth from the Dent Site, Colorado.* Ms. on file, Department of Anthropology, University of Northern Colorado, Greeley.

Gould, F. N., and R. B. Shaw
    1983   *Grass Systematics.* Texas A&M University Press, College Station.

Hoope, K. A.
    2004   Late Mammoth Herd Structure, Migration Patterns and Clovis Hunting Strategies Inferred from Isotopic Analysis of Multiple Death Assemblages. *Paleobiology* 30 (1):129–145.

Kondo, R., and T. Peason
    1981   Opal Phytoliths in Tree Leaves (Part 2): Opal Phytoliths in Dicotyledonous Angiosperm Tree Leaves. *Research Bulletin, Obihivo University* 12:217–229.

Kondo, R., and T. Sumida
    1978   The Study of Opal Phytoliths of Tree Leaves (Part 1): Opal Phytoliths in Gymnosperm and Monocotyledonous Angiosperm Tree Leaves. *Journal of the Science of Soil and Manure* 49 (2):138–144.

Mangenot, S.
    1968   Sur la Presence de Leucoplastes Chez les Végétaux Vasculaires Mycotrophes ou Parasites. *C. r. hebd. Séanc. Acad. Paris* 267:1193–1195.

Mauseth, James
    1988   *Plant Anatomy.* Benjamin Cummings, San Francisco.

Rovner, I.
    1971   Potential of Opal Phytoliths for Use in Paleocological Reconstruction. *Quaternary Research* 1:343–359.

Twiss, P. C.
    1987   Grass-Opal Phytoliths as Climatic Indicators of the Great Plains Pleistocene. In *Quatemary Environments of Kansas,* ed. W. C. Johnson, 179–188. Kansas Geological Survey Guidebook, Series 5, Lawrence.

PART THREE

NEW RESEARCH IN THE COLORADO ROCKY MOUNTAINS

CHAPTER SEVEN

Linda Scott Cummings, R. A. Varney, and Reid A. Bryson

Building a Picture of the Landscape Using Close-Interval Pollen Sampling and Archaeoclimatic Modeling

AN EXAMPLE FROM THE KIBRIDGE-YAMPA PALEOINDIAN SITE, NORTHWESTERN COLORADO

Understanding the past environment is made more difficult because no modern analogs exist for many of the previous vegetation communities or environmental systems. Vegetation communities when Paleoindians lived on the North American continent were governed by climatic conditions and an earth-sun relationship that do not exist on earth today. Therefore, rather than simply examining pollen records to provide information concerning the plants that were present, we have found it more insightful to incorporate archaeoclimatic modeling to understand the variations in seasonal temperature and precipitation that affected local plants and animals. Once the model is created, it is essential that pollen or other proxy records be consulted to "ground truth" the model. That is to say, models are excellent tools, but they should not be considered a substitute for data. Examining data at the closest interval possible provides considerably more information concerning local vegetation than does examining data averaged over long periods of time.

RELEVANCE OF MODELS AND MICRO-BOTANIC RECORDS TO PEOPLE

The "average" life span of a human living during prehistory has often been calculated at 35 years. This does not suggest that the average person lived to age 35 but rather that when infant mortality and other factors often leading to an early death were figured into the equation, the calculated expected life span was approximately 35 years. People who survived early childhood had a good chance of living into their 50s or perhaps longer, establishing what we will use as a life span for purposes of this discussion. Decisions on where to live were typically made on seasonal, annual, or decadal scales. Animal migrations are often seasonal. Plants are annuals, biennials, or perennials, with shrubs and some trees living 50 to several hundred years. These comparisons are necessary to establish a good sampling interval to understand the paleoenvironment. If decisions were made over relatively short periods of time (seasonally, annually, or perhaps decadally), then examination of the paleoenvironmental record every 200–500 years seems very inappropriate.

Previous pollen studies were considered sufficient if an individual sample represented a few hundred years. In fact, the vast majority of stratigraphic pollen and phytolith analyses for North America are based on a sampling interval that yields data every few hundred years, although bogs and lakes yield samples at 100-year intervals more often than sediment columns do. A survey of pollen records depicted in *Pollen Records of Late-Quaternary North American Sediments* (Bryant and Holloway 1985) displays sampling intervals ranging from a hundred to several hundred or even a thousand years for most of the records. The purpose in examining these records was to establish trends in vegetation representing paleoenvironmental conditions, usually documenting retreat of the glaciers or perhaps onset or conclusion of the middle Holocene period. Other studies referenced in that survey were conducted to provide general information concerning local and regional vegetation as part of the paleoenvironmental interpretation of the landscape used as the setting for human populations. Much of this work has assumed either relatively stable vegetation communities through time or gradual changes in vegetation communities, so sampling interval was assigned little importance. Rather, sampling intervals of 10 cm were adopted as convenient.

Although pollen sampling of very short vertical intervals (1 to 2 cm), separated by sediments not sampled, has been recommended for many years (Scott 1980), the recommendation has rarely been followed. Spacing samples at 5 to 10 cm intervals in a stratigraphic column has been the norm in many studies to accommodate small budgets for paleoenvironmental work. Unfortunately, this has often resulted in archaeologists collecting an entire block of 5 cm or 10 cm cubes, averaging large quantities of sediments, rather than collecting discrete 1 or 2 cm layers and then selecting samples 5 to 10 cm apart for analysis. One of the shortcomings of small budgets for laying a foundation for the archaeological record is that they do not recognize or give importance to understanding variations in the past environment, which provides a baseline for all life in the area. Plant and animal communities, and human populations, are reliant on the underlying environmental conditions, which have never been stable. Therefore, it is of paramount importance to understand the past climatic and environmental records in detail.

To be relevant to human occupation, reconstructed paleoenvironmental records must examine the finest or shortest time intervals possible to obtain a record of local and regional vegetation. The days of collecting samples at 10 cm intervals and worse, of averaging 10 cm blocks of sediment, should be gone. These time averages merely smear the paleoenvironmental record over a period of several hundred years, a time too long to be relevant to human activity in the area.

THE STRATIGRAPHIC POLLEN RECORD AT KIBRIDGE-YAMPA

The KibRidge-Yampa site is located immediately outside the eastern boundary of Dinosaur National Monument in northwestern Colorado (Figure 7.1). Deposition in the area sampled stratigraphically for pollen is anchored at the base by an age of approximately 11,200 radiocarbon years before present (RCYBP), while the uppermost age suggests that the top of the deposit sampled represents deposition at approximately 10,000 RCYBP. Paleoindian tools, including Folsom projectile points and bases of probable Goshen points, scrapers, Cody biface tool fragments, and other tools, were recovered by the archaeologists excavating the site (Hauck and Hauck 2002:162–167).

The stratigraphic pollen record generated from these sediments provides a unique record of past vegetation in the area. Twenty-eight pollen samples were collected as 2 cm high samples at 5 cm intervals from two separate areas in the site to sample the entire vertical record available. These two stratigraphic columns were later combined into a single stratigraphic record, based on stratigraphic contexts noted at the site. Radiocarbon ages, which vary from 11,290 RCYBP to 10,200 RCYBP, are either charcoal or bulk sediment dates, the latter of which provide only the most minimal standard for applying a date to the stratigraphic record. Dates from Contexts 15 (10,200 to 11,290 RCYBP) and 4 (10,200 RCYBP) were charcoal dates, while the age of 10,540 RCYBP, reported for Context 10, is a bulk soil date. Examining this record in its totality provides a detailed record of local and regional vegetation. Assuming continuous and even deposition through time, which undoubtedly did not occur, this record provides a look at the past environment approximately every 43 years. Because deposition is not anticipated to be constant, some intervals are less than 40 years while others are greater.

On the pollen diagram, archaeological components are noted, as are radiocarbon ages and sample numbers. All pollen taxa observed in these samples are

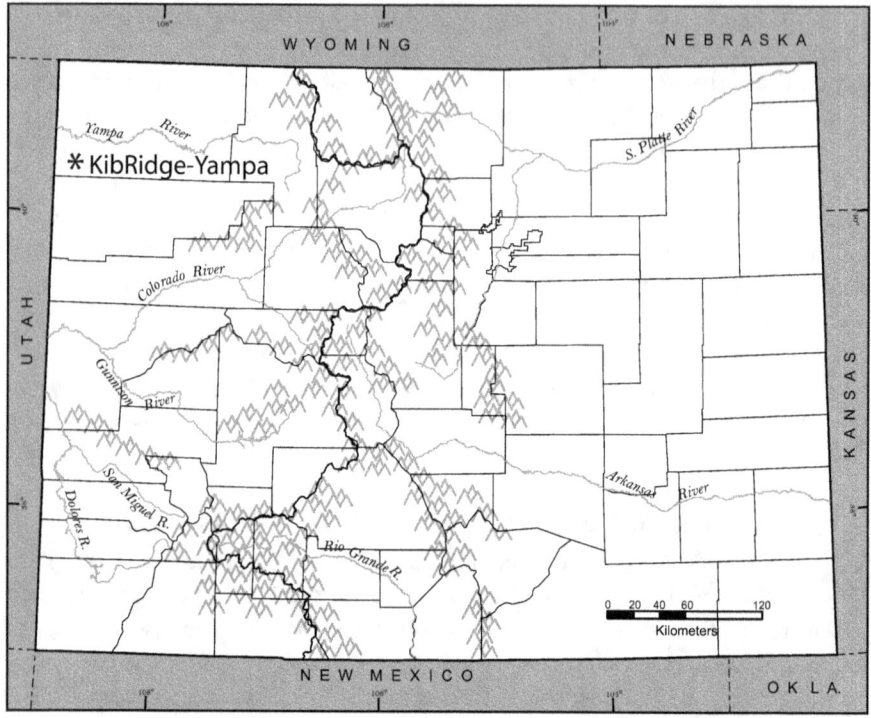

7.1. Location of KibRidge-Yampa site in northeastern Colorado. Map produced from a base map by James Doerner, University of Northern Colorado.

represented on the diagram; none is lumped under "other herbaceous plants." Consistency or change in the pollen record within an individual context, or stratigraphic layer, is important to note. Contexts were labeled by archaeologists using numbers but are not necessarily observed in numeric sequence from the bottom to the top of the record. The stratigraphic profile in the portion of the site sampled for pollen includes the sequence of contexts in order from the base to the top of the available record, in this order: 15, 14, 11, 3, 10, 13, 4, 2, and 1 (Figure 7.2). This does not reflect inversion of deposits, presence of any specific hiatus, or other unusual depositional events but merely indicates the excavation of the site over several years and the presence of some deposits in most of the excavation units and other deposits more rarely in other excavation units. Hence, when the contexts (or stratigraphic layers) were numbered, they were numbered in the order in which they were encountered, not necessarily the order in which they were deposited.

The lowest context (15) is marked by a very large quantity (more than 50 percent) of *Betula* pollen (Figure 7.2), indicating a dense stand of birch in the vicinity of this site approximately 11,200 RCYBP, according to the radiocarbon age associated with this context. The pollen record for this context, dominated

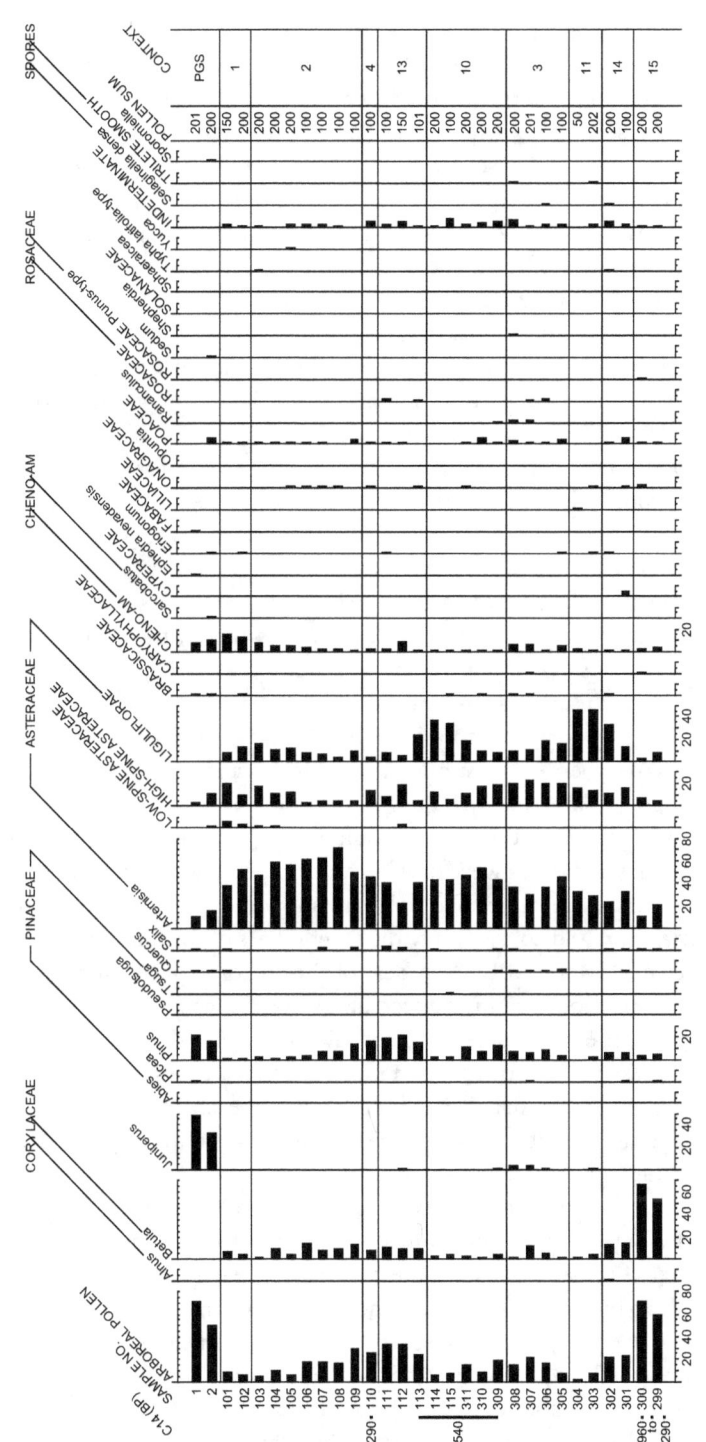

7.2. Combined stratigraphic pollen diagram from KibRidge-Yampa site.

by *Betula* pollen, is a far departure not only from modern vegetation but also from the remainder of the pollen record from the late Pleistocene for this site. Local growth of a large quantity of birch trees indicates the probability of a local spring or seep. The *Artemisia* pollen frequencies are similar to those of today but different from those of the rest of the late Pleistocene in this lowest context. Liguliflorae pollen, representing members of the chicory tribe of the sunflower family—which includes dandelion, chicory, and related plants—is another important component of the pollen record in the late Pleistocene and also might be associated with the presence of a local spring or seep.

Moving up in the diagram (and more recently in time) from Context 15 to Context 14, it is obvious from the rapid decline in *Betula* pollen that the birch population receded toward the bottoms of the drainages, that local springs and seeps dried out considerably, or both. Therefore, sediments in Context 15 represent pollen (and sediment) deposition over a period of several years because they contain pollen from plants that pollinate during the spring (birch), summer (most of the record), and fall (sagebrush—*Artemisia*), representing the entire growing season. The severe decline in birch trees suggests that during the accumulation of Context 14, birch trees grew much more sparsely and only in the bottoms of the drainages rather than more densely throughout the drainage. In addition, it indicates that seeps and springs in this area were drying rapidly. Indeed, openness of vegetation is underscored by increases in *Artemisia*, High-spine Asteraceae, and Liguliflorae pollen and to a lesser extent Poaceae pollen, reflecting sagebrush, various members of the sunflower family, chicory tribe plants, and grasses probably representing open, park vegetation.

By Context 11 the birch population had shrunk even farther, suggesting further drying. Pines were rare, as was juniper, and the vegetation communities on the landscape continued to open, supporting more sagebrush (represented by *Artemisia*) and considerably more members of the chicory tribe (Liguliflorae) of the sunflower family. Members of the chicory tribe, which includes chicory, native dandelion, and introduced dandelion, among other plants, tended to outcompete other members of the sunflower family during this time period and in the presence of more surface moisture than is present today. When environmental conditions dried out, members of the chicory tribe were replaced by other plants that tolerate more xeric conditions. Grasses were not particularly abundant.

The transition to Context 3, which overlies Context 11, was abrupt, once again suggesting the possibility of a depositional hiatus or deflation of the Context 11 upper surface. Context 3 was marked by increases in trees in general, including birch, juniper, and pines, although the vegetation was still typical of open areas, with widely spaced trees or clumps of trees. Sagebrush became even more abundant as part of the understory during this interval, becoming a dominant member of the local vegetation community. Members of the High-spine Asteraceae pollen group were abundant, and members of the chicory tribe

(Liguliflorae) were far less abundant, suggesting a reduction in available moisture on the ground. Cheno-am pollen became slightly more abundant in this interval, indicating the presence of either herbaceous or shrubby members of this group of plants, perhaps the xeric saltbush and related shrubs. Grasses continued to be a relatively sparse part of the local vegetation community.

Context 10, which yielded an age of 10,540 RCYBP on soil humates, is very similar to Context 3 in pollen content in the lower samples. Context 10 is represented by three samples from Location 300 and two samples at Location 100. Differences in pollen frequencies between these two groups of samples might reflect differences in vegetation slope or aspect or vegetation changes partway through accumulation of sediments for this context. Therefore, this context is a composite of pollen samples from two different areas of the site that exhibited sediments attributed to Context 10. The elevated Liguliflorae pollen frequency in the upper samples, offset by reductions in *Pinus* pollen, suggests open parkland that supported members of the chicory tribe of the sunflower family growing with other herbaceous plants that included grasses, members of the sunflower family, and sagebrush.

Context 13, which overlies Context 10, exhibits a return to slightly more *Betula* and *Pinus* pollen, indicating more trees distributed across the landscape or perhaps more clumps of trees in the vicinity of this site. Interestingly, very little *Juniperus* or *Quercus* pollen was observed in this level, indicating sparse local juniper and oak. The quantity of sagebrush declined, as did the quantity of Liguliflorae pollen, indicating reductions in local sagebrush and plants of the chicory tribe in the local vegetation. Only High-spine Asteraceae and Cheno-am pollen were elevated in one of the samples from this context, suggesting the possibility of fluctuations in the local understory plant population. Context 4 is a thin lens of human occupation that yielded a radiocarbon age of 10,260 RCYBP. The pollen record for this context is intermediate between that of the lower Context 13 and overlying Context 2.

Context 2 records a declining continuation of the birch population and a decline in the pine population, along with an increase in, and then stabilization of, the sagebrush population. The upper portion of this context includes increases in members of the sunflower family, including plants in the chicory tribe, as well as plants in the Cheno-am group. Sagebrush appeared to be the dominant vegetation, although birch continued to grow in the drainages.

The upper portion of the Paleoindian occupation is represented by Context 1, with an extrapolated age of 10,000 RCYBP or slightly younger. Birch remained on the landscape, and pines remained relatively sparse. Sagebrush was giving way to members of the High-spine Asteraceae and Cheno-am groups. Liguliflorae pollen declined. There, at the abrupt end of the stratigraphic deposits (at the present ground surface), vegetation communities reflected are not similar to those of today. There is no modern analog for this type of vegetation community, nor should there be, as climatic regimes during this period are not present today.

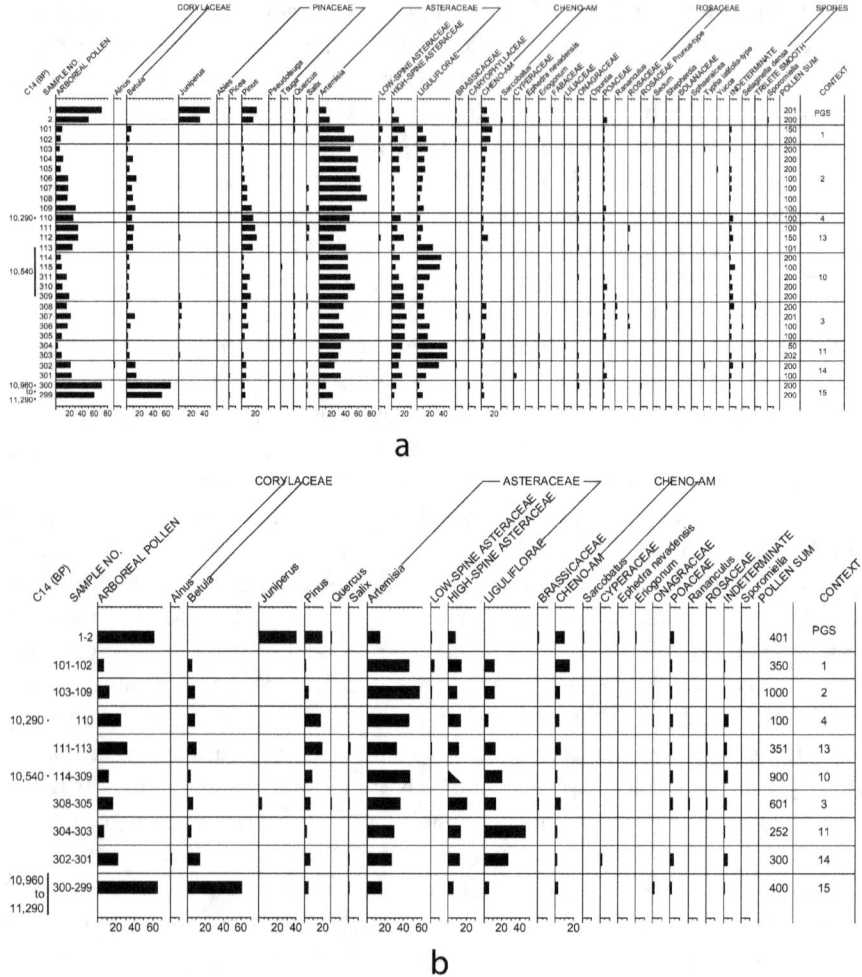

7.3. Comparison of sampling strategies: (a) combined stratigraphic pollen diagram, 43-year sampling strategy; (b) combined stratigraphic pollen diagram, stratum sampling strategy.

CLOSE-INTERVAL SAMPLING VERSUS STRATIGRAPHIC LAYER SAMPLING

One of the first assumptions of geomorphologists, geoarchaeologists, and many archaeologists is that a single context, layer, or stratigraphic unit represents uniform depositional conditions and that uniform depositional conditions indicate stability or stasis in the vegetation community. While to some people this makes sense, to plants on the ground, other factors are often as important or even more important. If this premise were true, no difference should exist in the pollen records from samples collected within a stratum or context, although an abrupt difference should be visible between strata or contexts. This is simply not

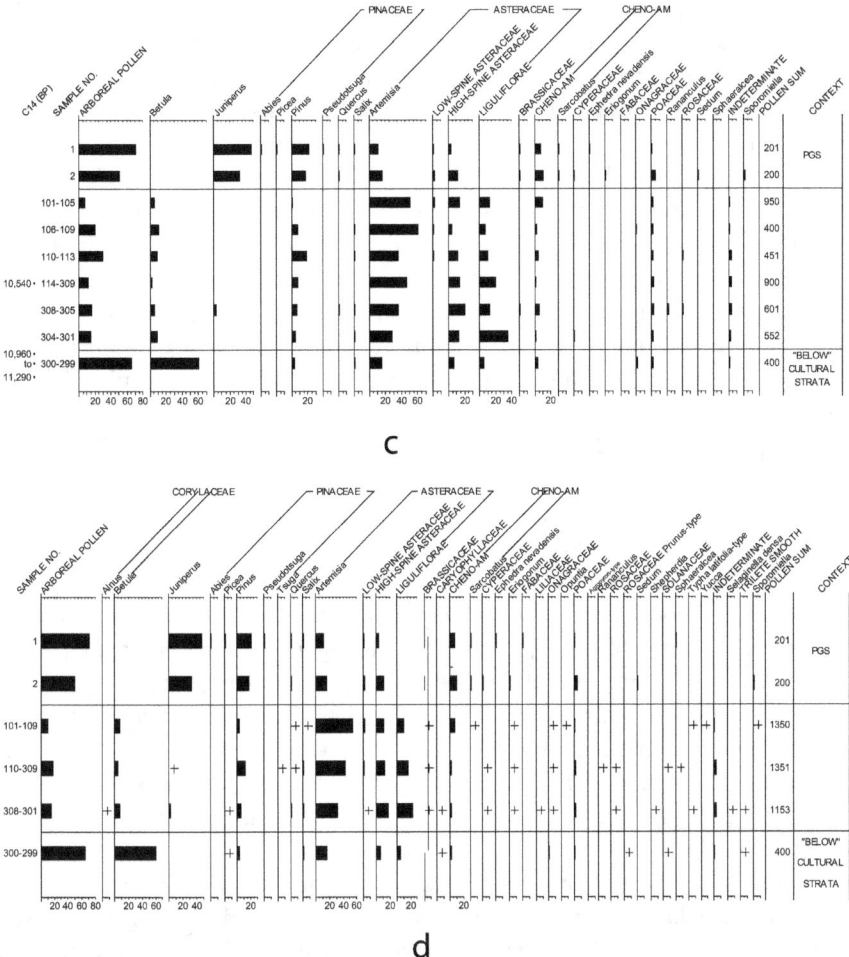

7.3—continued. (c) combined stratigraphic pollen diagram, 175-year sampling strategy; (d) combined stratigraphic pollen diagram, 400-year sampling strategy.

the case. Therefore, using a sampling strategy that collects and examines only one pollen sample per stratum, layer, or context has the potential of averaging a more complex record or eliminating portions of that record. This is demonstrated in Figure 7.3b (combined stratigraphic pollen diagram–stratum sampling strategy).

Using the mathematical construct of combining individual pollen samples into a single aggregate sample for each stratum reduces the original pollen counts per stratum (100, 900, 601, and so on) at KibRidge-Yampa to uniform 200 pollen grain counts, then calculates percentages including pollen types observed as 0.5 percent or more of the record. Certainly, this mathematical construct, which simulates the sampling strategy of taking one large sample per stratum, simplifies the pollen record, losing much detail. Many pollen types observed as small quantities in the original pollen record are now eliminated. This means that information concerning the presence of these plants as part of the local vegetation community is lost. Note in particular the changes in evidence for birch, juniper, oak, sagebrush, High-spine Asteraceae, and Liguliflorae pollen. Much of the interpretive evidence is lost, even with this relatively "minor" change in sampling strategy. With simplification of the record comes loss of variability and a tendency to interpret small differences as "insignificant."

Budgets sometimes rule the project, and an archaeologist elects to try to obtain a pollen sample every approximately 200 or more years or perhaps is simply unaware of the time depth represented by individual samples. For the purpose of this mathematical construct, we calculated a record of one sample every approximately 175 years (Figure 7.3c) irrespective of stratum, although two modern surface controls were present. This mathematical construct most closely approximates the sampling strategy of "sampling a block 10 cm × 10 cm × 10 cm" continuously through a column. Information lost using this sampling strategy is even more pronounced. The pollen record appears simplistic, suggesting very little change in local vegetation in the period between 11,200 and 10,000 RCYBP, with the exceptions of the large quantity of *Betula* pollen noted at the base of the record, reduction in Liguliflorae pollen, and the ever-increasing quantities of *Artemisia* pollen. This record suggests a fairly simplistic interpretation of a decline in chicory tribe plants, replaced primarily by sagebrush and a reduction in birches. The detail of fluctuations in quantities of Liguliflorae pollen is lost almost entirely, and with this loss comes a loss in the interpretation of available moisture for the plants.

Some budgets are even more severe, restricting the number of stratigraphic samples and yielding only one modern surface control and three or four subsurface samples. This sampling strategy is represented by Figure 7.3d (400 year). It is possible to see three elements to this pollen diagram. The lowest sample contains more *Betula* pollen than others, but it is not as noticeable as in other diagrams because of averaging. The rest of the period of Paleoindian occupation is one where sagebrush was more abundant than it is today, and little juniper or pine pollen was present, suggesting that the junipers and pines visible as scattered trees across the landscape are a phenomenon that developed later in the Holocene. Liguliflorae pollen was more abundant during the Paleoindian occupation, indicating the presence of more members of the chicory tribe compared with today, but no pattern of their increases and declines is visible. Birch was present throughout the Paleoindian occupation. This pollen record is likely to be dismissed as "insignificant" or meaningless. The data are averaged too far to provide an interpretable base. Commitment to sample collection at this level is perhaps as valueless as no commitment at all in understanding the paleoenvironmental record.

Interpretation of the stratigraphic pollen record, utilization of archaeoclimatic modeling, and comparison of these tools depend on close-interval pollen sampling. Examination of mathematical constructs simulating typical archaeological stratigraphic sampling designs elucidates the importance of close-interval sampling.

CLIMATIC MODELING

New answers for understanding Paleoindian environments must be sought outside modern analogs. We cannot look to today's landscape anywhere on this continent to find analogs for these vegetation communities and this environment. Understanding the past climate is often dependent on more than just review of a single stratigraphic pollen or phytolith record. The COHMAP model (COHMAP Members 1988), as originally published, provided a modeled climate for the past 18,000 years at 3,000-year intervals—clearly intervals too long for comparison with human activity but informative, nevertheless, concerning conditions that affected climate and vegetation. The COHMAP models highlighted numerous factors affecting climate that should have produced different vegetation communities over the past 18,000 years at least.

The entire seasonal cycle of solar radiation was considerably different during the early Holocene than either today or at the last glacial maximum (18,000 RCYBP). This may be attributed to both the eccentricity of the earth's orbit and the obliquity of the earth's rotational axis. Much attention has been focused on models of orbital eccentricity, obliquity of the rotational axis of the earth, and resulting monthly and annual insolation values (Barnosky 1986; COHMAP Members 1988; Davis, Sheppard, and Robertson 1986; Kutzbach 1987; Kutzbach and Guetter 1986; Webb et al. 1987; Wright 1984). While many have contributed to the formulation of a climatic model to explain paleoenvironmental changes over the past 18,000 years, a succinct statement of the model is presented by the COHMAP Members (1988).

Boundary conditions important to the formation of this model for North America include (1) the location and depth of the Laurentide ice sheet; (2) the June–August (or July) and December–February (or January) solar radiation for the Northern Hemisphere, expressed as a percentage difference from solar radiation at present; (3) global mean annual sea-surface temperatures, also expressed as a percentage difference from present; (4) excess glacial-age aerosol, expressed on an arbitrary scale; and 5) atmospheric carbon dioxide concentration, expressed in parts per million (Bryson and Bryson 1998). Particularly important factors for this model include the fact that summer solar radiation or insolation was approximately 8 percent greater than present at its maximum (11,000 to 10,000 RCYBP), and winter solar radiation or insolation was approximately 8 percent less than present at its minimum, which occurred near 9,000 RCYBP (Bryson and Bryson 1998). These factors are determined through models of obliquity of the earth's rotational axis. As the Northern Hemisphere tilts more toward the sun, summer

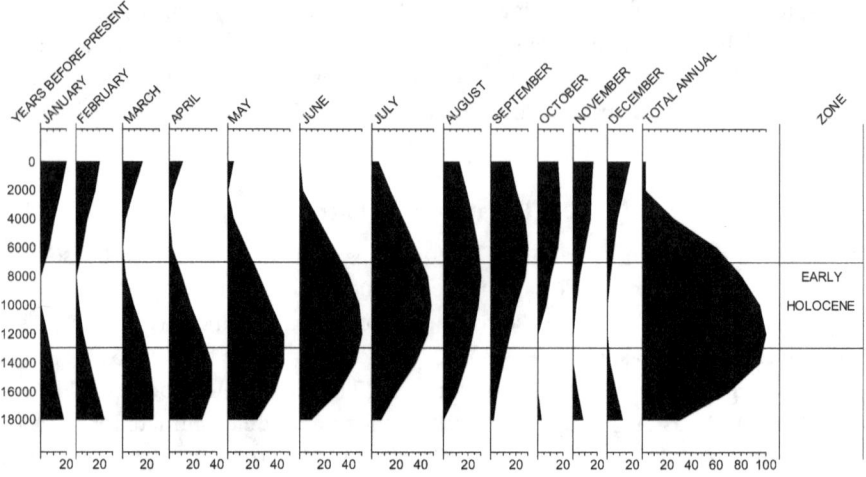

7.4. *Monthly and annual insolation, last glacial maximum through the present.*

solar radiation or insolation will increase and winter solar radiation will decrease. This results in an intensification of seasonal climatic difference.

Also important is orbital eccentricity. Perihelion, or the time when the earth is closest to the sun, now occurs in winter for the Northern Hemisphere. Between 15,000 and 9,000 RCYBP, however, perihelion occurred during the summer months. At the same time, axial tilt increased, combining with perihelion during summer to increase seasonality in the Northern Hemisphere and decrease seasonality in the Southern Hemisphere. Seasonal extremes in solar radiation noted near 9,000 RCYBP decreased through the Holocene toward modern values. Summer warming, which began by 12,000 RCYBP, reached a maximum around 9,000 RCYBP as a result of increased summer insolation. At this time, summer temperatures in western North America are estimated to be 2–4°C warmer than at present, and winters were probably correspondingly colder. By 6,000 RCYBP, summer temperatures were 2–4°C higher throughout the continental interior of North America, although winters should have ameliorated (COHMAP Members 1988).

Between approximately 12,000 and 6,000 RCYBP, the Northern Hemisphere received greater solar radiation in the summer and less in the winter than it does presently, resulting in greater seasonality. Climatic changes included changes in wind direction and velocity. Between 18,000 and 12,000 RCYBP, the western United States experienced easterly rather than westerly winds because the Laurentide ice sheet had split the winter jet stream. By approximately 12,000 RCYBP, this was no longer the case (COHMAP Members 1988). Paleoclimatic model simulations for the early Holocene show an intensification of the northeastern Pacific Subtropical High, bringing dry, warm air to the northwestern United States in summer. This pattern of circulation apparently increased summer drought during the early Holocene relative to present conditions, reducing effective moisture for vegetation and resulting in warmer, drier summers. This warming pattern of the Anathermal is noted to be a summer phenomenon, with winters colder than present (Kutzbach 1987). Strong westerly winds are postulated around 6,000 RCYBP across the Midwest, and a strong northeastern Pacific Subtropical High continued during the summer months off the West Coast. Prairies are postulated to have expanded to their maximums across the American Midwest by 6,000 RCYBP as a result of increased summer warmth (COHMAP Members 1988).

Davis, Sheppard, and Robertson (1986) explain differences in vegetation response between low-elevation and high-elevation sites in terms of monthly insolation (Figure 7.4). They have postulated that increases in insolation during the summer months, specifically July, significantly influence low-elevation vegetation boundaries, while high-elevation vegetation boundaries appear to be more influenced by fall, specifically September, insolation. This may explain why evidence of warming is often recovered in earlier deposits at lower elevations and in later or more recent deposits at high elevations. In the Snake River Basin of Idaho, the increase in the shadscale (*Atriplex*) community reached its maximum between 10,000 and 8,000 RCYBP, which coincides with the maximum July insolation. This model also indicates that summer temperatures increased during the Anathermal or early Holocene, while winter temperatures did not.

Resolution of the COHMAP model on 3,000-year intervals is not conducive to explaining vegetation change on a scale relevant to human occupation. Therefore, Bryson and Bryson (1994) developed archaeoclimatic modeling in the early 1990s. Their aim was to produce a model of climatic conditions for the past 14,000 years, with 200-year averages of the data, which provides considerably more detail in the environmental model than the COHMAP model, with 3,000-year intervals.

THE ARCHAEOCLIMATIC MODEL AND COMPARISONS TO THE STRATIGRAPHIC POLLEN RECORD

Development of macrophysical climate models was instrumental in creating archaeoclimatic models of past climates for specific locations (Bryson and Bryson 1998). Modeled mean temperature and precipitation can be examined for each month with 200-year averages (for instance, January or July temperatures or precipitation can be modeled for each 200-year interval for the past 14,000 radiocarbon years [Bryson and Bryson n.d.:1]). In addition, these parameters can be used to generate a "water budget," comparing precipitation and potential evapotranspiration, or to model wind speed and direction, storm intensity and frequency, snowfall, and other climatic factors.

Boundary conditions (conditions that define boundaries) important to the formation of modeling for North America include (1) radiation reflected from the ice or show in the world; (2) the summer and winter half-year's solar radiation averaged over the entire hemisphere (hemispheric average incoming radiation at the top of the atmosphere); (3) global average annual surface temperature; and

(4) the transparency of the atmosphere, as modulated by volcanic activity (Bryson and Bryson 1998). The more extreme seasonality noted in the late Pleistocene and early Holocene is a result of the changing earth-sun angle during the seasons. In the late Pleistocene and early Holocene, the earth was nearing perigee (closest to the sun) during Northern Hemisphere summers, resulting in relatively hotter summers, and apogee (furthest from the sun) during the winter, resulting in colder winters. Currently, the Northern Hemisphere is at perigee during the winter and apogee during the summer, resulting in more moderate seasonality. This effect, termed precession, has a period of roughly 23,000 years.

An archaeoclimatic model is constructed by incorporating the conditions outlined here to determine the insolation at the upper surface of the atmosphere for the past 40,000 years. Then, through a well-documented record of volcanic activity, an index of volcanic aerosols in the atmosphere, based on the number of radiocarbon dated volcanic events per century (by far the primary agent preventing insolation striking the upper surface of the atmosphere from reaching the surface of the earth), is calculated for the 40,000-year period. Volcanic activity records are considerably more reliable for the past 14,000 years than for the full potential 40,000 years, and this time period is more applicable to North American archaeology and Holocene geomorphology, so the models are usually restricted to the period from 14,000 RCYBP to modern. The information on insolation and energy budgets and the position of restrictive elements in the atmosphere (the jet stream and mostly permanently positioned high and low pressure zones) are compared statistically to 30-year average climatic data for a specific area. Small adjustments in the effect of the previously mentioned restrictive elements in the atmosphere are made until the model explains over 98 percent (usually over 99.5 percent) of the observed climatic averages. As noted, data points in the model reflect 200-year averages for climatic data and have been and are continuing to be ground-truthed through comparison with stratigraphic pollen and phytolith records, which indicate a high degree of reliability in the model (Bryson and Bryson 1994). Stratigraphic pollen records, such as those in this study, continue to provide "ground-truthing" or empirical evidence for evaluating these models.

The goal of archaeoclimatic modeling is to generate models of temperature, precipitation, seasonal distribution of precipitation ("march of precipitation"), precipitation intensity, water balance, an index of aridity, snowfall, and much more for a specific locality—incorporating topography, distance from major bodies of water, and other factors of local climate by the use of local weather averages. Simply put, if a modern 30-year record (e.g., from January 1961 through December 1990) is available for a specific area, the past can be modeled. The modules used in the model, combined with the local 30-year climate record, provide this ability to model the past climate for individual localities. Modern records already introduce all local boundary conditions of topography, distance from major bodies of water, and the like, since they are local records and the local weather is influenced by these same conditions.

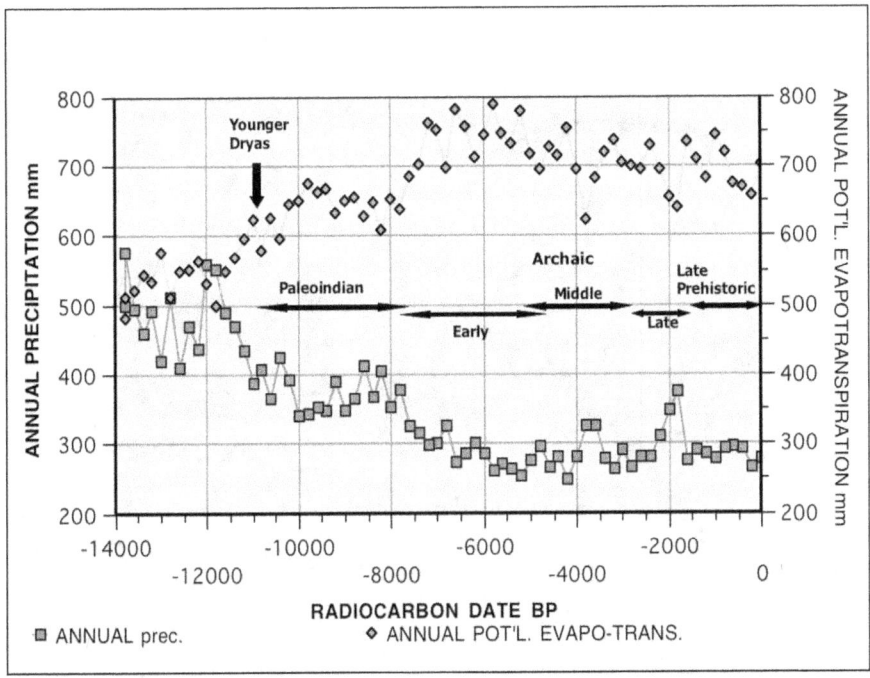

7.5. Modeled water balance history, Dinosaur National Monument, Colorado.

The simplest look at the past environment and the archaeoclimatic model is obtained by studying the modeled water balance history (Figure 7.5). The modeled water balance history obtained for Dinosaur National Monument, the closest weather station for which the 1961–1990 climatic normal data were available, produces an interesting archaeoclimatic model. Comparison of this model with the pollen record is best affected by applying frequencies for *Betula*, Liguliflorae, *Artemisia*, Low-spine Asteraceae, and High-spine Asteraceae pollen. Birch is most abundant at the base of the record, then it declines. Trees became more abundant as *Artemisia* became less abundant. Liguliflorae pollen indicates the presence of herbaceous plants in the chicory tribe of the sunflower family—similar in form to the low-growing dandelions and taller chicory that grow today. Grasses were not particularly abundant, and sedges, growing either in drainages or with the grasses, were even less abundant. There are two periods of increase in Liguliflorae pollen, which represent plants that grow well with increased moisture. Members of this group of plants are short-lived and respond quickly to changing conditions. The archaeoclimatic model shows two periods of increased precipitation and decreased potential evapotranspiration between 11,200 and 11,000 RCYBP, at 10,800 and 10,400 RCYBP. These episodes are appropriately spaced to be represented by the increases in Liguliflorae pollen (Figure 7.6).

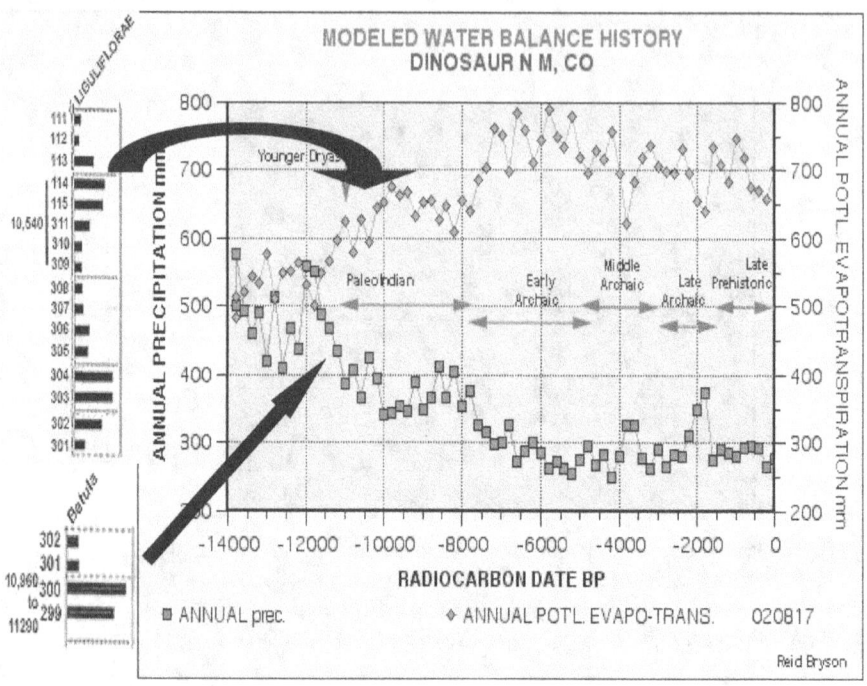

7.6. *Modeled water balance history, Dinosaur National Monument, Colorado, compared to portions of the pollen diagram.*

Temperatures are modeled to have increased fairly steadily during the period between approximately 11,200 and 10,000 RCYBP (Figure 7.7), as expected. This is a well-known period of change, with glaciers retreating. Also, this interval is modeled to have experienced decreasing snowfall (Figure 7.8), although, given the modeled fluctuations, decreases were greater during other periods. Precipitation is also modeled to have been greater during this period than it is today (Figure 7.9), which is in agreement with the recovery of large quantities of *Betula* pollen, indicating the presence of large stands of birch trees in this area. The modeled annual march of precipitation, showing the distribution of precipitation throughout the year using monthly averages (Figure 7.10), models a much different distribution of precipitation during the year than that observed today. Significantly more precipitation is modeled for the late-winter and early-spring months than occurs today. The fall peak in precipitation is modeled to occur one month earlier (September rather than October), and August is modeled to have been the driest month throughout most of the prehistoric period examined. These factors are expected to result in different vegetation for that time period than is noted today. In fact, the pollen record indicates the vegetation was quite different, with birches retreating from the area about or shortly after 11,000 RCYBP. Sagebrush became much more abundant than it is today and probably was

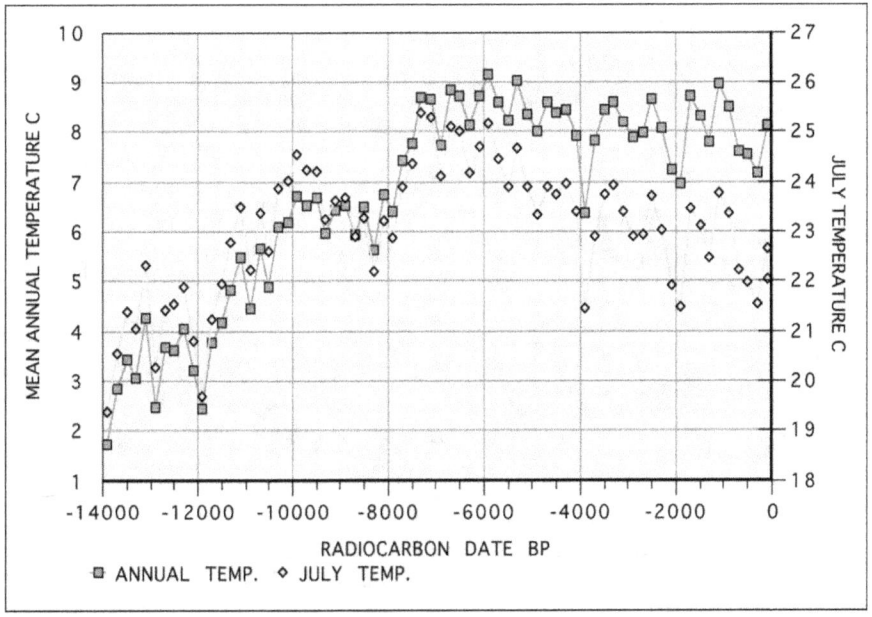

7.7. Modeled temperature history, Dinosaur National Monument, Colorado.

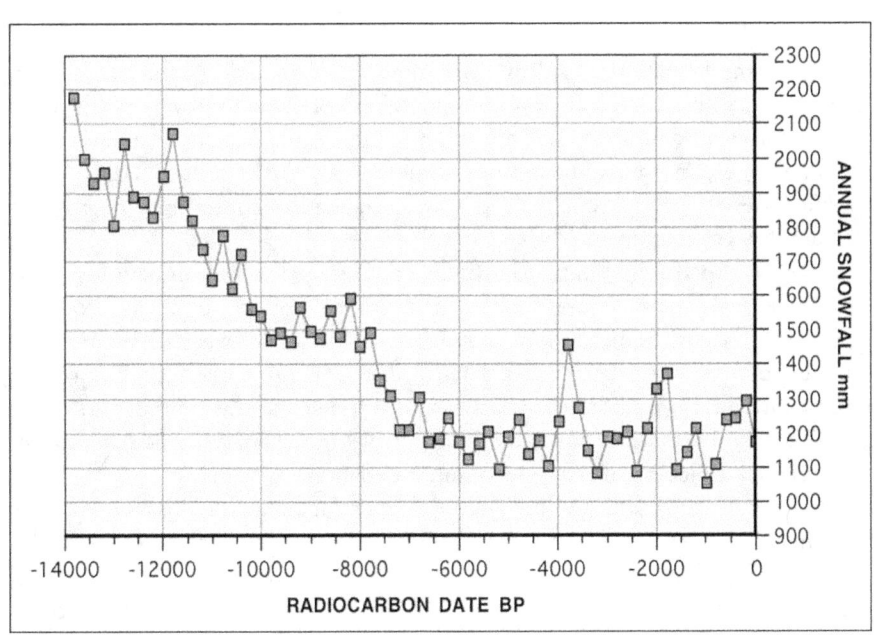

7.8. Modeled snowfall history, Dinosaur National Monument, Colorado.

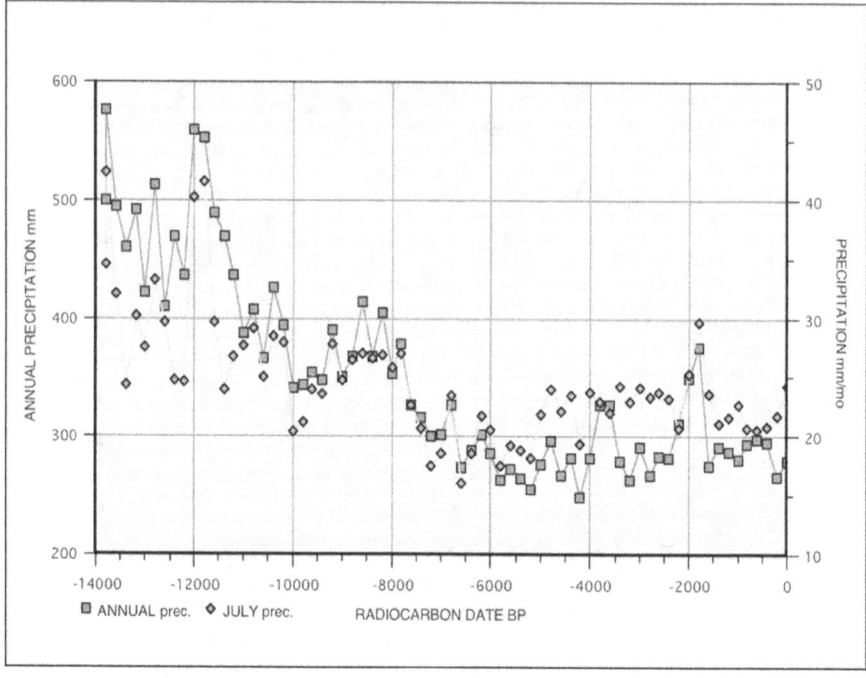

7.9. *Modeled precipitation history, Dinosaur National Monument, Colorado.*

denser on the landscape, resulting in a more lush vegetation community than that of today. In addition, herbaceous members of the sunflower family were much more abundant than they are today, contributing to a lush, green look to the landscape. Pines were moderately abundant, especially around 11,300 RCYBP. Junipers were nearly absent from the local vegetation community during the Paleoindian occupation.

We have the tools at hand to provide excellent paleoenvironmental records through examination of closely spaced stratigraphic pollen samples and comparison with archaeoclimatic models. Examination of various elements of the archaeoclimatic models, beyond just water balance, allows a look at modeled distribution of precipitation throughout the year, not just modeled average annual precipitation. It is possible, by using all the tools available on the analysis end of a project, to construct a picture of the environment that both explains what is observed in the microfossil record and provides the basis for understanding some of the reasons for changes in that environment. However, without a properly executed, well-thought-out sampling strategy based on human decision-making time spans, we will continue in the same old rut of examining paleoenvironmental records at gross intervals, repeating analyses without ever creating a detailed interpretation of the conditions of the past or building a reliable picture of the landscape on which people lived. Comparison of records of plant micro- and macrofossils with

BUILDING A PICTURE OF THE LANDSCAPE USING CLOSE-INTERVAL POLLEN SAMPLING

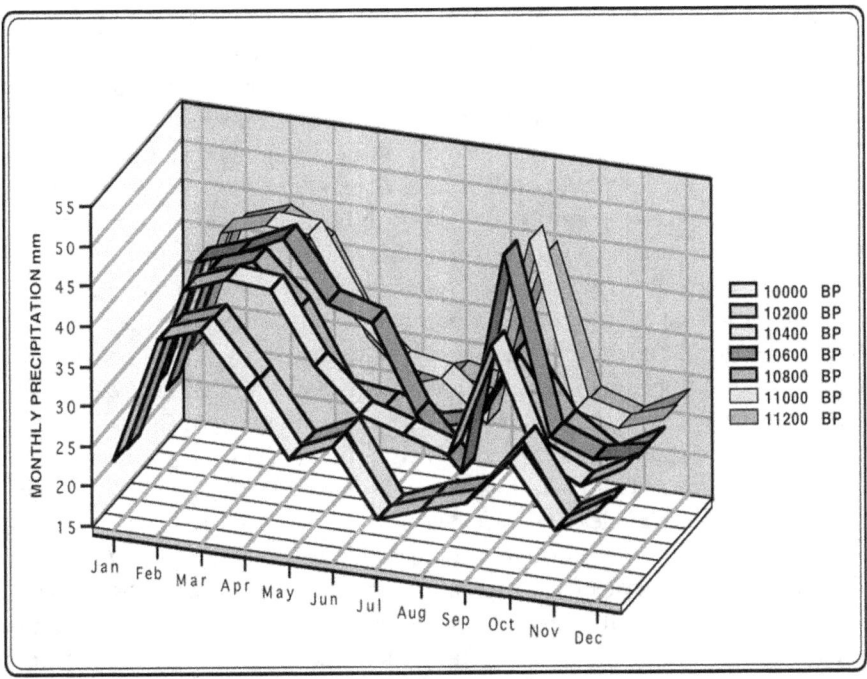

7.10. *March of precipitation from 10,000 to 11,200 RCYBP and modern. Modern values are represented by the front (bottom) ribbon, followed by the 10,000 values, and so on, until the back (top) ribbon, which represents 11,200 RCYBP.*

archaeoclimatic models allows researchers to ask more questions of the data and to formulate more hypotheses.

CONCLUSIONS

Using closely spaced stratigraphic pollen samples and comparing the record of vegetation generated from that analysis with an archaeoclimatic model has resulted in an interpretation of the past climate at the KibRidge-Yampa Paleoindian site that is much more complex than would be available from a stratigraphic record of pollen samples spaced at 10 cm intervals. During the Paleoindian occupation of this area, winters were several degrees centigrade colder than present and summers were several degrees centigrade warmer. This had an impact on the local plant population, which in turn was important in supporting animal populations.

The pollen record begins toward the end of a period (11,290 to 10,960 RCYBP) of positive water balance that supported birch trees in the drainages at least and perhaps also on the north-facing slopes of hills and other areas. These birch trees apparently grew close together, forming thickets that provided a specific habitat for animals and other plants. Along with birches, willows also grew in the drainages. Spruce and pines grew farther from this area, as their pollen is present in very small quantities and both pollen types are readily transported on the wind.

The local vegetation understory was apparently fairly restricted, probably by shade, and included sagebrush in open, sunny areas; members of the sunflower family; members of the chicory tribe of the sunflower family that grow in shady, moist areas; members of the pink family; Cheno-ams; grasses; and a member of the evening primrose family that grows in open areas. After approximately 10,900 RCYBP, the birch and willow thickets receded significantly, probably to the bottoms of drainages. This resulted in an opening of local vegetation communities and permitted encroachment of sagebrush and members of the sunflower family. The local understory vegetation also included a variety of low-growing plants typical of open parks of the time that included at least members of the chicory tribe, mustards, sedges, wild buckwheat, and grasses. The local understory vegetation probably looked like a grassy parkland, with sagebrush visible as the shrubby element living within a grassy or green understory.

Conditions are modeled to have become slightly wetter at 10,800 and again at 10,400 RCYBP, probably through a combination of increased precipitation and decreased potential evapotranspiration, resulting in an increase in the chicory tribe population. This increase in chicory tribe plants would have the effect of increasing the density of the understory vegetation, making the area look more lush and green and providing food for small herbivores. Rabbits were probably far more abundant locally during intervals with elevated Liguliflorae pollen frequencies. Precipitation probably declined, resulting in slightly drier conditions and fewer plants of the chicory tribe forming the green understory. This reduced food for rabbits and other small grazers and probably resulted in more bare, brown patches on the landscape between the sagebrush. Sagebrush became slightly more abundant. Cheno-ams were most abundant during intervals that appear to have been drier, suggesting that saltbush (and perhaps related) shrubs were becoming more abundant on the landscape. Members of the mustard family were part of the local understory community, providing good spring grazing fodder. Grasses were present but not particularly abundant. As conditions became drier, juniper and pine pollen became more noticeable in the record, suggesting either an increase in these trees on the landscape or the possibility that local vegetation became sparser and long-distance wind transport was responsible for the presence of the juniper and increased pine frequencies. Shrubby and perhaps herbaceous members of the rose family grew locally, probably in the drainages. *Shepherdia* pollen was noted only once in this record, indicating that buffaloberry shrubs probably grew in the drainages during at least the drier intervals of the early Holocene.

The next interval that appears to have been slightly wetter is associated with Context 10 (Location 100). This entire context is anchored by a soil humate date of 10,540 RCYBP. Comparison with the archaeoclimatic model suggests the moist interval occurred around 10,400 RCYBP. Vegetation at this time is very similar to that during the earlier moist interval around 10,800 RCYBP. Describing the vegetation (using pollen analysis) during two moist intervals, separated by a drier interval, within this tightly dated range of 10,800 to 10,400 RCYBP is possible only through close interval sampling. Viewing the pollen record and comparing it with the archaeoclimatic model results in a picture of the local landscape of slightly larger populations of rabbits and grazers of members of the chicory tribe of the sunflower family at two times, interspersed with a drier interval that supported a larger ratio of sagebrush and other shrubby members of the sunflower family that would have been browsed by deer.

Although bison have been observed to nibble the tips of shrubs, they are not now observed to be browsers by preference (Gear personal communication, 2006). Woods bison feed on willow, sedges, forbs, and grasses in the summer. In winter, they often move toward wet sedge meadows and lakeshores, feeding on grasses and sedges, or to the forest, where they feed on lichens (Northwest Territories Wildlife Division 2005). Wet areas that supported birch and willow in the drainages near the KibRidge-Yampa Paleoindian site would have provided a good habitat for woods bison, although there is no faunal evidence at the site. As the climate changed and these vegetation communities shrank, the bison population would have been affected. These changes in the local vegetation record provide information to interpret fluctuations in local animal populations through time, which would, in turn, have had an effect on hunter-gatherer populations in the area.

Between 10,400 and 10,290 RCYBP, plants in the chicory tribe declined in abundance again, but sagebrush did not increase. Instead, this time period is marked by increases in *Betula*, *Salix*, and *Pinus* pollen, indicating increases in local birch and willow trees, as well as pines. This interval apparently experienced a slight increase in moisture, which is modeled on the precipitation model (Figure 7.9). After this interval sagebrush increased in frequency, apparently competing better in the climatic conditions than the plants better adapted to wetter conditions that sagebrush replaced. According to the archaeoclimatic models, precipitation declined in the spring, which would have resulted in drier conditions for delicate forbs.

This study of modeled climate, combined with a close-interval stratigraphic pollen record of vegetation in the vicinity of the KibRidge-Yampa Paleoindian site, stands as an example of the interpretive depth possible through use of these analytical tools. Without all these analytical elements, this picture would not be as complete or rich in detail. The quantum leap in sampling strategy that has created this rich environmental mosaic depends on close-interval sampling in the field by field archaeologists, then relies on excellent laboratory and analytical techniques.

Acknowledgments. The close-interval pollen sampling undertaken at the KibRidge-Yampa Paleoindian site was conducted under a State Historical Fund

Grant Award from the Colorado Historical Society (number 2000-01-081), with matching funds provided by the Paleo Research Institute. Excavation of the KibRidge-Yampa Paleoindian site during the summer of 2000, which exposed the stratigraphic column faces sampled for pollen, was directed by Dr. Richard Hauck and was funded under the same grant, with matching funds coming from the Archaeological Environmental Research Corporation.

REFERENCES CITED

Barnosky, C. W.
    1986   Responses of Vegetation to Climatic Changes of Different Duration in the Late Neogene. *Trends in Ecology and Evolution* 2:247–250.

Bryant, V. M., Jr., and R. G. Holloway (eds.)
    1985   *Pollen Records of Late-Quaternary North American Sediments.* American Association of Stratigraphic Palynologists Foundation, Dallas, TX.

Bryson, R. U., and R. A. Bryson
    n.d.   *The Modeled Climate History of Green River, Wyoming Since the Last Glacial Maximum.* Ms. in possession of the authors.
    1994   A Comparison of Cultural Evidence and Simulated Holocene Climates of the Pacific Northwest. *Abstracts of the 59th Annual Meeting, Society for American Archaeology,* Anaheim, CA, 29.
    1998   Application of a Global Volcanicity Time-Series in Site-Specific High-Resolution Paleoclimate Modeling for the Past Forty Millennia. In *Water, Environment and Society in Times of Climate Change,* ed. A. Issar and N. Brown, 1–19. Kluwer, Dordrecht.

COHMAP Members
    1988   Climatic Changes of the Last 18,000 Years: Observations and Model Simulations. *Science* 241 (August):1043–1052.

Davis, O. K., J. C. Sheppard, and S. Robertson
    1986   Contrasting Climatic Histories for the Snake River Plain, Idaho, Resulting from Multiple Thermal Maxima. *Quaternary Research* 26:321–339.

Hauck, F. R., and M. R. Hauck
    2002   KibRidge-Yampa Paleoindian Occupation Site (5MF3687): Preliminary Archaeological Excavations (1993–2001) in Northwestern Colorado. *Archaeological Research Institute General Series* 4. Bountiful, UT.

Kutzbach, J. E.
    1987   Model Simulations of the Climatic Patterns during the Deglaciation of North America. In *North America and Adjacent Oceans during the Last Deglacitation,* ed. W. F. Ruddiman and H. E. Wright Jr., 425–446. Geological Society of America Bulletin K-3, Boulder, CO.

Kutzbach, J. E., and P. J. Guetter
    1986   The Influence of Changing Orbital Parameters and Surface Boundary Conditions on Climate Situations over the past 18,000 Years. *Journal of the Atmospheric Sciences* 43(16):1726–1759.

Northwest Territories Wildlife Division
   2005   *NWT Wood Bison.* Retrieved January 4, 2006, from Northwest Territories Wildlife Division on the World Wide Web: http://www.nwtwildlife.rwed.gov.nt.ca/ Publications/speciesatriskweb/woodbison.htm.

Scott, L. J.
   1980   *Manual for Pollen and Macrofloral Sampling.* Palynological Analysts, Montrose, CO.

Webb, Thompson, III, A. Street Perrott, and J. E. Kutzbach
   1987   Late Quaternary Paleoclimatic Data and Climate Models. *Episodes* 10:4–6.

Wright, H. E., Jr.
   1984   Sensitivity and Response Time of Natural Systems to Climatic Change in the Late Quaternary. *Quaternary Science Reviews* 3:91–131.

CHAPTER EIGHT

Todd A. Surovell and Nicole M. Waguespack

Folsom Hearth-Centered Use of Space at Barger Gulch, Locality B

This chapter concerns organization and use of hearth space at a Folsom residential site in the mountains (Middle Park) of north-central Colorado. Based on ethnoarchaeological and ethnographic observations of hunter-gatherer camps, it has been well established that hearths frequently served as focal activity loci (Binford 1978, 1983; O'Connell, Hawkes, and Blurton Jones 1991; Walters 1988; Yellen 1977). Fires not only aided in the performance of specific activities (e.g., cooking, wood working, or mastic preparation) but also provided micro-environmental enhancements in heat and light that often made areas adjacent to hearth features preferred working environments. Prehistorically, this pattern is evident in the form of hearth-centered activity areas, identified by high-density clusters of artifacts and bone in association with hearth features (e.g., Audouze and Enloe 1997; Gamble 1991; Leroi-Gourhan and Brézillon 1966, 1972; Simek 1984, 1987;

Stapert 1989, 1990, 1991–1992, 2003; Stevenson 1985, 1991). Yet with few exceptions, hearth-centered activity areas are uncommon from Folsom contexts, and those that have been proposed (e.g., Frison 1982; Jodry 1999; Jodry and Stanford 1992; Smith and McNees 1990) are only minimally described, with the sole exception of possible hearth-centered activity areas at the Mountaineer site (Stiger 2006). This observation serves as the primary inspiration for this study, in which we describe spatial patterning in a high-density Folsom hearth-centered activity area from Locality B of the Barger Gulch site in Middle Park, Colorado.

Although it is safe to assume Folsom peoples utilized fire, clear, unambiguous archaeological evidence of hearth features from Folsom contexts are rare. In fact, substantially more hearths are likely known from middle Paleolithic contexts (e.g., Gamble 1999:255–260; Simek 1987; Stapert 1990; Weiner et al. 1995) than from the entire sample of excavated Folsom sites. Certainly, in contrast to the comparably aged Magdalenian record of Western Europe, there are, as of yet, no Folsom Pincevents or Verberies with well-preserved and meticulously excavated stone-ringed or gravel-lined hearths surrounded by intact patterned distributions of stones and bones. While numerous factors are likely contributors, the scarcity of Folsom hearths may be in part a product of excavation bias. For example, it seems likely that excavated portions of the Lindenmeier site must have contained cultural fire features, but only scant evidence of the presence of hearths is provided in the available literature (Wilmsen and Roberts 1984:60). In discussing Frank Roberts's field notes, Wilmsen (Wilmsen and Roberts 1984:24) reported: "More serious limitations are imposed by absence of data for some classes of material remains. Roberts noted the presence of charcoal in many squares, but he gave no information about relative densities and rarely recorded the presence of hearths or firepits." Poor excavation quality (by modern standards) and limited documentation, therefore, may contribute to the relative archaeological scarcity of Folsom hearths, although this problem is certainly not unique to Folsom archaeology.

The record for recently excavated Folsom sites is more clearly documented but remains plagued by ambiguous and disparate lines of evidence. Table 8.1 presents a compilation of proposed hearth features from Folsom contexts. By our estimate, a minimum of twenty-six possible hearth features have been identified. Although this is a fairly large number considering the number of Folsom campsites that have been excavated, in only a few cases do the authors report the presence of a hearth or hearths with confidence (e.g., Dibble and Lorrain 1968; Frison 1982, 1984; Hofman 1995). Folsom hearths are often indicated by either very shallow charcoal-stained pits or surface stains of charcoal, such as those reported from Agate Basin (Frison 1982) and Rattlesnake Pass (Smith and McNees 1990). In other cases they are identified as clusters of burned artifacts, bone, or both, such as those at Bobtail Wolf (Root 2000) and Cattle Guard (Jodry 1999; Jodry and Stanford 1992). Ash is rare, only reported from Waugh (Hofman 1995) and Bonfire Shelter (Dibble and Lorrain 1968). Oxidation is only reported for the Hanson site in association with numerous possible hearth features (Frison

Table 8.1. Hearths Reported from Folsom Contexts.

Site (Locality)	n hearths	Size (cm)	Pit Depth (cm)	Burned Artifacts or Bone	Oxidation	Charcoal	Ash	References
Agate Basin (Area 2)	1	≈30 (diam.)	8	?	N	N	N	Frison 1982:39–45
Agate Basin (Area 2)	1 poss.	?	na	?	N	N	N	Frison 1982:39–45
Agate Basin (Area 3, Lower Folsom Comp)	1	≈75 (diam.)	6	?	N	Very Little	N	Frison 1982:71
Agate Basin, Area 3 (Upper Folsom Comp)	1	≈75 (diam.)	13.1	Y	N	N	N	Frison 1982:74
Bobtail Wolf (Block 2, Late Folsom Comp)	3 poss.	?	na	Y	N	N	N	Root 2000:120
Bobtail Wolf (Block 4, 2000:183–184 Late Folsom Comp)	1 poss.	?	na	Y	N	N	N	Root, MacDonald, and Emerson
Bobtail Wolf (Block 6, Early Folsom Comp)	1 poss.	?	na	Y	N	N	N	Root and Emerson 2000:213
Big Black (Block 2, Late Folsom Comp)	1 poss.	?	na	Y	N	N	N	William 2000:246
Big Black (Block 2, Early Folsom Comp)	1 poss.	65 × 40	na	N	N	N	N	William 2000:145–149
Bonfire Shelter	1	≈60 (length)	<2	?	?	Y	Y	Dibble and Lorrain 1968:30–33
Carter/Kerr-McGee	1	65 × 83	6	Y	N	Y	N	Frison 1984:300
Hanson	Many poss.	?	?	Y	Y	Little	N	Frison and Bradley 1980:9–10

continued on next page

Table 8.1—continued

Site (Locality)	n hearths	Size (cm)	Pit Depth (cm)	Burned Artifacts or Bone	Oxidation	Charcoal	Ash	References
Indian Creek (Upstream Local)	1	?	?	N	N	Y	N	Davis and Greiser 1992:266
Lindenmeier	2	?	?	?	?	?	?	Wilmsen and Roberts 1984:60
Mountaineer	1 poss.	55–60 (diam.)	10	N	N	Y	N	Stiger 2006:325
Mountaineer	1 poss.	≈50–60 (diam.)	?	Y	N	?	N	Stiger 2006:324
Rattlesnake Pass	1	≈60 (diam.)	na	Y	N	Y	N	Smith and McNees 1990:275–276
Rattlesnake Pass	1	≈300 × 100	na	?	N	Y	N	Smith and McNees 1990:275–278
Stewart's Cattleguard Stanford 1992	4–7	?	na	Y	N	N	N	Jodry 1999:262–324; Jodry and
Waugh	1	60 × 100	N	N	?	Y	Y	Hofman 1995:425–428

and Bradley 1980:9–10) and for Rattlesnake Pass (Smith and McNees 1990:275–276) and may be indicated by the "baked sediment" and "fire-scorched earth" reported for hearths from Waugh and Bonfire, respectively (Hofman 1995:425; Dibble and Lorrain 1968:33). Finally, only one hearth feature ringed with stones has been reported, the "interior hearth" at Mountaineer (Stiger 2006). At this site, the Folsom occupation occurs on a weathered bedrock surface littered with large stones, and it is unclear that the proposed hearth stones truly served that purpose (Stiger 2006:figure 9).

Based on this brief survey of Folsom hearth data, we agree with Hofman (1995:429) that Folsom hearths were most likely surface features, and, like Jodry and Stanford (1992:155), we suggest that Folsom hearths are unlikely to be preserved in many open-air contexts because ash and charcoal are easily dispersed by wind and water. If fire features oxidize underlying sediments, then reddening should be preserved in uneroded contexts, but given the rarity of oxidation, even this more reliable indicator of burning cannot be depended upon. Unfortunately, we suspect that if Folsom hearths were placed under the same scrutiny as many claims for the controlled use of fire from the lower Paleolithic (e.g., Weiner et al. 1998), very few cases would stand up to muster. This is not because we believe Folsom people did not make and use hearths; we accept as a foregone conclusion that Folsom hunter-gatherers were masterful fire producers and users. Nor are we arguing that many of the hearths that have been reported are not cultural fire features. Instead, we suggest that in many cases the identification of Folsom hearth features may, by necessity, have to rely on less reliable indicators of burning, such as the spatial clustering of burned cultural materials and associated artifact distributions. While natural post-occupational burning, as well as cleaning and dumping of hearth contents potentially complicate the identification of hearth features through spatial data, the very nature of the Folsom archaeological record suggests that reliance on clear visual evidence encountered during excavation (e.g., soil oxidization and stone features) is not sufficient. Quite simply, it seems logical to assume that Folsom peoples utilized hearths but that evidence attesting to their use is less readily identifiable than in other archaeological contexts.

After a brief description of the Folsom deposits at Barger Gulch, Locality B, we discuss methods employed to identify the presence of a hearth at the site. Next, we compare the composition of the lithic assemblages associated and not associated with the hearth. The final series of analyses looks at fine-grained spatial patterns in the hearth area aimed primarily at exploring whether the hearth was situated in an inside or an outside space. Our goals are to provide detailed spatial analysis and interpretation of a single Folsom hearth and its related activity areas to provide insight into the spatial organization of Folsom residential site occupations, to provide a methodological framework for identifying hearth features applicable to other Folsom archaeological contexts, and to establish a record of quantitatively defined hearth features suitable for multi-site and multi-feature comparison.

BARGER GULCH, LOCALITY B

The Barger Gulch site includes a series of archaeological localities adjacent to Barger Gulch, a perennial, spring-fed southern tributary of the Colorado River in Middle Park, Colorado (Surovell et al. 2003; Waguespack et al. 2002). We have identified eight Paleoindian localities in the northern portion of the drainage near its confluence with the Colorado. In 1988, Naze (1994) investigated an additional Folsom occupation at the Crying Woman site, approximately 3.5 km upstream from our work. The high density of Paleoindian archaeology associated with Barger Gulch is mimicked by the Middle Park region as a whole, where more than seventy-five Paleoindian sites or localities are known (Naze 1986; Kornfeld 1998, personal communication; Kornfeld and Frison 2000).

Locality B of the Barger Gulch site (herein referred to as BGB) is a shallowly buried Folsom campsite situated on a high eastern terrace of Barger Gulch, approximately 30 m above current stream level at an elevation of 2,323 m (7,620 ft) above sea level. Throughout the 2002 field season we excavated a total of 51 m^2, including a 40 m^2 contiguous excavation block. The excavated lithic assemblage totals 19,658 artifacts, including over 150 flake tools, 35 cores and core fragments, 14 bifaces, 8 preforms, 40 channel flakes, and 13 Folsom projectile points. The projectile point assemblage is dominated by basal fragments, with only one tip recovered to date. The assemblage is dominated by local Troublesome Formation Chert (a.k.a. Kremmling Chert), representing 98.6 percent of all items. Nonlocal raw materials include Trout Creek Chert available approximately 90 km to the south and Black Forest Petrified Wood, outcropping approximately 150 km to the southeast.

The cultural materials vary in depth from surface exposure to approximately 75 cm beneath the surface, and because the site sits on a relative topographic high, the archaeological deposits have likely never been deeply buried. Roots, rootlets, and krotovinas are regular occurrences in the deposits, and considerable vertical artifact dispersal is present. The occupation surface, identified by a peak in vertical artifact densities, has been dispersed in places as much as 40 cm upward and 30 cm downward (Surovell et al. 2005). Therefore, some post-depositional artifact movement is evident, and by no means would we consider the cultural deposits a "living floor."

Villa (1982:282) has shown that vertical dispersal of artifacts with relatively little horizontal displacement is possible, and numerous patterns and analyses indicate that this is the case at BGB. For example, at the scale of individual excavation units, the assemblage is statistically identical through vertical space with respect to the proportion of lithic artifacts exhibiting burning, platforms, and cortex (Surovell et al. 2000). Also, across all excavation units, the number of artifacts found in upper excavation levels positively correlates with the number of artifacts from lower levels (Surovell et al. 2003; Waguespack et al. 2002). When combined with several vertical artifact refits cross-cutting stratigraphic levels, it is clear that artifacts from upper levels are derived from lower levels, and because

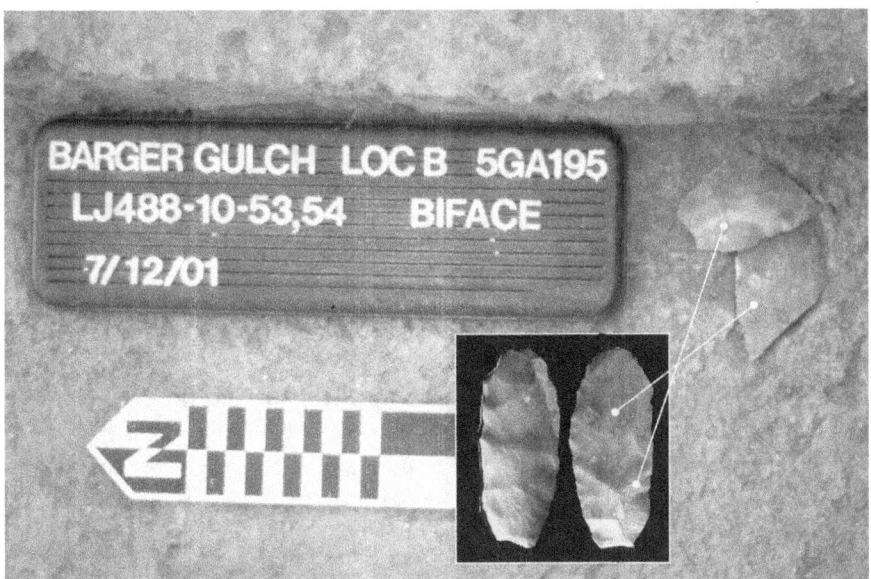

8.1. Two conjoining biface fragments in situ within the main excavation block. Inset shows both faces of the complete, conjoined biface. Inset is not shown to scale.

these patterns are detectable at the scale of excavation units, horizontal movement associated with vertical dispersal was likely on the scale of centimeters or decimeters rather than meters. Many additional spatial pattterns suggest that spatial relations remain intact. For example, we have recovered a tightly constrained cluster of nonlocal raw material related to a projectile point manufacture event (see Figure 8.11). This cluster includes more than 200 artifacts, of which more than 95 percent are smaller than 1 cm in maximum length. These tiny marginal pressure flakes should be very susceptible to lateral post-depositional movement, and yet they appear to have remained in place. Figure 8.1 shows two conjoining biface fragments recovered lying literally one on top of another, presumably how they were left when the site was abandoned.

In addition, by comparison of the lithic assemblage from BGB to Folsom assemblages from Agate Basin, Carter/Kerr-McGee, and Krmpotich, Surovell (2003) has shown that a single occupation is present, eliminating the possibility of an overlapping palimpsest of multiple site occupations. Based on high artifact densities, an overwhelming dominance of local raw material in the assemblage, and evidence attesting to the manufacture, use, resharpening, and discard of chipped-stone tools, we have argued that the site represents a long-term occupation, one that likely persisted for a period of multiple weeks to three months (Surovell 2003; Surovell et al. 2003; Waguespack et al. 2002). Although we have yet to recover any direct seasonality indicators, we have suggested that BGB represents a cold-season occupation where site inhabitants took advantage of the congruence of lithic raw material, water, fuel, and high densities of large ungulates wintering in the valley bottom (Surovell et al. 2003; Waguespack et al. 2002). Because the site appears to represent a single occupation, has excellent spatial integrity, and has produced large numbers of artifacts, it provides an excellent opportunity to examine the organization of Folsom spatial behavior at a very fine scale.

IDENTIFYING THE HEARTH

While there is clear evidence of burned cultural materials in the site assemblage, during excavations at BGB no unambiguous hearth features were identified. Burned lithics are found in virtually every excavation unit, flecks of charcoal are scattered throughout the deposits, and calcined bone fragments have been recovered. In the southeastern portion of our excavations, we have encountered somewhat linear concentrations of charcoal that we suspect represent burned roots from natural fires and occasional small, round clasts of what appear to be oxidized sediments. Based on temporal clustering in the population of charcoal radiocarbon dates (n=13), we have identified at least five natural burn events dating between 9,420 ± 50 and 6,880 ± 50 radiocarbon years before present (RCYBP) that passed over or near the excavation area following the Folsom occupation (Surovell et al. 2003). Given the number of natural burn events recorded in the deposits, the interpretation of the spatial distribution of burned material is by no means straightforward, but we nonetheless remain confident in our identification of at least one hearth feature preserved within the excavation block. Multiple lines of evidence support this contention. The hearth is identified on the basis of the spatial congruence of Folsom-age charcoal radiocarbon dates and high counts and frequencies of burned artifacts and bone.

From our 40 m² primary excavation block, we have mapped 2,857 chipped-stone artifacts. Figure 8.2a shows the distribution of burned piece-plotted artifacts overlain on all artifacts. Although burned artifacts are scattered throughout the excavations, a cluster, approximately 1.2 m in diameter, is present at approximately N 1479.25, E 2434.25. The cluster is also apparent in the distribution of small items recovered from screening (Figure 8.2b). This "hot spot" contains the greatest densities of burned artifacts and corresponds spatially to the highest artifact densities in the site. Excavation units (screened through ⅛" mesh) within 1 m of the hearth contain between 600 and 1,500 artifacts per m². While this pattern is typical of a hearth-centered activity area, whereby cultural debris becomes concentrated in work areas adjacent to hearth features, it could also be argued that more burned artifacts are present in this area simply because more artifacts are present. In other words, if the concentration of burned materials is a product of natural burn events, which resulted in a consistent proportion of all artifacts exhibiting signs of heat exposure, then units with more artifacts will necessarily contain greater numbers of burned artifacts. This possibility can be addressed

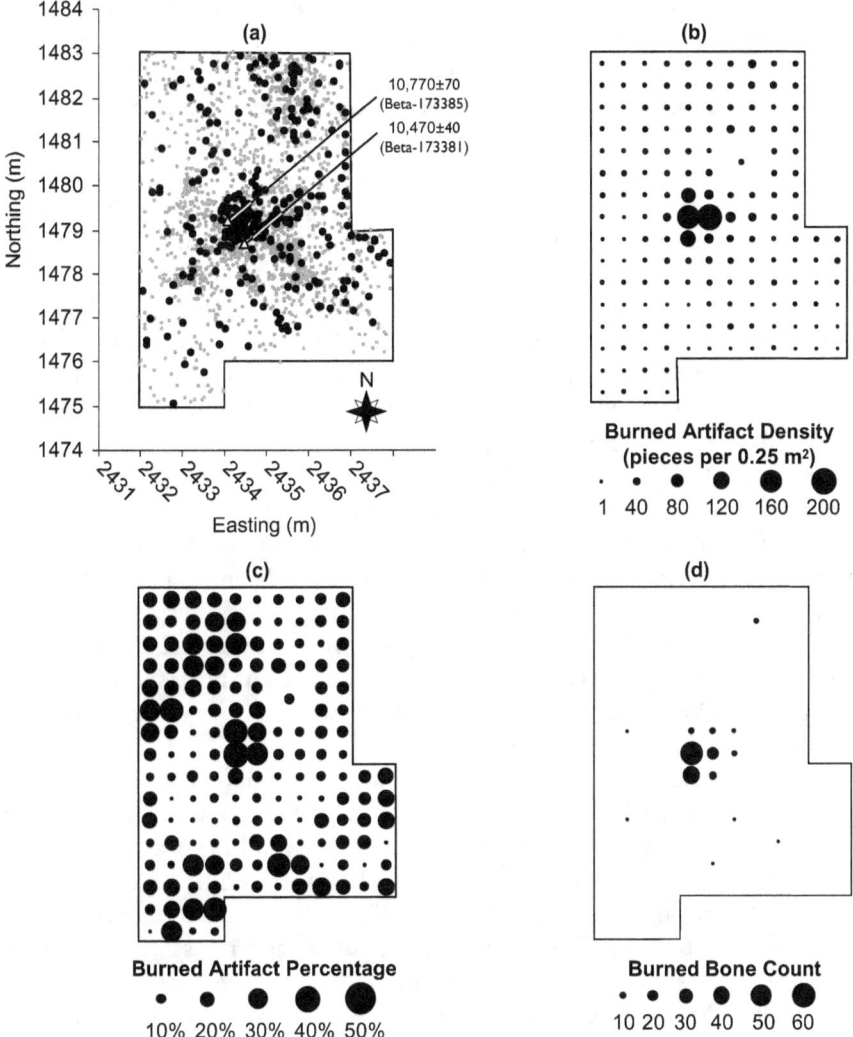

8.2. Distributions of burned materials from main excavation block of Barger Gulch, Locality B: (a) piece-plotted burned artifacts (black) mapped overlaid on all piece-plotted artifacts (gray). The positions of two charcoal samples yielding Folsom-aged radiocarbon dates are shown as white triangles. (b) Burned artifact density for all artifacts, including screen items by excavation unit or quad. (c) Percentage of burned artifacts for all artifacts by excavation unit or quad. (d) Counts of burned bone fragments by excavation unit or quad.

through the use of burn percentages as opposed to counts. If the concentration is a result of cultural burning, then the proposed hearth area should also contain relatively high percentages of burned artifacts.

When we look at percentages of burned artifacts across the excavation block, two patterns emerge (Figure 8.2c). First, the greatest burning percentages correspond exactly to our proposed hearth area. Second, immediately adjacent to the proposed hearth area, burn percentages are extremely low, but they increase in all directions in more distant areas. The zone of relatively low burn percentages takes on an oval shape, trending from southwest to northeast with dimensions of roughly 4 × 3 m. Given its regularity we argue that it is not likely to have been produced by differential fuel loads or heat intensities from natural fires.

Two additional lines of evidence provide support for the presence of a hearth in this area. Two charcoal samples recovered from the hearth area produced Folsom-age radiocarbon dates (10,470 ± 40 [Beta-173381] and 10,770 ± 70 [Beta-173385] RCYBP) (Figure 8.2a). Second, the highest counts of burned bone are also clustered within the proposed hearth area (Figure 8.2d). We are unable to estimate burned bone percentages because we have recovered very few unburned pieces of bone. However, we have argued elsewhere (Surovell et al. 2003; Waguespack et al. 2002) that enhancement in apatite crystallinity resulting from burning (Person et al. 1996; Shipman, Foster, and Schoeninger 1984; Stiner et al. 1995; Surovell and Stiner 2001) was the primary process responsible for the preservation of most of the bone from the site. If we are correct, then the burn event(s) recorded by burned bone most likely occurred during or shortly after the occupation, prior to the inferred loss of most of the faunal assemblage by mineral dissolution, subaerial weathering, or both.

Using multiple independent lines of evidence, we have identified the presence of a hearth at BGB based solely on post-excavation spatial analysis. During excavation we did not observe a pit, oxidation, or ash in this area. Dispersed flecks of charcoal were present, but this is true of the entire excavation area. Admittedly, spatially constrained dumping of hearth contents could also produce these patterns, but, as is shown later, many spatial patterns associated with the BGB hearth are similar to patterns recognized for hearth-centered activity areas from Paleolithic contexts. Perhaps the best verification of these patterns and interpretations will be replication of them from other Folsom contexts.

HEARTH-CENTERED USE OF SPACE, PART I: ARTIFACT REPRESENTATION

If spatial variation in the density of lithic materials is in part a reflection of people preferentially organizing their activities around sources of heat and light, we would expect artifact densities in hearth-centered activity areas to be higher than in areas more distant from hearth features. In this section, we first compare artifact densities by artifact type (e.g., debitage, tools, cores, points and performs, and bifaces) for zones associated and not associated with the hearth based on relative excavation areas. We then compare relative frequencies of artifact types for these two areas to determine if certain artifact classes are preferentially discarded in association with the hearth.

To perform these analyses, it is first necessary to define the hearth activity space. To do so, we rely primarily on visual inspection, a somewhat questionable technique but one that has proved useful for identifying coarse spatial patterns (Gregg, Kintigh, and Whallon 1991; Rigaud and Simek 1991). We then verify the "reality" of visually identified clusters using a simple algorithm similar to that used in nearest neighbor analysis (Carr 1984; Whallon 1973, 1974). From Figure 8.3a, two clusters of relatively high artifact densities are present within the excavation block. One of these clusters, in the center of the block, is associated with the hearth, and the second cluster is located in the northeastern portion of the block. We define the hearth activity space as a circle, with a radius of 1.93 m centered on the point E 2434.38, N 1479.00. This circle encompasses the majority of the hearth-associated cluster (Figure 8.3a).

Although numerous clustering techniques are available for partitioning point scatters into groups (e.g., Carr 1984; Koetje 1987; Simek 1984; Whallon 1984), the problem we face differs from the goals of traditional cluster analysis. As opposed to trying to define independently derived artifact clusters, we are instead attempting to define a cluster related to a particular point in space, the center of the hearth. A simple algorithm using inter-artifact distances was developed. The algorithm finds the total chain or web of artifacts lying within a particular distance of each other, beginning with the artifact lying closest to the center of the hearth (E 2434.25, N 1479.25). For example, if the inter-artifact distance is set to 12 cm, the program begins by finding all artifacts within a 12 cm distance of the artifact closest to the hearth center. It then finds all artifacts within 12 cm of those artifacts initially identified. This process is continued until no more artifacts can be added to the cluster. By plotting the inter-artifact distance versus total number of artifacts captured in the cluster, inflection points in the graph, where the slope of the curve dramatically drops, can be used to identify clusters of artifacts relatively isolated in space. If very few artifacts are added to the cluster when the maximum inter-artifact distance is increased, the cluster is more likely to be a true cluster rather than an artifact of the analysis, since a substantial spatial gap likely exists between the captured point scatter and the remaining points. A similar method for identifying good cluster solutions is used in K-means cluster analysis (e.g., Jodry 1999; Koetje 1987; Simek 1984).

When this algorithm is applied to the lithic scatter within the BGB excavation block, five inflection points are present in the curve relating inter-artifact distance to the number of artifacts in the cluster (Figure 8.3b). The cluster defined by a 14 cm inter-artifact distance corresponds well with that defined by visual inspection, although it extends slightly farther to the southeast (Figure 8.3c). It also excludes a number of artifacts in the northern and southern portions of our circular hearth-associated area. Nonetheless, the general correspondence of the two areas suggests that the area we have subjectively defined provides a reasonable approximation of the hearth-associated space.

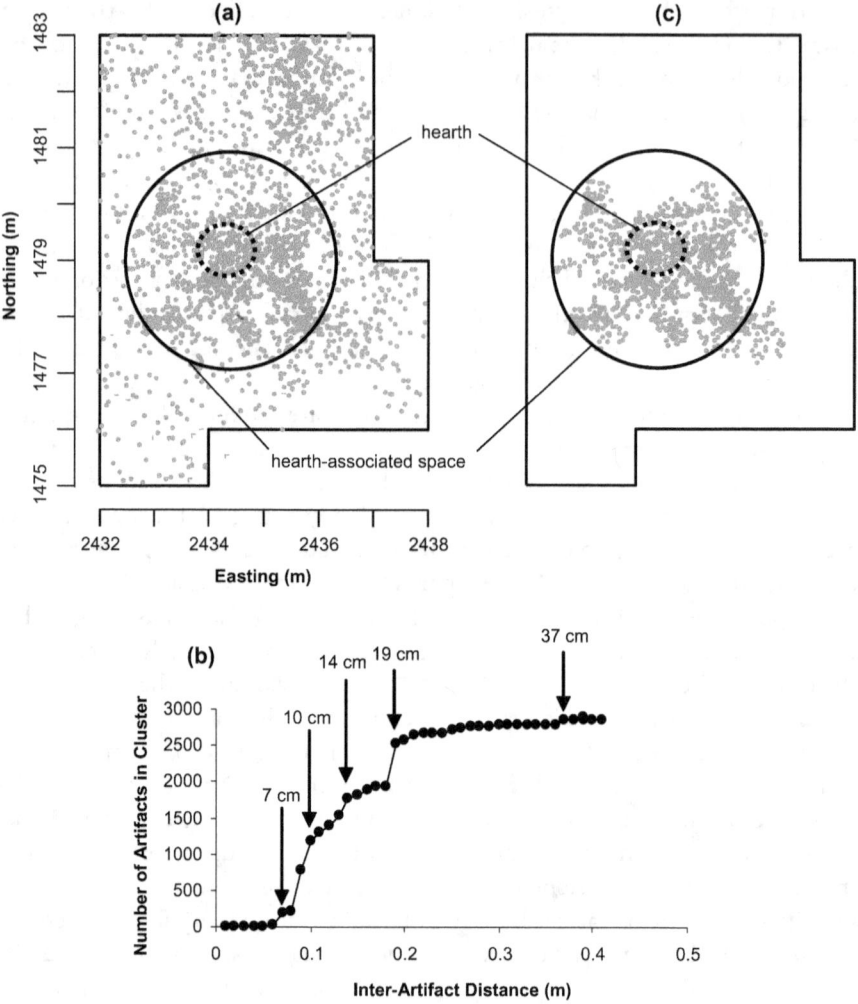

8.3. (a) Plan map of excavation block showing the position of the hearth and the spatial area defined by visual inspection as in association with the hearth. (b) Maximum inter-artifact distance versus the number of artifacts included within the defined hearth-centered cluster. Five inflection points in the graph, marked by arrows, represent best clustering solutions. (c) Plan map of excavation block showing correspondence between the defined hearth-associated space and the hearth-centered cluster defined using a 14 cm maximum inter-artifact distance.

The hearth-associated space encompasses 11.7 m^2, and the non-hearth-associated space includes 28.3 m^2. Based on excavation area alone, it is expected, therefore, that 29.3 percent of artifacts will be associated with the hearth, and 70.7 percent of artifacts will be outside the hearth area. Table 8.2 shows counts of piece-plotted artifacts for each spatial unit.

Table 8.2. Chi-Square Test Comparing Artifact Type Counts for Areas Associated and Not Associated with the Hearth Based on Relative Excavation Areas.

Artifact Type	Hearth-Associated Obs (Exp)		Not Hearth-Associated Obs (Exp)		Sum
Debitage	**1,689**	(783.7)*	990	(1895.3)*	2,679
Flake tools	**66**	(33.1)*	47	(79.9)*	113
Cores	8	(8.8)	22	(21.2)	30
Points and preforms	7	(4.1)	7	(9.9)	14
Bifaces	**11**	(5.3)*	7	(12.7)*	18
Sum	1,781		1,073		2,854

$\chi^2 = 1530.75$, df = 4, p << 0.001

Notes: Expected values calculated on the basis of relative excavation areas.
* Statistically significant deviation from the expected value following Everitt (1977:46–48). Values in bold face are those where a particular artifact class is overrepresented.

Artifact distributions are highly nonrandom, providing strong support for the presence of a hearth-centered activity area ($\chi^2 = 1536.2$, df = 4, p<<0.001). Contrary to expectations, 62.4 percent of piece-plotted artifacts are located *within* the hearth-associated space. By calculating adjusted standardized residuals, it is possible to identify which cells deviate significantly from their expected values (Everitt 1977:46–48). According to this analysis, all artifact classes are significantly overrepresented in the hearth area, with the exception of cores and projectile points–preforms (Table 8.2). Observed core frequencies almost perfectly match their expected frequencies. Points and preforms are present in greater frequencies than expected, but this difference is not statistically significant.

To directly compare the composition of lithic assemblages in the hearth area with those outside the hearth area, the analysis was repeated, but with expected values calculated based on the relative frequencies of artifacts in each area. Table 8.3 shows the observed and expected artifact counts for areas inside and outside the hearth-centered activity area. Artifact type frequencies differ significantly ($\chi^2 = 18.5$, df = 4, p = 0.001). Two artifact classes differ significantly from their expected values, debitage and cores (Table 8.3). Relative to other artifact classes, debitage is slightly overrepresented in the hearth-centered activity area, while cores are extremely underrepresented.

From these two analyses, one pattern is repeated—cores break from the trends defined by other artifact classes. Based on excavation area, they are present in their expected frequencies in the hearth area, but based on total artifact counts, they are dramatically underrepresented. This is particularly intriguing considering that debitage, a product of core reduction, is overrepresented. The discrepancy between cores and debitage could suggest that although cores were preferentially reduced in the hearth area, they were rarely discarded there. However, cores are not the only producers of debitage. Much of this debitage could have been produced by the reduction of bifaces as well, which are also overrepresented. This situation raises the possibility that there are relatively few cores compared

Table 8.3. Chi-Square Test Comparing Artifact Type Counts for Areas Associated and Not Associated with the Hearth Based on Artifact Counts.

Artifact Type	Hearth-Associated Obs (Exp)		Not Hearth-Associated Obs (Exp)		Sum
Debitage	**1,689**	(1671.8)*	990	(1007.2)*	2,679
Flake tools	66	(70.5)	47	(42.5)	113
Cores	8	(18.7)*	22	**(11.3)***	30
Points and preforms	7	(8.7)	7	(5.3)	14
Bifaces	11	(11.2)	7	(6.8)	18
Sum	1,781		1,073		2,854

$\chi^2 = 18.5$, df = 4, p = 0.001

Notes: Expected values calculated on the basis of relative artifact counts.
* Statistically significant deviation from the expected value following Everitt (1977:46–48). Values in bold face are those where a particular artifact class is overrepresented.

to flakes in the hearth zone because most of the hearth-related reduction was bifacial. Although debitage is also produced by tool edge maintenance, we are relying solely on piece-plotted artifacts (predominately pieces larger than 1 cm in maximum dimension), so we are confident that the majority of debitage included in the analysis was the product of primary reduction.

To distinguish between these possibilities, the debitage assemblage was apportioned into three categories: bifacial thinning flakes, core reduction flakes, and indeterminate flakes (those that could not be confidently assigned to either of the other two categories). If cores were discarded where they were reduced, then cores and core reduction flakes should show similar distributions. If cores were secondarily discarded, their distributions should be incongruent.

In Table 8.4 we present two chi-square tests comparing the frequencies of cores and core reduction flakes and bifaces (including points and preforms) and bifacial thinning flakes (including channel flakes). In this analysis cores are again underrepresented in the hearth area, while core reduction flakes are overrepresented. These differences are highly significant ($\chi^2 = 12.93$, df = 1, p = 0.0003). In contrast, bifaces and bifacial thinning flakes do not show significantly different distributions ($\chi^2 = 1.10$, df = 1, p = 0.294). This analysis demonstrates that although cores were commonly reduced in the hearth area, they were predominately discarded, stored in a different location, or both. In fact, the majority of the cores recovered cluster together in the northeastern portion of the excavation block (Figure 8.4). Four sets of conjoined core fragments link core specimens from the hearth area to this northeast core cluster (Figure 8.4), establishing the movement of cores between these two areas.

Numerous studies have shown that cleaning disproportionately affects large items (Bartram, Kroll, and Bunn 1991; Binford 1978; O'Connell 1987; Schiffer 1987; Simms 1988; Walters 1988), as small, unobtrusive items tend to remain in their location of initial discard while large items are often removed from work areas through deliberate cleaning. Cores are on average the largest artifact class

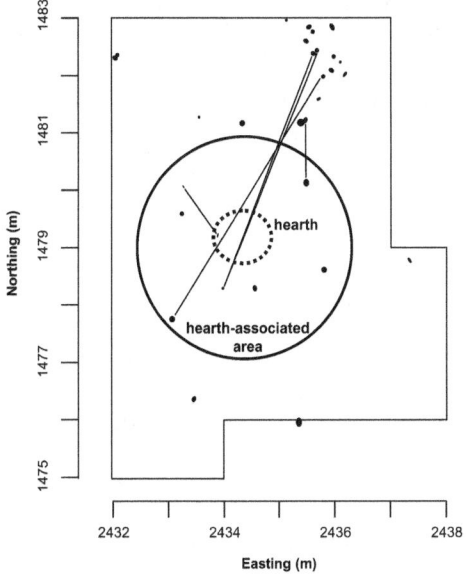

8.4. *Map of cores and core fragments recovered from primary excavation area. Lines connect conjoining core fragments.*

at Barger Gulch, which raises the question of whether cores have been removed from the hearth area simply because they are large artifacts more susceptible to cleaning activities. To test this hypothesis, the piece-plotted assemblage, excluding cores, was divided into five size classes for each spatial area (Table 8.5) to determine if other large-sized artifacts are also underrepresented in the hearth area.

A chi-square test shows no significant difference in the distribution of artifact size between the hearth and non-hearth areas ($\chi^2 = 5.527$, df = 4, p = 0.237). Therefore, among large artifacts, cores alone are found at higher proportions in the non-hearth-associated space. This provides no support for the cleaning hypothesis, implying that cores were removed from the hearth zone for some other reason.

There are numerous possible explanations for the removal of cores from the hearth area. By their very nature, cores have relatively long use lives and therefore would not necessarily be expected to be discarded at their use location (Bamforth and Becker 2000). A single core, for example, could be reduced at various locations within a site and be discarded at any of its possible use locations. However, the consideration that cores do appear to have been frequently reduced in the hearth vicinity, yet were deposited elsewhere implies that usable cores were removed from the hearth area and stored in a central location. If so, it would be expected that cores outside the hearth zone would be on average larger than those in the hearth area and, furthermore, that they should be spatially clustered. We have already shown that cores in our excavation block do show a distinctly clustered distribution, with fifteen of the thirty cores from the excavation block occurring within an area of roughly 2 m² in the northeastern corner (Figure 8.4). Spatial patterns of core mass also support the second prediction. Cores not associated with the hearth average 149 g in mass, while those within the hearth zone average 97 g. This difference is highly significant ($t = 26.6$, df = 28, two-tailed p<<0.001).

The preceding analysis identifies clear differences between the artifact assemblage associated with the hearth and the assemblage from the remainder

Table 8.4. Chi-Square Tests comparing (1) Counts of Cores and Core Reduction Flakes and (2) Counts of Bifaces and Bifacial Thinning Flakes for the Areas Associated and Not Associated with the Hearth.

Artifact Type	Hearth-Associated Obs (Exp)	Not Hearth-Associated Obs (Exp)	Sum	χ^2	p
Cores	8 (17.6)	22 (12.4)	30		
Core reduction flakes	**691 (681.4)**	472 (481.6)	1,163		
Sum	699 494	1,193		12.93	0.0003
Bifaces, pts, and prefs	18 (20.7)	14 (11.3)	32		
BF thinning flakes*	**172 (169.3)**	90 (92.7)	262		
Sum	190	104	294	1.10	0.294

Notes: Expected values calculated on the basis of relative artifact counts.
* Includes channel flakes. Values in bold face are those where a particular artifact class is overrepresented. In the upper test, all deviations from expected values are significant. In the lower test, none of the deviations is significant.

Table 8.5. Chi-Square Test Comparing Artifact Size Class Counts for Areas Associated and Not Associated with the Hearth.

Artifact Size Class	Hearth-Associated Obs (Exp)	Not Hearth-Associated Obs (Exp)	Sum
>1 and ≤2.5 cm	**570 (556.4)**	322 (335.7)	892
>2.5 and ≤4 cm	167 (180.9)	**123 (109.1)**	290
>4 and ≤5.5 cm	**39 (36.2)**	19 (21.8)	58
>5.5 and ≤7 cm	8 (10)	**8 (6)**	16
> 7 cm	5 (5.6)	4 (3.4)	9
Sum	789	476	2,854

$\chi^2 = 5.527$, df = 4, p = 0.237

Notes: Expected values calculated on the basis of relative artifact counts. Values in bold face are those where a particular artifact class is overrepresented. None of the deviations from expected values is significant.

of the excavation area. Based on excavation area, all artifact classes, except cores and projectile points and preforms, are present in greater numbers than expected in the hearth area. Relative to other artifact classes, debitage is overrepresented and cores are extremely underrepresented in the hearth area. The spatial discrepancy between cores and the debitage produced through core reduction indicates that storage-discard of usable raw material nodules was spatially segregated from the area of tool production.

HEARTH-CENTERED USE OF SPACE, PART II: INSIDE OR OUTSIDE

In this section we focus on fine-grained spatial patterns only within the hearth-associated zone. As we have defined it, the hearth area includes 1,538 piece-plotted artifacts. Including screen counts from 50 × 50 cm quadrants, the total hearth-related assemblage includes approximately 8,300 artifacts.

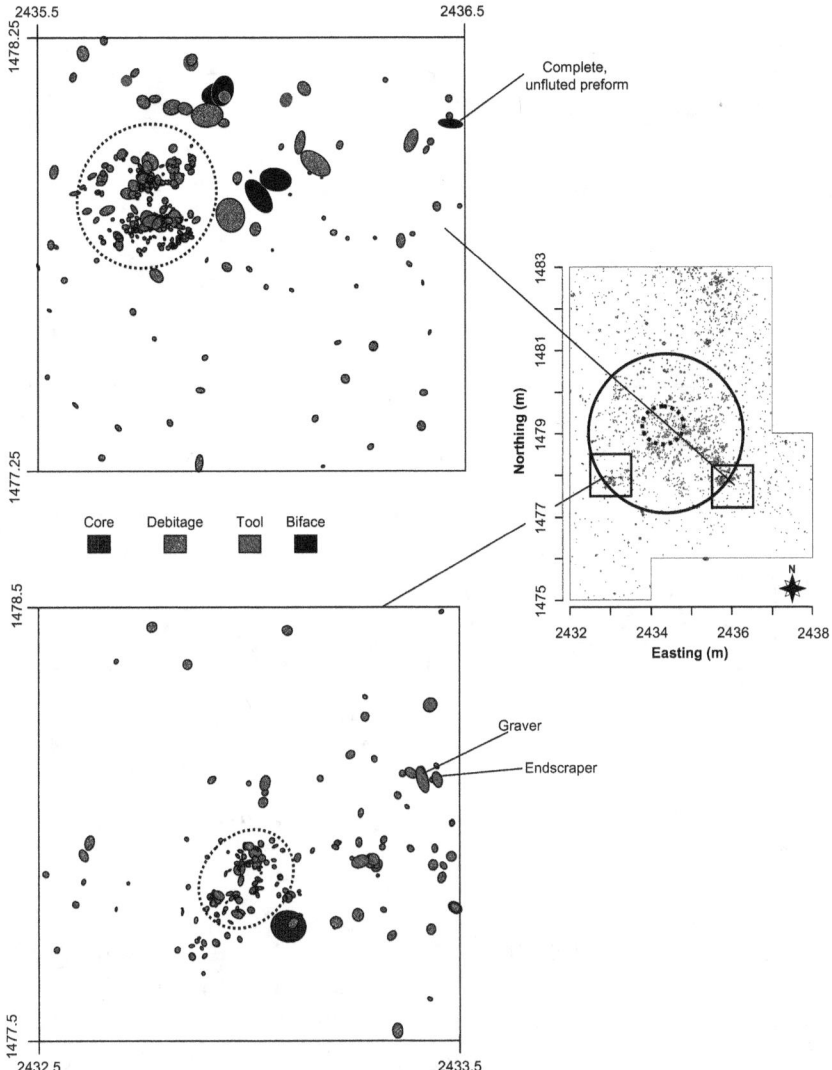

8.5. Plan maps of two bifurcated flake concentrations southeast (top) and southwest (bottom) of the hearth.

General Spatial Patterns

As is evident in Figure 8.3, artifacts are not concentrically distributed around the hearth; instead, they form a distinctive "X"-like pattern. The northern and eastern boundaries of the X-shaped cluster are somewhat smooth and curvilinear, but the southern and eastern boundaries are not (Figure 8.3c). The southeastern and southwestern extremes of the cluster are marked by discrete and bifurcated flake concentrations (Figure 8.5).

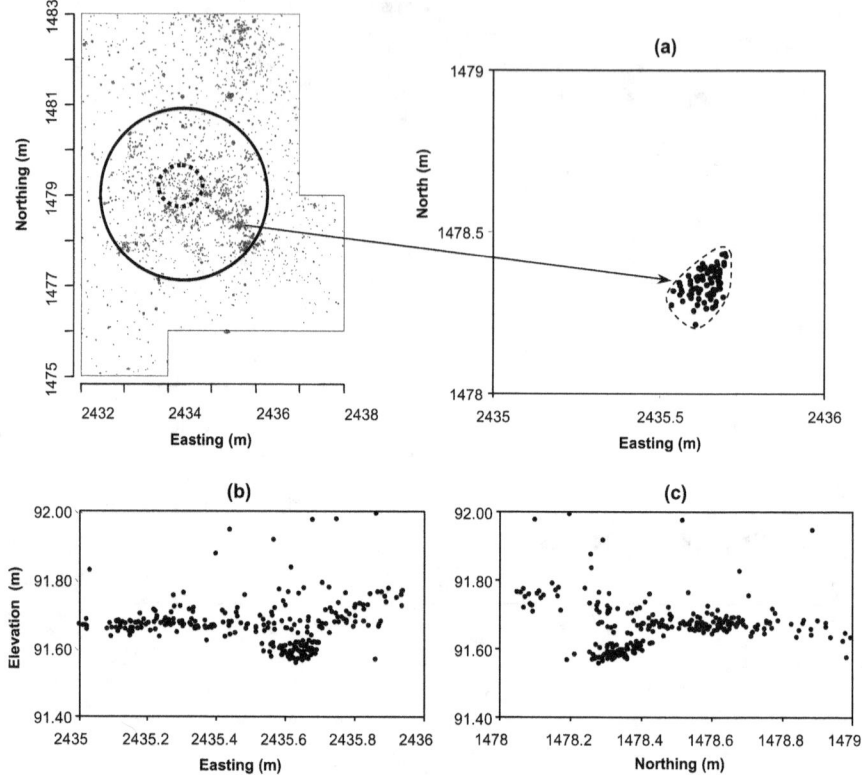

8.6. Maps of pit feature located to the southeast of the hearth. (a) Plan map. (b) and (c) Cross-sectional back plots.

These clusters fall on the boundary of the hearth zone, each lying approximately 2 m from the hearth center. The flake concentrations are roughly 20–25 cm in diameter, and each contains more than 400 artifacts. We do not know if these concentrations represent primary knapping debris, secondary dumping, or some other process, but given their similar configurations and spatial positions we suspect they were formed by a common process. This pattern may be repeated at the Area 2 Folsom component of the Agate Basin site, where two concentrations of debitage were mapped roughly 1.8 m from the center of a hearth (Frison 1982:figure 2.17). Numerous flake concentrations were also recovered at Bobtail Wolf and are generally interpreted to represent primary knapping debris (Root 2000:101–115).

A third debitage concentration in the hearth zone was recovered from what appears to be a shallow pit (Figure 8.6). The feature was undetectable geomorphologically, as the sediment filling the feature was indistinguishable from surrounding deposits. At the base of the feature, however, was a thin film of clay,

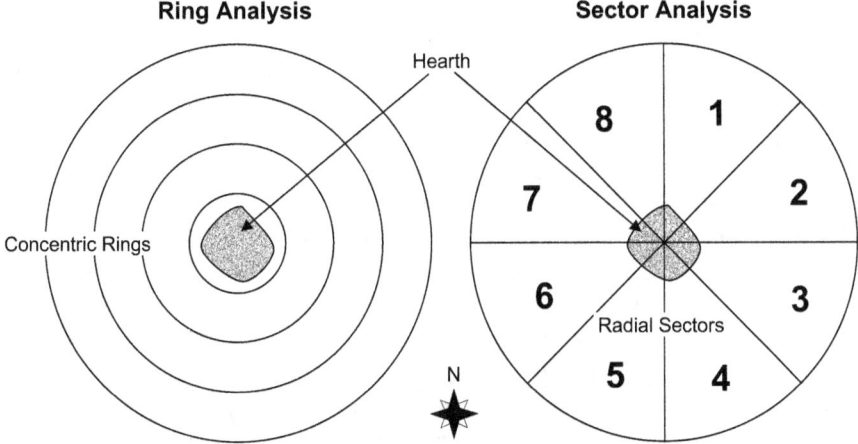

8.7. *Schematic representation of divisions of space used in ring and sector analysis.*

indicating that prior to being filled, standing water was present in the depression, causing clays to settle downward. The depression was filled with 434 unmodified flakes, 433 of Troublesome Formation Chert (a.k.a. Kremmling Chert) and 1 of Trout Creek Chert. Spatially reconstructed using backplots of artifacts, it is oblong in shape, measuring approximately 30 cm in length, 16 cm in width, and 7 cm in depth. The long axis is oriented southwest to northeast and is vertically separated from the overlying occupation surface by approximately 5 cm of sterile sediment. While caches of artifacts for later retrieval are suggested for other Folsom sites (e.g., Hofman, Amick, and Rose 1990), such features are typically associated with large usable flake blanks, tools, or bifaces. A cache presents an unlikely interpretation given the local availability of lithic raw material and the contents of the pit itself. Consisting of relatively small flakes (the majority are <2 cm in maximum dimension), the feature may represent a small refuse pit where debitage was deposited. It is also possible that the artifacts recovered from the pit washed in from adjacent areas, but, if so, it is difficult to explain the gap of relatively sterile deposits separating the main occupation surface with those recovered from within the pit fill.

Ring Analysis

In this and the following section, we perform a series of analyses derived from the work of Dick Stapert (Stapert 1989, 1990, 1991–1992, 2003; Stapert and Johansen 1995–1996; Stapert and Street 1997; Stapert and Terberger 1989). Stapert's approach to the spatial analysis of hearth-centered activity areas is based on polar rather than cartesian space, reflecting the observation that human behavioral activities are typically concentrically oriented around hearths. Stapert refers to the suite of methods he has developed as the "ring and sector" method, whereby hearth-centered space is divided into radial sectors and concentric rings radiating out from the hearth center (Figure 8.7). The primary application of the ring and sector method is to determine whether a hearth was enclosed within a structure.

To perform ring analysis, the number of artifacts within each concentric ring is tallied. Next, a bar graph is made of artifact counts as a function of distance from the hearth center. This analysis can be done for complete rings or, if sufficient numbers of artifacts are present, by individual sectors. The former method is limited because it assumes that hearths are centrally located within perfectly circular structures. By performing the ring analysis for individual sectors, no such assumptions are necessary. Stapert (2003:7) has found that distinct types of distributions are produced by this analysis that can be attributed to the spatial location of hearths inside or outside of structures: "For some 30 palaeolithic or mesolithic sites in Europe analysed so far, we find either diagrams with one peak or diagrams with two or three peaks. . . . Multimodal diagrams seem to be characteristic for hearths inside tents. The tent walls served as a barrier, stopping centrifugal movements. Waste material tended to accumulate against the walls during occupation, thus creating a peak in the ring diagram."

In this framework, a hearth showing a single peak in artifact counts as a function of distance is generally interpreted as an open-air hearth pattern whereby artifacts preferentially accumulate within a drop zone (akin to Binford's [1978, 1983] outside hearth model). In a bimodal distribution, the peak closest to the hearth is interpreted as a drop zone, and the more distant peak is argued to represent artifacts pushed against tent walls, what Stapert (2003:7) calls the "barrier effect." A trimodal distribution is interpreted as indicating a drop zone, tent walls, and a door dump.

To apply Stapert's method to Barger Gulch, we must first define the hearth center. In the absence of a clear feature, for simplicity we defined the center of the hearth as N1479.25, E 2434.25, the center of the southwest quadrant of the excavation unit N 1479, E 2434. This point was chosen because this particular quadrant contains both the greatest number and the greatest percentage of burned chipped stone and bone. We then divided the space surrounding the hearth into eight sectors, each 45° in width. The space surrounding the hearth was also divided into concentric rings, the width of which varies for each analysis.

Figure 8.8 shows the ring diagrams for each of the eight sectors (as shown in Figure 8.7). Interestingly, all of the ring diagrams are multimodal when viewed at various scales. The diagrams range from showing regular distributions to being fairly noisy, with two to four modes present. Some commonalities, however, exist among all the diagrams. A peak in artifact counts is invariably located near the hearth, generally at distances ranging from 0.3 to 1 m. Following Stapert and Binford (1978, 1983), these modes likely represent drop zones in association with the hearth. The near-hearth mode is followed by a trough in artifact counts, located between 0.6 and 1.2 m, and a second peak 1.3

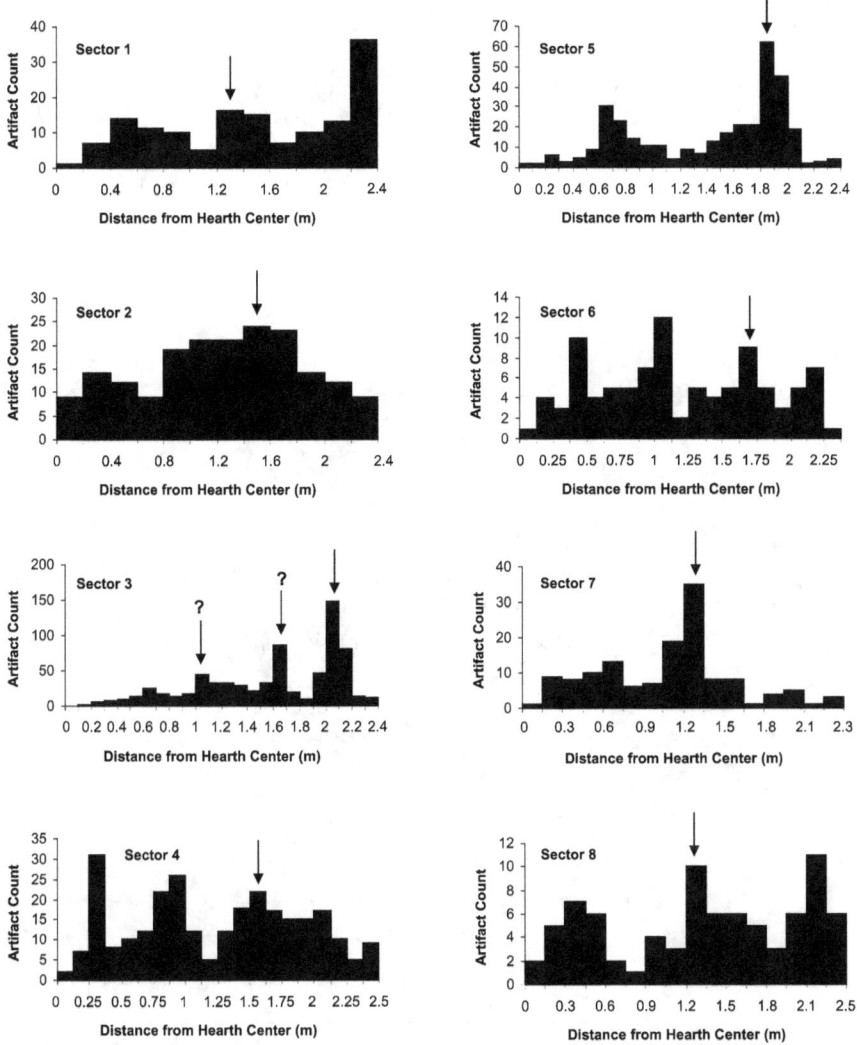

8.8. *Ring diagrams by sector for the hearth area showing artifact counts as a function of distance from the hearth. Arrows represent the postulated position of a "barrier effect," caused by artifacts pressed against the walls of a structure.*

to 1.8 m from the hearth center. The ring diagram from Sector 3 is particularly complex. This sector is characterized by the greatest number of artifacts and shows four distinct modes. Three of these modes are within 2 m of the hearth, and the fourth is at a distance of 2 to 2.1 m from the hearth center. The mode at 1.6–1.7 m is caused by the high density of artifacts within the pit feature discussed earlier (Figure 8.6), and the mode at 2–2.1 m is caused by one of the bifurcated artifact clusters (Figure 8.5).

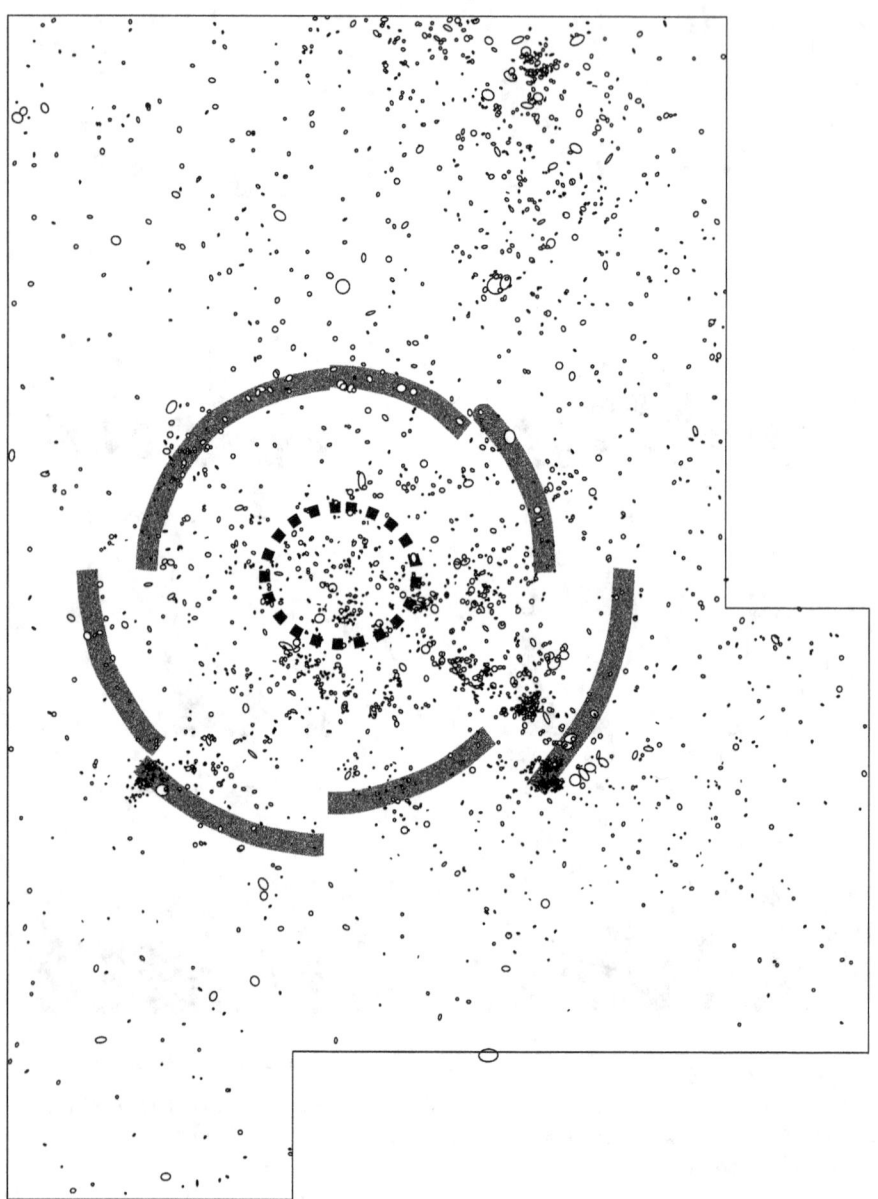

8.9. *Plan map of hypothesized barrier effect. Gray lines show reconstructed locations of possible structural walls. Dashed black line shows location of the hearth.*

If modes distant from the hearth center represent artifacts pushed against walls, Stapert's "barrier effect," then an interior hearth is suggested by the ring analysis for individual sectors. To identify the approximate location of a possible wall, for each ring diagram the first mode exceeding 1.2 m was identified (Figure

8.8). For Sector 4, the second mode exceeding 1.2 was used because the first mode is caused by the concentration of artifacts in a buried feature. By using the location of each mode, it is possible to reconstruct wall locations for a hypothetical structure (Figure 8.9). Using these estimates, the pit feature falls within the reconstructed walls.

The wall positions for the northern half (Sectors 7–8, 1–2) of the possible structure are consistently located between 1.275 and 1.5 m. On the southern half of the cluster (Sectors 3–6), the reconstructed wall positions are considerably more variable, ranging from 1.56 to 2.05 m from the hearth center. If this reconstruction is correct, the hearth sat within a semicircular structure roughly 3 × 4 m in size.

Two independent spatial patterns correlate well with the hypothesized structure. The oval of relatively low burning percentages discussed earlier is relatively congruent with the space defined by ring analysis (Figure 8.10a). Perhaps more striking is the congruence between that space and a contiguous cluster of Trout Creek Chert (Figure 8.10b). This cluster radiates outward in all directions from two excavation quads (N 1479.25 and 1479.75, E 2433.75), which contain the vast majority of Trout Creek artifacts. The cluster is skewed to primarily to the east and south (opposite of the slope of the ancient ground surface) and fills the space defined by ring analysis. We emphasize that we are not necessarily arguing for the presence of an interior hearth or a structure. Instead, we are proposing that this may have been the case. We have identified repeated spatial patterns, but only one of those, the possible "barrier effect," has any bearing on the existence of a structure. Also, in the next section we present evidence that might suggest that the hearth was located in an exterior space. We remain hopeful that our ongoing refitting analyses will shed additional light on these questions and that further excavation will reveal additional hearth-centered clusters for comparison. Although structures have been proposed for other Folsom sites (e.g., Frison and Bradley 1980; Frison 1982; Jodry 1999; Stiger 2006), the nature of the data available at this point in time is insufficient for meaningful comparison. The size of the possible structure we have identified, however, is consistent with that proposed for Area 2 of Agate Basin (Frison 1982:39–44).

Sector Analysis

Stapert has found that exterior hearths are often characterized by asymmetry in the distribution of tools, with tools concentrating on one side of the hearth, an effect he reasonably interprets to be a result of wind patterns (Stapert 1989, 1991–1992, 2003). People working around hearths typically position themselves on the upwind side to avoid smoke, and if there is a prevailing wind direction, most work will occur on one side of the hearth. Therefore, the distribution of primary refuse around an outside hearth should reflect the distribution of wind. For interior hearths, wind effects should be largely eliminated, and asymmetry associated with interior hearths is typically interpreted to represent division of behavioral activity space (Stapert 1989, 2003; Stapert and Street 1997).

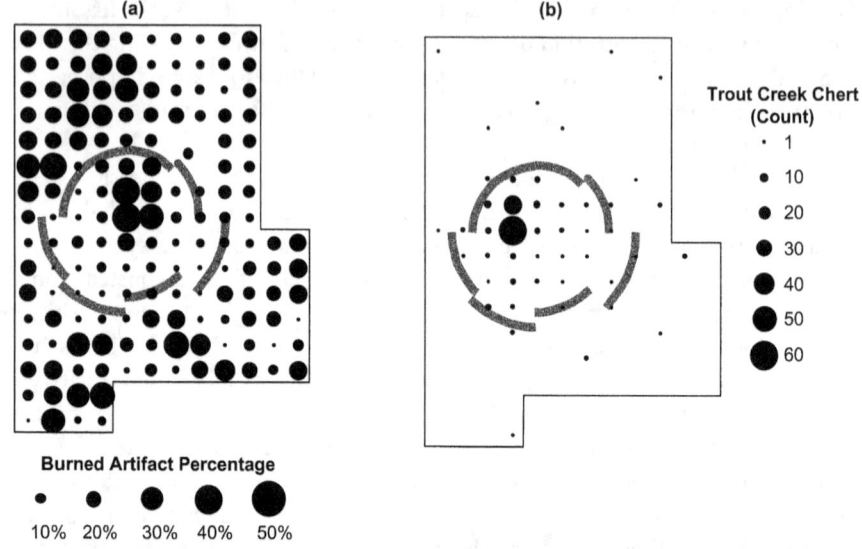

8.10. Plan maps of excavation block showing spatial congruence of the possible shelter reconstructed by ring and sector analysis and (a) an oval area of low percentages of burned artifacts and (b) a contiguous cluster of artifacts manufactured on Trout Creek Chert.

Table 8.6. Artifact Type Counts by Sector.

Sector	Bearing from Hearth Center (θ)	Debitage	Flake Tools	Points	Preforms	Bifaces	Channel Flakes	Cores	Sum
1	0≤ θ<45	107	9	0	0	0	0	2	118
2	45≤ θ<90	174	5	0	0	3	2	1	185
3	90≤ θ<135	684	8	1	0	6	3	1	703
4	135≤ θ<180	256	4	0	0	1	1	1	263
5	180≤ θ<225	320	9	0	0	3	3	2	337
6	225≤ θ<270	90	5	1	0	0	0	1	97
7	270≤ θ<315	105	16	4	1	2	6	2	136
8	315≤ θ<360	58	16	0	1	0	1	1	77

We divided the space surrounding the hearth at BGB into eight radial sectors (Figure 8.7). To perform the sector analysis, all piece-plotted artifacts within 2.25 m of the hearth were included. This distance includes some artifacts, particularly to the north and west, excluded from prior analyses, but their inclusion does not bias the results. Counts of artifact classes by sector are presented in Table 8.6, and radial sector diagrams are shown in Figure 8.11.

The half of the hearth composed of the four contiguous sectors containing the greatest numbers of artifacts was identified for each artifact class. Following Stapert (1989:29), this half of the hearth is referred to as the "richest half" and the opposite side as "the poorest half." Viewing artifact distributions this way

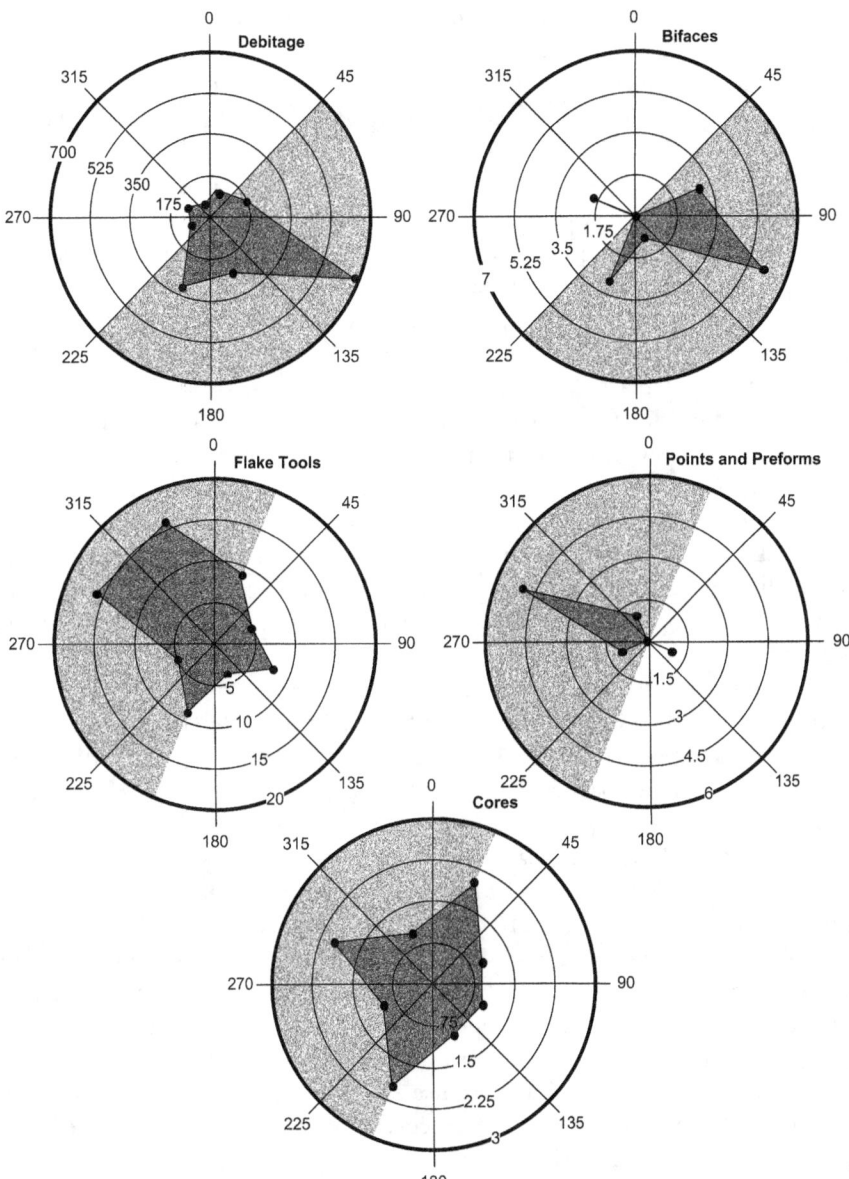

8.11. Sector diagrams of piece-plotted debitage, bifaces, flake tools, points and preforms, and cores. Artifact counts are plotted as the distance from the center of the graph, and artifact sector locations are plotted as the mean angle for the sector. Dark gray areas show the number of artifacts for each radial sector. The light gray areas show the "richest half" for each artifact class, defined as the four contiguous sectors containing the greatest numbers of artifacts.

produces a clear pattern. Debitage and bifaces are concentrated on the southeast side of the hearth, while flake tools, cores, and points and preforms are concentrated on the opposite side, on the northwest or west-northwest side of the hearth. All of these patterns are highly statistically significant with the exception of cores, which do not differ significantly from the expectation of equal association with both halves of the hearth ($\chi^2 = 0.09$, df = 1, p = 0.763). Cores are fairly consistently distributed around the hearth, with one or two present in all sectors.

Therefore, two groups of artifacts can be statistically discerned—those preferentially discarded on the northwest side of the hearth (flake tools and projectile points and preforms) and those preferentially discarded on the southeast side of the hearth (debitage and bifaces). Because of relatively large sample sizes, these patterns are particularly robust for debitage and flake tools, and, therefore, the remainder of the analysis will focus primarily on these two artifact classes. The dichotomous pattern we have identified separating debitage and flake tools is not unique to BGB. For example, in summarizing Leroi-Gourhan and Brézillon's (1972) spatial analysis of Pincevent, Section 36, Level IV(2), Simek (1984:60–61) noted, "Debitage tends to be concentrated with fire-cracked rock, on one side of the three central hearth features. The distributions of ocre (and stone tools) coincide on the opposite side. This pattern is repeated at all three central hearth locations."

Much has been written about the spatial patterns at Pincevent, particularly with respect to the presence of structures (e.g., Binford 1983; Carr 1991; Leroi-Gourhan and Brézillon 1966, 1972; Simek 1984; Simek and Larick 1983), but relatively few studies have addressed the incongruent distributions of debitage and tools. Leroi-Gourhan and Brézillon (1972) provide one explanation. They suggest that the Pincevent hearths are located at the doors of structures. The zones containing high frequencies of tools and concentrations of ochre are interior work spaces. These are abutted by relatively clean areas, interpreted to have been sleeping areas. On the opposite side of the hearth, debitage, bone, and fire-cracked rock are concentrated within an exterior, hearth-associated activity area. At greater distances are refuse zones, where artifacts are found in small piles thought to represent dumps (similar to the flake piles described earlier); and at even greater distances are diffuse refuse zones. In contrast, Binford (1983) and Stapert (1989) have argued that the Pincevent hearths were not associated with structures. Based on Binford's hearth model (1978, 1983) and ring and sector analysis, Stapert (1989) has argued that the sides of the hearth containing the majority of tools at Pincevent represent drop zones, while debitage and other waste is concentrated in a forward toss zone.

Of course, it is impossible to know a priori if debitage, tools, or both were discarded in their locations of production or use, and, of course, both debitage and tools could have been discarded in both primary and secondary contexts. Furthermore, while asymmetrical distributions around hearths are certainly expected for outside hearths in areas with prevailing winds, they might be

Table 8.7. Artifact Size Class Counts by Sector.

Sector	Bearing from Hearth Center (θ)	Size Class					Sum
		>1 to ≤2.5 cm	>2.5 to ≤4 cm	>4 to ≤5.5 cm	>5.5 to ≤7 cm	> 7 cm	
1	0≤ θ<45	64	30	14	3	4	115
2	45≤ θ<90	130	34	8	4	3	179
3	90≤ θ<135	399	129	31	7	8	574
4	135≤ θ<180	175	43	4	3	1	226
5	180≤ θ<225	241	43	6	2	4	296
6	225≤ θ<270	61	20	7	1	0	89
7	270≤ θ<315	85	38	8	1	1	133
8	315≤ θ<360	43	23	8	1	0	75

expected for interior hearths as well. Although the effects of wind are reduced or eliminated inside structures, hunter-gatherers and other mobile peoples commonly divided interior spaces into activity-specific areas (Binford 1983; Cribb 1991; Morgan 1881; Tanaka 1980:27) that could easily have produced asymmetrical patterns such as those observed at Barger Gulch or Pincevent.

If we begin with the hypothesis that the hearth at BGB is an outside hearth, then asymmetry in artifact distributions is likely best explained by prevailing wind direction. Based on sector analysis, three hypotheses are proposed: (1) based on the distribution of tools, prevailing winds were from the northwest, and debitage is concentrated in a forward toss zone; (2) based on the distribution of debitage, prevailing winds were from the southeast, and flake tools are concentrated in a forward toss zone; (3) prevailing winds cycled diurnally and were from both the northwest and the southeast. In this case, both debitage and flake tools were discarded in primary context.

Here we present a simple test of the drop and toss zone hypothesis. If drop and toss zones are present at Barger Gulch, they should be reflected by differences in artifact size distributions. Binford (1978, 1983:152–159) has suggested that toss zones will be dominated by large artifacts removed from work areas. Drop zones will be dominated by small artifacts that do not affect the usefulness of a space. Therefore, if drop and toss zones exist, we would expect to see spatial segregation between large and small items.

Counts of artifacts by size class are presented in Table 8.7, and Figure 8.12 shows radial sector diagrams by artifact size class. For all size classes, the greatest numbers of artifacts were recovered from Sector 3. The richest half for each size class varies from the northeast to the southeast half, with three size classes mimicking the distribution of debitage, the richest half being on the southeastern half of the hearth. Simple visual inspection would suggest that no drop and toss zones are present since all artifact sizes are distributed similarly around the hearth, but significant differences do exist. Based on total artifact counts (Table 8.6), the hearth area was divided into the richest (Sectors 2–5) and

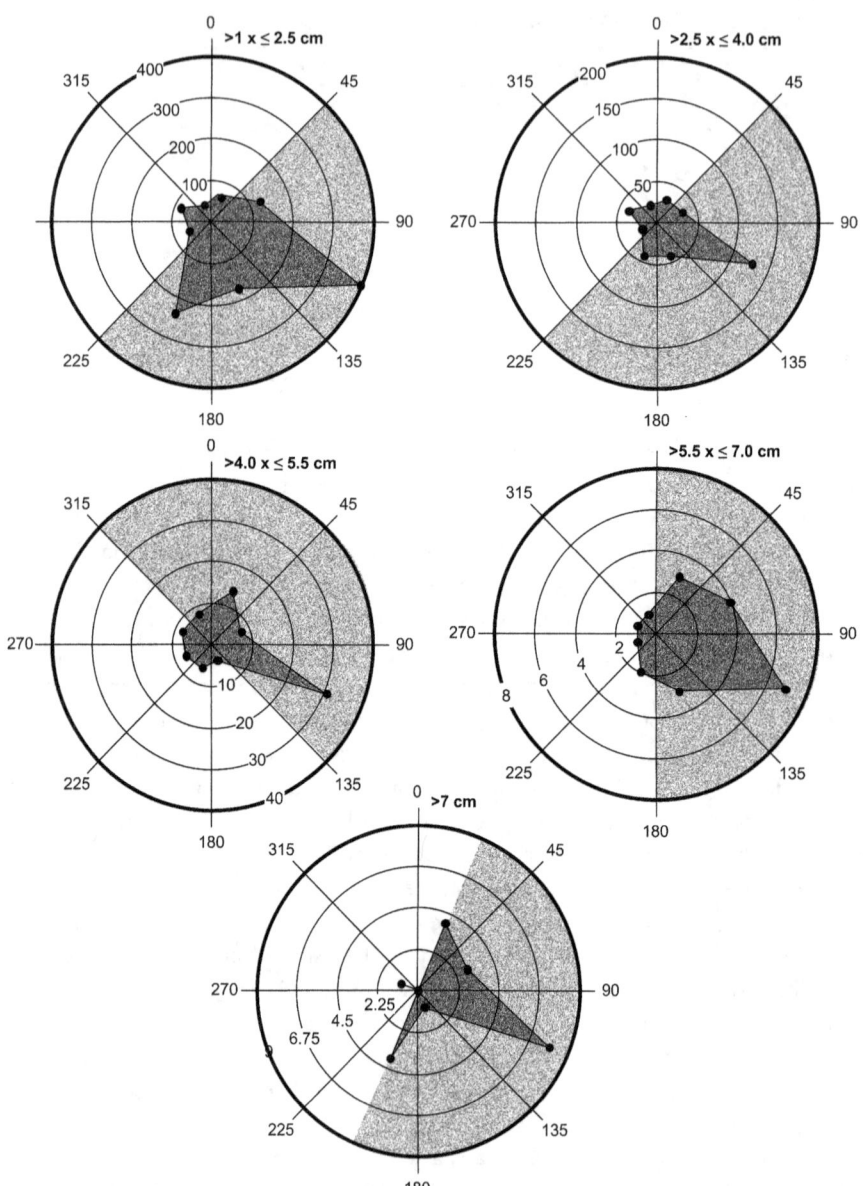

8.12. Sector diagrams of piece-plotted artifacts by size class. Artifact counts are plotted as the distance from the center of the graph, and artifact sector locations are plotted as the mean angle for the sector. Dark gray areas show the number of artifacts for each radial sector. The light gray areas show the "richest half" for each size class, defined as the four contiguous sectors containing the greatest numbers of artifacts.

Table 8.8. Chi-Square Test Comparing Artifact Size Classes for the Richest and Poorest Halves.

Hearth Half	Sectors	Size Class					Sum
		>1 to ≤2.5 cm Obs (Exp)	>2.5 to ≤4 cm Obs (Exp)	>4 to ≤5.5 cm Obs (Exp)	>5.5 to ≤7 cm Obs (Exp)	> 7 cm Obs (Exp)	
Richest half	2–5	945 (905)*	249 (272)*	49 (65)*	16 (17)	16 (16)	1,275
Poorest half	1, 6–8	253 (293)*	111 (88)*	37 (21)*	6 (5)	5 (5)	412
Sum		1,198	360	86	22	211,687	

$\chi^2 = 31.32$, df = 4, p << 0.001

Notes: Expected values calculated on the basis of relative artifact counts.
* Statistically significant deviation from the expected value following Everitt (1977:46–48). Values in bold face are those where a particular artifact class is overrepresented.

Table 8.9. Chi-Square Analysis of Tools and Large Artifacts.

Hearth Half	Sectors	Flake Tools Obs (Exp)	Other Artifacts >2.5 cm Obs (Exp)	Sum
Richest half	2–5	26 (45.4)	334 (314.5)	360
Poorest half	1, 6–8	**46 (26.5)**	164 (183.5)	210
Sum		72	498	570

$\chi^2 = 25.91$, df = 1, p << 0.001

Notes: Expected values calculated on the basis of relative artifact counts. Values in bold face are those where a particular artifact class is overrepresented. All observed values deviate significantly from expected.

poorest (Sectors 1, 6–8) halves, and artifact size class counts were tabulated for each (Table 8.8).

A chi-square test does provide some support for the drop and toss zone hypothesis (Table 8.8). Artifacts smaller than 2.5 cm are overrepresented on the richest side, and artifacts between 2.5 and 5.5 cm are overrepresented on the poorest half. The largest artifacts, those larger than 5.5 cm, are present in their expected frequencies. This patterning could provide support for a drop zone on the richest half of the hearth (southeastern) and a toss zone on the poorest half (the northwest), but, if so, it is only weakly developed. All artifact size classes are most common within Sector 3, and differences between observed and expected values do not exceed forty artifacts (2 percent of the total sample). Also, the artifacts that should have been the most likely to have been discarded in the toss zone (the largest pieces) are not overrepresented in the poorest half.

Can artifact size distributions account for the northwesterly concentration of tools? If tools were preferentially discarded on the northwestern side of the hearth within a toss zone, then the distribution of large artifacts and tools should be similar. Table 8.9 presents counts of flake tools and artifacts larger than 2.5 cm (excluding flake tools) for the richest and poorest halves of the hearth.

A chi-square test shows that tools and large artifacts have significantly different distributions ($\chi^2 = 25.91$, df = 1, p <<0.001). With respect to the distribution of flake tools, large artifacts are significantly underrepresented on the poorest half of the hearth. In other words, although large artifacts are present in greater frequencies than expected compared to the assemblage as a whole, compared to flake tools, large pieces are present in relatively small numbers. Therefore, artifact size differences between the richest and poorest halves alone cannot explain the northwesterly distribution of tools. There must be some other explanation, one unrelated to artifact size. This finding, we suggest, eliminates the possibility of both drop and toss zone hypotheses, unless one were to argue that only or primarily tools were tossed.

The directionally distinctive distribution of tools and debitage relative to the hearth cannot be explained solely by a simple drop and toss zone, which suggests that debitage and tools may have been discarded in their locations of use and production, respectively. If the hearth was located within an exterior space, one explanation is that winds most commonly blew from two opposing directions, northwest and southeast. Interestingly, winds in mountainous regions such as Middle Park often do cycle diurnally, and wind direction can be controlled by topography and valley orientation to a greater degree than atmospheric circulation (Banta and Cotton 1981; Whiteman 1982; Whiteman and McKee 1982). On calm nights, winds typically blow down valley axes. During the day, winds can blow upslope or in the direction of the prevailing winds above ridgetops. Therefore, the observed archaeological pattern could be a result of tool production and tool use occurring preferentially at different times of the day.

Barger Gulch sits within the greater valley of the Williams Fork (oriented southeast-northwest) near its junction with the Colorado River valley (oriented east-west). If winds cycled diurnally within the valley of the Williams Fork, they might be expected to blow from southeast to northwest from late evening to early morning and the reverse during the day. If so, it is possible that tool manufacture primarily took place in the evening, nighttime, or early morning, and tool use primarily occurred during the day. Unfortunately, we have been unable to locate any wind data from Middle Park, but because topography is the dominant control on mountain valley winds, wind patterns observed today should in theory be similar to those of the late Pleistocene. Therefore, it may be worthwhile in the future to collect wind data from the site. On the other hand, if this pattern is a product of wind direction, the same directional biases should be evident in other possible exterior hearth-centered activity areas at BGB (see Stapert 1989:30–34).

Alternatively, if the hearth was inside a structure, we may be seeing segregation of internal space, where reduction primarily took place on the southeast side of the hearth and discard and use occurred to its northwest. Patterns in tool discard location provide some support for this hypothesis. Here we performed a modified ring analysis. Rather than simply counting artifacts in concentric rings around the hearth, we calculated concentric artifact densities, taking into account the increasing area of successive rings. A comparison of the densities of flake tools and debitage concentrically around the hearth indicates that they are

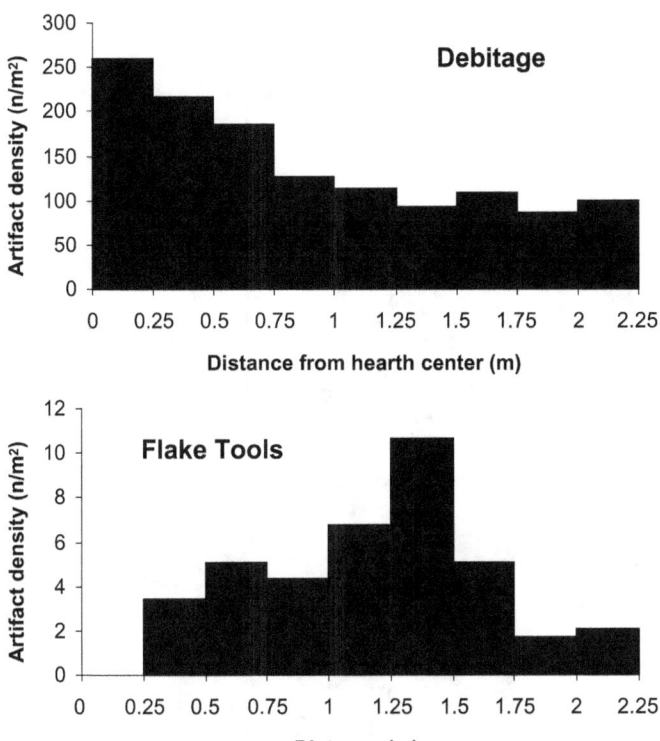

8.13. *Modified ring diagrams for piece-plotted debitage (top) and flake tools (bottom) showing the concentric densities of each artifact class as a function of distance from the center of the hearth.*

characterized by significantly different distributions (Kolmogorov-Smirnov test, $z = 1.538$, $p = 0.018$) (Figure 8.13).

Concentric debitage densities are maximized near the hearth center and drop smoothly at greater distances from the hearth. In contrast, concentric flake tool densities are very low directly adjacent to the hearth and peak at a maximum of 10.7 tools per m² at a distance of 1.25 to 1.5 m from the hearth center, highlighting again that the discard of debitage and the discard of flake tools were governed by different processes. A comparison of the distribution of flake tools to the possible wall positions reconstructed by ring analysis (Figure 8.14) shows excellent spatial congruence of the reconstructed wall segment and a high-density arc of tools in Sectors 7 and 8. If the hearth was inside a structure, then tools appear to have been preferentially discarded in a cluster against the northwestern wall.

SUMMARY

We began this chapter with a simple spatial analysis of burned materials from BGB. The spatial congruence of burned bone, lithics, and Folsom-age radiocarbon

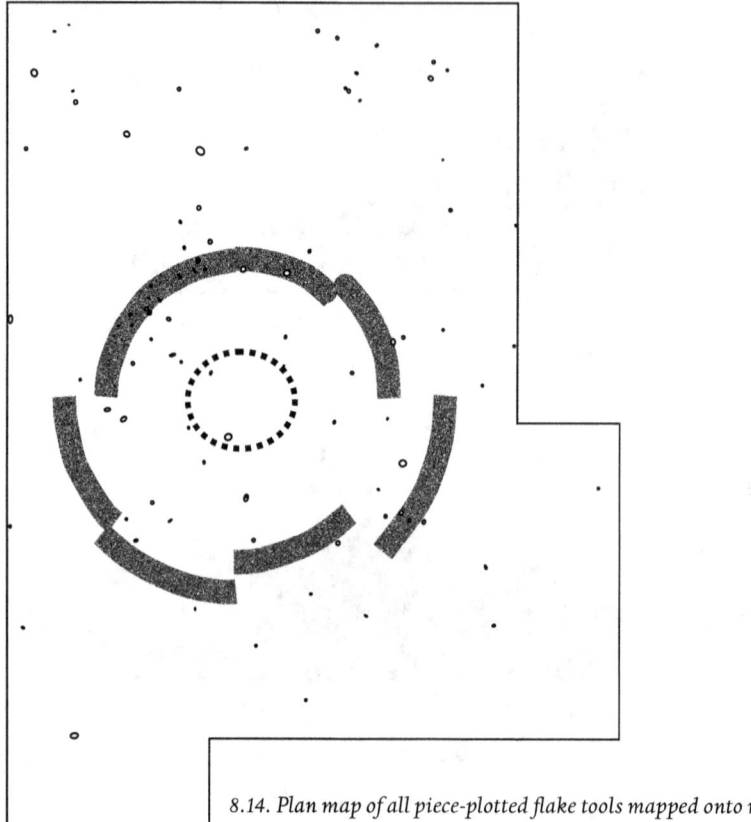

8.14. *Plan map of all piece-plotted flake tools mapped onto reconstructed structural walls.*

dates pointed to the presence of a hearth undetected during excavations. Analyses of artifact frequencies in the hearth- and non-hearth-associated areas further suggested the existence of a distinct hearth-centered activity area marked by high artifact densities. Unlike most other artifact classes, cores were not preferentially discarded in the hearth area despite being frequently reduced there. We suggest that cores were intentionally discarded and possibly stored in areas away from the hearth.

Within the hearth area, a series of spatial analyses was performed aimed primarily at addressing the question of whether the hearth was located within an interior or an exterior workspace. Bimodality in ring diagrams indicated the possibility of a structure roughly 4 × 3 m in size, with the hearth located on its northwest side. A discrete, contiguous cluster of Trout Creek Chert and an area of low burning percentages surrounding the hearth are spatially congruent with the hypothesized structure.

Using sector analysis, patterns in the discard of various artifact classes were identified. Debitage and bifaces appear preferentially discarded on the southeast side of the hearth, and flake tools and projectile points and preforms were preferentially discarded to its northwest. We argue that if the hearth was in an exterior space, wind direction, the presence of drop and toss zones, or both are the most likely explanations for these patterns. Alternatively, if the hearth was in an interior space, this pattern could emerge if different activities were preferentially performed at different locations within that space. In comparing the distribution of artifact sizes for both sides of the hearth, some support was found for the presence of a drop zone on its southeast and a toss zone on its northwest side. However, by comparing the hearth-centered distributions of large artifacts and flake tools, we demonstrated that size differences and, therefore, drop and toss zones alone do not sufficiently explain the preferential discard of tools on the northwest side. Two competing hypotheses remain. The preferential discard of different classes on opposite sides of the hearth can be explained by (1) a bimodal distribution in prevailing winds for an exterior hearth, or (2) the division of activity space inside a structure.

Distinguishing between these two hypotheses may be difficult. One simple approach could use spatial patterns in lithic refits to attempt to find further support for a barrier effect. Another approach might involve the excavation of a number of additional hearth-centered activity areas. For a series of contemporaneous exterior hearths, asymmetry in radial distributions of artifacts should consistently show preferential work, discard, or both on the same side of the hearth. Therefore, if a second contemporaneous hearth-centered activity area was excavated and artifacts were found to concentrate on a different side of the hearth, we could say with some confidence that at least one of these hearths sat within a structure.

Obviously, many questions remain regarding the organization of activities around the hearth at BGB. We have managed to identify a number of clear spatial patterns but have derived relatively few solid interpretations of these patterns, which returns us to the observation made at the start of this chapter. After almost eighty years of Folsom research, very few unequivocal examples of Folsom hearths and structures are known. Because both structures and hearths modify the physical landscape of archaeological sites, they should have predictable effects on archaeological spatial patterning. Hearths will leave evidence of burning beyond their direct products (e.g., charcoal and ash), and structures have walls, which should impede the movement of artifacts across space. Perhaps, then, we should be looking for hearths and structures not only in the ground but also in spatial patterning and associations among recovered artifacts.

Of course, if we assume (as we do) that hearths and structures were a component of Folsom residential occupations, by finding evidence of structures and hearths one could argue that simply establishing the presence of such features does not extend our knowledge of Folsom lifeways. However, abundant ethnoarchaeological and archaeological data have shown that the spatial associations within and between such features provide important opportunities to discern the nature of economic and social relationships among site occupants (e.g., Binford 1991; Boismier 1991; Enloe and David 1992; Gould and Yellen 1987; Henshaw 1999; Stapert 2003; Waguespack 2002; Whitelaw 1983, 1991; Yellen 1977). The identification of structures and hearth features is only the first step in this process. Jodry's (1999) work at Cattle Guard provides one excellent example of the utility of such data, and we hope the spatial analyses presented in this chapter will spur additional research in these areas. The hearth-associated spatial patterns observed at BGB provide one empirical framework potentially applicable to the identification of hearths and structures in other sites.

EPILOGUE

Since we originally wrote this manuscript in December 2003, we have spent two more seasons at the site. We have increased our excavations to 87 m², and the assemblage totals more than 50,000 pieces. We have also partially excavated two additional hearth-centered activity areas. The results of this new work do not substantially change any of our findings in this chapter. The center of the first hearth sits at approximately N 1481.6, E 2437.3 and shows typical hearth morphology, a charcoal-stained pit feature with associated sedimentary oxidation. This feature was at least 63 × 57 cm in length and width and 14 cm in depth. The presence of a hearth in the northeastern corner of the Main Block implies that some of the artifacts we considered to be unassociated with a hearth may in fact be within a separate hearth-centered activity area. Within a new excavation area we call the "East Block," the second hearth sits 15.5 m to the ESE of the central hearth in the Main Excavation Block, its center lying at N 1474.60, E 2449.01. Much like the central hearth in the Main Block, this feature did not show clear hearth morphology but was identified on the basis of very weak charcoal staining and strong clustering in burned lithics and bone.

While excavation and analyses of these areas are ongoing, spatial patterns associated with the East Block hearth appear similar to those of the hearth-centered activity area described in this chapter. From the little we have excavated, spatial patterns associated with the northeastern hearth-centered activity area in the Main Block appear to differ. While our agnosticism with regard to the presence of a structure in the center of the Main Block has not changed, we are optimistic that further excavation of these new areas will shed additional light on this issue. For example, artifacts appear to cluster preferentially to the north of the East Block hearth, suggesting that *at least* one of these hearths was in an inside space, assuming, of course, that they are contemporaneous. Also, from our preliminary analysis, it seems likely that we will eventually be able to identify classes of hearth-centered activity areas on the basis of repeated spatial patterning.

Acknowledgments. Our work at Barger Gulch has been performed in collaboration with Marcel Kornfeld and George Frison. Marcel gave us valuable input on many aspects of this chapter. Frank Rupp of the Kremmling office of the

Bureau of Land Management has been critical to the success of our work at the site. Likewise, we are extremely grateful to the Bruchez family for granting us access to the site via their property. It is rare that one gets a chance to thank two Bob Kellys, but we do. Bob Kelly (Department of Anthropology, University of Wyoming) has generously shared his thoughts on many of the spatial patterns and analyses we performed, and Bob Kelly (Department of Atmospheric Sciences, University of Wyoming) was kind enough to share his knowledge of winds in mountainous regions. We are grateful to Dick Stapert for sharing his work and thoughts with us. Without his simple and elegant approach to the analysis of hearth-centered activity areas, this chapter would have taken a very different form. Fine-grained spatial analyses would not be possible without fine-grained, careful excavation, and we have our excellent field crews to thank for that. Thanks to Bonnie Pitblado and Bob Brunswig for the invitation to contribute to this volume. Bonnie also provided valuable comments that improved the manuscript. This work was funded by the Colorado State Historical Fund (grant no. 2001-02-122), the National Science Foundation (NSF grant no. 0450759), the George C. Frison Institute of Archaeology, the Colorado Bureau of Land Management (Kremmling Field Office), and the Emil Haury Research Fund for Archaeology (University of Arizona).

REFERENCES CITED

Audouze, F., and J. G. Enloe
    1997   High Resolution Archaeology at Verberie: Limits and Interpretations. *World Archaeology* 29:195–207.

Bamforth, D. B., and M. S. Becker
    2000   Core/Biface Ratios, Mobility, Refitting, and Artifact Use-Lives: A Paleoindian Example. *Plains Anthropologist* 45:273–290.

Banta, R., and W. R. Cotton
    1981   An Analysis of the Structure of Local Wind Systems in a Broad Mountain Basin. *Journal of Applied Meteorology* 20:1255–1266.

Bartram, L. A., E. Kroll, and H. Bunn
    1991   Variability in Camp Structure and Bone Food Refuse Patterning at Kua San Hunter-Gatherer Camps. In *The Interpretation of Archaeological Spatial Patterning*, ed. E. M. Kroll and T. D. Price, 77–148. Plenum, New York.

Binford, L. R.
    1978   Dimensional Analysis of Behavior and Site Structure: Learning from an Eskimo Hunting Stand. *American Antiquity* 43:330–661.
    1983   *In Pursuit of the Past: Decoding the Archaeological Record*. Thames and Hudson, New York.
    1991   When the Going Gets Tough: Nunamiut Local Groups, Camping Patterns and Economic Organisation. In *Ethnoarchaeological Approaches to Mobile Campsites*, ed. C. S. Gamble and W. A. Boismier, 25–138. International Monographs in Prehistory, Ann Arbor, MI.

Boismier, W. A.
   1991   Site Formation among Sub-Arctic Peoples: An Ethnohistorical Approach. In *Ethnoarchaeological Approaches to Mobile Campsites*, ed. C. S. Gamble and W. A. Boismier, 189–214. International Monographs in Prehistory, Ann Arbor, MI.

Carr, C.
   1984   The Nature of Organization of Intrasite Archaeological Records and Spatial Analytic Approaches to Their Investigation. In *Advances in Archaeological Method and Theory 7*, ed. M. B. Schiffer, 103–221. Academic, New York.
   1991   Left in the Dust: Contextual Information in Model-Focused Archaeology. In *The Interpretation of Archaeological Spatial Patterning*, ed. E. M. Kroll and T. D. Price, 221–256. Plenum, New York.

Cribb, R.L.D.
   1991   Mobile Villages: The Structure and Organisation of Nomadic Pastoral Campsites in the Near East. In *Ethnoarchaeological Approaches to Mobile Campsites*, ed. C. S. Gamble and W. A. Boismier, 371–394. International Monographs in Prehistory, Ann Arbor, MI.

Davis, L. B., and S. T. Greiser
   1992   Indian Creek Paleoindians: Early Occupation of the Elkhorn Mountains' Southeast Flank, West-Central Montana. In *Ice Age Hunters of the Rockies*, ed. D. J. Stanford and J. S. Day, 225–283. Denver Museum of Natural History and University Press of Colorado, Niwot.

Dibble, D. S., and D. Lorrain
   1968   *Bonfire Shelter: A Stratified Bison Kill Site, Val Verde County, Texas*. Miscellaneous Papers 4, Texas Memorial Museum, University of Texas, Austin.

Enloe, J. G., and F. David
   1992   Food Sharing in the Paleolithic. In *Piecing Together the Past: Applications of Refitting Studies in Archaeology*, ed. J. Hofman and J. Enloe, 296–315. BAR International Series 578, London.

Everitt, B.
   1977   *The Analysis of Contingency Tables*. Chapman and Hall, London.

Frison, G. C.
   1982   Folsom Components. In *The Agate Basin Site: A Record of the Paleoindian Occupation of the Northwestern High Plains*, ed. G. C. Frison and D. J. Stanford, 37–76. Academic, New York.
   1984   The Carter/Kerr-McGee Paleoindian Site: Cultural Resource Management and Archaeological Research. *American Antiquity* 49:288–314.

Frison, G. C., and B. A. Bradley
   1980   *Folsom Tools and Technology at the Hanson Site, Wyoming*. University of New Mexico Press, Albuquerque.

Gamble, C.
   1991   An Introduction to the Living Spaces of Mobile Peoples. In *Ethnoarchaeological Approaches to Mobile Campsites*, ed. C. S. Gamble and W. A. Boismier, 1–23. International Monographs in Prehistory, Ann Arbor, MI.
   1999   *The Paleolithic Societies of Europe*. Cambridge University Press, Cambridge.

Gould, R. A., and J. E. Yellen
1987 Man the Hunted: Determinants of Household Spacing in Desert and Tropical Foraging Societies. *Journal of Anthropological Archaeology* 6:77–103.

Gregg, S. A., K. W. Kintigh, and R. Whallon
1991 Linking Ethnoarchaeological Interpretation and Archaeological Data. In *The Interpretation of Archaeological Spatial Patterning*, ed. E. M. Kroll and T. D. Price, 149–196. Plenum, New York.

Henshaw, A. S.
1999 Location and Appropriation in the Arctic: An Integrative Zooarchaeological Approach to Historic Inuit Household Economies. *Journal of Anthropological Archaeology* 18:79–118.

Hofman, J. L.
1995 Dating Folsom Occupations on the Southern Plains: The Lipscomb and Waugh Sites. *Journal of Field Archaeology* 22:421–437.

Hofman, J. L., D. S. Amick, and R. O. Rose
1990 Shifting Sands: A Folsom-Midland Assemblage from a Campsite in Western Texas. *Plains Anthropologist* 35:221–253.

Jodry, M.A.B.
1999 *Folsom Technological and Socioeconomic Strategies: Views from Stewart's Cattle Guard and the Upper Rio Grande Basin, Colorado.* Unpublished Ph.D. dissertation, American University, Washington DC.

Jodry, M.A.B., and D. J. Stanford
1992 Stewart's Cattle Guard Site: An Analysis of Bison Remains in a Folsom Kill-Butchery Campsite. In *Ice Age Hunters of the Rockies*, ed. D. J. Stanford and J. S. Day, 101–168. Denver Museum of Natural History and University Press of Colorado, Niwot.

Koetje, T. A.
1987 *Spatial Patterns in Magdalenian Open Air from the Isle Valley, Southwestern France.* BAR International Series 346, Oxford.

Kornfeld, M. (ed.)
1998 *Early Prehistory of Middle Park: The 1997 Project and Summary of Paleoindian Archaeology.* Technical Report 15a, Department of Anthropology, University of Wyoming, Laramie.

Kornfeld, M., and G. C. Frison
2000 Paleoindian Occupation of the High Country: The Case of Middle Park, Colorado. *Plains Anthropologist* 45:129–153.

Leroi-Gourhan, A., and M. Brézillon
1966 L'Habitation Magdalénienne No. 1 de Pincevent près de Montereau (Seine-et-Marne). *Gallia Préhistoire* 9:263–385.
1972 Fouilles de Pincevent: Essai d'Analyse Ethnographique d'un Habitat Magdalénien,. *Gallia Préhistoire* 7th Supplement, C.N.R.S., Paris.

Morgan, L. H.
　1881　*Houses and House-Life of the American Aborigines*. Contributions to North American Ethnology, Vol. 4. Government Printing Office, Washington DC.

Naze, B. S.
　1986　The Folsom Occupation of Middle Park, Colorado. *Southwestern Lore* 52 (4):1–32.
　1994　*The Crying Woman Site: A Record of Prehistoric Human Habitation in the Colorado Rockies*. Unpublished master's thesis, Colorado State University, Fort Collins.

O'Connell, J. F.
　1987　Alywara Site Structure and Its Archaeological Implications. *American Antiquity* 52:74–108.

O'Connell, J. F., K. Hawkes, and N. Blurton Jones
　1991　Distribution of Refuse-Producing Activities at Hadza Base Camps: Implications for Analyses of Archaeological Site Structure. In *The Interpretation of Archaeological Spatial Patterning*, ed. E. M. Kroll and T. D. Price, 61–76. Plenum, New York.

Person, A., H. Bocherens, A. Mariotti, and M. Renard
　1996　Diagenetic Evolution and Experimental Heating of Bone Phosphate. *Palaeogeography, Palaeoclimatology, Palaeoecology* 126:135–149.

Rigaud, J.-P., and J. F. Simek
　1991　Interpreting Spatial Patterns at the Grotte XV: A Multiple-Method Approach. In *The Interpretation of Archaeological Spatial Patterning*, ed. E. M. Kroll and T. D. Price, 199–220. Plenum, New York.

Root, M. J.
　2000　Excavations in the Western Terrace Area: Excavation Block 2. In *The Archaeology of the Bobtail Wolf Site*, ed. M. J. Root, 85–138. Washington State University Press, Pullman.

Root, M. J., and A. M. Emerson
　2000　The Northeast Terrace: Excavation Block 6. In *The Archaeology of the Bobtail Wolf Site*, ed. M. J. Root, 201–222. Washington State University Press, Pullman.

Root, M. J., D. H. MacDonald, and A. M. Emerson
　2000　The Southern Rise and Southern Terrace Area: Excavation Block 4. In *The Archaeology of the Bobtail Wolf Site*, ed. M. J. Root, 139–200. Washington State University Press, Pullman.

Schiffer, M. B.
　1987　*Formation Processes of the Archaeological Record*. University of New Mexico Press, Albuquerque.

Shipman, P., G. Foster, and M. Schoeninger
　1984　Burnt Bones and Teeth: An Experimental Study of Color, Morphology, Crystal Structure and Shrinkage. *Journal of Archaeological Science* 11:307–325.

Simek, J. F.
　1984　*A K-Means Approach to the Analysis of Spatial Structure in Upper Paleolithic Habitation Sites*. BAR International Series 205, Oxford.

1987 Spatial Order and Behavioural Change in the French Paleolithic. *Antiquity* 61: 25–40.

Simek, J. F., and R. R. Larick
1983 The Recognition of Multiple Spatial Patterns: A Case Study from the French Upper Paleolithic. *Journal of Archaeological Science* 10:165–180.

Simms, S. R.
1988 The Archaeological Structure of a Bedouin Camp. *Journal of Archaeological Science* 15:197–211.

Smith, C. S., and L. M. McNees
1990 Rattlesnake Pass Site: A Folsom Occupation in South-Central Wyoming. *Plains Anthropologist* 35:273–289.

Stapert, D.
1989 The Ring and Sector Method: Intrasite Spatial Analysis of Stone Age Sites, with Special Reference to Pincevent. *Palaeohistoria* 31:1–57.
1990 Middle Paleolithic Dwellings: Fact or Fiction? Some Applications of the Ring and Sector Method. *Palaeohistoria* 32:1–19.
1991– Intrasite Spatial Analysis and the Maglemosian Site of Barmose I. *Palaeohisto-*
1992 *ria* 33–34:31–51.
2003 Towards Dynamic Models of Stone Age Settlements. In *Perceived Landscapes and Built Environments: The Cultural Geography of Late Paleolithic Eurasia*, ed. S. A. Vasil'ev, O. Soffer, and J. Kozlowski. BAR International Series 1122, 5–16, Oxford.

Stapert, D., and L. Johansen
1995– Ring & Sector Analysis, and Site 'It" on Greenland. *Palaeohistoria* 37–38:29–
1996 69.

Stapert, D., and M. Street
1997 High Resolution or Optimum Resolution? Spatial Analysis of the Federmesser Site at Andernach, Germany. *World Archaeology* 29:172–194.

Stapert, D., and T. Terberger
1989 Gonnersdörf Concentration III: Investigating the Possibility of Multiple Occupations. *Palaeohistoria* 31:59–95.

Stevenson, M. G.
1985 The Formation of Artifact Assemblages at Workshop/Habitation Sites: Models from Peace Point in Northern Alberta. *American Antiquity* 50 (1):63–81.
1991 Beyond the Formation of Hearth-Associated Assemblages. In *The Interpretation of Archaeological Spatial Patterning*, ed. E. M. Kroll and T. D. Price, 269–299. Plenum, New York.

Stiger, M.
2006 A Folsom Structure in the Colorado Mountains. *American Antiquity* 71 (2):321–351.

Stiner, M. C., S. L. Kuhn, S. Weiner, and O. Bar-Yosef
1995 Differential Burning, Recrystallization, and Fragmentation of Archaeological Bone. *Journal of Archaeological Science* 22:223–237.

Surovell, T. A.
   2003   *The Behavioral Ecology of Folsom Lithic Technology.* Unpublished Ph.D. dissertation, University of Arizona, Tucson.

Surovell, T. A., and M. C. Stiner
   2001   Standardizing Infra-Red Measures of Bone Mineral Crystallinity: An Experimental Approach. *Journal of Archaeological Science* 28:633–642.

Surovell, T. A., N. M. Waguespack, M. Kornfeld, and G. C. Frison
   2003   *The First Five Field Seasons at Barger Gulch, Locality B, Middle Park, Colorado.* Technical Report 26, George C. Frison Institute of Archaeology and Anthropology, University of Wyoming, Laramie.

Surovell, T. A., N. M. Waguespack, J. H. Mayer, M. Kornfeld, and G. C. Frison
   2005   Shallow Site Archaeology: Artifact Dispersal, Stratigraphy, and Radiocarbon Dating at Barger Gulch, Locality B, Middle Park, Colorado. *Geoarchaeology* 20:627–649.

Surovell, T. A., N. M. Waguespack, S. Richings-Germain, M. Kornfeld, and G. C. Frison
   2000   *1999 Investigations at the Barger Gulch and Jerry Craig Sites, Middle Park, Colorado.* Technical Report 18a, George C. Frison Institute of Archaeology and Anthropology, University of Wyoming, Laramie.

Tanaka, J.
   1980   *The San: Hunter-Gatherers of the Kalahari.* Trans. D. W. Hughs. University of Tokyo Press, Tokyo.

Villa, P.
   1982   Conjoinable Pieces and Site Formation Processes. *American Antiquity* 47:276–290.

Waguespack, N. M.
   2002   Caribou Sharing and Storage: Refitting the Palangana Site. *Journal of Anthropological Archaeology* 21:396–417.

Waguespack, N. M., T. A. Surovell, M. Kornfeld, and G. C. Frison
   2002   *The 2001 Field Season at Barger Gulch, Locality B, Middle Park, Colorado.* Technical Report 20, George C. Frison Institute of Archaeology and Anthropology, University of Wyoming, Laramie.

Walters, I.
   1988   Fire and Bones: Patterns of Discard. In *Archaeology with Ethnography: An Australian Perspective,* ed. B. Meehan and R. Jones, 215–221. Department of Prehistory, Research School of Pacific Studies, Australian National University, Canberra.

Weiner, S., S. Scheigl, P. Goldberg, and O. Bar-Yosef
   1995   Mineral Assemblages in Kebara and Hayonim Caves, Israel: Excavation Strategies, Bone Preservation, and Wood Ash Remains. *Israel Journal of Chemistry* 35:143–154.

Weiner, S., Q. Xu, P. Goldberg, J. Liu, and O. Bar-Yosef
   1998   Evidence for the Use of Fire at Zhoukoudian, China. *Science* 281:251–253.

Whallon, R., Jr.
 1973 Spatial Analysis of Occupation Floors I: Application of Dimensional Analysis of Variance. *American Antiquity* 38 (3):266–278.
 1974 Spatial Analysis of Occupation Floors II: The Application of Nearest Neighbor Analysis. *American Antiquity* 39 (1):16–34.
 1984 Unconstrained Clustering for the Analysis of Spatial Distributions in Archaeology. In *Intrasite Spatial Analysis in Archaeology*, ed. H. J. Hietala, 242–277. Cambridge University Press, Cambridge.

Whitelaw, T.
 1983 People and Space in Hunter-Gatherer Camps: A Generalising Approach in Ethnoarchaeology. *Archaeological Review from Cambridge* 2 (2):48–66.
 1991 Some Dimensions of Variability in the Social Organization of Community Space among Foragers. In *Ethnoarchaeological Approaches to Mobile Campsites*, ed. C. S. Gamble and W. A. Boismier, 131–188. International Monographs in Prehistory, Ann Arbor, MI.

Whiteman, C. D.
 1982 Breakup of Temperature Inversions in Deep Mountain Valleys: Part I. Observations. *Journal of Applied Meteorology* 21:270–289.

Whiteman, C. D., and T. B. McKee
 1982 Breakup of Temperature Inversions in Deep Mountain Valleys: Part II. Thermodynamic Model. *Journal of Applied Meteorology* 21:290–302.

William, J. D. (ed.)
 2000 *The Big Black Site (32DU955C): A Folsom Complex Workshop in the Knife River Flint Quarry Area, North Dakota.* Washington State University Press, Pullman.

Wilmsen, E. M., and F.H.H. Roberts Jr.
 1984 *Lindenmeier, 1934–1974: Concluding Report on Investigations.* Smithsonian Contributions to Anthropology 24. Smithsonian Institution Press, Washington, DC.

Yellen, J. E.
 1977 *Archaeological Approaches to the Present: Models for Reconstructing the Past.* Academic, New York.

CHAPTER NINE

Robert H. Brunswig

Paleoindian Cultural Landscapes and Archaeology of North-Central Colorado's Southern Rockies

This chapter summarizes the current status of Paleoindian archaeology in north-central Colorado's southern Rocky Mountains. A significant increase in archaeological activity in the past two decades has resulted in major advances of our understanding of that region's earliest inhabitants. Increasingly clear patterns of Colorado mountain colonization, seasonal transhumant migratory cycles, and economic adaptations are emerging from a rapidly expanding Paleoindian database.

NORTH-CENTRAL COLORADO MOUNTAIN PHYSIOGRAPHY

The north-central Colorado region of the southern Rocky Mountain physiographic province encompasses several environmental zones on either side of the Continental Divide, occurring within several minor mountain ranges, dozens

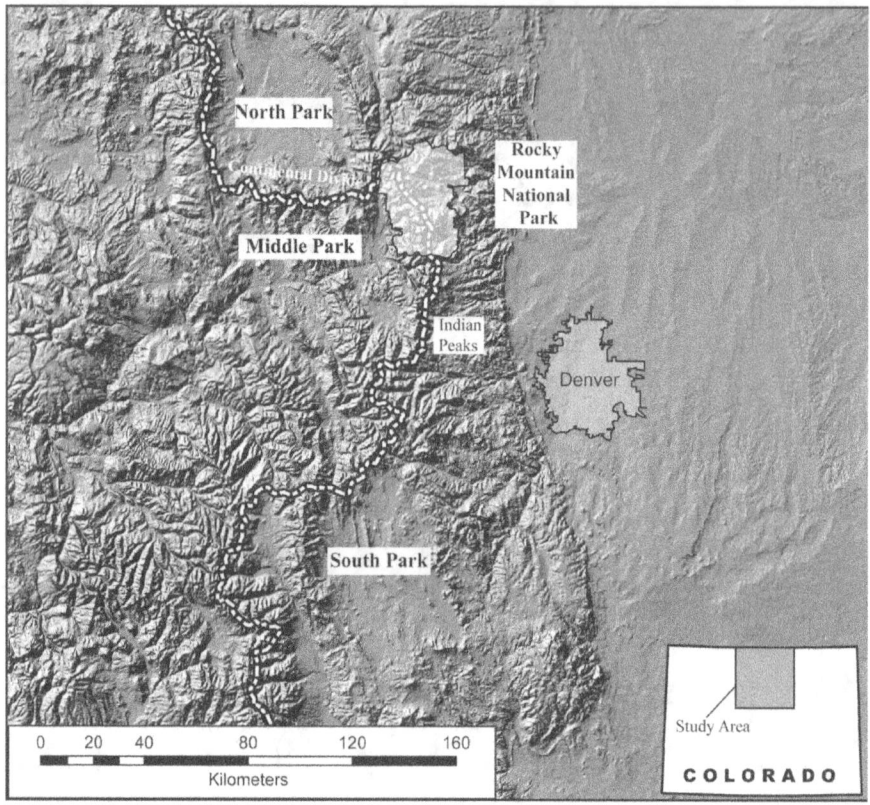

9.1. *Physiographic map showing Colorado's north-central and central mountain regions, with identified major interior montane parks and valleys. The dashed line represents the Continental Divide.*

of smaller river valleys, and two large parkland basin valleys (Middle Park and North Park) (Figure 9.1).

From north to south, the province's north-central Colorado region extends from the Wyoming border to an east-west line from Clear Creek east of the Continental Divide to the Blue River west of the divide. From east to west, the region begins with the eastern Front Range foothills-mountain boundary and extends west to the Park and Gore mountain ranges. Its eastern half consists of several smaller mountain ranges, including the Rawahs, Medicine Bows, Never Summer, Mummy, and Indian Peaks, with interspersed small river valleys, all making up the Colorado Front Range. The region's western section is dominated by two large parkland valleys, Middle Park and North Park, separated to the south and north, respectively, by the Rabbit Ears Range. The Continental Divide (Figure 9.1) winds through the region, starting at its northwest corner, departing in its southwest corner, and making an easterly U-turn near its center.

HYDROLOGY AND GEOLOGY

The region is home to headwaters of two of Colorado's great river systems, the Colorado and North Platte. North Park and its surrounding peaks, situated east of the Continental Divide, are headwaters to the North Platte, which flows northward out of the state into Wyoming. To the south, Middle Park, located west of the divide, is drained by an upper segment of the Colorado River, with originating headwaters in adjacent Rocky Mountain National Park's Kawuneeche Valley. Both North Park and South Park are large parkland basins dominated by rolling hills, elongated ridgelines, and complex secondary and tertiary stream networks that supply the North Platte and Colorado rivers.

Geologically, North Park and South Park were formed from the same ancient (Jurassic and Cretaceous) sedimentary basin, subsequently filled by 50 million years of post-Cretaceous sedimentation. However, both park valleys retain significant exposures of earlier geologic deposits (Harder 1957; Izlett 1967, 1975). The east-west–trending Rabbit Ears Range, which today separates the once common basin, was formed during the Laramide Orogeny by the tectonically induced rise of the Rockies (McMillan, Heller, and Wing 2006; Tweto 1975).

Mountain ranges in the region are composed of diverse geologic formations exposed over 50 million years of Rocky Mountain uplift and erosion and more recent volcanic activity. Ancient pre-Cambrian granite and schist are particularly dominant in the east, while sedimentary, meta-sedimentary, and volcanic rock types dominate in central and western areas.

Primary and secondary geological sources in both parks and adjacent mountains provide some of the southern Rocky Mountains' finest-quality stone-tool materials. Rock outcrops and secondary clast deposits of Jurassic and Cretaceous age (Sundance, Morrison, and Dakota formations) are interlaced with lithic-tool–quality sandstone and quartzite, among which Windy Ridge (or Dakota) quartzite is known to have been extensively mined and utilized by prehistoric hunter-gatherers (Bamforth 1994, 1998). Particularly rich tool materials are found in Tertiary-, Miocene-, and Pliocene-era sedimentary and volcanic formations, including the well-known Troublesome Formation Chert and chalcedony (also known as Kremmling Chert) and coarse to fine-quality chert, jasper, and porcellanite of the Table Mountain/Grouse Mountain Formation (Kornfeld, Frison, and White 2001; Metcalf et al. 1991; Miller 1991, 1998; White 1999). Paleocene-(Mississippian) age chert occurs as secondary gravel and cobbles in both Middle Park and North Park stream and river deposits and high ridgelines, the latter remnants of former river floodplains.

North Park and Middle Park also provide tool-quality Coalmont Formation petrified woods and less well-documented lithic materials derived from Dakota and Troublesome formations, most frequently occurring as secondary clast deposits (Brunswig 2006). Even western margins of Rocky Mountain National Park contain Miocene-era volcanic deposits, with lesser tool-quality andesite, rhyolite, and jasper known to have been prehistorically exploited for tools at a number of park sites (Brunswig 2005a; Steven 1975; Wahlstrom 1941, 1944; Wunderlich 2004; Wunderlich and Brunswig 2004).

ENVIRONMENTAL AND ECOLOGICAL CONTEXTS

As described in Chapter 1 (Doerner, this volume), regional environmental zones consist of alpine tundra, alpine-subalpine (or krummholz) ecotone, subalpine and montane (upper and lower) forests and meadows, and sagebrush steppe parkland (also see Brunswig 2005a:16–27). Plant ecosystems represented by mountain environmental zones not only provided life-sustaining forage for game animals but also dozens of plant species utilized by prehistoric humans for food, medicines, and, if ethno-historic records and modern Native American consultation studies are any indication, ceremonial and ritual practices (e.g., Bach 2003; Brett 2002; Brunswig 2003b, 2005a:16–27, 194–195, 2005b).

Major faunal species known to have been exploited by the region's past hunter-gatherers include bison, bighorn sheep, elk, mule deer, and pronghorn antelope (Brunswig 2005a:32–41). Although moose have been recently introduced to Middle Park, North Park, and Rocky Mountain National Park's Kawuneeche Valley, there is little evidence they were present in significant numbers in prehistoric times. Bison are the only prehistoric species now extinct from the region, having been eradicated by Euro-American hunting in the late nineteenth century (Brunswig 2005a:33–36; Meany and Van Vuren 1993).

Each environmental zone possesses its own unique set of perennially or seasonally available faunal and floral resources used by past hunter-gatherer populations, subject to differing paleoclimatic-paleoecological conditions that prevailed in successive Paleoindian periods (Chapters 1 and 7, this volume).

HISTORY OF NORTH-CENTRAL COLORADO MOUNTAIN RESEARCH

The north-central Colorado Rockies have a rich history of archaeological research. Over more than a half century, an impressive body of archaeological studies has been accumulated by private research centers (Benedict 1981, 1985, 1990, 1996; Benedict and Olson 1978; Cassells 2000; Pitblado 2000); student thesis and dissertation projects from the Universities of Denver (Yelm 1935; Lux 2004), Colorado-Boulder (Husted 1962), Colorado-Denver (Elinoff 2002), Colorado State (Naze 1994), Wyoming (White 1999; Daniele 2003), Arkansas (Rohe 2003), Wisconsin (Cassells 1995), and Northern Colorado (Wunderlich 2004); university-based field projects (Northern Colorado [Brunswig 1999, 2000, 2001a, 2002a, 2002b], Wyoming [Kornfeld, ed., 1998; Kornfeld et al. 1999; Kornfeld and Frison 2000; Surovell 2003; Surovell et al. 2000, 2001a, 2001b, 2003, 2005], and Colorado-Boulder [Bamforth 1994, 1998]); and government land agency–private cultural resource management (CRM) projects (e.g., Burney et al. 1979; Lischka et al. 1983; Metcalf et al. 1991; Wheeler and Burney 1984).

A recent and extensive contribution to the region's research record was a five-year (1998–2002) archaeological inventory program in Rocky Mountain National Park (RMNP), conducted as part of the National Park Service's Systemwide Archeological Inventory Program (SAIP) (Brunswig 1999, 2000, 2001a, 2002a, 2002b, 2005a). Over the life of the project, 430 archaeological sites representing more than 500 prehistoric cultural components (some sites were multicomponent) were recorded. SAIP field surveys resulted in 100 percent surface coverage of 29,793 acres of the park's total 173,000 acres and sampled all environmental zones. To date, the SAIP project constitutes the most detailed large-area study of prehistoric landscapes and forms an important data source for reconstruction of the region's Paleoindian record.

With the exception of SAIP and a handful of more limited surveys in the Indian Peaks area, central Middle Park, and south-central North Park, overall archaeological coverage tends to be geographically limited and unevenly distributed, most often reflecting limited linear or specific location (site) oriented investigations mandated by state or federal CRM legal requirements. Until future archaeological surveys in adjacent areas outside RMNP reach levels of scope and intensity achieved in the SAIP project, direct comparison of site numbers, cultural affiliation, densities, and distributions with non-park mountain areas will be only broadly useful for a detailed reconstruction of Paleoindian settlement patterns. However, I believe the current record provides an excellent starting point for initial settlement modeling studies, as demonstrated in this chapter.

Although most archaeological investigations in the north-central Colorado mountains are characterized by small-area survey coverage or individual site excavations, they collectively represent significant advances in our understanding of the region's prehistoric settlement history. Of particular note are a quarter-century of high-altitude game drive studies and site excavations by James Benedict and his Center for Mountain Archeology (Ward, Colorado) and, since 1995, the University of Wyoming's sustained program of surveys and camp and bison bone bed (kill and processing) excavations in Middle Park, particularly at the Barger Gulch, Jerry Craig, and Upper and Lower Twin Mountain sites (e.g., Surovell and Waguespack, Chapter 8, this volume). Other notable Paleoindian-related research programs include this volume's co-editor's (Bonnie Pitblado) Caribou Lake excavations and my excavations at RMNP's Lawn Lake site. More recently, the University of Northern Colorado (UNC) initiated a long-term survey and testing program on Bureau of Land Management lands in North Park that has been successful in identifying previously unknown Paleoindian activities (Brunswig 2004c, 2006).

PALEOINDIAN CHRONOLOGY AND CULTURAL TAXONOMIES

Paleoindian occupations in Colorado's southern Rocky Mountains encompass a time span of nearly four millennia (11,300–7,500 radiocarbon years before present [RCYBP]). Until recently, archaeologists often divided the long-used Paleoindian

Table 9.1. Paleoindian Classification Framework.

Paleoindian Periods from Youngest to Oldest (based on Chenault 1999)

late Plano/late or terminal Paleoindian "Period" (largely undefined in Chenault 1999, but seen here as including a range of projectile point types with parallel-oblique flaking patterns)
    Angostura Complex
    James Allen–Frederick Complex
    Meserve Complex
    Lusk Complex
    Pryor Stemmed Complex

early Plano Period (complexes broadly defined as associated with parallel-transverse projectile point flaking patterns)
    Hell Gap Complex
    Agate Basin Complex
    Cody Complex
    Cody Variants–Kersey and Firstview complexes
    Foothills/Mountain Complex

Folsom Period
    Folsom Complex

Clovis Period
    Clovis Complex
    Goshen Complex

---

cultural "stage" taxon into three subdivisions, each with one or multiple inclusive and generally successive, but often temporally overlapping, culture complexes referred to as its early, middle (a.k.a. early Plano), and late (a.k.a. late Plano) periods. A 1999 prehistoric context overview for Colorado's South Platte drainage system, an area that partially includes this chapter's region, utilized a broadly defined stage-period classification system that blended commonly used Paleoindian period terms defined by their association with defined "techno-complexes" defined by projectile point types (e.g., Clovis, Folsom) with more generic chronological-culture periods encompassing multiple culture complexes, for example, early Plano, late Paleoindian (Chenault 1999; Table 9.1).

Paleoindian stage-period–based subdivisions shown in Table 9.1, although broad and subject to future modifications, were assembled from decades of archaeological data gathered in Colorado's plains and eastern Front Range foothills, the plains of the Dakotas, Nebraska, and Kansas, and the Northwest Plains and central Rocky Mountains of Wyoming and Montana (e.g., Benedict 1992; Chenault 1999; Frison 1991a; Hofman and Graham 1998). A number of researchers, based on evidence for establishment of an indigenous, mountain-based Paleoindian tradition by the end of the early Paleoindian Period between 10,000 and 9,500 RCYBP, have chosen to use the term "late Paleoindian" rather than Plano (with its plains connotation) when referring to post-Folsom Paleoindian cultural adaptations in the middle and southern Rocky Mountains (e.g., Brunswig 2001c, 2004b, 2005a; Pitblado 1999a, 2003:10–11).

Paleoindian cultural periods and complexes, defined largely by projectile point typologies and dated through site-based radiocarbon analyses, remain relatively coarse measures of long-term evolving technologies and associated social and subsistence adaptations in north-central Colorado's mountains. As pointed out by Sellet (1999, 2001) and others (Haynes 1992; Holliday 2000; Holliday, Johnson, and Stafford 1999; Jodry 1999:47; Pitblado 2003), no clear-cut isomorphic succession of projectile point types and their associated techno (technologically defined) complexes exists, except in the broadest diachronic sense. The frequently synchronic (overlapping) nature of Paleoindian radiocarbon chronologies associated with particular projectile point types, and occasionally defined in excavated, cultural strata and features, suggests varying degrees of contemporaneity. In some instances, chronological contemporaneity of projectile point types and techno-complexes can be explained by a variety of factors, for example, statistical deviations, radiocarbon reservoir fluctuations (the Suess effect), contamination of radiocarbon samples, ethnic or regional function-based variability in projectile point typological traits, and extensive "remodeling" of points by successive reuse and rejuvenation (resulting in a morphological variability of specific "types"). Other factors—such as projectile point function (differing use patterns in varied ecosystems and their respective resources), overlapping ethnic territories, migratory patterns, and continued utilization of old technological patterns (types) as newer or introduced types remained in service—also likely played an important role in chronological contemporaneity of differing projectile point types (for further discussion of this topic, see Pitblado, Chapter 10, this volume).

In an analysis of the Hell Gap site sequence, Sellet (1999, 2001) documented stratigraphic and chronological overlap of Paleoindian projectile point types and occupation surfaces associated with its Folsom (10,900–10,200 RCYBP), Goshen (Goshen-Plainview) (10,900–10,000 RCYBP), Agate Basin (10,500–10,000 RCYBP), Hell Gap (10,400–9,500 RCYBP), and James Allen–Frederick (9,350–7,900 RCYBP) complexes. Eighmy and LaBelle's (1996) statistical analysis of radiocarbon date chronologies supports temporal overlap and contemporaneity of many well-established Paleoindian complexes.

REGIONAL PALEOINDIAN DATABASE SOURCES

Data for this study were derived from a comprehensive search of archaeological records. Resources included on-line Internet consultation of the Colorado State Historic Preservation Office (SHPO) COMPASS computer database and on-site examination of SHPO paper site forms in Denver. Paleoindian site and artifact data from Rocky Mountain National Park were already available from databases, analytical studies, and publications produced by the University of Northern

Colorado's SAIP program. Numerous other site and project reports, including limited distribution (gray literature) and more widely distributed published (journals, monographs) sources, were also consulted.

All north-central Colorado Paleoindian data—including such variables as site UTM (Universal Transverse Mercator) locations, environmental contexts, cultural components, site type, and others—were assembled in a master Excel™ spreadsheet database, converted to a dBase IV™ file format, and imported into an ArcGIS™ (Geographic Information System) mapping project. Other GIS data layers included geo-referenced U.S. Geological Survey Quadrangle DEMs (Digital Elevation Models), 1-meter-resolution aerial photography maps, and spatial data files for hydrology (steams, lakes, and similar features), land use (environmental-ecological polygons), and geology. The final GIS project provided basic components for the preliminary phase of settlement pattern modeling and visual representations (seen in following map figures) throughout the north-central Colorado mountain region's Paleoindian periods.

Database searches provided evidence for 137 Paleoindian sites and 8 isolated finds (in the form of diagnostic projectile points). Of that number, 141 definitive Paleoindian components with known cultural periods, based on specific projectile point types, were identified. An additional 57 sites and isolated finds were classed as "indeterminate Paleoindian." Indeterminate Paleoindian refers to sites or isolated finds that produced projectile point fragments considered Paleoindian in origin but lacking sufficient physical traits for definitive type assignments. The classification also included 9 sites with radiocarbon dates of Paleoindian age but having no directly associated Paleoindian material culture. All indeterminate components defined by artifact evidence were placed within the late Paleoindian Period based on their possession of projectile point fragments with parallel (transverse or oblique) flaking patterns.

The term "component," as used here, refers to evidence of a single occupation, or closely successive occupations, belonging to a specific cultural period at a particular locality. For purposes of analysis, isolated finds were treated in this study as single components. The term "multicomponent" refers to a site having more than one Paleoindian complex–projectile point type. Some Paleoindian sites classified as single component are actually multicomponent in the sense that they possess additional non-Paleoindian components. However, since this chapter deals only with Paleoindian occupations, designations of single or multicomponent refer only to each site or isolated find's Paleoindian affiliation. Figure 9.2 shows an ArcGIS-generated map of the region's 141 diagnostic and 57 indeterminate Paleoindian components. Some sites with multiple components have multiple, overlaid symbols representing the presence of different, successive cultural complexes at the same locality. Because of the complex and frequently overlapping nature of the figure's map symbols, no attempt was made to define them for each cultural complex, since the figure is intended only to illustrate the overall spatial patterning of Paleoindian Stage components.

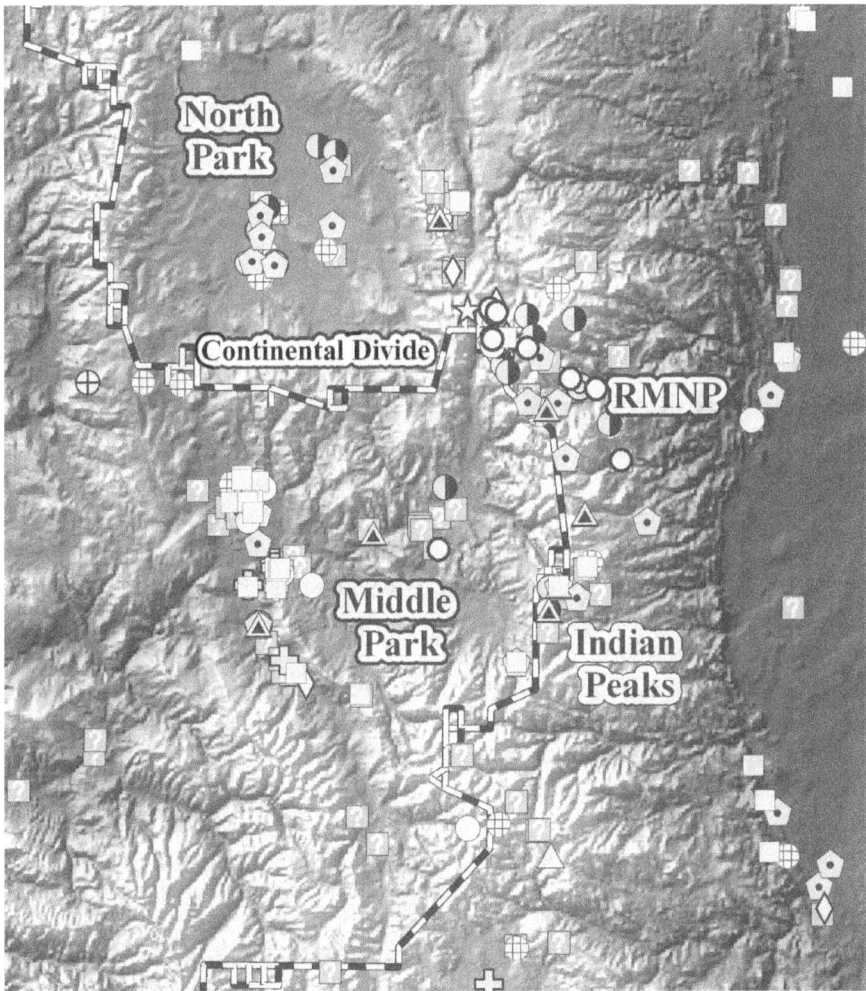

9.2. GIS map showing locations of all Paleoindian components in the north-central Colorado mountain region. Circles with dark borders are Clovis, circles with light borders are Goshen-Plainview, and light squares are Folsom.

NORTH-CENTRAL COLORADO MOUNTAIN PALEOINDIAN SETTLEMENT PATTERNING

The Early Paleoindian Period

The early Paleoindian Period encompasses three successive, but chronologically (radiocarbon) overlapping, techno-complexes: Clovis, Goshen-Plainview, and Folsom. Each is defined by morphologically similar (in a broad sense) projectile point types and nondiagnostic stone-tool assemblages associated with seasonally migratory hunting-gathering lifestyles. Table 9.2 shows site and isolated

Table 9.2. Distribution of Early Paleoindian Components by Environmental Zone.

Environmental Zone	Clovis	Goshen-Plainview	Folsom	Indeterminate Paleoindian
Alpine	4	—	—	1 (radiocarbon date-based)
Alpine-subalpine ecotone	—	—	3	—
Subalpine	1	1	1	—
Montane	3	—	1	—
Sage steppe (parkland)	1	9	14	—
Total sites and isolated find components	9	10	19	1

find component numbers of the three early Paleoindian techno-complexes (e.g., "periods") within the region and their locations within its five primary environmental zones. Table 9.2 is followed by Figure 9.3, which shows the distribution of early Paleoindian site and isolated find components in the region.

Clovis. The Clovis Complex (11,300–10,900 RCYBP) represents the earliest undisputed appearance of humans in North America (Stanford 1991). It is technologically defined by the presence of Clovis projectile points, represented by a range of small to large lanceolate-shaped projectile points, normally with some degree of basal fluting (Bradley 1993:252–254). Economic evidence for Clovis occupations is frequently grounded in hunting and scavenging of late Pleistocene fauna, including larger megafauna such as the Columbian mammoth (Cassells 1997:50). Documented Clovis sites in Colorado and Wyoming nearly always consist of small hunting camps or isolated projectile point finds, with the rare mammoth kill site (see Brunswig, Chapter 3, this volume). Although remains of late Ice Age (Pleistocene) megafauna (and associated Clovis artifacts) are more frequently preserved in the archaeological record than smaller species and are more likely to be discovered because of their size-based visibility, it remains likely that the hunting of larger Ice Age species (mammoth, bison, horse, and camel) was socially and economically important, if not central, to most Clovis hunter-gatherer bands, particularly in the western United States.

A survey of documented Colorado Clovis sites or isolated point finds (Brunswig 2007) shows that approximately forty Clovis sites or isolated finds have been officially reported and recorded in the Colorado State SHPO database (also see Chenault 1999:57–62; Jodry 1999:86–87; Reed and Metcalf 1999:56; Schroedl 1991). Several Clovis artifacts have been identified within Rocky Mountain National Park, but only two other Clovis components are documented in the region outside the park.

Shared Clovis toolkit traits across continental North America, and within Colorado, suggest the existence of a series of broadly similar adaptations to late Pleistocene environmental conditions (Meltzer 1993). Kelly and Todd (1988) have

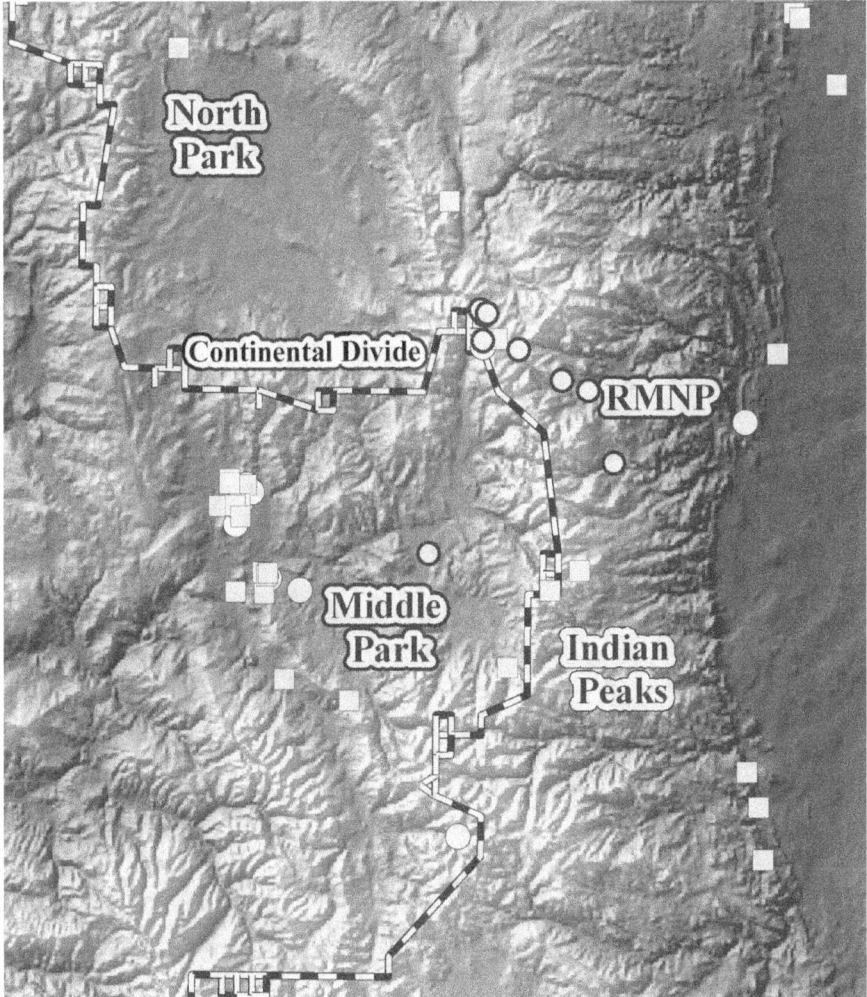

9.3. *GIS map distribution of early Paleoindian components. Circles with dark borders are Clovis, circles with light borders are Goshen-Plainview, and light squares are Folsom.*

proposed that this broadly shared toolkit and subsistence pattern was a result of a relatively rapid (<500 years?) spread of Clovis peoples throughout North America and a need for a generalized, flexible technological base and subsistence system designed to cope with late Pleistocene climatic and environmental uncertainty.

The Clovis Period, particularly in its later phases, was characterized by dramatic environmental change characterized by accelerating deglaciation of continental glaciers following the last (Pinedale) glacial maximum (Brunswig 2004a, 2005a:44–48, in prep; Doerner 2004, 2005, Chapter 1, this volume). Glaciers and annually persistent tundra snowfields in many Colorado mountain areas would have blocked most passes and hindered migratory access of game herds and humans to high-altitude summer pastures throughout most of Clovis times. Near the end of the Clovis Period, rapid and dramatic warming at 11,100–10,900 RCYBP appears to have resulted in substantial deglaciation of most mountain glacial cirques and col valleys in north-central Colorado's Rockies (Brunswig 2005a:45–50; Doerner, Chapter 1, this volume).

Although Clovis groups may have been technologically capable of living and moving in mid-elevations along either side of Colorado's Continental Divide, they may have had limited incentive to do so early in their occupation of the region. Initially, coming into the country for the first time, they would have been unfamiliar with mountain-based economic resources, and Terminal Pleistocene climatic conditions may have made the higher-altitude mountain areas less attractive or even physically inaccessible. As a result, early Clovis groups would have chosen to concentrate their economic activities on the procurement of late Ice Age prey species in Colorado's lower mountain valleys, foothills, and eastern plains. Recent discoveries of Clovis artifacts, many at extremely high altitudes, suggest growing utilization of and familiarity with mountain territories, particularly by late Clovis times.

The majority of Clovis finds in the region are from Rocky Mountain National Park, possibly as a result of extensive coverage by large-scale SAIP archaeological surveys from 1998 to 2002. Seven complete or partial Clovis projectile points have been documented (Brunswig 2001c, 2003a, 2005a:106–107). In 1932 a Clovis projectile point base was recovered from Trail Ridge in alpine tundra (Husted 1965:496). From 1998 through 2002, University of Northern Colorado surveys in RMNP recovered a complete Clovis point from the subalpine zone in La Poudre Pass and two point fragments from alpine tundra sites from Specimen Mountain and Bighorn Flats. A Clovis point and base fragment were also documented from lower montane zone sites east of the Continental Divide. Finally, in 2003 RMNP archaeologist William Butler retrieved a complete Clovis point from the University of Colorado museum, where it had been stored as part of Husted's 1962 master's thesis–related artifact collection from the park in the early 1960s. The specimen had come from a major multicomponent alpine tundra site overlooking the park's Milner Pass.

It is notable that five Clovis artifacts were found in modern alpine tundra or in upper subalpine forest-meadow ecosystems where Clovis-age tree lines are believed to have been 50 to 75 m. lower than at present (Brunswig 2005a:48–49). The presence of Clovis artifacts at high elevations indicates that significant deglaciation had occurred by late Clovis times and that tundra areas previously covered by permanent snowfields were accessible during summer months.

Goshen-Plainview. The Goshen, or Goshen-Plainview, Complex (11,100–8,000 RCYBP) represents an immediately post-Clovis cultural complex initially defined in stratigraphic deposits at Wyoming's Hell Gap site (Gilmore et al. 1999:63; Irwin-

Williams et al. 1971; Pitblado 1999a:170–176, 2003:104–107) and later at Montana's single-component Mill Iron site (Frison 1988:84–89, 1991a:41, 368, 1992b; Frison, Haynes, and Larson 1996; Stafford 1990). The complex and its defining Goshen projectile point type—a lanceolate point lacking the common, partial basal fluting of earlier Clovis points or the three-quarter flutes of slightly later to contemporary Folsom points—remains a focus of typological and cultural discussion.

Goshen, at least in its early stages, has been proposed as a transitional technological development between Clovis and Folsom, although radiocarbon dates suggest temporal overlap with termination of the former and initiation of the latter. Recent discussions on Goshen projectile points have pointed to their technological-typological similarity with Plainview points, primarily associated with southern plains sites. Pitblado (1999a, 2003) and others (Frison 1992b; Frison, Haynes, and Larson 1996; Haynes 1991) have suggested a technical (and possible cultural) relationship between Goshen and Plainview. In 1996 the term Goshen-Plainview was coined in an attempt to deal with close typological similarities between the two types (Frison, Haynes, and Larson 1996:206). Goshen component radiocarbon dates of the central and southern Rockies tend to be earlier than Plainview components in the southern plains, but there is significant overlap between their respective chronologies, with radiocarbon dated Goshen occupations ranging between 11,100–10,100 RCYBP and Plainview occupations tending to cluster later, ca. 10,000–8,000 RCYBP (e.g., Holliday 1997, 2000). It is conceivable the two types represent a lengthy evolutionary history of variations of a single projectile point style over an extraordinary span of time (3,000 or more years), but it is also possible the two types are not directly related in a "cultural" sense but rather in only a technological sense. Sellet (2001:52–53) also pointed out typological similarities between the Midland projectile type (once believed to be an unfluted Folsom variant) and suggests the three "types" might represent a single geographically and chronologically diverse typological style. This study follows Frison, Haynes, and Larson (1996:206) and Pitblado (2003:104–107) in using the term "Goshen-Plainview" when referring to early Paleoindian Period unfluted, lanceolate points with concave bases, a tendency toward parallel-traverse flaking, and generally straight, parallel lower blade edges.

Only ten Goshen-Plainview components have been identified in the region. Seven are in the lower-elevation parkland environmental zone (Middle Park, Grand County), and two were found in the upper subalpine zone (RMNP and at the region's southern edge near the Summit-Park counties boundary). The relative lack of Goshen-Plainview occupations may be related to the fact that, prior to University of Wyoming Middle Park investigations begun in 1995, earlier field archaeologists, lacking familiarity with the Goshen-Plainview type, may have misidentified points with morphologically similar McKean Lanceolate (Middle Archaic) and other less-well-known Paleoindian and non-Paleoindian types. Future reinvestigation of pre-1995 reported site materials may result in identification of additional Goshen-Plainview components.

Largely as a result of University of Wyoming field studies, Goshen-Plainview components, as noted earlier, are best known from Middle Park (Kornfeld 1998; Kornfeld et al. 1999; Kornfeld and Frison 2000). All seven of Middle Park's Goshen-Plainview component sites are concentrated in two locations: in the Barger Gulch area immediately south of the Colorado River and in and around Little Wolford and Twin Mountain several miles north of Kremmling. To date, the only excavated site with a Goshen-Plainview occupation is Upper Twin Mountain (5GA1513), a single-event bison kill in an upper-mountain slope slump depression. Remains of fifteen adult bison (*Bison bison antiquus*) were recovered with four Goshen-Plainview points, butchering tools, and flake debitage (Kornfeld 1998, 1999:663–670; Kornfeld and Frison 2000:144–147). Its two radiocarbon dates (10,470 ± 50 and 10,240 ± 70 RCYBP) (Kornfeld et al. 1999:658) suggest radiocarbon contemporaneity of Twin Mountain's Goshen-Plainview component with Middle Park's only dated Folsom site, Barger Gulch (discussed later). Upper Twin Mountain's excavators (Kornfeld et al. 1999:672; Kornfeld and Frison 2000:144, 147), citing bison season-of-death analyses, believe the kill took place in late fall–early winter and that its perpetrators were engaged in "the acquisition of surplus meat for permanent residence. Together with the archaeological evidence demonstrating a late fall/early winter bison procurement, a year-round occupation of Middle Park during Paleoindian times is implied because hunter-gatherers would not likely be at such a high, isolated, difficult to reach location at this late date if they planned to leave for the winter."

Only two Goshen-Plainview sites are found in high-altitude areas. One (5ST695) is a small lithic scatter camp with a chert Goshen-Plainview point, situated on a subalpine terrace of a Snake River headwaters tributary on the region's southern boundary. The second is a small subalpine camp (5GA2537), also with a single Goshen-Plainview projectile point, located in Rocky Mountain National Park's Milner Pass (Brunswig 2001a:41–42). Its location in the pass would have allowed access to four alternative routes (Milner Pass itself, the adjacent Cache la Poudre River headwaters valley, Fall River Pass, Forest Canyon Pass, and Trail Ridge) over the Continental Divide from the Kawuneeche Valley into Middle Park. Its presence indicates those passes were open to human transit for a time after the Clovis Period and may have remained open until onset of the Younger Dryas glacial climatic episode (Satanta Peak) around 10,800 RCYBP.

Folsom. The Folsom Cultural Complex, 10,900–10,000 RCYBP, chronologically overlaps later phases of the Goshen-Plainview Complex during a time of climatic-environmental transition between the colder Pleistocene and the warmer Holocene. By Folsom times, mammoth had become extinct in the western mountains and plains. Most Folsom sites, including several in Middle Park, appear to have been associated with hunting of small *Bison bison antiquus* herds (Gilmore et al. 1999:64). Folsom hunting technology is distinguished by the manufacture and use of fine-quality fluted, lanceolate projectile points with distinctive concave bases (Cassells 1997:71–72). Although the late Ice Age bison species *Bison antiquus* is considered to have been an economic mainstay of many Folsom groups in the western plains and mountains, faunal assemblages from sites such as Lindenmeier in the Front Range foothills provide evidence that smaller game species like pronghorn, rabbit, and turtle were also hunted (Gilmore et al. 1999:64; Wilmsen and Roberts 1978). A mixed-game subsistence strategy would likely have been practiced in Colorado's southern Rockies, where game species such as elk, mule deer, bighorn sheep, rabbits, sage grouse, and seasonally migratory ducks and geese would have supplemented bison hunting.

Although Folsom sites have often been thought to occur more commonly in the plains, substantial evidence indicates that Colorado's intermontane parks were home to Folsom hunter-gatherer bands, exemplified by a growing number of bison kill sites, processing camps, and possibly even longer-term cold-season camps. Archaeological evidence for extensive mountain resource utilization is seen in an expanding list of Folsom sites in the San Luis Valley (Jodry 1999:91–96), South Park (Lincoln et al. 2003:12–13, 21–22), the Gunnison Basin (Stiger 2006), Middle Park (Kornfeld and Frison 2000; Kornfeld et al. 1999; Naze 1986; Surovell et al. 2001a, 2001b), and North Park (Brunswig 2004c; Lischka et al.1983:59). In addition to a strong Folsom presence in intermontane park valleys, small camps and isolated finds occur in many smaller valleys and lower-elevation mountain slopes, although they are extremely rare in higher-elevation subalpine and alpine zones (Brunswig 2004a, 2004b, 2005a:72–73, in prep).

Nineteen Folsom sites and isolated finds are documented from the north-central Colorado mountains: four in high-altitude alpine and subalpine zones (Boulder and Larimer counties), one in the montane zone (Summit County), and fourteen in Middle Park (Grand County) and North Park (Jackson County) parkland zones (Table 9.2). However, all but one of the parkland sites was located in Middle Park.

The rarity of high-altitude Folsom sites is interesting. Benedict (2000a:162–164, figure 5.4b) recently documented a Folsom point in a private artifact collection from the Fourth of July Mine site near Arapaho Pass, but it was heavily reworked and may have been transported to the site by a later group. The only other high-altitude sites are an alpine-subalpine ecotone camp (5BL72) in the Indian Peaks Wilderness and two subalpine camps, one (5GA2209) near Ute Pass in southern Grand County's Williams Fork Range and the second (5LR17) on a west branch of the Laramie River south of the Wyoming-Colorado border. Finally, a lower-elevation montane zone camp (5ST300) is situated on a terrace of the Blue River in northern Summit County. Despite extensive archaeological surveys in Rocky Mountain National Park, only a single Folsom artifact has been identified, a reworked, heat-warped projectile point from a large multicomponent camp (5LR2) in the upper subalpine-alpine ecotone of Forest Canyon Pass.

I have suggested elsewhere that most alpine tundra areas in the southern Rocky Mountains may have been largely denied to Folsom hunting bands (and summer migratory herbivores) because of glacial conditions and persistent snowfield cover associated with the Younger Dryas climatic episode between 10,900 and 10,200 RCYBP (Brunswig 2001c, 2004a, 2005a). Jodry (1999:60–62) expressed a similar view when she remarked on the general lack of higher-altitude (>3100 m) Folsom sites in Colorado's Upper Rio Grande Basin. However, in the lower-elevation parklands of Middle Park and North Park, there is evidence that Folsom groups hunted small bison and other game and may have even been year-round residents (discussed later; also see Kornfeld et al. 1999; Surovell et al. 2003; Surovell and Waguespack, Chapter 8, this volume).

To date, no Folsom bison kills have been identified in those intermontane parks, only open camps. One, Hay Springs (5GA295), north of Little Wolford Mountain, contains a bison bone bed producing Folsom, Goshen-Plainview, and Cody artifacts, none definitively associated with the kill. Hay Springs is one of fourteen Paleoindian sites and two isolated finds within a large 88 km² area surrounding Little Wolford Mountain and Twin Mountain north of Kremmling, Colorado (Kornfeld and Frison 2000; Naze 1986, 1994). Of those, a minimum of six and possibly as many as thirteen have Folsom components, while two Folsom isolated points are also known.

The region's best-documented Folsom site is Middle Park's Barger Gulch's Locality B, the subject of this volume's Chapter 8 by Todd Surovell and Nicole Waguespack. Barger Gulch (5GA195) is a series of six prehistoric activity localities scattered over an extensive area of eroded hill ridges, slopes, drainage swales, and upper stream terraces south of the Colorado River. Its localities and isolated finds extend over 1.6 km². Three localities contain Folsom components, including A (a large quarry workshop with Folsom and other, late Paleoindian (Cody, Hell Gap–Western Stemmed, and James Allen–Frederick) components; B (a large Folsom camp site, the subject of Chapter 8, this volume); and C (a small Folsom camp).

In a report on excavations at Locality B, Surovell and colleagues (2003:10) suggested that the Barger Gulch localities represent the normal equivalent of archaeological sites and isolated finds, noting that the word "site" should be interpreted "synonymously with locality because the entities that are referred to as localities within the Barger Gulch site, aside from the two localities referred to as isolated projectile points, are large (hundreds to thousands of m² in area) spatially discrete concentrations of artifacts on the landscape and would fit most archaeologists' concept of site . . . [although] these sites share a single site designation, that of 5GA195."

Locality B, situated on a finger ridge overlooking a secondary tributary of Barger Gulch, has been under excavation by the University of Wyoming since 1997 (Danielle 2003; Kornfeld 1998:54; Kornfeld, Frison, and White 2001; Surrovell et al. 2000, 2001a, 2001b, 2003, 2005; Surrovell and Waguespack, Chapter 8, this volume). By the summer of 2003, 51 m² had been excavated and around 20,000 artifacts (a total that includes lithic debitage) had been recovered and analyzed. Its surface finds extend over at least 7,000 m², although the site's cultural deposits are thin (5–10 cm), shallow (30–50 cm below the surface), and have been subject to post-depositional vertical transport. Even so, the deposits are extensive and highly concentrated in some areas, reflecting a large camp with spatially discrete activity areas. One such concentration, around a hearth, is described and analyzed by Surovell and Waguespack in Chapter 8 of this volume. Radiocarbon dates of 10,770 ± 70 and 10,470 ± 40 RCYBP (averaged to 10,540 ± 35 RCYBP) were obtained from charcoal and are believed to represent a single-event occupation (Surovell et al. 2003:64). Thirteen whole or partial Folsom points, several preforms, game processing tools (e.g., scrapers and knives), and thousands of tool-manufacturing flakes have been recovered. Lithic-tool materials are almost exclusively made of local chert and quartzite. Although animal bone has been recovered, it has, so far, been too fragmented and deteriorated for species identification.

Two other Folsom sites, 5GA1208 (Crying Woman) and 5GA2246, are located west-southwest of Barger Gulch. Crying Woman, located near a spring in upper Barger Gulch, 2.7 km southwest of the Barger Gulch site complex, was subjected to limited test excavation by Naze for his 1994 master's thesis. Site 5GA2246 is an extensive lithic scatter with Folsom and later Paleoindian components, situated on a west-facing ridge slope overlooking the Blue River Valley, 6.5 km southwest of the Barger Gulch sites. A final Folsom component is believed to be present at Middle Park's Hay Gulch site (5GA1609), where test excavations revealed a buried hearth radiocarbon dated to 10,020 ± 90 RCYBP (Harrison et al. 2000). The relative abundance of Folsom components in central Middle Park prompted Cassells (1997:74) to suggest its Folsom site density was "equivalent to the San Luis Valley and exceeds portions of the plains commonly thought of as prime Folsom territory, such as the Llano Estacado far to the south and east in Texas, or in the Rio Grande Valley of New Mexico." University of Wyoming investigations at Barger Gulch and in the Little Wolford Mountain–Twin Mountain area go far in supporting that assessment.

The Late Paleoindian Period in the North-Central Rockies

The region's Goshen-Plainview and Folsom occupations are succeeded by cultural complexes belonging to the late Paleoindian Period. Earlier, primarily plains- and foothills-focused literature frequently divided what is referred to here as the late Paleoindian Period into two subperiods: early and late Plano, with occasionally an intermediate mid-Plano period added. Archaeological evidence accumulated over the past three decades suggests the existence of an evolving dichotomy of post-Folsom plains-adapted versus mountain-adapted cultural traditions, encouraged and driven by early Holocene climatic change (Benedict 1992; Black 1991; Brunswig 2001c; Frison 1992a, 1997; Husted 1969, 1995).

Current models of climate change in the central and southern Rockies point to establishment of warmer and moister than present conditions between 10,000–8,500 RCYBP, succeeded by continued warm conditions but with gradually decreasing effective precipitation patterns from 8,500 to 7,000 RCYBP (Brunswig

2005a:50–55; Cummings and Moutoux 1998; Cummings, Varney, and Bryson, Chapter 7, this volume; Doerner, Chapter 1, this volume; Doerner and Brunswig in prep; Elias 1985:35; Mayer et al. 2005). Early Holocene moisture increase and summer-season warming appear to have led to opening of high tundra pastures for warm-season migratory game animals and development of increasingly mountain-adapted Paleoindian populations, sometimes collectively referred to as Foothills-Mountain or Mountain Paleoindian traditions (Brunswig 2001c:437–447; Frison 1992a, 1997; Pitblado 1999a, 2003, Chapter 10, this volume).

Although detailed evidence for late Paleoindian Period (10,250–7,000 RCYBP) occupations in Colorado's southern Rocky Mountains is only now emerging, their radiocarbon chronology and evolutionary patterning of technological traits can be partially extrapolated from research in other western and central U.S. regions. In the broadest terms, the late Paleoindian Period is defined by a series of overlapping culture techno-complexes (with defining projectile point types) based on archaeological evidence assembled over three-quarters of a century of research in the northwest plains and foothills of Wyoming and Montana, the northern and central Great Plains, and the western and southern plains. The southern Rockies also contain rare evidence for external cultural interaction with the northern Southwest and the eastern Great Basin.

A recent synthetic study of southern Rocky Mountain projectile point types by Bonnie Pitblado (1999a, 2003, Chapter 10, this volume) initiated a serious effort to understand late Paleoindian settlement and culture-evolutionary patterns in Colorado's mountains, plains, and western plateaus. Pitblado's research and that by Benedict, Frison, Husted, Jodry, Kornfeld, and me, among others, provides a substantial emerging body of evidence for construction of an increasingly reliable chronological-cultural framework for later Paleoindian occupations of the southern Rockies. Based on those individuals' studies and recent data generated by UNC's SAIP program, I (Brunswig in press) have suggested consideration of a culture-chronological framework that broadly divides the late Paleoindian Period of Colorado's southern Rockies into two successive and overlapping early and late cultural phases (Table 9.3).

Late Paleoindian Projectile Point Types and Typologies. Mountain-based late Paleoindian occupations have, until recently, been largely referenced to Plano Paleoindian site assemblages from the Great Plains. Those occupations were often interpreted as representing hunter-gatherer bands focused on subsistence strategies emphasizing bison hunting, although bison appear to have become increasingly scarce (late Plano times) as climatic conditions deteriorated on the plains in the terminal centuries of the late Paleoindian Period.

In general, plains-based complexes were classified by association with projectile point types manufactured using a bifacial thinning technique that removed long, narrow flakes in parallel rows across both blade faces, referred to as parallel or collateral flaking. Resulting projectile points present an appear-

Table 9.3. Late Paleoindian Period, with Proposed Early and Late Phases (10,250–7,000 RCYBP). Individual Chronologies (date ranges) Based on Pitblado (1999a, 2003).

Culture Complex (Phase) (defined by one or more projectile point types)	Uncalibrated Radiocarbon Date Range
Early Phase (10,250–8,500 RCYBP)	
Great Basin Stemmed (rare, intrusive from the west?)	10,700–7,550
Agate Basin (rare, intrusive from the plains?)	10,430–9,350
Cody Complex (Scottsbluff I/II [rare], Eden, Firstview, San Jon, Kersey parallel-transverse point types (with some parallel-oblique examples)	9,400–8,300
Lovell Constricted	9,350–7,700
James Allen–Frederick	9,350–7,900
Angostura	9,700–7,550
Late Phase (ca. 8,500–7,000 RCYBP)	
Late continuation of James Allen–Frederick, Angostura, and Lovell Constricted and the appearance of Pryor Stemmed types (commonly, but not always, parallel-oblique flaked)	8,450–7,500/7,000
Concave-Based Stemmed	8,200–8,000
Deception Creek (defined and present in limited instances in far western areas of the southern Rockies and the Colorado Plateau)	8,500–7,500

ance (in most cases) of a series of horizontal lines of more or less continuous flake scars extending from their tips to their bases. Early Plano complexes (Hell Gap, Agate Basin, Alberta, Cody) applied the flaking technique in a way that nearly always created a series of flake scars transverse (blade edge to blade edge) to point lengths, while late Plano complexes such as James Allen–Frederick, Angostura, and many Lovell Constricted and Pryor Stemmed projectile points present more angled or parallel-oblique flake scar patterning. However, the existence of parallel-transverse or parallel-oblique patterning is not always a reliable diagnostic feature for all earlier or later late Paleoindian projectile point types. Some individual projectile point specimens with typological traits characteristic of earlier late Paleoindian complexes most frequently exhibit angled (parallel-oblique) flake scar patterning. However, some examples exhibit both parallel-transverse and parallel-oblique patterns on different sections of the same artifact. A similar mix of transverse and oblique flaking pattern can also be a case, although perhaps less commonly, of later projectile point types defined by possession of parallel-oblique flaking.

Growing typological and archaeological evidence suggests that both early (Cody) and later (James Allen–Frederick, Angostura, and Lovell Constricted–Pryor Stemmed) projectile point types, some previously considered almost exclusively Plano in geographic context, were common in the Rocky Mountains as well. Evidence suggests those types were undergoing stylistic modifications (regionalization) leading to stylistically differentiated mountain subtypes or variants, subtypes that remain to be fully defined. Although sufficient mountain projectile point assemblages have yet to be thoroughly analyzed for intratype variation, I am inclined to favor a working hypothesis that there may have been earlier use of parallel-oblique flaking in the Colorado Rockies, as opposed to parallel-transverse flaking, than in more easterly plains regions.

Although she does not apply her observations to specific point types, Pitblado (2003:188–191, table 8.6) noted a strong bias for parallel-oblique flaking (45.38 percent) versus parallel-transverse flaking (23.84 percent) in late Paleoindian projectile points of the Rocky Mountains (130), while plains points (206) exhibited a bias for parallel-transverse types (43.68 percent) versus parallel-oblique types (17.96 percent). Without knowing what proportion of her point study group constituted types normally defined as having one flaking pattern or the other but that instead exhibited the alternate pattern, we cannot judge if earlier parallel-transverse defined types, such as Cody, were actually departing or evolving away from their "normally established" pattern (parallel-transverse) in mountain areas.

Given the limited number of mountain Paleoindian radiocarbon dated sites and lack of detailed analyses of a large sample population of different projectile point types, this hypothesis may remain speculative for some time. It is suggested, in light of limited evidence, that parallel-oblique flaking as a stylistic technique *may* have initially been a "mountain-evolved" pattern that emerged in the earlier centuries of late Paleoindian times and was subsequently adopted by more easterly plains and foothills (Plano) populations. Minimally, that spread could have taken place in early Cody (9,300 RCYBP) times and been transmitted east, northeast, and southeast from the central and southern Rockies into the northwest plains, High Plains, and Great Plains in the guise of the late Plano complexes, an evolutionary pattern contrary to most current belief. In addition to what may have been early emergence of parallel-oblique flaking in mountain point-manufacturing technologies, a series of stemmed projectile point types (many with parallel-oblique flaking patterns) appears typologically analogous to Western Stemmed Tradition types of the Great Basin (Bryan 1988; Tuohy and Layton 1977), among which the Great Basin Stemmed type may be the best represented in Colorado's southern Rockies, although even there it appears rarely (see Pitblado 2003:92–99). Two other late Paleoindian types, Pryor Stemmed and Lovell Constricted, found in the region in limited numbers (so far), were initially defined in the central Rocky Mountains and foothills (Frison 1992a; Frison and Grey 1980; Pitblado 2003:99–100).

As described by Pitblado (1999a, 2003), late Paleoindian mountain (and other western U.S.) point types are broadly separable into two typological categories: (1) those with some degree of lower blade stemming, and (2) unstemmed lanceolate points with parallel lower blade edges. Stemmed point types include Hell Gap, Alberta, Western Stemmed types (generally lumped here under Great Basin Stemmed), Cody Complex–associated types or type variants-subtypes (Scottsbluff, Kersey, Firstview, San Jon, and Eden), and two morphologically related Foothills-Mountain types, Lovell Constricted and Pryor Stemmed.

Hell Gap (10,450–9,350 RCYBP) points are generally lanceolate, with a long-converging, unshouldered stem and a convex to straight base. Its blade faces generally exhibit parallel-transverse flaking patterns. Western Stemmed types (see Pitblado 2003:92–97) are subsumed here under the generalized Great Basin Stemmed (GBS) "type." Dated at various Great Basin sites between ca. 10,700 and 7,550 RCYBP, GBS points exhibit traits that broadly overlap with Hell Gap and are frequently classified as the Hell Gap type by many archaeologists working in the Rockies. They are lanceolate to nearly teardrop in outline, although they tend to be wider than most Hell Gap points. GBS stems are relatively long (up to 40 percent of total length), their bases range from rounded convex to lightly rounded, and blade flaking patterns range from random to parallel—either transverse, oblique, or both in the same point. Identification of Hell Gap points in the southern Rockies is somewhat problematic, particularly since many examples exhibit traits that overlap with those of Great Basin Stemmed examples.

Recent University of Wyoming publications refer to Hell Gap components at Middle Park sites, describing them as "Hell Gap or Western Stemmed" (Kornfeld and Frison 2000:147; Kornfeld, Frison, and White 2001:32–33). I classified two stemmed points stored in the Rocky Mountain National Park museum as Great Basin Stemmed, although, except for a lack of parallel-transverse flaking, they might fit within the range of documented Hell Gap points from eastern plains sites. All stemmed points from the north-central Colorado mountain region that broadly fit the Hell Gap and GBS type descriptions were, for the purposes of this study, lumped into a more generic Hell Gap–GBS type classification.

Alberta points (9,900–8,600 RCYBP) are a stemmed type with pronounced shoulders separating the stem from the upper blade body and tend to resemble slightly later Cody stemmed point types, but often with more pronounced shoulders. Alberta points appear to be extremely rare in most southern Rocky Mountain regions (Brunswig in prep).

Cody Complex point types include two variations (I and II) of the short-stemmed, shouldered, and (generally) parallel-transverse flaked Scottsbluff type; two, possibly three, lower stem-to-length ratio Scottsbluff-variant types (Kersey, Firstview, San Jon); and the narrow, subtly stemmed Eden type. Pitblado's (2003:81–87, Chapter 10, this volume) analysis of western late Paleoindian projectile point collections (plains, foothills, mountains, Great Basin) separates what are usually seen as Cody types into Scottsbluff and Eden-Firstview type categories. My own admittedly limited experience with Cody (sometimes referred to as "Cody-like" by University of Wyoming Middle Park researchers, e.g., Kornfeld and Frison 2000:139) projectile point types from the Colorado Rockies suggests that lumping all the Scottsbluff types (subtypes) into a generalized Cody category, pending more detailed analyses of those types from mountain locations in the future, is a reasonable approach for their inclusion in this study. Combining the various types as a single Cody phenomenon makes little difference in terms of chronological provenance, as a Scottsbluff radiocarbon chronology (9,400–8,300 RCYBP) and an integrated Eden-Firstview-Kersey chronology (9,500–8,200 RCYBP) are essentially identical (Pitblado 2003:84–87). I do see a distinction between the larger, wider Scottsbluff-Kersey-Firstview point types and the narrower, less robust Eden type and have differentiated them as Cody and Cody-Eden for GIS analysis.

Two other stemmed point types, considered core to Frison's central Rocky Mountain–defined Foothills-Mountain Tradition, are Lovell Constricted and Pryor Stemmed. Both are morphologically similar and may constitute parts of a single evolutionary, single typological continuum, with Lovell Constricted (9,350–7,700 RCYBP) representing the earlier portion of that continuum and Pryor Stemmed (8,450–7,800 RCYBP) the latest (Pitblado 2003:97–100). Lovell Constricted points are characterized by moderately to steeply converging lower blade edges in their lowest parts, displaying either subtle, short stems or more abrupt, lightly shouldered stems. Blade face flaking patterns range from random to parallel-oblique, and their bases are slightly in-curving to moderately concave. Pryor Stemmed points resemble Lovell Constricted points in their short lower stems but have straighter, less convergent lower blade edges. Blade flaking patterns (random to parallel-oblique) are identical in both, although their bases tend to be flatter and less concave.

Late Paleoindian unstemmed lanceolate point types include Agate Basin, James Allen (sometimes referred to as Jimmy Allen), Frederick, Lusk, and Angostura. The Agate Basin point type (10,500–9,600 RCYBP) is well established as the fossil-index artifact of a prominent early Plano cultural complex that directly succeeds, or even overlaps (in radiocarbon years), Folsom. It is rarely found in Colorado's southern Rockies, although it is certainly present. Morphologically, it tends to have a high length-to-width ratio, with its lower half to third converging to a well-rounded to slightly concave base. Its most common, but not universal, blade face flaking pattern is parallel-transverse.

James Allen, Frederick, Angostura, and Lusk points constitute slightly later (than Cody) lanceolate, unstemmed types in the region. All four are broadly similar in overall morphology and flaking patterns. James Allen and Frederick types, as noted by Pitblado (2003:112), exhibit traits that justify placing them in the same type class, which she simply calls Jimmy Allen–Frederick (as of publication of this volume, again simply Jimmy Allen but encompassing Frederick [Pitblado, Chapter 10, this volume]). The generalized James Allen–Frederick point type (shortened to JAF from here on) has a 9,350–7,900 RCYBP date range and is lanceolate in form, commonly with an in-tapering lower third, although some examples abruptly out-taper near the base, producing a slightly "eared" effect. Its base varies from slightly concave to deeply concave, and its blade faces nearly always exhibit parallel-oblique scar patterns, although blade sections sometimes display a more random pattern. Lower blade edges tend to be slightly ground down.

Angostura points (9,700–7,550 RCYBP), which include the essentially identical Lusk type, are also lanceolate in shape but have a more tapered, convergent lower blade area and a thinner cross-section than JAF. Angostura bases range from nearly

Table 9.4. Distribution of Late Paleoindian Components by Environmental Zones.

Environmental Zone	Hell Gap/ GBS	Agate Basin	Cody	James Allen– Frederick	Ango- stura	Lovell Con- stricted	Pryor Stemmed	Indeterminate Late Paleoindian
Alpine	—	—	2	10	6	1	2	7
Alpine- subalpine ecotone	2	1	11	10	4	—	3	12
Subalpine	—	1	2	1	2	—	—	4
Montane	—	1	—	1	1	1	—	11
Sage steppe (parkland)	2	—	12	15	6	3	2	23
Total of all sites and isolated finds	4	3	27	37	19	5	7	56

flat to moderately concave, and blade face flaking patterns vary from parallel-transverse to parallel-oblique, with a greater tendency for the latter. Frison (1997: 87–91) includes Angostura as part of the central Rocky Mountain's Foothills-Mountain Tradition, although there are a number of Angostura component sites in plains regions, including its type-site in South Dakota (Wheeler 1995). Pitblado (2003:132, Chapter 10, this volume), based on analysis of 589 Paleoindian projectile points from the eastern plains to the Great Basin, found Angostura to be the dominant type in the southern Rocky Mountains of Colorado and Utah.

Late Paleoindian Settlement Patterns. Table 9.4 presents data on all late Paleoindian culture components for sites and isolated finds and associated environmental zones in the north-central Colorado mountains.

The table documents 102 late Paleoindian components with diagnostic projectile points from the project area. Another 56 indeterminate components are considered late Paleoindian in affiliation, defined (as noted earlier) by their possession of projectile point fragments with transverse parallel, oblique, or both parallel flaking patterns or consisting of site components producing radiocarbon dates (8) falling within the late Paleoindian time range.

Computer database and literature records show that earlier late Paleoindian components are rare, with only 7 documented. Three were recovered from the alpine-subalpine ecotone zone, 1 from the subalpine forest zone, 1 from the montane zone (Agate Basin), and 2 from sagebrush steppe/parkland. Figure 9.4 shows a GIS map projection of earlier late Paleoindian component locations. Two Agate Basin components (points) finds occur in Rocky Mountain National Park, one from the large multicomponent Forest Canyon Pass (5LR2) site and a second (isolated find 5LR10266) from nearby La Poudre Pass.

Later late Paleoindian components represent a major increase in overall numbers and a more balanced spatial distribution in regional environmental

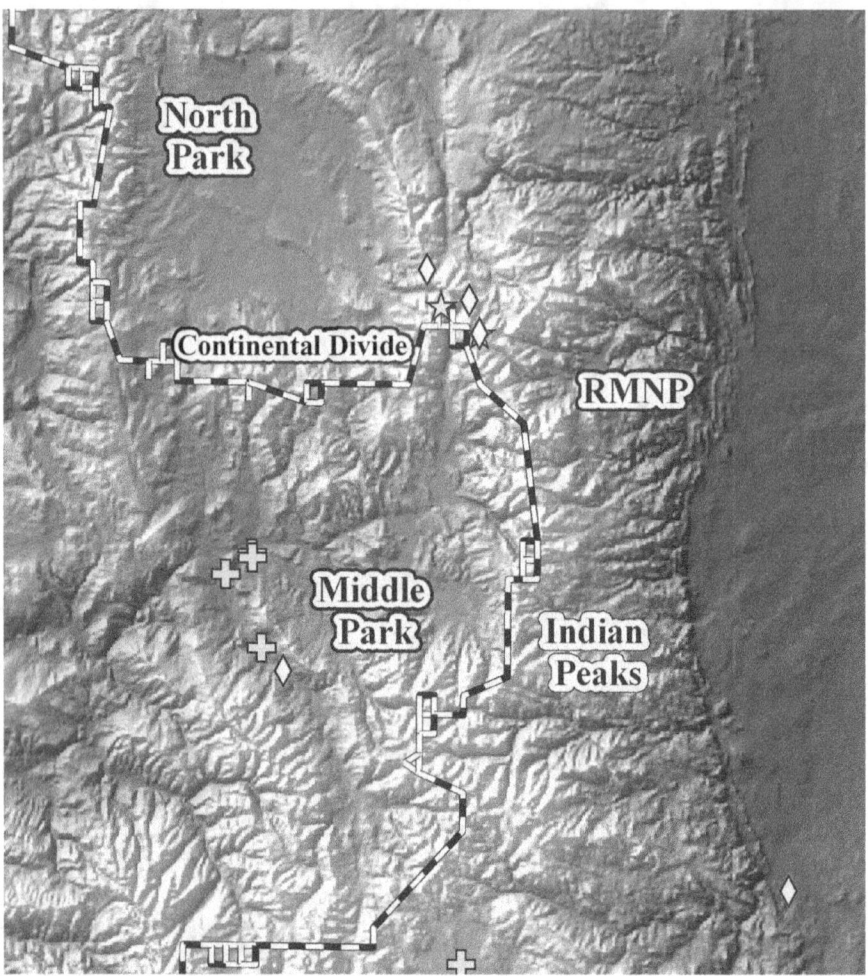

9.4. Locations of earlier late Paleoindian sites and isolated finds. Diamonds represent Agate Basin components. Crosses are Hell Gap/Great Basin Stemmed localities. The single star at the northwest corner of Rocky Mountain National Park is the Thunder Pass site (5GA319), where a Hell Gap/Great Basin Stemmed point was recovered by Husted in 1960.

zones. They are particularly well represented at opposite ends of the environmental zone spectrum: in high-altitude alpine tundra/alpine/subalpine ecotone and lower-elevation sagebrush steppe parkland. Of later late Paleoindian complexes, a majority (48 percent) of Cody components occurred in alpine tundra and alpine-subalpine ecotone zones, followed closely by those in sagebrush steppe parklands (44 percent). Only two Cody components were reported from the subalpine zone and none from the montane zone. Figure 9.5 presents a GIS map projection of locations and distributions of all regional Cody components.

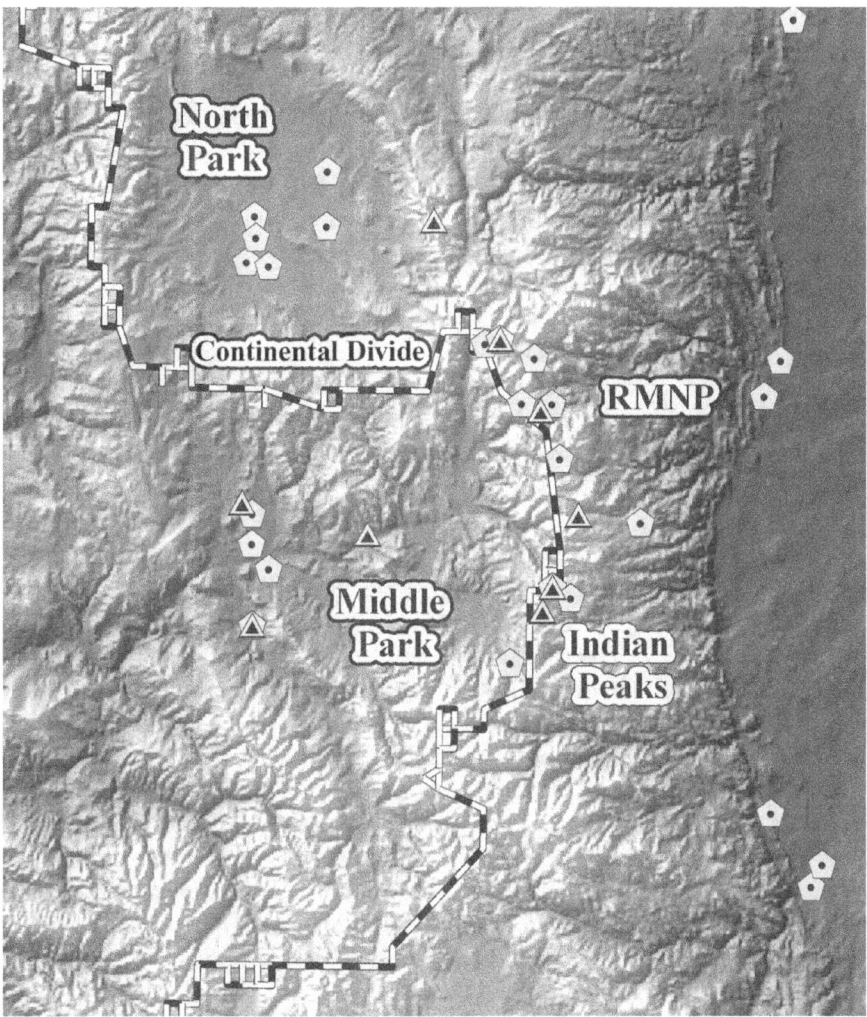

9.5. Site distribution of Cody components in the north-central Colorado Rockies. Pentagons with center dots are Cody components with Scottsbluff-Kersey-Firstview type variants (subtypes), while double triangles represent sites with Cody-Eden points.

Viewed collectively, slightly later JAF (37) and Angostura (19) components occur most frequently in high-altitude (alpine tundra and alpine-subalpine ecotone) localities (54 percent), followed by ones (37.5 percent) in sagebrush steppe parkland. The high frequency of both Cody and JAF/Angostura high-altitude summer occupations, coupled with significant numbers of lower-elevation basin valley site points, supports a working hypothesis that they represent evidence of former transhumant seasonal rounds between interior basins (fall-winter-spring) and mountain tundra (summer) (a topic discussed later). It may also be significant that regional JAF components heavily outnumber Angostura components (37 to 19), although I suspect both types were likely in use around the same time frame and may reflect at least some overlapping co-occupation of the region by ethnically related and territorially contiguous populations (see Pitblado 1999b, 2003, Chapter 10, this volume, for more on this issue).

Intriguingly, Pitblado (2003:129–133, table 6.2, figures 6.1 and 6.2), also basing her analysis on site components rather than absolute numbers of projectile points per site, found the opposite pattern in her study of multi-regional southern Rocky Mountain Paleoindian projectile points (she documented thirteen JAF components in the southern Rockies versus twenty-eight Angostura components in that region). Tabulation of my north-central Colorado mountain region data using projectile point *numbers* for all components possessing one or both of the two types showed JAF specimen totals (67) substantially outnumbering Angostura (17). For comparative data on individual specimens from Pitblado's study, see Chapter 10, this volume (Table 10.3). It is unclear whether the differences are a result of a more localized, regional bias of prehistoric populations for JAF over Angostura point styles or of inaccurate point type identifications (e.g., a tendency of some mountain archaeologists to type artifacts as JAF because they are more familiar with that type than with Angostura). Close morphological similarity of the two types, particularly aggravated when dealing with fragmented tools, tends to render their identification as one or the other type problematic.

The overall number and frequency of JAF components, again subject to archaeological report type misidentification, *do* broadly agree with Pitblado's (2003:135–138, table 6.4, and Chapter 10, this volume) finding that JAF components throughout the southern Rockies occur most commonly (69.23 percent) in *higher-elevation* zones. James Allen–Frederick component data for the north-central Colorado region show that 56.8 percent of JAF components were found in subalpine to alpine environmental zones versus 43.5 percent occurring in lower-elevation montane and parkland zones. Angostura component data provide a similar pattern, with 63.2 percent occurring in subalpine through alpine tundra zones and only 36.8 percent located in lower-elevation montane and parkland zones. Finally, limited numbers of Lovell Constricted (5) and Pryor Stemmed (7) components show a bias of Pryor Stemmed for upper-elevation zones (71.4 percent) and a lower-elevation zones bias (80 percent) for Lovell Constricted. However, numbers for the latter two types are too small to make a realistic assessment of trends. Figure 9.6 shows a GIS projection of all regional post-Cody late Paleoindian complex locations.

A highly significant pattern that emerges in later late Paleoindian site location distributions is the virtually equal number of high-altitude (summer hunting) locales versus those found in lower-elevation valley and parkland basin settings.

Late Paleoindian Cultural Landscapes. This subsection describes some of the more important late Paleoindian sites in the north-central Colorado region. Its

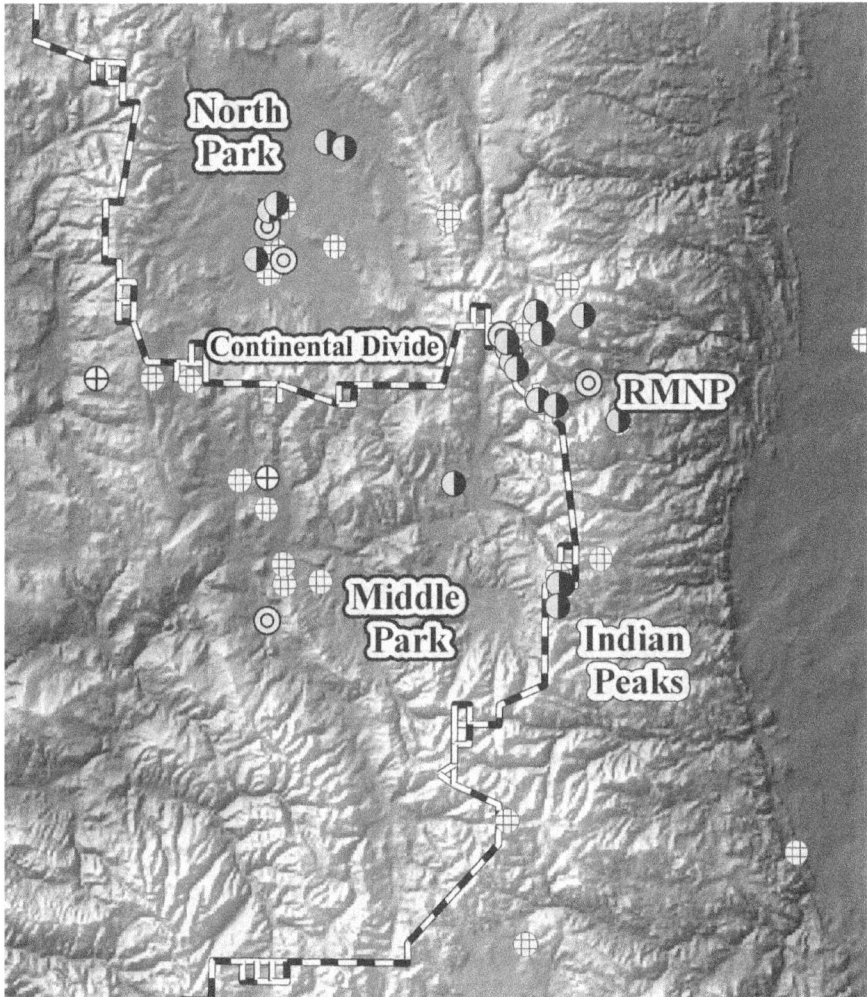

9.6. Site distribution of post-Cody late Paleoindian components. Bisected half-dark circles are Angostura, hatched circles are James Allen–Frederick, double circles are Lovell Constricted, and cross circles are Pryor Stemmed.

intent is to provide the reader with a sense of the nature of those sites and their cultural-ecological contexts in relation to our emerging picture of evolving later Paleoindian land-use and settlement patterns.

Aside from earlier noted, rare Agate Basin and Hell Gap/Great Basin Stemmed components, the current inventory of Cody sites and isolated finds indicates a substantial increase in Paleoindian activity in Colorado's north-central mountains. That activity appears to rise dramatically from Cody times to the end of the late Paleoindian Period around 7,500 RCYBP. Late Paleoindian site settings range from the parklands of Middle Park and North Park to the alpine tundra of the Indian Peaks Wilderness and Rocky Mountain National Park.

In the intermountain parkland basin of Middle Park, the University of Wyoming team recorded a Cody component at Middle Park's Barger Gulch's (5GA195) Locality A quarry and a lithic workshop site. Of even greater significance was their excavation of a Cody bison kill with a later JAF component at the Jerry Craig site (5GA639). So far, Jerry Craig represents the region's only known Cody bison kill (Kornfeld and Frison 2000:138–141; Logan et al. 1998; Richings 1998; Surovell et al. 2000). It was found buried in a steep erosion-slump depression on the east slope of Little Wolford Mountain. The site's organic-enriched cultural deposits contained fragmented bison bone, including teeth and mandibles, as well as lithic butchering tools, tool-manufacturing–rejuvenation waste flakes, and projectile points described as Cody or Cody-like. Its eleven projectile points included examples of JAF, and at least one of its points classed as Cody exhibited parallel-oblique flake patterning (Kornfeld and Frison 2000:139–141, figure 6; Richings 1998). Jerry Craig bone bed organics produced an early Cody radiocarbon date of 9310 ± 50 RCYBP (Kornfeld 1998:53). Analyzed bison skeletal elements were interpreted as indicating the presence of a minimum of five adult bison between 1.5 and 2.5 years. Tooth eruption and wear study results were found consistent with a late-summer to early-fall kill (August–September) (Logan et al. 1998:18–20).

Wyoming research also documented twenty-eight parallel-oblique flaked, lanceolate, concave base points identified as JAF in a local private collection originating from a Williams Fork Reservoir quarry and campsite (5GA1995) (Kornfeld and Frison 2000; Wiesend and Frison 1998).

In adjacent North Park, UNC test excavations at 5JA1183, a small hill bench campsite overlooking a spring-fed creek, uncovered cultural deposits radiocarbon dated at $9,340 \pm 40$ RCYBP (Brunswig 2006). An earlier survey recovered a Cody stemmed (Kersey subtype) point from the site's surface (O'Neil and Harrison 2000:18, 29).

Twenty kilometers west of 5JA1183, UNC recorded an extensive multicomponent site, 5JA1475, along one of the valley's most dominating landscape features, the east-west–trending Pederson Ridge (Brunswig 2004c, 2006). In profile, the undulating ridge is characterized by flat stretches periodically broken by U-shaped erosion gaps. Several such gaps along the site's 2 km length were found to contain loose masonry features (rock blinds and short walls) designed to conceal hunters waiting to ambush game directed up ridge slope drainage swales into ridge gap kill zones. One of the site's gap drives is associated with a Cody point tip fragment (impact fractured), and two game processing areas contained late Paleoindian point fragments, one diagnosed as Cody and a second as indeterminate Paleoindian (based on a point fragment with parallel-oblique flaking).

Late Paleoindian sites and isolated finds are particularly abundant in high-altitude environmental zones. A number of high-altitude sites have been identified in the Indian Peaks area (west of Boulder), including the Fourth of July Mine site (5BL153) (Benedict 2000a:163–164, figures 5.4, 5.5y, z, 5.8), the Devil's Thumb game drive (5BL3440) (Benedict 2000b:18–19, 36–54, 79, figures 2.19l, 2.28a–c), the Devil's Thumb Valley site (5BL6904) (Kindig 2000:112, figure 3.13h), the Fourth of July site (5BL120) (Benedict 1981:62–92), and Caribou Lake (5GA22) (Benedict 1985; Pitblado 1999b, 2000), all representing late Paleoindian hunting base camps and game processing areas.

The Fourth of July site (5BL120) is a subalpine-alpine ecotone camp situated on a terminal glacial moraine near the Fourth of July game drive (Benedict 1981:62–92). Limited test excavations uncovered parallel-oblique flaked James Allen point fragments and a partial parallel-oblique flaked Pryor Stemmed point. Charcoal from a hearth was radiocarbon dated to 5,960 ± 85 RCYBP and 6,045 ± 120 RCYBP, dates too young for late Paleoindian occupation or possibly representing younger carbon contamination. Benedict (1985) initially interpreted the chronological-cultural inconsistency (similar Paleoindian point types are dated elsewhere prior to 7,500 RCYBP) as indicating late survival of late Paleoindian flaking styles. However, reinvestigation of the site's stratigraphy and archaeology resulted in retrieval of a ca. 8,290-year-old radiocarbon date associated with microflakes from deep deposits, prompting Benedict (2005:829–831) to revise his earlier late Paleoindian projectile point trait "survival" interpretation to one associating the points with the older and more archaeologically consistent date.

Caribou Lake is situated in a protected cirque valley in a small upper alpine–subalpine ecotone meadow 90 m northwest of Caribou Lake's north shore, immediately west of Arapaho Pass. It was tested in 1970–1971 by Benedict (1985), revealing shallowly buried (10–20 cm) cultural materials, including a projectile point base with parallel-transverse to parallel-oblique flaking he provisionally assigned to the Cody Complex. Associated hearth charcoal provided a radiocarbon date of 8,460 ± 140 RCYBP, late in Cody times. Subsequent excavations (1995–1996) by Pitblado (1999b, 2000) recovered a parallel-oblique flaked point base, a parallel-oblique flaked point tip, and a complete lanceolate, indented base, parallel-oblique flaked projectile point. The complete point and two point fragments were identified as belonging to the JAF point type, as was the earlier Benedict-recovered point base (Pitblado 2000:153). Her excavations produced hearth charcoal associated with the points' cultural deposits that was radiocarbon dated at 9,080 ± 75 RCYBP, 7,985 ± 75 RCYBP, and 7,940 ± 70 RCYBP. The earliest date was suggested to be potentially unreliable (e.g., representing an old-wood problem), while an average of the two later dates, 7,955 RCYBP, was advanced as most representative of the points' and associated hearth's date of use (Pitblado 2000:139–140).

Devil's Thumb Pass game drive produced the best evidence to date of direct late Paleoindian association with high-altitude hunting features (Benedict 2000b:18–19, 36–47, 49–51, 53–54, figures 2.19l, 2.28a–c). The game drive is a complex of low wall and cairn alignments with strategically situated rock-wall blinds, all scattered within a sloping ridge and swale landscape in alpine-subalpine ecotone and lower tundra zones. One of its several lithic scatters produced surface finds of Cody-Eden, Angostura, and JAF points and point fragments in a lower ridge slope swale. A discontinuous 340-m-long alignment of low rock walls and cairns (wall C) is believed associated with the ambush of game maneuvered into the swale by waiting hunters. A C-shaped rock blind (No. 5) located in the swale's center is believed to have been an important structural element of the drive system. Granite weathering analysis of drive wall stones suggests it may have been constructed around 10,000 RCYBP, consistent with chronologies of the recovered Paleoindian point types. Excavation of the central swale's blind resulted in recovery of charcoal-enriched soil radiocarbon dated to the late Archaic (2,155 RCYBP), suggesting it had either been built or later reused at that time. Two main lithic concentrations on either side of the swale (A and B) were surface collected and tested, although only one (B) produced reasonably intact cultural deposits. Lithic material from both points and excavated waste flakes were exclusively from local sources (within 75 km), most being Kremmling Chert or Table Mountain Jasper from Middle Park.

Another high-altitude camp with a JAF component, 5ST87, is located on a small tundra bench 3 km southwest of Argentine Pass at the extreme southern boundary of the region (Marcotte and Mayo 1978). The Carey Lake site (5LR230) is located north of Rocky Mountain National Park, in the Rawah Wilderness's alpine-subalpine ecotone zone. Morris and Metcalf (1991) reported several late Paleoindian points from Carey Lake, including six point fragments, most with parallel-oblique flaking patterns. One of its points was identified by Pitblado (2003:84) as Cody (Eden-Firstview), while others represent unidentified Paleoindian types.

As a result of large-scale archaeological inventory surveys by the University of Northern Colorado, the region's highest known density of late Paleoindian sites and isolated finds is in Rocky Mountain National Park. The park has thirty late Paleoindian site components and four isolated point finds. Locations of those components are shown in Figure 9.7.

Nearly half (47.1 percent) of RMNP's thirty-four late Paleoindian components are situated above tree line on sites associated with what are inferred as warm-season tundra hunting territories (Brunswig 2004b, 2005a:231–293). Most are multicomponent, including late Paleoindian occupations and those of later post-Paleoindian groups. Alpine tundra site types with late Paleoindian components include constructed game drives with rock-hunting features and game processing–tool refurbishment camps. Ten sites (29.4 percent) have been identified as alpine-subalpine ecotone hunting base camps, located within easy access of tundra hunting grounds. The park's remaining eight late Paleoindian components (23.5 percent) are located in subalpine or montane environmental zones.

The park's only known buried, stratified Paleoindian component is at the upper subalpine zone Lawn Lake (5LR318) site. Lawn Lake was test excavated by

9.7. Distribution of late Paleoindian cultural components in Rocky Mountain National Park. The Continental Divide is marked by the undulating black-white line and the park boundary by the dashed line. The locations of late Paleoindian site concentrations discussed later are labeled as Mt. Ida sites and Bighorn Flats sites. The park's only excavated Paleoindian site, Lawn Lake, is also labeled on the figure map.

UNC in 2000 (Brunswig 2001d, 2004a, 2005a:111). Incorporated in its basal cultural deposits was a late Paleoindian Angostura projectile base directly associated with hearth charcoal radiocarbon dated at 8,000 ± 170 RCYBP (Brunswig 2001b:10–11). Excavation also recovered charcoal from upper Paleoindian deposits radiocarbon dated at 7,160 ± 40 RCYBP. A surface-recovered JAF projectile point base was also found at Lawn Lake. Excavation of its late Paleoindian deposits produced game processing tools, lithic waste flakes, and metate fragments, suggesting they likely represent a series of periodic short-term, warm-season hunting base camps between 8,000 and 7,200 RCYBP.

Of five multicomponent RMNP sites with Paleoindian components, one in particular, Forest Canyon Pass (5LR2), has the most impressive array of late Paleoindian components (5), including Hell Gap/Great Basin Stemmed, Agate Basin, Cody (Firstview-Kersey and Eden types), JAF, and Pryor Stemmed complexes. It produced one of the park's two known Agate Basin points and two of its three documented Hell Gap/Great Basin Stemmed points. The site also has the distinction of having produced one of two Cody knives found in RMNP, the second coming from an alpine-subalpine ecotone camp (5BL53) south of Longs Peak. Two of the park's well-known game drives, Flattop Game Drive (5LR6) and Trail Ridge Game Drive (5LR15), produced late Paleoindian projectile point fragments, with Flattop having Cody-Eden and JAF projectile points and Trail Ridge having yielded a probable Cody point (Benedict 1996:12–15; Brunswig 2004a, 2005a:283; Doerner and Brunswig in prep).

A significant aspect of Rocky Mountain National Park's late Paleoindian sites is their tendency to concentrate in alpine-subalpine ecotone and adjacent alpine tundra areas. Site concentrations are particularly well represented along the Continental Divide from Mount Ida Ridge to the southern edge of Bighorn Flats (Figure 9.6). The Mount Ida–Bighorn Continental Divide ridgeline extends, with only a short break, for 18 km from Milner Pass in the north to Andrews Pass in the south, representing the largest expanse of open alpine tundra in the region. One cluster of five sites occurs in Bighorn Flats (tundra) and adjacent Tonahutu Creek headwaters (alpine-subalpine ecotone, an area of approximately 9.8 km^2 (Figure 9.8).

Two Bighorn-Tonahutu sites are located on tundra, one just below Sprague Pass on a southwest-facing upper slope bench of Sprague Mountain and the second in a tundra boulder field at the southwestern edge of Bighorn Flats (Figure 9.8). Three others, considered to have served as base (or staging) camps, are situated on low alpine-subalpine ecotone ridges between upper headwater tributaries of Tonahutu Creek. Flattop Mountain, which extends east from the southwestern edge of Bighorn Flats (see Figure 9.8), has the earlier noted Flattop Game Drive with late Paleoindian components.

The five Bighorn-Tonahutu sites constitute a hypothesized warm-season (summer–early-fall) hunting territory with short-term, secondary base (staging) camps in protective alpine-subalpine ecotone, tundra hunting localities, and open tundra game processing camps (see later discussion). Detailed descriptions of the Bighorn Hunting System were published in Brunswig (2004b, 2005a:268–280) and are the subject of a forthcoming monograph (Doerner and Brunswig in prep).

A second late Paleoindian hunting system is located along the Continental Divide on Mount Ida Ridge, northwest of Bighorn Flats (Figure 9.9). Much of Mount Ida Ridge has steep talus cliffs, dropping into glacial cirque valleys on the east and long, less dramatic tundra grass meadow slopes on the west. Its topog-

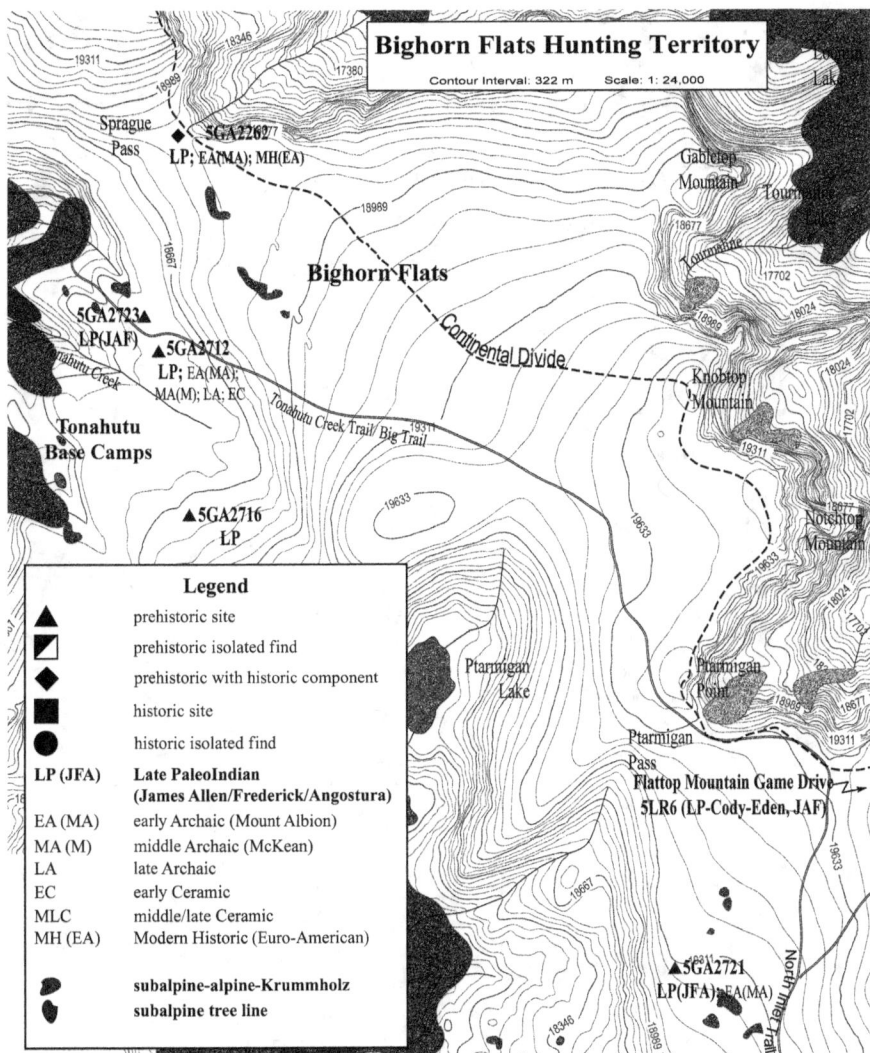

9.8. Sites with late Paleoindian components in the Bighorn Flats hunting territory. Three of the sites are located in the Tonahutu Creek headwaters in alpine-subalpine ecotone and are labeled base (hunt staging) camps. Two hunting/game processing camps are located at the northern and southern ends of Bighorn Flats tundra. The flats, a major summer grazing territory for elk and bighorn sheep, provide excellent terrain for maneuvering game into ambush points.

raphy provides ideal grazing for elk and bighorn sheep, and its landscape is well suited for maneuvering game animals into planned, constructed (blinds and drift walls) kill areas (game drives) and natural ambush concealment features.

Mount Ida Ridge has two sites with late Paleoindian components, 5GA1095 and 5GA2002, each with associated game drive features, including rock cairn

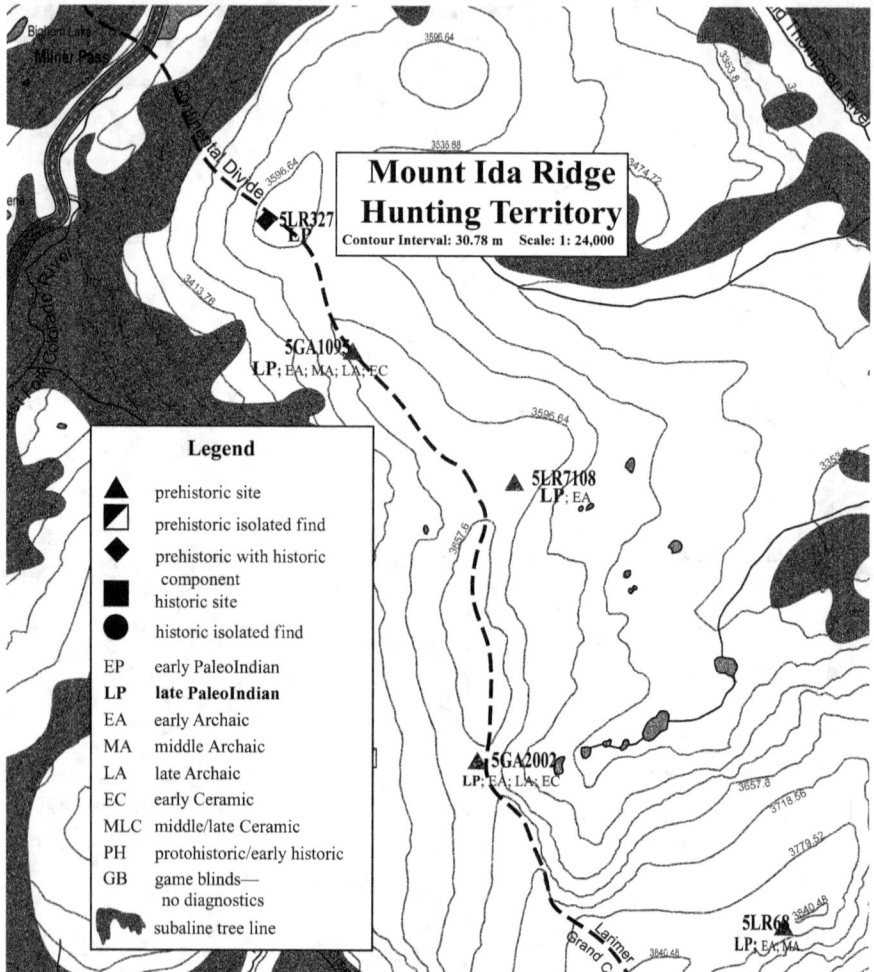

9.9. Map showing distribution of prehistoric sites in the Mount Ida Ridge hunting territory. Miler and Forest Canyon passes are shown in the upper left and center. Sites with late Paleoindian components are marked with the letters LMP (Late Mountain Paleoindian) to the right of the site symbol.

lines, rock-wall "observation pits," rock-wall alignments, and rock-wall hunting blinds (Figure 9.9). Three game processing–tool refurbishment camps (5LR68, 5LR327, and 5LR7108) are located on or adjacent to the main ridge on tundra slopes, knolls, and benches (Figure 9.9).

Site 5GA2002 was first recorded by Benedict (1995) and later systematically explored by UNC (Brunswig 2002a, 2002b, 2004b, 2005a:258–264). It is an extensive system of hunting features and lithic-tool (game processing) concentrations believed to have been intended to hunt both elk and bighorn. Its artifact assemblage included an Angostura projectile point fragment, suggesting the site had been used since late Paleoindian times. A second game drive system, 5GA1095, was also initially recorded by (Benedict 1987:1–27, appendixes A–C) and later reinvestigated by UNC (Brunswig 2004b, 2005a:264–267). It was also found to contain evidence of multiple cultural components ranging over several thousand years, beginning in late Paleoindian (Angostura) times.

Evidence from both Indian Peaks and Rocky Mountain National Park points to initiation of high-altitude hunting systems by late Paleoindian Cody times, a tradition that included constructed game drive– and natural terrain–aided ambush tactics. As I (and others) have discussed elsewhere (see previous citations), Native American hunters employed diverse and sophisticated high-altitude hunting systems from very early times, assisted by a logistical support subsystem of base and staging camps (Tonahutu) and secondary processing camps (Bighorn Flats, Mount Ida, Indian Peaks). As those systems were developed and modified through time, hunting bands based in the southern Rockies successfully and consistently acquired high-value game resources in the mid- to late-summer months when the tundra would have been snow-free and open to foraging herbivores.

PALEOINDIAN LITHIC MATERIAL SOURCES AND TYPES

This section deals with north-central Colorado mountain region Paleoindian projectile point lithic material sources. The purpose of identifying projectile point material sources is to determine patterning in local lithic material usage versus exotic source materials use. Knowledge of such patterns provides important information on past Paleoindian behaviors related to lithic procurement and, provisionally, indigenous residence or seasonal in-migration from outside the region.

Given the eclectic nature of available research sources, reliable (or sometimes any) information on projectile point materials (including their most probable sources) proved sporadic at best. The most complete sources were UNC's SAIP artifact studies (all lithic assemblages were systematically sourced and identified) and artifact analyses from the University of Wyoming's Middle Park project sites (Brunswig 2001b, 2001d, 2004a, 2005a:180–181, appendixes E and F, in prep; Kornfeld and Frison 2000; Kornfeld, Frison, and White 2001; Kornfeld et al. 1999; Surovell et al. 2000, 2003; White 1999; Wunderlich 2004; Wunderlich and Brunswig 2004). Wherever possible, projectile point material types and sources were extracted from site reports, Colorado SHPO site forms, and other lithic source publications (cf. Bamforth 2006; Black 1999). Limited lithic data were also gleaned from publications on sites with Paleoindian components in the Indian Peaks area (Benedict 1981, 1985, 2000a, 2000b; Pitblado 1999b, 2000). Altogether, material source data for 151 regional Paleoindian projectile points were compiled.

For the purposes of this study, lithic sources of individual Paleoindian projectile points (of known types) were classified as local and nonlocal. Local materials are defined as those occurring within the north-central Colorado mountain region's boundaries, as defined at the start of this chapter. GIS analyses of distance to documented quarry or lithic outcrop sites from individual Paleoindian sites showed that most local sources occurred within a 70 km radius of those sites. Nonlocal sources are defined as lithic materials known to have come from outside the region. Excellent to fair-quality lithic-tool materials are particularly abundant in North Park and Middle Park's parkland basins.

Consultation of Colorado SHPO computer files found at least twenty-four recorded quarry sites in Middle Park and thirteen in North Park, many associated with primary rock outcrops and prehistoric quarry pits. Personal communications with archaeologists working in the two parks and my own experience with Rocky Mountain National Park lithic sources, as well as with those in Middle Park and North Park, suggest to me that many more quarries and lithic workshops remain to be identified. Information on known regional geological sources containing lithic-quality tool materials was presented in the earlier hydrology and geology section and is not repeated here.

Table 9.5 summarizes material source and techno-complex type distributions of 151 type-identified Paleoindian projectile points in the north-central Colorado Rockies.

Figure 9.10 shows the relative percentages of projectile point types manufactured of local or nonlocal lithic materials. The sample population (151 points) is small and highly variable by point types and their associated cultural complexes. With that proviso in mind, the overall pattern and long-term trend are still suggestive. Even at the very beginning of regional Paleoindian colonization, when Clovis bands were initially moving into Colorado's mountain regions, local projectile point material use was predominant, at 62.4 percent. After Clovis, Goshen-Plainview and Folsom populations were almost exclusively relying on regional lithic sources, 100 percent and 95.7 percent, respectively. The late Paleoindian Period began with a mixed picture of local versus nonlocal usage, with 100 percent local material represented for Hell Gap/Great Basin Stemmed points but only 50 percent for Agate Basin. However, the current sample of two points for each type/complex has no statistical relevance. Sample sizes for Cody and later Paleoindian point types are much better but still limited for adequate statistical inference. The Cody frequency of local material use, 79.2 percent, is impressive, but subsequent point types/complexes are even higher, ranging from 93.3 percent (Angostura) to 100 percent (Lovell Constricted and Pryor Stemmed. The single-largest sample of source material identified point types/complexes, JAF, at 57 points, has 96.5 percent made of local stone.

Although current lithic source data do not represent a statistically viable sample for strong statistical inferences of long-term Paleoindian lithic procurement behavior, their overall pattern is compelling. As early as Clovis times, hunter-gatherer populations in the north-central Colorado Rockies were familiar with and systematically exploited interior mountain tool resources. Indigenous

Table 9.5. Local versus Nonlocal Sources of Paleoindian Projectile Point Materials by Type/Complex.

	Clovis	Goshen-Plainview	Folsom	Hell Gap/GBS	Agate Basin	Cody	Angostura	James Allen-Frederick	Lovell Constricted	Pryor Stemmed
Local										
Kremmling Chert–North Park/Middle Park	3	11	20	1	2	12	3	26	1	1
Table Mountain Chert/Jasper/Porcellanite–North Park/Middle Park	2	2	—	—	—	3	1	3	1	2
Dakota/Windy Ridge Quartzite–North Park/Middle Park	—	1	2	1	—	4	10	22	—	2
Local Mississippian Chert–North Park/Middle Park	—	—	—	—	—	—	—	3	—	—
Ignimbrite–North Park/Middle Park	—	—	—	—	—	—	—	1	—	—
Totals	5	13	22	2	1	19	14	55	2	5
Nonlocal										
Perker–Palmer Divide petrified wood–Front Range foothills	1	—	—	—	1	—	—	—	—	—
Mississippian/Hartville Chert–southern Wyoming	1	—	1	—	—	—	—	1	—	—
Mississippian/Hartville Quartzite–southern Wyoming	-	—	—	—	—	2	1	1	—	—
Bridger Formation/Tiger Chert–Southwest Wyoming–Northwest Colorado	-	—	—	—	1	1	—	—	—	—
SW Wyoming oolitic coquina–1 Southwest Wyoming	—	—	—	—	—	1	—	—	—	—
Flattop Chert–northeastern Colorado plains	-	—	—	—	—	1	—	—	—	—
Totals	3	—	1	—	1	5	1	2	—	—

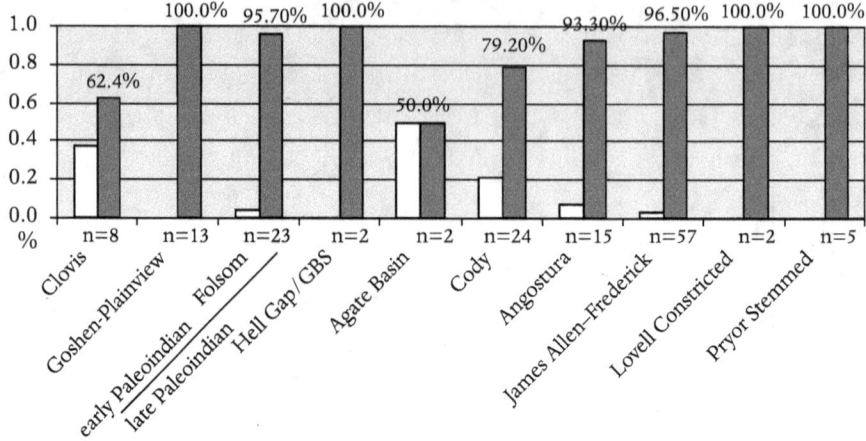

9.10. Bar chart showing relative percentages of local (dark) versus nonlocal (white) projectile point materials by projectile point type/complex.

use of mountain-based lithic materials by native populations became increasingly common after the Clovis era and quickly became the overwhelming source of raw materials for Paleoindian projectile points.

CONCLUSION

Current archaeological data for the southern Rocky Mountains' north-central Colorado region show initial in-migration of hunter-gatherers during the Clovis Period between 11,300 and 10,900 RCYBP. Although Clovis mountain populations appear to have been sparse, their presence at high-altitude tundra localities, including important passes in Rocky Mountain National Park, and their extensive use of mountain lithic sources suggest good access to high-altitude mountain areas. Importantly, that access included many passes previously blocked by late Pleistocene glaciers and permanent snowfields and indicates impressive familiarity with the region's terrain and resources.

Subsequent Goshen-Plainview and Folsom populations (10,900–10,250 RCYBP) continued an overall pattern of mountain adaptation, focusing on mountain game hunting, particularly of Ice Age *Bison bison antiquus*, in intermontane park valleys. Available evidence minimally indicates Goshen-Plainview autumn through early-winter hunting of bison and establishment of Goshen-Plainview and Folsom extended cold-season camps in protected areas near central Middle Park's Colorado River. Exploitation of high-altitude tundra pastures during warm-season months does not appear to have been common and may well have been prohibited by modest mountain glaciation and expansion of permanent snowfields during the Younger Dryas cold episode after 10,800 RCYBP.

With the end of Younger Dryas cold and the disappearance of Goshen-Plainview/Folsom occupations ca. 10,250 RCYBP, there may have been a span of several centuries when the region was sparsely occupied and mainly visited by outside Paleoindian hunter-gatherer bands. Evidence for the two archaeological complexes believed to chronologically follow the region's early Paleoindian Period Goshen-Plainview and Folsom occupations, Hell Gap/Great Basin Stemmed and Agate Basin (10,250–9,400 RCYBP), is rare, and no examples of their presence exist higher than the region's subalpine zone (greater than ca. 3,500 m). This apparent "gap" in occupation has yet to be explained. Its possible existence has been remarked upon by Kornfeld and Frison (2000:147). It is also conceivable that another, yet unidentified or recognized Paleoindian complex may fill the void or that later Paleoindian complexes and projectile point types such as Cody (Eden-Firstview) represent early-phase late Paleoindian time period occupations occurring at earlier-than-suspected dates.

By 9,400 RCYBP or slightly later, warmer and moister than-modern climatic conditions were established. At that time, late Paleoindian Period occupations in the form of Cody Complex components increased and are associated with late-summer/fall bison hunting in the region's mountain parks (at least Middle Park). At the same time, a seasonal transhumance cycle characterized by warm-season high-altitude tundra hunting and fall/early-winter (cool-season) hunting in parkland basins may have been established. Broadly similar seasonal transhumance behavior has been hypothesized for the middle Rocky Mountains based on research results at Osprey Beach, an early Cody site on Yellowstone Lake (Johnson, Reeves, and Shortt 2004:142–145, 156).

From Cody times to the end of the region's Paleoindian stage, an overwhelming utilization of local lithic resources for projectile points and other tools supports existence of a fully indigenous, mountain-based cultural tradition. Subsequent developments of late Paleoindian mountain lifestyles continued the earlier Cody-established seasonal transhumance pattern of summer high-altitude game hunting and fall-winter intermontane park occupations by hunter-gatherers employing closely related Angostura and JAF projectile point technologies.

After 8,500 RCYBP, continued regional warmth appears to have been accompanied by a gradual reduction in effective moisture. Regional human population losses may have either declined or begun to focus more intensively on summer-season tundra game resources, supplemented by winter hunting of lower-elevation parkland game. Parkland bison numbers in particular may have declined in the most recent late Paleoindian centuries as well but were probably present in smaller numbers than previously and were still hunted, but with less intensity and frequency. The relative scarcity of Lovell Constricted and Pryor Stemmed Foothills-Mountain projectile point types in the region may reflect either lower human population densities in the last millennium of the late Paleoindian Period or the possibility that those types were less commonly used than chronologically contemporaneous JAF and Angostura projectile point types.

REFERENCES CITED

Bach, D.
- 2003 *Floral Inventory and Ethnographic Analysis of Native American Plant Uses at 5LR7095.* Report to the University of Northern Colorado Department of Anthropology, Greeley, and Rocky Mountain National Park, Estes Park, by High Plains Macrobotanical Services, Laramie, WY.

Bamforth, D. B.
- 1994 The Windy Ridge Quartzite Quarry: Hunter-Gatherer Mining on the Continental Divide. In *Abstracts of the 59th Annual Meeting of the Society for American Archaeology,* 18–19. Anaheim, CA.
- 1998 *Survey and Test Excavations at 5GA872, the Windy Ridge Quartzite Quarry.* Report to the U.S. Forest Service, Medicine Bow–Arapaho National Forests, Department of Anthropology, University of Colorado, Boulder.
- 2006 The Windy Ridge Quartzite Quarry: Hunter-Gatherer Mining and Hunter-Gatherer Land Use on the North American Continental Divide. *World Archaeology* 38(3):511–527.

Benedict, J. B.
- 1981 The Fourth of July Valley: Glacial Geology and Archeology of the Timberline Ecotone. *Center for Mountain Archaeology Research Report 2,* Ward, CO.
- 1985 Arapaho Pass: Glacial Geology and Archeology of the Crest of the Colorado Front Range. *Center for Mountain Archaeology Research Report 3,* Ward, CO.
- 1987 A Fasting Bed and Game Drive Site on the Continental Divide in the Colorado Front Range. *Southwestern Lore* 53(3):1–27.
- 1990 Archeology of the Coney Valley. *Center for Mountain Archaeology Research Report 5,* Ward, CO.
- 1992 Along the Great Divide: Paleoindian Archaeology of the High Colorado Front Range. In *Ice Age Hunters of the Rockies,* ed. D. J. Stanford and J. S. Day, 343–359. Denver Museum of Natural History and University Press of Colorado, Niwot.
- 1995 *Colorado Cultural Resource Cultural Component Site Form for 5GA2002.* Ms. on file at the Colorado Office of Archaeology and Historic Preservation, Denver.
- 1996 The Game Drives of Rocky Mountain National Park. *Center for Mountain Archeology Research Report 7,* Ward, CO.
- 2000a Excavations at the Fourth of July Mine Site. In *This Land of Shining Mountains: Archeological Studies in Colorado's Indian Peaks Wilderness Area,* ed. E. S. Cassells, 159–188. *Center for Mountain Archaeology Research Report 8,* Ward, CO.
- 2000b Game Drives of the Devil's Thumb Pass Area. In *This Land of Shining Mountains: Archaeological Studies in Colorado's Indian Peaks Wilderness Area,* ed. E. S. Cassells, 18–95. *Center for Mountain Archaeology Research Report 8,* Ward, CO.
- 2005 Rethinking the Fourth of July Valley Site: A Study in Periglacial Geoarchaeology. *Geoarchaeology* 20 (8):797–836.

Benedict, J. B., and B. L. Olson
- 1978 The Mount Albion Complex: A Study of Prehistoric Man and the Altithermal. *Center for Mountain Archaeology Research Report 1,* Ward, CO.

Black, K. D.
- 1991 Archaic Continuity in the Colorado Rockies: The Mountain Tradition. *Plains Anthropologist* 36 (133):1–29.
- 1999 Lithic Sources in the Rocky Mountains of Colorado. In *Intermountain Archaeology*, ed. D. B. Madsen and M. D. Metcalf, 132–147. University of Utah Press, Salt Lake City.

Bradley, B. A.
- 1993 Paleo-Indian Flaked Stone Technology in the North American High Plains. In *From Kostenki to Clovis: Upper Paleolithic–Paleo-Indian Adaptations*, ed. O. Soffer and N. D. Praslov, 251–262. Plenum, New York.

Brett, J. A.
- 2002 *Ethnographic Assessment and Documentation of Rocky Mountain National Park*. Ms. on file at the Rocky Mountain National Park Museum, Estes Park, CO.

Brunswig, R. H.
- 1999 *Report on 1998 Archeological Surveys in Rocky Mountain National Park by the University of Northern Colorado*. Ms. on file, Department of Anthropology, University of Northern Colorado, Greeley.
- 2000 *Report on 1999 Archeological Surveys in Rocky Mountain National Park by the University of Northern Colorado*. Ms. on file, Department of Anthropology, University of Northern Colorado, Greeley.
- 2001a *Report on 2000 Archeological Surveys in Rocky Mountain National Park by the University of Northern Colorado*. Ms. on file, Department of Anthropology, University of Northern Colorado, Greeley.
- 2001b New Evidence of Paleoindian Occupations in Rocky Mountain National Park, North-Central Colorado. *Current Research in the Pleistocene* 18:10–12.
- 2001c Late Pleistocene/Early Holocene Landscapes and Paleoindian Economic Systems in Colorado's Southern Rocky Mountains. In *Presenting the First Peoples: Proceedings of the 1998 CHACMOOL Conference*, ed. J. Gillespie, S. Tupukka, and C. de Mille, 427–451. Archaeological Association of the University of Calgary, Alberta.
- 2001d *Lawn Lake (5LR318): Results of an Archeological Mitigation Research Project at a High Altitude Prehistoric Site in Rocky Mountain National Park*. Ms. on file, Department of Anthropology, University of Northern Colorado, Greeley.
- 2002a *Report on 2001 Archeological Surveys in Rocky Mountain National Park by the University of Northern Colorado*. Ms. on file, Department of Anthropology, University of Northern Colorado, Greeley.
- 2002b *University of Northern Colorado 2002 Archeological Investigations in Rocky Mountain National Park, North Central Colorado*. Ms. on file, Department of Anthropology, University of Northern Colorado, Greeley.
- 2003a Clovis-Age Artifacts from Rocky Mountain National Park and Vicinity, North Central Colorado. *Current Research in the Pleistocene* 20:7–9.
- 2003b *Archeological, Ethnographic, and Historic Investigations of the 5LR7095 Rock Feature Complex Site, Rocky Mountain National Park, North Central Colorado*. Report to and on file at Rocky Mountain National Park, National Park Service, Estes Park, CO, by the Department of Anthropology, University of Northern Colorado, Greeley.

2004a Paleoindian Colonization of Colorado's Southern Rockies: New Evidence from Rocky Mountain National Park and Adjacent Areas. In *Ancient and Historic Lifeways of North America's Rocky Mountains: Proceedings of the 2003 Rocky Mountain Anthropological Conference*, ed. R. H. Brunswig and W. B. Butler, 265–283. Available digitally from the Department of Anthropology, University of Northern Colorado, Greeley.

2004b Hunting Systems and Seasonal Migratory Patterns through Time in Rocky Mountain National Park. In *Ancient and Historic Lifeways of North America's Rocky Mountains: Proceedings of the 2003 Rocky Mountain Anthropological Conference*, ed. R. H. Brunswig and W. B. Butler, 393–410. Available digitally from the Department of Anthropology, University of Northern Colorado, Greeley.

2004c *Preliminary Report of a 2003 Archaeological Survey of 5JA1475 (Pederson Ridge), North Park, Colorado: Report to the Bureau of Land Management, Kremmling Field Office*. Ms. on file, Department of Anthropology, University of Northern Colorado, Greeley.

2005a *Prehistoric, Protohistoric, and Early Historic Native American Archeology of Rocky Mountain National Park: Final Report of Systemwide Archeological Inventory Program Investigations by the University of Northern Colorado (1998–2002)*. Report on file, Department of Anthropology, University of Northern Colorado, Greeley.

2005b Art and Cultural Landscapes in the Terminal Ice Age and Early Holocene: Contrasts and Parallels in America's Southern Rockies and Europe's Pyrenees. In *Art for Archaeology's Sake: Material Culture and Style across the Disciplines*, ed. A. Waters-Rist, C. Cluney, C. McNamee, and L. Steinbrenner, 252–268. Archaeological Association of the University of Calgary, Alberta.

2006 *2005 Archaeological Field Investigations of 5JA1475 (Pederson Ridge), 5JA1183 (Jo's Site), 5JA1666, and 5JA1667 in North Park (Jackson County), Colorado: Report to the Bureau of Land Management, Kremmling Field Office*. Ms. on file, Department of Anthropology, University of Northern Colorado, Greeley.

in press End of One World—Beginning of Another: Cultural and Environmental Changes at the Pleistocene-Holocene Boundary in Europe's Western Pyrenees and America's Southern Rocky Mountains. In *Apocalypse Then and Now: Archaeology and Worlds' Ends, Proceedings of the 2002 Chacmool Conference*, ed. L. Steinbrenner and M. Peuramaki-Brown. Department of Archaeology, University of Calgary, Alberta.

ms *Change and Adaptation in Late Ice Age–Early Holocene Colorado: Paleoindian Environments and Lifestyles of the Southern Rocky Mountains*. Anthropology Program, University of Northern Colorado, Greeley.

Bryan, A. L.
1988 The Relationship of the Stemmed Point and the Fluted Point in the Great Basin. In *Early Occupation in Far Western North America: The Clovis-Archaic Interface*, ed. J. Willig, C. M. Aiken, and J. L. Fagan, 53–74. Nevada State Museum, Anthropological Paper 21, Carson City.

Burney, M. S., C. Coe, C. Colle, and T. J. Lennon
1979 *Windy Gap: An Archaeological Study of Aboriginal Sites within the Windy Gap Dam, Reservoir, and Pipeline Project Near Granby*. Report to and on file at the Northern Colorado Water Conservancy District, Western Cultural Resource Management, Boulder.

Cassells, E. S.
1995 Hunting the Open High Country: Prehistoric Game Driving in the Colorado Alpine Tundra. Ph.D. dissertation, University of Wisconsin, Madison.
1997 The Archaeology of Colorado, 2nd ed. Johnson Books, Boulder.

Cassells, E. S. (ed.)
2000 This Land of Shining Mountains: Archeological Studies in Colorado's Indian Peaks Wilderness Area. *Center for Mountain Archeology Research Report* 8, Ward, CO.

Chenault, M. L.
1999 Chapter 4: Paleoindian Stage. In *Colorado Prehistory: A Context for the Platte River Basin*, ed. K. P. Gilmore, M. Tate, M. L. Chenault, B. Clark, T. McBride, and M. Wood, 51–90. Colorado Council of Professional Archaeologists, Denver.

Cummings, L. S., and T. E. Moutoux
1998 Pollen Analysis at the Jerry Craig (5GA639) and Lower Twin Mountain (5GA186) Sites and a Paleoenvironmental Summary of the Paleoindian Period in the Middle Park, Colorado. In *Early Prehistory of Middle Park: The 1997 Project and Summary of Paleoindian Archaeology*, ed. M. Kornfeld, 95–102. Technical Report 15a, Department of Anthropology, University of Wyoming, Laramie.

Daniele, J. R.
2003 *The Barger Gulch Locality B Formal Tool Assemblage: A Use-Wear Analysis*. Unpublished master's thesis, University of Wyoming, Laramie.

Doerner, J.
2004 Paleoenvironmental Interpretations of Holocene Records from Rocky Mountain National Park. In *Ancient and Historic Lifeways of North America's Rocky Mountains: Proceedings of the 2003 Rocky Mountain Anthropological Conference*, ed. R. H. Brunswig and W. B. Butler, 170–179. Available digitally from the Department of Anthropology, University of Northern Colorado, Greeley.
2005 *A High-Resolution Paleotemperature Record from Poudre Pass Fen, Rocky Mountain National Park, USA*. Report to and on file at Rocky Mountain National Park, by the Department of Geography, University of Northern Colorado, Greeley.

Doerner, J., and R. H. Brunswig
in prep Modeling Paleoenvironmental and Archeological Landscapes of Ancient Game Drive Systems in Rocky Mountain National Park, North Central Colorado. Ms. in progress on file in the Departments of Geography and Anthropology, University of Northern Colorado, Greeley.

Eighmy, J. L., and J. M. LaBelle
1996 Radiocarbon Dating of Twenty Seven Plains Complexes and Phases. *Plains Anthropologist* 41:53–69.

Elias, S. A.
1985 Paleoenvironmental Interpretations of Holocene Insect Fossil Assemblages from Four High-Altitude Sites in the Front Range, Colorado, U.S.A. *Arctic and Alpine Research* 17 (1):31–48.

Elinoff, L.
- 2002 *Oral Tradition and the Archaeological Record: An Integral Partnership in Understanding the Human Past of the Rocky Mountain National Park Region.* Unpublished master's thesis, University of Colorado, Denver.

Frison, G. C.
- 1988 Paleoindian Subsistence and Settlement during Post-Clovis Times in the Northwestern Plains, the Adjacent Mountain Ranges, and Intermontane Basins. In *America Before Columbus: Ice-Age Origins, University of Pittsburgh, Department of Anthropology, Ethnology Monographs* 12, ed. R. C. Carlisle, 83–106. Pittsburgh, PA.
- 1991a *Prehistoric Hunters of the High Plains*, 2nd ed. Academic, San Diego.
- 1991b The Goshen Paleoindian Complex: New Data for Paleoindian Research. In *Clovis: Origins and Adaptations*, ed. R. Bonnichsen and K. L. Turnmire, 81–118. Center for the Study of the First Americans, Corvallis, OR.
- 1992a The Foothills-Mountains and the Open Plains: The Dichotomy in Paleoindian Subsistence Strategies between Two Ecosystems. In *Ice Age Hunters of the Rockies*, ed. D. J. Stanford and J. S. Day, 323–342. Denver Museum of Natural History and University Press of Colorado, Niwot.
- 1992b The Goshen Cultural Complex—Where Does It Fit in the Paleoindian Cultural Sequence? *Research and Exploration* 8 (4):494–496. Laramie, WY.
- 1997 The Foothill-Mountain Late Paleoindian and Early Plains Archaic Chronology and Subsistence. In *Changing Perspectives of the Archaic in the Northwest Plains and Rocky Mountains*, ed. M. L. Larson and J. E. Francis, 84–105. University of South Dakota Press, Vermillion.

Frison, G. C. (ed.)
- 1996 *The Mill Iron Site.* University of New Mexico Press, Albuquerque.

Frison, G. C. and D.C. Grey
- 1980 Pryor Stemmed: A Specialized Late Paleoindian Ecological Adaptation. *Plains Anthropologist* 25(87):27–46.

Frison, G. C., C. V. Haynes Jr., and M. L. Larson
- 1996 Discussion and Conclusions. In *The Mill Iron Site*, ed. G. C. Frison, 205–216. University of New Mexico Press, Albuquerque.

Gilmore, K., M. Tate, M. Chenault, B. Clark, T. McBride, and M. Wood
- 1999 *Colorado Prehistory: A Context for the Platte River Basin.* Colorado Council of Professional Archaeologists, Denver.

Harder, B. P. (ed.)
- 1957 *Guidebook to the Geology of North and Middle Park Basins, Colorado.* Rocky Mountain Association of Geologists, Denver.

Harrison, C. A., B. P. O'Neil, B. L. Olson, L. Simmons, T. H. Simmons, M. J. Tate, and T. C. Tucker
- 2000 *Wolford Mountain Dam and Reservoir Project: Results of Phase I and Phase II Excavations at Seven Sites in Grand County, Colorado.* Report to and on file at the Colorado Water Conservancy, by Powers Elevation, Inc., Denver.

Haynes, C. V., Jr.
- 1991 Geoarchaeological and Paleohydrological Evidence for a Clovis-Age Drought in North America and Its Bearing on Extinction. *Quaternary Research* 35:438–450.
- 1992 Contributions of Radiocarbon Dating to the Geochronology of the Peopling of the Americas. In *^{14}C Dating and Peopling of the New World*, ed. R. E. Taylor, A. Long, and R. S. Kra, 355–374. Springer-Verlag, New York.
- 1993 Clovis-Folsom Geochronology and Climatic Change. In *From Kostenki to Clovis: Upper Paleolithic–Paleo-Indian Adaptations*, ed. O. Soffer and N. D. Praslov, 219–236. Plenum, New York.

Hofman, J. L., and R. W. Graham
- 1998 The Paleo-Indian Cultures of the Great Plains. In *Archaeology on the Great Plains*, ed. W. R. Woods, 87–139. University of Kansas Press, Lawrence.

Holliday, V. T.
- 1997 *Paleoindian Geoarchaeology of the Southern High Plains*. University of Texas Press, Austin.
- 2000 The Evolution of Paleoindian Geochronology and Typology on the Great Plains. *Geoarchaeology* 15 (3):227–290.

Holliday, V. T., E. Johnson, and T. W. Stafford Jr.
- 1999 AMS Radiocarbon Dating of the Type Plainview and Firstview (Paleoindian) Assemblages: The Agony and the Ecstasy. *American Antiquity* 64 (3):444–454.

Husted, W. M.
- 1962 A Proposed Archaeological Chronology for Rocky Mountain National Park. Unpublished master's thesis, University of Colorado, Boulder.
- 1965 Early Occupation of the Colorado Front Range. *American Antiquity* 30 (4):494–498.
- 1969 Bighorn Canyon Archaeology. *Smithsonian Publications in Salvage Archaeology* 12, Washington, DC.
- 1995 The Western Macrotradition Twenty-Seven Years Later. *Archaeology in Montana* 36 (1):37–92.

Irwin-Williams, C., H. C. Irwin, G. A. Agogino, and C. V. Haynes Jr.
- 1971 Hell Gap: Paleo-Indian Occupation on the High Plains. *Plains Anthropologist* 18:40–52.

Izlett, G. A.
- 1967 Geology of the Hot Sulphur Springs Quadrangle, Grand County, Colorado. *U.S. Geological Survey Professional Paper* 586. U.S. Government Printing Office, Washington, DC.
- 1975 Late Cenozoic Sedimentation and Deformation in Northern Colorado and Adjoining Areas. In *Cenozoic History of the Southern Rocky Mountains*, ed. C. F. Curtis, 179–209. Geological Society of America Memoir 144, Denver.

Jodry, M. A.
- 1999 The Paleoindian Stage. In *Colorado Prehistory: A Context for the Rio Grande Basin*, ed. M. A. Martorano, T. Hoefer, M. A. Jodry, V. Spero, and M. L. Taylor, 45–114. Colorado Council of Professional Archaeologists, Denver.

Johnson, A., B.O.K. Reeves, and M. W. Shortt
  2004   *Osprey Beach: A Cody Complex Camp on Yellowstone Lake.* Lifeways of Canada Limited, Calgary, Alberta.

Kelly, R. L., and L. C. Todd
  1988   Coming into the Country: Early Paleoindian Hunting and Mobility. *American Antiquity* 53 (2):231–244.

Kindig, J. M.
  2000   Two Ceramic Sites in the Devil's Thumb Valley. In *This Land of Shining Mountains: Archeological Studies in Colorado's Indian Peaks Wilderness Area,* ed. E. Steve Cassells, 95–123. Center for Mountain Archeology Research Report 8, Ward, CO.

Kornfeld, M.
  1998   Summary of Paleoindian Archaeology in Middle Park. In *Early Prehistory of Middle Park: The 1997 Project and Summary of Paleoindian Archaeology,* ed. M. Kornfeld, 49–55. Technical Report 15a, Department of Anthropology, University of Wyoming, Laramie.

Kornfeld, M. (ed.)
  1998   *Early Prehistory of Middle Park: The 1997 Project and Summary of Paleoindian Archaeology.* Technical Report 15a, Department of Anthropology, University of Wyoming, Laramie.

Kornfeld, M., and G. C. Frison
  2000   Paleoindian Occupation of the High Country: The Case of Middle Park, Colorado. *Plains Anthropologist* 45 (172):129–153.

Kornfeld, M., G. C. Frison, M. L. Larson, J. C. Miller, and J. Saysette
  1999   Paleoindian Bison Procurement and Paleoenvironments in Middle Park of Colorado. *Geoarchaeology* 14 (7):655–674.

Kornfeld, M., G. C. Frison, and P. White
  2001   Paleoindian Occupation of Barger Gulch and the Use of Troublesome Formation Chert. *Current Research in the Pleistocene* 18:32–34.

Lincoln, T., E. Friedman, R. H. Brunswig, S. Bender, J. Della Salla, and J. Klawon
  2003   *South Park Archaeology Project: Final Report of Archaeological Investigations Conducted in 2000 and 2001, South Park, Colorado.* Ms. on file, Department of Anthropology, University of Northern Colorado, Greeley.

Lischka, J. J., M. E. Miller, R. B. Reynolds, D. Dahms, K. Joyner-McGuire, and D. McGuire
  1983   An Archaeological Inventory in North Park, Jackson County, Colorado. *Bureau of Land Management Cultural Resource Series* 14, Denver.

Logan, J., J. Durr, M. G. Hill, C. Lee, and V. McMillan
  1998   Jerry Craig Site, 5GA639, a Cody Complex Site in Colorado. In *Early Prehistory of Middle Park: The 1997 Project and Summary of Paleoindian Archaeology,* ed. M. Kornfeld, 11–24. Technical Report 15a, Department of Anthropology, University of Wyoming, Laramie.

Lux, T. A.
2004 *Archeological Investigation of Ancient Trails in Rocky Mountain National Park, North Central Colorado*. Unpublished master's thesis, University of Denver.

Marcotte, J. R., and D. Mayo
1978 Archaeological Surveillance during Construction Activities at the Argentine Pass Site, Summit County, Colorado. *Reports of the Laboratory of Public Archaeology* 19. Department of Anthropology, Colorado State University, Fort Collins.

Mayer, J. H., T. A. Surovell, N. M. Waguespack, M. Kornfeld, R. G. Reider, and G. C. Frison
2005 Paleoindian Environmental Change and Landscape Response in Barger Gulch, Middle Park, Colorado. *Geoarchaeology* 20 (6):599–625.

McMillan, M. E., P. L. Heller, and S. L. Wing
2006 History and Causes of Post-Laramide Relief in the Rocky Mountain Orogenic Plateau. *Geological Society of America Bulletin* 118 (3–4):393–405.

Meany, C. A., and D. Van Vuren
1993 Recent Distribution of Bison in Colorado West of the Great Plains. *Proceedings of the Denver Museum of Natural History* 3 (4):1–10.

Meltzer, D. J.
1993 Is There a Clovis Adaptation? In *From Kostenki to Clovis: Upper Paleolithic-Paleo-Indian Adaptations*, ed. O. Soffer and N. D. Praslov, 293–310. Plenum, New York.

Metcalf, M. D., R. J. Rood, P. K. O'Brien, and B. R. Overturf
1991 *Kremmling Chert Procurement in the Middle Park Area, Colorado: 5GA1144 and 5GA1172*. Ms. on file at J. F. Sato and Associates, Golden, CO.

Miller, J. C.
1991 Lithic Sources. In *Prehistoric Hunters of the High Plains*, 2nd ed., by G. C. Frison, 449–476. Academic, New York.
1998 Latest Pleistocene and Holocene Geology and Geoarchaeology of Middle Park. In *Early Prehistory of Middle Park: The 1997 Project and Summary of Paleoindian Archaeology*, ed. M. Kornfeld, 70–94. Technical Report 15a, Department of Anthropology, University of Wyoming, Laramie.

Morris, E. A., and M. Metcalf
1991 *Twenty-Two Years of Archaeological Survey in the Rawah Area, Medicine Bow Mountains, Northern Colorado*. Paper presented at the 1st Biennial Rocky Mountain Anthropology Conference, Jackson, WY.

Naze, B. S.
1986 The Folsom Occupation of Middle Park, Colorado. *Southwestern Lore* 52 (4):1–32.
1994 *The Crying Woman Site: A Record of Prehistoric Human Habitation in the Colorado Rockies*. Unpublished master's thesis, Colorado State University, Fort Collins.

O'Neil, B., and C. Harrison
2000 *Class III Cultural Resources Inventory: Middle and North Parks Grazing Impact Assessments, Grand and Jackson Counties, Colorado*. Ms. on file, Grand River Institute, Grand Junction, CO.

Pitblado, B. L.
 1999a Late Paleoindian Occupation of the Southern Rocky Mountains: Projectile Points and Land Use in the High Country. Ph.D. dissertation, University of Arizona, Tucson.
 1999b New ^{14}C Dates and Obliquely Flaked Projectile Points from a High-Altitude Paleoindian Site, Colorado Rocky Mountains. *Current Research in the Pleistocene* 16:65–66.
 2000 Living the High Life in Colorado: Late Paleoindian Occupation of the Caribou Lake Site. In *This Land of Shining Mountains: Archeological Studies in Colorado's Indian Peaks Wilderness Area,* ed. E. S. Cassells, 124–158. Center for Mountain Archaeology Research Report 8, Ward, CO.
 2003 *Late Paleoindian Occupation of the Southern Rocky Mountains.* University Press of Colorado, Boulder.

Reed, A. D. and M. D. Metcalf
 1999 *Colorado Prehistory: A Context for the Northern Colorado River Basin.* Colorado Council of Professional Archaeologists, Denver.

Richings, S.
 1998 Jerry Craig Site Projectile Point Assemblage. In *Early Prehistory of Middle Park: The 1997 Project and Summary of Paleoindian Archaeology,* ed. M. Kornfeld, 25–33. Technical Report 15a, Department of Anthropology, University of Wyoming, Laramie.

Rohe, C. M.
 2003 *Reading the Landscape: A Location Model for Prehistoric Sites in Rocky Mountain National Park.* Unpublished master's thesis, University of Arkansas, Fayetteville.

Schroedl, A. R.
 1991 Paleo-Indian Occupation in the Eastern Great Basin and Northern Colorado Plateau. *Utah Archaeology* 4(1):1–15.

Sellet, F.
 1999 *A Dynamic View of Paleoindian Assemblages at the Hell Gap Site, Wyoming: Reconstructing Lithic Technological Systems.* Ph.D. dissertation, Southern Methodist University, Dallas, TX.
 2001 A Changing Perspective on Paleoindian Chronology and Typology: A View from the Northwestern Plains. *Arctic Anthropology* 38 (2):48–63.

Stafford, M. D.
 1990 *The Powars II Site (48PL330): A Paleoindian Red Ochre Mine in Eastern Wyoming.* Unpublished master's thesis, University of Wyoming, Laramie.

Stanford, D.
 1991 Clovis Origins and Adaptations: An Introductory Perspective. In *Clovis Origins and Adaptations,* ed. R. Bonnichsen and K. L. Turnmire, 1–14, Center for the Study of the First Americans, Corvallis, OR.

Steven, T. A.
 1975 Middle Tertiary Volcanic Field in the Southern Rocky Mountains. In *Cenozoic History of the Southern Rocky Mountains,* ed. C. F. Curtis, 75–94. Geological Society of America Memoir, Denver.

Stiger, M.
  2006 A Folsom Structure in the Colorado Mountains. *American Antiquity* 71 (2):321–351.

Surovell, T. A
  2003 Occupation Span and Site Reoccupation. In *The First Five Field Seasons at Barger Gulch, Locality B, Middle Park, Colorado.* Technical Report 26:119–129. George C. Frison Institute of Archaeology and Anthropology, University of Wyoming, Laramie.

Surovell, T. A., N. M. Waguespack, M. Kornfeld, and G. C. Frison
  2001a The 2000 Field Season at Barger Gulch Locality B, Middle Park, Colorado. *Technical Report* 19c. George C. Frison Institute of Archaeology and Anthropology, University of Wyoming, Laramie.
  2001b Barger Gulch Locality B: A Folsom Site in Middle Park, Colorado. *Current Research in the Pleistocene* 18:58–60.
  2003 The First Five Field Seasons at Barger Gulch, Locality B, Middle Park, Colorado. *Technical Report* 26. George C. Frison Institute of Archaeology and Anthropology, University of Wyoming, Laramie.

Surovell, T. A., N. M. Waguespack, J. H. Mayer, M. Kornfeld, and G. C. Frison
  2005 Shallow Site Archaeology: Artifact Dispersal, Stratigraphy, and Radiocarbon Dating at the Barger Gulch Locality B Folsom Site, Middle Park, Colorado. *Geoarchaeology* 20 (6):627–649.

Surovell, T. A., N. M. Waguespack, S. Richings-Germain, M. Kornfeld, and G. C. Frison
  2000 1999 Investigations at the Barger Gulch and Jerry Craig Sites, Middle Park, Colorado. *Technical Report* 18a. George C. Frison Institute of Archaeology and Anthropology, University of Wyoming, Laramie.

Tuohy, D. R., and T. N. Layton
  1977 Towards the Establishment of a New Series of Great Basin Projectile Points. *Nevada Archaeological Survey Reports* 10 (6):1–5.

Tweto, O.
  1975 Laramide (Late Cretaceous–Early Tertiary) Orogeny in the Southern Rocky Mountains. In *Cenozoic History of the Southern Rocky Mountains*, ed. C. F. Curtis, 1–44. Geological Society of America Memoir 144, Denver.

Wahlstrom, E. E.
  1941 Hydrothermal Deposits in the Specimen Mountain Volcanics, Rocky Mountain National Park. *American Mineralogist* 26:551–571.
  1944 Structure and Petrology of Specimen Mountain. *Geological Society of America Bulletin* 55:77–90.

Wheeler, C. W., and M. S. Burney
  1984 *Windy Gap: Aboriginal Adaptation to Middle Park.* Report to and on file at the Northern Colorado Water Conservancy District, by Western Cultural Resource Management, Boulder.

Wheeler, R. P.
 1995 Archeological Investigations in Three Reservoir Areas in South Dakota and Wyoming: Part I, Angostura Reservoir. *Reprints in Anthropology* 46, Lincoln, NE.

White, P. M.
 1999 *Getting the High Altitude Stone: Lithic Technology at the Barger Gulch Site (5GA195).* Unpublished master's thesis, University of Wyoming, Laramie.

Wiesend, C. M., and G. C. Frison
 1998 Parallel-Obliquely Flaked Projectile Points from the Phillips–Williams Fork Reservoir Site (5GA1955) in Middle Park, Colorado. *Southwestern Lore* 64 (1): 8–21.

Wilmsen, E. N., and F.H.H. Roberts Jr.
 1978 Lindenmeier, 1934–1974: Concluding Report on Investigations. *Smithsonian Contributions to Anthropology* 24, Washington, DC.

Wunderlich, R.
 2004 *Material Sourcing Studies of Lithic Assemblages in Rocky Mountain National Park.* Undergraduate thesis, University of Northern Colorado, Greeley.

Wunderlich, R., and R. H. Brunswig
 2004 Material Sourcing Studies of Prehistoric Lithic Assemblages in Rocky Mountain National Park. In *Ancient and Historic Lifeways of North America's Rocky Mountains: Proceedings of the 2003 Rocky Mountain Anthropological Conference*, ed. R. H. Brunswig and W. B. Butler, 214–223. Available electronically from the Department of Anthropology, University of Northern Colorado, Greeley.

Yelm, M.
 1935 *Archaeological Survey of Rocky Mountain National Park–Eastern Foothill Districts.* Unpublished master's thesis, University of Denver.

CHAPTER TEN

Bonnie L. Pitblado

Angostura, Jimmy Allen, Foothills-Mountain

Clarifying Terminology for Late Paleoindian Southern Rocky Mountain Spear Points

In 2003, I published a book on my research into late Paleoindian use of the southern Rocky Mountains. The research was based on detailed, hands-on analyses of 589 late Paleoindian spear points from 414 sites all over Colorado and Utah. The study area included the focal region of the southern Rockies that constitutes a substantial portion of the two states and, for comparative "big picture" purposes, the adjacent Plains and Far West (Colorado Plateau and Great Basin).

As I illustrated, photographed, and measured specimen after specimen, it quickly became clear that I would need to develop a projectile point typology that could capture the variability present in Rocky Mountain assemblages. That variability represented an obvious departure from the well-established Plains post-Folsom Paleoindian sequence (e.g., Frison 1991; Haynes 1992): Agate Basin, Hell Gap, Alberta, Scottsbluff, and Eden. Following Alex Krieger's (1944) approach,

I proposed two newly conceived (although not strictly new) types: "Angostura" and "Jimmy Allen/Frederick." Both, as elaborated later, came to play crucial roles in my characterization of late Paleoindian chronology and early human use of the southern Rocky Mountains.

Since I published my typology and conclusions, researchers have in at least two cases attempted to apply "Angostura" and "Jimmy Allen/Frederick" as I defined them to new projectile point data sets, only to produce results seemingly contradictory to mine (Brunswig, Chapter 9, this volume; Larson 2005). Other researchers, occasionally publicly (e.g., Jodry 2005) and sometimes in one-on-one conversation, have raised important questions both about my choice of terms and about how those terms relate to others invoked in the Rocky Mountain late Paleoindian literature—especially "Foothills-Mountain" (e.g., Frison 1991). This chapter's overarching goal is to address these issues and others in an effort to clarify how we all might fruitfully approach the southern Rocky Mountain Paleoindian record.

Chapter 10 will (1) define "Angostura" and what I will, as of this writing, call simply "Jimmy Allen" (rather than the longer "Jimmy Allen–Frederick") to give fieldworkers type descriptions they can apply to late Paleoindian finds in the southern Rockies and to give researchers terms with which to explore new analytical problems; (2) explain why I labeled the types as I did and offer retrospective thoughts about whether the terms are appropriate and, if not, how they should be modified; (3) demonstrate that the two types—however we label them—are morphologically and even mathematically quite different from one another; (4) present results that show why it matters that we distinguish between the two types in the southern Rocky Mountains; (5) compare my term "Angostura" with George Frison's "Foothills-Mountain" because some have used and continue to perceive them as synonymous when they are not; and (6) offer thoughts on seemingly contradictory results obtained by my colleague Robert Brunswig and reported in Chapter 9 of this volume for the late Paleoindian record in the north-central Colorado Rockies.

ANGOSTURA VERSUS JIMMY ALLEN

I want to be clear from the start that Angostura and Jimmy Allen are by no means the only two late Paleoindian point types found in the southern Rockies, nor is either of them found in the Rockies to their complete exclusion elsewhere. Other types that occur in the southern Rockies include components of the traditional Plains late Paleoindian sequence (e.g., Agate Basin, Hell Gap, Eden, and Scottsbluff) and its Great Basin counterpart (Great Basin Stemmed series). However, these point types (and a few others) are rarer in the southern Rockies than either of the two that are the focus of this manuscript, and they all play a comparatively minor role in my interpretation of what people were doing in those mountains ca. 10,000–7,500 radiocarbon years before present (RCYBP). For details on late Paleoindian projectile points from the southern Rockies other than Angostura and Jimmy Allen, I refer readers to my dissertation (1999) and book (2003).

Both my proposed "Angostura" and "Jimmy Allen" late Paleoindian types describe specimens with a lanceolate form and a typically parallel-oblique (but sometimes collateral or irregular) flaking pattern. They are therefore as similar to one another as are, say, Clovis and Folsom points, which share a lanceolate form, concave base, parallel to collateral flaking patterns, and flutes up one or both faces. As with Clovis and Folsom, however, the differences between Angostura and Jimmy Allen projectile point forms, production strategies, and geographic distributions outweigh their similarities.

Because this is the case, lumping the two types together and considering them to be one—or failing to properly distinguish one from the other—could lead to interpretive problems. Although it is hard to predict the form those problems might take, I see potential for them to parallel misguided interpretations of fluted points from 1927 (when Folsom was recognized, named, and generalized to include all points with flutes) to 1938 (when excavators at Blackwater Draw recognized Clovis as chronologically and otherwise distinct from Folsom). For a decade or so, our archaeological forebears viewed Folsom and Clovis points—or, as they sometimes referred to them, "true Folsoms" and "generalized Folsoms"—as manifestations of a single, chronologically equivalent type (e.g., Dixon 1999; Meltzer 1993). I would like us to avoid such errors in the southern Rockies.

In making the decision to assign the mostly obliquely flaked lanceolate assemblage of late Paleoindian specimens to two types rather than one, or three, or eight, I followed as closely as I could Krieger's (1944) still generally accepted and often-quoted (although, I would argue, far less often followed) "typological method." Table 10.1 juxtaposes the six steps in Krieger's methodology (cited nearly verbatim) with my application thereof to (mostly) obliquely flaked lanceolate forms.

Literature searches conducted cursorily in step three and more thoroughly in step four of my typological adventure revealed nineteen published sites with secure radiocarbon dates associated with projectile points I call Angostura and six with specimens I classify as Jimmy Allen. The nineteen Angostura dates suggest a median age of 8,790 RCYBP and an age range of 9,700–7,550 RCYBP. Fourteen of the previously recorded sites (74 percent) are in the Rockies, three (16 percent) are on the Plains, and one—the Angostura type-site—is in the Black Hills, a dome mountain Plains "island" with a Rocky Mountain–like environment (Hunt 1967; Osborn and Kornfeld 2003). The six Jimmy Allen sites have a median age of 8,780 RCYBP (essentially identical to the median for Angostura) and a range of 9,350–7,900 RCYBP. Four of the six Jimmy Allen sites are in the mountains (a rather meaningless 66 percent, given the small sample size). Of those, two are in the highest Rockies and two in the low foothills. The remaining two Jimmy Allen sites, including the type-site, are on the Wyoming Plains.

Previously recorded data used to develop my "tentative types" did not and do not suggest that what I came to call Angostura and Jimmy Allen are chronologically

Table 10.1. Krieger's (1944) "Typological Method" Steps and Pitblado's (1999) Application of Those Steps to Lanceolate Late Paleoindian Projectile Points from Colorado and Utah.

Krieger (1944:279–282) Step	Pitblado's (1999) Application
1. Sort specimens into major groups that look as though they were made with the same or similar structural patterns in mind. Create groups that contrast strongly.	Initial sort reveals two groups of lanceolate points: (1) thick, narrow specimens that converge to a slightly concave base, and (2) thin, wide specimens with parallel to divergent bases that show marked concavity.
2. Break down working patterns further according to differences consistent within some, but not all, like specimens in each pattern.	Conduct further sorts on the basis of flaking pattern (e.g., parallel-oblique, collateral), and the corner form (rounded vs. sharp), and basal side outline.
3. Recombine groups obtained in step two based on a study of distributions, taking into account geographic, temporal, and associational occurrence of the groups. Create "tentative types" that show "cohesiveness of elements proven through the use of archaeological data rather than simply supposed."	Use literature to roughly evaluate known occurrences of points similar to those represented in the study assemblage. Finding: if grouped by the initial sort (step one)—but not the more extensive sort (step two)—there appears to be chronological overlap between (1) and (2) but likely differences in geographic distribution and "associational occurrences."
4. Test "tentative types" using whatever further information is available. Check persistency with which elements of proposed types occur again and again, in the same essential pattern with the same variations.	Closely examine differences between "tentative types" (1) and (2). Examine all published radiocarbon dates and locations of known occurrences, and begin experimenting with research database to see if differences in the latter are consistent with the former. Persistency appears to hold.
5. Name and describe types based on a site or locative term; supply line drawings and photographs to make variations clear.	Name types "Angostura" (1) and "Jimmy Allen/ Frederick" (2) on the basis of their original type-sites; publish type names and detailed descriptions, drawings, and photographs (Pitblado 1999, 2003). As of this chapter, drop the "Frederick" but keep the type.
6. Employ typological knowledge in the reconstruction of cultural relationships. When sufficient data are available, the plotting of type distributions in space, time, and association may reveal consistency in the way certain types tend to fall together in site after site.	Use the new types to draw conclusions about the behavior of late Paleoindians who used the southern Rockies, where the two types occur so frequently.

distinct, like Folsom and Clovis. On the contrary, the data suggest these types were made and used contemporaneously. On the other hand, the extant data did hint at differences in geographic distribution. Thick, narrow lanceolate points appeared to occur commonly in Rocky Mountain settings and only occasionally on the Plains. Thinner, wider specimens were a little more common on the

Plains and were characterized in Frison's (1991:38–79) often-quoted, often-photocopied Paleoindian cultural chronology as a terminal Plains Paleoindian manifestation called the "Frederick Complex" (originally defined at the Hell Gap site [Irwin 1968]). Frison (1991:66) characterized points of the "Frederick Complex" as (1) younger than and technologically distinct from Cody, (2) bearing a "close similarity to specimens known as James Allen," and (3) distinct from but contemporary with points made by members of "Foothills-Mountain Paleoindian Groups."

In addition to helping me ascertain the likelihood that my two groups of lanceolate late Paleoindian points might reflect real variability in geographic space, Frison (1991; also see Frison 1973, 1976, 1983, 1988, 1992, 1998) also provided support for the notion that the two types might differ in terms of their "associations" (Krieger 1944:280). Frison perceives his "Foothills-Mountain Groups," a concept that, as I explain later, encompasses—but exceeds the scope of—my "Angostura," as representing a unique and mutually exclusive adaptive trajectory vis-à-vis that unfolding on the Plains at the same time and represented at its terminus by what Frison calls the "Frederick Complex." Frison's "Foothills-Mountain Paleoindians" were generalized hunter-gatherers; their Plains contemporaries were bison hunters—and, as he views them, ne'er the two did meet. The "associational" differences that support Frison's contention include differences in both faunal and non–projectile point artifact assemblages at Foothills-Mountain (including what I call Angostura) and Plains (including what I call Jimmy Allen) sites.

In short, what few published, relevant data were available in the mid-1990s, when I undertook my study of late Paleoindian points in the southern Rocky Mountains, revealed likely and rather provocative differences in two of the three dimensions that Krieger argued may—indeed must—bolster an argument for labeling a group of similar artifacts as a "type" proper. They likewise helped fulfill Krieger's (1944:281) requirement that types reflect a "cohesiveness of elements" not "simply supposed through a set of assumptions" but shown through the use of "archaeological data." This accomplished, I felt justified in offering the type descriptions that appear in my dissertation and book, which I present here as a foundation for the discussion that follows and which I maintain—à la Krieger—not only look different but are different.

Angostura

Angostura projectile points as I define them are lanceolate bifaces with flaking patterns that range from, most typically, parallel-oblique to collateral to irregular and very rarely, horizontal, with some specimens showing different patterns on opposite faces (Figure 10.1). The basal sides of the points converge toward the base, which is usually slightly concave in outline (Figure 10.2). As with virtually all Paleoindian spear points, the basal edges of finished Angostura points are ground. In longitudinal cross-section, Angostura points are usually

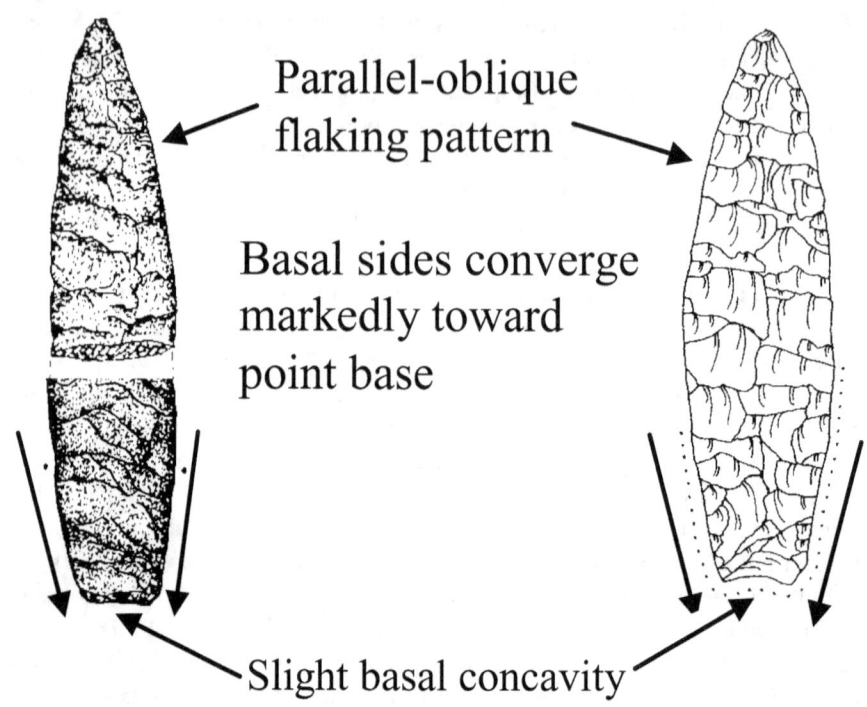

10.1. Left, *Angostura point tip and base from the type (Ray Long) site, Angostura Reservoir, Black Hills, South Dakota. Right, Angostura projectile point from 5MF625, Moffat County, Colorado (illustrated by the author; courtesy, Henderson Museum, University of Colorado, Boulder). Key diagnostic features are indicated with arrows. Dots/stippling delineate the extent of basal grinding. Ray Long specimens are reprinted from the Bureau of Reclamation–sponsored publication* Archaeological Investigations in Three Reservoir Areas in South Dakota and Wyoming, Part I, Angostura Reservoir, *by Richard Page Wheeler, 380, figure 47 b (point tip) and l (point base).*

symmetrical but are not uncommonly "D-shaped," "twisted," or otherwise asymmetrical.

I labeled this class of projectile points "Angostura" because the term is the chronologically earliest moniker I could find in the literature describing specimens that fit the description given here. Richard Wheeler (1995 [reprinted from 1954]:449) showed photographs and line drawings (e.g., Figure 10.1) of specimens he characterized as "distinctive, slender, lanceolate, diagonally rippled flaked dart-points with narrow and slightly concave or straight base and ground lateral edges." He noted further that "Angostura points have been reported from Texas, Nebraska, Wyoming, Montana, Idaho, Saskatchewan, and the Northwest Territories . . . and are similar to, but separable from, Agate Basin points" (Wheeler 1995 [1954]:450). He also cited radiocarbon dates bracketed by those I noted previously for the type.

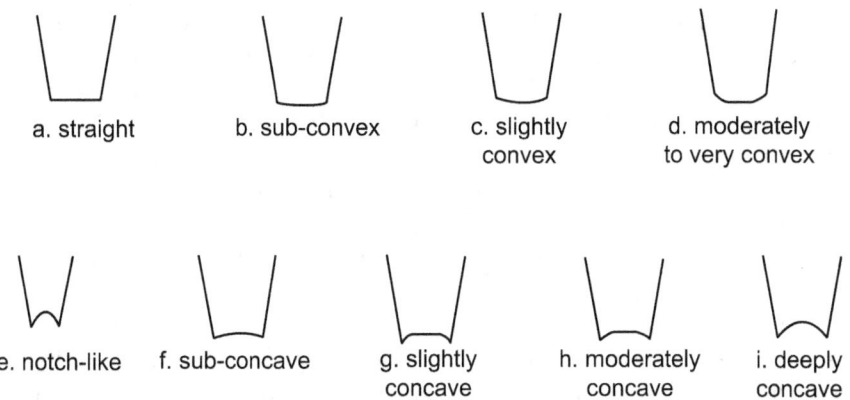

10.2. *Qualitative variants of basal convexity/concavity as expressed in specimens with convergent basal sides (Pitblado 1999). Absolute basal convexity or concavity of each specimen in the study assemblage was also recorded (in mm).*

Other projectile point labels floating around out there describe apparently similar projectile points, including Lusk (Greene 1967, 1968; Irwin 1968), Alder-Ruby Valley (Davis, Aaberg, and Greiser 1988; Davis et al. 1989), and Barton Gulch–Hardinger-Metzal (Davis, Aaberg, and Greiser 1988). All of these labels, however, were introduced after Wheeler proposed the term "Angostura," and none has yet been sufficiently described and illustrated in the literature that I could make a determination of whether one or more of them could be appropriately applied to my southern Rocky Mountain material. They were all, therefore, poor contenders to fulfill my labeling needs. "Foothills-Mountain" (sensu Frison 1991) is also an ill-advised choice of terms for reasons I explain later in this chapter.

The reason some have questioned my use of the term Angostura is that it has been argued to represent a "wastebasket" typological class. Marie Wormington (1957:140) noted this—and, in fact, perpetuated the problem—in her still relevant typological opus, saying, "This term [Angostura] is rapidly, and most unfortunately, replacing Yuma as a name to be applied indiscriminately to all lanceolate points." She perpetuated the problem by publishing a photo of a specimen not from the type-site but instead from Nebraska, while at the same time expressly accepting Wheeler's classification as appropriate. She concluded, almost rightly (Wormington 1957:140–141), that the term Angostura "should be applied only to points that have the same shape and general thickness and the parallel flaking that characterizes those from the type station." To have been entirely correct, she should have said "parallel-oblique flaking" rather than "parallel flaking," given her recognition that most of the points from the Ray Long "type station" exhibit this trait. I think she simply forgot the "oblique" in that sentence, an omission that may have further confused those looking to her for typological guidance.

My view is that it is not Wheeler's fault if his rather carefully conceived type has been misconstrued by other workers. Researchers have argued for years about whether "x" specimen is "really Clovis" (often in the case of specimens found ten states away from the Clovis type-site in New Mexico). Terms like "Plainview" and "Midland" have caused even more consternation among workers looking to place their finds in an appropriate chronological and geographic context. Yet Paleoindian archaeologists continue to use those terms because we understand their referents and can effectively employ them as foundations for discussions all can follow.

I believe it is more productive to reclaim a perfectly good old label and clarify its usage than to choose the only other course of action available: proposing yet another label for my colleagues to wrap their minds around—with no guarantee they would do a better job of it than they did with the "old" Angostura. In the final analysis, it does not make a lot of difference whether we call convergent-base, obliquely flaked, lanceolate points "Angostura," "Type X," "Sue," or "convergent-base, obliquely flaked lanceolate points" (CBOFLP for short). What does matter is that when we invoke the label (any label) as a Kriegerian type, we do so understanding that we are referring to a particular point form that has been convincingly associated with a particular time frame, geographic distribution, and set of material cultural associations. I will continue working on the "convincingly" part of that sentence throughout the rest of this chapter.

Jimmy Allen

Jimmy Allen points are lanceolate in form and typically show a well-executed parallel-oblique flaking pattern. Whereas Angostura points converge toward the base, Jimmy Allen points almost always show ever-so-slightly convergent to more typically parallel, or slightly converging, or even flaring (slightly concave) basal sides. Their bases proper also tend to show a more pronounced basal concavity than Angostura (Figure 10.2), although some share Angostura's less markedly concave base. Whereas Angostura specimens are narrow and relatively thick, Jimmy Allen specimens are wide and thin (Figure 10.3).

This description nicely captures the type descriptions for both Jimmy (James) Allen (Mulloy 1959) and Frederick (Irwin 1968; Irwin-Williams et al. 1973). Most who have weighed in on the issue consider the two so similar as to represent one and the same type, including Frison (1991:66). I concur, given that there are no demonstrable differences in geographic distribution or time frame between the two and that morphological differences mentioned by Irwin (1968:215) are clearly "minor" ones (sensu Bamforth 1991). Because I see them as so similar, in my 1999 and 2003 publications I juxtaposed the terms to label the type "Jimmy Allen/Frederick." As much as I still embrace my term "Angostura," however, I now regret assigning its wider, thinner, parallel-based counterparts an unduly cumbersome name. To recognize Mulloy's (1959) earlier contribution of the term Jimmy Allen to the literature, as well as the term's greater familiarity to most

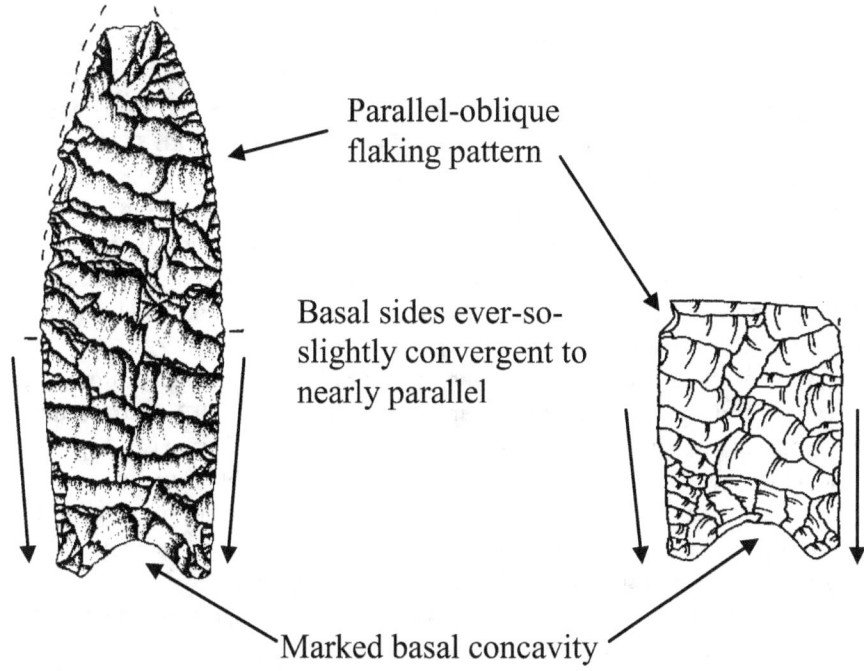

10.3. Left, *Jimmy Allen projectile point from the type-site, Laramie Basin, southern Wyoming. Right, Jimmy Allen point from Rocky Mountain National Park (specimen 14232), Larimer County, Colorado (illustrated by the author; courtesy, Rocky Mountain National Park, Estes Park, Colorado). Both specimens are ground along their basal sides. Type-site sketch reprinted from George C. Frison's* Prehistoric Hunters of the High Plains, *2nd ed. (1991), 63, with permission from Elsevier Press and George Frison.*

archaeologists, I hereby drop "Frederick" from my type label (although not the description), leaving it as simply "Jimmy Allen."

Distinguishing Angostura from Jimmy Allen in the Southern Rocky Mountains

To this point, I have explained the differences in geographic distribution of Angostura and Jimmy Allen sites recorded prior to my work and overviewed the major distinctions between the shapes and dimensions of Angostura and Jimmy Allen points. I also offered illustrations intended to visually convey key morphological differences. Here I delve back into a subset (just the Angostura and Jimmy Allen points) of my original Colorado-Utah database to demonstrate just how different the two types are in practice. In the paragraphs that follow, I overview qualitative and quantitative variables that clearly distinguish a population of sixty-five Angostura points from forty-nine Jimmy Allen points and offer a mathematical function that can discriminate between the two types with up to 98 percent accuracy.

Beginning with three key qualitative differences between the two types, I note first that Jimmy Allen points in my sample are more likely than Angostura to express the parallel-oblique flaking pattern—and Angostura is highly likely to show the pattern. Eighty-two percent of Jimmy Allen points from the entire study region of Colorado and Utah are obliquely flaked, compared with 57 percent of the Angostura points. Angostura, for its part, is more likely than Jimmy Allen to express a collateral flaking pattern (18 percent of specimens do) or an irregular one (12 percent). The difference in flaking patterns is statistically significant (Pearson chi-square = 10.960, df = 3, p = 0.012) and undoubtedly underlies the characterization of Jimmy Allen (by me and others) as possessing "well-executed flaking" when compared with some Angostura specimens.

Another clear vector of variability between Angostura and Jimmy Allen specimens from the project area is their basal outline (Figure 10.2). In my sample, 60 percent of Angostura points exhibit a sub- or slightly concave base, 22 percent a moderately or deeply concave base, and 18 percent straight bases. Jimmy Allen specimens have moderately or deeply concave bases 58 percent of the time and sub- to slightly concave bases in 40 percent of cases, and only 1 specimen of 114 has a base best characterized as straight (often, anomalous base shapes are the result of reworking, captured in other observations). Again, the difference in the two populations is statistically significant (Pearson chi-square = 17.628; df = 2; p = 0.000), reinforcing just how strong a predictor an obliquely flaked lanceolate projectile point's basal outline is of its type affiliation.

A final qualitative observation that clearly distinguishes our two classes of obliquely flaked lanceolate points from one another is basal side outline, a characterization of whether basal sides converge toward the base proper, diverge, are straight, or flare. Ninety-eight percent of points I categorized as Angostura converge toward their base; the other 2 percent (a single specimen) show basal sides closer to parallel. In stark contrast, Jimmy Allen points have convergent basal sides 14 percent of the time (and in those few instances the convergence is much less pronounced than in the typical Angostura artifact), parallel basal sides in 55 percent of cases, divergent basal sides with 18 percent frequency, and flared basal sides 12 percent of the time. Although the cross-tabulation that produces these results yields a number of cells with small frequencies, there is no doubt that in this case the chi-square significance test results are valid (Pearson's chi-square = 84.319; df = 3; p = 0.000). Angostura and Jimmy Allen bases differ dramatically from one another, both in the type description and in my Colorado-Utah sample.

Measurements, too, reveal stark differences between the Angostura and Jimmy Allen points I examined. Table 10.2 compares mean values for three key quantitative observations: basal width (distance from basal corner to corner), maximum width, and maximum thickness.

In each case, a t-test shows the apparent difference in central tendency to be statistically significant ($p < 0.01$). This demonstrates quantitatively what the type

Table 10.2. Mean Values (mm), Basal Width, Maximum Width, and Maximum Thickness.*

Type	Basal Width	Maximum Width	Maximum Thickness
Angostura (n = 65)	14.09	20.77	6.57
Jimmy Allen (n = 49)	21.35	22.46	5.85

* To be included in my 589-point sample, a specimen had to have a complete base and a maximum length at least equal to three-quarters of its basal width. Thus, a specimen did not have to be complete to be sampled, but it did have to have a sufficiently large basal fragment that a suite of measurements (Pitblado 2003, chapter 4) could be taken.

descriptions suggest verbally: that Angostura points are narrower and thicker overall than their Jimmy Allen counterparts and that their widths decrease markedly toward their bases (i.e., "converge").

In an effort to explore whether there might be an easy way for fieldworkers to objectively classify lanceolate points they can narrow down to the Angostura or Jimmy Allen types (i.e., lanceolate points with parallel-oblique flaking, basal grinding, and so forth), I conducted a discriminant function analysis (DFA) of the quantitative variables I measured for all the points of these two types in my Colorado-Utah sample. While the statistics and qualitative findings presented earlier show numerous differences between Angostura and Jimmy Allen points that register as statistically significant, the DFA shows that just *two* simple measurements—basal width and maximum width—can predict the type of any Angostura or Jimmy Allen point in my sample with 97–98 percent accuracy (assuming one is trying to discriminate only between those two types and is not evaluating, say, an Eden point). Figure 10.4 is a scatterplot of the basal width (x-axis) and maximum width (y-axis) of all 114 Angostura and Jimmy Allen points in my sample.

Visually, it is evident that basal and maximum width alone separate points of the two types with little discernible overlap. The DFA yields the algebraic function that mathematically best distinguishes the two clusters. Here, that function can be expressed as $L = -1.816 + 0.584(BW) - 0.383(MW)$, with L an object's discriminant score. The discriminant scores of the 114 specimens subjected to the DFA (the "developmental sample") range from -3.953 to 4.532. Specimens with $L < 0.53$ are classified as Angostura; where $L > 0.53$, the function predicts a specimen is Jimmy Allen. Applying this formula and a cutoff value of 0.53 results in the classification of two (of 65) points that I called Angostura as Jimmy Allen (an accuracy rate of 97 percent) and one (of 49) points that I called Jimmy Allen as Angostura (98 percent accuracy).

To be invoked as an effective predictive tool *outside* of the test assemblage, it is important to validate a function's discriminatory power on a new sample of Angostura, Jimmy Allen, or both, projectile points—one not included in the calculation of the function in the first place. I do not have access to as many specimens as I would like to test the function as rigorously as would be ideal. However, I do have available an assemblage of 21 projectile points that I classify

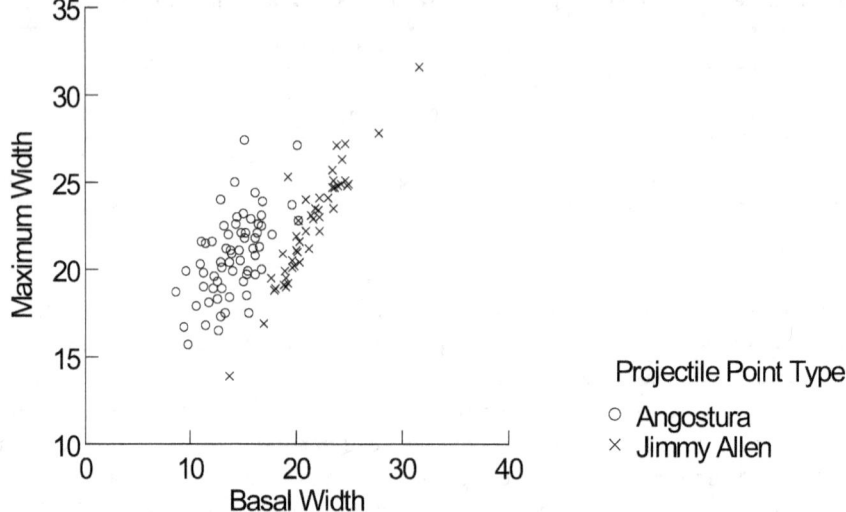

10.4. Scatterplot of basal and maximum widths (in mm) of Angostura and Jimmy Allen points in the Colorado-Utah sample. Note the lack of overlap between the two populations.

as Angostura from both excavated and surface contexts of the Chance Gulch late Paleoindian site, located in the Gunnison Basin of Colorado (e.g., Pitblado 2002). A suite of radiocarbon dates indicates an age for the Angostura component of the site of 8,000 RCYBP, well within the range I indicated earlier for the type (e.g., Stamm, Pitblado, and Camp 2004).

I began my test by measuring the basal and maximum widths of the 21 test specimens. I then plotted them, along with the 114 original specimens, on a second scatterplot (Figure 10.5). Visually, the graph suggests that the points I called Angostura based on their apparent conformance with the type description also cluster this way on the basis of their basal and maximum widths. To confirm what the graph suggests, I plugged the basal and maximum width values of the test specimens into the function calculated from the 114-point developmental sample: $L = -1.816 + 0.584(BW) - 0.383(MW)$. This yielded discriminant scores for the test assemblage ranging from -2.339 to 0.325. All twenty-one scores are lower than the 0.53 cutoff value of the developmental sample and thus represent—according to the DFA function—"Angostura" points.

Why We Should Care about Differentiating Angostura and Jimmy Allen Sites

All right, so Angostura and Jimmy Allen are really different from one another morphologically, and locations of previously known sites with these point types suggest there may be important differences in the physical distribution of the specimens across the Intermountain West and High Plains. Here I briefly overview what I argued in much more depth in my 1999 and 2003 publi-

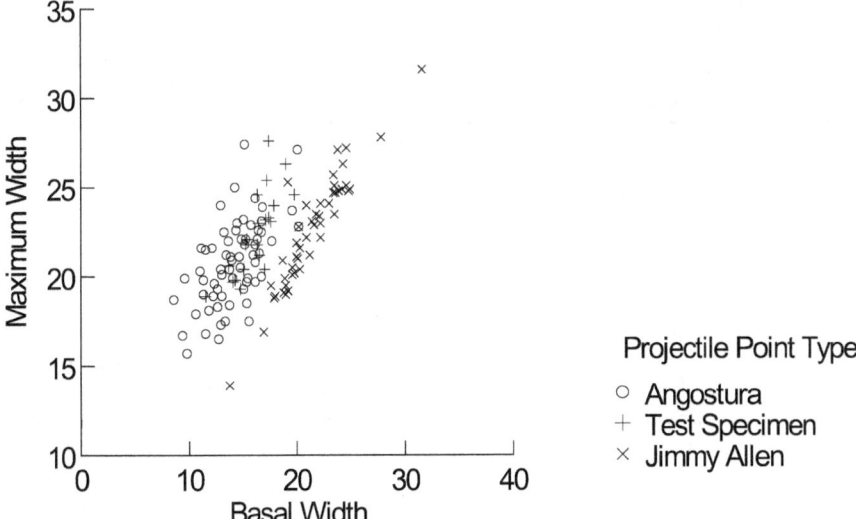

10.5. *Scatterplot showing the basal width (BW) and maximum width (MW) (in mm) of Angostura and Jimmy Allen points in the original 114-point sample and the test assemblage of 21 points assigned to "Angostura" from the Chance Gulch site (5GN817), Gunnison Basin, Colorado. Note that the test specimens cluster visually with the Angostura points from the original sample.*

cations: Angostura and Jimmy Allen are very differently distributed across the Plains and southern Rocky Mountains of my study area.

In short, Angostura points proved the consummate late Paleoindian point type represented in the southern Rockies within my sample assemblage. Of all the sites in my 414-site database that produced one or more Angostura points, 67 percent were recovered in the southern Rockies and only 5 percent on the Plains (and a very few others in the Far West). Jimmy Allen was the second-most-common point type in the southern Rockies, although they were found at only half as many Colorado Rocky Mountain sites as were their Angostura counterparts (15 Jimmy Allen sites versus 28 Angostura) (Table 10.3). In a clear departure from Angostura's distribution, sites with Jimmy Allen points were also common on the Colorado Plains—as common, in fact, as sites we might expect to dominate Plains late Paleoindian assemblages: Eden. In the Colorado Plains portion of my study assemblage, 20 sites each produced Jimmy Allen and Eden projectile points (compared with just 5 Plains localities that yielded a single Angostura point apiece).

Also of interest are different distributions of Angostura and Jimmy Allen sites within the southern Rocky Mountains, although sample sizes are small and these findings must be considered tentative until substantiated with more data. Of the twenty-eight Rocky Mountain sites that yielded Angostura points, all environmental zones were represented. The specimens occurred most commonly

Table 10.3. Angostura (Ang) and Jimmy Allen (JA) Projectile Points from the Rocky Mountains and Plains of Colorado.

Site No.	Site Name	Elevation (meters)	Rockies/ Plains	Point Type	No. of Points	Published References*
5ST87		3,597	Rockies	JA	1	Marcotte and Mayo 1978
5BL161		3,499	Rockies	Ang	1	
RMNP 6205		3,477	Rockies	Ang	1	
5LR6		3,463	Rockies	JA	1	Benedict 1996; Brunswig 2002
5BL80		3,455	Rockies	JA	1	
5GA22	Caribou Lake	3,444	Rockies	JA	3	Benedict 1974, 1985; Pitblado 2000
5HN154		3,420	Rockies	Ang	1	
5BL120	Fourth of July	3,415	Rockies	Ang	4	Benedict 1981, 2005
5BL120	Fourth of July	3,415	Rockies	JA	1	Benedict 1981, 2005
5GA56		3,415	Rockies	Ang	1	
5LR1733		3,398	Rockies	JA	1	
5LR230	Carey Lake	3,371	Rockies	JA	3	Morris and Metcalf 1993
5LR2		3,347	Rockies	Ang	2	Brunswig 2001
5LR2		3,347	Rockies	JA	1	Brunswig 2001
LM IF 94-1		3,338	Rockies	JA	1	
RMNP 169		2,972	Rockies	Ang	1	
5GN2151		2,606	Rockies	Ang	1	
5SM1456		2,548	Rockies	Ang	1	
5DL201		2,524	Rockies	Ang	1	
5GA1384		2,511	Rockies	JA	1	
5JA405		2,486	Rockies	Ang	1	
5DL691		2,445	Rockies	Ang	1	
5GN2133		2,414	Rockies	Ang	1	
5GN1835	Tenderfoot	2,340	Rockies	Ang	1	Stiger 2001
SD SZ	private collection	2,338	Rockies	JA	1	
SD M1	private collection	2,332	Rockies	Ang	2	
5DL775		2,322	Rockies	Ang	2	
5MT6660		2,283	Rockies	Ang	1	
McC 21	private collection	2,274	Rockies	Ang	2	
5MT7013		2,237	Rockies	Ang	1	
5MT5353		2,234	Rockies	Ang	1	
McC 20	private collection	2,204	Rockies	Ang	1	
McC 20	private collection	2,204	Rockies	JA	1	
5MT6468		2,121	Rockies	Ang	1	
5MT4690		2,091	Rockies	Ang	1	
5MF625	Cathedral Butte	2,076	Rockies	Ang	8	Stucky 1977
5MF633	Badger Skull	2,057	Rockies	Ang	1	Stucky 1977
MF 15M		2,057	Rockies	Ang	1	
McC 86	private collection	1,951	Rockies	JA	1	
McC 32	private collection	1,933	Rockies	Ang	1	
BT 1	private collection	1,911	Plains	JA	1	
5MF2918		1,836	Rockies	JA	1	

continued on next page

Table 10.3—*continued*

Site No.	Site Name	Elevation (meters)	Rockies/ Plains	Point Type	No. of Points	Published References*
McC 41	private collection	1,829	Rockies	Ang	2	
5MF3687	KibRidge-Yampa	1,780	Rockies	JA	1	Hauck and Hauck 2002
RL H	private collection	1,737	Plains	JA	1	
RL V	private collection	1,737	Plains	JA	1	
RL Russell	private collection	1,725	Plains	JA	1	
BF 10	private collection	1,672	Plains	JA	1	
BF 11	private collection	1,615	Plains	JA	3	
RL Pritchett	private collection	1,469	Plains	JA	1	
MT 193C	private collection	1,379	Plains	Ang	1	
MT 206D	private collection	1,379	Plains	JA	1	
TP 33755	private collection	1,372	Plains	JA	1	
TP 34/27	private collection	1,290	Plains	JA	1	
TP 27/18P	private collection	1,288	Plains	JA	1	
TP 75435	private collection	1,280	Plains	JA	1	
TP 9534	private collection	1,250	Plains	Ang	1	
TP 85335	private collection	1,231	Plains	Ang	1	
TP 1653	private collection	1,219	Plains	Ang	1	
TP 25753	private collection	1,219	Plains	Ang	1	
TP 7528	private collection	1,219	Plains	JA	1	
TP 75325	private collection	1,219	Plains	JA	1	
TP 95119	private collection	1,219	Plains	JA	1	
TP R+4	private collection	1,219	Plains	JA	1	
TP R-17	private collection	1,219	Plains	JA	1	
TP R-18	private collection	1,219	Plains	JA	1	
TP R-4	private collection	1,219	Plains	JA	1	
MT 48.16	private collection	1,097	Plains	JA	2	

* Artifacts in private collections do not have published references. Unless otherwise noted, sites with Smithsonian trinomial designations are either not fully reported (but are instead simply documented on site forms in Colorado Office of Archaeology and Historic Preservation [OAHP] files in Denver) or are reported in unpublished CRM (cultural resource management) reports on file at OAHP. Report titles can be accessed via OAHP's online COMPASS database (access can be arranged through OAHP personnel).

Note: Point types per Pitblado (1999, 2003) and assigned by Pitblado. Type assignments may or may not differ from other published references. This table does not include the few Jimmy Allen and Angostura specimens from the far western parts of the Colorado-Utah study area. Sites are listed by elevation, from highest to lowest.

(n = 11) in parklands (settings like those of Middle Park or the San Luis Valley). The low foothills yielded the next-greatest number of Angostura-producing sites (n = 7). The montane, subalpine, and alpine zones each contributed three sites to the Angostura database, and one was in an unknown environmental zone. The fifteen Jimmy Allen sites in the Colorado Rocky Mountain database, however, were best represented in the high subalpine zone (n = 6) and were not documented in the foothills. Three Jimmy Allen sites were located in parks, two in the highest alpine zone, one in the moderately high montane belt, and three in unknown environmental zones.

These data suggest a tendency for Jimmy Allen sites to be found (1) most commonly in the very high reaches of the Rocky Mountains (the subalpine and alpine zones) and (2) infrequently in the lowest mountain zone, the foothills. Angostura sites, on the other hand, according to these limited data, are found (1) most often in low, open settings but (2) throughout all the zones of the Rockies at least some of the time (a scan of the "elevation" column of Table 10.3 from top to bottom reinforces visually that Angostura occurs from high to low elevations of the Colorado Rockies). A check of absolute elevations of Rocky Mountain sites yielding projectile points of the two types shows a mean value of 2,484 m for Angostura and 2,915 m for Jimmy Allen. The difference is statistically significant at the 95 percent confidence level (pooled-variance $t = -2.142$, $df = 39$, $p = 0.038$) and confirms a tendency within the sample data set for Jimmy Allen sites to occur at higher elevations than Angostura.

This makes it all the more interesting that Jimmy Allen sites *also* occur with significant frequency on the Colorado Plains, while Angostura specimens do not. An interpretation I have posed as a hypothesis for testing is that Angostura projectile points index late Paleoindian groups who had made a full-time commitment to the Rocky Mountains, spending the entire year moving from environmental zone to environmental zone. With an adaptation like the historic Ute (including the pre-horse Ute), they would have occupied lower elevations of the foothills (and perhaps parks) during cold months and higher zones—in smaller groups—in milder months (e.g., Simmons 2000). If this reconstruction is accurate, then makers of Angostura points are virtually, by definition, a particular manifestation of the "Foothills-Mountain groups" Frison has long argued occupied the Rockies after 10,000 RCYBP.

Jimmy Allen points, with their dual occurrence on the Plains and in the Rockies—together with what appears to be an emphasis on the very highest Rockies—perhaps index late Paleoindian groups who migrated seasonally *between* the two regions. If that is the case, they must have used the Rockies primarily in the summer months, when the highest elevations would have been accessible. If we eventually learn that Jimmy Allen occurs equally often in lower mountain settings, we need not conclude that the very same groups migrated from region to region but rather that members of some cohesive unit occupied the Rockies and Plains and were sufficiently culturally united that they shared a projectile point technology.

This sort of adaptation would hardly be unprecedented: Folsom bison hunters used both the Plains and the Rockies extensively (even, as Jodry [e.g., 1999] has shown at the Black Mountain Folsom site, the very high southern Rockies). Additional data should help clarify which mountain zones Jimmy Allen point makers occupied, when, and what they were doing there. I suspect we will eventually find that like Folsom before them and some Shoshone much later (Trenholm and Carley 1964), Jimmy Allen folk were big-game hunters who pursued bison on the plains, bison in mountain parks, and bison, elk, and mountain sheep at very high elevations when conditions permitted.

10.6. Diagnostic artifacts from the Medicine Lodge Creek site, Bighorn Basin, Wyoming. Photo reprinted from George C. Frison's Prehistoric Hunters of the High Plains, 2nd ed. (1991), 70 (fig. 2.33), with permission from Elsevier Press and George Frison. Original photo caption: "Foothill-Mountain Paleoindian points (a–l, o–v), and a Cody point (m), and Cody knife (n) from the Medicine Lodge Creek site."

ANGOSTURA VERSUS "FOOTHILLS-MOUNTAIN PALEOINDIAN GROUPS"

Two paragraphs ago, I said that if my interpretation of the distribution of Angostura projectile points in the southern Rocky Mountains is correct, then makers of Angostura points must be a particular manifestation of the "Foothills-Mountain groups" Frison has long argued occupied the Rockies after 10,000 years ago. This statement captures the difference between Frison's "Foothills-Mountain" concept and my term "Angostura": his phrase describes an adaptation that he notes is characterized by many projectile point types; my term describes a particular projectile point type that I believe represents an adaptation akin to that Frison is trying to capture. A glance at figure 2.33 of Frison's 1991 volume (my Figure 10.6) helps clarify why our two terms are not equivalent.

As Frison sees it, all but the two Cody points from Medicine Lodge Creek are "Foothills-Mountain Points." That includes quite a few specimens (b, c, e, f, g, h, i, j, and k) that conform to my Angostura type, as well as a number that clearly do not. Those that do not include two stemmed specimens (r, s) that would be lost at a Great Basin Stemmed site, a specimen that could be justifiably classified as Jimmy Allen (v) (I have seen this specimen, and the flaking pattern is more parallel-oblique than parallel-horizontal), and a few other miscellaneous specimens. A "Foothills-Mountain Point," by this conception, can be defined as any diagnostic late Paleoindian projectile point except Cody found at a Rocky Mountain site, including points of types associated with the Far West and the Plains.

As long as we understand that this is what we mean when we use the term "Foothills-Mountain Points," we are on safe—if not particularly useful—ground. However, I have observed a tendency for archaeologists working in the southern Rocky Mountains to use the term "Foothills-Mountain Point" as if it were a true projectile point type (the term appears frequently on Colorado site forms in the "diagnostic artifacts" field). When archaeologists do that, all they can be safely assumed to be communicating is that they found a point they know *is* late Paleoindian, *is not* Cody—and that is it. In many cases, especially in southern Colorado—where we have few, if any, sites with the highly variable array of diagnostic late Paleoindian projectile points of Medicine Lodge Creek—they are really talking about an Angostura point. For reasons that should now be abundantly clear, by saying they found an *Angostura* point (or, if it sits better, "a point that nut-case Pitblado would call Angostura—but I hate the term"), they are communicating something more specific and meaningful.

Frison's "Foothills-Mountain" concept, I believe, accurately describes an *adaptation* some late Paleoindian people made to year-round life in the Rocky Mountains. In the southern Rocky Mountains, those people made Angostura points. The fact that a hefty percentage of the points at Medicine Lodge Creek (and other sites in Wyoming and Montana) are Angostura suggests that the type is probably a good index of a true, year-round adaptation there as well. Frison (1991) knows perfectly well that the Cody points at Medicine Lodge Creek are not "Foothills-Mountain" (i.e., they do not index occupation of that foothills site by mountain-adapted people), which is why he set them aside in his figure caption (see his quoted caption in Figure 10.6).

But we can go further employing the same logic: the two Great Basin Stemmed points and the Jimmy Allen point also are not "Foothills-Mountain Points"—they are Great Basin Stemmed and Jimmy Allen points. As Cody is to the plains, Great Basin Stemmed is to, well, the Great Basin. And as Cody is to the plains, Jimmy Allen is to the plains *and* the mountains, as I have tried to show in this chapter. To me, Medicine Lodge Creek is a fascinating site precisely because of the phenomenal variability in the projectile point assemblage. Cramming all that variability into any one type label—"Foothills-Mountain Point" or any other—is unhelpful, almost certainly not a reflection of how Frison himself views the assemblage, and not a convention we should adopt in the southern Rocky Mountains. So, friends, in the same way you resist the urge to record a gorgeous Eden point's type as "Plains late Paleoindian," when you find an Angostura point, why not label it as such rather than the more generic, less informative, never-intended-to-be-a-Kriegerian-point-type "Foothills-Mountain"?

EVALUATING BRUNSWIG'S EVALUATION OF ANGOSTURA AND JIMMY ALLEN IN THE NORTH-CENTRAL COLORADO ROCKIES

In Chapter 9 of this book, Bob Brunswig presents an excellent and exhaustive study of Paleoindian projectile points from north-central Colorado. This is precisely the sort of work I hoped would follow publication of the data in my dissertation and book because it independently tests the ideas and models I offered therein. For his study, Brunswig created a database of Paleoindian projectile points by compiling existing paper and electronic resources for sites with Paleoindian components within the study area. He started with the Colorado Office of Archaeology and Historic Preservation's COMPASS computerized site database and then added data derived from other databases, publications of the University of Northern Colorado's Systemwide Archeological Inventory Program, "gray literature" CRM reports, and published manuscripts.

Brunswig reports data summarized from these sources according to Paleoindian projectile point type(s) present. Of greatest interest to me and of greatest relevance to this chapter, of course, are his late Paleoindian findings, especially those of Angostura and Jimmy Allen points. In contrast to what my research and results would predict, Brunswig observes that in his study area—geographically a subset of mine—sites yielding Jimmy Allen points were more common than sites yielding Angostura points (37 to 19). In my study, the ratio in the Colorado Rockies was almost precisely the opposite (28 sites with Angostura points, 15 with Jimmy Allen). In terms of the presence of *individual* specimens—data I did not report in my 1999 and 2003 publications to avoid biasing interpretations of type distributions across the landscape by including sites with widely disparate numbers of projectile points (but see Table 10.3)—Brunswig records for his project area a very high absolute number of Jimmy Allen points (67). This total is far higher than the 19 individual Angostura specimens (exactly 1 Angostura spear point per Angostura component) he reports for his project area. These results again appear to run counter to my own, which suggest that Angostura, numerically and in other respects, is the consummate southern Rocky Mountain late Paleoindian point type.

Examining next the distribution of Jimmy Allen and Angostura components across the various environmental zones of his project area, Brunswig reports that 57 percent of Jimmy Allen points occur in "higher-elevation zones" and the remaining 43 percent in "lower-elevation" zones. Sites with Angostura specimens are similarly distributed in his study area, he notes, with 63 percent in "high-elevation" zones and 37 percent at "lower elevations." In my study, readers will recall from my earlier discussion, Angostura points were most common in mountain parks, second-most-common in foothills settings, and present in smaller and roughly equal percentages in the montane, subalpine, and alpine zones. Jimmy Allen points occurred by far most frequently in the subalpine zone, never in the foothills, and infrequently in mid-altitude parks and montane settings. In my sample, Jimmy Allen is tightly (although not exclusively) associated with the high Rockies, Angostura with all Rocky Mountain environmental zones—from lowest to highest.

So what is going on here? Why the apparent discrepancies in Brunswig's findings versus mine in geographically overlapping areas? In addressing that question, we must first and foremost explore how comparable the two investigations really are. In short, it appears from Brunswig's description of his study area that, environmentally, it is not strictly comparable to mine and that this structural difference could, in fact, account for much (maybe even all) of the variability in our results. Mountain environmental zones in Brunswig's study area include alpine tundra, the alpine-subalpine ecotone, subalpine, montane (upper and lower), and sagebrush steppe parkland (see his Chapter 9 discussion of "Environmental and Ecological Contexts"). This list encompasses all of the zones I delineated for the "southern Rockies" portion of my study area except one: the foothills—the lowest of the major Rocky Mountain environmental zones. Additionally, Brunswig classifies his montane zone as a "lower-elevation" zone, whereas in my study area I considered this zone of ponderosa pines, Douglas firs, and aspens to be "high elevation."

In a related vein, Brunswig's various map figures reflect a study region that includes a much greater ratio of higher-elevation mountain settings to lower than did mine, which encompassed *all* of the southern Rocky Mountains of Colorado, from the tops of the state's many "fourteeners" (mountains greater than 14,000 feet in elevation) to the lowest Foothills-Plains and Foothills–Colorado Plateau ecotones (and, indeed, eastward across the plains to the state's modern physiographic border). This means that in Brunswig's study area, relative to mine, there was an inherently much greater chance that projectile points of any type, from any time period, would derive from higher-elevation zones than from lower zones, simply because the project area was so heavily biased in this direction as to entirely preclude the inclusion of piñon-juniper woodlands.

Yet, in my study the foothills contributed the second-greatest number of Angostura sites to the total documented (mountain parks were first), and they were the *only* zone not to contribute even a single site to the Jimmy Allen site total. The foothills, then, played—and play—a pivotal role in distinguishing the distributions of the two projectile point types in the context of my study; yet this zone is not part of Brunswig's project area. Because this critical environment is missing, there is simply no basis for comparing the distribution of point types in Brunswig's project area and the Rocky Mountain portion of mine. As well, Brunswig's study cannot speak to what I see as the most noteworthy difference between Angostura and Jimmy Allen: Jimmy Allen occurs with equally high frequency in the Colorado Rockies and on the Colorado Plains, whereas Angostura occurs only in the mountains and almost never on the plains.

Although the structure of the two studies renders it essentially impossible to know if they do or do not support different interpretations of late Paleoindian use of the southern Rocky Mountains in all their variable-elevation glory, Brunswig

(p. 284) makes an extremely important observation relevant to the framing of future studies when he points out that there could be a "tendency of some mountain archaeologists to type artifacts as JAF [Jimmy Allen–Frederick] because they are more familiar with that type than with Angostura." Close morphological similarity of the two types, particularly aggravated when dealing with fragmented tools, tends to render their identification as one or the other type problematic.

I am confident that Brunswig is correct in suggesting that there has been a bias on the part of mountain fieldworkers to call any specimen with parallel-oblique flaking "Jimmy Allen." When I began my collections research a decade ago, I quickly learned that what site forms and reports referred to as late Paleoindian specimens from mountain contexts often bore little relationship to what I saw when I actually tracked down projectile points for examination—if, in fact, I could track them down, something that was distressingly frequently impossible. To illustrate the extent of the problem, in early 2006 I obtained from OAHP an electronic database (derived from the same master COMPASS site database that provided much of Brunswig's data) of all Paleoindian localities in Colorado. Using the "find" feature in Microsoft Excel™, I determined that those records mention "Jimmy Allen or "James Allen" points twenty-one times. The term "Frederick" is used twice, "Foothills-Mountain" or "Foothill-Mountain" twice (both for sites recorded by one firm in 2002), and "Angostura" in zero cases.

Of these twenty-six late Paleoindian sites with specifically mentioned obliquely flaked, lanceolate point types, eighteen were recorded sufficiently long ago that they were contenders for my original study—which began the same way, with Colorado OAHP site files (then available only in paper format). Each of those eighteen had been designated either Jimmy Allen or Frederick. Of the eighteen, however, only six found their way into my final database, which means that in fully two-thirds of cases, projectile points were not collected at the time they were found, had been lost and could not be examined, or were not—in my eyes—late Paleoindian at all. Of the six I did include in my database, I only agreed with the "Jimmy Allen" designation in three cases. In two cases I called the points Angostura, and one was of an indeterminate type.

The conclusion I draw from this exercise is that while state site files and other secondary reports of finds (e.g., "gray literature") include a plethora of important information, references to point types (especially when lacking associated high-quality artifact photographs or illustrations) must be viewed—and used in analytical studies—extremely critically. Sites recorded prior to publication of my work are, as Brunswig suspected and my brief examination suggests, highly likely (100 percent likely!) to use the term "Jimmy Allen" to describe finds of obliquely flaked lanceolate points, if such specimens are given a name at all. But those type affiliations are in most cases unsupportable, either because the evidence is now unavailable for reevaluation or because they were assigned as a default to specimens a hands-on evaluation and a larger frame of reference indicate may be better classified as Angostura.

As for Brunswig's suggestion that "close morphological similarity" exists between Jimmy Allen and Angostura, exacerbated when points are fragmentary, I hope this chapter has helped show what my previous publications may not have stressed strongly enough: this is simply not the case. Even very small basal fragments almost always possess the key diagnostic features that will support a designation of Jimmy Allen or Angostura—they are either thin, wide, and nearly parallel-based; or they are thick, narrow, and convergent-based. If a fieldworker doubts an assessment, measuring basal width and maximum width and plugging them into the function I presented previously should resolve the matter. If a base is not present, a projectile point tip or blade is almost never diagnostic anyway.

CONCLUSIONS

I wrote this chapter with a number of goals in mind, among them to clarify differences among the terms Angostura, Jimmy Allen, and Foothills-Mountain and explore reasons why studies attempting to apply my terms have produced seemingly different results than mine. To summarize without belaboring the point, I adopted the type labels "Angostura" and "Jimmy Allen" according to Krieger's (1944) classical typological method, not according to arbitrary differences in projectile point morphology or technology. At the same time, however, the morphological and technological differences between the two types *are* quantifiable, statistically significant, and easily recognizable—even in two dimensions (basal and maximum width can be measured from a typical plan view line drawing or photograph). I chose the labels I did to respect and honor their earliest scientifically supportable use in the archaeological literature.

Application of the type labels to my 114-specimen assemblage from the southern Rocky Mountains suggests that their geographic distributions differ in two respects—one I consider very well supported, the other more limited by sample size and thus a more tentative conclusion. Angostura points are to me as clear a manifestation of Frison's "Foothills-Mountain" adaptation as we could hope to see. Their disproportionately high presence in the mountains and not in adjacent lowland regions suggests that their makers lived in the southern Rockies on a sustained, year-round basis, subsisting through generalized hunting and gathering. Jimmy Allen, in rather stark contrast, occurred almost equally frequently in my sample assemblage in the mountains and on the plains and appears to represent—in a pattern akin to Folsom, for example—a more specialized big-game hunting adaptation than does Angostura.

In my sample (and here is where sample size issues render the following conclusion more tentative), Jimmy Allen occurred more often at high elevations—where elk and bighorn sheep are common in summer and early fall—than in the foothills, indicating that makers of Jimmy Allen points may have used the mountains on a seasonal basis, spending cooler months hunting on the High Plains. It seems prudent to leave open the possibility that as more Jimmy Allen sites are definitively recognized, we may also document a significant presence in parklands (as Brunswig's data suggest and mine do not contradict), which could mean that some groups wintered there. Parks are, after all, as the distribution of Folsom in Colorado attests, a good choice for big-game hunters targeting the bison and elk that sometimes congregate there.

Relevant to this issue may be Brunswig's finding that the Jimmy Allen sites in his largely high-altitude project area yielded significantly more projectile point specimens per site than did Angostura sites (67 Jimmy Allen specimens from 37 sites, 19 Angostura points from as many localities). This archaeological signature—although not particularly reflected in my data (see Table 10.3)—could be taken as support for the view that Jimmy Allen hunters in the north-central Colorado Rockies were using the sorts of communal big-game hunting strategies typically associated with Plains Paleoindians (and most Plains people thereafter), a hunting strategy that requires and leaves behind multiple weapons at single sites. The solitary nature of all of Brunswig's Angostura point finds, on the other hand, is more consistent with a scenario of opportunistic hunting by smaller groups of people—and perhaps of game less likely to congregate in large herds.

Attempts to apply my terms, I suspect, have been hampered by problems related to interpretation of what I meant by them—the inspiration for this chapter, which attempts to clarify what may not have been clear in previous publications. One good example: my term Angostura is not equivalent to Frison's "Foothills-Mountain," which upon close inspection can be shown to be a terrific description of a very real late Paleoindian adaptation but a very poor choice of label for a projectile point type (an application I am certain Frison did not intend but that has proliferated anyway). There are also problems related to comparability of data sets. In Brunswig's case, the lowest mountain elevations so crucial to demonstrating differences between Angostura and Jimmy Allen are not present for assessment. Without low-elevation mountain settings, the distributional distinction I observed between Angostura and Jimmy Allen in the southern Rockies not only will not but structurally *cannot* be replicated.

I believe that with my (re)introduction of the term "Angostura," we now have a typological toolkit available that, if used in the sense in which it is proffered, can help us learn more about late Paleoindian use of the southern Rocky Mountains than we know today. I have offered a broad-brush interpretation of how makers of Angostura and Jimmy Allen points, respectively, used the southern Rocky Mountains during the same era in prehistory. However, I would certainly like to develop a more detailed understanding of what, in each case, an annual trek across the landscape entailed. Assigning sites to the appropriate class provides some basis for framing appropriate research questions. Old-fashioned analyses of stone raw material sources, seasonality, subsistence remains, and intra-site use of space will help provide the answers.

Acknowledgments. I thank Jim Benedict and George Frison for reviewing and offering valuable suggestions for improving this manuscript and Bob Brunswig for offering me the opportunity not only to write this chapter but to help compile this book. The research reported here was funded primarily by the National Science Foundation (SBR-9624373). The American Alpine Club, Arizona-Nevada Academy of Sciences, Colorado Mountain Club, Colorado State University Foundation, Explorers Club, Graduate Women in Science/Sigma Delta Epsilon, Hyatt Corporation, Marshall Foundation of Tucson, and the University of Arizona Department of Anthropology, College of Social and Behavioral Sciences, and Graduate College also funded portions of the research that culminated in this chapter.

REFERENCES CITED

Bamforth, D. B.
- 1991 Flintknapping Skill, Communal Hunting, and Paleoindian Projectile Point Typology. *Plains Anthropologist* 36 (137):309–322.

Benedict, J. B.
- 1974 Early Occupation of the Caribou Lake Site, Colorado Front Range. *Plains Anthropologist* 19 (63):1–4.
- 1981 *The Fourth of July Valley: Glacial Geology and Archeology of the Timberline Ecotone.* Center for Mountain Archeology, Research Report 2, Ward, CO.
- 1985 *Arapaho Pass: Glacial Geology and Archeology at the Crest of the Colorado Front Range.* Center for Mountain Archeology, Research Report 3, Ward, CO.
- 1996 *The Game Drives of Rocky Mountain National Park.* Center for Mountain Archeology, Research Report 7, Ward, CO.
- 2005 Rethinking the Fourth of July Valley Site: A Study in Glacial and Periglacial Geoarchaeology. *Geoarchaeology* 20 (8):797–836.

Brunswig, R. H.
- 2001 *Report on 2000 Archaeological Surveys in Rocky Mountain National Park by the University of Northern Colorado (ROMO-R98-0804).* Department of Anthropology, University of Northern Colorado, Greeley.
- 2002 *Report on 2001 Archaeological Surveys in Rocky Mountain National Park by the University of Northern Colorado (ROMO-R98-0804).* Department of Anthropology, University of Northern Colorado, Greeley.

Davis, L. B., S. A. Aaberg, W. P. Eckerle, J. W. Fisher Jr., and S. T. Greiser
- 1989 Montane Paleoindian Occupation of the Barton Gulch Site, Ruby Valley, Southwestern Montana. *Current Research in the Pleistocene* 6:7–9.

Davis, L. B., S. A. Aaberg, and S. T. Greiser
- 1988 Paleoindians in Transmontane Southwestern Montana: The Barton Gulch Occupations, Ruby River Drainage. *Current Research in the Pleistocene* 5:9–11.

Dixon, J. E.
- 1999 *Bones, Boats, and Bison: Archaeology and the First Colonization of Western North America.* University of New Mexico Press, Albuquerque.

Frison, G. C.
- 1973 Early Period Marginal Cultural Groups in Northern Wyoming. *Plains Anthropologist* 18 (62, Parts 1 and 2):300–312.

1976   The Chronology of Paleoindian and Altithermal Cultures in the Big Horn Basin, Wyoming. In *Cultural Change and Continuity, Essays in Honor of James Bennett Griffin*, ed. C. E. Cleland, 147–173. Academic, New York.

1983   The Lookingbill Site, Wyoming, 48FR308. *Tebiwa* 20:1–16.

1988   Paleoindian Subsistence and Settlement during Post-Clovis Times on the Northwestern Plains, the Adjacent Mountain Ranges, and Intermontane Basins. In *America Before Columbus: Ice-Age Origins*, ed. R. C. Carlisle, 83–106. Ethnology Monographs 12, University of Pittsburgh, Department of Anthropology.

1991   *Prehistoric Hunters of the High Plains*, 2nd ed. Academic, New York.

1992   The Foothills-Mountains and the Open Plains: The Dichotomy in Paleoindian Subsistence Strategies between Two Ecosystems. In *Ice Age Hunters of the Rockies*, ed. D. J. Stanford and J. S. Day, 323–342. Denver Museum of Natural History and University Press of Colorado, Niwot.

1998   The Paleoindian in the Bighorn Mountains, Wyoming. *Abstracts of the 63rd Annual Meeting of the Society for American Archaeology*, Seattle, WA.

Greene, A. M.

1967   *The Betty Greene Site: A Late Paleo-Indian Site in Eastern Wyoming*. Unpublished master's thesis, University of Pennsylvania, Philadelphia.

1968   Age and Archaeological Association of Oblique Flaked Projectile Points at the Betty Greene Site, Eastern Wyoming. *Abstracts of Papers*, 33rd Annual Meeting, Society for American Archaeology, Santa Fe, NM.

Hauck, F. R., and M. R. Hauck

2002   *KibRidge-Yampa Paleoindian Occupation Site (5MF3687), Preliminary Excavations in Northwestern Colorado*. Archaeological Research Institute General Study Series 4, Bountiful, UT.

Haynes, C. V.

1992   Contributions of Radiocarbon Dating to the Geochronology of the Peopling of the New World. In *Radiocarbon after Four Decades*, ed. R. E. Taylor, A. Long, and R. S. Kra, 355–374. Springer-Verlag, New York.

Hunt, C. B.

1967   *Physiography of the United States*. W. H. Freeman, San Francisco.

Irwin, H. T.

1968   *The Itama: Late Pleistocene Inhabitants of the Plains of the United States and Canada and the American Southwest*. Unpublished Ph.D. dissertation, Harvard University, Cambridge, MA.

Irwin-Williams, C., H. Irwin, G. A. Agogino, and C. V. Haynes Jr.

1973   Hell Gap: Paleo-Indian Occupation on the High Plains. *Plains Anthropologist* 18:40–52.

Jodry, M. A.

1999   *Folsom Technological and Socioeconomic Strategies: View from Stewart's Cattle Guard and the Upper Rio Grande Basin, Colorado*. University Microfilms, Ann Arbor, MI.

2005   Recent Research in the Northern Rio Grande Valley. Paper presented at the 7th Biennial Rocky Mountain Anthropological Conference, Park City, UT.

Krieger, A. D.
　1944　The Typological Concept. *American Antiquity* 9 (3):271–288.

Larson, M. L.
　2005　*The Paleoindian to Archaic Transition: The Northwestern Plains and Central Rocky Mountains.* Paper presented at the 70th Annual Meeting of the Society for American Archaeology, Salt Lake City, UT.

Marcotte, J. R., and D. Mayo
　1978　*Archaeological Surveillance during Construction Activities at the Argentine Pass Site, Summit County, Colorado.* Reports of the Laboratory of Public Archaeology 19, Colorado State University, Fort Collins.

Meltzer, D. J.
　1993　*Search for the First Americans.* Smithsonian Exploring the Ancient World Series, ed. J. A. Sabloff. Smithsonian Books, Washington, DC.

Morris, E. A., and M. D. Metcalf
　1993　Twenty-Two Years of Archaeological Survey in the Rawah Area, Medicine Bow Mountains, Northern Colorado. *Abstracts of Papers*, First Biennial Rocky Mountain Anthropology Conference, Jackson, WY.

Mulloy, W. T.
　1959　The James Allen Site Near Laramie, Wyoming. *American Antiquity* 25(1):112–116.

Osborn, A. J., and M. Kornfeld
　2003　Biogeographical Islands and Ecological Patches: Seeing the Great Plains from the Inside Out. In *Islands on the Plains: Ecological, Social and Ritual Use of Landscapes*, ed. M. Kornfeld and A. J. Osborn, 1–18. University of Utah Press, Salt Lake City.

Pitblado, B. L.
　1999　*Late Paleoindian Occupation of the Southern Rocky Mountains.* Ph.D. dissertation, University of Arizona, Tucson, and University Microfilms, Ann Arbor, MI.
　2002　The Chance Gulch Late Paleoindian Site, Gunnison Basin, Colorado. *Current Research in the Pleistocene* 19:74–76.
　2003　*Late Paleoindian Occupation of the Southern Rocky Mountains.* University Press of Colorado, Niwot.

Simmons, V. M.
　2000　*The Ute Indians of Utah, Colorado, and New Mexico.* University Press of Colorado, Niwot.

Stamm, J. F., B. Pitblado, and B. A. Camp
　2004　The Geology and Soils of the Chance Gulch Archaeological Site Near Gunnison, Colorado. *Mountain Geologist* 41 (2):63–74.

Stiger, M. A.
　2001　*Hunter-Gatherer Archaeology of the Colorado High Country.* University Press of Colorado, Niwot.

Stucky, R. K.
　1977　*Archaeological Survey of the Sand Wash Basin, Northwestern Colorado.* Unpublished master's thesis, University of Colorado, Boulder.

Trenholm, V. C., and M. Carley
    1964   *The Shoshonis: Sentinels of the Rockies.* University of Oklahoma Press, Norman.

Wheeler, R. P.
    1995   *Archaeological Investigations in Three Reservoir Areas in South Dakota and Wyoming, Part I, Angostura Reservoir.* Reprints in Anthropology 46. J&L Reprint Co., Lincoln, NE.

Wormington, H. M.
    1957   Ancient Man in North America. *Denver Museum of Natural History Popular Series* 4, Denver.

AFTERWORD

George C. Frison

A Wyoming Archaeologist's Past and Present View of Wyoming and Colorado Paleoindian Archaeology

Within the lower forty-eight states, Wyoming claims the questionable distinction of being the leading contender as the last frontier in North American archaeology. If it were not for the proven association of extinct animals and humans at the Folsom and Blackwater Draw sites in the late 1920s, which, over a decade later, drew attention to several Paleoindian (then "Early Man") bison kills in Wyoming, this status would probably have been maintained longer than it was. Other than these bison kills, there was little to attract the attention of archaeologists, as did the Anasazi in the Southwest and Plains villages along the Missouri River to the east. Late Prehistoric–age bison jumps aroused some interest but little incentive to engage in research. Tipi rings were plentiful but of even lower priority than bison jumps.

On the other hand, my family established connections pertaining to Colorado archaeology in a strictly avocational sense nearly 100 years ago. Lacking adequate educational facilities in relatively isolated northern Wyoming in the first two decades of the twentieth century, my grandparents sent two of my uncles to school in Fort Collins, Colorado. One uncle, Robert Frison, had already developed a strong avocational interest in archaeology that eventually led to contacts with the Coffin family in Fort Collins who, in 1924, discovered the Lindenmeier Folsom site. Robert Frison learned of the Lindenmier site through contacts with the Coffins and maintained a lively interest in the site investigations. This eventually resulted in contact with Frank H.H. Roberts of the Smithsonian Institution, who was native to northern Colorado and served as the principal investigator at the Lindenmeier site in the 1930s. This contact would prove valuable in later years.

In 1953, I had the good fortune to make the acquaintance of Roy Coffin in Fort Collins. He gave me a copy of his account of the Lindenmeier site discovery (Coffin 1937), immediately arousing my interest in the Folsom projectile points I had read about but never seen. However, his interests extended well beyond Lindenmeier and Folsom. He showed me a collection of nearly 2,000 corner-notched bow-and-arrow points he had dug from a bone bed in a late Prehistoric-age bison corral in southern Wyoming, close to the Big Laramie River. This site had close affinities to another bison kill site about 30 km to the east, which I excavated in the late 1970s (Bupp 1981).

In 1941 a sheepherder, William Spencer of Edgemont, South Dakota, showed Robert Frison, who then lived in Newcastle, Wyoming, several broken and complete projectile points he claimed to have found among large bones eroding out of an arroyo bank in eastern Wyoming close to the Edgemont area. Frison visited the site with Spencer and agreed with his account of the association of the bones and projectile points. Frison had not seen any counterparts to these points but intuitively believed they could be quite old. His earlier contacts with Frank Roberts paid dividends when he, along with his brother H. B. Roberts, who lived in the Fort Collins area, and R. Frison tested the location in 1942 that later became known as the Agate Basin site (48N0201) (Roberts 1943). World War II postponed further work by Roberts until 1961, and bad health kept him from completing a final report. I worked at the site at various times from 1973 to 1980 and took the University of Wyoming collections to the Smithsonian Institution in 1980. Dennis Stanford and I worked with the University of Wyoming materials and the Roberts collection and produced a site report. The Agate Basin site proved to be a major Paleoindian site with Folsom, Agate Basin, and Hell Gap components (Frison and Stanford 1982).

My avocational interests in archaeology began during the Dust Bowl days of the 1930s and, except for the World War II years, continued until I finally decided to take the necessary steps in the early 1960s to pursue an academic career. While still avocational, I took a collection of perishable late Archaic artifacts I had recovered in 1953 in a dry cave site in northern Wyoming (Frison 1965) to William Mulloy, the first anthropologist hired at the University of Wyoming in 1948. He suggested I show them to H. Marie Wormington at the Denver Museum of

Natural History. In retrospect, this was the beginning of a long and rewarding relationship. She became a great cohort and, along with her husband, George Volk, a good friend. Marie knew everyone involved in Paleoindian studies and was always willing to put in a good word for those she believed demonstrated future potential.

During this same time period, through Marie Wormington, I became acquainted with Earl Morris, who lived in Boulder, Colorado. He expressed great interest in my Wyoming cave site materials and noted many similarities between them and his Basketmaker materials from the Southwest. He encouraged me to keep him informed of any new discoveries, which resulted in an exchange of letters for some time afterward.

In addition to my own interactions with Colorado archaeologists, both avocational and professional, there were other Colorado-Wyoming connections and interactions. During his long tenure at the University of Denver, E. B. Renaud had both a direct and an indirect influence on Wyoming archaeology. He made several surveys into Wyoming (Renaud 1932, 1936a, 1936b, 1938, 1940). In his seventh report of activities during the summer of 1935, he surveyed and recorded many sites in southwestern Wyoming along the Black's Fork of the Green River. It was there that he began to fall victim to his European background in archaeology (Renaud 1936a). Noting the similarity of many artifacts to European Paleolithic artifacts, he became convinced they were of the same age. Renaud's tenth report (1938) is devoted to his "Black's Fork Culture." He took a large sample of his artifacts—to which he applied European terms including Clactonian, Mousterian, and coup-de-poing—to Europe to show to his European colleagues, who agreed with his claims of morphological similarities to materials of the European Paleolithic.

In his twelfth report, Renaud (1940) described his final research on the Black's Fork materials. During August 1938, Dr. Ernest Antevs of the Carnegie Institution joined the Renaud expedition and recorded the terrace sequence at several locations along the Black's Fork River (Renaud 1940:10–13, 18–19). During June 1938, Dr. E. H. Stevens of the Colorado School of Mines joined the expedition and submitted a short geological report (Renaud 1940:14–17). Renaud was no doubt seriously searching for geological evidence to support his claims of great antiquity for his Black's Fork Culture.

The claims of great age for the Black's Fork Culture were viewed as suspect by archaeologists working in the Great Basin and Northwest Plains, and they were finally laid to rest by Floyd Sharrock (1966) as the result of excavations at the Pine Spring site (48SW101) and his revisiting of many of Renaud's sites. It is easy to understand why Renaud emphasized the similarities to European Paleolithic artifacts, but he ultimately lacked the geological evidence needed to uphold the claims he spent so much of his career defending.

Renaud's surveys covered a large share of Wyoming. Many of his efforts were spent recording rock art. He was particularly and understandably impressed by the pictographs in the Castle Gardens District in central Wyoming (Renaud 1936b:9–19). He described ceramics from eastern Wyoming (1932:58–63) and visited quarry sites in the Spanish Diggings area (1932:31–36).

In a related yet different vein, one of Renaud's students and earlier assistants with a 1937 degree from the University of Denver, Ted C. Sowers, became involved with the 1939 Wyoming Archaeological Survey funded by the Work Projects Administration (WPA) (Sowers 1941). Among other activities, Sowers conducted massive excavations at Dinwoodie Cave and campsite on the Wind River Indian Reservation in northwestern Wyoming, recovering hundreds of artifacts. Unfortunately, the disposition of the artifacts created a long-lasting controversy between archaeologists and the Native Americans on the reservation. Most artifacts were accidentally misplaced in a storage facility and were not discovered until over a half-century later. Charles Reher, archaeologist at the University of Wyoming, was allowed to view and photograph the collection, but the Native Americans refused his request to properly analyze and study the materials. There is one alleged claim that the Native Americans buried the entire collection somewhere in the mountains on the Wind River Indian Reservation. This is particularly unfortunate because the photographs indicate several late Paleoindian and early Archaic projectile points that would probably enhance our knowledge of the Foothill-Mountain Paleoindian and early Archaic occupants of the Wind River Mountains.

Sowers also excavated a site known as Medicine Creek Cave in northeastern Wyoming. This site is a long crevice over a meter wide originally containing nearly 2 meters of sediment that covered most of its major attraction, a large rock-art panel. The sediments also contained a flaked stone assemblage (Sowers 1941). William Buckles studied the rock art for his master's thesis at the University of Colorado (Buckles 1964). In addition, Sowers excavated for a short time at the Spanish Diggings site in eastern Wyoming but was forced to cease operations when WPA funding ended. A total of nearly $50,000 was expended on this Wyoming Archaeological Survey, a considerable sum even by present standards.

In his master's thesis at the University of Colorado, Wilfred Husted (1962) proposed an archaeological chronology for Rocky Mountain National Park based on projectile points and pottery. A short time later (1962–1964) Husted, then with the Smithsonian Missouri River Basin Survey, was the principal investigator of several cave sites in Bighorn River Canyon on both sides of the Montana-Wyoming line. These sites produced evidence of late Paleoindian occupations from which he named two projectile point types, Pryor Stemmed and Lovell Constricted. The former was named after the Pryor Mountains in southern Montana and the latter after the town by that name in northern Wyoming (Husted 1969). Pryor Stemmed is widespread over western Wyoming and southern Montana (Frison and Grey 1980), with numerous dates around 8,000 radiocarbon years before present (RCYBP). At present, I believe Lovell Constricted is represented by too few specimens in reliable contexts to make a valid claim as a point type.

AFTERWORD

During 1966, Husted took a leave of absence from the Smithsonian Missouri River Basin Survey and became the principal investigator at Mummy Cave along the North Fork of the Shoshone River, close to the eastern boundary of Yellowstone National Park. The site provided well-preserved stratigraphy along with radiocarbon dates from late Paleoindian to late Prehistoric. It demonstrated clearly the abrupt change from late Paleoindian lanceolate projectile points to those of the side-notched early Plains Archaic (Wedel, Husted, and Moss 1968). Harold McCracken was the director of the Buffalo Bill Historical Center in Cody, Wyoming, at the time and initiated work at Mummy Cave in 1963. Husted was hired to direct excavations at the site during 1966, the final year at the site. The final Mummy Cave report, completed in 1968, was not formally published until more than three decades later (Husted and Edgar 2002). Fortunately, a few copies of the 1968 report were circulated for archaeologists working in the area to use as a reference.

Wayne Powars from the Kersey area in Colorado was a teacher and coach at Sunrise, Wyoming, in the 1920s when the iron mine there was a major supplier of ore to the Colorado Fuel and Iron furnaces in Pueblo, Colorado. In 1935, Powars was on the excavation crew at the Lindenmeier site (Roberts 1936:2). He and his father, F. W. Powars, discovered and excavated the Powars Folsom site near Kersey, Colorado, in 1935 (Roberts 1937:69–72). While in Sunrise, Wayne Powars discovered what was later identified as a large assemblage of Paleoindian points and tools recovered on a steep talus slope formed by a railroad cut through red ochre deposits at the western edge of the Sunrise Mine.

Powars later moved to the Washington, D.C., area and eventually took his collection to Dr. Dennis Stanford, the Paleoindian archaeologist at the Smithsonian Institution. Powars was hesitant to divulge the exact site location, resulting in a fruitless search for the location by Stanford and me. In the early 1990s Powars returned to the area for a class reunion and discovered that the site was about to be destroyed by mine reclamation operations. Immediately following a desperate phone call from Powars, Wyoming State Archaeologist Mark Miller and I managed at the last moment to prevent total site destruction. Two articles (Tankersley et al. 1995; Stafford et al. 2003) present brief descriptions of the site and the Paleoindian artifacts recovered. All Paleoindian projectile point types found at the Sunrise Mine (Powars II) site are also present at the nearby Hell Gap site (Irwin-Williams et al. 1973), along with red ochre in nearly all cultural levels, probably from the Powars II site. The ochre is high quality and extremely difficult to remove from any medium it contacts.

Marie Wormington continued to exert a strong influence on Paleoindian studies in Wyoming. She was the mentor of two young Colorado archaeologists, Cynthia and Henry Irwin. In addition, she claimed, and rightly so, to have strongly influenced C. Vance Haynes Jr. to become involved in what would become geoarchaeological studies. This trio, along with George A. Agogino— hired to replace William Mulloy, who took a leave of absence from the University of Wyoming to join Thor Heyerdahl on his late 1950s Easter Island expedition—conducted two field seasons at the Union Pacific (UP) Mammoth Site in central Wyoming (Irwin, Irwin, and Agogino 1962) in conjunction with excavations at the Hell Gap site in eastern Wyoming from 1962–1966 (Irwin-Williams et al. 1973). Dennis Stanford received his initiation into Paleoindian archaeology at the UP Mammoth Site.

The Hell Gap site was central to establishing the chronology and radiocarbon ages of known and recognized Plains Paleoindian cultural complexes. I wanted to initiate limited additional excavations at the site in the early 1980s but waited for several years before Cynthia Irwin-Williams replied favorably to my proposal to acquire the Hell Gap collection from Harvard University. I looked forward to a cooperative effort, but her untimely death brought an unfortunate end to such a possibility. We needed her input to resolve questions and eliminate some of the guesswork about field notes and numerous other items concerning the site during Harvard's five years of investigations. Hell Gap is an outstanding example of why it is so important not to leave a massive site collection of artifacts and data for a later generation of researchers to analyze and interpret.

In 1973, James Michener was working on his Colorado novel, *Centennial*. At the time, I was testing the Hanson Folsom site (Frison and Bradley 1980) and the Colby Mammoth Site (Frison and Todd 1986) when I got a call from Marie Wormington telling me that Michener wanted to see a Paleoindian excavation in progress. She brought not only James Michener but also the flintknapper Bruce Bradley, whose talents in lithic technology were quickly recognized. Later, I took Bradley to the Jones-Miller Hell Gap site in eastern Colorado, where Dennis Stanford (1978) was excavating. Stanford was also impressed with Bradley's expertise in lithic technology. Bruce Bradley was destined to become an important element of both Stanford's and my Paleoindian studies through the years.

Bradley and Stanford (1982) performed a study of the eastern Colorado Claypool site projectile points and tools (Dick and Mountain 1960) and others recovered several years later (Stanford and Albanese 1975). Bradley pursued his observations of Cody lithic technology with several experimental specimens (Bradley and Stanford 1982:415–419). I firmly believe all students interested in Paleoindian projectile point typology and lithic technology should be familiar with this study. It demonstrates that what are sometimes perceived as two distinct projectile point types can actually be a single type terminated at different stages of manufacture. Bradley was also able to differentiate between what he named Alberta-Cody and Eden-Scottsbluff lithic technology at the Horner site (Frison and Bradley 1982). This is important because there is a 1,000-year separation between the two. Bradley (unpublished) also pointed out that a technological difference between most Casper Hell Gap site projectile points (Frison 1974) and Jones-Miller Hell Gap site points (Stanford 1978) was the result of the Casper points having been terminated at an earlier production stage than those from Jones-Miller.

William Mulloy excavated the James Allen bison kill site near Laramie, Wyoming, in 1951, 1953, and 1954 (Mulloy 1959). Joe Ben Wheat performed excavations at the Olsen-Chubbuck site in 1958 and 1960 (Wheat 1972) and later at the Jurgens bison kill site in northern Colorado in 1968 and 1970 (Wheat 1979). In 1971, I excavated the Casper bison kill site at the town by the same name (Frison 1974). In 1973 and 1974, Dennis Stanford excavated at the Jones-Miller bison kill in eastern Colorado (Stanford 1978, 1979) and in 1979 at the Frasca bison kill site in northeastern Colorado (Fulgham and Stanford 1982). In 1976 I excavated the Carter/Kerr-McGee bison kill in central Wyoming (Frison 1984), and during 1976 and 1977 I reinvestigated the Horner bison kill in northwest Wyoming (Frison and Todd 1987). In 1979 and 1980, I conducted a reinvestigation of the Agate Basin site (Frison and Stanford 1982). At the time, it appeared that Paleoindian archaeology in the American West was centered on Colorado and Wyoming bison kill sites. The large weaponry and tool assemblages these sites produced delighted typologists and lithic technologists, and faunal assemblages provided a seemingly endless database for bone technologists, bison taxonomists, and taphonomists. During this period, Marie Wormington kept close contact with all the sites and the archaeologists involved and acted as a clearinghouse for collecting and disseminating information. It was an exciting time, and I reflect back on it as the halcyon days of Paleoindian archaeology. I should also mention the Hudson-Meng site in western Nebraska because the investigator, Larry Agenbroad (1978), was part of the same loop of investigators.

Marie Wormington remained in the background during this time, but she was always ready to exert her influence in the best interests of Paleoindian studies. I was privileged to dedicate the Horner site (48PA29) book (Frison and Todd 1987) to Marie, especially because of her influence in making sense of the Cody Cultural Complex and placing the "Yuma" designation in its proper perspective (Wormington 1948).

A subtle change in Paleoindian studies began to appear during a 1988 symposium honoring Wormington at the Denver Museum of Natural History. Publication of the results of the symposium confirmed an awareness of a different trend in Paleoindian studies (Stanford and Day 1992) that in many ways presaged this present volume. Interest was taking a definite turn to the higher elevations, intermontane basins, and areas peripheral to the Plains (e.g., Benedict 1992; Davis and Greiser 1992; Jodry and Stanford 1992).

I was always able to claim common ground with Joe Ben Wheat because we both came into professional archaeology from an avocational background. He once pointed out the frustration of avocationals trying to gain status by a process of osmosis through associating with professionals and attending professional meetings. His influence was a strong determinant in my decision to leave the ranching business and pursue the academic route.

Wheat's Olsen-Chubbuck site monograph (1972) opened the door to the application of taphonomic principles to Paleoindian-age bone beds and to the beginning of a better realization of their potential to reveal cultural information. I searched the literature in 1982 and could find no review of that monograph. Fred Hadleigh West started his *Quarterly Review of Archaeology* in 1980, and I decided that might be the opportune time to write a review (Frison 1982). By this time, with the help of paleontologists, the aging of *B. antiquus* by tooth eruption and thereby the establishment of annual age groups was on fairly solid ground (Reher 1974). I had to argue against Joe Ben's interpretation of three age classes of bison and his belief that Olsen-Chubbuck was a spring kill. Tooth eruption of Olsen-Chubbuck calves (Frison 1991:figure 5.9 a, b) argues for a late-summer–early-fall kill.

In early July 1989, I received a phone call from James Chase of Granby, Colorado, inquiring if I might be interested in examining large bones eroding out of a hillside near Kremmling, Colorado. I was unable to resist such a tempting possibility, and before noon the next day we were looking at scattered bones on a talus slope, apparently the result of someone digging through the bones in search of artifacts. At first I thought the bones might be bison of recent age, but a closer look confirmed they were too large to be modern bison. Frank Rupp, the district Bureau of Land Management archaeologist in Kremmling, was extremely cooperative and approved an exploratory excavation. The site was named the Upper Twin Mountain site (5GA15), and it was situated at 2,500 m elevation. It proved to be a late-fall to early-winter bison kill with a date of 10,400–10,000 RCYBP (Todd, Rapson, and Hoffman 1996:165–169). The small assemblage of associated projectile points appears related to the poorly understood Goshen-Plainview type (Kornfeld et al. 1999:670). The bison procurement strategy involved is conjectural. The bones were contained in the bottom of a slump scar that may or may not have been the actual kill location.

Ralph and Ruth Phillips were long-term, dedicated artifact collectors in Middle Park. They discovered a small area just above the lowest water level on the Williams Fork Reservoir exposed only before rising water levels covered the location. The site produced a concentration of late Paleoindian points I believed were significant enough that I helped a student prepare a short paper for publication (Wiesend and Frison 1998). Ralph and Ruth Phillips were pleased at the interest in their collections and offered to reveal other Paleoindian point discovery locations in Middle Park.

For several years, another Middle Park resident collected an occasional late Paleoindian point eroding out of a bank of a small arroyo along a livestock trail. The man, Jerry Craig, finally agreed to divulge the location and later helped with test excavations. The Jerry Craig site (5GA639) appears to have Cody Complex affiliations with a 9,000-year age and may eventually prove to be a large bison kill (Kornfeld and Frison 2000). The bison bones are in a badly deteriorated condition, but we hope to eventually recover enough intact materials to make a seasonality determination. These two sites have had a profound effect on my recent thinking concerning *Bison antiquus* at higher elevations in Paleoindian times.

Jim Chase was well-known in the Middle Park area, and, especially after the investigation of the Upper Twin Mountain bison kill, he continually sought evidence of reported Paleoindian projectile point finds. Evidence of Folsom is widespread in Middle Park, and the end result of several surveys at the present time is the Barger Gulch Folsom site (Surovell and Waguespack, Chapter 8, this volume). It has expectations of being a large Folsom site with good integrity, and, with continuation of the present strategy of excavation and analysis, it should provide many future years of research and an expanded base of information on Folsom. Jerry Craig and Jim Chase, together with Ralph and Ruth Phillips, are prime examples of avocationals providing significant information to professionals. In addition, during the last few years, I became acquainted with several avocationals at the annual Stone Age Fair in Loveland, Colorado. It is worth the trip to watch and discuss flintknapping with Bob Patten. Better yet, look through his 2005 book on Folsom technology.

The preceding pages present my reflections on Colorado and Wyoming archaeology and the manner in which it flavors my thoughts on the contents of this volume. Perhaps I should begin by expressing my thoughts on projectile point typology. My basic philosophy is very much along the lines of a lumper rather than a splitter. The designation Foothills-Mountain Paleoindian was intended to convey the concept of ecological adaptations rather than projectile point types. I am forced to admit that in the fifteen years since it was proposed (Frison 1992), the distinction between Foothills-Mountain and Plains Paleoindian has become less clear, but I believe it is still a useful concept (see applications in Chapters 9 and 10, this volume). New data may or may not alter the situation.

High-altitude archaeology and Foothills-Mountain Paleoindian gradually gained recognition through projectile points that did not fit into the classic Plains Paleoindian cultural sequence known from Hell Gap and other related sites. I support any quantitative means to separate projectile point types, but only after close observation of the site assemblages used in determining late Paleoindian types, including Angostura, James Allen, Frederick, Lusk, and Pryor Stemmed. Points from the Barton Gulch site (Davis, Aaberg, and Greiser 1988) and the proposed Alder Complex (see Frison 1991:figures 2.40, 2.41) and a point from Southsider Cave (48BH363) in the Bighorn Mountains (Frison 1991:figure 2.38 b) simply add to the confusion. I could easily cite a number of others.

The Jimmy Allen and Angostura separation (Pitblado 2003, Chapter 10, this volume) may prove more useful for the Southern Rockies than for the Northern Rockies. The latter area produces a wide variety of poorly defined and poorly investigated variants that include as-yet-unnamed lanceolate, fish-tailed late Paleoindian points from the Lookingbill site (48FR308) (Frison 1983:figure 4b–d) and others that may or may not be related to Haskett further west (Butler 1965). Other projectile points from the Medicine Lodge Creek site (48BH499) (Frison 1991:figure 2.33) further demonstrate the problem (see discussion in Pitblado, Chapter 10, this volume). Eden and Scottsbluff projectile points have appeared at higher elevations, but some may be the Cody-Alberta variation as seen at the Horner site. On the other hand, we may have to seriously rethink the Cody Complex based on the results of the investigation of the Osprey Beach site on Yellowstone Lake in Yellowstone National Park (Johnson, Reeves, and Short 2004).

This volume clearly demonstrates that Paleoindian archaeology is dependent on a multidisciplinary approach for meaningful results. Some level of understanding past ecological conditions at the same time and before human groups were present is crucial for interpreting past human activities. Continual refinement of the methodologies involved in past environmental studies enhances archaeologists' abilities to better interpret their data. Chapter 7 of this volume is on track to provide better climatic data by focusing on shorter intervals than past studies have done (although, ideally, the intervals need to be even shorter). Climatic changes from year to year can dramatically change plant and animal procurement strategies.

Many pollen grains have passed under Linda Scott Cummings's microscope since she was the pollen analyst (and camp cook) in 1970 at the Jurgens site (Scott 1979; Wheat 1979:3). I was first able to have serious discussions with Reid Bryson (coauthor, with Linda Scott Cummings and R. A. Varney, of Chapter 7, this volume) at the 1974 meeting of the American Quaternary Association in Madison, Wisconsin. Bryson claims I had a strong influence in channeling his research interests into archaeologically related studies. If so, I believe I did a good thing.

I admit some relief at not having to consider chronological changes in the Folsom and late Paleoindian periods based on radiocarbon dates from the Gunnison Basin and Rocky Mountain National Park areas. From my own experience, I know it hurts to be forced to admit to having made bad decisions based on interpretation of our data, but good science dictates no other choice. I am not familiar with the Gunnison, Colorado, area, but from what I read and heard from the 2005 meeting of the Rocky Mountain Conference, it appears a rich area for Paleoindian research.

I have followed many kilometers of rock alignments, stone cairns, and postholes (Frison 1981, 2004:81–90; see also Brink and Rollans 1990). Some are recent enough to contain remnants of wooden components. Some are parts of game drive systems, and some are not. Stone alignments leading to a drop-off or a corral containing a bone bed are clearly related to animal procurement. On the other hand, and for unexplained reasons, similar alignments sometimes appear to lead nowhere. Some animals, such as bison, pronghorn, and mountain sheep, are more amenable to driving than deer or elk. However, all of these species react differently to similar stimuli, all of which a hunter must be aware.

Human hunting is learned behavior, and no single hunting strategy can be universally applied. All species commonly hunted prehistorically—whether wood rats, jackrabbits, white-tailed deer, mule deer, mountain sheep, elk, bison, mammoths, or others—exhibit behavior patterns unique to the species. Of equal importance is knowledge of hunting territory. Animal behavior can change rapidly in response to external conditions, such as topography, weather, and vegetation, and in response to internal changes within the species, such as breeding, birthing, and age. In addition, weaponry effectiveness places restrictions on a procurement strategy. Finally, supernatural restrictions are important, but they can be difficult to perceive in the archaeological record. Nonetheless, shaman activity is strongly indicated at the 10,000-year-old Jones-Miller bison kill site in eastern Colorado (Stanford 1979). The body of knowledge acquired by, and at the disposal of, prehistoric hunters was impressive to say the least and was necessary for their survival (see Frison 2004).

Most archaeologists involved with reconstructing mammoth hunting, myself included, tend to assume the unaffirmable but likely fact that mammoths emulated the family structure of modern African elephants. If this was the case, confronting or ambushing a mammoth family with Clovis weaponry was dangerous. Unlike a modern firearm, a Clovis projectile will produce a lethal wound to an elephant if properly placed, but in a situation of direct confrontation it stands little chance of accomplishing more than invoking the wrath of a matriarch elephant ready to protect her family. A much better strategy is for one or more experienced hunters to track the elephant family and, at the opportune time, inflict a wound that will cause the animal to weaken and eventually lay down. The waiting game is more productive and less dangerous than confrontation. This mammoth hunting strategy is more in line with the seasonality evidence proposed by Daniel Fisher and David Fox (Chapter 4, this volume) than the killing of an entire family. I see no mention of grizzlies, which were around at that time and were unpredictable and dangerous (see Storer and Tevis 1996). Good hunters are not foolish hunters who take unnecessary chances that can deny their families a subsistence base.

Human butchering and processing versus carnivore and other evidence on mammoth and other large mammal bones has been a controversial topic that led to a major conference but few conclusions other than that some marks on bone reflect unequivocal human activity and some are the result of other activities, with a vast amount of unidentifiable evidence in between (see Bonnichsen and Sorg 1989). I remember looking with Joe Ben Wheat at part of a late Pleistocene horse mandible from Little Box Elder Cave in central Wyoming (Anderson 1968) with wear patterns over a broken edge. We were almost convinced it was the result of human tool activity, but later we concluded that the wear patterns on this and some other bones were likely the result of marmots and other small mammals crawling over the bones for hundreds of years.

After studying the skeletal material and making several statements about butchering marks on bones and bone- and stone-tool use on *B. antiquus* at the Casper Hell Gap site (Frison 1974:35–57), I started taking closer looks at carnivore-ravished elk and other large mammal carcasses and realized too many of my claims for tool use were the results of carnivore activity. I next engaged in experimental butchering with stone tools. I practiced butchering on freshly killed elephants and will only mention briefly some observations I believe are pertinent to mammoth butchering. First, a freshly killed elephant is easier to butcher than one allowed to cool. Second, the hide of an African elephant is thicker than a mammoth of the same age, and cutting the hide is the most difficult task of the entire butchering process. Third, a quartzite tool with a grainy cutting edge will cut more elephant hide than a chert tool, and a tool with an edge too dull to cut hide can still be functional for most of the remaining butchering process. Fourth, elephant long bones are relatively easy to disarticulate compared with those of other large mammals (Frison 1989). Unfortunately, the Colby Mammoth Kill site bones were too badly deteriorated to retain tool marks compared with the Dent site bones Jeff Saunders analyzed (Chapter 5, this volume).

I look at the aerial views of the Dent site (Brunswig, Chapter 3, this volume), the Colby site, and Blackwater Draw and get the impression that all three were locations favorable for plucking off a mammoth or two and were exploited for this purpose, possibly over a long period of time.

For several reasons, I decided the Upper Twin Mountain bison kill (5GA15) in Middle Park, Colorado (Kornfeld et al. 1999), would be my last fieldwork in the position of principal investigator. The last day of fieldwork was a warm, cloudless, windless, late September day, with the aspen leaves turning and traces of the first snowfall lingering above timberline. Earlier in the day we recovered the mandibles from a young bison in a missing age group. We were elated because we knew it would help establish the seasonality of the kill. Finally, we recovered the base of a Goshen-Plainview point in good context among the bones. It could not get any better than this, and it leaves me with a good feeling that covers three-quarters of a century of association with Wyoming and Colorado archaeology, archaeologists, and avocationalists.

REFERENCES CITED

Agenbroad, L. D.
    1978   *The Hudson-Meng Site: An Alberta Bison Kill in the Nebraska High Plains.* University Press of America, Washington, DC.

Anderson, E.
    1968   Fauna of Little Boxelder Cave, Converse County, Wyoming. *University of Colorado Studies, Series on Earth Sciences* 6:1–59, Boulder.

Benedict, J. B.
    1992   Along the Great Divide: Paleoindian Archaeology of the High Colorado Front Range. In *Ice Age Hunters of the Rockies*, ed. D. J. Stanford and J. S. Day, 343–362. Denver Museum of Natural History and University Press of Colorado, Niwot.

Bonnichsen, R., and M. H. Sorg (eds.)
    1989   *Bone Modification.* Center for the Study of the First Americans, Institute for Quaternary Studies, University of Maine, Orono.

Bradley, B. A., and D. J. Stanford
1982   The Claypool Study. In *The Horner Site: The Type Site of the Cody Complex*, ed. G. C. Frison and L. C. Todd, appendix 2:405–434. Academic, Orlando, FL.

Brink, J. W., and M. Rollans
1990   Thoughts on the Structure and Function of Drive Lane Systems at Communal Buffalo Jumps. In *Hunters of the Recent Past*, ed. L. B. Davis and B.O.K. Reeves, 152–163. Unwin Hyman, London.

Buckles, W. G.
1964   *An Analysis of Primitive Rock Art at Medicine Creek Cave, Wyoming and Its Cultural and Chronological Relationships to the Prehistory of the Plains*. Unpublished master's thesis, University of Colorado, Boulder.

Bupp, S. L.
1981   *The Willow Springs Bison Pound: 48AB130*. Unpublished master's thesis, University of Wyoming, Laramie.

Butler, B. R.
1965   A Report on Investigations of an Early Man Site Near Lake Channel, Southern Idaho. *Tebiwa* 8 (2):1–14.

Coffin, R. G.
1937   *Northern Colorado's First Settlers*. Department of Geology, Colorado State College, Fort Collins.

Davis, L. B., S. A. Aaberg, and S. T. Greiser
1988   Paleoindians in Transmontane Southwestern Montana: The Barton Gulch Occupations, Ruby River Drainage. *Current Research in the Pleistocene* 5:9–11.

Davis, L. B., and S. T. Greiser
1992   Indian Creek Paleoindians: Early Occupation of the Elkhorn Mountains' Southeast Flank, West-Central Montana. In *Ice Age Hunters of the Rockies*, ed. D. J. Stanford and J. S. Day, 225–283. Denver Museum of Natural History and University Press of Colorado, Niwot.

Dick, H. W., and B. Mountain
1960   The Claypool Site: A Cody Complex Site in Northeastern Colorado. *American Antiquity* 26 (2):223–235.

Frison, G. C.
1965   Spring Creek Cave, Wyoming. *American Antiquity* 31 (1):81–94.
1974   *The Casper Site: A Hell Gap Bison Kill on the High Plains*. Academic, New York.
1981   Linear Arrangements of Cairns in Wyoming and Montana. In *Megaliths to Medicine Wheels: Boulder Structures in Archaeology*, ed. M. Wilson, K. L. Road, and K. J. Hardy, 133–147. Proceedings of the Eleventh Chacmool Conference, Department of Anthropology, University of Calgary, Alberta.
1982   Taphonomic Analysis in Archaeology. *Quarterly Review of Archaeology* 3 (3):13.
1983   The Lookingbill Site, Wyoming 48FR308. *Tebiwa* 20:1–16.
1984   The Carter/Kerr-McGee Paleoindian Site: Cultural Resource Management and Archaeological Research. *American Antiquity* 49 (2):288–314.
1989   Experimental Use of Clovis Weaponry and Tools on African Elephants. *American Antiquity* 54 (4):766–784.

1991   *Prehistoric Hunters of the High Plains*, 2nd ed. Academic, San Diego.

1992   The Foothills-Mountains and the Open Plains: The Dichotomy in Paleoindian Subsistence Strategies between Two Ecosystems. In *Ice Age Hunters of the Rockies*, ed. D. J. Stanford and J. S. Day, 323–342. Denver Museum of Natural History and University Press of Colorado, Niwot.

2004   *Survival by Hunting: Prehistoric Human Hunters and Animal Prey*. University of California Press, Berkeley.

Frison, G. C., and B. A. Bradley

1980   *Folsom Tools and Technology at the Hanson Site, Wyoming*. University of New Mexico Press, Albuquerque.

1982   Projectile Points and Specialized Bifaces from the Horner Site. In *The Horner Site: The Type Site of the Cody Cultural Complex*, ed. G. C. Frison and D. J. Stanford, 199–231. Academic, Orlando, FL.

Frison, G. C., and D. C. Grey

1980   Pryor Stemmed: A Specialized Paleo-Indian Ecological Adaptation. *Plains Anthropologist* 25 (87):27–46.

Frison, G. C., and D. J. Stanford

1982   *The Agate Basin Site: A Record of the Paleoindian Occupation of the North American High Plains*. Academic, New York.

Frison, G. C., and L. C. Todd

1986   *The Colby Mammoth Site: Taphonomy and Archaeology of a Clovis Kill in Northern Wyoming*. University of New Mexico Press, Albuquerque.

1987   *The Horner Site: The Type Site of the Cody Complex*. Academic, Orlando, FL.

Fulgham, T., and D. Stanford

1982   The Frasca Site: A Preliminary Report. *Southwestern Lore* 48 (1):1–9.

Husted, W. M.

1962   A Proposed Archaeological Chronology for Rocky Mountain National Park Based on Projectile Points and Pottery. Unpublished master's thesis, University of Colorado, Boulder.

1969   *Bighorn Canyon Archaeology*. Smithsonian River Basin Surveys, Publications in Salvage Archaeology 12, Washington, DC.

Husted, W. M., and R. Edgar

2002   *The Archaeology of Mummy Cave, Wyoming: An Introduction to Shoshonean Prehistory*. Southeast Archaeological Center, Technical Reports Series 9. U.S. Department of the Interior, National Park Service, Midwest Archaeological Center, Lincoln, NE.

Irwin, C., H. T. Irwin, and G. A. Agogino

1962   Ice-Age Man vs. Mammoth in Wyoming. *National Geographic* 121 (6):828–837.

Irwin-Williams, C., H. T. Irwin, G. Agogino, and C. V. Haynes Jr.

1973   Hell Gap: Paleo-Indian Occupation of the High Plains. *Plains Anthropologist* 18 (59):40–53.

Jodry, M. A., and D. J. Stanford

1992   Stewart's Cattle Guard Site: An Analysis of Bison Remains in a Folsom Kill-Butchery Campsite. In *Ice Age Hunters of the Rockies*, ed. D. J. Stanford and J.

S. Day, 101–168. Denver Museum of Natural History and University Press of Colorado, Niwot.

Johnson, A., B.O.K. Reeves, and M. W. Short
2004   Osprey Beach 48YE409/410: A Cody Complex Camp on Yellowstone Lake. Yellowstone Center for Resources, Yellowstone National Park, Mammoth, WY.

Kornfeld, M., and G. C. Frison
2000   Paleoindian Occupation of the High Country: The Case of Middle Park, Colorado. *Plains Anthropologist* 45 (172):129–153.

Kornfeld, M., G. C. Frison, M. L. Larson, J. C. Miller, and J. Saysette
1999   Paleoindian Bison Procurement and Paleoenvironments in Middle Park of Colorado. *Geoarchaeology* 14:655–674.

Mulloy, W. T.
1959   The James Allen Site Near Laramie, Wyoming. *American Antiquity* 25 (1):112–116.

Patten, B.
2005   *Peoples of the Flute*. Stone Dagger, Denver.

Pitblado, B. L.
2003   *Late Paleoindian Occupation of the Southern Rocky Mountains*. University Press of Colorado, Boulder.

Reher, C. A.
1974   Population Study of the Casper Site Bison. In *The Casper Site: A Hell Gap Bison Kill on the High Plains*, ed. G. C. Frison, 113–124. Academic, New York.

Renaud, E. B.
1932   *Archaeological Survey of Eastern Wyoming*. University of Denver.
1936a *Archaeological Survey of the High Western Plains*, Seventh Report. Department of Anthropology, University of Denver.
1936b *Archaeological Survey of the High Western Plains*, Eighth Report. Department of Anthropology, University of Denver.
1937   *Archaeological Survey of the High Western Plains*, Ninth Report. Department of Anthropology, University of Denver.
1938   *Archaeological Survey of the High Western Plains*, Tenth Report. Department of Anthropology, University of Denver.
1940   *Archaeological Survey of the Western High Plains*, Twelfth Report. Department of Anthropology, University of Denver.

Roberts, F.H.H.
1936   Additional Information on the Folsom Complex. *Smithsonian Miscellaneous Collections* 95:1–38.
1937   New Developments in the Problem of the Folsom Complex. In *Explorations and Field-Work of the Smithsonian Institution in 1936*, 69–74. Smithsonian Institution, Washington, DC.
1943   A New Site. *American Antiquity* 8:100.

Scott, L.
1979 Jurgens Site Palynological Analysis. In *The Jurgens Site*, by J. B. Wheat, 149–151. Plains Anthropologist Memoir 15.

Sharrock, F. W.
1966 *Prehistoric Occupation Patterns in Southwest Wyoming and Cultural Relationships with the Great Basin and Plains Culture Areas*. University of Utah, Anthropological Papers 77, Salt Lake City.

Sowers, T. C.
1941 *Wyoming Archaeological Survey*. University of Wyoming, Laramie.

Stafford, M. D., G. C. Frison, D. J. Stanford, and G. M. Zeimens
2003 Digging for the Color of Life: Paleoindian Red Ochre Mining at the Powars II Site, Platte County, Wyoming. *Geoarchaeology* 18 (1):71–90.

Stanford, D. J.
1978 The Jones-Miller Site: An Example of Hell Gap Bison Procurement Strategy. In *Bison Procurement and Utilization: A Symposium*, ed. L. B. Davis and M. Wilson, 90–97. Plains Anthropologist Memoir 14.
1979 Bison Kill by Ice Age Hunters. *National Geographic* 155 (1):114–121.

Stanford, D. J., and J. P. Albanese
1975 Preliminary Results of the Smithsonian Institution Excavation at the Claypool Site, Washington County, Colorado. *Southwestern Lore* 41 (4):22–28.

Stanford, D. J., and J. S. Day (eds.)
1992 *Ice Age Hunters of the Rockies*. Denver Museum of Natural History and University Press of Colorado, Niwot.

Storer, T. I., and L. P. Tevis Jr.
1996 *California Grizzly*. Berkeley, University of California Press.

Tankersley, K. B., K. O. Tankersley, N. R. Shaffer, M. D. Hess, J. S. Benz, M. D. Stafford, G. M. Zeimens, and G. C. Frison
1995 They Have a Rock That Bleeds: Sunrise Red Ochre and Its Early Paleoindian Occurrence at the Hell Gap Site, Wyoming. *Plains Anthropologist* 40 (152):185–194.

Todd, L. C., D. J. Rapson, and J. L. Hoffman
1996 Dentition Studies of the Mill Iron and Other Early Paleoindian *Bison* Bone Bed Sites. In *The Mill Iron Site*, ed. G. C. Frison, 145–175. University of New Mexico Press, Albuquerque.

Wedel, W. R., W. M. Husted, and J. Moss
1968 Mummy Cave: Prehistoric Record from the Rocky Mountains of Wyoming. *Science* 160:184–186.

Wheat, J. B.
1972 *The Olsen-Chubbuck Site: A Paleoindian Bison Kill*. Society for American Archaeology Memoir 26, Washington, DC.
1979 The Jurgens Site. *Plains Anthropologist* 24 (84, pt. 2):1–153.

Wiesend, C. M., and G. C. Frison
    1998   Parallel-Obliquely Flaked Projectile Points from the Phillips-Williams Fork Reservoir Site (5GA1955) in Middle Park, Colorado. *Southwestern Lore* 64 (1): 8–21.

Wormington, H. M.
    1948   A Proposed Revision of Yuma Point Terminology. In *Proceedings, Colorado Museum of Natural History* 18:2. Colorado Museum of Natural History, Denver.

INDEX

Page numbers in italics indicate illustrations.

African elephant: cheek teeth, 124; experimental butchery of, 111; herd organization, 101–102, 124; *Loxodonta africana*, 155; social and economic behaviors of, 114, 116. See also Bunching; elephant; *Loxodonta africana*
African Elephant (Equivalent) Years (AEY), 101, 129, 155, *159*
Agenbroad, Larry, 345
Agogino, George, 48, 90, 108, 343–344
Albert, Rosa Maria, xvi, 5
Alamosa State College, Colorado, 44
Alberta projectile points, 279–281
Alder-Ruby Valley, 317
Alignments: rock, 289–290, 348; rock-wall, 290; stone, 348. See also Cairns
Alpine zone, 14–16, 50, 64, 65; alpine-subapline transition, 52, 275, 283 (*see also* Krummholz

ecotone); Folsom sites in, 275; glaciers, 12; Range zonation, 14; tundra, 264, 272, 284–286, 288; Upper, 273, 325, 326, 329; vegetation, 16. See also Subalpine zone
Altithermal, 26
American Cordillera, 20
Anasazi, 339
Anathermal, 207
Anderson, Harold, 41, 44
Anderson, Perry, 41, 44
Andrews, Brian, 56
Andrews Pass, 292
Angostura: basal variation, 317; bases, 282–283; Chance Gulch site, 60; Cultural Complex, 279, 282–283, 285–286; defined, 315–316; distribution, 287; projectile points, 56, 60, 282, 290, 295–297, 299; qualitative distinctions from

INDEX

Jimmy Allen, 319–320; quantitative distinctions from Jimmy Allen, 320–322, *322*; type-site (Ray Long), 313, *316*, 317; typological methods, 314, 332
Antelope (pronghorn), 264, 275, 348
Antevs, Ernest, 341
Arapaho Pass, 50, 275, 289
"Arapaho Peak" advance, 20
Arapaho Valley, Colorado, 20
Archaic, 47; Crescent Shelter site, 53; early, 51, 59, 342–343; late, 290, 340; middle, 273
Argentine Pass site, Colorado, 51
Arkansas River, 13
Artiodactyl, 53
"Audubon" advance, 20
Avocational archaeologist, 49, 61. See also Collector

Barger Gulch site, Colorado, *13*; Kremmling, 59; Locality A, 288; Locality B (BGB), 60, 223; Middle Park, 220; Mountaineer site, 5, 6, 56; University of Wyoming Research Program, 59–60; Williams Fork Reservoir, 248. See also Debitage assemblages; Hearth; Ring analysis; Sector anaylsis
"Barrier effect," 238–241, 251
Barton Gulch site, Montana, 317, 347
Basketmaker, 341
Beaver Meadows, 27
Beaver Meadows site, Colorado, 29
Benedict, James, xvii, xviii, 2, 6, 18, 62, 64, 275; Caribou Lake, 59, 289; Center for Mountain Archeology, 48, 50, 58, 265; Holocene glacial expansion of, 20
Bernhardt site, Colorado, 92
Bifacial artifacts: Angostura, 315; burial related, 53; caches, 237; Cody, 197; conjoinable, 224–225, *225;* density 228; distribution at Locality B, 244; knives, 53; Late Paleoindian thinning, 278; reduction/thinning, 231–232, 234; sector diagram of, *243,* 250
Biggs, William, 49
Bighorn Basin, 327
Bighorn Flats, 272, 292, 295
Bighorn Range, 347
Bighorn River Canyon, 342
Bighorn sheep, 264, 275, 293–294, 332. See also Mountain sheep
Bighorn-Tonahutu sites, Colorado, 292
Bilgery, Father Conrad, 2, 42, 157; Dent excavation, 87–89; redeposition hypothesis, 95, 105; remarks, 113
Bison: *Bison antiquus*, 60, 274–275, 296; *Bison taylori*, 44; bone bed, 265, 276; Carter/Kerr-McGee site, 345; Casper site, 345; Cody, 288, 299; corral, 340, 348; Frasca site, 345; Horner site, 345; hunting, 264, 278, 298; Ice-Age, 270; James Allen site, 345; Jerry Craig site, 346; Jones-Miller site, 345, 349; jump, 339, 348; Jurgens site, 345; KibRidge-Yampa site, 215; kill sites, 340; modern, 346; Olsen-Chubbuck site, 346; procurement, 274, 276; Upper Twin Mountain site, 274, 275, 288, 346, 347, 350; woods, 215
Black Forest petrified wood, 224
Black Hills, 313, 316
Black, Kevin, 62–63
Black Mountain site, Colorado, *43,* 55, 64, 326
"Black's Fork Culture," 341
Blackwater Draw site, New Mexico, 313, 339, 350; "accumulated" faunal assemblage, 104; bone damage, 179; Paleoindian "firsts," 1, 2, 39, 41, 42; mammoth age profiles, 156; *Mammuthus columbi*, 158
Blue Mesa Reservoir, 51
Blue Range, 262
Bobtail Wolf site, North Dakota, 220, 236
Boiling pit, 51
Bone apatite, 90, 228
Bone artifacts, 265, 276, 340, 348; bison, 59; bone bed, 48; Jerry Craig site, 60, 288; Jones-Miller site, 49; Jurgens site, 49; Lamb Spring site, 52; Olsen-Chubbuck site, 345; Upper Twin Mountain site, 60. See also Dent site
Bone collagen, 52–53, 158
Bone gelatin, 49
Bones. *See individual elements by name*
Bonfire Shelter site, Texas, 220
Bow-and-arrow points, 340
Bradley, Bruce, 344
Breternitz, David, 52
Brown, Barnum, 88
Brunswig, Robert, 5–6, 62; Angostura, 312, 329–332; Bighorn Hunting System, 292; Dent, 123, 135, 138, 146, 148, 157, 179; Jerry Craig site, 60; Mountain Paleoindian adaptations, 65; University of Northern Colorado South Park/South Platte Research Program, 57
Buckles, William, 342
Buffalo Pass, 17
Bunching, 114
Bureau of Land Management (BLM), 61, 265, 346
Bureau of Reclamation, 316
Burton, Robert, 2, 49
Butchery (elephant): by Efe people, 164; experimental, 162, 174; by Valley Bisa people, 172; by Nunamiut, 160; Folsom, 47
Butchery (mammoth), at Dent, 156, 162, 177
Butchery (mastodon), 146
Butterfly Lake, 20
Bryson, Reid, 5, 278, 348

358

Cache, 46, 237
Cache la Poudre River, 274
Cairns: rock, 290, 348; stone, 348. *See also* Alignments
Calcium oxylate crystals, 185, 187
Calculus, mammoth tooth, 185–188, 190, 191
Camel, 45, 270
Carey Lake site, Colorado, 51, 290
Caribou, Nunamiut butchery of, 160–162
Caribou Lake site, *43*, 50–51, 64, 265, 289; Benedict and Center for Mountain Archeology, 58–59
Caribou Lake Valley, Colorado, 20
Carnegie Museum, Pennsylvania, 100, 160, 179
Carter/Kerr-McGee site, Wyoming, 225, 345
Casper site, Wyoming, 344–345, 349
Cassells, Steve, 40, 277; Dent, 95, 110, 113
Cattle Guard site. *See* Stewart's Cattle Guard site
Center for Mountain Archeology, Colorado. *See* Benedict, James
Ceramics, 342
Chalcedony, 106, 263
Chance Gulch site, Colorado: Angostura projectile points, 56–57, 322, 323; location, *43*; Post-Folsom, 65
Channel flakes. *See* Lithics
Chert, 106, 263, 274, 277, 550. *See also individual chert types by name*
Chase, James (Jim), 346–347
Chipped-stone, chipped stone. *See* Lithics
Chloridoideae, 188
Chubbuck, Jerry, 49
Claypool site, Colorado, 3, 42, *43*, 44–45, 344
Clear Creek Range, 262
Cleveland Museum, Ohio, 100, 160, 179
Clovis sites: Blackwater Draw, 2; Claypool, 3; Dent, 2; Drake, 46; Haystack Cave, 46; Lange-Ferguson, 110; Little Clovis, 46
Cody sites: Barger Gulch, 276; Carey Lake, 51; Caribou Lake, 50; Claypool, 44; Crescent Rockshelter, 53; Frasca, 50; Frazier, 49; Hay Springs, 276; Jerry Craig, 60; Jurgens, 49; KibRidge-Yampa, 197; Lamb Springs, 52; Osprey Beach, 299; Wilbur Thomas Shelter, 52
Coffin, A. Lynn (son), 43
Coffin, Judge Claude C. (father), 43
Coffin, Roy, 340
Coffin family, 43–44, 340
COHMAP model, 205, 207
Colby site, Wyoming, 111, 156, 344, 350
Collagen: acetone-insoluble, 90; acid-insoluble, 90; bone, 52, 53, 158; hoof, 49
Collector (of artifacts), 41, 44, 46, 60–62, 65, 162. *See also* Avocational archaeologist
Collins, C. K., 43
Collins, Michael, 48
Colorado Archaeological Society, 47

Colorado Historical Society, 63
Colorado Office of Archaeology and Historic Preservation (OAHP), 325, 331
Colorado Piedmont, 88, 92, 116
Colorado River, 47, 242, 248, 263, 274, 276, 298
Colorado State Historic Preservation Office, 267
Columbian mammoth, 102, 114, 270
COMPASS computerized database, State Historic Preservation Office of Colorado, 267, 325, 329, 331
Continental Divide, 13, *18*, 41, 261, 263, 272, 274, 291; Mount Ida–Bighorn, 292
Cores, 29; bog, 57–58; lithic, 233–234, 243–244, 250; sediment, 92, 96–98
Corral, bison, 340
Cotter, John, 41, 44, 177
Craig, Jerry, 346–347
Crania (cranium), 161
Crescent Rockshelter site, Colorado, *43*, 53, 65
Cretaceous, 92, 93, 263; Foxhills formation, 92–94
Crying Woman site, Colorado, 47, 224
Cultural Resource Management (CRM), 47, 264, 325
Cummings, Linda Scott. *See* Scott Cummings, Linda

Davis, Owen, 55
Dawson, Jerry, 47
Debitage assemblages: Agate Basin site, 48; Barger Gulch site, Locality B, 60, 228, 231–232, 234, 236–237, 276; Barger Gulch site ring analysis, 249–250; Barger Gulch site sector analysis, 243–245, 250; Chance Gulch site, 56; 5BL3440 site, 58; Mountaineer site, 56; Upper Twin Mountain site, 274
Deer, 215, 348; mule, 264, 275, 348; white-tailed, 348
Dentin, incremental features: first-order, 124–125; oxygen isotope variation, 127; second-order, 126; third-order, 126
Dent site, xv; actualistic butchery, 162; experimental butchery, 162; elephant social behavior, 114; ethnoarchaeological butchery, 162, 164; excavation film, 89; fluting/channel flakes, 109; geoarchaeological, 88–92, 94, 95, 96; herd protective instincts, 114; human versus natural death, 112–113; hydraulic coring of, 96–98, 108–110; local fauna, 100–105; mammoth migration route, 114; matriarchal use wear, 106; refluting flakes, 109
Devil's Thumb Game Drive site (5BL3440), Colorado, 58–59, 64, 289
Devil's Thumb Valley site (5BL6904), Colorado, 58–59, 64, 289
Devlin Lake, 18, 21
Devlin Lake site, Colorado, 28

Dinosaur National Monument, 197, *198*, 206, 209–212
Dinwoodie Cave site, Wyoming, 342
DNA, mitochondrial, 51
Drake, Orvil, 46
Drake site, Colorado, *43*, 46
Dreier, Becky, 49
Dreier, Wayne, 49
Dutton and Selby sites, Colorado, *43*, 45

"Eastern Survey of Colorado" ("Archaeological Survey of Colorado," "High Plains Archaeological Survey"), 41. *See also* Renaud, E. B.
Echo Lake, 18, 22–25, 29
Echo Lake site, Colorado, 18, 22–25, 29
Eden projectile points, 60, 280, 281, 282, 292, 311, 312, 321, 323, 328, 347; Eden-Firstview projectile points, 281, 290, 299; Eden-Firstview-Kersey chronology, 282; Eden-Scottsbluff lithic technology, 344
Edwards Plateau chert, 47
Efe people, 164
Elephant: African, *101*–102, 111, 114, 116, 155, 158, 349–350; Asiatic, 162; Dent site, 124, 125, 158; Efe use, 164; elephantids, 145, 156, 159, 172; Indian, 111; modern elephant, 125, 126, 174, 176; Valley Bisa processing, 162, 172. *See also Loxodonta Africana*
Elk, 275; Bighorn Flats and Mount Ida Ridge, *293*–295; Casper site, 349; Jimmy Allen site, 326, 332–333; teeth, 53
Elk Creek site, Colorado, 52
Enamel, 128
Escapule site, Arizona, 113

Fall River Pass, 271
Femur (femora), 110, 157, 163, 168–171, 174–175, 177, 178
Flakes. *See* Lithics
Flattop chert, 106
Flattop Mountain, 292
Flattop Mountain Game Drive site, Colorado, 292, *293*
Figgins, J. D. (Jesse), 42; Colorado Museum of Natural History, 87–89, 100; Dent excavation, 105–106, 109–110, 113, 157
Firstview projectile points, 49, 280, 281; Firstview-Kersey, 292. *See also* Eden projectile points
Fisher, Daniel, xvi, 103, 117
5GA1095 site, Colorado, *293*, 294, 295
5GA2002 site, Colorado, *293*, 294
5GA2209 site, Colorado, 275
5GA2246 site, Colorado, 277
5LR17 site, Colorado, 275

5LR68 site, Colorado, 294
5LR327 site, Colorado, 294
5LR7108 site, Colorado, 294
5MF625 site, Colorado, 316
Folsom sites: Barger Gulch, 5; Black Mountain, 55; Crying Woman, 277; 5GA2246, 277; Hay Springs, 276; Lindenmeier, 39; Linger, 42; Powars, 42; Reddin, 47; Zapata, 42
Foot bones. *See* Metatarsals
Foothills-Mountain Tradition, 50, 282–283. *See also* Mountain Paleoindian Tradition
Forest Canyon Pass, 274, 275, 283, 292, 294
Forward, Paul, 49
Fourth of July Mine site, Colorado, 275, 289
Fourth of July Valley site, Colorado, 17, 289
Fossil beetle, 12, 21, 28, 29
Fossil insect, 21, 26, 28, 29
Fossil pollen, 26
Frasca, Charles, 49
Frasca site, Colorado, *43*, 345
Friesenhahn site, Texas, 104
Frazier, Frank, 48–49, 89, 93, 105, 113
Frazier River Valley, 18
Frazier site, Colorado, 49
Frison, George C., xvi, xviii, 3, 63, 273, 278; Foothills-Mountain Tradition, 282, 283, 312, 315, 327–328, 332–333; tool marks, 111, 162, 174
Frison, Robert, 340
Fulgham, T., 49

Game drive systems, 265, *293*, 348; sites, 289, 292, 293
Gantt, Erik, 44
Garner, Frank, xv, 87, 105, 108, 115
Gastropods, 96
Gelatin, 49, 90
George C. Frison Institute of Archaeology, 253
Gordon Creek burial site, Colorado, 53, *43*
Gore Range, 262
Goshen projectile points, 60, 197, 267, 272–273
Goshen-Plainview projectile points, 59–60, 267, 269, 271, 272–274, 276, 277, 296, 298–299
Gouges, 165–169, 171, 173–178; crescentic, 165–166, 168, 173, 174, 177
Grasslands, 14
Great Basin Stemmed (GBS) projectile points, 52, 280, 281, 287, 292, 296, 299, 312, 327, 328
Great Sand Dunes, Colorado, 46
Ground-stone, 46. *See also* Groundstone
Groundstone, 56. *See also* Ground-stone
Gulf of Mexico, 13
Gunnison Basin, Colorado: Folsom archaeology in, 275, 322–323, 348; Mountaineer site, 3, 56, 60; Paleoindian Research Programs, 55–57, 59–60, 62; quartzite sourcing, 57; Upper, 46

INDEX

Haas and Banewicz (heating extraction) technique, 90–91
Hackle marks, 163–165, 167
Hanson site, Wyoming, 220
Hartville chert, 107, 108
Haskett projectile points, 347
Hay Gulch site, Colorado, 277
Hay Springs site, Colorado, 276
Haynes, C. Vance, xv, 48, 89, 92, 93–96
Haynes, Gary, 102, 115
Haystack Cave site, Colorado, 43, 46
Hearth: artifact distributions, 228–229; Barger Gulch site, Locality B, 5, 60; Caribou Lake site, 50, 59; Elk Creek site, 52; Folsom hearth indicators, 223, 228; Fourth of July Valley site, 50, 58; hearth-centered activities, 220; hearths reported from Folsom contexts, 221–222; Kezar Basin site, 51; One-Two-Three site, 46–47; Ponderosa/Soap Creek site, 51; spatial patterning, 227. *See also* Barger Gulch site, Locality B; Debitage assemblages; Fire features; Ring analysis, Sector analysis; Unlined hearth
Hematite, 53
Henderson Museum, University of Colorado, 316
Heyerdahl, Thor, 344
Hofman, Jack, 48
Hogback Valley, 53
Holliday, Vance T., 49, 95
Horse, 45, 65, 270, 326, 349
Hourglass Cave site, Colorado, 43, 51–53
Howarter, Frederick, 88–89
Hudson-Meng site, Nebraska, 345
Human remains, Paleoindian-aged, 53
Hurst, C. T., xviii, 44, 46, 47, 62
Husted, Wilfred, 2, 50, 62, 64–65; Clovis, 272, 278; master's thesis, 342; Mummy Cave site, 343
Hwange National Park, Zimbabwe, 102

Illium (illia), 156, 161
Indian Peaks region, 19–20, 64; Center for Mountain Archeology and the Indian Peaks Wilderness Area Research, 58; Wilderness Area, 6, 21, 54, 275, 288–289, 295
Innominate(s), 161
Intermontane zone, 13, 275; parks, 262, 276, 299; park valleys, 298
Irwin, Cynthia, 2, 53, 343; as Irwin-Williams, 344
Irwin, Henry, 49, 53, 343
Ivory, 46, 168

Jackrabbit. *See* Rabbit
Jasper, 46. *See also individual jasper types by name*
Jerry Craig site, Colorado, 43, 60, 265, 288, 346–347

Jodry, Pegi (Margaret), 5, 22; Clovis, 46; excavations, 47, 49, 55, 252; Folsom, 63, 276
Jones, Robert, Jr., 48
Jones-Miller site, Colorado, 3, 43, 48–49, 344–345
Judge, Jim, 48
Jurgens site, Colorado, 2–3, 43, 49–50, 345, 348
James Allen site, Colorado, 47, 50–51. *See also* Jimmy Allen, Jimmy Allen-Frederick
Jimmy Allen, Jimmy Allen-Frederick (JAF): Argentine Pass site, 51, 52; Carey Lake site, 1, 52; Crescent Rockshelter site, 53; Crying Woman site, 47, 52; defined, 318, 319; Fourth of July Valley site, 50; geographic distributions, 326; Jerry Craig site, 60; Lawn Lake site, 57; qualitative distinctions from Angostura, 319–320; quantitative distinctions from Angostura, 320–322; Soderquist Ranch site, 52. *See also* Angostura

Kawuneeche Valley, 264
Kersey strath, 94; Terrace, xv, 48, 92, 94
Kezar Basin site, Colorado, 51
KibRidge-Yampa site, Colorado, 5, 197, 198, 203, 213, 215
Knife River flint, 108
Kornfeld, Marcel, 3, 49, 62, 252, 299
Kremmling, chert. *See* Troublesome Formation chert
Krmpotich site, Wyoming, 225
Krummholz ecotone, 15. *See also* Alpine zone

La Poudre Pass, 17, 26, 272, 283
La Poudre Pass Bog site, Colorado, 26
Lake Isabelle Bog site, Colorado, 26
Lamb Spring site, Colorado, 21, 45, 52
Lange-Ferguson site, South Dakota, 110, 111, 156
Larson, Mary Lou, 3, 49, 62
Laurentide ice sheet, 205
Lawn Lake site, Colorado, 57–58, 265
Lehner site, Arizona, 158
Lindenmeier site, Colorado, 3, 39, 42–44, 47–48, 62
Linger site, Colorado, 42, 43, 44, 47
Lithics, 46, 52, 107; bifacial knife, 53; bifacial thinning flakes, 232, 234, 278; channel flakes, 56, 224, 232, 234; core reduction flakes, 232, 234; end scraper, 53; fluting flake, 109; hide abrader, 53; microflakes, 58–59, 289; pressure flakes, 108, 225; refitting, 55; refluting flakes, 109; scraper, 52; tool manufacturing flakes, 277; tool manufacturing–core rejuvenation flakes, 52, 288; use-wear analysis, 55; utilized flakes, 53; waste flakes, 290–291
Little Box Elder Cave site, Wyoming, 349
Little Clovis site, Colorado, 46
"Little Ice Age," 20, 27, 29, 31

361

INDEX

Little Wolford Mountain, 60, 276, 277, 278
Llano Estacado, 277
Loch Vale, 19
LoDaiska site, Colorado, 43, 53, 65
Lookingbill site, Wyoming, 347
Lost Park Meadow, 29
Lower Twin Mountain, 59
Lower Twin Mountain site, Colorado, 60, 265
Loxodonta africana, 155, 158, 176. See also African elephant
Lusk projectile points, 317
Lutz, Bruce, 46

Malde, Harold, 105
Mammoth, 5, 42, 45, 46, 52, 89, 90–92, 94–95, 98, 99, 100–102; Clovis site, 46; Columbian, 102; Dent site, diet, 100; *Mammuthus columbi* (See also Columbian mammoth), 102; *Mammuthus imperator*, 158; *Mammuthus primigenius*, 102, 126; skeleton, 44; tusks, 125, 131, 133, 139; Zapata site, 46
Mandible(s): bison, 350; horse, 349; mammoth, 155, 158, 160, 161, 162, 185, 188, 191, 288
Martin, Duane, 47
Mary Jane site, Colorado, 18, 21, 28
McCracken, Harold, 343
McKean projectile points, 273
Medicine Bow Range, 262
Medicine Lodge Creek site, Wyoming, 327, 328, 347
"Medieval" warming, 29
Megafauna, 1, 4, 45, 115, 144, 270
Meltzer, David, 56
Metacarpals, 161
Metatarsals, 161
Metcalf Archaeological Consultants, 62
Metcalf, Mike, 51, 62
Miami site, Texas, 104
Michener, James, 344
Midland projectile points, 273, 318
Miller, Jack, 48
Miller, Mark, 343
Milner Pass, 272, 274, 292
Minimum number of individuals (MNI), 101
Montane zone, 275, 283, 284, 290, 325, 329, 330; lower, 12, 14, 264, 272, 286, 330; upper, 14, 264, 330
Moraine, 16, 20, 21, 289
Morris, Earl, 341
Morris, Elizabeth, 50, 51, 62
Mount Evans, 18, 22, 25, 28
Mount Ida Pond, 26
Mount Ida Ridge, 292–295
Mountain, Bert, 44
Mountain Branch of the Western Macrotradition, xvii

Mountain Paleoindian Tradition, 278
Mountain sheep, 264, 293, 326, 332, 348. See also Bighorn sheep
Mountaineer site, Colorado, 56
Mule deer. See Deer
Mulloy, William, 340, 343, 345
Mummy Cave site, Wyoming, 343
Mummy Range, 262
Murchison Falls, Uganda, 101
Murray Springs site, Arizona, 156

Naco site, Arizona, 113
National Park Systemwide Archaeological Inventory Program (SAIP), 265, 268, 272, 278, 295
Naze, Brian, 47
Never Summer Range, 262
Nunamiut hunters, 160, 163

Ochre, 244, 343
Obliquely flaked projectile points, 58, 313, 318, 320, 331
O-H apatite, 90. See also Bone apatite
Olsen-Chubbuck site, Colorado, 2, 3, 43, 345–346
One-Two-Three site, Colorado, 46–47
Opal. See Phytolith
Opuntia sp., 104, 185, 187
Osprey Beach site, Wyoming, 299, 349
Oxygen isotope analysis, in tusk, 124

Pacific Subtropical High, 206–207
Paleolithic, 6, 42, 220, 223, 228, 341
Panicoideae, 188
Parallel-horizontal flaking. See Angostura; Jimmy Allen
Parallel-oblique flaked projectile points. See Angostura; Jimmy Allen
Parallel transverse flaking. See Angostura; Jimmy Allen
Park Range, 262
Patten, Bob, 347
Pawnee Creek, 49
Pawnee National Grassland, xvi, 57
Pederson Ridge, 288
Phillips, Ralph, 346–347
Phillips, Ruth, 346–347
Phytolith, opal, 104, 187; chloridoid, 187–188, 190–191; festucoid, 187–188, 190–191; panicoid, 187–188, 190–191
Pictographs, 342. See also Rock art
Pinedale: glaciers, 16–18, 20, 21; glacial maximum, 271
Pitblado, Bonnie L., 6, 56–57, 65, 278, 286, 289; Caribou Lake, 58, 59; research, 61, 62
Plano, 266, 277, 278–280, 282

Platte River: Northern, 263; Southern, 44, *45*, 57, 87, 266; Upper, 16. *See also* Dent
Pleistocene, 11; mammals, 11
Postholes, 348
Powars, F. W., 343
Powars, John, 44, 343
Powars site, Colorado, 44, 343
Powars II site, Wyoming. *See* Sunrise Mine site
Ponderosa / Soap Creek site, Colorado, *43*, 51–52
Prickly pear. *See Opuntia* sp.
Proboscidean, 114. *See also* Elephant
Projectile points. *See individual types by name*
Pronghorn. *See* Antelope
Pryor Stemmed projectile points, 279
"Ptarmigan" advance, 20

Quaternary, 4, 11–12, 17, 19–20, 30, 196, 348
Quarry, 59, 157, 296; Barger Gulch, 276, 288; jasper, 46; Spanish Diggings, 342; quartzite, 56
Quartzite: sand, 95; sourcing, 57; quarries, 56
"QUEST" Paleoindian Research Program, 56. *See also* Southern Methodist University

Rabbit, 214, 215, 275; jackrabbits, 348
Rabbit Ears Range, 262, 263
Rat, wood, 348
Rattlesnake Pass site, Wyoming, 220, 223
Rawah Range, 262
Rawah Wilderness Area, 50, 290
Ray Long site, South Dakota, 316, 317
Reddin site, Colorado, *43*, 47
Redrock Lake site, Colorado, 25–27
Reher, Charles, 342
Renaud, E. B., 2, 6, 341, 342; artifacts, 61, 62; survey, 40–42. *See also* "Eastern Survey of Colorado"
Rio Grande Valley, 277. *See also* Upper Rio Grande Basin
Ring analysis, 237, *239*, 241–243, 246, 249
Riparian, 14, 190
Roberts, Frank H. H., 43–44, 47–48, 220, 340
Rock alignment. *See* Stone alignment
Rock art, 341; panel, 342. *See also* Pictographs
Runberg site, Colorado, *43*, 51, 52, 65
Rupp, Frank, 346
Ryan, Michael, 87

San Jon projectile points, 280, 281
San Juan National Forest, 61
San Luis Valley, 5, 41, 44, *54*, 59, 62–64; Clovis, 46; Folsom, 47–48, 275, 277, 325; Smithsonian Institution, 54, 55, 59
Sandia Cave site, New Mexico, 105, 108
Satanta Peak, 274
"Satanta Peak" advance, 19, 20
Sawatch Range, 51

Scapula(e), 110, 160, 162–167, 171–173, 177
Schreger bands, *131*, 137
Sclerochronology, 127
Scott Cummings, Linda, xvi, 2, 4, 5, 55, 65, 348; as Scott (Cummings), 49
Scottsbluff projectile points, 52–53, 347
Sector analysis, *237, 239*, 241–246, 249, 250
Selby and Dutton sites, Colorado, *43*, 45
Sharrock, Floyd, 341
Shoshone, 65, 326
Shoshone River, 343
Siberia, 28, 126
Sigurd, Olsen, 49
Skeletons. *See individual elements by name*
Sky Pond, 19, 22
Slocum terrace, 95, 97, 110
Soderquist Ranch site, Colorado, *43*, 52
South Park, 41, *54*, 64, 263, 275; University of Northern Colorado South Park/South Platte Research Programs, 57, 61; Walker-Buchanan, Patty 61; Yelm, Mary Elizabeth (Betty), 62
Southern Methodist University (SMU), 55–56
Sowers, Ted C., 342
Smithsonian Institution, 40, 44–49, 54, 62, 63; Bureau of American Ethnology, 43–44; Paleoindian/Paleoecology Program, 54, 55; Smithsonian Missouri River Basin Survey, 342
Spanish Diggings, Wyoming, 342
Spelunkers, 51
Spencer, William, 340
Spero, Vince, 55
Spikard, Linda, 89, 157
Sprague: Mountain, 292; Pass, 292
Stanford, Dennis, 44, 49, 340, 343–345
Stevens, E. H., 341
Stewart's Cattle Guard site, 47, 220, 252
Stone Age Fair, Colorado, 347
Stone alignment, 348
Strontium ratios, 104, 115; signatures, 115
Subalpine zone, 14, 15–16, 50, 55, 57, 272, 274, 275, 284, 286, 299, 325–326, 329; alpine-subalpine ecotone, 283, 284, 285, 290, *293*, 330; sites at, 275, 289, 292, 294; subalpine-alpine ecotone, 52; upper forest, 21, 29; upper forest meadow, 272; 273, 283, 290. *See also* Alpine zone
Sunrise Mine (Powars II) site, 343
Sutherland, Gene, 44
Surovell, Todd, 5–6

Table Mountain jasper, 290
Tandem Accelerator Mass Spectroscopy (TAMS), 90, 91
Tarryall Mountains, 22
Tenderfoot Mountain site, Colorado, 56
Thunder Pass Site, Colorado, 284

Tibia(e), 110, 157, 160, 162–163, 170–171, 175–176, 177
Tipi rings, 339
Tonahutu Creek, 292, 293
Total bone carbon, 90
Trail Ridge Game Drive site, Colorado, 271, 292
"Triple Lakes": advance, 20; moraine, 20
Troublesome Formation chert, 224, 237, 263, 290
Trout Creek chert, 224, 237, 250
Turtle, 275
Twin Mountain, 274, 276, 277. See also Lower Twin Mountain site; Upper Twin Mountain site

Ulna(e), 110, 157, 160, 162–163, 165, 168, 171, 173–174, 177
Union Pacific (UP) Mammoth site, Wyoming, 344
University of Colorado, Institute of Arctic and Alpine Research, 55
University of Northern Colorado (UNC), South Park/South Platte Research Programs, 57, 61
Unlined hearth, 51, 52. See also Hearth
University of Wyoming, Middle Park Archaeological Program, 59–62
Upper Rio Grande: Basin, 276; drainage, 41, 54. See also Rio Grande Valley
Upper Twin Mountain site, Colorado, 43, 58, 60, 274, 346, 347, 350
Utah State University, Rocky Mountain Paleoindian Research Program, 56
Ute, 65, 326
Ute Pass, 275

Valley Bisa, Zambia, 162; elephant butchery, 172; Efe people, 164
Vertebrae, 160, 161
Volk, George, 105, 341

Waco site, Texas, 104, 114, 147
Walker-Buchanan, Patty, 61
Waguespack, Nicole, 5–6
Waugh site, Oklahoma, 220–223
Wedel, Waldo, 45, 52
West, Fred Hadleigh, 346
Western State College (WSC), Colorado, 44, 46, 55
Wheat, Joe Ben, 2, 5–6, 49, 55, 89, 96; Dent, 105, 107; "Kersey," 50; Olsen-Chubbuck, 2, 49, 345
White-tailed deer. See Deer
Wilbur Thomas Shelter site, Colorado, 52
Williams Fork Reservoir, 288, 346
Wilmsen, Edwin, 48
Wind River Indian Reservation, 342
Wolford Mountain, 59–60, 274, 276–277, 288
Wood rat. See Rat, wood
Wood bison. See Bison
Worman, F. V., 44
Wormington, H. Marie: Agate Basin site, 48; Dent site, 89, 105, 108, 115, 157; Jurgens site, 49; matriarch of Paleoindian studies, 2, 5, 62, 63; typologies, 317, 340–341, 343–344, 345; Yuma, 41
Wyoming Archaeological Survey by Work Projects Administration (WPA), 342

Xerothermic, 28, 29

Yellowstone Lake, Wyoming, 299, 348
Yellowstone National Park, 343, 348
Yelm, Mary Elizabeth (Betty), 41
York, Robert, 61
Younger Dryas chronozone, 19, 22, 28
Yuma, 41–42, 65, 317, 345

Zapata site, Colorado, 42, 43, 44, 46, 47
Zimbabwe. See Hwange National Park

www.ingramcontent.com/pod-product-compliance
Lightning Source LLC
Chambersburg PA
CBHW071146070526
44584CB00019B/2679